D1457603

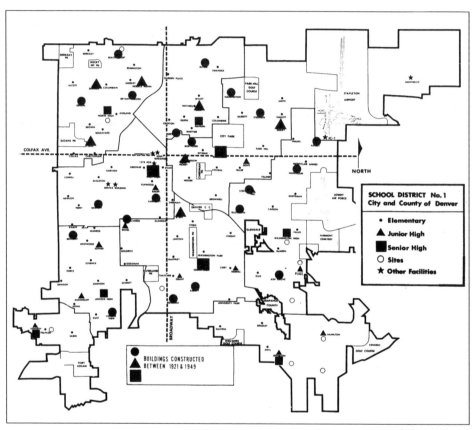

This map shows the location of Denver Public Schools in the late 1960s when debates about busing started to tear apart the district and the city.

The Denver School Busing Wars
1967–1995

Volume Two of the
History of Denver Public Schools

By Phil Goodstein

Denver
New Social Publications
2020

In memory of Daniel Lowenstein, 1957–2019:
A great friend, a marvelous artist, and someone who did not let
his days in Denver Public Schools interfere with his learning.

Laura Givens designed the cover based on a photo of South High
School by Phil Goodstein. The design shows how during the 1970s, de-
bates over busing blotted out all other educational concerns, including
the griffin perched atop South High School. It looks down on the back
cover. Tom Torgove shot the picture of the author on the back cover.

The Denver School Busing Wars
1967–1995
Volume two of the three-volume *The History of Denver Public Schools*

New Social Publications
Box 18026; Denver, Colorado 80218
(303)333-1095
capitolhillbooks.com for information about books
from New Social Publications

Printed in Denver, Colorado
First Edition: April 2020

Library of Congress Control Number 2020902167
ISBN 978–0–9860748–5–1
ISBN 0–9860748–5–3

Contents

Abbreviations

414 14th Street: DPS headquarters from 1923 to 1975

900 Grant Street: DPS headquarters beginning in 1975

AAU: Amateur Athletic Union

ACLU: American Civil Liberties Union

AFL: American Federation of Labor

AFT: American Federation of Teachers

AP: Advanced Placement

ASA: Administrations and Supervisors Association

ATU: Amalgamated Transit Union

BAC: Budget Advisory Council

BCL: Blair–Caldwell Library

BN: Board News

BSC: Budget Steering Committee

CANS: Citizens Association for Neighborhood Schools

CBLP: Colorado Black Leadership Profiles

CCR: Commission on Community Relations

CDE: Colorado Department of Education

CDM: collaborative decision-making

CEA: Colorado Education Association

CEC: Community Education Council

CHS: Colorado Historical Society, History Colorado

CI: Classroom Interests

CIC: CDM Improvement Council

CIO: Congress of Industrial Organizations

CJ: Cervi's Journal

CL: Colorado Lawyer

Cmq: Communiqué

CORE: Congress of Racial Equality

CSJ: Colorado School Journal

CT: Colorado Teacher

CU: University of Colorado

DBJ: Denver Business Journal

DCTA: Denver Classroom Teachers Association

DESCI: Denver School Employees Senior Citizens Incorporated

DFT: Denver Federation of Teachers.

DIA: Denver International Airport

DP: Denver Post

DPL: Denver Public Library

DPS: Denver Public Schools

DSIAC: District School Improvement and Accountability Council

DU: University of Denver

DURA: Denver Urban Renewal Authority

GCCC: Glendale Cherry Creek Chronicle

GP: Griebenaw Papers

GPHN: Greater Park Hill News

GW: George Washington High School

HDN: Historic Denver News

IJN: Intermountain Jewish News

KKK: Ku Klux Klan

KRMA: Channel Six

LCH: Life on Capitol Hill

LDF: Legal Defense Fund

LWV: League of Women Voters

MALDEF: Mexican-American Legal Defense and Educational Fund

Metro: Metropolitan State University

NAACP: National Association for the Advancement of Colored People

NDT: North Denver Tribune

NEA: National Education Association

NSAC: North Side Alumni Center

NYT: New York Times

P&R: Proficiency and Review

PHAC: Park Hill Action Committee

PLUS: People Let's Unite for Schools

PPV: Parent Point of View

PR: A press release

PTA: Parent–Teacher Association

QM: Quality Matters

RMH: Rocky Mountain Herald

RMN: Rocky Mountain News

RTD: Regional Transportation District

SB: Superintendent's Bulletin

SCJ: Straight Creek Journal

SCOPE: Steele–Crofton Organization of Parents and Educators

Seventeenth Street: Denver's commanding business boulevard. Used to emphasize the power of the city's leading banks and corporate interests.

SIAC: School Improvement and Accountability Council

SN: Superintendent's Newsletter

SR: The Superintendent Reports

SRv: School Review

UCD: University of Colorado Denver

UNC: University of Northern Colorado

Who's: Who's Who

WPP: Washington Park Profile

YMCA: Young Men's Christian Association

Introduction

"Schools should be the most beautiful place in every town and village—so beautiful that punishment for undutiful children should be barred from going to school the following day," stated playwright/social critic Oscar Wilde. Denver once tried to follow this advice with schoolhouses that were nothing less than temples of education. This had been true from the time East Denver School District #1, serving the city to the east of Cherry Creek, opened its first true schoolhouse in 1873. Buildings educating children were statements of community pride.

The policy continued in the 20th century on the formation of School District #1 of the City and County of Denver on December 1, 1902. Denver Public Schools (DPS) stressed that its schoolhouses were outstanding examples of civic design. This especially stood out in the 1920s when an ambitious building campaign made schoolhouses the premier landmarks of many neighborhoods. The city's foremost architects crafted them. Included were stately new homes for East, West, and South high schools.

Not everybody believed beautiful buildings guaranteed outstanding education. The *Denver Post* continually ripped the school board, claiming its spending on the ornate edifices was extremely wasteful. In exposés, the paper showed questionable real estate deals linked to the erection of new schoolhouses. What was more, there was never a consensus about what went on in the classrooms.

There was nothing unique about this. Virtually from the time the first free public schools emerged in the United States during the decades before the Civil War, ideologues bitterly clashed about the purpose of the schools and what instructors should teach in them. The mixed view on schools came out in another Oscar Wilde quip: "Education is an admirable thing, but it is well to remember, from time to time, that nothing that is worthwhile can be taught." For that matter, far from fearing exclusion from a schoolhouse as a punishment, many youngsters saw it as a welcome break from a dreary, weary routine. At the same time Wilde stated "you can never be overdressed or overeducated," he also defined education as "a process which makes one rogue cleverer than another."

1

The irony of Wilde has always been beyond the scope of DPS and earnest believers in educational uplift. Far and away, proponents of schools have been voices of the establishment. By the middle of the 20th century, the Mile High consensus was that District #1 was a model system that had succeeded in educating a literate community. Insofar as there was dissension during the 1950s and 1960s, it was over whether DPS provided equal quality education to one and all, especially African-American youngsters. Divisions on this question tore the city apart in 1969 amidst intense controversies over busing students across town in the name of desegregation.

Opponents of busing swept the May 1969 balloting for the school board. Their victory came two years after Kenneth K. Oberholtzer retired as superintendent of District #1 — he had held the post for 20 years. The emergence of public education in Denver and the evolution of DPS from its origins through the Oberholtzer era are covered in *The Denver School Book*, the first part in this three-volume history of Denver Public Schools. Besides focusing on busing controversies, including how the federal courts oversaw DPS from 1969 to 1995, *The Denver School Busing Wars* reviews contemporaneous developments during those years.

Included is the rise of the Denver Classroom Teachers Association (DCTA) as a union and how and why the teachers went on strike in 1969. Also told is the way the school board declared war on all of the district's pre–World War I buildings and launched an aggressive construction campaign to replace them in the 1970s. All of this relates to the interaction between the schools, busing, suburban growth, and the city's general political, social, and economic development. Volume three, *Schools for a New Century*, will cover developments since the end of the court school busing order in 1995.

The dates of the volumes are not hard and fast. There is an immense overlap in developments. For example, *The Denver School Book* talks about the role of KRMA, Channel Six. DPS launched it in 1956 as a district-owned and operated educational television station. In 1987, the district spun off the frequency to a nonprofit. I include what happened in volume one, though the separation between Channel Six and DPS is 20 years after the official end of the study.

Similarly, to understand debates over busing, the first three chapters review racial relations and school board politics prior to 1967. Then, I have left other actions between 1967 and 1995, such as the creation of the Career Education Center, the rise of charter schools, and the impact of Padres Unidos, a group decrying the way the system has sometimes dealt with Latino youngsters, to volume three. *Schools for a New Century* will also discuss such topics of the 1960s, 1970s, and 1980s as the district's endless efforts to lower the dropout rate while creating such places as the Metropolitan Youth Education Center for students who had trouble in the regular secondary schools.

After much reflection, I also decided to put the sweeping changes at Manual High School in volume three. During the busing era, it was the shining example of what happened when well-prepared white students occupied what had been a black academy. The end of busing saw the collapse of Manual's academic achievements. In the early 21st century, the district essentially destroyed the program.

Prior to the emergence of School District #1 of the City and County of Denver on December 1, 1902, there had been other school districts in the city, including #17 for the North Side. Like the old East Denver District #1, District #17 took pride in its schoolhouses such as the new Boulevard School in 1891 on the west side of the 2300 block of Federal Boulevard. The pictured building came down in 1964. Part of a 1904 wing survives. It became condominiums in the 1980s.

Given the lack of any hard dividing line between the volumes, some repetition has been necessary between them. In the current study, for example, I have occasionally traced some of the people and developments I outlined in *The Denver School Book*. Ideally, by mentioning the same point in the different tomes, the text helps readers refresh their memories and see the larger picture.

In volume one, I outlined the construction and development of the district's schools prior to 1967. In introducing schools in this study, I have tried to give the address when first mentioning a building. If the specific location is important vis-à-vis the text, I might repeat the address. Given that DPS has rebuilt some schools such as Columbian and Mitchell at slightly different locations, addresses reflect the location of the building at the time I refer to it. A comprehensive index in volume three will list all of the mentioned schools.

Changing names present a problem. Not only did the district redesignate some of its buildings in the 1920s and 1930s such as Corona School (846 Corona Street) into Moore School, Clayton School (1140 Columbine Street) into Stevens School, Villa Park School (845 Hazel Court) into Eagleton School, and Hyde Park School (3620 Franklin Street) into Wyatt School, but the city has relabeled some key roads.

Daniel Lowenstein, 1957–2019, drew pictures of some of the people in this volume.

In particular, Jackson Street, where Barrett School opened in 1960 at 2900 Jackson Street, has become Richard Allen Court. In 1980, city hall declared 32nd Avenue east of Downing Street "Martin Luther King Boulevard." It subsequently named 23rd Street "Park Avenue West." To avoid confusion, I often give both the past and present names of the road to which I am referring.

The result has been a three-prong approach. Part of the emphasis is on the specific developments of the school board and administration. This includes focusing on elections to the board of education and the continuity and change within the way the district has been run. Next to this is a look at specific buildings, educators, and the general role of instructors in making schools what they are. This, in turn, links up to debates about the nature of American public schools, Denver developments, and society at large.

The endeavor is bulky enough as it is. I have deliberately cut back on topics that deserve monographs of their own, such as the convoluted world of DPS labor organizations. While I pay an immense amount of attention to the litigation over school busing, that is not the subject of this book. Legal scholars have written extensively over the meaning of *Keyes* v. *School District #1*, the 1973 landmark decision of the United States Supreme Court upholding Mile High busing. My purpose is to outline its importance vis-à-vis DPS and its impact on the community. I will let others write the extensive volume the case merits. While there are passing mentions of school sports, theater, and art programs, I have not given them the full attention they require. In volume three, I will look at the continuing debates over the importance of instruction on art and music while outlining the rise and achievements of the Denver School of the Arts at Montview Boulevard and Poplar Street.

For the most part, I have sought to use original photos and copies of documents in addition to enlivening the text with archival shots of the city's historic schoolhouses. Here and there, I have drawn on images printed in some of my other volumes. Not all of the graphics are as good as I wish they could be. Unfortunately, I have not discovered better images, particularly of demolished buildings and some of the key actors in school developments. There is no outstanding, affordable collection of pictures of Denver since World War II.

Over the years, photographer John Schoenwalter, who started shooting in the city in the 1970s, shared some of his images. He died after a long battle with prostrate cancer and Parkinson's Disease in October 2019. Tom Torgove has allowed me to use pictures he has taken of leading politicians while giving me moral support and sometimes acting as my chauffeur. Jason Bosch particularly helped with contemporary photography of schools in Montbello and Green Valley Ranch.

While I was working on this volume, Daniel Lowenstein also died. A product of DPS, he was an immensely talented artist who painted murals, designed sculptures, and drew sketches of people at street fairs. In my recent books, he transformed poor original pictures of people and places into original artwork. In early 2019, he came down with an aggressive case of cancer of the esophagus that killed him in August. I consider the drawings by him in this book as part of the legacy of his many contributions to the city. Gregorio Alcaro contributed his artistic skills in drawing some of the people mentioned in the text. As always, Laura Givens has done her outstanding job designing the cover.

Given that I am a product of Denver Public Schools, parts of this book are inescapably autobiographical. Not only do I devote a good deal of attention to Park Hill as the neighborhood at the center of integration fights during the 1960s, but that is where I grew up. I entered kindergarten at Park Hill School, 5050 19th Avenue, in September 1957. From there I proceeded to Smiley Junior High, 2540 Holly Street. I graduated from East High, 1545 Detroit Street, in 1970. My time at East was simultaneous to the years when Robert D. Gilberts was superintendent of DPS from 1967 to 1970.

A schoolboy does not have a grasp of the dynamics of what is actually occurring where he attends classes. If anything, the schools deliberately sought to cloak the outside world from students. Far more than any encouragement of education as a

DENVER PUBLIC SCHOOLS

EAST HIGH SCHOOL

This Certifies That

PHILIP H. GOODSTEIN

HAS COMPLETED THE REQUIREMENTS FOR GRADUATION AS PRESCRIBED BY THE BOARD OF EDUCATION OF SCHOOL DISTRICT NO. 1 IN THE CITY AND COUNTY OF DENVER AND STATE OF COLORADO, AND IS ENTITLED TO THIS

DIPLOMA

GIVEN THIS FIRST DAY OF JUNE, ONE THOUSAND NINE HUNDRED AND SEVENTY

PRESIDENT, BOARD OF EDUCATION

SECRETARY, BOARD OF EDUCATION

PRINCIPAL

SUPERINTENDENT

The author graduated from East High in 1970, right before the full turbulence of school busing hit Denver Public Schools.

marvelous product for its own sake or a nurturing of independent-minded learning, what I primarily recall of my schooldays are tyrannical administrators, petty-minded teachers, and a brain-deadening routine. There was a general feeling of a lack of freedom. In protest, I emerged as a student activist, especially combating the powers that be while I was at East High. This bias naturally slants the book.

For the most part, I hated school. I found it far more a confining, restrictive, sterile environment than a place exploring ideas and the nature of the world. If anything, especially at Smiley, the administration acted to keep students isolated from current events. In retrospect, I have been among the many pupils who have identified with the Pink Floyd's 1979 song "Another Brick in the Wall," with the refrain "we don't need no education, we don't need no thought control" in response to sadistic schoolmasters. The words have resonated with generations of students. The song's reception reflects how schools frequently have more been institutions designed to control and limit youth than help them understand society and the possibilities of transforming it.

Already while in high school, I had a perception that alternatives were possible. This was the high tide of the 1960s when East High was a national model of a seemingly liberal school with progressive, alternative programs. During my last semester, for example, it was a pioneer in introducing Senior Seminar, an offering through which some seniors were able to get off of campus and explore the community. I was too much involved with student politics and the college prep program at East, including taking a couple of Advanced Placement classes, to participate in it.

Generally, my years at East were a miserable time. I constantly clashed with my counselor. Every time she suggested a program, it was a wrong turn. But I was not an ideal student who was an echo, brilliantly repeating what teachers wanted to hear. On the contrary, I was convinced there had to be a better way while I paid little attention to classes in which I had no interest. Via independent reading, I probed alternative views about the schools and the nature of education.

A keynote of debates over busing and DPS during the 1960s, 1970s, 1980s, and 1990s, was a thorough avoidance of the question of the exact purpose of the schools and whether even the best of them were the ideal way to help children learn. This is a background theme in the book. So is the relationship between socioeconomic status and school success. Time and again, that subject was present during the school busing wars in reviews that showed the very unequal achievements of students whereby white youngsters, particularly those from affluent, white families, did much better than did youngsters of color who lived in economically distressed circumstances.

At no time during the fights over integration did either proponents or foes of the program directly address the assertion that schools are not institutions independent of the larger society; rather, schools are part and parcel of the status quo. By its very nature, the school system favors those who have grown up in an atmosphere treasuring literacy and who have generally done well within the financial system. Schools filled with the sons and daughters of successful college graduates have tended to be far more conducive to academic achievement than those populated by youngsters whose parents have never made it through high school. In a word,

Photo by Phil Goodstein

The author attended Park Hill School, 5050 19th Avenue from 1957 to 1964. Developments at the school at that time laid the foundation for the busing upheavals that swept Denver beginning in 1969.

schools are the embodiment of the social, economic, racial, and ethnic divisions of the wider world.

Given that there is a rich literature about the nature of the interaction between the schools and the larger society, I do not probe this point in detail. For the purpose of the immediate study, the goal is to portray the actual operations of School District #1 of the City and County of Denver from the time school integration became a hot topic in 1967 until the United States District Court ceased its oversight of DPS at the end of the 1995–96 schoolyear.

Back in 1969, during the tumultuous school board election turning on the issue of desegregation, I was among those who fervently believed that school busing in the name of equal educational opportunity was a sure-fire means to achieve racial justice. The opponents of busing readily resorted to racist innuendos and had but the most limited if not cynical view of the schools and the busing issue. Even so, they proved correct in many ways: busing alone was no means to transform the schools or society. Far from providing better education for all, it actually harmed many students and programs while it drastically divided the community.

A prime failure of busing, as pointed out by radical critics of the day such as the Black Panthers and the Chicano Crusade for Justice, was that proponents did not realize the extreme class, ethnic, and social divisions within the community. Busing ideologues premised their program on the essential equality of all within the values of the affluent, white upper-middle class. The tensions enveloping the city during the busing era showed the fragile nature of this illusion.

In part, I have become extremely critical of busing simply in terms of what it did to the children the program impacted. It made them get on buses at an early hour, bringing them home late. Busing schedules came to define much of the schoolday. Having found myself constantly manipulated while in school and recruited for projects that no adult with the most basic commonsense would agree to undertake, I have no use for programs that seek to exploit youngsters, treating them as mindless puppets. For example, part of my extreme doubts about the nature of corporate America go back to when I was in Junior Achievement at East High. More than anything, it taught me about the cynical nature of business and efforts to create unnecessary products, selling them to gullible customers.

But personal impressions are thoroughly inadequate. In researching and writing about the topic, I have sought to provide the same critical vigor in dealing with developments on other topics, times, and locations. I pay great heed to Park Hill because it was the hotbed of support for school busing and integration. In probing what occurred there, I have applied the same standards as I give to other schools and different parts of the city. While numerous people have shared their memories about their DPS experience, especially as students and teachers, I have primarily relied on the standard sources of the historian in printed documents, newspaper accounts, school studies and memoranda, and the incredibly long, detailed record of the court litigation surrounding District #1 during this epoch.

Instead of footnotes, I have added essays on sources at the end of each chapter. The notes for the introduction list the major sources on the school busing wars. A detailed bibliography will be in volume three. Two sources on which I have continually drawn are the web sites of Great Schools and SchoolDigger. Both survey the enrollment of contemporary schools, listing their racial and socioeconomic composition. Often they present different numbers. As with many internet sources, they are amazingly imprecise in giving exact dates. For that matter, I have tended to steer away from the internet given its rapidly changing character and what a site says one day might well be different the next. Even with that said, I wish to complement the web school news service Chalkbeat for having far and away the best overall reportage on area schools during the modern era.

Acknowledgements

Over the years, I have been part of the Naysayers. It is a small group that gathers monthly for dinner. Those present critically discuss current and past Mile High developments. The club calls itself the "Naysayers" since corporate Denver, echoed by the major media, have tended to dismiss as "naysayers" those who have questioned the direction of the community and various booster projects.

Among those who sporadically showed up at Naysayer meetings from around 2008 to 2012 was Rita Montero. She served on the school board from 1995 to 1999 when she was usually at odds with the other members of the seven-person elected agency overseeing DPS. In the process, she not only shared many stories about her experiences, but urged me to write a history of the school district.

A close friend of Montero, Dorolyn Griebenaw, joined her in lobbying for a book on DPS. Back in the 1990s and early 2000s, Griebenaw was a leader

ART BRANSCOMBE
GOOD NEWS for Schools
Vote May 19, for School Board
2287 Bellaire, Denver, CO 80207

Courtesy Carla Branscombe

In 1987, Art Branscombe, who had covered education issues for the Denver Post for 22 years unsuccessfully ran for the school board.

of the District School Improvement and Accountability Council (DSIAC). This was a citizens' agency that was supposed to assure that the school system indeed educated children. Even before emerging as its head, Griebenaw was something of the committee's record keeper. In the early 21st century, she gained possession of old PTA records when nobody at the central school headquarters showed any interest in keeping or saving them when they were stashed in a basement that flooded after a water pipe broke. She has readily shared her holdings with me. I cite them as GP, the Griebenaw Papers. Her encouragement and records have been vital in making this study possible.

Posthumous thanks go to Carla Branscombe who died in 2017. She was the widow of Art Branscombe. With his first wife Bea, he was a most active journalist during the second half of the 20th century. Among his beats was covering DPS for the *Denver Post*. A resident of Park Hill, he was a leading figure in its pro-integration citizens group, the Park Hill Action Committee, an organization growing into Greater Park Hill Community Incorporated. With Bea, he sought to write a comprehensive history of Park Hill, focusing on integration battles. Other than many newspaper articles in the *Greater Park Hill News*, the monthly sheet of Greater Park Hill Community Incorporated, they never completed it. They left behind an amazingly rich archive on both Park Hill and DPS.

When I started work on my book *Park Hill Promise* in 2011, a lengthy portrait of the neighborhood to the east of Colorado Boulevard and north of Colfax Avenue, Carla Branscombe opened her basement to me where the records were stored. Denver Public Library subsequently acquired the papers. Since I used them before the complete reorganization of the collection, I am unable to cite specific file folders when referring to the holding.

The Western History Department of the library, the permanent location of the Branscombe papers, also houses many of the records of DPS. In addition to numerous cartons donated by the district, filled with folders about individual schools, the main library has copies of the minutes of school board meetings, and many of the seemingly endless studies the district has conducted of its programs. Additionally, the library has uneven collections of numerous DPS publications.

Librarians there have been of utmost assistance in helping me find some of the DPS records. They have also been of endless help in pulling other records about

the city. Without them, this volume would not have been possible. Besides those
at the Western History Department, special thanks goes to Terry Nelson of the
research collections at Denver Public Library's Blair-Caldwell branch where she
oversees the collection on the African-American West. Nelson has also chatted
about her DPS experiences.

There are scattered records about DPS in the Auraria Archives. The collections
of Doris Banks, Minoru Yasui, and Rich Castro contain immense materials on
the schools, including the integration fights of the 1960s and 1970s. Archivist
Rosemary Evetts, who retired in July 2019, readily welcomed me. She struggled
with the vandal-like dictates from the library administration to dispose of other
crucial collections dealing with Denver such as the papers of John Carroll, Wally
Wahlberg, and Byron Johnson.

Unfortunately, the Stephen Hart Library of the Colorado Historical Society
has drastically cut back its hours. In 2010, the organization changed its name to
History Colorado. I still use Colorado Historical Society to refer to photos I had
previously procured from it or to collections I consulted in its archives.

Another treasure chest about DPS is at the special collections/archives of the
University of Denver (DU) at Penrose Library/Anderson Commons. At one time,
DU history professor Ted Crane focused on the history and nature of the schools.
Some of his students wrote excellent theses and dissertations about DPS. He saw
the DU library obtain the papers of DPS superintendents Jesse Newlon (1920–27),

Photo by Phil Goodstein

*East, West, North, and South high schools have alumni rooms that are small
museums packed with materials and memorabilia on the schools. Shown is a
collection of West High apparel at that school's alumni center. At the bottom are
bound issues of* The Rodeo, *the student newspaper.*

and Archie Threlkeld (1927–37). Most of the library's holdings deal with DPS prior to the busing upheavals. The special collections staff was most accommodating in allowing me access to these materials. They were crucial to volume one of this series. The archives and special collections of the University of Colorado at Norlin Library welcomed me to look at the papers on the Keyes case and the holdings donated by Herrick Roth, once the executive director of the Colorado Federation of Teachers.

I also wish to remember Kenton Forrest. Once a science teacher in Jefferson County Public Schools, he probed how Denver worked in numerous publications. While he primarily dealt with the history of railroads and streetcars, serving as the archivist of the Colorado Railroad Museum, he was also most interested in the schools. In 1989, with Gene McKeever and Raymond "Ray" McAllister, he put together *History of the Public Schools of Denver*. Primarily a listing of the different buildings that have educated Denver students, it is indispensable background material about district facilities. I had a copy at my fingertips while writing this study, consulting it constantly. Forrest passed away in 2018. On occasion, Ray McAllister has discussed his role in the work and the schools. Included is his wide-ranging knowledge of the physical plant of the district. His son, Daniel, has shown himself an eager member of the younger generation wishing to enhance the schools.

Besides sharing records about DPS, Dorolyn Griebenaw and her husband Don, a former DPS instructor, have sporadically invited me to luncheons with some of their acquaintances who have dealt with school issues. Sherry Eastlund, another leader of DSIAC, and Kristen Tourangeau, who was also part of the group, have shared their experiences in DPS as students, mothers, and activists. At times, Jeannie Kaplan, who was on the school board from 2005 to 2013, attended the events. She has given me her take on DPS in the 21st century.

Incidentally, the PTA materials of the Griebenaw Papers are of extremely uneven quality. In places, they are simply listings of social affairs conducted by school PTAs. In other instances, they are notebooks filled with newspaper clippings. Unfortunately, many of the articles are not identified by date or source. Where possible, I have tried to give specific page numbers of newspaper articles. This has not always been possible in clipping files. Many newspaper articles archived on the internet, likewise, lack specific page numbers.

Despite the lack of specific citations, immense thanks goes to the PTA volunteers who put together the group's notebooks. The collection of miscellaneous articles and brochures about the schools has been amazingly helpful in understanding many of the issues concerning DPS. As such, the seemingly arcane and forgotten materials of yesterday are crucial in helping make sense of what has happened. They illustrate the necessity of saving such documents. It is incumbent on places such as DPL and the Auraria Archives to gather, catalogue, and keep such records.

CJ Backus has given me moral support and helped with research, particularly of genealogical questions. Additionally, she reviewed the text. Proofreaders/editors Maxine Lankford, Dinah Land, Ruth Vanderkooi, Jane Lane, and Sunny Maynard have kept me from making too many grammatical and logical blunders.

Photo by Phil Goodstein

*In 1956, KRMA, Channel Six, went on the air as a DPS owned and operated
television station. In 1992, it occupied what had been the studio of Channel Nine at
the southwest corner of West 11th Avenue and Bannock Street. The* Denver School
Book *traces its origins and evolution into being Rocky Mountain Public Media.*

Bill Robinson, a 1948 East graduate, has backed my work while constantly
debating with me about Denver history. He arranged for me to speak to a luncheon
group of East alumni. People there reflected on their Mile High schooldays. So
have those gathering at North High, West High, and South High alumni events.
Members of the groups running the alumni associations have been most supportive.
They have opened up their records to me. East historian Dick Nelson has further
shared his immense research on and knowledge of DPS. Jim McNally, the historian
of Manual High School, has readily chatted about its rich heritage. Unfortunately,
I cannot recall the name of the librarian of Bromwell School who helped me during
research in 2000–01 when he provided me with copies of photos of members of
the board of education.

Joe DeRose, a graduate of North, went on to teach in DPS. He has always had a
good word, sharing his diverse and colorful experiences. Sheila Corwin Robinson
spent time at East in 1969–70 from George Washington during my senior year at
East. She became an instructor, reflecting on what she has seen in different districts.
Ed Augden, once a teacher at George Washington, has likewise shared his memories.
Jimi O'Connor has continually filled me in about his days as a junior high/middle
school teacher and counselor and what he experienced in volunteering for many
district ventures. Countless others, when talking about growing up in Denver,
often refer to the schools. They have given me their happy and horrid memories
of attending Denver Public Schools.

Booksellers Holly Brooks, Lois Harvey, Nicole Sullivan, Ron and Nina Else,
and the people at Tattered Cover have boosted my efforts by buying and marketing
my books. Thanks also go to Leanne Vargas, Angel Garcia, Gregorio Alcaro, Linda

Walker, Katie and Steve Fisher, Caroline Green, Susan Decker, Mike Davenport, Joanne Roll, Doug Gerash, Jim Peiker, Charlotte Rocha, Charlie Salzman, Steve Kosmicki, Kirk Peffers, Larry Ambrose, Mary Van Meter, Isaac Solano, Dave Parce, John Wren, Jerene Dildine, Phil and Janet Lutz, Patricia Moore, Charline Porter, Madyson Dreiling, Miller Hudson, Jessica Abbeg, Ashlie Woods, Dave Felice, Karen Gonzales, Rob Weil, and Orville Spriggs. Most of all, thanks go to those buying my books and coming on my tours. Their response shows me that many recognize the city's heritage is key to shaping its future.

Phil Goodstein
Denver
April 1, 2020

A Note on Sources:

There are mentions about the relationship between economic class, school achievement, and the quest for equal educational opportunity in *School Book*, 2, 6, 169, 272, 355. *WW*, January 22, 2020, discovered anew the correlation between economic affluence and school success. *New Yorker*, September 30, 2019, pp. 76–77, emphasized how colleges more reflect the social and class stratification of society than reward merit. Neil Postman, *The End of Education* (New York: Vintage, 1996), ix–x, ponders educational debates. He argues they must focus on the purpose of the schools rather than simply on how they are administered and whom they teach and how.

DP, November 3, 2017, p. 14A, observed the passing of Carla Branscombe. A private obituary of Kenton Forrest was in *DP*, September 22, 2018, p. 20A. His work on the schools with Gene McKeever and Raymond McAllister is *History of the Public Schools of Denver* (Denver: Tramway Press, 1989).

Major works on the impact of busing on DPS are primarily unpublished graduate works or articles in legal journals. Mary Jean Taylor, "Leadership Responses to Desegregation in the Denver Public Schools, A Historical Study: 1959–1977" (Ph.D. dissertation, DU, 1990), includes interviews with members of the school board, allowing them to give their version about what happened during the 1960s and 1970s. Another good graduate study is Frederick D. Watson, "Removing the Barricades from the Northern Schoolhouse Door: School Desegregation in Denver" (Ph.D. dissertation, CU, 1993). Sharon Bailey, who served on the school board and was a member of the DPS administration working on racial issues, wrote "Journey Full Circle: A Historical Analysis of *Keyes* v. *School District #1*" (Ph.D. dissertation, UCD 1998). For the most part, it draws on the existing literature, bringing a public administration viewpoint into the discussion of the rise and fall of school busing in Denver. The work is especially good on the end of busing. Harriet Elaine Glosson Adair, "Trends in School Desegregation: An Historical Case Study of Desegregation in Dayton, Ohio; Denver, Colorado; Los Angeles, California; and Seattle, Washington; 1954–1985" (Ed.D. dissertation, Brigham Young University, 1986), is of little value.

Jessica and Jeffery Pearson trace the legal origins of the school busing case, *Keyes* v. *School District #1*, in Howard I. Kalodner and James J. Fishman, eds., *Limits of Justice* (Cambridge: Ballinger, 1978), 167–222. The study was originally written for the United States Civil Rights Commission in 1976, a copy of which is in FF 1:15 of the Rachel Noel papers, ARL 117, at BCL. In part, the authors followed James Meadow, "It Has Been Five Long Hard Years," *CJ*, May 8, 1974, pp. 23–26. Filled with numerous little errors about names and dates, the latter is a polemic against opponents of busing. Despite its faults, it is a basic introduction. Citizens Association for Neighborhood Schools, *Education by Judicial Fiat* ([Denver]: [CANS], [1974]), is a politically charged blast against the inanities and undemocratic nature of court-ordered busing. A good capsule review of the controversy is in *PPV*, 1:1 (1981), pp. 3–4.

A retrospection on the school busing wars is by Natasha Gardner, "The Legacy of Denver's Forced School Busing Era," *5280*, June 2018. Also see William M. Beaney, "The Keyes Case in Perspective," an article from the July 26, 1974, *DU Law Review*; a copy is in FF 2:3 of the Rachel Noel Papers.

Rachel F. Moran has written law review articles about the integration campaign including "Untoward Consequences: The Ironic Legacy of *Keyes* v. *School District #1*," *DU Law Review*, 90:5 (October 2013), 1209–29. The contribution was part of a special issue "Forty Years Since *Keyes* v. *School District #1*." It stemmed from a two-and-a-half day seminar at the DU College of Law held in conjunction with the university's College of Education and others interested in the area's legal history.

Tom Romero introduced the journal, 1023–58. He has written various articles in law journals emphasizing the landmark status of the Keyes case, particularly looking at the concept of Denver as a "tri-ethnic" district with the important Hispanic dimension of the city, esp. 1046. Also see his "The Keyes to Reclaiming the Racial History of the Roberts Court," *Michigan Journal of Race & Law*, 20:2 (2015), 415–40.

There is passing mention of the Denver experience in R. Stephen Browning, ed., *From Brown to Bradley: School Desegregation 1954–74* (Cincinnati: Jefferson Law Book Company, 1975), 141, 148, 149, 152, 155. Gary Orfield, *Must We Bus?* (Washington: Brookings Institution, 1978), examines the national debate over busing as the closing chapter of the Civil Rights Revolution. It stresses how the Keyes case was central to federal litigation during the 1970s in defining the nature of a de facto segregated school district, xvi, 2, 15.

James Fishman and Lawrence Straus, "Endless Journey: Integration and the Provision of Equal Educational Opportunity in Denver's Public Schools: A Study of *Keyes* v. *School District #1*," *Howard Law Journal*, 36 (1987), 627–727, highlights the legal dimension of the controversy. The article is reprinted as chap. 5 of Barbara Flicker, ed., *Justice and School Systems* (Philadelphia: Temple University Press, 1990), 185–232. The study is somewhat sloppy, being the product of outsiders who focus on the legal history of the case. Generally, I have cited pages from *Justice and School Systems* though I occasionally refer to the original law journal article. Flicker comments on the importance of the Keyes case, 10–12. Maurice Mitchell, "The Desegregation of Denver's Public Schools," *Center Magazine*, November-December 1978, pp. 67–76, is the retrospective of the chairman of the court-appointed Community Education Council about how well court-ordered desegregation worked.

Chapter One

Promise and Prejudice

O n October 3, 1859, Owen Goldrick taught the first school lessons in the nascent Mile High City. Two years later, Denver had its first public school classes. As the city expanded to a community of 133,859 residents in 1900, there were numerous different school districts serving the diverse parts of the city. They consolidated into District #1 of Denver Public Schools of the City and County of Denver on December 1, 1902, the birth date of the City and County of Denver.

From the beginning, there were passionate debates over the schools. Settlers saw them as crucial to Denver's destiny. At times the district flourished. During other periods, taxpayers, suffering from economic reverses, moaned that the school system was a costly drain on public resources. DPS counted around 25,000 students on the formation of District #1. After a period of stagnation during the early 1910s, enrollment started to climb as Denver's population surged to 415,786 in the mid-20th century. In 1950, 51,866 students were enrolled in DPS. A decade later, there were 90,518 students in a city of 493,887. Membership peaked in 1968 at 96,848 by which time the last of the baby boomers were in the classrooms.

From the beginning, DPS emphasized it was far more than a system simply instructing youngsters in the basics. Already in the 19th century, Superintendent Aaron Gove (1874–1904) argued that moral education was just as important as any book learning. The schools additionally had a major social-welfare role. Gove insisted that students from economically comfortable families learn the necessity of community service and helping their less fortunate classmates.

The schools also played a major role in Americanization programs. By the beginning of the 20th century, Denver was a major industrial city. Numerous immigrants worked in factories and smelters. Many were from southern and eastern Europe. The schools reached out to the youngsters of such families. The prime necessity was teaching them English. Additionally, the schools emphasized

American versions of hygiene, diet, and behavior. Ideally, students took these lessons home, helping educate their parents. DPS also connected with adults through evening programs. Until at least World War II, it offered classes on English as a second language and how to gain citizenship.

Often administrators were extremely insensitive to the traditions of children from other countries and cultures. The nation's supposed melting pot was based on the values of the existing social-economic elite, people overwhelmingly of northern European, especially English, origins. Not surprisingly, performance in affluent schools, where parents were often high school if not college graduates, was much better than in schools overwhelmingly populated by poorly educated newcomers. Until World War II, it was not unusual for students to leave school after eighth grade for the workforce. Not until the return of peace did a high school diploma become a goal for all students.

During the first half of the 20th century, self-proclaimed "patriots" emphasized the schools. Often such individuals were extremely intolerant. They demanded the schools observe a kind of flag worship to instill youths with a narrow brand of citizenship. Others fought back, insisting the schools were the heart of democracy. By learning together, students of all backgrounds came to know and appreciate each other. This, integration advocates argued, was the heart of the country's future.

As was the case across the country, DPS slanted its curriculum to the values of a White Anglo-Saxon Protestant culture. This especially came out in intelligence tests (IQ). Educators used them not just to measure perception and students' ability to answer a broad array of questions, but also to gauge how much pupils knew about some of the mores and customs that were part and parcel of the dominant racial-religious-economic group. When children of immigrants and racial and ethnic minorities scored poorly on the IQ tests, the patriots cited this as evidence of the inferior character of those who were not of Anglo-Saxon stock.

Racial Concerns

As Denver burgeoned, DPS emphasized neighborhood schools. It drew attendance zones to bring together youngsters living close to schoolhouses. Names of schools sometimes reflected geographical locations such as University Park (2300 South St. Paul Street), Barnum (85 Hooker Street), Washington Park (1125 South Race Street), Swansea (4650 Columbine Street) and Montclair (1151 Newport Street). Four of the city's five high schools had outright geographical designations: East (1545 Detroit Street), North (2960 Speer Boulevard), South (1700 Louisiana Avenue), and West (951 Elati Street). The fifth, Manual Training High School (1700 28th Avenue), a program launched in 1893, was a magnet school for youngsters in East Denver who wanted a vigorous trade or scientific education opposed to the college preparatory program at the heart of East High.

Given the neighborhood orientation of the schools, African-American children naturally predominated in the schools in and around greater Five Points. This refers to the five-pointed intersection where 26th Avenue comes together with 27th Street, Welton Street, and Washington Street. Once a middle-class white section, Five

Photo by Phil Goodstein

The Rossonian Hotel, at the southeast corner of Five Points, the intersection of 26th Avenue with Washington, Welton, and 27th streets, was a center of black culture in the mid-20th century when Five Points was the heart of African-American Denver.

Points became increasingly black in the early 20th century. Neighborhood schools included Ebert at 23rd Street (Park Avenue West) and Tremont Place, Crofton at 24th and Arapahoe streets, Gilpin at 29th and California streets, and Whittier at 25th Avenue and Downing Street. As black settlement spread to the east of Downing Street after World War II, particularly to the north of 20th avenue, such schools as Mitchell at 32nd Avenue (Martin Luther King Boulevard) and Lafayette Street, and the nearby Cole Junior High at 3240 Humboldt Street also increasingly had a large percentage of black students. Eventually, so did Manual. By the end of World War I, Manual, then at 27th Avenue and Franklin Street, was a general high school with all of the city's high schools having manual training programs. In 1952, the institute officially became Manual High School.

Denver's black population exploded during World War II. Growth continued after the return of peace. From 6,836 African-Americans in 1940, 2.4 percent of the city's population, the number was 15,049 ten years later, 3.6 percent. Black Denver doubled to 30,251 by 1960, 6.1 percent. By 1970, there were 47,011 African-American inhabitants, 9.1 percent of the Mile High City's population.

In part, the growth of black Denver stemmed from the Air Force. The recently established branch of the military moved its Finance Center (subsequently the

Finance and Accounting Center) from St. Louis to an old military medical depot at
3800 York Street in 1951. Many black careerists then found themselves transferred
to town. After leaving the service, they stayed in Denver. Despite Mile High racial
tensions, they found the city a far better place than where they had previously
lived—most hailed from the South.

Besides jobs in the military, many African-Americans took jobs in the federal
civil service at the time when Denver touted itself as second to Washington in the
per capita number of federal employees. In the process, the newcomers fit in well
with the existing black community, one led by professionals and successful real
estate investors. Even at that, in touring Denver during World War II, Roy Wilkins,
the field secretary of the National Association for the Advancement of Colored
People, had dismissed the town as just another racist community.

The rapid growth of the African-American population increasingly transformed
sections of northeast Denver into overwhelmingly black enclaves. While there had
never been an official Jim Crow line in the city, some came to insist there was such
a de facto border near Vine and Race streets to the north of 18th Avenue. Others
placed it at Gilpin Street or as far east as York Street. The lack of agreement showed
the nebulous nature of such a division.

Early on, schools reflected the population of those living close to them.
The original Fairmont School, at West Second Avenue and Elati Street,
which held its first classes in 1883, was an integrated academy. It drew in
the children of the wealthy living in Victorian homes in what became the
Baker neighborhood, the offspring of blue-collar workers who dwelt close
to Santa Fe Drive, and those living in poverty along the South Platte River.

Regardless of the location, African-Americans increasingly moved to the east of that limit as the black population surged after World War II. In the course of the 1950s, blacks moved all the way east to Colorado Boulevard to the north of City Park. In the process, such schools as Harrington, 3230 38th Avenue, and Columbine, at the northeast corner of 28th Avenue and Columbine Street, came to have large black enrollments.

The African-American community had extremely mixed views about the nature of the school system. Some treasured it. Graduates looked back, praising teachers for instilling them with the necessity of hard work and mastering subjects as a road to success. Usually these were members of old middle-class Denver families who had made their way through the schools. The buildings, they remembered, were all integrated. DPS did not have any black schools as such. Places like Manual and Cole were mini-United Nations with an amazingly wide variety of students from numerous different cultures, races, and backgrounds.

Opposed to this outlook, other African-Americans moaned that DPS was a racist system. They complained that buildings, furniture, and textbooks in black schools were old. In some cases, textbooks were nonexistent. (At times, DPS informally gave old textbooks to parochial schools.) This, civil rights activists claimed, was a result of bias: burgeoning white suburban areas got the new school buildings, furniture, and books; black Denver got the castoffs. Frequently, those who complained the most about how black Denver got the short straw from DPS were newcomers to the community. They had attended segregated schools elsewhere and interpreted DPS through that experience.

There was nothing new about such complaints. There had been a class and ethnic divide in DPS from the beginning. In part, this reflected economics. Regardless of how much money the school district received, administrators, teachers, and parents continually complained it was not enough. A prime purpose of the Parent–Teacher Association (PTA) was to help raise additional funds for supplementary programs. Alas, poverty-stricken residents, including European immigrants living in Swansea, Elyria, Globeville, and parts of North and West Denver, could not provide such funds in contrast to economically comfortable parts of town.

Parents sacrificed and saved to assure the success of their children. Time and again, supporters of education insisted that while nice buildings, comfortable furniture, and excellent books and libraries helped, it was the student who had to do the learning. Others faulted teachers. They viewed schools as essentially educational factories. In the same manner that assembly-line workers manufacture commodities, the role of instructors was to pour knowledge into the heads of students. As such, racism and ineptitude on the part of teachers and administrators was why students did worse in black and poor schools than in middle-class white schools.

No group more embraced this outlook than the National Association for the Advancement of Colored People (NAACP). Since at least the 1930s, it had nationally targeted the schools as at the heart of the country's shameful discriminatory system. Particularly in the South, not only were public schools legally segregated, but facilities for black students were overwhelmingly much worse than schools for whites. Nor was this just the case in the South. School segregation was everywhere. Illustrative is that the lead defendant in the landmark 1954 decision of the United States Supreme Court, *Brown* v. *Board of Education*, was the school district in Topeka, Kansas. By having equal integrated schools, the NAACP argued, blacks would truly have equal opportunity to fulfill the promise of American life. The Supreme Court agreed in its *Brown* ruling.

As the civil rights movement started to convulse the country in the 1950s, Mile High African-Americans embraced it. Since the time of the emergence of a Denver branch of the NAACP in 1915, they had protested the discriminatory practices of city hall and elite Denver. The wealthy were blatantly racist. Their leading social organizations, particularly the Denver Club, the Denver Athletic Club, and the Denver Country Club, not only banned blacks from membership, they also did not allow Jews into their ranks. Leading department stores refused to sell to African-Americans or hire them. Premier theaters exiled black patrons into distant balconies.

Nor did DPS escape the growing anger of black Denver. Long subject to discrimination and unfair practices that judged them based on the color of their skin, activists saw everything through a lens of racism. They attacked DPS as being essentially an inequitable system. Not only did it segregate black students, but it hired few black teachers.

Author's collection

Arapahoe School, at the west corner of 18th and Arapahoe streets, was the city's first true schoolhouse. In getting money for it in 1873, the district promised there was to be no racial discrimination in Denver Public Schools.

Besides temples of education, DPS once had small, utilitarian schoolhouses. Pictured is 29th Street School. Located at 29th and Blake streets, it served a blue-collar neighborhood from1879 to 1913.

In 1957, Juanita Gray, a black activist, raised these points when she unsuccessfully sought a place on the school board. By this time, she loudly demanded civil rights and equal educational opportunity for the city's black youngsters. Besides being a vice president of the Mile High PTA who was a saleswoman for a management company, Gray was also a coordinator for the city's Commission on Community Relations (CCR).

Mayor Quigg Newton had created this agency in 1947 as the Mayor's Committee on Human Relations. The goal was for people of good will to come together to calm simmering racial, ethnic, and religious tensions. In 1951, the body became the Commission on Human Relations. It adopted the moniker as the Commission on Community Relations in 1959. Twenty-five years later, the city branded it the Agency for Human Rights and Community Relations. From its beginnings, the committee sought to redress racial and ethnic disparities within the schools.

An Integrated District

At the same time the NAACP and black Denver decried racism and the lack of equal educational opportunity in the schools, the country rediscovered poverty in the 1960s. Not just people of color suffered from inadequate nutrition, ramshackle housing, and a lack of skills, resources, and jobs. So did many whites. Lack of money hurt a sizable percentage of senior citizens. Nor was poverty simply an urban problem. There were massive swathes of people living in straitened circumstances across rural America. Such individuals were particularly lost when redevelopment pushed them out of their homes whereupon they drifted to urban areas. The upheavals of the day forced Washington to recognize widespread pauperism when President Lyndon Johnson declared war on poverty in January 1964.

Schools were on the front line of the battle against poverty. Educators knew that many children came from families where decent lodging and adequate meals were a daily struggle. Already in the 19th century, East Denver School District #1 had programs reaching out to children lacking shelter, clothing, and food. So did some of the other districts that consolidated in 1902 to form District #1 of the City and County of Denver.

During much of the first two-thirds of the 20th century, there were often two different systems within District #1: schools where the bulk of the enrollment came from middle-class backgrounds and those filled with immigrants and blue-collar workers of all races. Those attending North, West, and Manual high schools, for example, openly complained that they received second-rate treatment compared to what they branded the city's two "rich" high schools, East and South.

A racial dimension was part of the divide. Since the opening of the city's first true schoolhouse in 1873, Arapahoe School at the west corner of 18th and Arapahoe streets, the system was ostensibly non-discriminatory. Classes were open to all youngsters from ages six to 21 who lived in East Denver. As the city's population exploded from 4,759 in 1870 to 35,629 in 1880 to 106,713 in 1890, numerous other schools joined Arapahoe School. Given the class stratification of the city, some

Courtesy Chuck Woehl

A few black faces are present in this 1976 picture of male alumni of Bromwell School at Fourth Avenue and Columbine Street shortly before the demolition of a building that had been an integrated school during the first half of the 20th century.

schools primarily educated the children of the poor, including blacks and ethnic immigrants. Others, reflecting their locations, were filled with children of those who had gained economic success.

The sons and daughters of the financial elite were among those in public school classrooms. As East Denver District #1 rapidly grew in the 1870s and 1880s, it supplanted some private programs. At least until the era of school busing beginning in 1969, the offspring of the community's richest denizens frequently attended DPS. Most parents considered District #1's programs superior to those of private or religious schools. Besides emphasizing class ties and the morals of the ruling class, such elite private institutes as Graland, Randell, and Kent schools nurtured struggling students, youngsters who might get lost or fail in the public school system.

After the opening of Arapahoe School, there were no racially exclusive public schools. Given that blacks lived in all parts of town, their children showed up in schoolhouses across the community. Included were the children of black farmers who dwelt in still rural parts of the community. Some black servants lived on Capitol Hill. Their children went to such places as Morey Junior High at 14th Avenue and Clarkson Street and East High. Likewise, some African-Americans showed up in the classrooms of West High School. Into the 1950s, both Cole and Manual were naturally integrated schools, pulling in the sons and daughters of many white blue-collar workers who lived nearby. During the mid-20th century, the two schools also had visible populations of youngsters of Hispanic and Japanese heritage.

Adolph "Pat" Panek (1901–81) was among those welcoming black students to East. He was a foremost coach who led numerous teams to state championships during his tenure between 1936 and 1966. The coach saw there were many outstanding African-American athletes. Wanting them for his teams, he managed to get top athletes to East regardless of the school's attendance border with Manual. In 1982, East named its new gym for Panek.

At one time, there were a sizable number of African-American youngsters at Bromwell School at Fourth Avenue and Columbine Street in what became the elite Cherry Creek North area. Early on, many African-American truck gardeners settled there. So did some blacks who were maids and gardeners for the wealthy living in the nearby Country Club neighborhood. Additionally, a few black professionals dwelt near Bromwell.

Beginning in the 1930s, an increasingly visible Latino population grew in North Denver where their children started to fill the classrooms at places such as Lake Junior High, West 18th Avenue and Lowell Boulevard, and North High School. Within a few years, there were also many Hispanos at West High and Baker Junior High School, West Fifth Avenue and Fox Street.

Despite such ostensible integration, after World War II the racial divide within DPS appeared greater than ever. Given the failure of schools in poverty-stricken neighborhoods to turn out sterling scholars, black parents increasingly complained that the schools in their parts of town were inferior to those in places such as Park Hill and South Denver. DPS, they insisted, had to offer their children equal educational opportunity. Ideally, by receiving it, the next generation would grow up fulfilling the American dream.

Even while a loud section of the African-American community argued as much, black Denver was never a homogenous whole. Some were well satisfied with the schools. There were also parents, both black and white, who seemingly did not care. They did not participate in school activities. Not surprisingly, their children often were poor pupils who suffered disciplinary lapses.

The Culture of Poverty

This led to the debates over poverty during the 1960s. It was not enough simply to declare war on poverty with programs designed to improve housing, transportation, job training, and nutrition for the bottom fifth of the population; backers argued it was also necessary to redress a "culture of poverty." This soon became a highly contentious term. Being poor, sociologists argued, was more than simply lacking money and decent job skills. It was often a way of life. The thrift ethic and actions constantly protecting against setbacks and preparing for tomorrow were frequently absent from those mired in rotten jobs and even worse housing. Such individuals were so beaten down by the system that they did not believe anything the government or uplifters offered them. If anything, they feared all authorities. As such, they were even more in dread of being called into the principal's office for a conference about their children at school than was any errant student. Observing that youngsters growing up in poverty were far more likely to be poor as adults than were their middle-class counterparts, commentators focused on such phenomena, talking about the "cycle of poverty."

Evidence of this was the lack of participation of many poor parents in school activities. Historically, those engulfed in economic problems, especially individuals fearing persecution on account of their race, religion, ethnicity, or immigration status, shied from the limelight and civic involvement. Voter turnout was often quite low in sections filled with people living in poverty. Many low-income residents more feared the government as a coercive force than saw it as an instrument of the populace to help one and all.

Educators realized this. There was not only a culture of poverty, but also a culture of learning. Studies repeatedly showed that the sons and daughters of college graduates did much better in school than the children of poverty-stricken families where nobody had ever graduated from high school. Having books in the home, including having parents who regularly read to and with their children and took them to cultural performances, greatly improved literacy among youngsters. Time and again, pedagogues struggled about how to imbue such values in those who seemingly came from a different world than the middle class for whom the schools were geared. Indeed, some households had no books. The parents never read. Therefore, they never read to and with their children.

Such explanations were nothing but rationalizations. Or so many civil rights advocates argued. "Culture of poverty," they loudly declared, was actually a racist excuse to explain the way the federal government came to turn its back on the War on Poverty when leaders of the Richard Nixon administration called for a "benign neglect" of those who were not part of mainstream, middle-class America. If

In 1878, 24th Street School opened at the south corner of 24th and Walnut streets. Some called it the "School of All Nations" and the "57 Varieties School," since the academy was filled with students of numerous different ethnic, racial, and religious backgrounds. Generally, all were from low-income families. DPS abandoned the building for a new home at 24th and Arapahoe streets in 1919. After fire ravaged the old schoolhouse in 1933, workers brought it down the next year.

anything, talk about the "culture of poverty" was a cloak for the way the schools continued to provide better educations for the rich than the poor.

Both factors, a culture of poverty and the racism of the system, were part and parcel of the school upheavals of the 1960s. At that time, in tune with the War on Poverty, Denver sought to lift up residents who lived in the core of the city. This included urban renewal programs. Those whom they targeted often greatly feared and opposed them. What urban renewal actually meant, they understood, was the destruction of their lodging, stores, neighborhoods, and everyday existence. In contrast, others embraced the War on Poverty. If nothing else, they saw it as a personal opportunity to gain jobs within the system. Before long, many young black and Hispanic activists were intermeshed with Denver Opportunity, the agency charged with conducting the Mile High War on Poverty.

There was a chasm between the crusade of middle-class black Denver for equality of educational opportunity and the War on Poverty. Promoters of better schools for African-Americans paid little heed to the culture of poverty as they decried the racism of DPS. The district, they proclaimed, had to eliminate its existing discriminatory practices. Ideally, having their children go to school with the sons and daughters of the affluent white middle class, backers of the Denver NAACP declared, was the ideal means to guarantee educational success.

There was virtually no link between the Mile High campaign for equal educational opportunity and the Poor People's Campaign of 1968, an effort Martin Luther King was planning at the time of his murder. A prime goal of the Poor People's Campaign was to show that abstract civil rights and equal opportunity were not enough. It was necessary to change a society where a large portion of the population lived in miserable, low-income circumstances. This meant a transformation of the economic system.

While the War on Poverty sputtered away during the 1970s, the push for equal educational opportunity was more urgent than ever. The federal courts agreed. After having ordered the end of school segregation in the South, they turned their attention to the North. In 1969, Denver became the first non-southern city in the country subject to a federal court order mandating integration. The United States Supreme Court emphasized this in 1973 in a landmark case, *Keyes* v. *School District #1*, when it ruled that Denver's de facto school segregation was just as illegal as the outright de jure segregation of the old Confederacy. These upheavals came after Kenneth K. Oberholtzer had retired as superintendent in 1967 after 20 years of being the commanding leader of District #1.

A Note on Sources:

The views of Aaron Gove are in *School Book*, 74–78, 80–85, the social responsibility of the schools, 77, 344, and Americanization programs, 70, 163, 164, 165, 203, 333, 457. The volume emphasizes the patriotic emphasis of DPS, 195, 197, 226, 303, 335, 455–56, 457, 458, and the employment of IQ tests, 12, 332, 333. Lecile B. Hull, *December Festivals* (Denver: DPS, 1954), is a booklet for the schools sponsored by the Anti-Defamation League. It observes not all students were white Christians and that the district must be aware of the different beliefs and backgrounds of its pupils.

A comprehensive volume on the history of black Denver is direly needed. Ronald J. Stephens, La Wanna M. Larson, and the Black American West Museum, *African Americans of Denver* (Charleston, SC: Arcadia, 2008), is a beginning. So is Laura M. Mauck, *Five Points Neighborhood of Denver* (Charleston, SC: Arcadia, 2001), an introduction to that area. I deal with the rise of black Denver in *DIA*, chap. 1. *Curtis Park*, 27, 146–240, 332, 380, focuses on the evolution of Five Points.

Pearson, "Denver Case," 168–71, outlines the changing racial demographics of Denver and the middle-class orientation of the black community. My *DIA*, chap. 2, includes an overview of the busing wars. People interviewed in the video by Michael Bird, *A Sense of Self: Growing up in Five Points* (n.p.: Birdhaus Media, 2015), stress the excellent nature of neighborhood schools. They argue instructors cared greatly about pupils and instilled them with discipline taught them the necessity of hard work. Among those speaking out in the video was Terry Nelson. She expanded on her remarks, especially the outstanding character of pre-busing Manual High School, in a conversation on August 28, 2019. Charline Porter echoed her on September 8, 2019, recalling she always attended integrated schools in the pre-busing era. Porter, a fourth-generation Denverite, emphasized the split between settled families and newcomers to black Denver in the way they viewed the schools.

DPL has an eight-box holding of the records of the Commission on Community Relations, WH 903. The introduction to the collection traces the origins and evolution of the agency. Minoru Yasui headed the organization from 1967 to 1983. His papers, including a good deal of materials from the agency, are at the Auraria Archives.

Colorado: The Superstar State (Baton Rouge: Moran Publishing Company, 1979), 33–34, features the accomplishments of Pat Panek. *SB*, October 3, 1966, p. 20, observed his retirement. *SN*, May 12, 1982, p. 65, told of East's naming the gym for him. Thomas Hornsby Ferril, *I Hate Thursday* (New York: Harper & Brothers, 1946), 231, reflected on the relations between East and Manual and the way East recruited black athletes from the Manual attendance area. East historian Richard Nelson discussed that point during a chat on April 17, 2019. He mentions Panek in *Flights of Angels* (Denver: East High School, 2004), 93–94, 112.

Michael Harrington, *The Other America* (New York: Penguin, 1962), is the classic statement about the widespread presence of poverty in the United States during the early 1960s. He deals with the culture of poverty, 91, 99–100, 105–10. Julian E. Zelizer, *The Fierce Urgency of Now: Lyndon Johnson, Congress, and the Battle for the Great Society* (New York: Penguin, 2015), is an overview of the origins of the War on Poverty and how it fit into the social programs of the 1960s. Chalkbeat, October 4, 2019, reported the continuing correlation between economic affluence and school success. *WW*, January 22, 2020, echoed the finding.

Orfield, *Must We Bus?* 61, 88, stresses the class dimension of school integration. He cites Frederick Mosteller and Daniel P. Moynihan, eds., *On Equality of Educational Opportunity* (New York: Random House, 1972), a volume dealing with this crucial part of debates over schools. Clinton B. Allison, ed., *Without Consensus: Issues in American Education* (Boston: Allyn and Bacon, 1973), 53–77, focuses on the connection between class and educational success. Linsey McGoey, *No Such Thing as a Free Gift: The Gates Foundation and the Price of Philanthropy* (London: Verso, 2015), 124, 129, glances at the evolving discussions about the links between poverty and poor educational performance. Veteran DPS teacher Anna Noble observed how parental involvement and PTA donations accentuate the class divisions between schools, *DP*, January 30, 2020, p. 8C YourHub.

A work remains to be written about the War on Poverty and the Great Society in Denver. I touch on the subjects in *DIA*, 131, 145, 147, 185, *North Side Story*, 86, 112, 195, 249, 333, *West Side*, 4, 192, 219, 224, 228, 231, 238, 242, 244, 245, 248, 270, 278, 312, 370, 371, 372, and *Civic Center*, 289. *DP*, October 19, 1969, pp. 6–7 Contemporary, focused on DPS efforts to fight poverty.

Chapter Two

A New Era

When Denver Public Schools opened for classes in September 1967, the district had a new superintendent. That April, the school board had signed Robert D. Gilberts to a five-year contract to lead the system. He replaced the retiring Kenneth K. Oberholtzer who had been in charge of the schools since 1947.

Oberholtzer had been a commanding administrator. There was never any question that he made crucial decisions concerning DPS ranging from curriculum to building plans to shaping attendance zones. The school board overwhelmingly supported him. Members repeatedly stated they had not been elected to run the schools; they were in office to see that the schools were well run. While now and then a member questioned Oberholtzer's specific decisions, those on the board readily agreed DPS was a top-notch, well-administered system under an outstanding pedagogue.

A native of Carbon, Indiana, born on December 22, 1903, Oberholtzer graduated from high school in Tulsa in 1920 where his father, Edison E. Oberholtzer (1880–1954), was superintendent of schools from 1913 to 1923. The senior Oberholtzer next headed the Houston school district from 1923 until his retirement in 1950. Along the way, Edison Oberholtzer was the founding president of the University of Houston in 1927, an academy which was initially part of the Houston school district.

Oberholtzer junior followed his father to Texas after earning his bachelor's degree from the University of Illinois. The young man's first teaching post was in Bellville, Texas. He quickly emerged as a principal and then superintendent. In 1926, he took charge of the schools of El Campo, Texas. The future DPS leader headed the Lubbock school system from 1934 to 1937. The educator then served as superintendent of schools in Long Beach, California, a community of 200,000 outside of Los Angeles. During World War II, Oberholtzer was a lieutenant colonel, helping the Army select military instructors and school materials. On occasion, some referred to him as "The Silver Fox."

Back in 1928, Oberholtzer gained a master's in education from Texas A&M. He took the post in Long Beach the same year he earned a doctorate from Columbia Teachers College, writing about "American Agricultural Problems in the Social Studies" as his dissertation. Jesse Newlon, DPS superintendent from 1920 to 1927, was his advisor. By this time, Newlon was a central part

Birlauft & Steen

Kenneth K. Oberholtzer was DPS superintendent from 1947 to 1967.

of what was known as the Columbia Teachers College Ring. Teachers College at Columbia University in New York City was then the country's foremost institution of higher learning that focused on elementary and secondary education. The leaders of Teachers College consciously sought to place graduates as superintendents across the country. Not only was Newlon an alumnus of Teachers College, but so were his successors as superintendent, Archie Threlkeld (1927–37), Alexander Stoddard (1937–39), and Charles Greene (1939–47). Oberholtzer's father had worked closely with Newlon in various enterprises, particularly in the National Education Association (NEA).

DPS brought in Oberholtzer to revive the system. District #1 had been in something of a rut since the early 1930s. The Depression had severely impacted it. In the face of the financial collapse, DPS undertook no new construction while it scraped to pay off its huge bonded indebtedness. Superintendent Charles Greene did little to provide leadership during his eight years in office when the schools were more or less stagnant.

Oberholtzer quickly took charge. He established close personal connections with members of the board of education. The governing body consisted of seven members. Voters selected them for staggered six-year terms on the first Monday of May in odd-numbered years.

The superintendent courted leaders of the PTA. The Columbia graduate also engaged in a wide-ranging civic activism. He served on the boards of the Denver Art Museum, University of Denver, and the Denver Council of Churches. Personally, he was a 33rd-degree Mason and a Rotarian. Numerous colleges and civic associations bestowed honors on him. In 1950, *Time* put Oberholtzer on its cover as the model educator of a big city school system.

As had his predecessors, Oberholtzer subjected students to an endless testing regimen. Generally, the results were excellent. Testing, however, was not the defining mark of the schools. Time and again, pedagogues explained that tests were essentially measuring devices. They showed how well students had learned.

As such, they were simply a tool. Besides academics, the district emphasized the physical well-being of students with health examinations. It additionally called for an informal moral education whereby graduates emerged as the responsible citizens of the next generation.

The superintendent had an outstanding publicity machine. The city's two daily newspapers, the *Denver Post* and the *Rocky Mountain News*, regularly featured Oberholtzer's achievements, praising him as a foremost national educator. On occasion, Oberholtzer was on network television as a champion of public schools. He was highly visible. Almost every evening he was at a reception, a school dedication, a PTA meeting, or a gathering of a club or board with which he was affiliated. As such, concerned citizens could approach him and try to convince him of their views. They rarely got him to change his mind.

In 1950, Oberholtzer reached out to the public, launching a triennial public opinion survey, *Denver Looks at Its Schools*. It showed the citizenry firmly backed Oberholtzer's administration. He accentuated the performance of the schools with another survey published every three years or so, *Denver Public Schools Look at Themselves*. The booklet emphasized the excellent scores DPS students achieved on standardized tests. Given Oberholtzer's wide involvement in national educational groups, including a term as the president of the American Association of School Administrators, generally DPS had a pristine reputation across the country.

On two occasions, Oberholtzer passed on the chance to become United States Commissioner of Education, an office that was the forerunner of Secretary of Education. He also said no to an offer to take charge of the Chicago Public Schools. In June 1963, DPS affirmed its commitment to Oberholtzer's leadership when it extended his contract from 1964 to July 31, 1967. At that time, it hiked his salary

Photo by Phil Goodstein

Flat-roofed buildings were a hallmark of many of the schools DPS erected in the 1950s under Superintendent Kenneth K. Oberholtzer. Shown is Godsman, 2120 West Arkansas Avenue, which held its first classes in 1958.

from $27,400 to $29,500. Soon he was receiving $32,500. As such, he was the highest paid public official in the state.

The *Post* and *News* both expressed concern when Oberholtzer's contract neared its expiration. The superintendent was set to turn 65 in December 1968, a seemingly mandatory retirement date. Backers loudly expressed hope he could stay on with the district past his 65th birthday. He said no to the suggestion in December 1966 when he announced he was retiring at the end of the schoolyear. After stepping down, Oberholtzer relocated to Danville, California. Later, he dwelt in Walnut Creek, California, where he died on December 17, 1993, days before his 90th birthday on December 17, 1993. Florence Craver, whom he had married October 22, 1928, survived him. She saw that he was buried in Tulsa.

Author's collection

In promoting bond issues in 1948, 1952, and 1955, DPS stressed that the city's aggressive annexation policies made it urgent to build schoolhouses to serve rapidly growing parts of the city. School Review *was a DPS paper informing the public of the district's plans and achievements. It appeared sporadically from 1919 into the 1970s. This issue dates from 1955.*

Among Oberholtzer's achievements was an aggressive building program. On October 11, 1948, he convinced taxpayers to authorize a $21 million bond issue. New construction was direly needed. Not only were many of the city's schoolhouses old, dating from the 19th century, but Denver had started aggressively annexing real estate in 1941. New sections of the city rapidly filled in after World War II. The city did not require developers benefiting from burgeoning growth to set aside land for schools and help pay for the buildings to educate the children of settlers. Instead, DPS accepted the obligation. The district was blunt about this. It told voters they had to say yes to the bond issue because "Schools Must Follow the Moving Vans."

Denver's population soared during and after World War II. By 1960, it was home to 493,887 dwellers. A decade later, the census bureau counted 514,678 residents. The rapid growth especially impacted DPS.

In many instances, no sooner were new schools open than they were packed to capacity. The district soon needed more money for expansions and additional schools. Voters readily authorized a $30 million bond on October 6, 1952. A $28.5 million bond followed on December 6, 1955. Ideally, it was to provide enough space to last the growing district for another decade. The bond issues included funds to replace, expand, or remodel some of the 19th-century schoolhouses such as Gilpin, opened in 1881 at 29th and Stout streets, Mitchell, which occupied a new home in 1898–99 at 32nd Avenue (Martin Luther King Boulevard) and Lafayette Street, and Columbine, dating from 1893 at 28th Avenue and Columbine Street.

The 1955 bond issue additionally provided sums to build three new high schools: George Washington at 655 South Monaco Street Parkway, Thomas Jefferson at 3950 South Holly Street, and Abraham Lincoln at 2285 South Federal Boulevard. All opened in 1960. Additionally, there were new junior highs: Merrill, 1561 South Monroe Street, opened in 1952; Kepner, 911 South Hazel Court, dated from 1953; Hill, 451 Clermont Street, held its first classes in 1956; Kunsmiller, 2250 South Quitman Street, built in 1957; and Rishel, 451 South Tejon Street, opening in 1959. As with the elementary schools, they had attendance borders where, ideally, students could walk to them.

When Oberholtzer arrived in 1947, enrollment was at 48,171. The number had been flat since 1932 when DPS had a membership of 47,107. By the time he left, there were 96,435 students in the schools. In addition to new buildings, there were numerous portable units around schoolhouses. These were large, trailer-like facilities that usually had two classrooms. The district moved them around as demand dictated.

Even this was not enough. As baby boomers descended on the schools, some buildings were on double sessions. This referred to having two separate school sessions during the day. Morning classes lasted from about 7:00 AM to noon. The afternoon classes stretched from shortly after noon to past 5:00 PM. Overcrowding was a fact of life. Students endlessly had to wait in line, especially for lunch. They also had to rush constantly around junior highs and high schools to get from one room to another during passing periods in extremely crowded hallways.

A Hierarchical Administration

Oberholtzer ran an extremely hierarchical administration. Many teachers cowered in fear of him and his assistants. Reflecting the views of the superintendent's office developed by the Columbia Teachers College Ring, he operated on the premise that the superior was always right. In the 1950s, deputy superintendent Roy Hindermann, assisted by assistant superintendent Peter Holm, dealt with the everyday bureaucracy of the district and the complaints and concerns of instructors. Graham Miller, who had been with DPS since 1938, was assistant superintendent for business. He went on sick leave in 1962. Six months later he retired. Edgar Olander replaced him. By this time, Charles Armstrong was assistant superintendent of planning—Holm had retired at age 65 in 1960 a few weeks before his death.

Part of a family that had been part of DPS since the early 20th century, Armstrong was once an instructor at Grant Junior High (South Pearl Street and

GP

As superintendent, Kenneth K. Oberholtzer, bottom right, ran a tight, hierarchical administration. Among his key aides was assistant superintendent Peter Holm, left. LeRoy Fisher, the secretary of the school board, is second from the left, next to Kenneth R. Gher, the assistant secretary, in this shot dating from the late 1950s.

Mexico Avenue), before teaching at South. After service as an officer during World War II, Armstrong was in the front office as a teacher supervisor. Before long, he was in charge of building planning. As such, he oversaw much of the district's massive construction program of the 1950s. In particular, he was the key figure coordinating the erection of Thomas Jefferson, George Washington, and Abraham Lincoln high schools. Eventually, members of the Armstrong family taught in the district for more than 100 years. They were interrelated to the Lort family, another clan producing generations of DPS teachers, administrators, and architects.

Now and then, Oberholtzer appeared unsure of policy. In such instances, he deferred decisions to the board. In most cases, it listened to him. Administrative reports to the board usually had recommendations about what choice members should make.

To encourage academically talented youths, Oberholtzer saw that DPS had a tracking system whereby bright students were placed in accelerated classes. This culminated in the senior year of high school when qualified students were allowed to take college-level Advanced Placement courses. To encourage top academic performers, high schools awarded pupils in accelerated and college courses extra points on their grades. An "A" in them was worth 5.2 points on a scale of four; a "B" was 3.9. Hence, while 4.0 was a straight-A average, outstanding students often had a grade-point average of more than 4.5.

The tracking system was relatively inflexible. Once a student was in a specific track, he usually remained in it. While teachers sometimes placed an advanced student back in regular classes if he failed to do the work in the accelerated courses, it was quite rare for a pupil whom instructors and counselors had branded "average" to rise to the accelerated courses. Whereas 40 percent of the white students in the district took at least one course in the advanced track, only 11.5 percent of the black students did so. A count showed about 7 percent of Hispanos were in the advanced track. In part, this reflected the way the district relied on culturally biased IQ tests in determining the placement of students.

Members of the black community who were concerned about schools realized that not all African-Americans grew up in a culture valuing learning and scholarship. At times, bright youngsters of color deliberately did not speak up in class, fearful of being mocked by their fellows as know-it-alls. Other black students were sure the system was automatically rigged against them. As such, they had no desire to participate in it.

The district reached out to students with learning difficulties. In addition to special education programs for youngsters with physical and mental problems, it placed those having trouble with coursework in modified sections. To show that all graduates had a basic command of the curriculum, in 1960 Oberholtzer introduced the Proficiency and Review (P&R) test. A student had to pass it to gain his diploma.

The P&R consisted of four parts, emphasizing English, basic arithmetic, spelling, and reading comprehension. Generally, it was geared to a sixth grade level. By the 1970s, the district started giving it to those in ninth grade. Students who failed had repeated opportunities to retake the test while the schools offered them tutoring. Should they pass some, but not all of the parts, they did not have to repeat the sections they had successfully completed. Sporadically, amidst scares that the schools were failing society, the board increased the rigor of the test. Then, when complaints about dropouts came to the fore, DPS tended to make it easier for students to pass it. Rumors were heard that some principals opened test packages, doctoring the results, before the tests were sent to the grading center.

By the time they ended their senior year, 98 percent of students had mastered the P&R. Those who failed to do so simply received a completion certificate rather than a diploma. Many pupils who had failed P&R dropped out before 12th grade.

In addition to working to get dropouts back into school, the district stressed adult education, particularly at Emily Griffith Opportunity School at 1250 Welton Street. Among its many programs, Opportunity School was the home of the district's television station, Channel Six, KRMA. DPS broadcast instructional classes on it geared to elementary students. Additionally, the station aired many general educational programs. The call letters meant "Knowledge for the Rocky Mountain Area."

Besides the regular schoolday, District #1 had classes in the evenings and a summer school. Buildings were frequently open after hours for recreation programs serving the entire community. The district collaborated with the city to operate summer recreation programs at selected elementaries and park playgrounds.

Photo by Phil Goodstein

Hyde Park School, 3620 Franklin Street, opened in 1888. Within a few years, it had a sizable number of black students. DPS renamed the building in 1932 for veteran principal George W. Wyatt.

A Jim Crow World

By the time he was in high school in Tulsa, Oberholtzer lived in the world of Jim Crow. In 1921, a year after he received his diploma, an extremely violent riot ripped Tulsa. A well-armed and coordinated white mob destroyed most of the African-American business section of the community, possibly killing more than 100 blacks. Apparently, the event never registered on the young man. On the contrary, Oberholtzer accepted the Jim Crow policies of the Texas schools where he taught and worked as an administrator after getting his bachelor's degree. For the most part, he unquestioningly nurtured a world of racial separation.

Even at that, in Denver Oberholtzer joined a premier congregation advocating racial brotherhood, Montview Boulevard Presbyterian Church at Montview Boulevard and Dahlia Street in the heart of Park Hill. But Oberholtzer did not stand out in its initiatives. On the contrary, he appeared unconsciously to accept the southern mores of his youth. This haunted his decisions as the head of DPS. Among his legacies was leaving the district with an extremely disjointed, explosive racial situation.

In 1868, responding to protests from racists, East Denver School District #1, the entity providing education for children living to the east of Cherry Creek, kicked children of color out of its classrooms. Working with Zion Baptist and Shorter Methodist, the city's two pioneer African-American churches, DPS created a Jim Crow academy for black students. The school lasted five years. Its demise stemmed from black protests and voting clout. In particular, in 1873 the district needed more money to open Arapahoe School. Whites were deeply divided on authorizing additional funds. To push through the tax hike, backers asked blacks to vote for the measure. African-Americans made it clear they would endorse school taxes only if there was no racial discrimination at the promised new schoolhouse.

Henceforth, there was no official discrimination against black students. Not surprisingly, they primarily attended schools close to the African-American pockets of Denver. An 1890 census counted 336 black boys and girls in East Denver District #1, a little more than 3 percent of the total enrollment. The survey showed there were 88 African-Americans at 24th Street School (Crofton) then at 24th and Walnut streets, 39 at Ebert when it was near 20th Avenue and Logan Street, 49 at Whittier, close to 24th Avenue and Marion Street, and 46 at Hyde Park (Wyatt), 3620 Franklin Street. Given that there was no official Jim Crow in the city and blacks lived in many different parts of the community, here and there blacks showed up in small numbers in schools throughout the district.

Even so, there was always something of a racial edge in DPS. This especially stood out after World War I. Particularly mealy-mouthed was Jesse Newlon, superintendent from 1920 to 1927. He was a personification of Progressive Education, a popular trend which argued schools had to prepare students for life as active, informed citizens of a democracy.

Newlon served when the Ku Klux Klan was riding high in the city. A self-styled liberal Republican, the superintendent had problems with the group. In

Author's collection

In the 1920s, Superintendent Jesse Newlon and the KKK agreed there must be an American flag in every classroom, showing the district's commitment to patriotism. This is from the old Bryant School at the northeast corner of West 36th Avenue and Shoshone Street.

correspondence, he called for a community mobilization to defeat it across the country. Locally, however, he failed to speak out against the KKK. He was particularly hurt when its two candidates won seats on the school board in 1925 opposed to the good old boys of 17th Street whom he preferred.

Even so, Newlon and the Klan were at one in insisting schools had to be bastions of Americanism. Included was placing an American flag in every classroom. Students began the day by reciting the Pledge of Allegiance. The schools stressed flag ceremonies, treating Old Glory as a veritable holy icon.

The Klan heralded such policies and Newlon. It highlighted his speech of September 2, 1924, delivered to teachers at the beginning of the schoolyear. To assure "civic and moral training," the pedagogue insisted that teachers stress ethics. Not abstract learning, but the spiritual welfare of students was the district's foremost concern. Neither Newlon nor the Klan, showed much ethical concern when it came to treating black students as full and equal members of the community.

In particular, on March 27, 1924, the superintendent blatantly violated the letter and the spirit of the Colorado Constitution when he ordered principals to segregate all school social functions based on race. As such, the patriotic Newlon ignored the mandates of the state's basic document prohibiting any racial discrimination. He acted in response to tensions at Morey Junior High and Manual High. In particular, he banned an African-American girl from enrolling in a swimming class at Morey. The order further was a means of excluding young black women from social functions at Manual. African-Americans responded with outrage, suing the district. The Denver District Court upheld the superintendent. In 1927, the Colorado Supreme Court, citing constitutional protections, ordered DPS to cease and desist from such practices.

This was about the time Columbia Teachers College recruited Newlon to New York to oversee its model school. There he once more projected himself on the cutting edge of liberalism and tolerance. He gained acclaim in 1935 for his nationally broadcast address to the summer convention of the National Education Association. There Newlon condemned the passivity of teachers in Germany for readily collaborating with the Nazis. Even at that, he never condemned racism within DPS nor within the NEA, of which he served as president in 1924–25.

Black Denver was highly conscious of Newlon's policies. Long subjected to racism, many African-Americans saw it everywhere. They also agreed with white Denver after World War II: everything old was automatically bad. In the years after the return of peace, a new generation under Mayor Quigg Newton (1947–55) committed itself to rebuilding Denver on the basis of someplace else. DPS embraced the outlook, announcing the necessity of replacing its 19th-century buildings. Generally, civil rights activists heralded this initiative, observing that the oldest schoolhouses were mostly in black neighborhoods.

Many of the city's early school buildings were definitely showing their age. Heating systems were not always efficient while the acoustics were terrible in some classrooms. Not until after World War II did all buildings have modern electric lights. The structures often lacked gymnasiums, auditoriums, and lunchrooms.

Harry McWhirter Barrett
Elementary School

Barrett School opened in 1960 at the northeast corner of 29th Avenue and Jackson Street. Eventually, the United States Supreme Court ruled its erection and attendance borders were the epitome of the Jim Crow policies practiced in DPS under Superintendent Kenneth K. Oberholtzer.

As a way of showing it was committed to equal educational opportunity, in 1951 the district opened a new home for Gilpin School at 30th and California streets. Manual students occupied a replacement home at 28th Avenue and Gilpin Street in 1953. Major additions transformed Mitchell (1958 and 1964), Whittier (1964), Columbine (1959 and 1961), Wyatt (1957), and Harrington (1950 and 1963) into modern structures.

Most of all, District #1 erected a new building for children living north of City Park to the west of Colorado Boulevard, Harry M. Barrett School, at the northeast corner of 29th Avenue and Jackson Street. It opened in 1960, causing mass outrage among many aspiring middle-class African-Americans. They vehemently protested in 1958 when the district committed itself to the schoolhouse that remembered a former principal of East High.

Prior to the opening of Barrett, children living in the area had the option of attending either the mostly white, affluent Park Hill School, at 19th Avenue and Elm Street, or the seemingly old, much poorer and increasingly black Columbine School at 28th Avenue and Columbine Street. Many African-Americans had preferred their children ride the bus to Park Hill. They saw Barrett as a Jim Crow academy to keep African-Americans out of that distinguished institute. Among those stating as much was Rachel Noel. Her protests personified the massive black unease with DPS.

A Note on Sources:

Back in the 1990s, former congressman and CU regent Byron Johnson emphasized that the role of board members is not to run a district, but to assure it is properly run. *School Book*, esp. 340–44, 349–61, 463–64, reviews Kenneth Oberholtzer's years as superintendent. Among the prime sources I drew upon was Patricia Ann Shikes, "Three Denver School Superintendents" (Ph.D. dissertation, DU, 1987), 216–309. Peggy Lynn Schwartzkopf, "Collective Bargaining in Denver Public

Education: A Historical Perspective from 1946 to 1976" (Ph.D. dissertation, UCD, 1993), 223–25, emphasizes Oberholtzer's efficiency and ability to project himself as the all-encompassing administrator. She calls him "The Silver Fox," 3. *RMN*, June 20, 1963, reported the renewal of Oberholtzer's contract.

School Book, 90, 353, 354, 355, 358, glances at Peter Holm, and Roy Hindermann, 352–53, 354, 355, 358, 437. On August 7, 2019, Phil Lutz, the son-in-law of Charles Armstrong, recalled the assistant superintendent. Armstrong's daughter, Janet Lutz, chatted about the educator and the Armstrong family's DPS links on September 7, 2019.

In an interview in *Our Neighborhood Schools*, part of a four-disk video by Dick Alweis, *Rebels Remembered* (n.p.: Ruth Denny producer, 2000, 2011), retired DPS Superintendent Evie Dennis emphasized that some black children did not want to be known as being smart. Anna Jo Haynes, her daughter Happy Haynes, and others interviewed in the program likewise observed how many black youngsters were afraid of being known as scholars, fearful of being mocked by their peers. The video additionally reports the alienation and lack of engagement of some black students.

On January 9, 2018, Jimi O'Connor discussed the evolution of the P&R examination and the impact of busing on the system's testing policies. I mention the origins of P&R in *School Book*, 350–52.

Randy Krehbiel, *Tulsa, 1921* (Norman: University of Oklahoma Press, 2019), discusses the destructive riot in Tulsa the year after Oberholtzer graduated from high school there. Wilber Fiske Stone, *History of Colorado* (Chicago: S. J. Clarke Publishing 1918), 1:588–89, mentions the East Denver District #1 Jim Crow school for blacks. Marian Talmadge and Iris Gilmore, *Barney Ford, Black Baron* (New York: Dodd, Mead, 1973), 192–93, touches on the fights over school integration and links them to the financing of Arapahoe School.

Samuel James Mathieson, "A History of the Public Schools in Colorado, 1859–1880" (Ed.D. dissertation, DU, 1963), 191–92, stresses how whites, led by former territorial Governor John Evans, insisted on the necessity of having a unitary school district. The 1890 *DPS Report*, 44, looks at black enrollment. *Jones* v. *Newlon*, 253 P 386, discusses the racist practices in DPS stemming from the decisions of Superintendent Jesse Newlon. Tom Romero looked at that case in reviewing the origins and legacy of the Denver school busing litigation in *DU Law Review*, 90:5 (October 2013), 1025.

School Book, examines the origins, expansions, and replacements of Whittier, 63–65, 304–06; Gilpin, 62, 304–05, 400; Mitchell, 64, 65, 400, 415, 451; Wyatt, 374, 384, 400; Columbine, 114–15, 257, 400; and Manual, 400–02. The study deals with Barrett, 381, 398.

Chapter Three

Rachel Noel

B orn Rachel Louise Bassette on January 15, 1918, in Hampton, Virginia, Rachel Noel was the daughter of a lawyer and a teacher. Her parents raised her with the expectation that she was going to be a success and contribute to the community. After gaining her bachelor's with a teaching degree from Hampton Institute, a historic black college in her home town, she earned a master's in sociology from Fisk University, a prestigious African-American school in Nashville, Tennessee. She came to Denver with her husband, physician Edmond Noel, in November 1949. After World War II service, he had completed his residency in St. Louis. The couple moved to Denver, seeing it as a city of opportunity. He joined the staff of the newly opened Rose Hospital. Subsequently, he operated a clinic at 28th Avenue and Race Street. Edmond and Rachel Noel fit in with a well-educated African-American professional class. It, along with a business elite, had provided direction for black Denver since the 19th century. Like Edmond Noel, many black leaders were veterans.

Edmond and Rachel Noel were soon active in a variety of community pursuits. After dwelling at 2253 Vine Street, in 1958 the couple erected their dream house at 2601 Adams Street, directly north of the City Park Golf Course. This became a favored location for the black professional class. Even at that, the family moved there only after a white seller had disposed of the lot to the light-skinned African-American city councilman Elvin Caldwell, a man the landowner thought was white. Previously, the Noels had wanted to move to Monaco Street Parkway. The city's informal Jim Crow system made that impossible. On occupying their new home, the Noels were the first black family on the block.

Taking advantage of the option of having their children go to Park Hill School rather than Columbine School, the couple sent their son, Edmond Jr. "Buddy," and daughter, Angela "Angie," to Park Hill. Buddy especially enjoyed riding the bus as an adventure. It gave him a chance to get to know others on the bus. At times, waiting for the bus after school saw him engage in mischief.

The youngster observed Park Hill School was much better supplied than Wyman School, at 16th Avenue and Williams Street, where he had previously attended classes. Most of all, Buddy found his sixth grade teacher at Park Hill, Beulah Glesner, the best instructor he encountered in his life. She was a veteran of the district who had come to DPS from her home state of North Dakota. In 1958, she was among the inaugural winners of the teacher of the year award from the newly established Denver Teacher Award Foundation.

Drawing by Daniel Lowenstein

Rachel Noel gained election to the school board in 1965. The first black on the body, she was in the vanguard of pushing school integration.

As more black children rode the bus to Park Hill School, the academy acted to segregate them. On getting off the bus, they were often herded to the auditorium until the start of classes. At the end of the school day, they likewise went to the auditorium until they got on the bus. Some stayed in their homerooms after classes until the bus bell sounded.

Early on, Rachel Noel was involved with the Commission on Community Relations, the city agency working to check discrimination and promote racial understanding. She worked closely with the man who became the head of the commission, Minoru Yasui, with the goal of bringing people together. If they got to know each other personally, Noel was sure that members of different races could live together in harmony. Repeatedly, she stressed that school integration was not a panacea. It was simply a most practical step the community could take to ease tensions and erase the country's heritage of slavery and discrimination.

Noel projected a fundamental humanity. She drew on her genteel heritage as a black from Virginia who had the obligation to treat one and all with respect while serving the community. At times, Noel became frustrated by the endless opposition she encountered.

As a young mother, Rachel Noel especially stressed education. She came to head the health committee of the Colorado PTA. Additionally, she avidly supported the Girl Scouts. A major lament of her youth was that she had not been able to join the Girl Scouts because there was no chapter for blacks where she had grown up. In college, Noel involved herself with the Girl Scouts when she worked at the Southwest Settlement House in Washington, D.C. (Settlement houses were a continuing legacy of the Progressive Era of before World War I. At that time, affluent young men and women went to poverty-stricken areas with the goal of

GP

As controversies about busing roiled Denver, the PTA was a naturally integrated
body. Here is its executive board in 1962–63.

helping locals improve their lives through uplift efforts, living at community centers
that were known as settlement houses.) In the process, Noel promoted the Girl
Scouts in a poor black section of Washington. In Denver, after leading a group
of Brownies and Girl Scout Troop 509, she emerged as the vice president of the
Mile Hi Council of the Girl Scouts. For a while she was on the national council
of the Girl Scouts.

The Denver Classroom Teachers Association (DCTA), the Mile High affiliate of
both the Colorado Education Association and the National Education Association,
honored Noel in 1963 with its Eddy Award, a citation given "for dedicated service to
the cause of education." This was illustrative of the woman's widespread outreach
on numerous school initiatives. At that time, the DCTA was more a professional
group heralding the cooperation between teachers, the administration, and the
community than the teachers union it soon became.

Illustrative of Noel's educational commitment was her role in forming the
Community Study Hall Association in October 1964. This was a volunteer effort.
The goal was to provide safe, quiet, friendly places where students, particularly
those in grades four, five, and six, could go to do homework in the evening, receiving
refreshments and tutoring assistance. Study halls were often in churches close to
schools. Ideally, the program got youngsters out of loud, crowded homes with
blaring televisions.

Before long, the Study Hall Association was part of DPS. The initiative
urged high school students to volunteer as tutors. During the 1970s, the program

operated out of the Irving Street Center at 1521 Irving Street in the old Cheltenham School. A predecessor of the effort in the 1950s had specially sought to reach out to Spanish-American youngsters.

Along with other middle-class blacks who were sure that excellent education was the key to lifelong success, Noel was outraged by the construction of Barrett School, seeing it as a means of segregating black pupils there while keeping Park Hill a white school. Even at that, she was the inaugural chairwoman of the Barrett School advisory committee, an informal body composed of the principal, teachers, and parents. Immediately, she expressed concern that her fifth-grade daughter Angie was getting the same lessons at Barrett that she had received as a fourth grader at Park Hill the previous year.

In response to the perceived segregation embodied by Barrett School, Noel took the lead in demanding equality of educational opportunity in DPS. The system, she loudly stated, must not open any more racially segregated academies. By the early 1960s, she was the foremost African-American advocate of ending DPS's informal Jim Crow system. If black and white children went to school together, she repeatedly declared, the world would become a better place. This was in tune with the credo of champions of integration everyplace: by attending classes with each other, youngsters of different backgrounds would grasp diversity and judge people based on who they are rather than their race, religion, or ethnicity.

With All Deliberate Speed

Noel attacked the Jim Crow practices in DPS right as the Civil Rights Revolution was sweeping the country. Besides a branch of the NAACP that had functioned since 1915, the Congress of Racial Equality (CORE) had recently re-established a Mile High presence. Unlike the NAACP, which primarily depended on the courts and political system in redressing discrimination, CORE often engaged in direct action such as militant picket lines and civil disobedience to keep the racist system from operating as usual.

CORE sometimes questioned the entire social-political order that made endemic and legal racism possible. Its national head, James Farmer, was once a member of the Socialist Party who later was part of the Richard Nixon administration. In contrast, in many ways, the NAACP was a champion of the establishment. The nation's oldest and largest civil rights organization, it aimed for complete equality regardless of race or ethnicity. Unlike black radicals, who constantly lampooned the system as the embodiment of racism that viciously exploited poor African-American workers and farmers, the NAACP primarily desired success within the economic order. To make sure black youngsters were able to achieve their full potential, it demanded an equal school system.

Since the 1930s, through its Legal Defense and Educational Fund, usually simply known as the Legal Defense Fund (LDF), the NAACP had targeted discrimination in education as the most legally vulnerable part of Jim Crow. Its greatest victory came in 1954 when its lawyers convinced the Supreme Court to overturn the doctrine of separate but equal in the landmark *Brown* v. *Board of Education* case. Henceforth,

A few white faces showed up in early Barrett School. This shot is from the school's dedication booklet in 1961.

the court ordered, school authorities must proceed with "all deliberate speed" to desegregate school systems. It never adequately defined precisely what this meant.

The *Brown* case centered on racist practices in Topeka, Kansas. The presence of discrimination there was indicative. Jim Crow was not limited to the South. It was everywhere. As the Civil Rights Revolution exploded, the demand for equal schooling was a prime plank of those wishing to destroy a long-entrenched racist order.

In crusading for equal educational opportunity, the NAACP and other voices of integration paid little heed to educational reformers of the 1960s who argued that the public school system was a dysfunctional machine that ground down students and destroyed individualism and a love of learning. On the contrary, the NAACP and advocates of equal educational opportunity took the schools at surface appearance: they were preparing youngsters for successful careers. The reason blacks trailed behind in educational achievement was because districts had systematically starved schools in African-American communities. The solution was the complete equality of schools in all districts. Federal court judges, citing the *Brown* precedent, repeatedly affirmed this was the law of the land.

This especially hit home in Denver. During the entire controversy over school integration, both advocates and opponents of busing to achieve equal educational opportunity agreed about the existing nature of the school system. They not only accepted it, but they paid no heed to the correlation between success in school and family background and affluence. People like Noel were sure DPS offered white children outstanding educations. More than anything, she and her cohorts insisted the district must quit discriminating against blacks and offer African-American children the same fine programs it provided to whites.

Both the NAACP and CORE demanded more blacks in elected and appointed political offices. They argued this was both a sign of recognition and a way by which people of color could assure the government actually assisted all citizens rather than being a discriminatory, oppressive force against blacks and others who were not white. A way to begin, especially vis-à-vis Denver Public Schools, was putting Rachel Noel on the school board.

A Glance at the School Board

This was the situation when board member Frank Traylor died on September 16, 1963. The six surviving members of the agency were responsible for naming the replacement. They deeply divided over whom they should appoint. This reflected the changing nature of the board.

In 1917, at the behest of the Chamber of Commerce, with the full support of the PTA, the legislature expanded the board of District #1 from five to seven members. (The school district is a county agency. As such, it is under the purview of the state whereby the legislature has the power to determine the size of the school board and the date of elections.)

In part, the Chamber acted to pack the body against three of the existing five members who opposed business as usual. The expansion of the board worked. Soon backers of the Chamber dominated the agency, often consisting of all seven members. Into the 1950s, the Chamber usually caucused with the PTA and other civic groups prior to board elections. Other than for a few exceptions, from 1917 to the late 1950s, all of its candidates won.

Frank Traylor was born in Coffeen, Illinois, on July 31, 1889. He grew up in Denver, earning his diploma from East High. After succeeding as a paint salesman, he became a director of Benjamin Moore Paints. On the side, he dedicated himself to youth work, being a major backer of the YMCA and the Boy Scouts. He had joined the school board in May 1947, right after that year's election when incumbent Howard Patience resigned.

Apparently, this was a cynical move. Patience had mentioned nothing of his impending departure from the board prior to the balloting. Had he quit before the polling, voters would have chosen his replacement. Rather, by waiting until the returns were in, he allowed the others on the body to name Traylor as his successor.

The new member easily kept his seat in 1949, gaining re-election in 1955 and 1961. Traylor emerged as board president in 1957. In that post, he was the director who arranged for DPS to name its three planned new high schools for great presidents: George Washington, Abraham Lincoln, and Thomas Jefferson. In 1961, Traylor left the post of board president, serving as vice president until his death.

A month before Traylor joined the school board, DPS had hired Kenneth Oberholtzer as superintendent. The new member worked closely with the district's leader. So did the others on the bureau. Traylor and associates were convinced that DPS had an outstanding manager in Oberholtzer.

In 1959, Palmer Burch seemingly upset the apple cart. A native of Ordway, Colorado, born on March 27, 1907, he had been part of Horace Bennett & Company since 1931. This was a leading commercial real estate agency and downtown landlord. After winning a seat in the Colorado House of Representatives in 1946,

Author's collection

In 1959, Palmer Burch gained election to the school board as an outsider. He dominated the board for the next eight years.

Burch quickly rose in the Republican Party. He was the unsuccessful GOP contender for governor in 1958 against incumbent Stephen McNichols.

The previous year, Burch pushed a bill through the legislature changing the date of Denver school board elections. The act moved them to the third Tuesday of May, combining them with municipal polling. As such, the Denver election commission rather than the secretary of the board of education was responsible for conducting the contests. The goal was to produce more interest and participation in the balloting. Until then, many voters ignored the school polling, seeing it as nothing more than the ratification of the decisions of the insider nominating clique of the Chamber of Commerce/PTA.

As had previously been the case, all board seats were at-large. Victors were those who received a plurality for the two or three seats open every two years. There was no provision for runoffs or proportional representation. Nor was there any requirement that members represent any specific part of the city.

On the heels of the change, Burch, a Hilltop resident who dwelt at 395 Fairfax Street, easily led the race for the three open seats in the 1959 school board election. He was at the top of the 16 contenders, getting 60,092 votes. The other victors were incumbents Francis Bain, 37,067, and Isadore Samuels, 31,366.

Bain was a baker who had gained appointment to the board in 1949. His father-in-law, Stephen Knight Jr., had previously been on the board as had Stephen Knight Sr., his grandfather-in-law. From 1961 to 1973, Bain's wife, Jean, was in the legislature where she served on the House education committee. Samuels was a life insurance agent and Chamber of Commerce activist who had won election to the board in 1947. He and Bain were firm backers of Oberholtzer. Burch, in contrast, sometimes questioned the superintendent's policies.

Lois Babbitt Heath gained election as president of the school board in 1961. A social worker and Red Cross executive who dwelt in an elite section of Park Hill at 2212 Ash Street, she had joined the board in 1951 as something of a representative of the PTA. On gaining re-election in 1957, she declared the district was a smooth-running system where she expected no turbulence during her second term. With her husband Raymond, she subsequently dwelt at 1955 Glencoe Street.

Heath took charge of the school board right after the 1961 election. In the contest, Frank Traylor easily kept his place on the board, gaining 27,601 votes. The 40-year-old Jackson F. "Jack" Fuller, came in second for the two open seats, 24,047, out of 14 candidates. He ousted incumbent Irene Saliman, 22,419, another

PTA representative on the board. The new member lived across the street from Heath, dwelling at 2090 Ash Street.

An applications engineer with General Electric, Fuller was born in Salt Lake City on October 9, 1920, coming to Denver as a boy. After graduating from East High, he made his way through CU, gaining his bachelor's in engineering in 1944. A young father at the time of his election, he served as scoutmaster of a Cub Scout troop which gathered at Park Hill Methodist Church. His wife was the Republican district captain. Back in 1959, Fuller had come in fourth for the school board. In office, he never quite fit in with the traditional, high-society orientation of the board.

Lela S. Gilbert finished fourth in the 1961 contest, 21,438, trailed by Herbert Wolff, 8,345. After gaining appointment to the state House of Representatives in 1957 as a Democrat, Gilbert had won election to the body in 1958 and 1960. Shortly before the school board polling, she had switched to the Republicans. In the balloting, the Denver Classroom Teachers Association backed Jackson Fuller and A. Edgar Benton. The professional organization specifically opposed returning Frank Traylor and Irene Saliman to the board.

Auburn Edgar "Ed" Benton was a third victor in 1961. He won a two-year vacancy election in a field of nine to fill the seat of Earl J. Boyd, a dentist, who had died in January 1961. Born in Colorado Springs on July 12, 1926, he invari-

Photo by Phil Goodstein

Park Hill has projected itself as Denver's most sophisticated neighborhood. Activists in the area especially focused on the schools. At times, Park Hill had one or two residents who served on the board of education. Shown is the area's elite 17th Avenue Parkway looking east from the Forest Street Parkway.

Photo by Tom Torgove

After his election to the school board in 1961, Ed Benton was in the lead of shaking up the body. He remained an observer of school and city politics into the 2010s.

ably went by Ed Benton. As a student at Colorado College, he was on the debate team, partnering with future civil rights attorney Irving Andrews. A job with the commanding law firm of Holme Roberts & Owen brought Benton to Denver in 1952 shortly after he had passed the bar. Eventually, he was a partner in the firm.

After originally settling at 1244 Lafayette Street, Benton moved to 2831 South Mabry Way to the west of Loretto Heights College. This was a change—he was the first person from a newly developing part of the city to get a place on the school board. For the most part, board members lived on Capitol Hill, Park Hill, in the Country Club neighborhood, or affluent parts of South Denver. Saliman had been an exception, dwelling at 1531 Lowell Boulevard along the West Colfax corridor.

Benton decisively won the two year term with 12,765 ballots. Jack R. Ashton came in second, 9,145. Black activist Juanita Gray was number three, 6,742. Aaron J. Shwayder, 6,686, and Bernard Campbell, 6,205, followed. At the bottom were C. Elroy Shilkles, 4,919, Dorothy B. Bonar, 3,481, Warren C. Isberg, 2,021, and Matt A. Nieminen, 1,073. Altogether, about 50,000 participated in the balloting compared to an average of 15,000 to 16,000 voters between 1951 and 1957, prior to moving the date of the school board contests.

The victor was an activist within the Democratic Party. It helped him win the seat. At first, Benton was discouraged when few people showed up at his campaign events. As he prospered as an attorney, he moved in 1964 to an elite home adjacent to Cheesman Park and Botanic Gardens at 901 Race Street. He was caught up in the idealism of the times. Included was a commitment to civil rights and the need for DPS to reach out to people of color.

Along with Burch, Benton sometimes intently questioned the policies of Oberholtzer. Used to deference, the superintendent was not always happy with their implied challenges. Oversight became more intense after Rachel Noel joined Benton and Burch on the board in 1965. The district's chief had long sought to avoid conflict and was unhappy with having to deal with seemingly hostile board members. In part, this was among the reasons why he announced his impending retirement in December 1966.

Replacing Frank Traylor

When Traylor died in September 1963, the six surviving board members deadlocked over whom to name to replace him. The *Denver Post* loudly heralded the bid of Rachel Noel to join the body. At a time when civil rights were roiling the country, she was the ideal person to replace Traylor, a woman of color who had a distinguished record as a supporter of the schools. Nobody more loudly expressed this view than Art Branscombe, an editorial writer at the *Post* who was a strong integration activist. He convinced *Post* editor Palmer Hoyt to endorse Noel for the school board.

By this time, Noel had an informal circle of backers. Included was school board member Ed Benton. Anna Jo Haynes, who came to establish herself as a foremost force in early childhood education, was a friend and supporter of Noel. Most of all, Noel's husband, Edmond, advised and encouraged her efforts. City Councilman Elvin Caldwell and state Senator George Brown, the area's foremost elected African-American politicians, were other close contacts, urging Noel on in her school board ambitions.

In contrast to the views of the *Post*, three members of the board were unenthusiastic about Noel's bid. They opposed her precisely because she was black and had challenged existing DPS policies. Additionally, they viewed her as too friendly to organized labor. This was at a time when the Denver Federation of Teachers (DFT) was making noise about gaining union recognition for instructors while the DCTA was evolving from a professional association into a teachers union.

The board remained divided three-to-three on naming Traylor's successor until February 26, 1964, when it selected Robert Stuart McCollum for the post. The new member was the epitome of the establishment. Born in Denver in 1916, he attended Deerfield, an elite New England prep school. He proceeded to Amherst for his bachelor's degree. After World War II, he took charge of his parents' auto distributorship. By this time, he was a major figure in the Junior Chamber of Commerce. At the behest of his good friend Quigg Newton, mayor between 1947 and 1955, McCollum won office as the city council representative for southeast Denver in 1951. Four years later, he did not seek re-election. Before long, he joined the administration of Mayor Will F. Nicholson (1955–59). Next he headed to Washington to work for the State Department. Along the way, he failed in a run for Congress in 1956 as a Republican against incumbent Byron Rogers.

Back in Denver, despite having no background in higher education, McCollum joined DU in 1960 as its vice chancellor. Chester Alter, the president of the Rotary Club in 1958–59, was then the chancellor of the school—McCollum was a fellow member of the most influential central Denver Rotary Club. In addition to loudly supporting the Cold War, as a university official McCollum urged a universal fallout shelter program. Colleges, he insisted, must not advocate "socialistic welfare programs." On the contrary, they had to use their prestige to show business that schools enhanced the economy.

McCollum created close ties between DU and the Denver Police Department. Community service included being a director of the Adult Education Council, a coalition pushing for a literate community. Rachel Noel was a fellow director.

From the beginning, McCollum stressed his membership on the school board was an interim appointment whereby he would not seek to hold the post in 1965. He was subsequently a major figure in the city's disastrous and deceitful campaign to host the 1976 Winter Olympics. The former board member passed away in early 1987.

Park Hill Schools

The appointment of McCollum aggravated racial tensions. The board's failure to tap Noel, loud voices of black Denver argued, showed DPS was essentially a racist system. They observed that the construction of Barrett School was not alone. Under Oberholtzer, DPS had repeatedly gerrymandered school borders whereby it segregated black students from white students. This was not only the case with trying to keep blacks out of Park Hill School, but the district also sought to exclude African-Americans from Stedman School at 2950 Dexter Street. The goal, civil rights activists charged, was to keep blacks west of Colorado Boulevard.

This was to no avail by the early 1960s when black Denver was rapidly growing. As had previous generations of whites, African-Americans saw Park Hill as an address of distinction. This is the neighborhood directly east of City Park. Generally, it came to mean the area north of Colfax Avenue to at least 38th Avenue from Colorado Boulevard to Quebec Street if not all the way to Syracuse Street. The prime section was between Colfax and 26th avenues from Colorado Boulevard to Monaco Street Parkway. Beginning in the late 19th century, the area filled in with the substantial homes of the city's professionals and business leaders. For years, Park Hill projected itself as essentially equal to if not superior to the Country Club neighborhood.

As Denver boomed after World War II, new sections of Park Hill popped up, particularly to the north of 32nd Avenue (Martin Luther King Boulevard). They were not nearly as ornate as old Park Hill. Included were many apartments and duplexes. Additionally, there were numerous large, sprawling ranch-style houses. In 1972, when it carved the city into statistical planning units, the planning office labeled the section north of 32nd Avenue as Northeast Park Hill. It called the spread from 26th Avenue to 32nd Avenue North Park Hill. South Park Hill made up the mile between Colfax and 26th avenues. For the most part, veterans and their families occupied the residences of new Park Hill.

By the mid-1960s, a massive black influx had transformed much of Park Hill, particularly to the north of 26th Avenue. This part of the neighborhood went from being virtually all white to predominantly black. A review of the area reported the number of blacks in North Park Hill had increased by 67 percent a year between 1960 and 1967. The 1970 census counted North Park Hill and Northeast Park Hill as overwhelmingly African-American. In the process, such places as Hallett School, 2950 Jasmine Street, opened in 1951, and Smith School, 3590 Jasmine Street, dating from 1955, became filled with black faces. In 1960, for example, DPS counted virtually no blacks at Smith; by 1966, 80 percent of the school's 1,248 students were African-Americans. During that period, the section east of Colorado

In the 1960s, besides 35 classrooms, Smith School, 3590 Jasmine Street, had 12 portable units. The enrollment was mostly African-American.

Boulevard and north of 32nd Avenue went from fewer than 1 percent black to 66.1 percent African-American.

From the beginning, both Smith and Hallett were overcrowded and on split sessions. Smith, recalling veteran educator Margaret Mendenhall Smith, had opened with 690 seats. At one point, it had a membership nearly twice that number. At its peak enrollment in the mid-1960s, Smith had 35 classrooms, and 12 mobile units. The last filled virtually all of the playing fields.

The overcrowding was not a product of racism. The two new schools had already been packed when the student body was predominantly white. For that matter, schools were overcrowded everywhere in the 1950s and well into the 1960s with baby boomers. In a majority of cases, schools in newly emerging white parts of the city were overcrowded, had portable units, and were often on split sessions.

Given the way they had long been treated and subjected to systematic public and private discrimination, African-Americans readily saw everything as a matter of black and white. Past and present racism taught them they could never trust the system. In response to the fight over Barrett, they were especially vigilant in 1962 when Superintendent Oberholtzer called for the construction of a new home for Gove Junior High School at the southwest corner of 32nd Avenue and Colorado Boulevard.

DPS had owned the land for years. Already in the early 1950s, Oberholtzer had suggested it as the site for a replacement building for Gove. The schoolhouse, along the west side of the 1300 block of Colorado Boulevard, dated from 1911. It saluted Aaron Gove, superintendent from 1874 to 1904. Virtually from the time DPS had transformed the beaux-arts building from a grammar school (grades one through eight) to a junior high in 1917 (grades seven, eight, and nine), there had been calls for abandoning the schoolhouse since it was unsuited for the needs of modern education. Not only was the gymnasium right above the auditorium, but many of the fixtures in the school were not modified—they had been designed for children who were about five to ten years old. Almost from the beginning of Gove Junior High, the campus included "temporary" buildings that were something of permanent fixtures. The district carved old cloakrooms into classrooms, squeezing up to 40 students into tiny spaces. Even after Smiley Junior High opened in 1928 at 2540 Holly Street to take in students from Park Hill, helping relieve the overcrowded Gove, suggestions were endless that a new building was necessary for the junior high at 14th Avenue and Colorado Boulevard.

In proposing a new location for Gove, Oberholtzer observed that loud voices, especially in Park Hill, had repeatedly complained about the physical design of the overcrowded Gove. A new building would especially serve black Denver. As it was, children living near 32nd Avenue and Colorado Boulevard had to walk around one-and-a-half miles to get to either Cole Junior High at 32nd Avenue and Humboldt Street or Smiley Junior High at 25th Avenue and Holly Street when they did not go to Gove.

Black Denver vehemently said no to the proposed new Gove. The real purpose of the building, integration activists argued, was to keep Smiley the traditional, elite, white Park Hill academy. They much preferred to see their children walk or ride the bus to Smiley or old Gove rather than have them occupy a new Jim Crow schoolhouse designed to maintain the district's racist practices. The outcry was so severe that the superintendent retreated. He agreed that a consciousness of the racial balance of schools had to be taken into account in drawing attendance boundaries. Actually, Oberholtzer had already taken racial numbers into account, working to assure that some schools were overwhelmingly white; others were primarily black. Now, ideally, he would act to achieve integrated programs. Equality of educational opportunity, he conceded, had to be a prime goal of the district.

Already in 1961, an East Denver Citizens Committee had emerged. That March, it threatened to sue the school board for its cynical gerrymandering of attendance zones to isolate minority students. A recent revision of school borders, it argued, was unfair and did not make geographical sense. Though the group quickly went by the wayside, never filing the litigation, its action indicated a growing tension over perceived DPS racism.

Amidst the national civil rights movement, black Denver found racism everywhere. In 1960, for example, an Urban League study observed lingering racism in DPS. It argued Manual High School, which was primarily black, was not as academically challenging as the city's other schools. Increasingly, racial considerations haunted all school decisions and elections to the school board.

Allegra Saunders

Concern about racial divisions had not been part of the balloting in 1963 when voters elected two members to the board. Incumbent Ed Benton easily kept his place, winning a six-year term, when he received 61,661 votes, leading a field of five. Allegra Saunders, the city's foremost woman Democrat, joined him in gaining a seat.

While both school board and municipal elections were ostensibly nonpartisan, the Democratic and Republican parties constantly hovered in the background. This was especially the case after the traditional Chamber of Commerce–PTA coalition weakened in the 1950s. By 1963, the Republicans were in trouble. Their unofficial candidates had won city hall in 1955 (Will F. Nicholson) and 1959 (Richard Batterton). The Democratic contender, Thomas G. Currigan, ousted Batterton in 1963. Mile High voters had not put a Republican in Congress since 1944. The bulk of the city's members in the state legislature, all elected at-large, were Democrats. Even so, the Republicans had a majority on the school board. While victors in school contests usually had partisan links, they had to build personal and organizational connections to gain election.

Saunders was indicative of the strong political aspirations of many serving on the board. She ran as part of an informal Democratic slate with Benton, receiving 56,514 votes. The challenger ousted incumbent Lois Heath, 48,301. Former state Representative Lela Gilbert, who had run with Heath as something of the de facto Republican ticket, was number four, 38,909. Attorney Martin G. Dumont, an independent, trailed the field, 17,160.

In part, voters said no to Heath stemming from a controversy two years earlier. In the spring of 1961, DPS had denied tenure to Park Hill School first grade teacher

In 1963, Allegra Saunders, the city's foremost woman Democrat, won a seat on the school board.

Barbara Chapman. The instructor had suffered the measles while in college, leading to occasional health problems. Since the health of students came first, Heath insisted that DPS get rid of Chapman. A mass community outcry forced the board to reconsider its decision, leading it to grant Chapman tenure in May 1961. Heath still voted to deny her a position.

Additionally, Saunders won the election thanks to her excellent political connections. Her triumph was a vindication after she had lost her bid to stay in the state Senate in 1962. A native of Ottawa, Kansas, born Allegra J. Carson on April 13, 1909, Saunders came to Denver to attend the University of Denver, gaining a degree in journalism. On November 27, 1937, she wed George E. Saunders. Once sheriff of Larimer County, he settled in Denver in 1935 when Governor Edwin C. Johnson named him to fill a vacancy in the secretary of state's office—impeachment had removed George Saunders' predecessor from the post. In 1940, the former sheriff unsuccessfully sought to become governor against Republican incumbent Ralph Carr. Soon thereafter, George Saunders dedicated himself to business, running the extremely successful North Denver Furniture Company near West 39th Avenue and Tennyson Street. His wife, henceforth, was the political figure in the family.

During the 1940s, 1950s, and 1960s, Allegra Saunders was a leader of the Jane Jefferson Club, the woman's branch of the Democratic Party. She held numerous appointed posts on state boards, including on determining state standards and refugee resettlement. Additionally, she was on the Denver Public Library commission and a president of Sertoma International.

Illustrative of Saunders' record was her term on the board governing the Colorado State Home for Dependent and Neglected Children. Located near South Washington Street and Iliff Avenue, this was the state orphanage. Scandals repeatedly wracked it. Boys and girls staying there complained they were more treated as inmates in a penal institution than as young men and women entitled to dignity and respect. They publicized their plight in 1951. Sensational newspaper exposés and an outside evaluation confirmed many of their allegations. Saunders, who was then the head of the board, denied that anything was wrong.

In 1952, Saunders gained election to a six-year term as Denver's representative on the state board of education. This is the body directing the Colorado Department of Education, the agency charged with overseeing the state's schools. Each congressional district has a seat on it. If there are an equal number of congressional districts, it additionally has an at-large member.

The politician quit the state board shortly before the expiration of her term when she won election to the state Senate in 1958. At this time, both Mile High Republicans and the Democrats sought to put at least one woman on their slates for the House of Representatives and the Senate. In the upper house, Saunders described herself as a housewife and an author.

The school board victor dwelt at 4840 Tennyson Street, across the street from the Willis Case Golf Course, in the Berkeley neighborhood. The residence was near the home of Dorothea Kunsmiller, 5086 Vrain Street, who had retired from the board in 1955 after 24 years in office. In the school board campaign, Saunders had projected herself as a candidate of change. The Denver Federation of Teachers endorsed her and Benton. The DCTA backed Benton and Heath. Both the DCTA and the DFT were vehemently opposed to Gilbert. On the school board, Saunders generally voted with Benton. This included backing the Special Study Committee on Equality of Educational Opportunity.

The Special Study Committee

As racial controversies pulsated, especially over the question of building a new home for Gove, Benton listened to black protests. He increasingly observed the complacency and racism among top administrators. Deputy Superintendent Roy Hindermann spoke about our "fuzzy-headed" children. Now and then, newspapers realized the DPS student body was extremely diverse, including youngsters who were not white and not from middle-class families.

The district, Benton insisted, had to examine its racial practices and its connections with African-American Denver. On June 27, 1962, he convinced the board to form the Special Study Committee on Equality of Educational Opportunity. It consisted of 32 members in addition to all members of the board of education, the superintendent, and the deputy superintendent. The body was to file its report by June 1, 1963. The board was to review it and act upon it by June 1, 1964.

The resolution creating the Special Study Committee specified the body was to have three residents from each of the city's eight high school areas. (For the purpose of the study, DPS combined South High and Thomas Jefferson as one high school area.) Six members of the staff were to join them. The board selected the public members out of more than 400 applicants. About a quarter of the members had direct connections with DPS as teachers or administrators.

In addition to looking at the abstract issue of equal educational opportunity, the commission was to probe other parts of the district including curriculum, the nature of instruction, the character of schoolhouses, the necessity for vocational education, the level of guidance and counseling, and the character of the administration. In some ways, it was a modern version of the review of District #1 conducted by the Bureau of Municipal Research in 1915–16. The Bureau was a New York agency of urban experts commissioned by the Tax Payers

Auraria Archives

In 1962 the school board named veteran attorney and powerbroker William W. "Bill" Grant III to chair the Special Study Committee on Equality of Educational Opportunity. He quit the post in March 1963 to run for mayor. This was his campaign photo/flyer.

Protective League, a Mile High organization composed of the city's largest and most powerful property and business owners. That probe had sought to reshape DPS as a streamlined agency guaranteed to work closely with 17th Street.

At the stipulation of the board, a prime powerbroker, William W. "Bill" Grant III, was chairman. Not only had his father been a prominent player at DPS, including serving on the school board from 1943 to 1949, but the appointee was the owner of Channel Four and had been the chairman of the Denver Democratic Party. Back in 1947, Bill Grant had been a key figure in making Quigg Newton mayor.

James D. Voorhees, an attorney who dwelt in the Country Club neighborhood at 170 Downing Street, was vice chairman. In some accounts, he projected himself as a Denver native; in other versions he was born in Haverford, Pennsylvania, attending elite eastern private schools, including Phillips Exeter Academy. After gaining his bachelor's from Yale in 1940, Voorhees served in the Navy during World War II, rising to the rank of lieutenant commander. Following the return of peace, he earned his law degree from Harvard in 1946. He specialized in natural resource law, especially oil and gas.

In 1947, Voorhees settled in the Mile High City, working in the legal department of Conoco, then headquartered in Denver. He went on to cofound the boutique law firm of Moran Reidy & Voorhees in 1956. In the 1980s, he joined the influential 17th Street firm of Davis Graham & Stubbs, a partnership closely linked with school issues. Active in the Junior Chamber of Commerce, Voorhees was a member of the University Club and the Denver Country Club.

Voorhees' mother was Elsa Denison, the daughter of Ella Denison. From 1921 to 1925, his grandmother had served on the school board—she is the namesake of Denison School, 1821 South Yates Street. Back in 1915, Ella Denison was as responsible as anybody for seeing that the Bureau of Municipal Research came to Denver to conduct its survey of DPS. In 1942, Voorhees married Mary Margaret Fuller. The couple showed up in the social directory. Personally, the attorney was very proud of his New York Dutch colonial heritage.

A self-styled conservative Republican, Voorhees was the father of three children attending DPS. There he expected them to be in the best classes. The lawyer, a legal and personal acquaintance of Ed Benton, took charge of the Special Study Committee after Grant quit the body in March 1963 when the owner of Channel Four launched an unsuccessful bid to win election as mayor. Back in 1951, Voorhees had failed in a run for the school board.

Irving P. Andrews, the premier black civil rights attorney in the city, was among those serving on the Special Study Committee. He eventually emerged as vice chairman of the group—he and Benton were close companions. James A. Atkins, an African-American activist and scholar who had studied civil rights and the level of racial tensions in the area, joined Andrews on the body. In 1968, Atkins put together a book for the Colorado Department of Education about the state's human relations record.

Roger Cisneros, a Latino attorney who had sought a place on the school board in 1959 and who had readily complained about the discrimination to which "Mexicans" were subjected, represented Hispanic Denver. So did Bernard "Bernie" Valdez, a former trade union activist who became a ranking city official and something of a voice of the Spanish-Surnamed community.

Suzanne Joshel, the wife of the man managing the nuclear bomb plant at Rocky Flats, likewise was on the Special Study Committee. A Holocaust survivor who lived on Hilltop, she was concerned about racism and anti-Semitism. As part of her campaign against discrimination in DPS, Rachel Noel also gained a place on the commission.

Considerably behind the original schedule, the group filed its report on February 29, 1964 — it was officially dated March 1, 1964. For the most part, the committee suggested voluntary measures to make equal educational opportunity a reality. This was the premise that all schools should have equal funding and programs. Ideally, such an approach allowed all children to compete on a level ground to achieve success in the existing money-driven society.

> Report and Recommendations
> to the
> Board of Education
> School District Number One
> Denver, Colorado
>
> *by*
> *A Special Study Committee*
> *on*
> *Equality of Educational Opportunity*
> *in the Denver Public Schools*
>
> MARCH 1, 1964

Author's collection
In 1964, the Special Study Committee on Equality of Educational Opportunity released its report, calling for DPS to be conscious of racial and ethnic considerations in shaping its policies and attendance borders.

The school board responded to the report by adopting Resolution 1222C. It required the district to ponder the racial implications whenever it modified the boundary of a neighborhood school. The measure implied that Oberholtzer had not previously done so as part of his de facto Jim Crow policies. Resolution 1222C was closely linked to Policy 5100 of 1964, specifying the necessity of racial awareness in DPS decisions. In part, the board passed Policy 5100 in response to federal legislation aiding schools as long as they did not discriminate.

The report of the Special Study Committee did not simply deal with racial balancing. It was an overall review of the district. Included were suggestions about the nature of the administration, the character of facilities, the quality of community relations, and the content of the curriculum. On May 6, 1964, Superintendent Oberholtzer officially responded to the report, vowing to study its recommendations and follow them in improving the district.

The 1965 Election

The report of the Special Study Committee and the civil rights efforts impacted the 1965 school board election. Robert McCollum kept his promise to step down from the agency. He and others saw that change was in the air. Neither Francis Bain nor Isadore Samuels sought to remain in office. Rather than asking voters for another six-year term, Palmer Burch stated he hoped to fill the two years left in the term of Traylor/McCollum.

Contenders included Reverend John Gerberding, the head of the Committee to Oppose Discrimination, a community group advocating brotherhood. He was something of a Democratic Party candidate. A 1943 graduate of Yale who received a divinity degree in 1948, he was the pastor of Epiphany Lutheran Church, 790 South Corona Street. He dwelt east of Washington Park at 831 South Williams Street. Prior to his bid for the school board, he had been president of the Young Democrats and a member of the Democratic Party central committee.

Sam Menin, a politically active civil rights and labor lawyer with a strong progressive agenda, threw his hat in the ring. Active with the American Civil Liberties Union (ACLU), he specifically attacked the administration of Oberholtzer as responsible for the petty bureaucratic rules of the district and its endless troubles. James Willis was another attorney seeking a place on the board. He lived at 5409 Montview Boulevard in the heart of elite Park Hill, sending his three sons to DPS. The previous year, Willis had unsuccessfully taken the district to court, claiming its use of race as a criterion for admission and drawing of school borders was an illegal, racist practice. He also turned his guns on Oberholtzer.

Lela Gilbert once more sought election to the board, targeting the teachers union. Accountant Wallace Sam also ran. A Denver native and product of DPS, he was among the early black settlers of Park Hill. The candidate had devoted himself to school issues for years, once having been a substitute in the district. Barbara Taplin and Howard Wallace were the radicals in the contest, campaigning as members of the Socialist Workers Party. Harry Haddock, a parent most active at Bromwell School, was another of those seeking a place. Twenty-two candidates sought the three open six-year seats; the other seven contenders vied for the two-year vacancy spot. KRMA, Channel Six, then owned and operated by DPS, televised some of the candidate debates as it had since going on the air in 1956.

Most of all, Rachel Noel ran. Her campaign was not only to vindicate her effort to gain appointment to the seat of the deceased Frank Traylor, but was also to show that black Denver had come of age whereby an African-American could win a place on the school board. From the beginning, she was the contender of the middle-class civil rights movement.

Noel rallied the black political and business elite to her campaign. The three co-chairs of the effort were state Senator George Brown, state Representative Isaac "Ike" Moore, and David Smith, a real estate agent who frequently sold houses in Park Hill to aspiring middle-class African-Americans. In the process, he introduced the new residents to their white neighbors. Some believed this was a cynical effort to spur white flight from the area.

The contender's support committee included black civil rights attorney Irving Andrew along with such leading African-American medical professionals as Bernard Gipson and Clarence Holmes. Rabbi Samuel Adelman, a prominent Denver cleric from the South, backed her as did Ben Bezoff, a legislator who became a close advisor of Mayor Bill McNichols. African-American businessmen Charles Cousins and McKinley Harris lent their support. Dolores Dickman, a stalwart of the labor movement and the Democratic Party in North Denver, joined the campaign.

James Voorhees, second from the left, chaired the Special Study Committee on Equality of Educational Opportunity in 1962–64. He went on to win election to the school board in 1965. Here he sits with fellow members of the DPS governing body in the course of 1965–67. John H. Amesse is on the left. Allegra Saunders is the third from the left. Next to her, in the back row, is Kenneth R. Gher, board secretary. Palmer Burch, president of the board, is next to him, flanked by Superintendent Kenneth K. Oberholtzer. The third from the right is Ed Benton next to Rachel Noel. Jackson F. Fuller is on the far right.

Future Governor Richard Lamm, then an attorney, also endorsed the drive. So did Five Points black political boss O. L. "Sonny" Lawson, joined by African-American preachers Wendell Liggins and Acen Phillips. Other backers included former CU president Robert Stearns, fixer attorney and Channel Four owner Bill Grant, Manager of Safety Dan Hoffman, and Hispanic civil rights activist Bernie Valdez.

The DCTA was in the lead of endorsing Noel for the board. It also backed Ernest E. Cronover, and Kenneth E. Valis. Melvin Coffee gained its nod for the two-year term. The DFT in contrast, backed LeRoy Cavnar, a teacher at Opportunity School, Noel, Gerberding, and Coffee. The Democrats made it known that Noel and Gerberding were the party's candidates. They also urged voters to back either Cavnar or attorney Sam Menin while the party was split between supporting Coffee and Robert M. Lucero for the two-year spot.

The Republicans emphasized the candidacies of John Amesse, James Voorhees, and Lela Gilbert plus Palmer Burch for the two-year term. The Administrators and Supervisors Association, a professional group among top-ranking DPS officials and principals, declared it was comfortable with Noel, Voorhees, Amesse, Stephen J. Knight Jr., and Burch. The *Post* especially pushed the Noel campaign. Besides endorsing Burch, the *News* urged voters to select Knight, Noel, and Voorhees.

Around 45,000 voters, about 20 percent of those eligible to cast ballots, trooped to the polls on May 18. Rachel Noel led the field for the three six-year terms, 20,379. James Voorhees, fresh from his leadership of the Special Study Committee, came in second, 19,155. Physician John H. Amesse finished third, 16,665. Stephen J. Knight Jr., who went on to win a place in 1967, was the number-four finisher, 14,150. Other contenders included city councilman Hoot Gibson, 3,313, and Wallace Sam, 1,518. Menin gained 2,382 votes. Both Republican Lela Gilbert, 6,469, and Democrat John Gerberding, 9,226, were also-rans. Harry Haddock was at 1,866. James Willis gained 1,870 votes.

Palmer Burch got the most ballots of any candidate, 25,025, overwhelming all of the others for the two-year spot who received 20,308 votes between them. The result left the board split between three Democrats (Benton, Saunders, and Noel), and three Republicans (Voorhees, Amesse, and Burch). Jackson Fuller was ostensibly an independent though his wife was a Republican district captain.

Photo by Phil Goodstein

The Denver Rotary Club has had intimate links with DPS. Among the organization's ventures was a sculpture, unveiled in 2006, The Player, in front of Coors Field at 20th and Blake streets.

John H. Amesse, who pronounced his name "Ah-Mess," was a Denver native, born in 1915, to a pioneer Mile High pediatrician, John W. Amesse. In 1941, following in his father's footsteps, he earned his medical degree from the University of Colorado. Besides medicine, the younger Amesse was involved in many community pursuits, foremost of which was being the president of the powerful Denver Rotary Club.

The Rotary Club had an amazingly wide reach in civic life. A former head of the group was Adolph Kunsmiller, the president of American National Bank. At one time, DPS deposited most of its sums in that financial institution. His wife, Dorothea Kunsmiller, was on the school board from 1931 to 1955. Superintendent Charles Greene (1939–47) was a leading Rotarian. Usually, the Rotary Club had a seat in the Chamber of Commerce–PTA caucus selecting candidates for the school board. At one point, Herrick Roth, the executive director of the Denver Federation of Teachers, argued that the Rotary Club actually ran DPS. Kenneth Oberholtzer was another Rotarian. So was William Berge who joined the school board in 1967.

Be that as it may, Amesse stood out in numerous other fields. An excellent singer, he was once part of the choir of Montview Presbyterian where he served as an elder and trustee—the church was the congregation of Kenneth Oberholtzer and other top DPS administrators. On the school board, Amesse backed the initiatives of Rachel Noel and Ed Benton, pushing for racial accommodation and equal educational opportunity.

Despite the triumph of Noel, nothing immediately changed on the board. Burch remained as president, a post he had held since 1963. Benton was vice president. Beneath the surface, the election, combined with mass campaigns for civil rights, started to transform the nature of the board and the direction of the district.

Noel and her backers were sure her victory was a great achievement, showing DPS was on its way to redressing past discrimination and assuring equal educational opportunity. The new board member made it clear she was comfortable with keeping Oberholtzer as superintendent and the general direction of DPS. As with much of the school equality push led nationally by the NAACP, Noel and middle-class black Denver did not seek to transform the nature of public education, which had generally failed black America, but to equalize it to assure black boys and girls got the same schooling offered to whites. Those of this viewpoint never addressed educational skeptics who argued that even the best of white schools had severe flaws. Critics likewise asserted the goal of the schools and society had to be more than equal opportunity. It must be a world nurturing all people, not simply rewarding those with the best school, business, and professional skills.

The NAACP and middle-class blacks ignored this perspective. They likewise paid no heed to differences in white schools. The children of white blue-collar workers invariably did not do as well as those of the upper-middle-class. More than ever, the Noel-civil rights goal was "equal educational opportunity." This was an old slogan, dating from the late 19th century. At that time, proponents defined it as the equal financing of all schools whereby those attending classes in poor districts had the same quality of instruction and buildings as did those who lived in wealthy areas. Back in 1946, when the Denver Federation of Teachers emerged as a group seeking to speak for DPS instructors, "equal educational opportunity" was among its demands.

Like Noel, most of black Denver agreed that under Oberholtzer, DPS was generally an excellent system, at least for white students. Not everybody thought as much. Four of the candidates in 1965 had outspokenly condemned the superintendent. Their opinions widely varied. Attorney Sam Menin, for example, lambasted the administrator as an embodiment of the corporate control of the schools. Others saw Oberholtzer as some kind of subversive for his continuing adherence to Progressive Education. This was a doctrine dating from the early 20th century that argued the schools had to be in tune with society. As such, schools

Photo by Phil Goodstein

During World War II, the military built a huge medical depot near the southeast corner of 40th Avenue and York Street. After the return of peace, the Air Force transformed the complex into its Finance Center. In the process, it brought many proud African-American airmen to Denver, some who made the city their home after getting out of the service. They were loud voices in demanding a unitary Denver Public School system free of all racial discrimination. Shown is the powerhouse of the Finance Center.

not only emphasized academics, but also nurtured the socialization of students and prepared them to fit into the wider world.

A Heritage of Racism and Opportunity

By the time of Noel's election to the board in 1965, the civil rights movement was at the peak of its success, including winning crucial national legislation that year. Locals observed that Colorado had never been part of Dixie. On the contrary, it had been a supporter of the Union during the Civil War. While racial tensions had buffeted the city, ostensibly Denver was a model non-discriminatory community. At an early date, Colorado adopted many progressive measures. As a requirement for admission to the union, the 1876 state constitution included the protections of the 1875 Civil Rights Act. For the most part, they were paper measures: victims of discrimination had to sue to gain vindication. Rarely did they get juries to side with them. Prosecutors did virtually nothing to enforce civil rights statutes.

By the time the civil rights explosion started to shake the South in the 1950s, Denver projected itself as a modern city that had jettisoned remnants of Jim Crow. Many in the black community furiously disagreed. They found themselves subjected to everyday racism. Nobody practiced and sanctioned it more than elite Denver. Only under the blows of the civil rights movement did premier stores start to hire blacks and allow them to purchase goods. Social and country clubs eased their rules, especially those which had banned blacks and Jews from membership. Banks continued to draw red lines around low-income, mostly minority areas, announcing they would not provide loans to those seeking to buy or improve homes in them. Many blacks realized that only through militant direct action could they achieve anything.

Not until 1935 did District #1 hire its first black instructor, Marie Anderson. While she eventually came to teach at Newlon School, 361 Vrain Street, in a rapidly developing section where she lived in southwest Denver after World War II, DPS mostly assigned black teachers to black schools. It argued African-American students learned better when they had black teachers instructing them. Likewise, black clerical and maintenance workers primarily were at schools with heavy African-American enrollments.

Combined with the mass agitation sweeping the country, DPS found itself forced to listen to black concerns that it was not a unitary district offering the same high-quality education to one and all. This especially resonated after Noel's election to the board. She immediately allied with Ed Benton in demanding DPS affirmatively address racial disparities in the schools. Fellow members James Voorhees and John Amesse also realized it was urgent for the board to listen to all of the community, not just the Chamber of Commerce. Allegra Saunders generally went along with them. In consequence, the new board was something Denver had not seen since the 1917 Chamber of Commerce takeover of the agency, a bureau not subservient to business as usual.

From the time it had created the Special Study Committee on Equality of Educational Opportunity, the board faced the problem of defining exactly what it meant by "equality of educational opportunity." The report of the committee did not answer that question. Around this time, the federal government, seeing that poor children were behind when they entered the schools, had created an early childhood education program to give them a "head start." The implication was that all youngsters were in a race for limited success.

To help guide the board about precisely how it could guarantee equality of educational opportunity, in 1966, under the impetus of Benton and Noel, the agency formed a follow-up group to the Special Study Committee, the Advisory Council on Equal Educational Opportunity. Virtually from when the Special Study Committee dissolved following the issuance of its 1964 report, there had been calls for a new, comparable, semi-permanent bureau. The composition of the Advisory Council was much like the Special Study Committee, filled with community and civil rights activists, most of whom had excellent ties with the business and political establishments. Members often had a visible moral vigor.

William G. "Bill" Berge chaired the Advisory Council. (The final "e" was silent in the pronunciation of his name.) Born in Cleveland on July 10, 1923, he came to Denver with his family when he was a lad. He made his way through Moore, Gove, and East before attending Dartmouth. During World War II, Berge served in the Army Air Forces. DU awarded him a law degree in 1950. By this time, he was part of high society. His marriage that summer was a major event of the social season. Future Episcopal Bishop Edwin Thayer performed it. Berge's bride, Nancy Roberts, was the daughter of a leading investment banker who was the vice president of the powerful real estate firm of Garrett–Bromfield & Company. The reception was at the Denver Country Club.

On joining the bar, Berge immediately emerged as a corporate lawyer. In 1955, he helped form the influential firm of Winner Berge Martin & Camfield. His partners included Fred Winner, who went on to become the chief judge of the United States District Court of Colorado, and Warren O. Martin who later served on the bench of the Denver District Court. Eventually, Berge was a specialist in eminent domain, helping the Denver Urban Renewal Authority condemn properties.

Board member James Voorhees, who had headed the Special Study Committee, was a close friend. Berge sent his three sons to DPS. Among the attorney's past service was being the head of an advisory council at Pitts School, 3509 South Glencoe Street, near his home at 3908 South Jasmine Street. Additionally, he had served on the committee helping create the public defender's office. The attorney was a big clubman, being a member of such groups as the Gyro Club, University Club, and Mile High Club.

On February 23, 1967, the Advisory Council formally presented its report. The enabling resolution had required it to end its operations on March 16, 1967. The body declared that not only must DPS educate all of the children in District #1, but "in judicious exercise of their wide powers of discretion," the members of the school board must "voluntarily promote racial and ethnic integration of our community." Listening to the council, the board affirmed that equal educational opportunity was a foremost district priority. As much as had been the case with the Special Study Committee's report, the document was extremely nebulous about how to achieve this goal. Given the extreme flux about exactly where the district was in terms of its policies, integration activists called for extending the life of the council, making it something of an on-going advisor to the board. The school board did not heed this recommendation. All the while, developments in Park Hill shaped the future of the district.

Park Hill Developments

While the Advisory Council debated the definition of equal educational opportunity and what policies DPS should adopt to assure it became a reality, the board had to address the changing character of Smiley Junior High. The school opened in 1928 at 2540 Holly Street near what was then the northeastern edge of residential development. It immediately stood out as a premier academy.

Photo by Phil Goodstein

Park Hill Methodist Church, along the north side of Montview Boulevard between Forest and Glencoe streets, was among the eight neighborhood congregations promoting integration in the 1960s when it was a stalwart of the Park Hill Action Committee. It continued to emphasize diversity into the 21st century.

Expansions followed in 1950, 1958, 1964, and 1966. The building recalled William H. Smiley, superintendent of schools from 1913 to 1916. By the mid-1960s, a majority of Smiley students were black. Given the failure to build a new home for Gove Junior High, it was also overcrowded. Changes at Smiley reflected upheavals in Park Hill as a whole.

In addition to blacks, who mostly settled in the new, modest northern half of Park Hill in the 1960s, a visible number of African-American professionals bought homes in the premier southern section of the neighborhood. Some whites responded by moving out; others proudly insisted Park Hill was their home. They were staying there, welcoming blacks to share their distinguished enclave.

Eight white churches worked to transform Park Hill into the country's premier integrated neighborhood. In 1960, after four years of meetings and calls for brotherhood, Montview Presbyterian, Blessed Sacrament Catholic, St. Thomas Episcopal, Park Hill Methodist, City Park Baptist, Messiah Lutheran, Park Hill Congregational, and Park Hill Christian joined forces to create the Park Hill Action Committee (PHAC). It was both a traditional improvement association and something of a social club, primarily reaching out to church members. Neighbors could join as individuals. Others automatically were members through church affiliations. Civil rights was a prime concern.

From the beginning, PHAC had a strong class bias. All residents of the area, it implied, had to be successful professionals who took immaculate care of their homes and lawns. By the mid-1960s, as ever more blacks poured into Park Hill, especially the northern half, PHAC became alarmed. The mass migration, it observed, threatened to resegregate the section. Nobody more agreed with this than some of the early black professionals who were proud Park Hill pioneers.

To prevent the resegregation of Park Hill and to make sure only affluent blacks were part of elite southern Park Hill, in the summer of 1965 PHAC issued what was known as the Blue Flyer. Officially entitled "The Facts on Housing for Negroes," it was printed on blue paper. The Northeast Park Hill Civic Association, the homeowner association dating from 1954 for parts of the northeastern section of the settlement, joined PHAC in the effort. The three-page statement, which backers of CORE helped circulate, insisted all of Denver must become an integrated city. The immigration of any more Negroes into Park Hill would undermine the neighborhood's desegregation success.

Loud voices of African-American Denver denounced the Blue Flyer. They saw it as nothing less than a new imposition of Jim Crow. Nor, they argued, did all blacks want to live in idyllic integrated areas. As had members of countless religious and ethnic groups since the 19th century who lived in distinctive enclaves, many blacks preferred to dwell close to other blacks, including being in proximity of churches and stores that especially reached out to them.

As it was, few listened to PHAC's suggestion that blacks move into other white neighborhoods. On the contrary, the drift of blacks continued to new sections of Park Hill. The new settlers of Park Hill reflected the black community as a whole, including individuals who lacked high school diplomas and had criminal records.

The changing racial composition of the neighborhood naturally impacted the schools. Not only did the enrollment at Smith and Hallett become mostly black, but Stedman went from being a white to a black academy. Increasing numbers of African-Americans showed up at Philips School, 6550 21st Avenue. Black faces returned to Park Hill School. Most of all, developments at Smiley showed the troubled character of school integration.

Improving Smiley

As African-Americans became the majority of the Smiley student body in the mid-1960s, parts of the school were integrated. Other sections were starkly segregated. Whites and blacks, joined by some Hispanos and a few Japanese-Americans, took music, art, gym, home economics, shop, and social studies classes together. In contrast, accelerated math, science, and English classes were often nearly if not completely white compared to blacks who predominated in both regular sections and modified classes.

To assure that black parents would not complain about discriminatory discipline, particularly against African-American boys, Smiley made a point of having a large black man, Dennis H. Small, as assistant principal, the official in charge of punishing on errant young men. Born in 1911, he was a veteran of DPS, having previously taught social studies at Horace Mann Junior High (4130 Navajo Street) and North High. From Smiley, Small went on to be the tough, no-nonsense principal of

Smiley Junior High opened in 1928 at 2540 Holly Street at what was then the northeast limits of the city's elite Park Hill neighborhood. As new sections of Park Hill filled with African-Americans in the early 1960s, the school became a center of fights for desegregation and equal educational opportunity. The picture shows what the school looked like before major expansions in 1950 and 1958.

Morey Junior High in 1967. Small subsequently joined the administration of the University of Colorado before returning to Smiley. He died on October 15, 1980. Back in the mid-1960s, he readily stared down one and all. He was just as ready to discipline straying black youths as any traditional white assistant principal.

Small was not alone. The district readily employed big black men as disciplinarians. By the 1970s, it also reached out to Latino men. For a while, it was seemingly impossible for a white man to advance to be an assistant principal given this form of affirmative action.

Without improving the schools and redressing segregation, Park Hill champions feared their area was doomed. Typical were the views of Dr. James Kent, an educational consultant to DPS. Studying Park Hill developments, he lamented the area was in the infant stage of emerging as a "black ghetto." It was not just a racial question, he observed, but also one of class. Many of the neighborhood's new black residents lacked the wealth and educational experiences that were hallmarks of white Park Hill.

The term "ghetto" also signified the bias of much of white Denver. For many, including whites in Park Hill and some African-Americans, "ghetto" was simply an urban area overwhelmingly filled with blacks. In the process, those lamenting the "ghetto" failed to observe the many fine middle-class houses blacks occupied to the west of Colorado Boulevard. In the white Park Hill view, the only way to keep the area from being a ghetto was by not having too many blacks live on any one block.

A way of assuring that Park Hill did not so become a ghetto was by making improvements at Smiley. It had upwards of 1,600 students. More were on the way with the development of Montbello, an emerging neighborhood to the northeast of Stapleton Airport. Developers of that area did not provide for secondary schools. Seemingly, they expected Smiley to handle those in seventh, eighth, and ninth grades.

To provide more room and improve Smiley, leaders of PHAC convinced DPS to put the school on split sessions for the fall of 1966. This essentially transformed it into two schools in one, each with an enrollment of around 800–900. Included was a whole new set of administrators. Ideally, the smaller size of the two separate programs assured that teachers paid more personal attention to students. Additionally, it allowed for enrichment classes in the mornings or afternoons for students who were out of school at those times of day. What was then the Museum of Natural History in City Park, for example, invited students over once a week in the afternoons as part of learning and volunteer sessions.

In advocating double sessions, Smiley champions paid no heed of what this did to the biological clocks of adolescents. Those who did not want to get to class by 7:00 AM and did not qualify for the afternoon session had the opportunity to ride

Photo by Phil Goodstein

In 1986, DPS named its new Montbello middle school for Martin Luther King. This was a belated recognition of the man. Following his assassination, violence had flared in some schools on April 5, 1968, when callous principals refused to recognize the extreme anger of black students on the murder of the foremost civil rights leader. Eventually, DPS declared Martin Luther King Middle School, a facility primarily filled with minority youths from low-income families, an early college as a way of showing that college was the system's primary goal. Here students from the school march in the 2019 Martin Luther King Day parade.

the bus to other schools. Few accepted. Far from stabilizing Smiley, the double sessions led to further white flight from the area.

Some left because conditions at Smiley became worse. This especially stood out on April 5, 1968, the day after the assassination of Martin Luther King. Far from seeing that the murder had touched a raw nerve of black America, Smiley's overbearing, conservative principal, Roy Rebrovick, insisted on classes as usual. The result was an explosion when black youths attacked and viciously beat some of their white schoolmates. A few believed this was their personal way of gaining their revenge for the killing.

Smiley was not alone. In other places, DPS principals saw it best to dismiss class rather than suffering from upheavals. Not until the violence was on the verge of getting out of hand did Rebrovick decide it was necessary to dismiss all pupils. Seeing that the PHAC-backed "improvements" at Smiley had made conditions worse, a Smiley Drastic Action Committee emerged. Demanding change, it staged a one-day student boycott of the school. In response, DPS transferred Rebrovick to Merrill Junior High for the 1968–69 schoolyear. It also returned Smiley to normal hours, showing that parents were not at all satisfied with PHAC, which had argued split sessions at the school were a great achievement. In part, the district was able to end split sessions thanks to the opening of Hamilton Junior High in January 1969 at 8600 Dartmouth Avenue in far southeast Denver. Students from Montbello now rode the bus to it rather than to Smiley.

DPS had imposed split sessions on Smiley in the name of making it, along with Baker Junior High (574 West Sixth Avenue), a "superior" school. In part, this was its response to the report of the Advisory Council on Equal Educational Opportunity. No more than "equal educational opportunity" was there a precise definition of what was a "superior school." Nor were there any agreed-upon ways to measure whether the reforms delivered as promised. Backers never reflected whether the district's action in imposing split sessions might well have caused more damage than assisted Smiley students.

Placing Smiley on split sessions occurred during Superintendent Kenneth K. Oberholtzer's last year in office. By the mid-1960s, the superintendent was clearly uncomfortable with the changing times. Seemingly, he got out of the district right before conditions got worse at Smiley and racial tensions increasingly overshadowed all aspects of the school system. The new superintendent, Robert D. Gilberts, had to deal with those problems.

A Note on Sources:

Jeanne Varnell, *Women of Consequence* (Boulder: Johnson, 1999), 192–96, features Rachel Noel. A profile in *RMN*, September 23, 1990, pp. 14–17M, heralded her achievements. OH-84 is an interview with her at the Western History Department of DPL. Side A of the first of three tapes emphasizes her family background. Besides a portrait of her in *RMN*, September 23, 1990, pp. 14–17M, there was a file on her in drawer 33 of the Branscombe papers. ARL 117 at the Blair–Caldwell Library is a collection of her papers. A niece, Phoebe A. Haddon, the dean of the University of Maryland School of Law, reflected on Noel as a civil rights pioneer, incorporating her contributions into the Keyes case in *DU Law Review*, 90:5 (October 2013), 1251–76. The article particularly focuses on Noel, 1273–75.

Billie Arlene Grant with Ernestine Smith and Gladys Smith, *Growing Up in Black Denver* (n.p.: n.p., 1988), 76–78, emphasizes Noel's importance. Her son, Buddy Noel, granted me an interview on September 13, 2019, reflecting on her career. During it, her stressed her genteel Virginia roots and fundamental humanity. FF 1:9 of the Noel papers has materials on her 1965 run for the school board, complete with a list of her backers.

There is an undated clipping in loose papers in GP from *RMN* in March 1963 by Marjorie Barrett emphasizing the work of Rachael Noel. It observes her commitment to the Girl Scouts and her receipt of the DCTA's Eddy Award. FF 1:42 of the DPS papers at DPL, WH 1990, has materials on the Community Study Hall Association. Also see FF 4:2 of the CCR papers, WH 903.

Watson, "Barricades," 92–94, outlines how Noel came to serve on the school board. I touch on her in *Curtis Park*, 206, 218. Laura Lefkowits effusively praised Noel as a civil rights pioneer during a talk at the January 27, 2018, meeting of Park Hill Neighbors for Equity in Education. *DP*, February 5, 2008, p. 1B, mourned her passing.

Buddy Noel shared his memories of being bused to Park Hill School in an interview on September 13, 2019. Journalist, historian, and novelist Sandra Dallas remembered Beulah Glesner as her outstanding sixth grade teacher at Park Hill in *Giving Credit*, 10:1 (May 2015). Volume three will discuss the rise of the Denver Teacher Award Foundation.

Noel gave her credo about integration in *Our Neighborhood Schools* in Alweis, *Rebels Remembered*. *The Nation*, September 23, 2019, p. 23, spelled out the integration faith in reducing prejudice and improving community relations.

Alweis, *Rebels Remembered*, emphasizes the activities of CORE within the context of the history of black Denver. For the most part, the video simply consists of interviews with some excellent footage of protest and solidarity marches. In passing, politicians, journalists, and community figures share their memories. They frequently repeat much of the folklore about the African-American community, the character of white racism, and the nature of the Ku Klux Klan in Denver. Claims are sometimes contradictory and unsupported by hard evidence. The effort fails to trace the specific origins of the first Denver branch of CORE and civil rights protests during World War II. I mention CORE and civil rights protests at that time in *Soup Lines*, 308, 436, *Curtis Park*, 213, 341, and *Park Hill*, 46, 158, 412, 455. There are portraits of the Denver NAACP in *Curtis Park*, 57, 156, 183, 190, 224, 340, 349, *Klan*, 24, 25, 27, 29, 30, 31, 34, 124, 248, and *Soup Lines*, 242, 304, 305, 308. Among the disks of *Rebels* Remembered is *Our Neighborhood Schools*. It features such black activists on educational issues as Rachel Noel, Jennie Rucker, Evie Dennis, Omar Blair, and Marie Greenwood.

Features on Lois Heath were in *DP*, April 28, 1957, p. 3A, and May 7, 1957, pp. 1, 3, and *RMN*, March 18, 1963, p. 14. She is in the 1958 *Who's*, 249. I mention her and Jackson Fuller in *Park Hill Promise*, 173. *DP*, December 29, 1965, p. 1

Zone 1, highlighted her many activities. Shikes, "Three Superintendents," 262, profiles her role on the board. *DP*, May 6, 1957, p. 1, and May 7, 1957, p. 1, and *RMN*, May 6, 1957, p. 5, looked at her re-election. Schwartzkopf, "Collective Bargaining," 120, paints Fuller as an outsider on the school board.

Voting returns, including precinct-by-precinct breakdowns, are in box 23 of the Doris Banks papers at the Auraria Archives. Where possible, I have relied on them. In other cases, I have followed newspaper reports. The records of the old Denver Election Commission have not always been accessible.

Shikes, "Three Superintendents," 267–68, 270, reviews board politics in the early 1960s and the role of Ed Benton. Also see Taylor, "Leadership," 52. In 1999, Benton granted me an interview, reminiscing about his board experiences. He followed up on it on August 14, 2019, when his daughter, Margaret, was present. In passing, she shared stories about him and the school busing wars in addition to recalling her days in DPS in the 1960s and 1970s.

There are some undated clippings about the 1961 school board race in the 1960–61 PTA Historian's Notebook in GP. *RMN*, May 3, 1961, and May 11, 1961, p. 5, outlined that year's campaign. It reported the results, May 17, 1961, p. 5.

During a September 13, 2019, interview, Buddy Noel recalled the circle supporting the campaigns of his mother. He especially stressed the roles of Ed Benton and Anna Jo Haynes as among those backing her drive for the school board and giving her moral support in office.

Taylor, "Leadership," 60–63, looks at the controversy leading to the appointment of Robert McCollum to the school board. Bailey, "Journey Full Circle," 78, mostly follows Taylor's study. The DU Archives have a file on McCollum. He is in the 1958 *Who's*, 367. I talk about his South Denver role in *University Park*, 61, and *Washington Park*, 266–68.

George Bardwell, *Park Hill Areas of Denver, 1950–1966* (Denver: CCR, 1966), reviewed the changing population character of North Park Hill while giving population statistics about black Denver, esp. 3. It emphasizes the massive changing character of the population of North Park Hill, 6. Also see Doral D. O'Dell, *The Park Hill Area of Denver: An Integrated Community?* (Denver: Denver Urban Observatory, 1973), and Pearson, "Denver Case," 171. A summary of the history of desegregation from the "Park Hill Perspective," is a document in FF 2:1 of the Noel papers. I give my take on the division of Park Hill between the new northern and old southern sections of the area in *Park Hill Promise*, 7, 8, 25, 30, 48, 53, 93, 409, 429, 431, 480. That book deals with the Blue Flyer, 46, 47.

FF 12:4 of the Yasui papers surveys the massive overcrowding in Park Hill schools and the changing racial composition of the area. *DP*, December 18, 1966, p. 5, recalled the controversy over the proposed new home of Gove; cf. Watson, "Barricades," 50, and James A. Atkins, *Human Relations in Colorado* (Denver: CDE, 1968), 190–91. *SB*, February 27, 1950, p. 2, mentioned plans to sell Gove Junior High. *SB*, September 8, 1952, p. 2, looked at the school's future amidst bond election promises to construct a new home for Gove. A May 14, 1976, DPS PR heralded the dedication of new Gove. DPS records on Gove are in FF 7:10–17 of its papers at DPL. My *Modern East Denver*, 55–61, discusses the junior high.

RMN, March 14, 1966, p. 5, emphasized the narrowing of the racial gap in high schools. Also see *RMN*, March 15, 1966, p. 28. The daily observed that elementary schools were more segregated than secondary schools, March 16, 1966, p. 23. *RMN*, January 2, 1964, p. 38, told about the Urban League study and black complaints about lingering discrimination in the schools. *RMN*, March 15, 1960, p. 20, observed the challenges before minority children in DPS. FF 4:7 of the CCR papers has the proposed litigation of the East Denver Citizens Committee, mentioning its attack on the racism of DPS and the gerrymandered nature of school attendance borders.

My *North Side Story*, 462, outlines the lives of George and Allegra Saunders. *Soup Lines*, 366, 386, 412, deals with George Saunders' political career. In *University Park*, 229, I tell of the upheavals at the State Home for Dependent Children. The 1958 *Who's*, 486, includes Allegra Saunders. Taylor, "Leadership," 60, 129–30, focuses on her role on the school board. *RMN*, May 18, 1963, p. 58, outlined that year's board election. It reported the results, May 22, 1963, p. 5. *RMN*, May 11, 1961, p. 5, reviewed the controversy over Barbara Chapman. She was my first grade teacher at Park Hill in 1958–59.

School Book, 183–85, probes the study financed by the Tax Payers Protective League. I deal with that organization in *Speer's Denver*, 352–56, 362–65. The five-volume review of DPS is Franklin Bobbitt et al., *Report of the School Survey: District One* (Denver: School Survey Committee, 1916).

An undated, unsigned typescript in the Mildred Biddick papers at DPL, WH, 695, "A Citizen Committee Studied Equality of Opportunity in the Denver Public Schools," traces the origins of the Special Study Committee. It looks at how DPS recruited members, and the way the commission functioned. Biddick was DPS's coordinator of the Special Study Committee and is the likely author of the document.

SB, November 13, 1962, p. 44, listed the members of the committee. A copy of the resolution creating it is in FF 21:16 of the Yasui papers. The holding has other materials on the schools. Box 21 is particularly filled with studies relating to the Special Study Committee, including drafts of its reports and the surveys it conducted. FF 21:37 includes the specific recommendations of the group. The study is in FF 21:38–39. Known as the Voorhees Report, it is officially *Report and Recommendations to the Denver Public Schools by the Special Study Committee on Equality of Educational Opportunity in the Denver Public Schools* (Denver: DPS, 1964). Atkins, *Human Relations*, 190–91, links the emergence of the Special Study Committee to the presence of de facto segregation in DPS.

My *Washington Park*, 156–57, touches on Bill Grant. *RMN*, March 21, 1963, announced his resignation from the Special Study Committee. George V. Kelly, *The Old Gray Mayors of Denver* (Boulder: Pruett, 1974), 163–70, focuses on Grant's run for mayor.

I have followed the biographical sketch of James Voorhees in the 1955 *Social Record*, 302. The best obituary of him was in the publication of *The Holland Society of New York*, 84 (Fall 2011). *DP*, December 13, 2010, p. 18A, also looked at Voorhees' life. On August 14, 2019, Ed Benton recalled Voorhees, stressing the high-society orientation of his fellow school board member.

John Kane reviewed the contributions of Irving P. Andrews in *CL*, 38:7 (July 2009), 31–35. I drew on it for my discussion of Andrews in *Curtis Park*, 340–41. On August 14, 2019, Ed Benton shared many stories about Andrews. I deal with Roger Cisneros in *Civic Center*, 128. On occasion, the late Pierre Wolfe chatted about his sister, Suzanne Joshel. Also see Alice Millett Bakemeier, *Hilltop Heritage* (Denver: Cranmer Park/Hilltop Civic Association, 1997), 134–35.

A copy of Policy 5100 is in an unnumbered folder in box 13 of the Banks papers. Materials on it are in FF 1:6 of the Noel papers. Watson, "Barricades," 65, highlights Policy 5100. Pearson, "Denver Case," 182, mentions it. Bailey, "Journey Full Circle," 228, prints it. *SRv*, February 1964, p. 4, and April 1964, pp. 1–2, outlined the nature of the Special Study Committee and the essence of its report. Superintendent Oberholtzer's response to the Special Study Committee report is in FF 21:30 of the Yasui papers. Also see FF 21:36 of that collection. FF 1:9 of the Noel papers has a document, "Two Years After," reflecting on what had happened since the report of the Special Study Committee.

School Book, 452–53, sketches the backgrounds of Francis Bain, and Isadore Samuels, 449, 450, 458, 459, 462. *RMN*, February 26, 1965, announced Bain was not seeking to stay on the board. On March 20, 1965, it observed Samuels was retiring from the agency. That article also focused on such contenders for the board as Samuel Menin, Wallace Sam, and James Willis. *RMN*, February 25, 1965, profiled John Gerberding when he announced his candidacy for the board. *RMN*, May 12, 1965, listed its picks. On May 19, 1965, p. 5, it reported the results of the election. The daily did not print the complete returns.

Schwartzkopf, "Collective Bargaining," 95, cites Herrick Roth's views of the Rotary Club, while observing DPS deposits at American National Bank. In *School Book*, 220, 221, 291, 300, 309, 315, 340, 342, 450–51, 458, I observe the impact of the Rotary Club on DPS. Rosemary Fetter, *First 100 Years* (Denver: Rotary Club, 2011), is the official centennial history of the Denver Rotary Club.

RMN, May 14, 1965, p. 18, looked at John Amesse's candidacy. I outline his career in *Modern East Denver*, 179, drawing on Taylor, "Leadership," 79, 112, 143, 165, 183, Fetter, *First 100 Years*, 87, 178, the 1966 *Who's*, 16, and *DP*, October 7, 1971, p. 3. FF 10:1 of the DPS papers is a personal scrapbook of the physician/school board member.

Edwin Ketchum, "A History of the Colorado Education Association" (M.A. thesis, DU, 1938), 54, reports the goal of "equal educational opportunity" in 1897 and its definition as equal school financing; cf. Carleton Washburne and Myron Stearns, *Better Schools* (New York: John Day, 1928), 91. Schwartzkopf, "Collective Bargaining," 92, lists "equal educational opportunity" as among the demands of the DFT.

Ivan Illich, *Deschooling Society* (New York: Harper & Row, 1970), and Paul Goodman, *Compulsory Mis-Education* (New York: Vintage, 1964), were typical volumes of the mid-20th century decrying the severe problems of supposedly good white schools. I touch on the educational critics of post–World War II America in *School Book*, 12, 20, 359.

DP, May 21, 1965, p. 29, reviewing the outcome of that year's school board election, reported the criticisms of Oberholtzer. *DP*, December 18, 1966, p. 5, recalled demands in 1950 to oust Oberholtzer since he was a proponent of Progressive Education. *School Book*, 4, 5, 90, 225, 228, 328, 333, 343, 349, 356, 359, 453, 454, reviews debates about and definitions of Progressive Education. *DP*, September 11, 1960, p. 30C, looked at the superintendent's achievements and the way he reacted to corporate criticism of DPS spending policies.

SRv, April 1966, p. 3, and *SB*, January 3, 1967, p. 65, mentioned plans for the Advisory Council on Equal Educational Opportunity. *Final Report and Recommendations to the Board of Education by the Advisory Council on Equality of Educational Opportunity* (Denver: DPS, 1967), is the Berge Report. The "keynote" statement is 94.

William Berge is in the 1955 *Social Record*, 19, the 1979 *Social Record*, 51, and the 1966 *Who's*, 41. *DP*, August 20, 1950, p. 1CS Sb, emphasized his wedding as a high-society event. *RMN*, March 26, 1967, p. 47, reported his run for the school board. *DP*, June 2, 1966, p. 3, had looked at his views on busing. *RMN*, June 8, 1995, p. 65A, reviewed his life.

In informal conversations, Jim McNally has recalled Dennis Small, particularly at Smiley. CJ Backus helped on genealogical research on Small. There is a smidgen on him as the Smiley disciplinarian in the Branscombe papers.

Park Hill News, September 14, 1966, p. 6, sketched James Kent and his analysis of Smiley and Park Hill. Also see *SB*, September 6, 1966, p. 1, and December 5, 1966, p. 53. Interviews with Art Branscombe and PHAC chairman Dick Young in *Our Neighborhood Schools* in Alweis, *Rebels Remembered*, emphasize fears that any black urban area was, by definition, a "ghetto." They tell how they fought to keep the neighborhood integrated.

The video further features the Smiley Drastic Action Committee. On occasion, Jim McNally has reflected on his experiences as a young instructor at Smiley in the late 1960s and the upheavals following the assassination of Martin Luther King. FF 21:1 of the Yasui papers has the DPS consultant's study promoting Smiley and Baker as "superior" schools. FF 21:32 has the specific recommendations for improving Smiley in 1966. I deal with the transformation of Smiley in *Park Hill Promise*, 98–107.

Chapter Four

Robert D. Gilberts

I n January 1967, a month after Kenneth K. Oberholtzer announced he was retiring on the termination of his contract on July 31, 1967, DPS launched a national search for his successor. Members of the board believed an outsider was necessary. After 20 years of Oberholtzer, the district required fresh blood. The senior personnel were either aging or had been too completely beholden to Oberholtzer to be his successor. Nobody recognized this more than deputy superintendent Roy Hindermann. He retired from DPS along with Oberholtzer at the end of the 1966–67 schoolyear.

After considering more than 100 candidates, in April 1967 the board unanimously named Robert D. "Bob" Gilberts to lead District #1 of the City and County of Denver, signing him to a five-year contract. Born on February 2, 1924, the new superintendent grew up in a small town in Wisconsin. After service in the Army from June 4, 1943, to January 30, 1946, he entered Wisconsin State University at Eau Claire, graduating in 1950. For a while, he studied to be an engineer. When he realized this was not his calling, he dropped out, going to work as a salesman for Oscar Mayer. His wife convinced him to return to college and get a teaching certificate. Gilberts went on to gain a master's of science from the University of Wisconsin in 1955, followed by a doctorate from the University of Wisconsin in 1961. Three years later, he took charge of Madison schools after having been superintendent in Oconomowoc, Wisconsin, a town of 10,000 residents. There were around 30,000 students in the Madison school district when Gilberts moved to the Wisconsin capital.

The 43-year-old Gilberts fit DPS's specifications: he had a doctorate, experience, was young enough whereby he could lead the district for the next 20 years, and had unanimous support among the board. He beat out semi-finalist Neil Sullivan, the superintendent of Berkeley, California, who was a national pioneer in pushing the integration of a northern school district.

Gilberts was married and the father of three teenage children. The new superintendent settled at 3112 South Monroe Street. His home was near where Oberholtzer had lived, close to the Wellshire Country Club—Park Hill advocates had wanted the superintendent to move to an integrated area, ideally their abode. Personally, Gilberts was an avid hunter and a fisherman. This was also in tune with DPS traditions. Since at least the day of Superintendent Jesse Newlon (1920–27), District #1 superintendents had projected themselves as devoted fishermen. Shortly before taking the Denver job, Gilberts had discovered skiing.

In part, DPS hired Gilberts because he emphasized discipline. In Madison, he insisted on an extremely hierarchical chain of command. Illustrative was what happened when a high school refused to hire a University of Wisconsin professor as a teacher when he failed to shave off his beard. Gilberts automatically upheld the principal even while he conceded, in response to a suit filed on behalf of the instructor by the American Civil Liberties Union, that the rule was ridiculous. This was fully in tune with the traditional role of the superintendent. Since at least the early 20th century, ideologues emphasized the superintendent's office must be the center of power. Superintendents had to act in such a manner that teachers realized that their superiors were always right.

The issue of the beard was also indicative. By the 1960s, many school administrators, including those in DPS, had a hysterical hatred of young men having facial hair or hair that grew beyond their ears. On many occasions, they ordered boys to go to a barber for a shave and haircut before allowing them into classes. Coaches automatically dismissed youths from sports teams if they refused to get a shave or cut their hair. Seemingly, having a beard, mustache, or hair growing over the ears was a sign of subversion. Districts also had rules governing the hair of male teachers. They likewise had strict dress codes, including the minimum length of the skirts of girls and women teachers. Far more than dress codes, Gilberts was highly concerned about the performance gap in Denver between schools filled with white middle-class youths and those populated by poor children of color. He was sure he could do something about that.

The new superintendent arrived at DPS when sprawl was overwhelming Denver. Since the completion of the buildings stemming from bond issues in 1948, 1952, and 1955, DPS had operated on a pay-as-you-go basis in financing new buildings. While the crunch of baby boomers was slowly easing at elementaries, junior highs and high schools were still packed. Even before Gilberts took charge of the district, the system had pondered creating educational parks to redress the problem. This was another reason it had hired him. In Madison, Gilberts had pushed for an educational park.

Rather than have youngsters attend neighborhood schools, proponents of educational parks argued that the district should group its buildings together. In the same way the corporate community increasingly preferred to isolate office buildings from the everyday world in office parks, the same should be true of the school system with what were known as educational centers or educational parks. By erecting multiple structures ranging from elementaries to high schools on large, well-landscaped campuses, DPS could provide a wide variety of programs, assuring excellent education for all. In passing, educational parks would make sure there were no racial disparities within the system. Open enrollment was to allow children from throughout the city to attend classes at educational parks. The Advisory Council had recommended educational centers as a way of making equal educational opportunity a reality. In its report, it officially labeled the parks "educational complexes."

Besides, DPS needed to resume its building program. New structures were not simply to provide classroom space for the rapidly growing district, but modern buildings had to replace seemingly obsolete edifices dating from before World War I. For the most part, children were to ride the

Drawing by Daniel Lowenstein

In 1967, DPS brought in Robert D. Gilberts as superintendent.

bus to get to the new facilities. Educational parks became a crucial issue in the 1967 school board race. That contest was a prelude to fights over busing that tore apart DPS during the next decade.

The 1967 School Board Election

The board hired Gilberts about a month before voters went to the polls on May 16, 1967, to elect two directors. Neither Jackson Fuller nor Palmer Burch sought to stay in office. Before long, Fuller relocated to Boulder where he emerged as a professor of electrical engineering at CU. He died in the university city in the early 21st century.

After leaving the school board, Burch increasingly focused his attention on the legislature. In the General Assembly, he essentially rewrote the state's school finance laws. Already in 1963, he had been a crucial figure in authorizing the establishment of Metropolitan State College as a commuter campus. In 1970, Burch won election as state treasurer, suffering defeat when he sought to retain his post four years later. The ex-board member died at age 83 in 1990.

By the time Burch and Fuller stepped down from the school board in 1967, loud whispers started to resonate about forced busing to achieve racial parity in the schools. The issue was in the background when candidates debated educational parks as they sought to fill the shoes of the two departing board members.

Proponents urged educational complexes as a solution to the continued overcrowding of the schools. They paid little heed to the changing demographics of the student body. By the mid-1960s, the birth rate had declined considerably. It was obvious that the number of students would soon decline. Against this, advocates of a greater Denver were sure that the city would continue to grow and annex suburban spreads direly in need of quality schools. DPS stressed this. With the full backing of city hall, it was sure that new schools near the edge of the city would encourage residents of unincorporated areas to petition to join the City and County of Denver.

Others had extreme problems with educational parks. They saw them more as a bureaucratic empire-building scheme than a path to educational excellence. Promoters, they observed, bluntly insisted that the complexes were to be as much a part of urban renewal plans and schemes to shape residential development as they were designed to enhance learning. The district, critics stated, needed to maintain its traditional system of neighborhood schools. Not only were schoolhouses located where most students could walk to them, but they were also something of community centers, complete with after-hour programs and meeting spaces. Youths used playgrounds at the schools during weekends. Residents identified with elementary schools as defining institutions in their parts of town. Nor were old buildings automatically bad. Many were distinguished landmarks. A great city took pride in its architectural heritage, including the schools that grew up with Denver in the years before World War I.

William Berge was among those championing traditional neighborhood schools. On the heels of his leadership of the Advisory Council, he announced for the school

GP

Some schools and functions were integrated such as this gathering of elementary student leaders in the early 1950s.

board in spring of 1967. Campaigning for office, he advocated voluntary busing for integration while vehemently opposing forced busing for that purpose.

Stephen J. Knight Jr. also sought a seat on the board. He was part of a dynasty. His great-grandfather, Stephen Knight Sr., and grandfather, Stephen Knight Jr., had been on the board during much of the first half of the 20th century. The son-in-law of Stephen Knight Jr., Francis Bain, had served on the board from 1949 to 1965.

Born in Denver on January 29, 1922, Stephen J. Knight Jr. graduated from East before receiving his bachelor's of science in electrical engineering from the Massachusetts Institute of Technology. Along the way, he served in the Navy and was the father of three children who attended DPS. Active in the Chamber of Commerce, he chaired its committee on educational finance. He ran Technical Equipment Corporation at 917 Acoma

Author's collection

Stephen J. Knight Jr. led the balloting in the 1967 school board election as an opponent of educational parks and forced busing for integration.

Street. The contender had unsuccessfully sought a spot on the school board in 1965. With his wife, Barbara Kendrick, the daughter of a pioneer office supplies dealer who had once run for the school board, he showed up in the social directory.

Knight had served on the Advisory Council with Berge. There he had differed with the attorney. Signing a minority report, Knight emphasized that Denver needed neighborhood schools. Were the district to make abstract integration its goal over quality education, it might destroy itself. At the least, an integration policy for the sake of integration could very well provoke white flight from the city's many fine and stable middle-class neighborhoods. Personally, Knight lived in Bonnie Brae at 3040 Exposition Avenue, a couple of blocks west of Knight School, a building opened in 1951 at 3245 Exposition Avenue. It recalled his grandfather and great-grandfather.

Both Berge and Knight had excellent political connections as they campaigned for the board. In particular, an informal coalition backed them. Included was the Republican Party. By this time, the party was split on civil rights. For the most part, it supported them in Washington, seeing them as a way of breaking the hold of the Dixiecrats in the Democratic Party. It also sought to appeal to the fears of individuals uncomfortable with the Civil Rights Revolution. The party's 1964 presidential candidate, Barry Goldwater, had done quite well in the South as an opponent of civil rights legislation. Typical of the action of the Colorado Republican Party is that its majority in the legislature shot down a 1967 measure putting the state on record in favor of school integration.

kate stonington...
you can trust her
with your children...
with your pocketbook

Democrat for State Board of Education

In 1967, Kate Stonington unsuccessfully sought a seat on the school board. This flyer is from her failed 1972 campaign for the state board of education.

Berge and Knight emerged as an unofficial team for the school board. Against the two, advocates of integration arranged a slate of attorney Jesse B. Sauceda, who lived at 4495 Lakeridge Drive, an exclusive road in southwest Denver, and Richard Kozelka, 2270 Ivanhoe Street, who had been pastor of Park Hill Congregational Church since 1959.

Sauceda had been a member of the Advisory Council. He was ready to allow the district to experiment with an educational park. Before committing itself to educational complexes, he insisted DPS first had to prove the success of the effort with a show facility. The candidate also insisted that DPS must return to its tradition of having architecturally distinguished buildings. Alas, he complained, the structures since World War II had been incredibly bland. As the chairman of the school committee of PHAC, Kozelka had been among those praising the imposition of split sessions at Smiley. Receiving the support of board members James Voorhees and Ed Benton, he emphasized the need for more vocational education and outreach to handicapped students.

A physician's wife and educational activist, Kate Stonington, was something of the traditional PTA/mothers' candidate. Active in the Democratic Party, she was also a backer of Speak Out on School Integration. This was a group insisting that Denver had to recognize the Civil Rights Revolution and redress past segregation policies in DPS.

A 50-year-old mother of five, who had been in Denver for 18 years, Stonington stepped down as the state president of the League of Women Voters to run for the board. A graduate of Bennington College in Vermont, she was also an active backer of the Skyline Urban Renewal Project, another issue on which voters had to decide in the May balloting. It called for destroying the heart of pre–World War I downtown along Larimer Street to encourage business development. Further, she pushed the creation of a new convention center. The former speaker of the Colorado House of Representatives, Allen Dines, co-chaired her campaign. In a word, Stonington was very much part of the establishment. The Democrats recognized this, handing her their endorsement along with Sauceda for the 1967 contest. (Kozelka was an independent.) In 1972, Stonington failed in her run for the state board of education, being defeated by Republican Robin Johnson.

The Democrats wavered about endorsing another member of their party in 1967, the 35-year-old Leonard Kopec of 3068 South Gray Street in southwest Denver. A computer programmer who was the father of three, he opposed busing. What the city needed, he claimed, was a strong fair housing ordinance. It was the solution to segregated school buildings, rather than busing or educational parks. Melvin Coffman, who ran a business college, Colorado Polytechnic, campaigned for a seat on his opposition to educational parks. He also stressed the need for more vocational education and outreach to "disadvantaged and displaced children."

Knight swept the balloting, 66,478. Berge was second, 56,688. Stonington was considerably behind, 42,627. The ticket of Sauceda, 18,542, and Kozelka, 11,390, had little dynamism. Coffman gained 16,997 votes. Kopec trailed the field at 9,574.

The 1967 Bond Election

The triumph of Knight and Berge assured that Republicans retained control of the school board—Voorhees and Amesse were also members of the GOP. Voorhees emerged as president of the board after the election, besting Benton for the post. The defeated contender was too much of a maverick for others on the board to name him, the senior figure on the agency, their chief. Allegra Saunders became vice president. Amesse and Voorhees more leaned to the pro-integration, educational park program of Noel and Benton than they did to the views of the newcomers. Saunders generally lined up with her fellow Democrats Benton and Noel.

Despite the result of the election, the school board remained committed to educational parks. Creating such complexes was a central component of a $32.5 million bond issue DPS asked voters to approve on November 14, 1967. Bill Grant, who had been the original chairman of the Special Study Committee in 1962, joined with aspiring politician and Denver Democratic Party chairman Dale Tooley to lead the campaign.

In the course of 1965–66, DPS had come up with a wish list for new facilities. The district estimated they would cost up to $65.5 million. The proposal assumed that educational parks were the wave of the future. It was also premised on the belief that enrollment would continue to soar. Back on May 19, 1966, the board had called for placing the matter before the voters before March 31, 1967.

The borrowing, the first proposed since 1955, was to provide for massive new construction, particularly in emerging parts of the city. Additionally, the district promised to replace all buildings dating before 1917, i.e., structures that were now at least 50 years old. In their place, educational parks were to provide space for those who had attended classes in the older buildings. This especially impacted parts of central and Old East Denver, areas where many African-Americans lived. It also applied to much of West Denver and parts of the North Side. Both of those areas were increasingly Latino. Rather than replacing the old schoolhouses as neighborhood facilities, educational parks were to be the site of the new schools. A side effect was to deprive neighborhoods of schoolhouses as gathering spots and places where young people could go and play. Instead, students would ride the bus to the complexes rather than walk to neighborhood buildings.

Backers of the bond issue bluntly declared that old was bad. Money was to destroy Whittier and Eagleton schools. Included was demolishing the 1889 wing of Moore School. In other places, the district announced it planned to sell old buildings, using the funds to help pay for educational parks.

In plugging the educational parks and the end of neighborhood schools, the district and bond supporters cited the report of the Advisory Council: educational parks would guarantee there was no more deliberate segregation of schools. The board conceded the creation of the facilities would require the additional busing of 4,500 to 5,000 students. By that time, about 10,000–12,000 students rode the bus where no buildings were in manageable walking distance of the homes of pupils. (DPS statistics on the number of students who rode the bus varied. In some counts, it was only about 4,000. In other instances, it was upwards of 14,000.)

Given the impending school board election and the need to replace Kenneth Oberholtzer, in early 1967 the district delayed the bond issue until the fall. It also reduced its ambitions, trimming the $65.5 million request to $44 million. Besides the $32.5 million bond issue, it expected a five-year hike in the mill levy to bring in the additional $11.5 million. The wide-ranging proposal promised to expand vocational education, particularly with job-training centers for dropouts in the northeast and southwest sections of the city as part of the recently created Metropolitan Youth Education Center. The agenda included a new administration headquarters, a high school athletic field, a warehouse, and a cultural art center for elementary schools.

Most of all, Superintendent Gilberts announced the passage of the bond would lead to a reorganization of the district's elementary schools. Targeting the central city and the northeastern part of town, including Park Hill, the district promised to use the money to transform eight elementary schools into either primary (kindergarten through third grade) or intermediate schools (grades four through six). This would allow more specialized programs. The superintendent conceded some busing was necessary to make the conversion work. It was not, he stressed, the ultimate solution to segregation.

The proposed division in elementary schools did not take into account the design of buildings. Generally, they included facilities for both young learners, approximately ages five through eight, and those who were nine through 12 years of age. It was often awkward to have the children of different ages use drinking fountains and lavatories designed for those who were younger or older.

Gilberts drew on the ideas of the day. As usual, Park Hill voices were quite loud. They talked about completely reshaping their neighborhood as a mini-school district. Ideally, all children from kindergarten through fourth grade would go to Smith, Stedman, or Hallett. Those in fifth grade were to attend Philips or Park Hill. Sixth graders in the neighborhood were to ride the bus to Knight School at 3245 Exposition Avenue. Despite the overcrowding of junior high schools, proponents

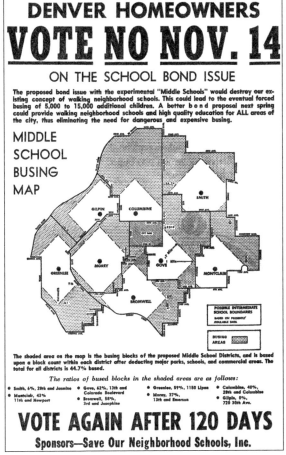

DENVER HOMEOWNERS
VOTE NO NOV. 14
ON THE SCHOOL BOND ISSUE

The proposed bond issue with the experimental "Middle Schools" would destroy our existing concept of walking neighborhood schools. This could lead to the eventual forced busing of 5,000 to 15,000 additional children. A better bond proposal next spring could provide walking neighborhood schools and high quality education for ALL areas of the city, thus eliminating the need for dangerous and expensive busing.

MIDDLE
SCHOOL
BUSING
MAP

The shaded area on the map is the busing blocks of the proposed Middle School Districts, and is based upon a block count within each district after deducting major parks, schools, and commercial areas. The total for all districts is 44.7% bused.

The ratios of bused blocks in the shaded areas are as follows:

- Smith, 6%, 28th and Jasmine
- Montclair, 43%, 11th and Newport
- Gove, 62%, 13th and Colorado Boulevard
- Bromwell, 58%, 3rd and Josephine
- Greenlee, 59%, 1150 Lipan
- Morey, 37%, 13th and Emerson
- Columbine, 40%, 28th and Columbine
- Gilpin, 0%, 720 30th Ave.

VOTE AGAIN AFTER 120 DAYS
Sponsors—Save Our Neighborhood Schools, Inc.

Doris Banks Papers, Auraria Archives

Advocates of neighborhood schools opposed the 1967 DPS bond issue. They claimed the request for money was not for physical improvements of the district, but a scheme to impose busing. The "Vote again after 120 days" was the promise DPS made that it would hold a new bond election at that time exclusively focusing on building needs if voters said no to educational parks in the November 1967 balloting. No such election was held.

of educational parks further suggested DPS close the troubled Cole Junior High School. New facilities would disperse its 1,500 students. The district, in turn, would convert the schoolhouse into its administrative headquarters.

As had been the case in the May school board balloting, tensions over racial integration haunted the bond campaign. An organized opposition emerged. DPS, skeptics told voters, could not be trusted. The bond was not for the needed expansion of schools, but a sub rosa scheme to transform the district. Educational parks were not about better schools, but were a conspiracy by those who made race and busing their primary concerns.

Keep **I**mproving **D**enver **S**chools

FOR

- UNCROWDED SCHOOLS
  62 Denver Public Schools are
  overcrowded
- NEW SCHOOLS
  4,000 Elementary School children have no neighborhood
  school—are bussed as far as 11
  miles a day.
- NEEDED FACILITIES
  17 schools have no lunchroom
  12 schools have no library
  18 have too small gymnasiums
  or no gymnasium at all
- VOCATIONAL EDUCATION
  Expanded facilities and program.

FOR

ALL THESE IMPROVEMENTS
costing only $5.00 per year in
property taxes on a house that
sells for about $15,000.

FOR

A BOND ISSUE SUPPORTED BY
Denver Chamber of Commerce,
Denver League of Women
Voters, Denver County Council
PTA, Denver Classroom Teach-
ers Association, American Le-
gion, Administrators and Super-
visors Association, Denver Fed-
eration of Teachers, Religious
Council on Human Relations for
Metropolitan Denver, and many
different neighborhood groups
in North, South, East, and West
Denver.

FOR

*Better schools make better citizens,
better property values, and a better
Denver for us all.*

Vote **FOR** Tuesday, November 14

Doris Banks Papers, Auraria Archives

*Backers supported the 1967 school bond
issue as a means of reducing the busing of
elementary school students by building more
neighborhood schools.*

Most of all, opponents decried the bond issue as a stealth measure. Essentially, they observed, it combined three completely different issues: the need for new and better facilities, the proposal for educational parks, and intermediate schools. Given that the board did not give voters a chance to weigh in on the redesign of the schools, it was best to reject the matter. Then, in 120 days, the time the board estimated it would take to organize and hold a new election, the electorate would have a chance to judge whether DPS deserved a building bond. (Despite the extremely diverse promises and purposes of the bond issue, debates over it did not include the suggestion of dividing the ballot into three separate issues.)

Proponents paid this no heed. If anything, they stressed the bond issue was a way to reduce the existing busing of elementary students by building more neighborhood schools. Virtually all were for new sections of the city that were primarily filled with white residents. Those who had previously walked to neighborhood schools in the central city, in turn, would find themselves riding the bus to educational parks.

No group was more outspoken in opposing the bond than the Junior Chamber of Commerce (the Jaycees). As the voting approached, its members leafleted the city, informing residents about the tax question's link with integration. A coalition emerged to defeat the bond issue, Save Our Neighborhood Schools. It ripped the bond issue as a Trojan Horse. While promising to build better schoolhouses, opponents declared, the proposal actually sought to rearrange the essence of the district. Backers of the bond included the Chamber of Commerce, the PTA, the Denver Classroom Teachers Association, the Denver Federation of Teachers, the American Legion, and the Religious Council on Human Relations.

The Jaycees' opposition was reflective of a breakdown of a corporate consensus on the schools. In advocating the bond issue, the Advisory Council had affirmed the necessity of business leadership of public opinion on the schools. In particular, it urged DPS create a "blue-ribbon panel." The school board, it suggested, should appoint this commission, filling it with top figures from 17th Street. It nominated possible members. Included was Ace Alexander, the kingpin of Denver Tramway, the private, profit-seeking operator of public transportation. His support was necessary, the group explained, because the educational park scheme called for depending on the city's bus system to haul many of the students to the isolated complexes. In making this point, advocates insisted there was to be no forced busing to educational parks. The group did not have any place on its blue-ribbon panel for labor officials or civil rights activists. As it was, the suggested committee never emerged.

In part, this reflected severe opposition to the bond proposal. For many voters, the question was not about bricks and mortar, but the direction of DPS. They did not buy the reorganization of the district mandated by the bond. Combined with racial unease, the populace rejected the tax by more than a two-to-one margin, 20,381–43,983. Many opposed the issue as a way of expressing their lack of confidence in the school board. The results shocked backers of the bond. They had been sure that public-spirited citizens would readily open their pocketbooks for schools even if they had qualms about the educational parks and the complete reshaping of elementary schools.

Despite the results, advocates of equal educational opportunity forged ahead. The need for better schools was urgent. This came out with the release of test scores in 1968. The results were only average. Under Oberholtzer, they had been above national norms. This was particularly the case in good, white, middle-class schools. Those in poverty-stricken neighborhoods, including places filled with poor whites and Hispanos, had never done as well as students from affluent families. Even

Photo by Phil Goodstein

Park Hill Congregational Church, at the northeast corner of 26th Avenue and Leyden Street, was among the Park Hill congregations promoting integration in the 1960s. It additionally was the home of a Community Study Hall. In 1967, its pastor, Richard Kozelka, unsuccessfully ran for the school board.

In 1960, DPS opened Thomas Jefferson as a joint junior high/high school program at 3950 South Holly Street, right across the city line from unincorporated Arapahoe County. A goal was to encourage those living outside of the City and County of Denver to agree to annexation so their children could attend the distinguished Denver Public School system.

before standardized tests had become a central component of DPS, the district had expressed concern prior to World War I about the miserable performance of Italian immigrants in North Denver schools. Now the attention was on how poorly black students performed, particularly in schools in and around Five Points.

Once more, civil rights advocates argued integration was the solution. In the process, they paid little heed to the traditional correlation between class, family background, and school success. The schools were geared to the middle-class achievement ethic. The places with poor test scores often had a low level of parental involvement. In other words, it was not just a question of racial composition, but the mixture between schools, social stratification, and the entire community.

This point was absent from the perspective of integration advocates. By making sure schools reflected the overall racial balance of the city, they argued all schools would be equal. Every academy would have the same quality textbooks, furniture, and supplies. Students would be from both rich and poor families. This, ideologues of desegregation insisted, would assure black children learned better. In contrast, many white parents, particularly those who were struggling economically, feared that by giving blacks more they would receive less. The integration scheme, they argued, would actually bring down the quality of the entire district, particularly in their children's neighborhood schools.

Amidst these controversies, DPS's élan faded. In contrast, that of the suburban Cherry Creek School District soared. Back in 1960, DPS had opened Thomas Jefferson High School at 3950 South Holly Street, directly across the street from unincorporated land in Arapahoe County. The hope was that residents would agree to be annexed by Denver so their children could attend DPS. Those living in the area close to Thomas Jefferson in Arapahoe County, in contrast, opted to join growing Cherry Hills Village—they did not want to be part of DPS.

Residents of this section of Arapahoe County supported the massive expansion of Cherry Creek High School at 9300 Union Avenue near the Cherry Creek Reservoir. Dating from 1955, Cherry Creek High School was the premier school of the southeastern suburbs. Soon it had more than 3,000 students. Increasingly, its teams triumphed in state-wide sports competitions. Those ranking the schools placed it ahead of East, George Washington, and South as the foremost high school in the region. (Despite the failure of Thomas Jefferson to induce annexations, DPS tried again when it opened John F. Kennedy in January 1966 at 2855 South Lamar Street as a joint junior high/high school. It was also close to the county line. Once more, residents preferred suburban schools rather than joining Denver.)

The Coleman Report

Champions of equal educational opportunity argued DPS could regain its edge over Cherry Creek and the suburbs by making integration a reality. The issue was urgent. If there were any doubts about this and the way desegregation promised better schools for all, proponents pointed to the Coleman Report. This referred to a study commissioned by the federal government in response to the 1964 Civil Rights Act. Lead author James S. Coleman submitted it in 1966, an investigation of the impact of racial mixing in public schools.

By this time, Coleman stood out as a critic of education as usual. He had previously blasted the mind-destroying nature of testing and high school bureaucracy. A solution was to get students out of their homes and provincial neighborhood schools. Years before he specifically addressed integration, he called for busing students across town to different sections of cities to assure they got a wider view of the world. The scholar additionally emphasized the class dimension of education. Writing at a time when Washington was conducting the War on Poverty, he stressed the correlation between school success, family backgrounds, and the education and affluence of parents.

Advocates mostly ignored Coleman's emphasis on the importance of economic class. Rather, they focused on his assertion that desegregation had produced "astonishing" results. The Coleman Report concluded that African-American youngsters did much better in predominantly white schools than they did in schools where most students were black.

Many African-Americans heralded the finding. "Quality education means integrated education," they declared. While they admitted that their children might not learn in racially mixed classrooms, they were convinced at least they would be taught—they were not sure this was the case in all-black schools. This was at the same time many middle-class blacks, particularly of old Denver families, praised their teachers who had instructed them when they had been in DPS during the previous generation. It also assumed that instructors in predominantly black schools, including African-American teachers, were incompetent or did not care.

Washington published the Coleman Report without submitting it to any peer reviews. Critics quickly pointed out there was no corroborating evidence or long-term investigations of the claims about the success of integration. They also ripped Coleman's shoddy methodology and poor sociology. Nonetheless, advocates of desegregation cited the Coleman Report as virtually holy writ. The simple racial mixture of children, they confidently announced, would assure a prosperous, post-racial society within a generation.

Among those who eventually came to question the findings of the Coleman Report was James S. Coleman. In the mid-1970s, when controversies over busing swept the country, he concluded that the racial mixture within schools really did not matter in defining educational success. The key measuring rod, he argued, was economic class and family background. As such, little was achieved by transferring inadequately prepared black children of low-income, poorly educated families, into affluent schools of the white middle-class.

The finding that racial integration was crucial to educational success did not originate with the Coleman Report. In the wake of the 1954 landmark Supreme Court *Brown* v. *Board of Education* decision, urban school districts in the North realized they might have a problem with de facto segregation. Since the *Brown* case, federal courts had repeatedly affirmed that quality education meant integrated education. They continued to focus on places, particularly in the South, with blatant de jure dual school systems. Even so, hints were heard

---

GENERAL APPRAISAL OF DENVER'S PUBLIC SCHOOLS

NEARLY SIX OF TEN DENVER RESIDENTS RATE THE CITY'S PUBLIC SCHOOLS "EXCELLENT" OR "GOOD". 1/ PARENTS OF CHILDREN ATTENDING THE SCHOOLS ARE EVEN MORE POSITIVE IN THEIR GENERAL APPRAISAL OF THE DISTRICT.

TABLE 1: RATING OF DENVER PUBLIC SCHOOLS.

QUESTION: "IN GENERAL, WOULD YOU SAY YOU THINK OF THE PUBLIC SCHOOLS IN THIS CITY AS EXCELLENT, GOOD, FAIR OR POOR?

	AS A % OF:	
THINK OF SCHOOLS AS:	ALL CITY	ALL PARENTS
EXCELLENT	17%	29%
GOOD	42	50
FAIR	15	14
POOR	4	2
DON'T KNOW; NO OPINION 2/.	22	5
TOTAL	100%	100%
(SAMPLE)	(597)	(405)

NOTABLY, ON A CITY-WIDE BASIS, PARENTS ARE MOST INCLINED TO RATE THE SCHOOLS GOOD-TO-EXCELLENT.

NEGRO AND SPANISH SUR-NAME PARENTS ARE SOMEWHAT MORE APT TO THINK OF THE SCHOOLS AS BEING ONLY "FAIR", BUT STILL ALMOST SEVEN OF TEN IN EACH OF THESE GROUPS SAY "EXCELLENT" OR "GOOD".

TABLE 1A: RATING OF DENVER PUBLIC SCHOOLS, BY SPANISH SUR-NAME AND NEGRO RESPONDENTS.

	AS A % OF:			
	SPANISH		NEGRO	
THINK OF SCHOOLS AS:	ALL	PARENTS	ALL	PARENTS
EXCELLENT	16%	21%	12%	15%
GOOD	37	48	49	54
FAIR	24	22	22	24
POOR	6	3	4	3
DON'T KNOW	17	6	13	4
TOTAL	100%	100%	100%	100%
(SAMPLE)	(201)	(199)	(199)	(203)

Auraria Archives

Though civil rights activists bewailed school segregation, residents were pleased with the schools. That was the conclusion of a public opinion survey in 1963–64 reported by the Special Study Committee on the Equality of Educational Opportunity.

that the Department of Justice would intervene in the North if it found glaring evidence of de facto segregation.

In response, school boards probed the issue in Detroit and New York. They agreed that it was best to have integrated education, but the districts did not make any moves to impose it. The lack of action impacted the 1964 Civil Rights Act. The measure specified the need for school desegregation. In part, this led Washington to commission the Coleman Report.

Heterogeneity was a buzzword of the day. Schools, proponents endlessly argued, should mirror the extreme diversity of the larger society. Even at that, proponents of integration did not see a place for alternative approaches and differing class and social attitudes in the schools. On the contrary, they agreed schools had to reflect the traditional values of discipline and achievement geared at middle-class success. The efforts did not necessarily involve more funding to help students of poverty-stricken backgrounds pay for the extra costs middle-class students usually met for field trips and additional books and instructional materials. As opposed to Washington funds providing supplementary educational programs for students attending schools in poverty-stricken areas, busing simply called for transporting such pupils across town.

At the high tide of the progress of the civil rights movement in the mid-1960s, integration advocates argued their programs could succeed through voluntary efforts. In particular, they called for open enrollment. This primarily meant allowing black youngsters to ride the bus to white schools. The board granted limited open enrollment in May 1964. Those applying to attend schools outside of their residential districts had to provide their own transportation. This automatically excluded many who lacked the funds to go to schools beyond walking distance. It was among the reasons the program did not produce the promised results. For the most part, students stayed in their neighborhood schools. In some instances, determined parents or students used open enrollment to go outside the assigned borders. Here and there, consequently, white children traveled outside of attendance borders so they did not have to attend so-called minority schools.

Not until 1968–69 was open enrollment fully in effect. By that time, the district provided "voluntary transportation" for those going to schools outside of their assigned district insofar as that enhanced integration. For a while, DPS used "voluntary transportation policy" as its euphemism for open enrollment and busing.

The district counted 1,245 applying to attend schools outside their attendance zones in 1968–69. The program required the system to bus 865 students: 573 blacks, 253 whites, and 39 Hispanos. The board further expanded open enrollment on November 21, 1968, to elementary students.

For the most part, open enrollment had a limited impact. During the 1969–70 school year, for example, about a dozen high school students, particularly at Thomas Jefferson and George Washington, jumped at the opportunity to go to East. Not only did this enhance East's white enrollment, but such adolescents were also getting out of what they considered to be extremely boring institutions. For the most part, children and families stuck with neighborhood schools. Busing schedules, opponents observed, meant students often could not participate in extracurricular activities.

Some desegregation backers opposed open enrollment. The schools, they declared, had to be universally integrated sites of equal educational opportunity. Voluntary actions by some concerned parents via open enrollment were not enough to assure this. In contrast, advocates argued open enrollment and busing were means by which DPS could relieve overcrowding, particularly in predominantly black schools in new Park Hill.

At this time, all schools throughout northeast Denver were bursting at the seams. Despite additions, replacements, and numerous portable units, DPS could not keep up with the demand as the last wave of baby boomers enrolled in elementaries. During the 1950s and into the 1960s, double sessions were common, including at such predominantly black schools in Old East Denver as Crofton, Ebert, Gilpin, Mitchell, and Whittier.

Some members of the school board, particularly those who were not enthusiastic about busing, stated the district's best option was further expansions of existing schools. New wings went up at Stedman and Hallett in 1966 and Park Hill School in 1969. Against this, integration advocates stated DPS could immediately redress overcrowding by putting black youngsters on buses and taking them to predominantly white schools in southeast Denver where space was available. They did not call for boys and girls to be transported from white sections to predominantly black schools.

In 1965, backers of the Congress of Racial Equality, joining with the Stedman PTA, urged the district to bus 113 students from the overcrowded Stedman to Carson (5420 First Avenue), Steck (425 Ash Street), and Ellsworth (27 South Garfield Street). These were overwhelmingly white schools with extra classroom space. Room in those schools reflected a generational pattern. During the 1950s and early 1960s, they had filled with the children of settlers. By the time the busing controversy heated up, the bulk of the youngsters in the enrollment zones of those schools were in junior high, high school, college, the military, or at work. Consequently, the enrollment of the schools declined whereby they had places for students from crowded buildings elsewhere in the district.

The Stedman Action Group observed that the school had a membership of 910, well beyond the building's capacity of around 750. In contrast, Carson, with 750 desks, had an enrollment of 660. Besides 15 students from Stedman, Carson also had 132 youngsters who lived in the emerging Hampden Heights in far southeast Denver, and 33 from the attendance district of McMeen School, 1000 South Holly Street.

Altogether, backers of desegregation observed, there were 576 spots available in southeast Denver. In 1966–67, busing proponents counted 169 empty seats at Carson, 100 at Ellis (1651 South Dahlia Street), 40 at Ellsworth, 54 at Slavens (3000 South Clayton Street), 98 at Steck, and 38 at University Park (2300 South St. Paul Street). There was no reason DPS could not transport African-American children to them to relieve overcrowding at predominantly black Park Hill schools. In the wake of such programs, DPS reported a total of 717 students in Carson in

1969. It listed 78 percent of them as white, 19.5 percent as black, .8 percent as Hispanic, and 1.7 percent as Asian.

The emphasis on schools in southeast Denver was revealing. Many in black Denver believed such academies were far and away superior to the schools in northeast and central Denver. They observed that the neighborhood schools African-American children attended were generally in low-income areas, places the affluent had fled years earlier. Back in their heydays, such institutes as Whittier, Gilpin, and Emerson (14th Avenue and Ogden Street) had been on the cutting edge of academic performance. They had succeeded when they educated children of affluent families and those who were committed to enlightenment. Time and again, teachers emphasized they were but one link in the chain connecting families with the larger society in determining the nature and success of an individual school.

At times, a sociological analysis was very much part of the demand for equal educational opportunity. In particular, black critics of DPS decried how, through a series of vocational aptitude tests, school counselors concluded that the overwhelming bulk of African-American students had no future except as blue-collar workers or as members of the military. As such, the schools kept youngsters out of classes providing them with advanced academic vigor and college preparation. Civil rights champions insisted the school system must provide all students the equal opportunity to advance within the economic system. A few went beyond this, insisting it was necessary to change the inequitable social-economic

Photo by Phil Goodstein

In the late 1960s, integration advocates argued the system should bus youngsters from northeast Denver to schools in southeast Denver that had additional classroom space. Among the proposed destinations was Ellis School, 1651 South Dahlia Street.

Photo by Phil Goodstein

In the late 1960s, the pictured Hallett School, 2950 Jasmine Street, had some success with a voluntary busing program that took black students from its attendance zone to University Park School at 2300 South St. Paul Street.

system. Included were calls to abolish the tracking system so there would be no distinction between bright and average students.

Even at that, a link between poverty and inferior educational performance frequently remained missing from the crusade for better schools. Integration proponents dismissed as a racist rationalization the explanation of educators who argued black children often failed to achieve the same academic distinction as did the children of the successful white upper-middle class in light of the unequal nature of American society and how the schools overwhelmingly catered to the white middle-class success ethic. On the contrary, civil rights champions declared, if DPS provided better schools for blacks, it would produce better results.

Time and again, the middle-class civil rights movement insisted all it wanted was equal opportunity, a fair and unbiased chance to compete within the existing system. Schools were the prime means to assure that the new generation could make the most of a post-racial, unbiased society rewarding merit. This meant that DPS must end its subtle forms of discrimination. Once more, the conclusion was that the best way immediately to improve schools was for blacks to ride the bus to the seemingly better white schools of southeast Denver.

CORE was most active in militant direct action for civil rights compared to the NAACP's legal strategy. Seeing they had the same goals, the groups cooperated. They formed a joint school council with the American GI Forum, a group composed of Hispanic veterans who demanded equality and respect, and the Jewish Anti-Defamation League.

The protests nudged DPS. Space increasingly became available in South Denver schools as new buildings opened in far southwest Denver during the late 1960s. Such was particularly the case in January 1968 when students took their first classes at Traylor at 2900 South Ivan Way in the West Bear Creek neighborhood. Before then, DPS had bused 411 students from the Traylor attendance area to University Park School, 2300 South St. Paul Street. Suddenly that schoolhouse, close to the University of Denver campus, had plenty of empty seats.

In 1962–63, DPS stated University Park School, with 30 classrooms on a 4.69-acre campus, had 1,020 desks with an enrollment of 1,003. In contrast, the 1970 school census listed 377 pupils living in its attendance zone. Many parents of University Park School students agreed the school should open its doors to black youngsters, especially from Hallett School. The result was a voluntary agreement in 1968 that brought some boys and girls from Hallett to University Park. To help them adjust, neighbors volunteered as host parents, assisting with transportation and logistics.

By the fall of 1969, University Park had 1,025 students: 89.9 percent of them were white, 7.5 percent were black, 1.2 percent Hispanic, and 1.4 percent Asian. Hallett, with a membership of 760, was 38.2 percent white, 58.4 percent black, 2.6 percent Hispanic, and .8 percent Asian. Efforts to link Hallett with Carson were not nearly as successful as were its ties with University Park School. Hallett parents also worked out an integration plan with Ellis School with the active involvement of host parents. Part of the program included having the guest pupil for dinner once a week. Parents in the Hallett area welcomed 11 white students from Ellis School who volunteered to go to the school in northeast Denver.

In 1970, amidst the intervention of the United States District Court in Denver integration issues, backers of Hallett convinced Judge William Doyle to exempt Hallett from the school busing order in light of its voluntary program. The Tenth Circuit Court of Appeals overturned the jurist, stating that there could be no exemptions to the requirement that DPS become a unitary district where all schools were treated alike. The ruling came shortly after the *Denver Post* had cited Hallett in 1973 as a shining example of the success of integration thanks to a committed community.

Ash Grove School, 1700 South Holly Street, was another school trying to make integration work with host parents. During much of the busing epoch until its shuttering in 1982, it offered kindergarten and grades four through six when it was paired with Hallett, kindergarten and grades one, two, and three. A DPS Desegregation Assistance Center popped up to assist the busing link of the two schools.

The Denver Council of Churches was among the organizations rallying for integration, urging the school board to make the recommendations of the Special Study Committee a reality. Listening to it and the demands of CORE, on January 20, 1966, the board authorized busing 117 students from Stedman to Carson, Evans (11th Avenue and Acoma Street), Teller (1150 Garfield Street), and Steck schools. In subsequent years, Stedman pupils also rode the bus across town to Denison (1821 South Yates Street), Force (1550 South Wolff Street), and Washington Park

(1125 South Race Street) schools. Back in 1970, as part of the first wave of court-ordered busing, DPS had sent 37 students from Stedman to Schenck (1300 South Lowell Boulevard).

The Noel Resolution

Right as debates on the Coleman Report and tensions on integration were becoming ever more taut, Martin Luther King was assassinated on April 4, 1968. By this time, DPS claimed to be very aware of growing racial tensions. It had an Office of School–Community Relations. Veteran teachers/administrators Lena Archuleta and Royce Forsyth supervised it. A prime goal was educating teachers about the growing racial antagonisms and why African-Americans had good reason for their rage.

The PTA worked closely with the schools, having an affiliated School–Community Relations Committee. Even before the death of King, the Office of School–Community Relations, working with the PTA, held forums about the specific problems faced by black youths. Included were sessions addressed by leading scholars. At them, there was a recognition that better job training and vows of equal educational opportunity were not enough. It was necessary to change the system to assure the young African-American men and women believed they had a future in middle-class America. At the same time, DPS geared up its emphasis on social work and mental health, seeing that sometimes students suffered problems from living in a crazy society.

The violence stemming from King's assassination, including in Denver schools, showed the district had to act. So argued Rachel Noel. DPS, she insisted, had conducted enough studies. In the wake of the killing of King, she pushed for what became known as Resolution 1490, the Noel Resolution. She drafted it the night of the death of King with fellow school board member Ed Benton. It ordered Superintendent Gilberts to draw up a proposal by September 30, 1968, to assure the complete equality of educational opportunity in the district. Insofar as busing was necessary to achieve this end, the motion authorized employing it to achieve racial justice.

Despite the turmoil following the assassination of Martin Luther King assassination, the board hesitated to adopt the Noel Resolution. On April 25, the majority voted to delay consideration of it at a session packed with advocates of the measure. In response, backers picketed the school headquarters and the homes of members of the board who were not committed to Resolution 1490. Black Educators United, a coalition of African-American teachers, threatened a mass boycott to force the administration to act. Both the Chamber of Commerce and city council urged the board to adopt the Noel Resolution. In contrast, many in the community feared it. Numerous speakers denounced it at packed public hearings at the auditoriums of Thomas Jefferson and Abraham Lincoln high schools.

As tensions were simmering, Benton and Noel convinced fellow board member John Amesse to endorse the measure. Just before the crucial board meeting on the resolution on May 16, 1968, board President James Voorhees threw his support to the Noel Resolution. He agreed to vote for it in exchange for writing the second

In 1951, DPS rebuilt University Park School, 2300 South St. Paul Street. The academy became the home of a pioneer busing program for integration in 1968.

half of the resolution, explaining the purposes of the declaration. (The first part of the Noel Resolution proper was two short paragraphs; part two, by Voorhees, was about three pages.)

Seeing which way the wind was blowing, Allegra Saunders also voted for the Noel Resolution, giving the pro-busing measure a five-to-two majority against the opposition of Bill Berge and Stephen J. Knight Jr. The last especially feared it, predicting special outreach to improve the education of black children could "incite riots." Seeing that victory was in the air, backers of the school boycott canceled the protest. Even at that, nearly half of the district's black children were out of school on May 16. Champions of the Noel Resolution asserted the measure would undoubtedly redress the division and violence sweeping the racially polarized city and country.

In many ways, there was nothing new about Resolution 1490. It built on the recommendations of the Special Study Committee, calling for the district to consider racial, ethnic, and social-economic differences when setting school attendance zones. The Noel Resolution stated that, once the board had pondered the superintendent's plans for equal educational opportunity, it would act to make the program a reality for the 1969–70 schoolyear.

Speak Out on School Integration was a community group heralding the Noel Resolution. George Bardwell, a statistician who taught at DU, chaired its steering committee. He frequently showed up as an expert witness who cited mathematical studies to support liberal programs. Prior to the Special Study Committee, he had worked with Noel on a school advisory probe of how the district could best allocate its resources. In the process, he started accumulating massive statistics about all aspects of the district.

Future school board members Omar Blair and Kay Schomp were members of the Speak Out governing body. So was Sheldon Steinhauser, the longtime head of the Anti-Defamation League. Dennis Gallagher, a rising, young North Denver politician who was a product of parochial schools, was among the few people in that part of town to support Speak Out and school integration.

Citizens for One Community was another backer of integration. It advocated busing insofar as transporting students between schools was necessary to achieve equal educational opportunity. Park Hill activists especially supported the group. In 1968, they were part of a Citizens for One Community picket line of DPS headquarters, demanding the adoption of the Noel Resolution. The next year, a white Park Hill activist, Helen Wolcott, took two daughters of black educator Anna Jo Haynes to Knight School as part of what Citizens for One Community called a "practice run" for racial balance right as tensions were soaring in the impending school board election.

Time and again, Citizens for One Community insisted Denver needed a multiracial coalition for the benefit of all. To show its inclusiveness, the group had three co-chairmen, a black, a white, and a Hispano. The organization stressed that a former Juvenile Court judge, a social worker, and cleric had joined hands to form it. Citizens for One Community purchased ads on 50 Yellow Cabs calling for "Integrate Grade Schools Now." The organization included a youth group, Students for One Community.

The Gilberts Plan

In response to Resolution 1490, Superintendent Robert D. Gilberts turned to two top functionaries, Joseph Brzeinski and Charles Armstrong. They drafted "Planning Quality Education—A Proposal for Integrating the Denver Public Schools." To present it simultaneously to the school board and the public, Gilberts went on the air of the district's television station, Channel Six, at 7:00 PM on October 10, 1968, to announce the city's desegregation initiative. The district, the superintendent informed viewers, was to overcome racial disparities by busing a limited number of students. For the most part, the undertaking was designed to take blacks, especially from Park Hill, to white schools where there was extra classroom space. (There was nowhere near the same eagerness for busing among blacks living west of Colorado Boulevard as its advocates in Park Hill.)

In the course of the next four years, during annual phases, Gilberts explained, his plan would slowly but surely integrate the district. The prime means was by allowing blacks to get on the bus and ride to white schools. White students had the opportunity to attend black schools. This required a considerable expansion of the district's bus fleet. In particular, the program called for spending $624,000 to acquire 30 new buses. The initiative mandated 2,700 youngsters ride the bus to school for desegregation in addition to the 13,000 whom the district already bused where no schools were in walking distance of students' homes.

The superintendent's suggestions additionally called for DPS to commit itself to a new building program modeled on the failed 1967 bond issue. The total bill, including construction, was $120 million. The board and media immediately labeled this the Gilberts Plan. Under it, ideally, all schools would have the same racial composition. As such, no whites would be bused to black schools since all schools would now have a ratio comparable to the total enrollment of about 64 percent white, 15 percent black, and 21 percent Latino.

To get whites into what were then black schools, the Gilberts Plan recommended magnet schools. These were outstanding programs pulling in students. Such had been among the suggestions of the 1966 report of the Advisory Council on Equality of Educational Opportunity. In particular, the Gilberts Plan called for transforming Manual into a college preparatory academy. Additionally, there was to be a DPS Astro-Aerospace Center focusing on advanced mathematics and space science along with a scientific-technological education program. The district was further to have a cultural arts facility, particularly reaching out to students who wished classes in music, acting, and television production. Complexes of elementary schools were to have shared cultural arts programs, reading clinics, academic facilities, pre-primary programs, and special education offerings. The assumption was that

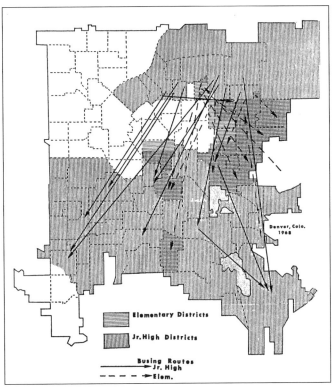

The integration plan of Superintendent Robert Gilberts, released in October 1968, primarily called for busing black students out of northeast Denver to the southeastern and southwestern parts of the community.

black and white families were alike and would be equally committed to having their children attend these distinctive programs.

By this time, Manual had an extremely problematic reputation. Academic performance was hideous. In many cases, all a student needed to do to graduate was to attend classes regularly and behave. Accusations flew that the principal manipulated the Proficiency and Review test to assure his students literally made the grade. Typical of the school is how it endlessly emphasized its outstanding basketball teams and excellence in the Junior Reserve Officers Training Corps program; academics came across as a secondary concern.

Even at that, alumni proudly rallied to Manual in response to suggestions DPS rename the place Martin Luther King High School. Not only was the new moniker to honor the civil rights leader, but it was to blot out the manual training heritage of the school. Protests against this effort to erase a crucial part of DPS's heritage led to the collapse of the suggestion. Not until 1986 did DPS get around to having an academy named for Martin Luther King when it dubbed its new middle school at 19535 46th Avenue in memory of the preacher. Additionally, Manual alumni loudly protested the defamation of the school, pointing to its many distinguished graduates. They hinted racism was why many so picked on their alma mater.

If a magnet for Manual were not enough, the Gilberts Plan also drastically revised high school borders. Under the new proposal, many blacks living in parts of new Park Hill were to go to George Washington rather than East. The document once more sought to make educational parks a reality. In some scenarios, virtually

Photo by Phil Goodstein

The Gilberts Plan called for transforming Manual High School, as seen from the southwest corner of 28th Avenue and Williams Street, into a college prep program, drawing in white students from across the city.

all students would be bused to educational parks/clusters, showing there was no racial edge to the district.

To emphasize the urgency of the effort, in 1969 the superintendent had DPS publish the test results from each school. Previously, the administration had only reported them by the district as a whole. Superintendent Oberholtzer argued it would not do to list them on a school-by-school basis because that might "hurt morale." The release of the scores of the individual schools showed what the district's former leader had been trying to hide.

The tests revealed the mass divisions within the city. Returns from some schools were outstanding—these were invariably in white, affluent parts of the city; other schools hovered at around the tenth percentile including such widely dispersed academies as Wyman (16th Avenue and Williams Street), Alcott (West 41st Avenue and Tennyson Street), and Alameda (West Byers Place and South Bannock Street).

In 1969, Alameda's enrollment was 46.2 percent white and 50.2 percent Hispanic. The district counted 80.2 percent of the students at Alcott as white, 2.1 percent were black, and 17.3 percent were Hispanic. The predominantly white Thatcher School (South Grant Street and Colorado Avenue) was another "low-achieving school," defined as having scores below the 40th percentile for either students in third or fifth grade. So was another South Denver academy, Lincoln School at South Pearl Street and Exposition Avenue. The survey, with a total of 48 "low-achieving schools," additionally listed such places in southwest Denver as Knapp (500 South Utica Street), Belmont (4407 Morrison Road), Munroe (3440 West Virginia Avenue), Westwood (3615 West Kentucky Avenue), and College View (2680 South Decatur Street). Some were primarily white; others had heavily Hispanic enrollments. Latino students predominated at other poorly performing schools such as Fairview (West 11th Avenue and Decatur Street), Eagleton (845 Hazel Court), Elmwood (720 Galapago Street), and Greenlee, (1150 Lipan Street). Emerson School on Capitol Hill, the majority of whose students were white, also was a low-achievement school. So was Stedman, mostly filled with black students in Park Hill.

Public Hearings

To hear what the community thought about the Gilberts Plan, the board held a series of public hearings. Thirty-nine signed up to speak at a session at South High on November 12, 1968. Among them were representatives of the Chamber of Commerce and the Jaycees. Both organizations endorsed the effort. The League of Women Voters (LWV) generally backed it, pointing out where it believed the school board could improve it. The American Civil Liberties Union also lined up behind the superintendent's suggestions.

In contrast, Jules Mondschein, an activist with PHAC who was a cochairman of Citizens for One Community, joined with liberal statistician George Bardwell of Speak Out on School Integration in criticizing the Gilberts Plan. The proposal, they argued, was essentially milquetoast. It was far more tokenism than an actual effort to provide true integration. Nor was the Denver Federation of Teachers happy about the Gilberts Plan. The measure, the union claimed, was simply a paper gesture, a pretend solution to problems in the district. The Park Hill Action Committee likewise stated the Gilberts Plan did not go far enough. Fred Thomas of the group loudly asserted that he and other African-Americans were "sick of gradualism."

The way members of Speak Out, PHAC, and Citizens for One Community attacked the Gilberts Plan reflected the polarized views on the schools. After years of discrimination, aggressive civil rights advocates insisted it was high time DPS take the drastic actions necessary to cut out the racial cancer that had long undermined the integrity of the district. Proponents of integration pointed out how few students had taken advantage of open enrollment. DPS needed a firm hand at the top relentlessly acting to make desegregation a reality.

Champions of neighborhood schools also blasted the Gilberts Plan. The proposal, opponents observed, failed since it did not forthrightly recognize that education was the purpose of the schools. The district had no business engaging in sociological schemes, programs far more likely to cause youngsters to experience trauma than learn. Busing, they lamented, more threatened to destroy a functioning system than produce educational excellence. It would make racial quotas, not academic achievement, DPS's foremost concern. Besides, if African-Americans were so enthusiastic about integration, they would have taken advantage of open enrollment to make it a reality. Their failure to do so showed that proponents of busing did not represent black Denver.

Other packed hearings followed. On November 26, 1968, for example, 80 spoke at a South High school board meeting lasting from 7:30 PM to 2:00 AM. Countless groups appeared, wishing to make their opinions known. The board held another tumultuous hearing on January 16, 1969. At noon that day, 100 advocates of integration, including blacks, whites, and Hispanos, picketed school headquarters to show their support for the Gilberts Plan. In the evening, self-professed members of the "Silent Majority" vehemently attacked the effort at a board session at South High. Opponents loudly proclaimed that the adoption of the Gilberts Plan meant "destroying neighborhood schools by forced busing." As such, those against the scheme insisted they were no longer the Silent Majority—they were making themselves heard. They branded busing advocates as nothing but the "Vocal Minority." (At this time, facing numerous tumultuous demonstrations, particularly against the Vietnam War, newly inaugurated President Richard Nixon claimed his backers were the "Silent Majority.")

After endless controversy, on April 24, 1969, by a five-to-two vote (Noel, Benton, Voorhees, Amesse, and Saunders opposed to Berge and Knight), the school board officially authorized the Gilberts Plan, Resolution 1531. Specifically, the measure ordered the implementation of busing of elementary students for desegregation for the new schoolyear.

Backers insisted the issue was equal educational opportunity. Busing was simply a tool to achieve it. There was nothing new about busing. Even before the arrival of the motor bus, horse-drawn vehicles had transported some students to school in semi-rural sections that came to encompass District #1 of the City and County of Denver.

On January 16, 1969, civil rights advocates picketed the DPS administration building at 414 14th Street.

Rapid growth after World War II forced the system once more to depend on busing, particularly for children living miles away from the closest schools. A 1949 report listed 2,626 children, out of an enrollment of 50,422, being transported to school daily on 18 buses. Additionally, there were two emergency buses. In 1960, DPS stated it had 42 buses, hauling 5,400 students to classes everyday when it reported a membership of 90,518.

The Religious Council on Human Relations, a backer of integration, pointed out that, by the time Superintendent Gilberts announced his plan, about half of the students at such schools as University Park, Knight, College View, and Garden Place (4425 Lincoln Street) already rode the bus to school. Approximately a quarter of those going to Berkeley (5025 Lowell Boulevard), Cory (1550 South Steele Street), Denison, Palmer (995 Grape Street), Pitts, Rosedale (2320 South Sherman Street), Ash Grove, Bradley (3051 South Elm Street), Carson, and Whiteman (451 Newport Street) also arrived via bus. Nearly 80 percent of the junior high students at Thomas Jefferson came to school on buses.

School buses also transported students to distinctive programs. Such was the case with those attending Evans School at West 11th Avenue and Acoma Street. Since the 1920s, it had classes educating students with severe seeing and hearing impairments. Boettcher School, 1900 Downing Street, a place opened in 1940, was a location for youngsters with extreme physical problems.

Busing was also part and parcel of many suburban and rural districts. Some, who moved out of Denver to keep their children from being bused, found their youngsters had to ride buses in the suburbs. Observing this, opponents of busing for integration invariably labeled the integration scheme "forced busing." Some advocates referred to it as "cross-town busing." Backers, observing the mass transportation of students in suburbs on buses further remarked, "It's not the bus—it's the color of the children that it's bringing to your neighborhood." For that matter, proponents of busing repeatedly stated busing was not the solution to the lack of equal educational opportunity; it was simply a tool to make that goal possible.

When Gilberts first outlined his plan, 10,062 of the district's 98,848 students were eligible for busing in addition to 500 who were enrolled in special education programs. DPS stated 5,582 elementary students rode the bus; there were 4,480 in junior high who depended on busing. No high school students were bused to school. Elementary students who lived more than a mile from their schools qualified for busing — 4,576 were eligible. The others were bused from 10 elementaries to schools far from their homes to alleviate overcrowding. Forty-one of the district's 93 elementaries received students who arrived on buses. Fifteen junior highs likewise had bused-in students. Only Smiley had students living in its attendance zone who rode the bus elsewhere. Garden Place and University Park had far and away the most students who arrived on bus, more than 500 a day. To handle the busing load, in 1969, right after committing itself to the Gilberts Plan, the school board authorized the purchase of 27 new school buses. The decision, opponents argued, showed the board was already committed to busing as outlined in the superintendent's program.

Back in 1962, when Park Hill civil rights proponents first incessantly raised the issue of the need for integration, leading voices of the Park Hill Action Committee emphasized they were against busing to achieve desegregation. In other words, the question was not busing; it was quality integrated education and who was riding the bus and why. Advocates so dismissed opponents as racists. Champions of neighborhood schools branded this as name-calling. They observed that, given its limited budget, DPS should be spending its money on better schools, not simply moving students about in the name of abstract equal educational opportunity.

School Board Meetings

Debates on busing impacted the nature of school board meetings. Until Palmer Burch convinced his fellow board members on January 20, 1965, to amend the bylaws to stipulate the body was to hold its monthly business meeting on the third Thursday of the month at 7:00 PM, the board had traditionally assembled on the third Thursday of the month at either 10:00 AM or 2:00 PM whereby working members of the public were unable to attend.

As was the case in most districts, board members tended to back the superintendent. They lacked the intimate, inside knowledge of the district. Some were lazy, not bothering to do independent reading and research about what was happening within DPS. Instead, they relied on the expertise of the administration. Usually, prior to the formal meeting, board members gathered in a work session where they hashed out the issues and decided how to proceed at the official meeting.

As controversy over busing escalated, the board room in the central administration building at 414 14th Street, which could accommodate about 100 people, was packed beyond capacity. At the peak of community concern over desegregation, upwards of 1,500 residents descended on school board meetings. To handle the crowds, the governing body moved its sessions to high school auditoriums. Before long, the board settled on South High as the best location for its meetings. This caused new problems.

South High students were the "Rebels." Confederate lore was part of the school. *The Confederate* was the name of the student newspaper. The yearbook was *Johnny Reb*. Prior to the construction of All City Stadium to the south of the high school in 1957 as the main location of DPS football contests, South athletes played at Rebel Field. Symbols celebrating the slaveholders' rebellion were scattered around the school.

Right about the time controversies over busing were simmering in 1965, students arranged for the installation of a terrazzo mosaic of Johnny Reb in the foyer of the school. Other Denver high schools responded by using the Johnny Reb logo in high school gyms where they displayed the symbols of all of the city's high schools. On top of this, the South student body overwhelmingly voted on November 21, 1967, to make the Stars and Bars, the Confederate battle flag, the school's official

CHS

No busing signs were common at school board meetings in the late 1960s when the subject of school integration convulsed the city.

banner. Supporters proudly flew it at football games. Confederate battle flags were on display in the auditorium.

Nothing in the school celebrated the fight for freedom. For that matter, it was impermissible for South students to be rebels in word or deed against an overbearing school administration. Only a revolt against the United States government in the name of defending slavery, in other words, was tolerated by the school.

Not until the 1990s did the South community start to grasp the obnoxious essence of such symbols and lore. It dropped the name *Johnny Reb* from the yearbook in 1991. The school newspaper became *The Gargoyle* four years later, observing the many gargoyles decorating the school. Even at that, the alumni association continued to label its newsletter *Confederate Alumni*. A rug cloaked the Johnny Reb mosaic in the foyer. Black students convinced the school board on February 19, 2009, that a griffin, rather than Johnny Reb, was the official symbol of the school. (A carving of a gigantic griffin hovers atop the main entry to South High.) By this time, the school was the most ethnically mixed academy in the area as the home of English as a second language program for students from around the world. The school's drum corps remained the Denver South Rebel Line.

This was well in the future. As the citizenry packed the South auditorium for school board meetings, civil rights activists loudly complained about the

Confederate symbolism. The school board responded by ordering custodians to remove or cover symbols celebrating the slave power's government. Meanwhile the board sought to limit citizen input.

An opportunity for the populace to address the board was part of the governing body's meetings. On occasion, the public loudly spoke out. Some who addressed the board droned on endlessly. Especially as clashes over busing came to a head, the board limited citizen comments to three minutes. A timekeeper rang a loud bell once the speaker passed the limit. Rules eventually required those wishing to speak to sign up at least 24 hours in advance of a meeting designed to receive public input. A group of five or more individuals had the right to cede their time to one

Photo by Phil Goodstein

A griffin guards the 1926-vintage South High School. Students there were long the Rebels, celebrating the slaveholders rebellion during the Civil War. Not until 2009 did those at South become the Griffins. Back in the late 1960s, the school board held many of its meeting in the school's auditorium.

speaker for a total of 15 minutes. Time limits were seemingly necessary. On occasion there were so many speakers and such pressing business that the sessions did not adjourn until 3:00 AM.

Gene Kane was a regular in speaking out at the public hearings. Vehemently anti-busing, he styled himself the representative of North Denver at school board meetings. Sporadically, he chaired meetings at Highland Park Presbyterian Church at West 29th Avenue and Julian Street where those present agreed busing did far more to hurt than help the schools and students.

Tensions at the school board meetings were often so extreme that some mocked the sessions as the "Thursday Night Fights." Fearful that passions might explode, police, dressed to look like janitors, were in the lobby outside the South auditorium. They never had to intervene during or after the gatherings.

So one and all could see the meetings, the board arranged for Channel Six to broadcast them. Instead of monthly meetings, the board convened more frequently. Most of the sessions remained at the administration headquarters. These were officially work sessions. As they had in the past, members frequently made decisions at them that they ratified at the official Thursday evening business meetings.

In 1992, the board declared the public could address it during a meeting on the first Thursday of the month. On the second Thursday, it had its work session. The third Thursday saw a legislative session where it set policy. School board elections remained heavily contested. No contest more decided the future of the district and busing than the 1969 balloting.

A Note on Sources:

Articles in *RMN*, April 16, 1967, p. 5, and April 21, 1967, p. 5, and *DP*, April 17, 1967, p. 11, told of the selection of Robert Gilberts as superintendent. Also see Taylor, "Leadership," 93–94, 154. There are clippings about the superintendent in FF 1:16 of the DPS papers. DPL additionally has a clipping file on Gilberts. Richard "Dick" Koeppe, Gilberts' right-hand man as DPS superintendent, shared his memories of the leader during an August 26, 2019, interview.

DP, April 23, 1967, p. 42, was a portrait of Gilberts' role in Madison from that city's newspaper, *Capital Times*. *DP*, October 22, 1967, p. 6 Contemporary, profiled his wife and personal life. Chalkbeat, January 29, 2020, and *DP*, March 7, 2020, p. 8A, observed continuing discrimination experienced by DPS teachers based on their hair styles. Watson, "Barricades," 78, outlines the push for educational parks.

I trace Palmer Burch's fate after he left the school board in *School Book*, 462–63. FF 2:17 of the Noel papers reports a posthumous award Metro bestowed on Burch in 1990 as something of the father of the school.

FF 21:13 of the Yasui papers has the report on the "Educational Complex" of the Advisory Council. A draft in FF 21:19, shows that "complex" had replaced "park" in writing the document. The study particularly stressed the urban renewal component of the program when it listed sites proposed for educational parks, pp. 24–31.

RMN, February 28, 1965, profiled Stephen J. Knight his announcing for the board in his unsuccessful race that year. Watson, "Barricades," 78–80, 113–14, emphasizes Knight's opposition to educational parks and active integration measures. A copy of Knight's minority opinion to the Berge Report is in FF 12:5 of the Yasui papers. *DP*, May 12, 1967, included an election supplement. On pp. 6–7, it specifically focused on candidates for the school board.

Pearson, "Denver Case," 183, discusses the legislature's rejection of the bill advocating the elimination of school segregation in 1967. *Park Hill Action News*, June 1966, heralded the school work of Richard Kozelka. On September 8, 2019, retired Park Hill Congregational pastor Phil Campbell recalled Kozelka and discussed the congregation's civil rights commitment.

Taylor, "Leadership," 95–97, fails to mention educational parks in her confused discussion of the 1967 school board election. *SB*, May 8, 1967, p. 133, listed the candidates. *DP*, May 17, 1967, pp. 1, 81, reviewed the contest. *DP*, May 24, 1967, p. 21B, reported Voorhees' election as president of the school board. Schwartzkopf, "Collective Bargaining," 184, argues that Benton was too much a maverick to gain the presidency of the board.

Materials on the 1967 bond issue, including flyers supporting and opposing it, are in box 8 of the Banks papers. *SRv*, October 1967, and November 1967, were both filled with articles touting how DPS planned to use the money from the bond. A discussion of the push for the 1967 bond issue, complete with educational parks and soaring enrollment, is pp. 39–53, of the 1966 Educational Complex report of the Advisory Council.

The Advisory Council's Educational Complex report, p. 36, suggested the Park Hill mini-district. It mentioned the possible closing of Cole, p. 37. A statement of Save Our Neighborhood Schools is in an unnumbered folder in box 13 of the Banks papers. The 1966 Advisory Council's Educational Complex report, pp. 53–54, stressed the need for corporate leadership, the Blue-Ribbon Panel, and the participation of Ace Alexander and Tramway.

RMN, November 5, 1967, p. 5, outlined the bond issue and Gilberts' advocacy of it. Watson, "Barricades," 82, emphasizes the surprise of bond backers on the rejection of the measure.

Dan Goe, principal of Cherry Creek High from 1969 to 1972, discussed the growth and prestige of that school during an April 24, 2018, conversation. There is mention of the Cherry Creek School District in *Perspectives in Arapahoe County* (n.p.: Arapahoe County Board of Commissioners, [ca. 1964]), 64–67. Tom Romero stresses the growth of the Cherry Creek district, linking it to the expansion of the suburbs and their desire to be separate from Denver and school busing in *DU Law Review*, 90:5 (October 2013), 1044.

James S. Coleman et al., *Equality of Educational Opportunity* (Washington: Government Printing Office, 1966), known as the "Coleman Report," was the key document heralding integration as a proven means of enhancing education. *Saturday Review*, January 20, 1968, pp. 57–58, 67–68, echoed the conclusions of the Coleman Report. Taylor, "Leadership," 98–99, tells of the impact of the study.

David Berliner and Bruce J. Biddle, *A Manufactured Crisis* (New York: Basic Books, 1995, 2015), 70–73, is a devastating critique of the Coleman Report and its extremely sloppy methodology. Goodman, *Compulsory Mis-Education*, 73, 151–52, observed Coleman's criticisms of the schools and his busing proposals in the years prior to the issuing of the Coleman Report.

McGoey, *No Free Gift*, 126, stresses the class emphasis of the Coleman Report. The book does not link it to debates over busing. Ibid., 129, observes how the poverty dimension about school problems quickly disappeared from debates over equal educational opportunity. Orfield, *Must We Bus?* 99, 106, 120, deals with the way Coleman emerged as a hero of opponents of busing in the 1970s.

Another highly discussed book of the day stressing class over abstract integration, was Christopher Jencks, *Inequality: A Reassessment of the Effect of Family and Schooling in America* (New York: Basic Books, 1972). The chapter by J. Harold Flannery on "De Jure Resegregation," in Browning, *From Brown to Bradley*, 149, hints that socioeconomic factors were far more important than racial differences in terms of defining school success and the workings of integration. Generally, this subject was absent from Denver integration debates. Even so, the Wilma Webb interview in *Our Neighborhood Schools* in Alweis, *Rebels Remembered*, argues that busing was not enough; equal opportunity required reforming the inequities of the economic system.

FF 21:16, 19, of the Yasui papers have materials on the desegregation studies of the 1950s in New York City and Detroit, and the 1964 Civil Rights Act's desegregation stipulations. The 1966 Educational Complex report of the Advisory Council, p. 47, makes this point. Ibid., pp. 7–8, 14, 17, emphasizes the need for heterogeneity in the schools.

The 1970 PTA Community Relations Notebook in GP has a resolution of the Religious Council on Human Relations, arguing "quality education means integrated education." There is no mention of busing controversies in the 1972–73 PTA History Notebook in GP, compiled at a period of extreme tensions on the subject. In contrast, the PTA newsletter, *Communiqué*, frequently commented about busing and the court order in 1981–82, e.g., May 1981, p. 3, November 1981, p. 5, December 1981, p. 7, and February 1982, p. 1.

SB, April 24, 1962, p. 122, May 11, 1964, p. 133, and April 11, 1966, p. 117, and October 13, 1969, p. 25, and *SRv*, October 1965, p. 4, April 1968, p. 1, April 1969, p. 1, and February 1970, p. 4, touch on open enrollment. *DP*, May 21, 1964, p. 1, told about the program. Also see FF 21:21 of the Yasui papers. *RMN*, January 6, 1966, p. 5, observed that few students accepted open enrollment. Meadow, "Hard Years," *CJ*, May 8, 1974, pp. 23–26, noted that open enrollment sometimes allowed whites to travel outside of the attendance district of minority schools. Art Branscombe makes this point in an interview in *Our Neighborhood Schools* in Alweis, *Rebels Remembered*. Pearson, "Denver Case," 182, 186, emphasizes the transportation problems associated with open enrollment.

In a January 9, 1969, letter to school board president James Voorhees, integration activist Doris Banks spelled out the problems with open enrollment and the need for a universally desegregated school system. A copy is in an unnumbered folder in box 13 of her papers. In a letter to the editor, *GPHN*, August 2019, p. 10, former school board member Marcia Johnson reflected on the extreme strain busing put on the lives and schedules of elementary students, including the problems with extracurricular activities.

SB, November 2, 1964, p. 33, mentioned a representative of the Denver Council of Churches speaking to the school board in favor of equal educational opportunity. *SB*, November 29, 1965, p. 49, reported Helen Wolcott, a white mother and backer of Stedman, urging DPS to bus students from Stedman. Also see *DP*, November 18, 1965, p. 3. *SB*, January 3, 1966, p. 65–66, told of the board's response and the suggestion of a new equality in educational opportunity committee. On January 24, 1966, p. 77, and January 31, 1966, p. 81, *SB* further discussed overcrowding in Park Hill schools and the options of busing and construction.

The pleas of the Stedman Action Group are in FF 21:25 of the Yasui papers. FF 21:43 counted the open seats in southeast Denver schools. Statistics about Carson, busing, and school capacity are also on p. 34 of the Educational Complex report of the Advisory Council.

Our Neighborhood Schools in Alweis, *Rebels Remembered*, spells out the civil rights argument that DPS was a racist system which failed to provide black youngsters with challenging courses and equal educational opportunity. As such, it asserts, the schools blocked the path of middle-class success for African-American youths. *New Yorker*, August 19, 2019, p. 20, looked at a 21st-century claim of black anti-racist Ibram Xolani Kendi that different perspectives in the black community provide an alternative way of measuring the success of African-Americans in the schools.

FF 6:94 of the DPS papers counted 411 students moving from University Park School to Traylor. I discuss University Park School and the integration program in *University Park*, 119. Phil Lutz who attended University Park School in the 1950s and whose wife once taught there, recalled the place on August 7, 2019.

SN, November 30, 1970, p. 25, touched on the busing of students from Stedman. FF 1:13 of the Rachel Noel papers focuses on the Hallett plan. The 1970 Community Relations PTA Notebook in GP observes efforts to link Carson and Hallett schools. FF 12:4 of the Yasui papers lists the extreme overcrowding of the schools and the busing at them in the mid-1960s.

DP, February 5, 1969, p. 1 Zone 2, highlighted host parents and integration efforts at Ellis. There are additional materials on them in an unnumbered folder in box 13 of the Banks papers. *DP*, July 1, 1973, p. 28, heralded Hallett as an integration success. I discuss the links of Hallett and University Park schools in *Park Hill Promise*, 95. The Ash Grove PTA collection at DPL, WH 923, includes mention of the host parents and efforts at desegregation. There is passing reference to the Desegregation Assistance Center in the 1978–79 PTA Notebook in GP.

GP has a notebook on "School–Community Relations" for 1967–68. It includes the programs of some of the forums DPS sponsored on that topic, complete with transcripts of speeches. The same collection has materials on the PTA committee on School–Community Relations. The box holding these materials additionally has literature on DPS's emphasis on mental health and social work in the 1960s.

FF 1:6 and 2:4 of the Noel papers include the Noel Resolution and reports about it. A copy of the document is also in FF 1:18 of the DPS papers. Rachel Noel and Ed Benton tell of the origins of the Noel Resolution in *Our Neighborhood Schools* in Alweis, *Rebels Remembered*. Included is the explanation of how James Voorhees wrote much of the explanatory section of the Noel Resolution. Robert Connery, *DU Law Review*, 90:5 (October 2013), 1098, states Noel and Benton drafted the resolution on the night of the murder of King.

Pearson, "Denver Case," 184, emphasizes the politics behind the adoption of the Noel Resolution. *RMN*, May 15, 1968, gave Rachel Noel's version of her resolution. Also see Watson, "Barricades," 94, 95, and the Educational Complex report of the Advisory Council, pp. 22–24. Materials on the Noel Resolution and the interrelationship between the schools and the city are in FF 40:18 of the Thomas Currigan papers at DPS, WH 929.

Information about Speak Out on School Integration is in the Banks papers, especially box 13. Included is a list of board members of the group. There are also flyers and programs of Speak Out in the 1970 Community Relations PTA Notebook in GP.

During a September 13, 2019, interview, Buddy Noel called my attention to George Bardwell's ties with Rachel Noel on the committee studying DPS's allocation of the district's resources. *Front Page Northeast Denver*, February 2019, p. 7, focused on Helen Wolcott's activism in Citizens for One Community. She shared her memories in informal conversations on February 14, 2019, and February 27, 2020. There are scattered materials on Citizens for One Community in an unnumbered folder in box 13 of the Banks papers. Drawing on an interview with the co-director of the group, Jules Mondschein, Pearson, "Denver Case," 184, outlines the origins and purpose of the organization, emphasizing its founders.

Planning Quality Education: A Proposal for Integrating the Denver Public Schools (Denver: DPS, 1968), is the Gilberts Plan. DPS also printed it in *SR*, November 1968, pp. 1–8. *SB*, October 7, 1968, p. 29, observed Gilberts' intention to present his integration proposal on Channel Six. All four pages of *SRv*, May 1969, were devoted to the Gilberts Plan and efforts to redress segregation. *DP*, January 17, 1969, p. 1, outlined the impact of the Gilberts Plan. Meadow, "Hard Years," pp. 23–26, emphasized the busing numbers. Orfield, *Must We Bus?* 16, focuses on the Gilberts Plan's limited busing requirements. Subsequent issues of *SR* into the mid-1970s had various DPS integration proposals.

The League of Women Voters, in collaboration with Speak Out on School Integration, put together an undated mimeographed brochure, ca. 1968–69, "As a Matter of Fact: A Guide for Discussion on Quality Integrated Education," outlining the Gilberts Plan. It argued that without the program, Denver would become a city of ghettos. A copy is in box 13 of the Banks papers. Robert Connery recalls PHAC's criticisms of the Gilberts Plan and the views of Fred Thomas in *DU Law Review*, 90:5 (October 2013), 1100.

Bel Kaufman, *Up the Down Stair Case* (New York: Avon, 1966), 122, observes the practice at many schools of passing students who simply showed up and behaved. During a January 9, 2018, interview, Jimi O'Connor charged that Manual principal James Ward had manipulated the results of the P&R test at the school. Jim McNally, *Denver's Manual High School* (Denver: n.p., 2016), 77–78, reviewed the controversy over changing the name of Manual. The Blair–Caldwell Library has a gallery featuring the many distinguished graduates of Manual, emphasizing the vigor of the school.

Meadow, "Hard Years," pp. 23–26, explained why Oberholtzer refused to publish test results on a school-by-school basis. There is mention of Gilberts listing the test results by school in a note by board member John Amesse in his scrapbook, FF 10:1 of the DPS papers. *DP*, May 11, 1969, p. 36, outlined the district's "low-achievement" schools. FF 1:10 of the Noel papers has a list of such schools.

SB, November 25, 1968, p. 49, and December 9, 1968, p. 57, looked at the hearings on the Gilberts Plan. *SB*, January 27, 1969, p. 77, observed the board had officially received *Planning Quality Education*. Also see Watson, "Barricades," 105, and *DP*, January 12, 1969, p. 1G. Calvin Trillin, "Doing the Right Thing," *New Yorker*, May 31, 1969, p. 85, especially played on the term "Vocal Minority."

SRv, January 1961, p. 2, looked at the size of the district's bus fleet and operations. *SB*, October 31, 1949, p. 4, sketched the scope of post–World War II busing. Orfield, *Must We Bus?* 128–29, puts the employment of busing in a national perspective. He notes its heavy use in rural and suburban districts while arguing that neighborhood schools in walking distance were an exception rather than the rule when the busing debates convulsed the country in the 1960s and 1970s.

DP, January 5, 1969, p. 23 Contemporary, had busing statistics. *DP*, April 12, 1962, contained letters from PHAC activists Ed Lupberger and Helen Wolcott in which they expressed their opposition to busing for integration. *DP*, May 15, 1969, p. 37, observed the link between DPS's purchasing new buses and the Gilberts Plan.

Jonathan Kozol quoted the remark about the color of the children on buses in *The Nation*, July 1, 2019, p. 3. In passing, he observed how Joe Biden was among the leading anti-busing Democrats in the country in the 1970s when he mocked blacks for wanting their children to share white culture. Meadow, "Hard Years," pp. 23–26, stressed the many children who rode the bus simply for transportation opposed to the hysteria around busing for racial integration.

On February 27, 2018, former school board member Rita Montero reflected on why and the way board members generally back the superintendent. She emphasized the committee meetings and pre-session caucuses where board members usually made their decisions.

DP, September 19, 2017, p. 1A, focused on South High as a diverse school filled with immigrants. My *Washington Park*, 127–29, deals with the controversy over South students being "Rebels." *School Book*, 88, 90, 236, 252, 254–55, traces the origins of the academy.

Dick Koeppe recalled the long, contentious board meetings at South High during an August 26, 2019, interview. In passing, he remarked about police officers being disguised as custodians at the school during what he called "hectic times." Dorolyn Griebenaw remembered Gene Kane in an e-mail of September 20, 2019.

SB, October 14, 1968, p. 25, emphasized the television broadcast of board meetings on integration. "Thursday Night Fights" was the mocking term for school board meetings used by board candidate Meyer Kadovitz, *DP*, May 2, 1979, p. 69. A copy of the December 10, 1992, guidelines for board meetings, outlining when the public could address it, is in the 1992–93 notebook in GP.

Chapter Five

A Pivotal Election

Two seats were open on the school board in the May 1969 elections when Ed Benton and Allegra Saunders sought to stay in office. The first firmly supported the Gilberts Plan and had excellent ties with integration advocates. Saunders was less enthusiastic about busing though she was officially committed to equal educational opportunity. Meanwhile, the Republican Party and conservative activists lined up a ticket against busing. Seeing that board members William G. Berge and Stephen J. Knight Jr., both Republicans, had severe questions about the Gilberts Plan, the GOP perceived that by winning the two open seats, it could reassert itself in municipal politics.

As the balloting neared, the board of education affirmed its commitment to integration and busing in early 1969. It passed Resolution 1520 on January 30. Initially considered on May 16, 1968, the measure declared DPS would do all in its power to assure that East and Smiley remained integrated. Included was changing the attendance borders of East, South, and George Washington. The effort bluntly assigned students based on race to assure more whites attended East. By 1969, only 50.1 percent of the high school's 2,562 students where white while 39.9 percent were black, 7.4 percent Hispanic, 1.9 percent Asian, and .1 percent Native American.

Resolution 1520 was indicative. As much as anything, saving East as an idyllic integrated high school was a prime goal of desegregation advocates, particularly whites living in the Country Club and elite Park Hill. Under the Gilberts Plan, according to a January 1969 scenario, East would go to a white enrollment of 70 percent while the number of blacks declined to 23 percent. Without the Gilberts Plan, backers feared, East would soon become a majority black school, following the downward path of Smiley.

To improve Smiley, DPS argued the junior high needed more white students. It so rearranged the boundaries between Smiley and Hill Junior High, 451 Clermont Street. At this time, Hill was the city's top-performing junior high. Students there,

Author's collection

In 1969, the school board adopted Resolution 1524. It ordered the improvement of the troubled Cole Junior High School, 3240 Humboldt Street. The measure did not provide any specific, tried-and-true means of making this a reality.

the Skyhawks, scored the 80th percentile on Iowa tests compared to the city's worst junior high, Cole, which was at 20 percent—very few of Cole's students were white. The district counted 97.2 percent of Hill's students as white in a building capable of teaching 1,485 pupils.

Smiley, with 1,635 students, 24.7 of whom were white, scored at 44 percent on the Iowa tests. Resolution 1520 saw the district bus 670 white students to Smiley from Hill, bringing in another 42 students to Smiley from Merrill Junior High where students averaged 77 percent on the tests in a student body that was 98.9 percent white. The program shipped 330 black Smiley students to Hill and 342 to Merrill. The action transformed Smiley back into a majority white school. In the fall of 1969, it reported that 61.2 percent of its 1,393 students were white, 30.4 percent were black, 6.9 percent were Hispanos, 1.4 percent were Asian, and .1 percent Native Americans.

Resolution 1524 mandated the improvement of Cole Junior High. This was an extremely troubled school. The 1969 school census listed 1.4 percent of its students as white, 72.1 percent black, 25 percent Hispanic, 1.2 percent Asian, and .3 percent Native American. (A different count about the same time said 5.3 percent of the Cole membership was white. DPS likewise listed different numbers as the exact racial compositions of East and Smiley. Frequently, its counts did not add up to 100 percent.) Enrollment at Cole hovered at around 1,500. In January 1969, a police riot at Franklin Street and 32nd Avenue (Martin Luther King Boulevard), near the eastern edge of the school, had marred a protest by the Black Panthers against perceived racial discrimination at the school. At that time, the Panthers' headquarters were at 3401 Franklin Street.

As tensions remained taut, 75 of Cole's 80 teachers signed a petition to the school board. They wanted stricter, tougher discipline. Included was having big men use paddles to cudgel errant boys. To assist in the imposition of corporal punishment, DPS added a second assistant principal to Cole. Students knew they needed to stay away from Room 115—it was the discipline room where assistant principals smacked them with the paddle. Here and there, accusations were heard of teachers hitting younger children. Advocates of corporal punishment never reflected that the boys who were beaten usually internalized that violence when they bullied and pummeled others. Not until at least the 1980s did DPS cease spanking students.

Jim Perrill

By the time the board had passed Resolution 1520, James "Jim" Perrill headed the drive to vote out the pro-integration school board. A native of Wilson, Kansas, born on August 11, 1924, he came to Denver to attend the University of Denver College of Law. Marriage led him to make the city his permanent home in 1951. In no time, he was politically well connected. For a while, he worked for the influential insurance defense law firm of Yegge Hall Treece & Evans.

After being an assistant United States attorney, Perrill gained a place as a judge on the Denver Municipal Court. Rising in the Republican Party, he connected with Richard Batterton. Mayor from 1959 to 1963, Batterton was the last Republican to win city hall. Perrill was his administrative assistant. From there the Kansas native returned to corporate insurance defense law. Despite the Lyndon Johnson sweep in 1964, that year Perrill won a seat in the state Senate.

As the 1968 balloting approached, Perrill decided not to seek re-election. Rather, he eyed what he thought was a far more influential post, a place on the school board. Personally, he presented himself as a racial liberal. Not only did his daughters attend the integrated Gove Junior High and East High, but personally,

---

James C. Perrill

James C. Perrill, 44; candidate for 6-year term on Denver Board of Education at May 20 election; Colorado state senator 1965-69; mayor's administrative assistant 1960-62; Denver municipal judge 1959-60; assistant U.S. attorney for Colorado 1956-59. Navy veteran of World War II.

Graduate University of Denver Law School and admitted to practice 1953; partner in law firm of Yegge, Hall, Treece and Evans.

Lives with wife, Marilyn, and two daughters at 1324 Birch Street; Pamela, 16, attends East High School, and Judith, 13, is a student at Gove Junior High School.

Want to help?

Pin and wear.

Help get the word out.

Help stop forced busing.

Help build necessary schools in all neighborhoods.

Dear Taxpayer–

To build schools in neighborhoods where they are needed...

To bring better schools to disadvantaged neighborhoods...

To end forced busing and support voluntary busing...

To develop programs to upgrade education, including high school training for jobs...

To communicate effectively with the community...

Those are my goals. They're why I'm running for the Denver Board of Education. With your support, I can win. Go to the polls May 20, 1969.

Phone 333-3334   James C. Perrill

In 1969, Jim Perrill mobilized the Republican Party in gaining a place on the school board as a vehement opponent of busing for desegregation.

he stated, he opposed all discrimination. Busing, however, was not the solution to educational problems suffered by African-Americans. They had to advance themselves economically. Once they had done so and become part of mainstream middle-class society, concerns about busing and discrimination would be passé.

Perrill's position was something of the community consensus. Polls showed that around three-fourths of the populace abstractly supported school integration and the equality of educational opportunity. However, they overwhelmingly opposed busing as the means to achieve these goals. Busing proponents, in contrast, argued blacks needed better education to advance economically.

Rather than addressing this point, Perrill saw that the Republican Party could make great headway by opposing busing. As opposed to the majorities the party had received in the city in the mid- and late 1950s, it had lost great ground in recent years. Busing, Perrill was sure, showed that the Democrats were out of touch with the feelings of the city's white majority. Another Republican stalwart, Franklin Kenny "Frank" Southworth, agreed with him, teaming up with Perrill on the anti-busing ticket.

Born in Denver in 1925 to an affluent family, Southworth graduated from East in 1943. He thereupon enlisted in the Army Air Forces. After the end of World

Photo by Phil Goodstein

Moralism was at the heart of the 1969 school board election over busing. Proponents decried the defeat of integration forces as a victory of hate over love. Seemingly, this mural on the north wall of Eagleton School, on West Ninth Avenue between Hazel Court and Hooker Street, painted in 2011, is a commentary on what happened.

War II, he studied at the University of Kentucky, receiving a degree in economics in 1950. Five years later he returned to Denver to work for Gulf Oil, focusing on its real estate holdings. After living at 1245 Leyden Street, he moved to new southeast Denver, settling at 1945 South Kearney Way about the time he formed a commercial construction firm in 1958.

Rising in the Republican Party, Southworth joined the cabinet of Mayor Batterton in 1960 as the manager of revenue, staying there until voters ousted Batterton from city hall in 1963. Southworth subsequently turned to commercial real estate, forming his own brokerage in 1966. Two years later, he was the state leader of the Ronald Reagan for president drive. He simultaneously eyed elective office. Opposition to busing, he was sure, would return Mile High Republicans to power. Former board member Palmer Burch prominently endorsed the slate of Perrill and Southworth.

More than anyone, Bill Daniels financed the anti-busing drive. He was an extremely wealthy, self-made cable television magnate. Having a strong political agenda, he pondered a run for governor. Daniels readily donated to candidates and causes he favored. The millionaire spread his money around to numerous charities and was a key backer of Republican reaction in the legislature in the 1970s and 1980s. Over the decades, he also advocated public financing of private schools. Eventually, DPS opened its doors to Daniels' Young Americans Bank, a financial institution designed to gear youth to the banking system.

The Busing Slate

Integration advocates aligned behind Benton and Monte Pascoe. In late 1968, advocates of equal educational opportunity saw the necessity of running two forthright champions of desegregation. A group of young lawyers sought to recruit such candidates. Allying with people around the Park Hill Action Committee and the circle giving moral support to Rachel Noel, the attorneys formed a committee to decide on a pro-busing ticket for the May contest.

At first, Benton declined to seek re-election. Those pushing the nominating caucus urged him to stay on the board. In late February, he committed himself to run again. By this time, Benton had poor relations with Allegra Saunders, refusing to back her re-election bid. Vice president of the board since 1967, she never took any lead in desegregation issues or showed much enthusiasm for them.

Opponents mocked Saunders as someone who did not know the difference between majority rule and always voting with the majority. This was an unfair portrait. Since 1965, she had often joined with Benton and Noel as a three-member minority on the board. Still, backers of Benton and the Noel Resolution did not believe she was dependable. They had trouble communicating with her, claiming Saunders lacked a clear understanding of the issues.

Rather than backing Saunders, supporters of Benton and the Gilberts Plan selected a close friend of Benton as his running mate, Donald Monte Pascoe. Going by the name Monte, the contender was born in Iowa, on January 4, 1935, coming with his family to Denver when he was in third grade. After graduating from East in 1953, he went to Dartmouth. Upon earning his bachelor's, he attended

Drawing by Claude Boyer

In 1969, corporate attorney Monte Pascoe, who lived close to Cheesman Park, joined with another corporate attorney, Ed Benton, who lived close to Cheesman Park, in running for the school board in the name of equal educational opportunity. Pascoe went on to be a cabinet member under Governor Richard Lamm before unsuccessfully running for mayor in 1983. He subsequently served on the water board.

Stanford Law School. In the course of the 1950s and 1960s, the California academy attracted such future Denver Democratic politicians as Gary Hart, Richard Lamm, and Craig Barnes.

Back in Denver, Pascoe specialized in water law. In 1960, he joined the most influential firm of what became Ireland Stapleton Pryor & Pascoe. Partners included Gail and Clarence Ireland, both of whom had served as Colorado attorney general, and Benjamin Stapleton Jr., the son of Mayor Benjamin Stapleton. In 1967, Pascoe had been among those advocating the controversial school bond issue. At both East and Dartmouth, Pascoe had been a star football player. The school board candidate was an elder at Superintendent Oberholtzer's old church, Montview Presbyterian.

Benton and Pascoe met by chance. Both were avid pedestrians who regularly walked from their homes near Cheesman Park to their downtown law offices. Henry Toll, another distinguished attorney, often joined them. His wife, Lydia, was active in numerous school pursuits, including serving a term as the president of the Denver PTA. The three usually walked to work together regardless of the weather.

Pascoe married Patricia Hill on August 3, 1957. A graduate of the old Aurora High School, she eventually earned a doctorate in English from the University of Denver. She was a teacher and educational specialist. The couple sent their children to DPS. Eventually, she had a political career in her own right, serving in the state Senate. Pat Pascoe went on to publish a study of pioneer feminist state Senator Helen Ring Robinson.

Backers of integration, including many in black Denver, figured Pascoe was ideal for the board. He was a lot like Benton and James Voorhees. The last was then president of the school board, another corporate lawyer living near the Country Club who backed equality of educational opportunity.

Pascoe additionally had close ties with the Democrats. In 1968, he especially supported the presidential campaign of Hubert Humphrey. But the party was deeply divided by the issue of busing. Its leadership never showed nearly the same enthusiasm for the pro-busing slate as the Republicans did in lining up behind Perrill and Southworth. Even so, the Democratic central committee donated $5,000 to the Benton-Pascoe campaign. It stated that 52 of its 71 district captains endorsed the pro-desegregation ticket. Mike Pomponio, the veteran Democratic boss of North Denver, was among those saying no to the effort. Nor did the Benton-Pascoe campaign gain much traction from Democrats in southwest Denver. Some Democrats in southeast Denver likewise were more favorable to the Perrill-Southworth campaign than the ticket of Benton and Pascoe.

As the balloting approached, the contest polarized the city. Leading Republican publicists loudly whispered about the black dimension of school busing. This was at the time that President Richard Nixon readily employed his Southern Strategy, an effort to pull old racist Southern Dixiecrats into the Republican Party while dividing the country on the basis of race, age, and cultural proclivities. In response, Pascoe and Benton claimed the high moral ground. "Doing the right thing isn't always easy, but it is always worth doing," they declared. Optimistically, they stated they were sure the citizens of Denver would not be beguiled by the race card in opposing the Gilberts Plan.

In part, Benton and Pascoe seized the high moral ground because voters failed to listen to their programmatic explanations of why busing was good for the community. If nothing else, the Gilberts Plan was necessary to preserve Denver as a city of fine middle-class residential neighborhoods. It would keep some sections, especially Park Hill and areas around East High, from becoming a supposed "ghetto." Besides, "today's school is a working model of tomorrow's society." As such, students needed to learn to work with each other in the classrooms whereby they would be cooperative teamplayers in the corporate world. The Chamber of Commerce, in backing the Benton-Pascoe election, agreed. In part, this reflected something of the uplift tone of backers of integration: it was to provide magic whereby poor blacks came to model themselves on middle-class whites.

A Question of Black and White

In many ways, the impending election was literally a matter of black and white. The city's largest ethnic group, Latinos, were mostly absent from the debate. In pondering the scope of the district, the Special Study Committee commissioned an independent public opinion survey of citizen attitudes about the schools. The poll, completed in October 1963, observed that no group had a more positive view of the schools than the Spanish-Surnamed. Sixteen percent of those questioned stated DPS was an "excellent" system. Another 37 percent rated it as good. Fair was the response of 24 percent. Only 6 percent branded it poor. Seventeen percent had no opinion. Support of the system was even greater among parents of those attending DPS. In this case, 21 percent of Latinos rated the district excellent with another 48 calling it good. This was generally in tune

Amidst the divisions over school integration, a militant Chicano community emerged. It had no truck with busing. Rather, it insisted people of Latin American heritage embrace a strong national consciousness. Here militants protest in 1969 in front of the then DPS headquarters at 414 14th Street.

with the community. Seventeen percent of all respondents called the system excellent and 42 percent branded it good. Among parents, the numbers were 29 percent excellent and 50 percent good.

Despite all the laments about racism, the survey also showed that black Denver embraced DPS. Twelve percent said the district was excellent (15 percent of the parents) and 49 percent called it good (54 percent of the parents.) In other words, at least in terms of popular perceptions, both African-American and Hispanic Denver were satisfied with DPS. Like the majority of those participating in the survey, members of the Spanish-American community were greatly opposed to busing in the name of abstract integration.

DPS conducted the survey right when Chicano radicalism was percolating. This referred to a tendency in the community that insisted on the militancy and independence of Latin Americans from mainstream society. Those of this slant employed the controversial term "Chicano" to denote their roots in Mexico and the fierce Indians of the American southwest. Individuals of such an outlook had no enthusiasm for school busing. The whole system, claimed their foremost leader, Rodolfo "Corky" Gonzales, was thoroughly racist. His nationalist organization, the Crusade for Justice, argued Latino children did not need to go to white schools and learn the values and history of "Anglos" (any white who was not of Spanish descent), but had to focus on their own rich heritage. If anything, they should study Spanish and learn the history of Latin America in school.

Gonzales did not think much of the Benton-Pascoe ticket. Nor was he enthusiastic about black supporters of integration. Their advocacy of it, he argued, was actually a sign of an inferiority complex. African-Americans, he argued, had so little faith in their own community, customs, and culture that they wanted to immerse their children in the world of the white middle class. (Back in 1965, Gonzales, who was then part of the Democratic establishment, had been among those prominently backing the campaign of Rachel Noel for the school board.)

The Chicano firebrand frightened the school board. A popular tale is that during a packed, contentious public hearing at South High School, Gonzales gained the speakers' podium, surrounded by his bodyguards/goons. He started lambasting the school board. Six of the members thereupon got up and left the stage. James Voorhees remained. Ignoring him, Gonzales harangued the audience. Generally, the Spanish-Surnamed community polarized between avid supporters of Gonzales and those who intensely hated him.

Right as the board of education campaign was escalating, a riot besmirched West High School on March 20, 1969. It stemmed from a walkout by some of the followers of Gonzales. As much as anything, the confrontation was a desperate cry for recognition by Latino youths. They knew something was wrong. Counselors did not urge them to go to college while teachers and authorities sometimes punished them for speaking Spanish.

Known by one and all as Corky, Gonzales capitalized on the way West did not reach out to Latino students. He targeted social studies teacher Harry B. Shafer. The instructor sometimes deliberately mispronounced the names of Hispanic pupils. When asked why Hispanos generally did not perform as well as "Anglos," he emphasized the links between class, culture, and academic success. Shafer also noted that diet was important to doing well in school. Chicano militants interpreted this as a claim that Spanish-American youngsters failed because they ate too many beans.

Communication on all sides was at a minimum while Gonzales exploited the unease. At this time, DPS listed West as having more than 1,900 students. It counted 56 percent of them as white, 9 percent as black, 34 percent as Hispanic, with the rest being Asian-Americans or Indians. On March 19, 1969, Chicano students linked to the Crusade for Justice informed West Principal Earl Paul of their concerns and plans to walk out of classes at 9:00 AM the next day. Instead of showing a willingness to resolve their problems, he alerted the police to expect trouble at the school.

The force massively responded when about 300 students at West left classes shortly after 9:00 AM. The youths thereupon marched three blocks south to Baker Junior High (574 West Sixth Avenue), getting about hundred or so pupils to join the protest. They thereupon returned to West, gathering near the main entrance. Some adults, including parents and Corky Gonzales, were present.

The police immediately ordered the crowd to get away from the building, herding protesters across the street to Sunken Gardens, a park directly east of the high school. Rather than recognizing that the protest showed that something had to be done, the school let the police employ the riot squad against the demonstrators.

The department had recently formed a special unit to deal with protests. This was the first time it had sent it into action. Sure enough, violence flared. The police beat participants in the protest. Some who fled the riot showed their anger by breaking windows of nearby cars and houses. Police Chief George Seaton, who was on the scene, lamented that the presence of many small children kept him from having his officers use tear gas against the mob and employ even more severe means of repression.

Militants branded the event the "blowout." This was a term popular among Chicano protestors in California where there had been a wave of school protests in March 1968. On the one hand, the walkout simply aggravated school problems; on the other, it forced the West administration to reach out to Latino students. Included was adding Mexican foods to the lunch menu.

While many white militants, including radical college students, rallied to the blowout, Gonzales and his backers had little in common with the middle-class blacks demanding desegregation. African-American Denver had previously clashed with Gonzales when he was the head of the city's War on Poverty. They claimed he ignored blacks for his ethnic cohorts. Some African-Americans were convinced Gonzales was a racist who had no more respect for them than did the worst white bigot. In part, their protests against his administration of the War on Poverty had forced Mayor Tom Currigan to dismiss Gonzales from the post on April 24, 1966. The Chicano leader responded by forming the Crusade for Justice. It pulled in many lower-middle-class Hispanos. That DPS had failed to reach out to students allured by Gonzales' militant nationalist rhetoric was indicative of a system unable to communicate with students, parents, or the community.

The Perrill-Southworth ticket played on the chaos at West. Its response, fully in tune with the policies of President Nixon, was to advocate more repression and a greater police presence. Nixon's hyped Silent Majority rallied to the anti-busing candidates. Backers of Perrill and Southworth feared for the future of the city and the school district. Given the unease of the country and the severe tensions shown by the West High blowout, unproven experiments with school busing were the last thing District #1 needed.

The Black Opposition

Some blacks had a far greater affinity for the politics of Corky Gonzales than they did for advocates of busing. The 1963 survey by the Special Study Committee showed that only about one half of black Denver supported busing for racial integration. Thirty-five percent of the African-Americans polled opposed the measure—43 percent of the parents were against it. Some voices in the African-American community became even louder in rejecting the Gilberts Plan as the controversy over busing escalated in 1969.

No group was more outspoken in dismissing busing as a utopian fantasy than the Black Panthers. The Mile High chapter of this self-avowed revolutionary organization, primarily composed of young, politically aware poor inner-city blacks, had emerged in late 1967. From the beginning, its members clashed with the police. Turning their attention to the schools, the Panthers stated they did not want integration whereby black students were overwhelmed by white culture. On the contrary, they argued the African-American community must have its own schools. "Uncle Toms," the Panthers insisted, were foolish to think the racist system would give blacks anything. Only by taking the initiative of educating their children about the proud traditions of African-Americans could the next generation of black Denver carry on the struggle. Blacks, the party argued, would gain very little by having their children overwhelmed by white middle-class culture in the sterile schools of suburbia. In reviewing the strife, the Panthers declared that the busing controversy was a sideshow, a "frivolous delay" to keep the city from addressing the need for community control whereby blacks would have a greater say in the schools their children attended.

Drawing by Gregorio Alcaro

Lauren R. Watson, a graduate of Manual, headed the Denver chapter of the Black Panthers. The group was outspoken in opposing school busing. What the African-American community needed, it argued, was its own schools emphasizing black pride and achievements.

Not just self-avowed black revolutionaries questioned busing. Future Nobel Prize laureate Toni Morrison, for example, stated what African-Americans needed was more money in neighborhood schools, allowing for better programs and teachers. This, she argued, was a far preferable option than simply placing black boys and girls in "some high school next to some white kids."

At the same time that middle-class Park Hill African-Americans pushed busing for integration, the Panthers operated a "freedom school." The curriculum touched on black history and achievements. The group asserted it could not trust the racist DPS to provide adequate programs for black children. Nor would African-Americans gain much of anything by going to white schools and being subjected to their racist culture.

The Panthers' perspective was comparable to traditional defenders of black colleges in the South. Since Reconstruction, these had been beacons of African-American civilization and intellectual development. During the civil rights upheavals, backers emphasized historic black colleges had to be preserved and enhanced against white culture. Similarly, locals had to defend the traditional neighborhood schools of northeast Denver opposed to schemes to destroy them in the name of busing and educational parks.

For that matter, a lot of blacks continued to support neighborhood schools. They did not believe the gains of busing were worth the disruption and racism stemming from the controversy. Besides, in local schools, the teachers knew the pupils and the needs of black Denver. Busing opponents did not think this would be the case if their children were bused across town to white schools.

Others, reflecting the wide divisions that had historically been part of black America's fight for freedom, argued that a lack of education was only part of the problem. It was also necessary to smash discrimination while redressing the abject poverty of much of the African-American community. Backers of busing replied that once the schools provided equal educational opportunity for all, blacks would quickly overcome the other problems and the legacy of slavery, racism, and discrimination.

For the most part, integration advocates paid little heed to the Panthers and the views of black supporters of neighborhood schools. As voting day approached, backers of Benton and Pascoe insisted Denver's soul was at stake. The *Denver Post* agreed, lining up behind the ticket. It repeatedly printed editorials endorsing the ticket.

Republicans for Benton and Pascoe was an ad hoc group rallying to the integration slate. Among its members were board members John Amesse and James Voorhees. Also signing on was future reactionary suburban Congressman William H. Armstrong, former board member Francis Bain, Hugh Catherwood of the Colorado Public Expenditure Council, oil tycoon Philip Anschutz, bankers

---

Dear Friends:

MAY 20 is the day all concerned citizens will go to the polls to select TWO SCHOOL BOARD MEMBERS that will represent the People of Denver on the Denver School Board. And we who are concerned will vote men in office that will set the destiny of children for those of us who ARE concerned as well as those who are not!

WHAT ARE WE REALLY CONCERNED ABOUT? Is it the BUSING OF OUR KIDS TO DIFFERENT SCHOOLS? Many feel that this is a necessary, temporary solution. We'll have to decide if some transportation of children is not the only temporary solution to keep the doors open until good men can find a lasting solution. Is integrating for the sake of integration? NO! Integrating is necessary for good education. Segregated schools in the south have proved to be one of the BIGGEST CAUSES OF SOME OF OUR PROBLEMS! LET'S NOT HAVE SEGREGATED SCHOOLS! LET'S NOT HAVE PERMANENT BUSING! LET'S HAVE QUALITY EDUCATION, NEIGHBORHOOD SCHOOLS, INTEGRATED SCHOOLS, AND SOME TEMPORARY INTEGRATED BUSING.

LET'S HAVE BENTON AND PASCOE.

THE BLACK CITIZENS FOR BENTON-PASCOE

Doris Banks Papers, Auraria Archives

In 1969, much of black Denver rallied to the campaign of two white 17th Street lawyers, Ed Benton and Monte Pascoe, for the school board in the name of assuring quality education.

Richard Kirk and Bob Priester, former CU president Robert Stearns, and architect James Sudler and his socially prominent wife Barbara. Future Colorado chief justice Luis Rovira and future board member Les Woodward were others who was part of Republicans for Benton and Pascoe. So were 17th Street lawyers Peter Holme Jr. and J. Churchill Owen.

Another attorney, Minoru Yasui, signed the ad of Republicans for Benton and Pascoe. Born in Oregon on October 19, 1916, of Japanese parents, Yasui was among those who loudly protested the racial profiling of the Franklin Roosevelt administration during World War II. The government responded by locking him up and stripping him of his citizenship. Eventually, he convinced the courts to overturn that ruling. In Denver, Yasui was a foremost exponent of brotherhood, overseeing the Commission on Community Relations from 1967 to 1983. Along the way, he also chaired the Metro Denver Urban Coalition, an effort to bring different constituencies together in the name of a united community.

Intently involved in the schools, Yasui had been a member of both the Special Study Committee and the Advisory Council. As controversies over school busing heated up, he saw that the Commission on Community Relations issued statements and studies urging a sane, peaceful dialogue about the issue. It also emphasized the necessity of the school board and the city preparing for the successful implementation of the Gilberts Plan.

Other candidates sought to make their voices heard in the campaign. Carl Barnhart pushed for compromise. In 1960, he had been the inaugural principal of Barrett School. After serving elsewhere in the system, he had gone on to head the education department at Loretto Heights College. He later was principal of College View Elementary, a school located close to Loretto Heights. Self-styled advocates of peace, accommodation, and good government backed him. Few voters did.

Bob Crider, a truckdriver who went on to win a seat on the board in 1971, campaigned for the office as an independent advocate of neighborhood schools. Nathan Singer and Wiley J. Smith were others on the ballot who argued busing was a road to disaster. Singer, an aeronautics engineer, was a dramatic speaker who peppered his talks with rhymes as he told audiences to "Be aware and vote with care." Edgar J. Scott, a Democrat, dropped out of the ten-candidate field on May 10, throwing his support to Benton and Pascoe.

Numerous groups emerged backing or opposing busing and desegregation or neighborhood schools. Illustrative was Denver Physicians for Better Schools. It endorsed Perrill and Southworth. Against it, there was a rival Doctors for Benton and Pascoe. Back in 1967, a Physicians, Surgeons, and Dentists' coalition emerged, backing that year's unsuccessful bond issue. Right as the balloting was approaching, a coalition of Mile High Catholic priests endorsed busing in the name of brotherhood.

The proliferation of groups also reflected that both supporters and foes of busing poured money into the race. By May, the Benton-Pascoe campaign had spent about $35,000 compared to $50,000 for the Perrill-Southworth ticket. This was quite a change. Usually, successful school board candidates spent fewer than a thousand dollars on campaigns. None of the other candidates had much

FOR–NEIGHBORHOOD SCHOOLS!

HELP ELECT
AND
VOTE FOR
FRANK K.
SOUTHWORTH
DENVER SCHOOL BOARD
MAY 20TH, 1969
12   OVER

*Frank Southworth led the pack in the May 1969 school board election, a
contest rejecting busing for integration.*

of a treasury. Incumbent Allegra Saunders, for example, stated her budget was
somewhere between $350 and $400. Carl Barnhart reported spending about $500.

Voters flocked to the polls on election day. Whereas school elections often had
a turnout of approximately 10 percent of the electorate, about 110,000 voters went
to the polls out of a total registration of 215,000. It was no contest. Southworth
gathered 75,596 ballots. Perrill was second, 73,932. Far behind was Benton with
31,098. Pascoe had 28,948. Carl Barnhart, 11,726, came in fifth. Saunders trailed
with 4,666, having shown no dynamism in the contest. Nathan Singer, 3,499, Wiley
J. Smith, 2,582, Bob Crider, 2,022, and Edgar Scott, 853 rounded out the field.

The pro-integration ticket managed to carry Park Hill and the heart of old
black Denver. Voters in the latter more backed Benton and Pascoe based on the
observation that "they're for us," as a flyer stated, than any enthusiasm about
busing. While Benton and Pascoe had expected to lose, the size of the landslide
staggered them. Even in parts of central Denver, which were supposed to benefit
from busing, voters backed Perrill and Southworth. Hispanic voters likewise lined
up behind the neighborhood schools slate. Nobody celebrated the triumph more
than cable television millionaire Bill Daniels. He hosted the victory party, heralding
the triumph of Southworth and Perrill as the salvation of the city.

After his defeat, Pascoe was more politically committed than ever, being among
those raising funds for the plaintiffs who sued Denver Public Schools in the wake
of the May 1969 school polling. In 1973, he emerged as the chairman of the state
Democratic Party. As such, he helped it elect Richard Lamm governor in 1974
while putting Gary Hart in the United States Senate. Pascoe went on to manage
Lamm's successful re-election bid in 1978. Along the way, he remained active in
school board politics, working to recruit pro-integration candidates for the agency.

Between 1980 and 1982, Pascoe was a member of the Lamm cabinet, directing
the Department of Natural Resources. He left the post to run for mayor in 1983.

The victor in the contest, Federico Peña, recognized Pascoe's service by naming him to the water board where he served until 1995. During his tenure, the failed school board candidate was a foremost advocate of building Two Forks Dam along the South Platte River in the name of enhancing the city's water supply. The Environmental Protection Agency vetoed it as destructive to the area's natural amenities.

Pascoe also came to serve on the board of Colorado School of Mines and as president of the Iliff School of Theology. He died from a stroke at age 71 on March 2, 2006. To remember him, that year Mayor John Hickenlooper created the Monte Pascoe Civic Leadership Award. Working with the Chamber of Commerce, the citation went to a Denver resident providing outstanding direction to the community.

Benton was a senior partner at Holme Roberts & Owen by the time of his retirement. By the 2010s, he was still bitter about the unscrupulous character of Jim Perrill. Saunders sought to return to the legislature in 1970 when she lost a primary bid for the Senate. Soon thereafter, she retired to Arizona with her husband. By the time of her death in 1995, she was mostly forgotten.

The school board gathered on May 23, 1969, to canvass the election results and swear in the new members. At it, Benton sulked, claiming that nefarious men of bad will had gained control of the board. The new four-member anti-busing majority selected William Berge as president. Stephen J. Knight Jr. was vice president.

This was simply the prelude. Voters had spoken, the four-member anti-busing majority declared. Denver was to have neighborhood schools. To assure this was the case, on June 9, 1969, the new board passed Resolution 1533. It rescinded resolutions 1520, 1524, and 1531. The Gilberts Plan was dead. Denver, the board announced, was not going to subject children to busing in the name of an unproven experiment to mix students simply because of their race. In the process, they created more commotion than foes or advocates of busing had imagined possible.

A Note on Sources:

Box 13 of the Banks papers and Box 12 of the DCTA papers at DPL, WH 2125, have materials on the 1969 school board election. Calvin Trillin, "Doing the Right Thing Isn't Always Easy," *New Yorker*, May 31, 1969, pp. 85–89, was a pro-integration account of the election, lamenting the defeat of Benton and Pascoe. In passing, he observes that theirs was a virtually hopeless campaign.

SB, February 10, 1969, pp. 85–86, and September 8, 1969, p. 5, and *SRv*, April 1969, p. 1, and May 1969, p. 1, and Watson, "Barricades," 107–08, outline the goals of resolutions 1520, 1524, and 1531. Copies of the resolutions are in FF 1:11 of the Noel papers. The May 1969 *SRv*, p. 4, stressed the Gilberts Plan. An unnumbered folder in Box 13 of the Banks papers has a racial census of junior high students, dealing with the impact of the school board's transfer of students between Smiley and Hill.

A copy of Resolution 1520 is in FF 1:29 of the DPS papers. *SB*, February 10, 1969, p. 86, mentioned it and the goal of preserving the racial and ethnic status quo at East while increasing the number of white students at Smiley; cf. *SB*, May 4,

1970. *SRv*, April 1969, pp. 2–3, outlined the plan to deal with the racial balance at East and Smiley. So did *SRv*, May 1969, pp. 2–3. *DP*, January 17, 1969, p. 1, and *RMN*, January 17, 1969, p. 8, explained efforts to assure East remained a predominantly white school. John Timmons, a liberal faculty member at East, celebrated the school as a great integration success in *CT*, March 1971, p. 2. Leo Good, a somewhat iconoclastic instructor and counselor at Smiley, praised how the adjusted attendance area helped the school flourish as a desegregated academy, *CT*, April 1971, p. 2. Timmons and Good were among my instructors at East and Smiley.

DP, January 17, 1969, p. 43, outlined problems at Cole. *SRv*, April 1969, p. 4, was the district's account of its efforts to redress difficulties at the school. Unidentified clippings in FF 2 of the Helen Anderson papers at the DU Archives, M016, discuss problems at Cole, the demand for fierce discipline and paddling, and the police clash with the Black Panthers near the school. *RMN*, April 22, 1978, had a story about a protest against authorities beating kindergartners at Greenlee School. *DP*, February 3, 1978, p. 2, observed continuing debates over schools employing spanking. *School Book*, 78–80, 84, 101, 118, 262, 359–61, mentions DPS's policy on corporal punishment.

Watson, "Barricades," 101, touches on the Black Panthers' views of busing and education. I glance at the group in *DIA*, 22–26, and *Curtis Park*, 212–16. The 1963 *Report and Recommendations to the Denver Public Schools by the Special Study Committee*, pp. 43–48, focused on attitudes about school desegregation and busing, including the views of black Denver. Also see FF 21:17 of the Yasui papers, which has the Research Services Incorporated survey of DPS, dated October 1963, which was originally a "confidential" study.

League of Women Voters, *Court-Ordered Desegregation of the Denver Public Schools* (Denver: LWV, 1974), is a short guide to what had happened during the first five years of busing conflicts. The LWV thoroughly revised the brochure in *The Composite View of Denver Desegregation* (Denver: LWV, 1986). Meadow, "Hard Years," *CJ*, May 8, 1974, pp. 23–26, reviewed developments. *SCJ*, December 16, 1976, pp. 4–5, argued neither the *Post* nor the *News* knew what was going on in DPS; consequently, their reportage of the whole controversy was hideous.

There is an outline of Perrill's racial views in Trillin, "Doing the Right Thing," p. 85. I trace his background in *Modern East Denver*, 44–46. There are biographical materials about Southworth in an unnumbered folder in Box 13 of the Banks papers and in the obituaries of him, *DP*, February 19, 2016, p. 16A, and February 21, 2016, p. 3B. *DP*, May 15, 1969, p. 37, observed Palmer Burch's endorsement of the Perrill-Southworth ticket. CANS, *Judicial Fiat*, 13, emphasized Bill Daniels' funding the anti-busing movement.

In passing Trillin, "Doing the Right Thing," p. 85, mocked Allegra Saunders' perspective on majority rule. In contrast, Schwartzkopf, "Collective Bargaining," 168, observes Saunders often was on the losing side of four-to-three votes on the board when she joined with Noel and Benton against the four-member Republican majority. Pearson, "Denver Case," 298, reports the polls noting community support of school integration along with the anti-busing sentiment.

Craig Barnes mentions the lawyers' committee focusing on candidates for the 1969 board election in *DU Law Review*, 90:5 (October 2013), 1062. *RMN*, March 1, 1969, p. 44, reported Benton deciding to seek re-election. *DP*, May 24, 1969, p. 4, focused on Monte Pascoe's run for the school board. *RMN*, May 4, 1969, p. 8, portrayed the candidate. A look at him when he ran for mayor is *RMN*, March 6, 1983, p. 14. *RMN*, March 3, 2006, p. 18A, reviewed his life. On August 14, 2019, Ed Benton shared his memories of walking to work with Monte Pascoe and Henry Toll.

RMN, May 19, 1969, p. 5, outlined the involvement of the Republicans and Democrats in the nonpartisan school board race. *DP*, May 15, 1969, p. 37, observed the opposition of Mike Pomponio and other leading Democratic captains to the Benton-Pascoe ticket.

Trillin, "Doing the Right Thing," pp. 86–87, emphasizes the argument that busing was supposed to prevent the development of a black Denver ghetto and how Benton and Pascoe came to embrace the "doing the right thing" slogan. Ibid., p. 88, observes the elitist tone of integrationist arguments and the idea that "today's school is a working model of tomorrow's society."

Trillin, "Doing the Right Thing," p. 88, looks at Corky Gonzales' role in the 1969 school board campaign and his argument that a black "inferiority complex" was behind African-American advocacy of busing. Craig Barnes relates the story about Gonzales lambasting the school board, erroneously claiming Gonzales was the head of La Raza Unida, *DU Law Review*, 90:5 (October 2013), 1062. Ernesto Vigil, *The Crusade for Justice: The Chicano Movement in Denver* (Madison: University of Wisconsin Press, 1999), is the major study of Gonzales. A book painting Gonzales as a manipulator if not a police agent and provocateur is Juan Haro, *The Ultimate Betrayal* (Pittsburgh: Dorrance Publishing, 1998).

I review the West High upheavals in *West Side*, 322–26. "Power Play," *WW*, March 7, 2019, pp. 9–13, reflected on them in discussing a play produced for the 50th anniversary of the protest, *Fire in the Streets*, by Tony Garcia, at Su Teatro. Performances of the play included lobby displays about what had happened during the event. FF 8:17 of the papers of CCR at DPL has a transcript of a 17-minute-long film about the protest created by CCR in December 1970. Mario T. Garcia and Sal Castro, *Blowout* (Chapel Hill: University of North Carolina Press, 2011), is the memoir of Sal Castro, the man most responsible for the California school blowouts.

Trillin, "Doing the Right Thing," p. 88, quotes "frivolous delay" and observes how black militants opposed busing. Wayne F. Cooper, *Claude McKay* (New York: Schocken, 1987), 332, 343, reflects on divisions in the civil rights movement, debates over integration, and the need for equal educational opportunity. The obituary of Toni Morrison, *DP*, August 7, 2019, p. 1A, observed her views on school integration.

Thomas Penn Johnson, "Angeline Smith Was Retiring," *Almagre Review*, 5 (Summer 2018), 37–44, is a haunting story about a most successful black high school in the pre-civil rights South. Teachers feared desegregation meant the destruction of the school's academic achievements whereby white teachers and administrators would overwhelm the African-American faculty.

There was a statement/advertisement of Republicans for Benton and Pascoe in *DP*, May 18, 1969, p. 40. It included a list of backers of the organization. *DP*, May 11, 1969, p. 3, told of Voorhees' endorsement of the Benton-Pascoe campaign.

Statements of the CCR on school desegregation are in an unnumbered folder in Box 13 of the Banks papers, especially a declaration of April 29, 1969, on the need to prepare for the successful implementation of the Gilberts Plan. CCR reviewed minority problems in DPS in FF 5:12 and 7:4 of its papers at DPL. I tell of Yasui's career in *DIA*, 7–8, *Soup Lines*, 444–46, and *Washington Park*, 83–84. Also see Barbara Annette Upp, "Minoru Yasui" (Ph.D. dissertation, University of Oregon, 1997). Bill Himmelmann, *A Train Runs Through It: Journey of a Lifetime* (Denver: Time Travelers, 2019), 60, emphasizes Yasui's role in the Urban Coalition.

RMN, May 19, 1969, p. 30, had an advertisement of Doctors for Benton and Pascoe. A copy of the declaration of Denver Physicians for Better Schools is in FF 13:9 of the Banks papers. The 1967 declaration of Physicians, Surgeons, and Dentists for the bond issue is in an unnumbered folder in Box 13 of the Banks papers. *DP*, May 15, 1969, p. 37, reviewed the financing of the 1969 school board race. *RMN*, May 17, 1969, p. 5, told of the Catholic priests endorsing busing.

Park Hill Action Committee News, May 1969, p. 4, looked at the campaign of Carl Barnhart. Trillin, "Doing the Right Thing," p. 86, highlighted the candidacy of Nathan Singer. *DP*, May 11, 1969, p. 3, reported Edgar Scott ending his school board bid.

DP, May 21, 1969, p. 14, emphasized the scope of the anti-busing sweep. Harold E. Jackson, "Discrimination and Busing: The Denver School Board Election of May 1969," *Rocky Mountain Social Science Journal*, 8:2 (October 1971), 101–08, is primarily filled with numbers based on statistical models. It includes a map of the results, 102. Trillin, "Doing the Right Thing," p. 88, observes the "They're for Us" flyer and the lack of enthusiasm for busing among much of African-American Denver. Ibid., p. 89, observes how Benton and Pascoe were shocked by the size of the vote against them.

DP, March 3, 2006, p. 6C, reviewed the career of Monte Pascoe. He is in the 1976 *Who's*, 316. During a chat on December 17, 2019, Miller Hudson remembered Monte Pascoe interviewing candidates for the school board in the 1970s. On occasion, Pat Pascoe has discussed him and her political career. Her monograph is *Helen Ring Robinson: Colorado Senator and Suffragist* (Boulder: University Press of Colorado, 2011). I mention Monte Pascoe's bid for city hall in *DIA*, 210, 217. Also see Taylor, "Leadership," 129. *LCH*, September 2018, p. 14, highlighted the Monte Pascoe Civil Leadership Award. During an informal conversation in January 2018, Ed Benton reviewed the 1969 campaign, especially his behavior at the meeting of the new board that swore in Perrill and Southworth.

Chapter Six

The Keyes Case

Integration advocates refused to concede defeat despite the results of the May 1969 school board election. They argued that the action of the new board, in reversing the district's commitment to desegregation, was blatantly illegal. The anti-busing majority's overturning of the Gilberts Plan was a complete rejection of the principle of equal educational opportunity stemming from the Supreme Court's landmark *Brown* v. *Board of Education* ruling.

Fred Thomas led the protest against the board's action. A native of Harlem, born on September 7, 1919, he was an outstanding student. Despite great achievements, he found himself constantly suffering discrimination because of his race. He was among the many African-Americans who proudly served in the military, glad to have an equal opportunity to succeed. As such, he stayed in the service after World War II, joining the new Air Force. In 1951, it brought him to Denver to work at the Finance Center.

During the 1950s, Thomas increasingly focused on civil rights. After leaving the military, he joined the federal Department of Health Education and Welfare as a civil rights specialist. From there he moved over to corporate America. After manufacturer Johns-Manville relocated its headquarters to Denver in 1971, he became its official in charge of corporate compliance with civil rights statutes.

In 1959, Thomas had moved to 2875 Bellaire Street in North Park Hill, being among the first African-Americans settling east of Colorado Boulevard. He proudly sent his children to Stedman School, which then had about a 90 percent white enrollment. Before long, other blacks followed him into the area. Within a few years, Stedman was about 90 percent black. Even while his son and daughter excelled in school, he complained teachers did not give them exacting enough

Drawing by Daniel Lowenstein

Fred Thomas led the protest of black Denver against the school board's decision to revoke the Gilberts Plan in June 1969. He was the instigator of litigation that saw the federal courts oversee Denver Public Schools for more than 25 years.

assignments. Nevertheless, they received good enough schooling whereby his son was a distinguished scholar at Dartmouth and his daughter went to Smith.

When Thomas complained about the lack of equal educational opportunity for black children in DPS in the mid-1960s, the district responded by sending him to a conference of the United States Civil Rights Commission on the subject. There he saw how other cities were reaching out to African-Americans. He was sure that Denver could do the same.

Thomas, who joined the predominantly white Park Hill Methodist Church, was on the ground floor of the Park Hill Action Committee, serving as its first black chairman in 1967. Along the way, he was among those endorsing the 1965 Blue Flyer, urging other blacks to stay out of Park Hill. As much as anything, he blamed DPS's racial assignment policies for the way blacks kept pouring into Park Hill— they wanted to have their children attend good Park Hill schools compared to what they believed were the inferior academies west of Colorado Boulevard. This was at the same time Thomas complained that his children's schools did not properly challenge them. He never addressed whether, as with numerous other groups, many blacks preferred to live in areas filled with fellow members of their race/nationality/religion.

The Harlem native was the first African-American on the board of Outward Bound. His political and social connections were endless. Whenever the political-economic establishment needed a black for a board, it often turned to him. Schools were always a foremost concern. Back in the mid-1960s, Thomas was on the Advisory Council on the Equality of Educational Opportunity. As controversies heated up over the Noel Resolution and Gilberts Plan, he was vice president of the Metro Denver Urban Coalition under Minoru Yasui, a top-down group urging racial reconciliation. In 1969, he was a prime champion of busing and the ticket of Benton and Pascoe.

When black rage soared in reaction to the triumph of Perrill and Southworth, Thomas announced he would be the lead plaintiff in suing the district after it repealed the Gilberts Plan. Right as Thomas was gathering support for the litigation and lining up finances and other plaintiffs, Governor John Love appointed the civil rights activist to the Colorado Commission on Higher Education. This was the first time the white elite had so recognized an African-American. Believing it was a great honor to both him personally and all of black Colorado, Thomas accepted

Photo by Phil Goodstein

DPS has named its Career Education Center, along the east side of the 2600 block of Eliot Street, for Fred Thomas, the community activist who put together the coalition suing the district in the wake of the 1969 school board election.

the position. Not wishing to endanger this achievement, he decided he was not going to be a plaintiff in suing DPS.

Wilfred Keyes

Still, Thomas did not back away from the fight for school busing. Rather, he recruited chiropractor Wilfred Keyes to lead those suing the school district. Thomas convinced seven other concerned citizens to join Keyes in filing the complaint: Christine A. Colley, Irman J. Jennings, Robert R. Wade, Edward J. Starks Jr., Josephine Perez, Maxine N. Becker, and Eugene R. Weiner. All had children in one of the 33 schools impacted by the Gilberts Plan.

To pay for the litigation, Thomas organized the Denver Equal Educational Opportunity Fund, serving as its treasurer. Seeing that the Mile High black community was willing to support the case, raising money for the lawsuit, the NAACP Legal Defense and Educational Fund offered its assistance. Then an autonomous civil rights organization usually simply known as the Legal Defense Fund (LDF), it had been the prime organization behind the lawsuits culminating in the *Brown* v. *Board of Education* decision. The group's lawyers were the most knowledgeable people in the country about federal law dealing with school desegregation.

Wilfred Keyes was a native of Kansas City, Missouri, born on April 14, 1925. After attending a Jim Crow school in his home town, he served in the Army during World War II. On the return of peace, he attended Washburn University in Topeka. He arrived in Denver in 1952 after gaining a degree as a chiropractor in Kansas City. In the Mile High City, Keyes signed on at the highly controversial Spears

Drawing by Daniel Lowenstein

Wilfred Keyes was the lead plaintiff in suing DPS in the wake of the May 1969 school board election and the reversal of the district's commitment to an integration plan.

Hospital at Ninth Avenue and Jersey Street. Its head and namesake, Dr. Leo Spears, claimed he could cure any and all diseases by chiropractic. Spears was frequently in court, unsuccessfully suing those who branded him a quack.

Keyes left Spears Hospital in the early 1960s. After being a janitor of Scott Surgical, a firm providing retail medical equipment, he went to work as an insurance salesman. As the battle over school busing mounted, he was in charge of the Learning Tree, a program for students with learning disabilities. He also had links to the Denver Board Retarded Children's School. After his daughter Christi was born around 1960, he became concerned about DPS.

As his daughter approached school age, Keyes lived at 2836 Humboldt Street in a middle-class black area. When he inspected the nearby Mitchell School, to which the district assigned his daughter, he found it old and dirty. Teachers told him that they received their books second-hand from schools in southeast Denver. When Keyes sought to relocate to southeast Denver, he discovered racism blocked his ability to buy a house there. DPS said no to his plea for open enrollment. Besides, DPS observed it had completed a modern wing of Mitchell in 1964.

In the hope of finding a better place for his two children, in 1967 Keyes relocated to 2651 Ivanhoe Street in North Park Hill. Though such nearby schools as Smith and Hallett were new, they were extremely overcrowded. Once more, the textbooks were old. To assure that his daughter Christi and son Mark had a chance at equal educational opportunity, he agreed to be the lead party in what became a long-lived and tumultuous lawsuit. Eventually, both of Keyes' children graduated from George Washington High School. The complaint, known as *Keyes* v. *School District #1*, charged DPS with operating an illegal dual system based on de facto segregation.

Craig Barnes

Even before Keyes emerged as the face of the lawsuit or the school board had specifically rejected the Gilberts Plan, Thomas moved to make sure the new board would not proceed with impunity. Shortly after the election, he consulted with Craig Shellenberg Barnes. A native of affluent white Park Hill, born on June 16, 1936, Barnes grew up in Arapahoe County while living with his family around the world. Along the way, he studied in Europe and Asia. In 1962, he earned his law degree from Stanford Law School. After a stint in the Peace Corps and service as a lieutenant in the military, he worked for the big, influential law firm of Holland & Hart between 1965 and 1968.

Originally a Republican, Barnes had switched to the Democrats in response to the civil rights upheavals and the Vietnam War. By the spring of 1969, he was pondering a life in academia or in the peace movement. Toward this end, he was working on a doctorate at the University of Denver's Graduate School of International Studies. Back in 1959, he had received a master's in international affairs from Tufts. By the time he took the Keyes case, Barnes had a small independent law office, Barnes & Jensen with Gerald L. Jensen, at 2430 South University Boulevard, near the DU campus, close to where he lived.

All the while, Barnes was part of a group of pro-integration lawyers who had campaigned for Benton and Pascoe. Additionally, he had been caught up in the enthusiasm of the 1968 Bobby Kennedy presidential campaign. Before long, he was the personification of the Mile High New Politics movement. This was the belief that the rising generation could successfully work within the system to redress problems and fulfill the promise of American life. In 1970, Barnes ousted the city's incumbent Democratic congressman, Byron Rogers, in a closely fought primary. Barnes badly lost in November to law-and-order, anti-busing district attorney Mike McKevitt. In part, both Barnes' emergence as a candidate against Rogers and defeat by McKevitt stemmed from his involvement in the school busing case. Barnes went on to be the founding head of the Colorado branch of Common Cause.

At the same time the May 1969 school board contest tore apart the city, Barnes was preparing to take his comprehensive examinations for his doctorate at DU. He never sat for them. Rather, he responded to the call to sue DPS after the victory of the ticket of Perrill and Southworth. A close political and legal associate, Robert T. "Bob" Connery, convinced him to try the case against DPS.

Connery, also a lawyer at Holland & Hart, was another part of the Park Hill crowd. After graduating from Yale in 1962, he taught the humanities for a year before earning his law degree from Harvard in 1966. From there, he joined the Denver firm. An avid bicyclist, he found his Park Hill home at 1944 Hudson Street ideally suited for his commute to Holland & Hart. Simultaneously, he became most active in the education committee of the Park Hill Action Committee. As fights over the Gilberts Plan heated up in 1968, Connery intently studied federal law concerning school integration. He styled himself an expert on the Coleman Report and the harm imposed on students and society by school segregation.

During discussions with Richard Kozelka of PHAC in November 1968, Connery pondered what advocates of integration could do if DPS failed to adopt a desegregation program. He mentioned the matter to Fred Thomas whom he knew through PHAC. By this time, Thomas was in contact with the NAACP Legal Defense Fund. As the May voting approached, Connery was among the integration advocates who considered a lawsuit to force DPS to act. He later claimed he never expected the district to fight the litigation so vehemently.

George Bardwell and Paul Klite assisted Connery in preparing for a possible suit prior to the balloting. The former, who had led Speak Out on School Integration, was a masterful statistician who gathered data on discrimination in the city and school system. Klite, a brilliant medical researcher who taught at the University of Colorado School of Medicine, devoted himself to collecting

Courtesy Susan Bardwell

George Bardwell, the head of Speak Out on School Integration, provided massive statistical data for those suing DPS as a racist district.

the evidence. He worked closely with Bardwell who provided the statistics; Klite explained what they meant. In 1971, Klite ran unsuccessfully for the school board, failing to gain the backing of advocates of integration.

The bitterness of the 1969 school board election helped polarize the city and create extremely bad feelings on all sides. When Connery had first mulled the suit prior to the balloting, other attorneys had convinced him to wait until voters had their say. After Perrill and Southworth overwhelming triumphed, he joined Barnes and others on the day after the election in drafting the complaint. Lawrence "Larry" Treece and Ed Kahn were other lawyers at Holland & Hart who assisted them. The latter, once the head of the Denver Young Democrats, later had a distinguished record in public service law.

Another white Park Hill attorney, Gerald "Jerry" Kopel, likewise argued civil rights advocates had strong grounds for a suit. Kopel was in and out of the Colorado House of Representatives between 1965 and 1993. Dick Young, a leader of PHAC and the Democratic Party, also contributed his legal skill in helping develop the case. So did Hal Haddon who went on to be a most successful trial attorney.

With Connery and Barnes taking responsibility, the plaintiffs asked the United States District Court for an injunction against the school board once it repealed the Gilberts Plan. They worked closely with Conrad Harper, a lawyer with the Legal Defense Fund. Barnes further had connections with the American Civil Liberties Union, a group which had expressed concern about school segregation. From the beginning, ACLU attorneys collaborated with the plaintiffs. (Back in 1966, the ACLU had expressed extreme concern about perceived racism within DPS. After pondering litigation against the district at that time, it decided not to take the legal initiative against the school system.)

Neither Barnes nor Connery was a veteran trial attorney with the skills to handle all aspects of the case. Barnes, in fact, had never tried a case. At Connery's suggestion, they turned to a mutual acquaintance with whom they had worked at Holland & Hart, Gordon Gray "Gordie" Greiner. He became the pivotal lawyer for the plaintiffs in the school integration case.

Born in Harvey, Illinois, a suburb to the south of Chicago, on September 7, 1934, Greiner moved frequently as a youth, attending 13 different schools before gaining his high school diploma in Evanston, Illinois. He earned both his bachelor's and law degrees from Northwestern. About the time he joined the bar, he visited

Colorado on his honeymoon. The young lawyer fell in love with the state. This led him to apply for a place with Holland & Hart. There he emerged as a highly skilled litigator, specializing in anti-trust cases.

Personally, Greiner, who lived on Lookout Mountain, described himself as a Goldwater Republican. Cleanly shaven and wearing a crew cut, he gloried in the material comforts of life. In 1968, he had energetically worked in the successful re-election campaign of conservative Republican United States Senator Peter Dominick who had once been part of Holland & Hart. In court, Greiner was low key, having little charisma but showing a masterful command of the facts and knowing exactly how to conduct a trial.

Greiner agreed to meet with Thomas and associates at the behest of Barnes and Connery. At first, he was highly skeptical of the plaintiffs' charges. The way busing advocates asked him for help, he reflected, showed their utter desperation. Still, he agreed to review the evidence. On doing so, he was impressed by the thorough research of the plaintiffs. Convinced that Keyes and company had a solid case, he educated himself on constitutional law as it applied to the schools.

Additionally, Greiner persuaded his colleagues at Holland & Hart to allow him to work on the case as part of the firm's wide-ranging pro bono activities. As he committed himself to the litigation, the lawyer changed his political views. Greiner divorced, grew a beard, and moved to Park Hill, embracing the neighborhood's trendy liberalism.

Thomas, Keyes, and associates had loudly stated their intention to sue if the school board repealed the Gilberts Plan. Despite this, their filing the suit in mid-June caught DPS by surprise. It quickly came out that the district's legal department was as confused and as witless about what was going on as was most of the school board and hierarchy. The litigation specifically named each of the members of the school board as defendants, including the three who backed the Gilberts Plan: Amesse, Voorhees, and Noel. The suit also named Superintendent Gilberts as a defendant.

Judge William E. Doyle

The case came before Judge William Edward Doyle. A Denver native, born on February 5, 1911, he originally attended Catholic schools before entering DPS. He graduated from West High in 1929 where he was a star football player while he also stood out as a boxer. A commitment to physical fitness was always part of his life. A new home of Baker Junior High and the massive expansion of the school's grounds in the mid-1950s destroyed Doyle's childhood house at 585 Elati Street.

After earning his bachelor's from the University of Colorado in 1934, Doyle headed to Washington, attending law school at George Washington University. After graduating in 1937, he went to work as an investigator for his brother-in-law, Denver District Attorney John Carroll. When he joined the bar in March 1938, Doyle moved up to being a deputy district attorney. During World War II, Doyle was a non-commissioned officer in the invasion of North Africa, moving with the Army to Italy, France, and Germany. By the time of his discharge in November 1945, he was a newly minted second lieutenant.

Both Carroll and Doyle had strong political ambitions. After failing in a run for the United States Senate in 1940, Carroll gained a place in the federal House of Representatives in 1946, again losing bids for the Senate in 1950 and 1954. Doyle, meanwhile, briefly filled a vacancy appointment on the bench of the Denver District Court in 1948–49. He moved over to work as chief deputy district attorney from 1949 to 1952. He failed to win election to the state Supreme Court in 1952.

Carroll finally got a seat in the Senate in 1956. Two years later, Doyle gained election to the Colorado Supreme Court. This was the situation in 1961 when Congress created a new judgeship for the United States District Court of Colorado. In response to Carroll's lobbying, President John F. Kennedy named Doyle to the federal bench.

The jurist generally was pro-prosecutorial in criminal cases. He adopted liberal stances on social and civil rights issues. Besides projecting himself as New Deal Democrat, Doyle was a Cold Warrior. This particularly came out in February 1968 when he presided at the trial of Denver's first draft card burner, North High graduate Mendel Cooper. Constantly clashing with Cooper's politically aware counsel, Walter Gerash, the jurist refused to allow Cooper to mount the defense of lesser evils. The Vietnam War, Gerash and Cooper argued, was a crime. The principles of Nuremberg required the populace to refuse to participate in such an atrocity.

The assertion, the judge stated, was ridiculous. He implied that his political views in support of the war supplanted the defense's appeal to international law. During the trial, he openly sided with the prosecution, even making a slit throat gesture to the jury whereby it knew the verdict the judge expected it to reach. The jury found Cooper guilty.

Around 11:45 PM on March 25, 1968, about a month after the Cooper trial, a bomb exploded at Doyle's home at 3501 Seventh Avenue Parkway. It damaged the porch and shattered a basement window. Doyle did not believe it had a political slant, explaining he had not recently received any hate letters or threats. He had been reading in bed at the time of the blast. In reflecting on what happened, he guessed the device had been thrown from a passing car as an act of vandalism rather than deliberate terror. Even so, his backers later claimed the bomb might have been aimed to protest his actions on the bench. Shortly after the explosion, his wife, a fellow lawyer whom he had married in 1939, separated from him, moving to Florida. Doyle, in turn, relocated to a distinctive modern house at 3555 Belcaro Drive in an elite section close to the Polo Club.

Though an alumnus of DPS, Doyle, a staunch Catholic, sent his children to parochial schools. In reflecting about the litigation, Craig Barnes stated the plaintiffs' had the "terrific luck" to get Doyle assigned to the case. The jurist was supposedly among the most liberal judges on the bench of the United States District Court in the country.

After the plaintiffs asked the court to issue a temporary injunction to force the district to proceed with busing in the fall according to the Gilberts Plan, Doyle held a hearing on July 17, 1969. Rachel Noel was the lead witness. Neither she nor any of the other advocates of judicial relief was able to cite specific instances of racial prejudice by District #1 during the past ten years. Instead, the plaintiffs focused on the cynical gerrymandering of attendance districts. More than ever, the relationship between Park Hill and Barrett schools was their prime example of how DPS worked to keep the races apart. According to both the *Brown v. Board of Education* case and the conclusions of the Coleman Report, this was ipso facto evidence of an illegal dual system that harmed black youngsters.

The hearing was wide ranging. The Legal Defense Fund helped lay out the nature of the evidence, arranging for experts to testify about the impact of segregation. The plaintiffs called past and present members of the school board. Retired Superintendent Oberholtzer took the stand. He conceded the district had acted to maintain a racial separation of black and white students in Park Hill School. Proponents of integration also produced evidence that the district had unsuccessfully sought to keep Stedman a white academy. In addition, they argued DPS had

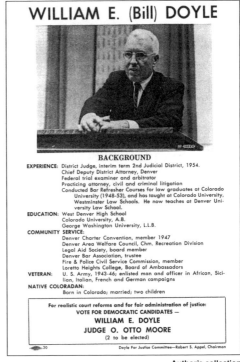

WILLIAM E. (Bill) DOYLE

BACKGROUND

EXPERIENCE: District Judge, interim term 2nd Judicial District, 1954.
Chief Deputy District Attorney, Denver
Federal trial examiner and arbitrator
Practicing attorney, civil and criminal litigation
Conducted Bar Refresher Courses for law graduates at Colorado University (1948-53), and has taught at Colorado University, Westminster Law Schools. He now teaches at Denver University Law School.

EDUCATION: West Denver High School
Colorado University, A.B.
George Washington University, L.L.B.

COMMUNITY SERVICE:
Denver Charter Convention, member 1947
Denver Area Welfare Council, Chm. Recreation Division
Legal Aid Society, board member
Denver Bar Association, trustee
Fire & Police Civil Service Commission, member
Loretto Heights College, Board of Ambassadors

VETERAN: U. S. Army, 1943-46; enlisted man and officer in African, Sicilian, Italian, French and German campaigns

NATIVE COLORADAN:
Born in Colorado; married; two children

For realistic court reforms and for fair administration of justice:
VOTE FOR DEMOCRATIC CANDIDATES —
WILLIAM E. DOYLE
JUDGE O. OTTO MOORE
(2 to be elected)

20   Doyle For Justice Committee—Robert S. Appel, Chairman

Author's collection

In 1958, William Doyle successfully campaigned for the Colorado Supreme Court as a New Deal Democrat. Three years later, he gained appointment to the bench of the United States District Court. He heard the litigation of Keyes *v.* School District #1.

neglected minority schools—the buildings were old and the district frequently failed to redress the physical problems at them.

Nor, the plaintiffs argued, was the tracking system a means of encouraging bright students to make the most of their academic abilities; it was a way to separate excellent white students from black students. National educational critics came to echo them, stating tracking programs did not produce educational marvels. If anything, tracking restricted the level of knowledge available to seemingly average students including those of ethnic and racial minorities. The overall result, the plaintiffs concluded, was that the schools of black Denver were separate and unequal from those of white Denver. Given the residential segregation of the city, the repeal of the Gilberts Plan meant a continuation of DPS's illegal Jim Crow practices.

DPS denied all charges. Yes, its lawyers admitted, Colorado Boulevard, two blocks east of Barrett School, was the attendance boundary. This was not because blacks lived west of Colorado Boulevard while whites dwelt to the east. Colorado Boulevard, they observed, was a very busy, dangerous arterial.

Back in 1951, DPS had sent upwards of 100 students from Columbine School at 28th Avenue and Columbine Street to Stedman at 30th Avenue and Dexter Street across Colorado Boulevard. It had explained the move was necessary to get Columbine off of double sessions. At that time, the district did not concern itself with the dangers of elementary students crossing Colorado Boulevard. Even when it made the arterial the eastern border of Barrett, DPS assigned children living east of Colorado Boulevard to Teller School, three blocks west of Colorado Boulevard at 12th Avenue and Garfield Street. Some children living west of Colorado Boulevard went to Steck School at Fourth Avenue and Albion Street, a block east of the speedway.

The defense also vehemently rejected the accusation that black schools were old and outdated. First of all, old did not mean bad. Denver was filled with beautiful, distinguished school buildings that dated from before World War I. Generations had thrived in them, including at Park Hill School, a structure built in 1901. (Back in 1967, a stated purpose of that year's bond issue was to allow DPS to get rid of all of its schoolhouses dating from before 1917.)

Nor were all supposedly black schools old. The Park Hill neighborhood, for example, included Smith and Hallett schools, both of which went up in the 1950s. The district had completed a new section of Mitchell in 1964. The same year it added a modern wing to Whittier. Back in 1951, it had opened a new home for Gilpin. Within the last 15 years, it had also vastly expanded and modernized Columbine. Most of all, it had built Barrett as a new facility — this was the specific school about which the plaintiffs so complained.

District #1 stressed the lack of the plaintiffs' evidence of specific acts of racial discrimination. That Keyes and associates were unable to produce it showed they were nothing but sore losers. Educational problems in the black community did not stem from inferior schools; busing would not solve them. DPS, the defense concluded, was a colorblind system. The attorneys for the district did not call any members of the board who had voted to rescind the Gilberts Plan.

Greiner rebutted the defense. He cited the report of the Special Study Committee for the Equality of Educational Opportunity of 1962–64 on the need for the district to be aware of racial concerns as it worked to provide equal educational opportunity. But until it adopted the Gilberts Plan, the school board had not carried through. If anything, it accentuated its blatant segregation practices in Park Hill, turning places like Smith and Hallett into black schools while it sought to preserve Park Hill and Philips schools as white.

The plaintiffs also emphasized the confusion of DPS's witnesses. Those testifying for the defense contradicted each other, giving varied explanations of the reasons for the district's actions. It was apparent that nobody in DPS had a complete mastery of exactly how the system operated. The lack of central coordination of the district was especially clear when teachers went on strike in November 1969. Observing the confusion of the superintendent's office, leaders of the DCTA, the teachers union, branded DPS headquarters at 414 14th Street "Fort Fumble."

Judge Doyle ruled that the plaintiffs had produced the preponderance of evidence. Surprised and offended by the amount of racial discrimination in the

Photo by Phil Goodstein

A bridge was once over Colorado Boulevard between 13th and 14th avenues by Gove Junior High School. DPS erected it in 1966, a year after a motorist killed two Gove students crossing the arterial during a gym class. Here the passageway looks east shortly before the demolition of the bridge in 2012 after wreckers razed the second home of Gove.

district, he granted the plaintiffs' request for the injunction on July 23, 1969. Resolutions 1520, 1524, and 1531, he declared, were "bona fide attempts" to redress past acts of segregation. Repeal of them was a huge step backwards. The plaintiffs had shown illegal de facto segregation existed. To redress it, the board must start busing for elementary schools in September based on the Gilberts Plan. It primarily impacted blacks living in Park Hill. The plaintiffs had emphasized that neighborhood, not specifically arguing that DPS was an illegal dual system through the entire community.

DPS immediately appealed. The defendants again emphasized there were no specific instances of proven discrimination. Nor had Judge Doyle concluded that DPS was a dual system automatically dividing students by race. Before plunging into the highly questionable world of busing, the court should hold a full trial.

On August 5, 1969, a three-judge panel of the Denver-based Tenth Circuit Court of Appeals granted DPS relief. It ordered Doyle to reconsider the matter. The District Court jurist responded on August 14, issuing a slightly revised decision. Still, he upheld the plaintiffs. Consequently, busing must begin in September.

Once more, DPS appealed. The Tenth Circuit Court again listened to it. On August 27, it vacated Doyle's order. The plaintiff had not shown that busing would redress the problem. With the impending opening of the schools, a hasty implementation of busing was far more likely to cause problems that bring benefits.

The plaintiffs responded by asking the United States Supreme Court for emergency relief. The clerk of the recessed court initially contacted Justice Byron White who oversaw the Tenth Circuit. A Colorado native, the judge was out of the capital, spending the summer near Craig, Colorado. The jurist demurred about listening to the appeal. Given that he had once handled some litigation for DPS while he was in private practice, White thought it would be a conflict of interest for him to rule on a case concerning the school district.

The clerk then sought to contact Justice Thurgood Marshall who was in Washington. When he was unable to reach him, he turned to the other justice who was in the capital, William Brennan. Reviewing the evidence, the jurist ordered the reinstatement of busing. The Tenth Circuit, Brennan stated, had "improvidently granted" the stay of execution. It was necessary, he ruled, to support the decision of the District Court particularly in a civil rights case raising constitutional issues. Given the massive resistance of DPS and how it had done everything to block the Gilberts Plan, the court had to force the district to act. Consequently, DPS was to begin busing for integration based on the Gilberts Plan with the opening of the schoolyear on September 2.

The school board knew better than to defy the Supreme Court. On August 31, it stated it would implement busing. The schoolyear so opened with DPS under court order. Specifically, busing took 2,830 pupils across town in the name of desegregation. For the most part, this meant transporting black elementary students to white neighborhoods. Few whites rode the bus in the name of integration. The order did not impact students in junior highs and high schools.

Bombings

Despite fears that the city would explode because of forced busing, the results were amazingly peaceful in September 1969. At the most, there was a great deal of confusion during the first few days since many students were not clear about bus schedules or which school they were supposed to attend. Once they arrived in the new schools, classes more or less flowed smoothly. In response to some disturbances, Superintendent Gilberts loudly stated it was "Our Responsibility" to redress tensions and have the schools be leaders in assuring Denver was a prosperous, collaborating community rather than have students and parents become victims of racial differences.

Still, there was mass resentment. Opponents of busing placed their hopes in a full-scale trial. Given the ascension of Richard Nixon to the White House and his appointments to the Supreme Court, they were sure the legal system would uphold the voters. The trial on the matter started before Judge Doyle on February 2, 1970.

As the showdown loomed, DPS had trouble finding the right lawyer to defend it. When civil rights advocates filed the litigation, S. Arthur Henry, who had been attorney for the board since 1933, was quite ill. He died in December 1970. The district reached out to Kenneth M. Wormwood to handle the case. He was a premier corporate attorney who specialized in insurance defense, i.e., he was not someone intimately familiar with the district and the intricacies of school and civil rights

CHS

Officials inspect the ruins of a bombing that destroyed about one-third of the DPS bus fleet on February 5, 1970.

law. Even so, he was an excellent litigator. Insurance defense attorneys are often outstanding in the courtroom.

While preparing for the trial, the lawyer took a break for a Christmas getaway in a mountain cabin near Evergreen. In early January, a park ranger discovered Wormwood's body there—the lawyer had died alone of a heart attack. In the wake of the death, at the behest of board member Bill Berge, a veteran attorney, the board hired another insurance defense attorney as its lead counsel, William K. Ris (1915–2003). Prior to recruiting Gordon Greiner as their trial attorney, the plaintiffs had pondered approaching Ris to handle the case given his reputation as an outstanding courtroom pleader.

Members of S. Arthur Henry's firm of Henry Cockrell Quinn & Creighton joined Ris in defending DPS. In particular, Thomas E. Creighton, Benjamin Craig, and Michael Jackson, were in the courtroom assisting Ris. Jackson, previously DPS's special assistant attorney, emerged as the attorney of District #1 in 1976.

Then, right as the trial was getting underway, two explosions, about four minutes apart, ripped the main DPS bus garage, the Hill Top, 2920 West Seventh Avenue at around 9:30 PM on Thursday, February 5, 1970. A series of 12 dynamite bombs, linked together and placed under the gas tanks of school buses, destroyed 25 buses and ravaged 15 more. The blasts also wrecked four trucks and damaged six automobiles. The arson squad of the fire department, inspecting the site, concluded that a professional skilled in explosives was responsible. The 40 buses made up about 30 percent of the district's total fleet of 126 buses.

Initially, DPS estimated the damage at $500,000. Next it claimed, taking depreciation into account, the bill was $300,000. Before long, it reduced the sum to $200,000. To keep the buses rolling for the everyday transportation of students, the district immediately leased about 20 buses from private operators in addition to acquiring four buses from the Jefferson County School District. Then, on March 19, 1970, the board resolved to buy 15 new buses and refurbish 23 more. Money to pay for them came from an $82,289 insurance settlement in addition to $71,232 from state emergency assistance funds. (The district had built the Hill Top complex in 1959. Between 1974 and 1976, it called the space, which included some nearby support offices, Riverfront. DPS spellings oscillated between branding the complex "Hill Top" and "Hilltop.")

At first, the police blamed the Crusade for Justice for the bombing, nabbing Baltazar Martinez, a militant Chicano from New Mexico who had ties to land nationalist Reis Lopez Tijerina. Not only did the authorities have no evidence against him, but it turned out that the report of a paramedic, claiming he had bandaged the hands of a possible suspect in the wake of the blast, cleared Martinez — there were no signs of injury to his hands. The police so quickly released him. Prosecutors never tried anybody for the crime.

Other bombings followed. Around 3:00 AM on February 22, the sound of breaking glass awakened board member Jim Perrill at his home at 1324 Birch Street.

RMN/DPL

Police sergeant Carrell Byrd stands on the porch of the home of Wilfred Keyes at 2651 Ivanhoe Street shortly after a bomb had badly damaged the residence on the evening of February 25, 1970.

Jumping out of bed, he discovered someone had thrown a Molotov cocktail through
the front window of his house. The device set the dining room on fire, causing
about $2,000 in damages, mostly from smoke. He and his family escaped uninjured.

Then, at 8:30 PM on February 25, 1970, lead plaintiff Wilfred Keyes heard
something land on the porch of his house at 2651 Ivanhoe Street. Going outside to
investigate, he saw a burning package. When he sought to extinguish it by pouring
water on it, the device exploded. The blast knocked down the front door and
broke 15 windows, spraying glass shards through the dwelling. The arson squad
determined the device was a pipe bomb filled with metal bearings comparable to
those found in shotgun shells. Keyes and his family were not seriously hurt. In
the wake of the attack, Keyes' wife wanted to move. He refused, stating the family
could not run away from the civil rights fight.

About this time, school board president Bill Berge reported receiving a bomb
threat. The police gave protection to him and other members of the board. In
response to the scare, a member of the board installed bullet-resistant windows
in his house. Nobody ever claimed responsibility for the bombings. At the most,
the prosecution of somebody the police described as "a stranger" did not result in
a conviction in the explosion at Keyes' home.

The Trial

Meanwhile, in the courtroom, the plaintiffs were extremely well organized.
During the two-week trial, they presented an impressive array of maps, charts,
graphs, and statistical analyses to prove their points. With the help of the Legal
Defense Fund and its lawyer Conrad Harper, they brought in numerous expert
witnesses. In the process, they once more showed the systematic and cynical efforts
by DPS to segregate schools through the manipulation of attendance boundaries.

Those suing DPS also produced evidence of some specific discriminatory
practices of the district such as allowing faculty and staff specialists the right to
decline to work with black youngsters. The plaintiffs additionally illustrated how,
to cloak the poor performance of schools filled with low-income children of color,
DPS cooked the books on the way it scored and reported the results of standardized
tests. In particular, the district added points to low-performing schools while
reducing the scores achieved at affluent, white, middle-class academies. Overall,
the plaintiffs painted the district as thoroughly racist. The city's public schools, they
argued, had produced quality education for whites and inferior schools for blacks.

Given that it had to bring in new attorneys at the last minute with the illness of
Henry and the passing of Wormwood, the district's case was not well prepared. The
plaintiffs had gathered a great deal of discovery materials. In the process, they were
able to show the thoroughly disorganized nature of the central administration—
different branches did not have the slightest idea of what other parts of the district
were doing. At times, numbers from one DPS report contradicted those from
another study.

In building their case, advocates of integration charged DPS with cynically
segregating black teachers and staff whom the administration usually assigned to

black schools. In 1968 for example, there were nine white and ten black teachers at Barrett, 16 blacks and 32 whites at Mitchell, 12 blacks and 39 whites at Whittier, 23 blacks and 73 whites at Smiley, 25 blacks and 93 whites at Manual, and 31 blacks and 51 whites at Cole. For the most part, the faculties at other schools were exclusively white. Here and there, DPS employed a few Hispanos, American Indians, and Asian-Americans as instructors.

DPS, Keyes and company insisted, had to become a unitary district with equal educational opportunity for all. It was both to be colorblind in that it did not give preference to any students because of race, and acutely conscious of color, reaching out to black and other minority students to assure they indeed received equal educational opportunity. (This was the same time the federal government, under the cynical leadership of Richard Nixon, called for affirmative action, programs designed to advance blacks, women, and others within the system.)

In presenting their case that DPS was a de facto segregated district, the plaintiffs again emphasized the division between Barrett and Park Hill schools. They returned to how DPS came to make Smith and Hallett black schools while seeking to preserve Park Hill and Philips as white schools. Additionally, Keyes produced evidence of a 1962 gerrymander between Cole and Smiley in the hope of preserving Smiley as a white school. At the same time, DPS sent many blacks to Morey Junior High as it endeavored to make Byers Junior High (150 South Pearl Street) the elite white school for the Country Club crowd. Generally, the plaintiffs introduced any and all questionable decisions, based on race DPS had made since at least when Kenneth Oberholtzer became superintendent in 1947.

In testifying for the defense, Oberholtzer stated he did not pay specific attention to racial issues when he authorized the construction of Barrett. The plaintiffs' case, he insisted, was purely post facto, trying to make a set of coincidences into a nefarious conspiracy. No such conscious discrimination, Oberholtzer swore, had existed during his 20 years at DPS. Publicly, Oberholtzer was silent on the controversy. Such past school board members as Palmer Burch and Irene Saliman, who had been on the board at the time DPS opened Barrett, denied the district had a specific racial goal in building it.

(Pictures show some white youngsters in early Barrett School. In an oral history in a video *Rebels Remembered*, a community member stated that the original school was integrated. In no time, white flight saw Barrett become virtually 100-percent black. In other words, changing residential patterns, not conscious discrimination, shaped the racial charter of Barrett. DPS did not raise this defense. For that matter, the anti-busing Citizens Association for Neighborhood Schools admitted early Barrett was 90 percent black.)

The district rebutted the claim that it had used portable units to assure segregation. Given the massive school crowding of the 1950s and 1960s, DPS used portable units everywhere. Once more, the defense concluded that the plaintiffs were sore losers whose program would not enhance education for either black or white students. Besides, the school board argued, DPS had engaged in "compensatory" education for poor and minority students. It had channeled Great Society funds into improving schools in poverty-stricken neighborhoods. The system was on the right path. Busing would not benefit students.

To show it was a unitary school system, early on District #1 saw that all high school athletes wore a "D" as their letter, standing for Denver High School. This included young women who succeeded in sports such as members of the Girls Athletic Association at East High in 1930.

After listening to the testimony and arguments, Doyle pondered the evidence for more than a month. He announced his decision on March 21, 1970. Reviewing actions by DPS over the last ten years, he ruled that District #1 had engaged in a cynical and systematic illegal program of de facto segregation limiting the educational opportunities of black students. The schools to which DPS assigned blacks were not equal to the schools given over the whites. Citing the poor academic and test performances in schools with overwhelmingly black enrollments, the jurist ruled DPS had at least 15 "inferior" schools in the core of the city. Their enrollment was overwhelmingly that of minority youngsters: blacks at Whittier, Stedman, Smith, Mitchell, Harrington, Hallett, and Columbine, and Hispanos at Greenlee, Fairview, Fairmont, Elmwood, and Bryant-Webster (3635 Quivas Street) — all elementaries. Additionally, Doyle stated the predominantly Latino Baker Junior High, the black Cole Junior High, and Manual were also "inferior" schools.

At times, Doyle sided with the defense. In particular, he denied that the erection of the new Manual High School in 1953 was a deliberate act of racism. On the contrary, the construction of the building showed that DPS did not always assign blacks to old and dilapidated school buildings. The district had constructed the new Manual in response to loud community demands, including from African-Americans. In other words, at times DPS listened to black Denver.

Nor did Judge Doyle have problems with the assignment of black teachers and staff to predominantly black schools. Evidence showed black students did better when they had black teachers as role models. But such findings did not redress the obvious illegal discriminatory acts of DPS. By repealing the Gilberts Plan, the board had engaged in "eye-closing and head-burying" practices. In summary, DPS had violated the constitutional rights of the plaintiffs. It was the duty of the court to remedy this injustice.

Before imposing means to correct the district's illegal behavior, Doyle asked for additional testimony about the specific ways to overcome the system's many problems. The plaintiffs and DPS once more clashed in front of him on this issue between May 11 and 19, 1970. In pondering what DPS could do to purge itself of its segregated nature, the judge showed himself favorable to some of the actions of the board from 1967 to 1969, including voluntary open enrollment and the basics of the Gilberts Plan. By all means, the district should continue efforts to improve the 15 "inferior" schools attended by blacks and Hispanos in the core city. The judge added two more "inferior" elementaries to his list on May 21.

In preparation for the hearing on what remedies DPS should undertake, the school board adopted Resolution 1562 on May 6, 1970. It vowed that the district was committed to assuring equal educational opportunity. The question was how to achieve it. Busing, it repeated, was not the solution.

After pondering the evidence and pleadings, Doyle ruled on May 21. The court, he announced, must impose drastic measures to cut out the racist cancer the trial had exposed. Unable to find a better alternative to busing, on June 11, the jurist ordered its implementation to create a unitary, desegregated system providing all students with equal educational opportunity. He called for an acceleration of the Gilberts Plan beginning in the fall. All elementary schools were to retain existing kindergartens based on neighborhood attendance districts. Otherwise, the buses were to roll in September. The order impacted 8,380 children in 20 schools.

Photo by Phil Goodstein

The United States Tenth Circuit Court of Appeals is based in Denver. Eventually, it came to occupy the old Post Office/Federal Courthouse, naming it in honor of Supreme Court Justice Byron White. The Circuit Court checked the busing rulings of the United States District Court during the busing litigation that began in the summer of 1969. Here the temple of justice is seen from 18th and Champa streets.

Photo by Phil Goodstein

In February 1969, Judge William Doyle heard the trial of whether DPS was an illegally segregated dual district in the new United States Courthouse at the north corner of 19th and Stout streets, a building dating from 1966.

The school board appealed Doyle's verdict and order. The plaintiffs also had qualms about the ruling, complaining it did not go far enough. Still, they were happy with the victory. They knew, given recent election results, they had no immediate chance of regaining control of the board of education. As such, they had to depend on the federal judiciary as opposed to what they believed was a racist district and electorate.

On June 11, 1971, a three-judge panel of the Tenth Circuit reviewed the Keyes case. Yes, it ruled, Doyle had properly concluded that, given the evidence, District #1 suffered from de facto segregation. It was not sure, however, that mandatory busing was the solution. Denver, it stated, did not have a dual system, one set of schools specifically for whites and another for blacks. Consequently, past Supreme Court decisions were inapplicable. It ordered Doyle to review whether busing was indeed the best means of redressing DPS's racial disparities. In the meantime, the busing order was to remain in place. Both sides turned to the United States Supreme Court to determine whether Doyle's remedy was appropriate. The NAACP Legal Defense Fund wrote the plaintiffs' application for the high court to review the case.

The Supreme Court Decision

The United States Supreme Court accepted the Keyes case on January 17, 1972, hearing it on October 12 of that year. The divided body handed down its decision, *Keyes* v. *School District #1*, on June 21, 1973. James "Jim" Nabrit III of the Legal Defense Fund joined Gordon Greiner in arguing the case for the plaintiffs. The attorneys asserted that unequal educational opportunity was illegal and a denial of the 14th Amendment. No lawyers had previously raised this point in federal litigation over desegregation. As he had since the time of the trial before Judge Doyle in February 1970, William Ris was the main counsel for DPS.

The plaintiffs insisted that the high court go beyond Judge Doyle's decision. The issue was not just segregation in Park Hill, but the entire nature of the district. Discrimination could not be contained to one neighborhood. The district's actions in Park Hill showed that DPS was an illegal dual system.

The Supreme Court agreed. Speaking for the majority, Justice William Brennan concluded that de facto segregation was just as illegal and insidious as de jure segregation. Seen in this light, Judge Doyle had not gone far enough. Given that District #1 had cynically sought to segregate its schools, a drastic remedy was necessary to transform DPS from a dual system into a unitary district. This required a comprehensive desegregation program. The ruling broke new legal ground. It declared that evidence of segregation in a specific part of a community was presumption of a segregated district. As such, it was necessary to redress the entire problem, not just a limited number of schools as had been the case with both the Gilberts Plan and Judge Doyle's busing order.

Given the school board's opposition to the proposed remedy in the Gilberts Plan, Brennan ordered the United States District Court to maintain supervision of the district to assure the system eliminated all vestiges of segregation. Additionally, DPS must aggressively recruit minority faculty and staff. The district's legal problems would not be over until such employees mirrored the composition of the student body and the city's population.

While agreeing with Brennan's remedy, Justice William O. Douglas observed his colleague missed the opportunity to make the Keyes case a prime part of constitutional law. Douglas insisted the court must state there is no difference between de jure and de facto segregation. By intervening in Denver, the court should set a national model to assure the urgent integration of all school systems.

The division between de facto and de jure segregation was very much part of the Keyes decision. The evidence about segregation in DPS, the justices agreed, was nebulous. There was no specific decision mandating segregation. Nor could the plaintiffs point out a uniform pattern of gerrymandering schools. In particular, DPS had never acted to segregate Hispanos from other students via a manipulation of school borders. Still, the way DPS had cynically drawn attendance lines between Park Hill and Barrett schools, the court decided, showed the presumption of segregation in the district as a whole. In other words, the combination of de facto and de jure segregation made it mandatory for the court to act and expand on Judge Doyle's ruling. Besides, regardless of the specific nature of DPS segregation, it was necessary for the court to order the end unequal educational opportunity.

Justice Lewis Powell was uneasy about the combination of de jure and de facto segregation. He wanted to keep a clear demarcation between them. Still, he agreed that District #1 was an illegally segregated system, but he did not believe busing was a satisfactory solution. School and residential populations are not stagnant. People often move to a specific location based on the nature of the schools. If faced with crude, court-ordered busing, many whites might move or take their children out of

District #1. A court diktat, consequently, could well increase segregation. Busing, Powell concluded, was a tool, not a solution to the vestiges of discrimination.

In contrast to Douglas and Powell, both of whom essentially approved of Justice Brennan's ruling, future Chief Justice William Rehnquist dissented. De jure and de facto segregation, he argued, were not the same. The plaintiffs had failed to make Denver's practices indistinguishable from the outright Jim Crow systems outlawed by the *Brown* decision. (A Supreme Court law clerk at the time of the *Brown* case, Rehnquist had opposed that ruling.) The specific gerrymandering in Park Hill did not justify mandatory busing throughout the district. Rehnquist's dissent was the first filed in a Supreme Court civil rights case since before it had handed down its unanimous 1954 *Brown* verdict.

Chief Justice Warren Burger and associate justices Harry Blackmun, Thurgood Marshall, and Potter Stewart backed Brennan. This was a compromise. Initially, Burger had sought to sidetrack the case. Others on the court turned on him for trying to make politics rather than justice the keynote of the decision.

United States Supreme Court

Associate Justice Lewis Powell warned, in supporting the plaintiffs in the Denver school integration case, Keyes v. School District #1, *that an arbitrary imposition of busing might lead to white flight from the city and even greater racial divisions within the schools.*

The ninth justice, Byron White, recused himself from the decision after reviewing the briefs and sitting in on the hearing. He cited the presence of William K. Ris as lead lawyer for DPS. White and Ris had been classmates together at the University of Colorado. Additionally, White once more pointed out his past professional connections with DPS whereby he did not believe it was appropriate for him to participate in the ruling.

Brennan's opinion was law. Judge Doyle faced the task of deciding exactly what it meant and how it was to be implemented. By the time he held hearings on this in late 1973 in the wake of the Supreme Court's verdict, racial tensions had swept through DPS. Some of Justice Powell's predictions were already becoming true. Anti-busing voices argued the quality of the district was declining in the face of racial pressures. Violence was part of the mix.

A Note on Sources:

There are considerable materials on Fred Thomas in the Branscombe papers. I drew on them in looking at him in *Park Hill Promise*, 414–16. Watson, "Barricades," 85, cites Thomas blaming DPS for too many blacks flocking to Park Hill.

Robert Connery observes Thomas' concerns that DPS did not have a challenging enough curriculum for his children and told of them attending Dartmouth and Smith in *DU Law Review*, 90:5 (October 2013), 1094. Ibid. mentions Thomas' attendance at the conference of the United States Commission on Civil Rights. There is 1967 correspondence between Thomas and United States Commissioner of Education Byron Hansted about Denver school integration in FF 1:9 of the Noel papers.

Richard Kluger, *Simple Justice* (New York: Knopf, 1976), is a thorough, pro-integration history of court school segregation cases, primarily focusing on *Brown* v. *Board of Education*. It mentions the Keyes case, complete with the involvement of the LDF, 768–69. Noah Feldman, *Scorpions* (New York: Twelve, 2010), 407–08, criticizes the vacuous nature of the *Brown* decision as to the precise means of enforcing it. The result, he argues, was turmoil over integration during the next generation.

C. Vann Woodward, *The Strange Career of Jim Crow* (New York: Oxford University Press, 1966), 142, 144–47, 152–63, is an excellent sketch of the Supreme Court's move toward requiring desegregation of schools and the turbulence the order encountered. In passing, the work observes the intense de facto segregation in the North, 182.

Watson, "Barricades," 123–79, reviews the Keyes litigation. Art and Bea Branscombe looked at Wilfred Keyes and his role in the lawsuit in *GPHN*, February 20, 1992, and June 17, 1999, p. 12. *RMN*, February 18, 1985, p. 10, reflected on how Keyes became the lead plaintiff.

Robert T. Connery gives his memories of his involvement in the Keyes case and his ties to Craig Barnes in *DU Law Review*, 90:5 (October 2013), 1083–1114. Included, 1101–02, is a look at the origins of the lawsuit and the attorney's discussions with Dick Kozelka. *GPHN*, May 1971, mentioned Connery's involvement with PHAC.

Pearson, "Denver Case," 186–87, traces the prehistory of the litigation over school busing, stressing the roles of Craig Barnes, Paul Klite, and George Bardwell. Over the years, Susan Bardwell, the daughter of George Bardwell, has recalled his wide-ranging civic activism. Her family has donated George Bardwell's papers to DU.

Bardwell provided the statistical overview for the plaintiffs in *Segregation: A Social Account* (Denver: Colorado Civil Rights Commission, [1971]). The work is virtually unreadable for anyone lacking a knowledge of advanced mathematics, being filled with countless formulas. It is most valuable for its appendix, listing enrollments and the ethnic distribution of the city's elementary schools from 1943 to 1968.

Pearson, "Denver Case," 187–88, traces the origins of the lawsuit, the role of the LDF, and how Gordon Greiner became the plaintiffs' lead attorney. Craig Barnes gives his version of the way Greiner joined the case, *DU Law Review*, 90:5 (October 2013), 1065. Connery remembers the lawyers who met about the possible suit in ibid., 1103–04. Barnes further reflects on his experiences in the case, "A Personal Memoir of Plaintiffs' Cocounsel," in ibid., 1059–81. *Growing Up True: Lessons of a Western Boyhood* (Golden: Fulcrum, 2001), is Barnes' autobiography. He is in the 1976 *Who's*, 22. I touch on his 1970 run for Congress in *Big Money*, 464–67.

DP, October 11, 2015, p. 4B, recalled Greiner's role in the *Keyes* case. William H. Hornby, *The Law Out West: Holland & Hart, 1947–1989* (Denver: Holland & Hart, 1989), 133–36, emphasizes Greiner, Holland & Hart's pro bono outreach, and the firm's involvement in the Keyes case. Far and away the best portrait of Greiner was in *CJ*, May 8, 1974, pp. 11–12.

Greiner donated his records on the Keyes case to the University of Colorado where there is a 68 box collection in two accessions, the Keyes papers, COU 931, in the archives at Norlin Library. Besides the transcripts of hearings and trials, the holding has plenty of the exhibits in the cases, clipping files, court pleadings, and research materials.

The Auraria Archives has an eight-box holding on Doyle. *RMN*, September 24, 1961, p. 32, profiled William Doyle when he joined the bench of the United States District Court. It once more looked at him when he was assigned the busing case, July 27, 1969, p. 5. John L. Kane Jr. and Harry F. Temker Jr., "William E. Doyle," *CL*, 27:7 (July 1998), 21–24, is an overview of the judge's career. Also see James K. Logan, ed., *The Federal Courts of the Tenth Circuit* (Denver: Tenth Circuit Court of Appeals, 1992), 69–71, 385, 411–18. Ibid., 385, 412–19, deals with the Keyes case. CANS, *Judicial Fiat*, 4, observes Doyle sent his children to private schools. I mention the Mendel Cooper case, drawing on the records of Walter Gerash, in *Big Money*, 439–44. *DP*, March 26, 1968, p. 17, and *RMN*, March 27, 1968, p. 8, reported the bombing of Doyle's home.

Craig Barnes remembers Judge Doyle in *DU Law Review*, 90:5 (October 2013), 1066. The same volume includes the reminiscences of two of Doyle's law clerks at the time of the Keyes case, Jane Michaels, 1115–20, and Gregory J. Hobbs Jr., 1121–37. DPS has a small holding from Jane Michaels, M2224. It primarily consists of copies of Judge Doyle's rulings concerning busing.

Pearson, "Denver Case," 188, emphasizes the role of LDF in shaping the plaintiffs' case. Connery recalls the hearing before Judge Doyle, *DU Law Review*, 90:5 (October 2013), 1111–13. Schwartzkopf, "Collective Bargaining," 199, mentions Fort Fumble. LWV, *Composite View*, 1–2, outlines the suit against DPS and the plaintiffs' claims. On August 26, 2019, Dick Koeppe recalled being a witness in the 1969 hearing before Doyle. He reflected on the court intervention in DPS, insisting the judge had made the right decision.

RMN, July 24, 1969, p. 5, reported Judge Doyle's decision. It told of the impending start of busing, July 17, 1969, p. 5, and the status of appeals, July 18, 1969, p. 8, and July 23, 1969, p. 8. *DP*, July 27, 1969, p. 49, printed the text of Judge Doyle's injunction which is *Keyes* v. *School District #1*, 303 FSupp 279. His revised order is 303 FSupp 289.

Fishman, "Endless Journey," 199, mentions how the plaintiffs in the school busing litigation attacked tracking. Jeannie Oakes criticizes tracking in *Phi Delta Kappan*, September 1986, pp. 12–17, and October 1986, pp. 148–53. Bailey, "Journey Full Circle," 39, is also insistent that tracking undermines integration. *Schools for a New Century* will analyze debates over tracking.

Pearson, "Denver Case," 197–98, looks at the decision of the Tenth Circuit. Connery observes how William Brennan came to review the Tenth Circuit's ruling in *DU Law Review*, 90:5 (October 2013), 1086. Compare Barnes' account in ibid, 1075.

SB, October 6, 1969, p. 21, had Gilberts' plea, "Our Responsibility." My *Modern East Denver*, 172, mentions Kenneth Wormwood, drawing on *CL*, July 1988, 1261–62. *CL*, July 2003, 59–62, looked at the achievements of William Ris and his representation of DPS in the *Keyes* case. Connery mentions how the plaintiffs had pondered approaching Ris to represent them, *DU Law Review*, 90:5 (October 2013), 1104.

DP, February 6, 1970, p. 1, and *RMN*, February 6, 1970, p. 1, February 7, 1970, p. 1, and February 8, 1970, p. 8, reported the bombing of the bus garage. *NYT*, February 6, 1970, summarized the school bus bombing. In 1995, Walter Gerash allowed me to review his file on Baltazar Martinez. *RMN*, February 9, 1970, pp 1, 5, told about the surrender and release of the suspect. *Oxford Encyclopedia of Latinos & Latinas in the United States* (Oxford: Oxford University Press, 2005), 4:235–36, emphasizes the importance of Reis Lopez Tijerina.

RMN, February 25, 1970, p. 9, and February 26, 1970, p. 5, and *DP*, February 25, 1970, p. 3, reported the bombing of the house of Wilfred Keyes. There is an interview with the wife of Wilfred Keyes in *Our Neighborhood Schools* in Alweis, *Rebels Remembered*, in which she mentioned the bombing and her urging her husband to move. My *Modern East Denver*, 45, observes the bombing of the home of Jim Perrill. *DP*, March 20, 1970, p. 37, and *SB*, March 30, 1970, p. 101, mentioned the bus purchase decision. Also see *SN*, September 8, 1970, p. 2, and November 30, 1970, p. 25.

Mark Whitman, *The Irony of Desegregation Law, 1955–1995* (Princeton: Markus Wiener Publishers, 1998), 185–87, and Meadow, "Hard Years," *CJ*, May 8, 1974, pp. 23–26, look at the trial. Pearson, "Denver Case," 220, stresses the well-prepared nature of the plaintiffs' case, emphasizing the role of LDF. *RMN*, February 4, 1970, p. 8, told of court testimony about the racially discriminatory practices of the district and the way faculty and staff could decide not to work with black students. On February 5, 1970, p. 8, the *News* stated a witness swore the district distorted the results of standardized tests to cloak the racial disparities of the district. *Our Neighborhood Schools*, in Alweis, *Rebels Remembered*, includes a discussion of Barrett School. One community member claimed it was initially 50 percent white. CANS, *Judicial Fiat*, 4, states Barrett was originally 90 percent black.

A 1962–63 census of black instructors in DPS is in FF 21:33 of the Yasui papers. There is a 1968 count in an unnumbered folder in Box 13 of the Banks papers. FF 5:10 of the DPS papers outlines the border adjustment between Columbine and Stedman schools. Watson, "Barricades," 49, stresses the boundary changes between Cole and Smiley, and Morey and Byers. On August 14, 2019, Margaret Benton recalled having to attend Byers Junior High in the late 1960s. She lived adjacent to Cheesman Park, close to Morey, but found herself sent to Byers through what she claimed was a cynical gerrymandering of the attendance zone between that school and Morey.

DP, February 20, 1970, p. 3, reported the testimony of Oberholtzer at the trial before Doyle. *DP*, July 27, 1969, p. 49, reviewed Oberholtzer's public silence on DPS racial controversies and quoted the views of Burch and Saliman on Barrett School. *RMN*, March 22, 1970, p. 8, and *DP*, March 22, 1970, p. 1, reported Doyle's decision in the school busing trial. His ruling is 313 FSupp 61; his specific order mandating busing is 313 FSupp 90.

SN, April 12, 1971, p. 47, mentioned Resolution 1562. *RMN*, April 17, 1970, p. 5, observed Doyle hearing evidence of plans for desegregation. Pearson, "Denver

Case," 194, looks at the May 1970 hearing before Judge Doyle. The article observes the exclusion of kindergartens from the integration order.

The January 21, 1971, *SR*, outlined Superintendent Howard Johnson's review of the status of the school busing suit and the impending ruling of the Tenth Circuit. Also see Johnson's paired busing scheme in the March 17, 1971, *SR*, pp. 1–8.

The Tenth Circuit decision modifying the ruling of Doyle is 445 F.2d 990. The Supreme Court order affirming Doyle's decision is 396 US 1215. The Supreme Court accepted the Keyes case, 404 US 1936. Pearson, "Denver Case," 198, looks at how the Supreme Court came to rule on the Keyes case, including the role of LDF.

Briefs in the Keyes case are in Philip B. Kurland and Gerhard Casper, eds., *Landmark Briefs and Arguments of the Supreme Court of the United States: Constitutional Law* (Washington: University Publications of America, 1977), 77:3–600. The crucial *Keyes* v. *School District #1* decision by the Supreme Court case is 413 US 189. A copy is in FF 1 of the Jane Michaels papers.

Mark Tushnet, "A Clerk's Eyeview of *Keyes* v. *School District #1*," *DU Law Review*, 90:5 (October 2013), 1139–49, are the memories of a clerk of Justice Thurgood Marshall. The article discusses the inside politics of how the court reached its decision on the case. Whitman, *Irony of Desegregation*, 187–94, is another examination of the politics of the Supreme Court and the way it came to rule on the Keyes case.

Pearson, "Denver Case," 198–201, outlines the arguments of the plaintiffs in reviewing Brennan's decision. Ibid., 188–89, stresses the role of James Nabrit and the LDF in the Supreme Court hearing and the novel nature of the claim that unequal educational opportunity was unconstitutional. Orfield, *Must We Bus?* 16–18, 27, stresses the landmark character of the ruling and the theory of the presumption of segregation. He interviewed Nabrit, giving the attorney's take on the case and its impact, 367.

There is a brief discussion of *Keyes* v. *School District #1*, fitting it into constitutional law, in Kermit L. Hall, ed., *The Oxford Companion to the Supreme Court of the United States* (New York: Oxford University Press, 2005), 558–59. Jeffrey Raffel mentions it in *Historical Dictionary of School Segregation and Desegregation: The American Experience* (Westport, CT: Greenwood Press, 1990), 139–41. There is a chapter on it in Whitman, *Irony of Desegregation*, 177–209. CANS, *Judicial Fiat*, 7, observes Byron White's recusing himself from the decision.

The article in *DU Law Review*, 90:5 (October 2013), 1144–48, by Mark Tushnet, stresses the combination of de facto and de jure segregation in leading the Supreme Court to decide in favor of the plaintiffs. He observes Powell's hesitancy to join the majority, 1145. Michael A. Olivas in ibid., 1161–62, stresses the trailblazing role of the Denver case in combining de jure and de facto segregation. Also see the views of Tom Romero, in ibid., 1029–30, and Phoebe A. Haddon, 1255.

Whitman, *Irony of Desegregation*, 201–22, includes Judge William O. Douglas' memorandum on the Keyes case. Ibid., has Brennan's memorandum. It prints Powell's opinion, 203–8, and Rehnquist's dissent, 208–09.

Chapter Seven

Violence

After implementing busing for selected elementary schools in 1969–70 based on the Gilberts Plan, the next schoolyear, on the order of the United States District Court, District #1 expanded the desegregation program to secondary schools. To facilitate it, DPS purchased 16 new school buses. The board complained about the cost. The money spent, advocates of neighborhood schools asserted, could be better used to improve what went on in the classrooms. Even as opponents of busing declared as much, they refused to apply for funds from the federal government available to enhance school transportation. Such money, the board asserted, would recognize the legitimacy of the court order and the right of Washington to interfere with local school decisions. When it became obvious that there was no way around the court busing order, DPS finally asked for federal money for more buses in 1974.

As it squabbled over the cost of busing, DPS did not have a well-crafted program of action to assure the success of expanded busing in the fall of 1970. The clumsy implementation of the effort resulted in tumultuous disturbances at South and George Washington high schools. Both had previously had the reputations of being excellent, college-oriented academies.

By 1970, many veteran teachers had fled to South High from other schools where the upheavals of the 1960s had changed the traditional, rigid hierarchies of the district. These instructors were comfortable in a place where students obeyed orders and strict discipline took care of any pupils questioning the status quo. The inflexible system was unable to handle the changed world produced by busing.

Realizing that busing might lead to school upheavals, in 1969 the district's Office of School–Community Relations had collaborated with the PTA and the Administrators and Supervisors Association, the organization representing DPS principals and senior front-office personnel, to address the possible impact of desegregation. It put together guidelines on how schools should deal with new students arriving on buses in the name of integration. Included were small orientation sessions, outreaches to parents, and efforts to have welcoming committees which assigned each new student a buddy/locker partner. The buddy

The architectural partnership of Fisher & Fisher designed South High School at South Gilpin Street and Louisiana Avenue. The building held its first classes in January 1926.

was to help introduce the new student to the school. Additionally, there were to be social affairs where the bused-in pupils got to know others in the student body. The guidelines further suggested that office personnel were to show themselves as warm and supportive, getting to know the new students early and urging them to ask for help when necessary. Virtually none of this was done with the new students at South in September 1970 under freshly installed principal Erick M. Holland.

In part, South made no effort to implement the program of the Office of School–Community Relations because of the district's last-minute legal appeals. Rather than seeing it had to make sure schools could accommodate the changed assignments stemming from busing, DPS had been so sure it would win appellate relief that it made no provision for what might happen if the courts ordered busing to proceed. In particular, it delayed telling students about what high school they were to attend, complete with bus schedules and orientations about what to expect in their changed settings. Not until August 21, 1970, about ten days before the start of classes, did the district inform parents of where their children had to go to school that fall.

Given the lack of such action on the part of the district or the leadership of South, many black students found themselves lost when they entered the high school. It was nothing like the places they had previously attended. Discipline and order were everywhere. Nor did South make sure that counselors were readily available to whom students could turn for assistance when they found themselves dumbfounded by the place.

Principal Holland, a veteran of the district who had a doctorate of education from the University of Denver, did not believe in coddling students. As such, he was completely unresponsive to pleas for help from lost, confused black youngsters. Punishment rather than support was his response when they found themselves baffled by the way South operated.

A native of Iowa born in 1922, Holland served in the Navy during World War II. He rose to the rank of commander in the reserves. A former teacher at West High, South's leader had been assistant principal at George Washington before taking the new post in 1970. He went on to lead John F. Kennedy High School from 1974 to 1986. The retired educator died at age 74 in 1997.

South High, in the long-standing tradition of District #1, was particularly severe in chastising students who were tardy. In the case of some of the transported black students, they could not help it: the district's busing schedule was not reliable and many of the adolescents had yet to master the transit system. This, ruled Holland and his cohorts, was no excuse. The pupils showed they were refractory by coming to school late. Those who ran in halls to make it to class on time were penalized for violating a no-running rule.

The principal's actions reflected the district as a whole and schools everywhere. By the late 1960s/early 1970s, schools were in crisis. Administrators insisted on enforcing extremely petty rules. Included were overbearing dress codes completely out of tune with the changing mores of the day. Only via unrelenting, unquestioning obedience, disciplinarians were sure, would students learn to conform and behave. This, far more than academic achievement or nurturing a love of learning, was the prime purpose of the schools. Dictatorial administrators made any challenges to unbending rules a punishable offense.

Many blacks were sure such policies reflected a racist administration. When they found it impossible to communicate with Principal Holland and others in the administration about their problems with the busing schedule and their being discombobulated by the school, African-American pupils banded together, going out on strike on October 2. The principal called in the police. Students, he loudly announced, must not rebel. He made no reflection that South students were the Rebels, celebrating those who had committed treason during the Civil War when they fought for slavery. Apparently, that was the only kind of rebellion the South leader tolerated.

Arbitrary chastisement did not solve the problems of black students. On the contrary, they became more rebellious as they lost class time and became further behind in their studies. In part, this reflected a most dubious DPS disciplinary policy: suspending errant students from classes. The punishment did not account for the fact that it might further alienate students and lead them to drop out once they discovered classes were completely beyond their comprehension. Indeed, the more class time they missed, the more the administration and teachers tended to mark them down for not keeping up with classwork.

In response to the administration's measures to increase the penalties against those who had struck, South students staged new walkouts on October 28–30. Once more, Holland called in the police. In tune with the policies of city hall, many of the officers showed themselves most ready to use physical violence against the protesters. In consequence, for a few days South was literally a police state with both uniformed and plainclothes officers patrolling all parts of the building.

Typical of the way Holland operated was that he suspended a couple of students in late October 1970 when they refused to leave a meeting with him after he had

South High students were once the Rebels. This did not include any tolerance for students rebelling against a rigid, unbending administration. While the school's mascot became the Griffin in 2009, the South's drum corps has remained the South Rebel Line. Here its members march in the 2020 Martin Luther King Day parade.

refused to redress their concerns. In response, led by South's head girl, pupils asked the school board to relieve Holland as someone who more endangered peace and learning at South than enhanced them. He remained as principal.

Civil rights groups provided assistance to South students. They helped black students create a youth chapter of the National Association for the Advancement of Colored People. Hispanos formed La Raza de Aztlan whose members described themselves as being Christian "by the grace of God." Ethnic and racial identity were vital since, with the approval of federal courts, they overshadowed all aspects of the district. They were also necessary because minority youths seemingly gained no respect, recognition, or assistance from the administration.

Many Hispanic students at West had the same concerns as blacks at South. In late October 1970, about 100 of them staged a sit-in at the school to protest the school's lack of equipment and facilities. Having learned from the blowout in the spring of 1969, the West administration at least claimed it was concerned. Students soon returned to class. There was no violence.

Eventually, South solved the transportation problems. Black students did not learn better at South than they had at previous schools. In part, this was because they were unprepared for the vigor of some of the classes. That problem especially haunted George Washington High School.

The George Washington Riot

Since it opened in the fall of 1960, George Washington had been integrated. Included were the sons and daughters of black military personnel at Lowry Air Force Base, a facility located to the southeast of South Quebec Street and Alameda Avenue from 1937–38 to 1996. Many such students were well behaved. Their parents frequently instilled something of a military discipline in them. At times, commanding officers of military posts transferred soldiers and airmen if they received complaints that the children of those in the service were out of control in schools. Some dismissed the sons and daughters of military personnel as "brats."

Besides Hilltop, Montclair, and much of central-southeast Denver, George Washington pulled in students living in eastern Park Hill, including along prestigious Monaco Street Parkway. By the mid-1960s, increasing numbers of blacks lived in the last area. While a few African-Americans showed up in advanced classes at the high school, for the most part they were in regular classes. Rarely did black students win academic awards. Altogether, they made up about 5 percent of the student body during the 1960s.

In contrast, many Jewish students shined at George Washington. They totaled about one-third of the enrollment. Some treasured the place as a veritable college preparatory academy. No school in the district had a greater number of Advanced Placement students, the bulk of whom passed the challenging examination at the end of the year. The high school likewise usually had the most National Merit Scholarship semifinalists in the district.

Pupils usually called George Washington "GW." They also referred to it as "George." At times, the school's football helmets simply read "George"; on other occasions they had "GW." Students were the Patriots. Their newspaper was *The Surveyor*. A popular logo for the school was the Jolly Green Giant. School colors were green and white.

The school had excellent test results. In 1968, it was at 76 percent of the median. Students at Manual scored 30 percent. East pupils were at 54 percent. In some ways, the last number was deceiving. About 40 percent of East was black. Internally, the school was highly segregated, especially in advanced classes. Generally, the best East students were fully equal to those at GW. In contrast, many blacks at East did quite poorly. In other words, integration was no magical solution to learning disparities. Many who opposed busing feared that rather than elevating blacks in white schools, the presence of poorly prepared blacks would bring down the quality of the white schools. Such, seemingly, is what happened at GW.

As at South, George Washington failed to make arrangements to welcome the 257 new black students whom the court had ordered to the school for the 1970–71 schoolyear. Some were seniors who had previously attended East. They often shared the prejudices of the Angels against the Patriots. East students were the Angels who were aware of the school's strong rivalry with GW. Integration advocates and the court had blocked DPS's suggestion that the high school busing order exempt seniors so they could earn their diploma from the school where they had spent the last two years. Doyle further rejected pleas that students in sixth and

George Washington High School opened in 1960 at 655 South Monaco Street Parkway.

ninth grades be allowed to stay in their old schools. Such a decision, he explained, would upset the racial balance of the busing order. In other words, abstract numbers, rather than a personal concern with students, was at the heart of the court order.

Some of the black students who were bused to GW were angry about being nothing more than pawns being manipulated in the name of abstract ideas. Not only were many of them nervous, so were most of the other youngsters bused to new schools in strange parts of the community. In the hope of calming their fears, community volunteers, with the blessings of the United States District Court, rode buses with the goal of reducing the trauma of the desegregation experiment.

Busing did not work well at GW. In part, this stemmed from DPS's lack of cooperation. It failed to allocate enough buses to bring the black students to the school. Routes were often highly convoluted and extremely slow. Some students arrived at school exhausted by the bus ride.

Nor did DPS provide transportation to all students it ordered to GW. Many had to rely on the privately owned operator of public transportation, Tramway. Its drivers complained the students were rowdy and sometimes refused to pay fares. Eventually, conditions were so bad that Tramway ceased service to the school in mid-October, canceling runs in the morning and afternoon right when students needed to get to and from the school. At the end of the month, under pressure from a court order and state regulators, Tramway resumed its regular service along Monaco Street Parkway.

Additionally, DPS announced it was providing more school buses for GW students. To get youngsters to the building on time, the district made high school hours ever earlier—the bulk of the buses were reserved for delivering elementary students to school around 8:30–8:45. This impacted the sleep patterns of adolescents who often had not completely awakened when they reported to school. Teachers then chastised students who sometimes fell asleep in class.

Though there was no Jim Crow at GW, even before the onset of busing blacks had often separated themselves from the whites. In particular, they occupied their own part of the lunchroom. At a time when race was seemingly everything, both blacks and whites frequently judged each other by the color of their skins. In a word, they were acting like adults amidst the racial hysteria dividing the city over busing. Generally, black students were no more eager to be forcefully bused than white parents were to have their children get on the buses.

There had already been black-white tensions at GW in 1968. That year, the administration called in the police in response to some racial assaults—the murder of Martin Luther King increased racial violence everywhere. There were few racial problems in 1969–70 when DPS counted 2,889 students at the school. It stated 94.4 percent of them were white, 4.4 percent black, .7 percent Hispanic, and .5 percent Asian. According to the district, GW had an official capacity for 2,520. At times, the school was on split sessions, including in 1969–70. Forced busing changed everything for the worse in September 1970.

By this time, GW was something of the embodiment of mass schooling. It had a most rigid dress code, insisting girls' skirts be at least knee length. The institute, according to physics teacher Buel C. Robinson, was an "assembly-line operation," providing an "impersonal, dehumanizing brand of education." Rather than have instructors and counselors work with a student, shaping his program, computers made key decisions concerning pupils' fates. Racial tensions aggravated this climate. Teachers found themselves caught in the middle.

Heritage 1971

Upheavals at George Washington High School in the fall of 1970 short-circuited the rising career of principal Jack Beardshear. Here he gives the peace symbol of the day as he seeks calm at the school.

Many of the new black students were not prepared for the high quality of the GW curriculum. As they had with their previous white students, the traditional instructors gave black learners exacting assignments. When the new pupils failed to perform adequately, the teachers gave them poor grades. Some youngsters had never been subject to such academic vigor. No more than at South did teachers and administrators at GW go out of their way to help new black students who were desperately lost. Receiving failing grades and taunted by white students, blacks increasingly claimed white instructors discriminated against them. They believed the teachers dismissed them as being hopelessly stupid.

As at South, strict discipline, complete with a reliance on the police, was the administration's means of dealing with disruptive black students. There were few efforts at active integration, school-sponsored programs to bring black and white students together whereby they got to know each other, share experiences, and see that they were a new generation who could move beyond the racism of their elders. On the contrary, racial divisions were omnipresent. Fights erupted between blacks and whites. Rather than grasping that something was terribly wrong, the administration increasingly relied on the police. Officers patrolled the halls. Many blacks feared and hated the men in blue, being sure that they would be punished by them for the color of their skin.

Tensions exploded in the cafeteria on Thursday, September 24, 1970. A black girl clashed with a white girl. After calling each other names, fisticuffs flew. Others joined the brawl that quickly became a race riot. In no time, the confrontation spread through the entire building. To make sure there was no more trouble that day, Principal Jack Beardshear, a rising star in DPS who had taken charge of George Washington at the beginning of the 1969–70 schoolyear, closed the building at 1:20 PM. Sixteen students were injured in the fray. The police arrested two blacks, including a non-student.

Conditions were no better the next day, Friday, September 25. Again, racial violence flared. The locus was the north courtyard and the student parking lot. At 11:45 AM, the administration closed the school. It saw there was a heavy police presence when the school reopened on Monday, September 28. Included were officers patrolling the halls with dogs.

Racial tensions remained. The school failed to redress their causes. This was the situation when, around 1:00 PM on Tuesday, October 20, a plainclothes officer discovered some black students playing a game of dice in a stairwell. Not only did he break it up, but he ordered a participant to submit to a search, convinced a young man had drugs on him. In response the students jumped the officer, or so he claimed. He responded by grabbing his pistol, firing two shots. This provoked another riot with some students throwing chairs through windows. Outside, particularly in the north courtyard, they vandalized the property.

As the school became completely out of control, the fire alarm sounded, leading to the evacuation of the building. The upheaval lasted for about two hours. At its worst, approximately 250 youths fought with the police. Nine people were hurt; eight were arrested.

The renewed violence led to the shuttering of GW for the next six schooldays. The school needed a week's peace since faculty members were terrified by what had occurred. Meeting together, they realized the need for active intervention, particularly in patrolling the hallways, parking lot, lunchroom, and restrooms.

Meanwhile, the school board was torn by debates over what it could and should do. This was particularly came out during its October 22 session. Seeing

NSAC

George Washington High School opened in 1960. Its students are the Patriots. For the bicentennial in 1976, its color guard accentuated the school's name.

the extreme tensions between the police and black students at GW, state Senator George Brown, the first African-American in the upper house of the General Assembly, called for disarming the police. He knew that, if faced with armed white police officers, especially those who were not in uniform, some black students might carry guns. Former school board member Ed Benton agreed. Listening to members of the black community, at the school board session he vehemently denounced turning GW into an armed camp patrolled by the police.

The school board did not listen to Benton. After it voted down, three-to-three, a resolution by Rachel Noel prohibiting an armed police occupation of the schools, particularly at GW, Benton announced he was not going to leave the board room/DPS headquarters until the board had reconsidered the matter. About 20 to 25 others joined him. Their sit-in lasted from the end of the board meeting at around 1:00 AM on Friday, October 23, until Sunday afternoon, complete with a fire department inspection of the premises in the middle of the night.

Benton and company ended their occupation after police chief George Seaton stated he would not specifically assign officers to schools. The head of the force additionally stated that if DPS hired any off-duty officers as security guards, such personnel must be in uniform. The police would not give up their weapons.

The school board also claimed victory in the dispute. President Bill Berge explained that the administration was giving the decision about stationing police in buildings to individual schools. In particular, this was to be a consensus of the faculty, staff, and parents. Not surprisingly, the overwhelming bulk of the GW faculty urged a police occupation of the academy. In response, Benton argued it was the lack of action by DPS, especially the school board, which was responsible for the chaos at George Washington. Nobody suggested metal detectors through which students had to pass to enter the schoolhouse.

With many teachers agreeing to go out of their way in assuming extra disciplinary responsibilities, the administration reopened the school on October 29, placing it back on split sessions. This meant that the 1,000 sophomores at GW took classes from 12:30 PM to 5:30 PM daily. The action separated them from 2,000 juniors and seniors who were in the building from around 7:00 AM to noon. All students had to have an identification card to get into the building.

From the time of the creation of junior high schools in 1917–18 to the establishment of middle schools in 1982, high schools were for grades ten, 11, and 12. Courses often mixed students of different grades together. As a consequence of the reorganization of GW, pupils found themselves placed in new classes with new teachers. Around 100 unarmed community volunteers and parents patrolled the hallways. The city's Commission on Community Relations had recruited and trained them for three-hour shifts. Additionally, DPS arranged for black security personnel to be visibly present at the school. To assure no more problems in the lunchroom, the school closed the cafeteria. It was not necessary, GW explained, since, with split sessions, students either got out of school around noon or started the schoolday shortly thereafter.

Though the presence of the police and volunteers, complete with the split sessions, saw the return of peace, many GW students lived in fear. Rumors circulated that some white girls did not eat breakfast or drink water before school because they were afraid to use the restrooms. Meanwhile, liberal champions of integration claimed that racism was the cause of the upheavals, particularly on the part of the faculty.

African-American political leaders agreed. Rather than blaming the administration or the school board, they targeted the faculty as responsible for the troubles. Consequently, they demanded outsiders supervise the instructors to guarantee they did not discriminate against black pupils. More than that, they insisted the teachers recognize that many of the black students were not prepared for GW's academic rigor. The solution was lowering standards. Included was eliminating Dickens and Shakespeare from tenth grade English classes since they were not part of the cultural heritage of black America. To reach out to African-American students, GW introduced a black studies program. Nobody claimed black youngsters got a better education at GW; many lamented white pupils received a worse one. (There was nothing unique about the school's changing curriculum. Across the country, there was an increasing de-emphasis in the 1970s on the classics and the traditional scope of English classes while ethnic studies programs soared.)

Seeing the commotion, Judge Doyle intervened. He ordered all faculty members to take five hours of classes annually about the need for desegregation. The instructors found this blatantly offensive. What was worse, overbearing, politically correct individuals conducted the sessions. Some of those paid to teach the teachers, including African-American activists who gloried in the power the court order had given them, readily branded the GW teachers as racists. Veteran instructors saw this nothing less than highly insulting brainwashing. Under the supervision of the United States District Court, they lamented, politics had supplanted education as the primary purpose of the school.

Officially, the sessions were "human relations" classes, part of "inservice" training for all instructors in the district. The courses were necessary, the court declared, to assure integration worked. Judge Doyle court further suggested DPS transfer veteran teachers to core-city schools, employ teacher aides, and extend the schoolyear. Further recommendations were the addition of early childhood education, classes in black and Latino history, and the provision of Spanish-language classes for students who were not proficient in English. While none of these measures were an immediate part of the desegregation ruling, DPS adopted most of them in subsequent years.

In the wake of the commotion, George Washington principal Jack Beardshear asked for a transfer at the end of the 1971–72 schoolyear. A Marine during World War II, he had previously been a teacher at Grant Junior High (1701 South Washington Street) and at East before emerging as principal at Baker and then assistant principal at East. The school's head was somewhat cynical and had a wry sense of humor. During the worst of the tensions at GW, he joked that he was often up all night with his good friend, Jim Beam. Beardshear was subsequently in the DPS office of pupil services. He retired to Stockton, California, in the 1980s. Born in Colorado on June 13, 1920, he died in California on February 12, 1991. After he left GW, the school never had the same élan as it had before busing.

George Washington was not alone in suffering educational upheavals. Racial violence swept Hamilton Junior High in the spring of 1971. In many ways, problems there showed DPS had not learned from what happened at South and GW. Once more, blacks bused into the building were unprepared for classes and found themselves lost and seemingly mistreated. As at South and GW, overbearing administrative measures were the response.

Back in the spring of 1970, some white parents complained their daughters were being viciously bullied and beaten by black girl gangs at Smiley. Such was the claim of anti-busing board member Frank Southworth who presented a parent petition calling for an armed policeman at the junior high. Black integration advocate Rachel Noel responded that she had not heard anything about such violence at Smiley. The board members' different views illustrated that advocates and foes of court-ordered busing seemingly lived in different worlds.

The superintendent's office reacted to the problems at places such as Smiley, Hamilton, George Washington, and South by considerably increasing the budget of the district's safety department. While DPS suffered severe financial shortages by the late 1970s, it continued to spend ever more on creating its own security system. Additionally, the police department regularly stationed officers at schools.

To prevent more problems, schools and teachers lowered their standards. So did the district as a whole. It greatly modified the Proficiency and Review test high school students had to pass to graduate. Advocates of equality of educational opportunity asserted many minorities failed it because of the seemingly racist core of the examination. Many students still struggled to pass the replacement test. An atmosphere encouraging a love of knowledge and self-directed learning was less part of the day-to-day operations of the system than it had ever been.

A Collapse of Confidence

The overall result was the collapse of confidence in the schools. District #1 enrollment had peaked in 1968 with 96,848 students—back in 1962, the system had predicted it would have 100,977 students by 1967. Membership dropped slightly to 96,634 in 1969 and 95,754 in 1970. Not only were baby boomers increasingly graduating from high school, but many parents so distrusted DPS that they started to leave the city for the suburbs. They did not want their children to attend classes in a district engulfed in crisis and court-ordered busing. (Among those who did not want his daughter getting on a bus was attorney Craig Barnes who had represented the plaintiffs in the initial Keyes litigation. He explained she had special needs that he did not believe DPS could provide.)

Others transferred their children to private schools. Such institutes rapidly grew. Back in the 1960s, Denver was home to about a handful of notable non-sectarian private academies. Included were such places for the elite as Kent School, Denver Country Day, and Graland. There were additionally many programs for early childhood education and some religious-based private day schools. The number of alternative programs exploded with the onset of busing. The 1970s particularly saw an increasing number of students in Jewish day academies. In part, the rise of Jewish day schools reflected a growing Zionist enthusiasm whereby American

Photo by Phil Goodstein

For years, Denver had but few private schools for secondary learners. Among them was Randell School. It started in 1923 as a preparatory academy for students who were unable to handle the East High curriculum. Anna Ragland Randell, a former West High teacher, conducted it at her home, the pictured 1600 Madison Street, until her death in 1941. The program, later Randell–Moore School, was subsequently along the south side of the 1700 block of 13th Avenue. In 1967, it moved to South Cook Street and Warren Avenue. It surged there in the 1970s when white parents increasingly enrolled their children in private schools to escape court-ordered busing.

Jews wanted to show their allegiance to Israel in contrast to their previous goal of blending in as full and equal American citizens.

Until the chaos at George Washington, Jewish Denver had been an extremely strong supporter of public schools. Many Jews had joined with blacks in the campaign for desegregation. Among them was Eugene R. Weiner, a co-plaintiff is the school busing case. In part, he joined it at the behest of Martha Radetsky. She was the widow of Ralph Radetsky, a key insider at both city hall and KOA Radio and Television (Channel Four). Long active in numerous civic causes, Martha Radetsky had been on the board of Speak Out on School Integration. During the early years of the Keyes case, she hosted fundraisers for the litigation at her deluxe home to the south of the Country Club.

Protestant day schools also became ever more popular. Besides mass unease with court-ordered busing, they reflected changing religious values. A strong Christian fundamentalism was sweeping the country. Ironically, the 1970s were also the time when the Catholic Archdiocese increasingly closed parochial schools, particularly in poor neighborhoods with heavy minority enrollments. In places where parochial schools remained open, some non-Catholics enrolled their children in them as alternatives to the troubled public schools. Additionally, the 1970s saw the rise of home schooling, another means by which parents could keep their children out of court-ordered busing.

The federal government encouraged the growth of private schools. It granted them ever greater funds. Per capita, they received about four times as much money from Washington as did public schools. Advocates argued private schools were crucial to the safety of children. Here they painted inner-city schools, i.e., those in minority and poverty-stricken neighborhoods, as extremely violent places. Ironically, when the first massive deadly school shooting in the country occurred, it was at Columbine High School on April 20, 1999, in an affluent Denver suburb.

Many subsequent school shootings were also in wealthy areas. Some cynics argued there were no shootings in supposedly tough, bad inner-city schools because the students were armed and would readily shoot back at any gunmen. A different explanation, according to retired East principal Robert Colwell, was that places like East had enough diversity and tolerance whereby there was room for every pupil whereby nobody had to resort to an insane, murderous rage against the school and fellow students. Others have seen school shootings as products of unhinged wrath against extremely restrictive institutions that more warp youngsters than nourish them.

Administrators replied to the shootings by increasingly turning buildings into something of besieged fortresses where they limited entry into the schoolhouses. The massive laments about school shootings paid virtually no heed to the busing debates of the 1970s. At that time, foes feared bringing black students to white schools would bring violence with them. Nothing ever substantiated this. Other than during the troubles of 1970–71, integrated schools were no more violent than segregated schools.

That was well in the future. Numbers showed the immediate results of the imposition of court-ordered busing. Enrollment was at 92,759 in 1971; 89,685

Author's collection

At one time, DPS openly emphasized students' familiarity with weapons. Pictured is the 1951 Rifle Team at South High.

in 1972, and 87,620 in 1973. The fall of 1974 saw 85,483 students. The district plunged to a membership of 77,670 in 1975. The drop was ominous. This was the first year of full-scale busing after the United States Supreme Court had upheld the Keyes decision whereby busing was expanded to most elementary schools. At times, students disappeared from DPS at an average of 80–100 a week. In one count, DPS went from 57 percent white in September 1973 to less than 50 percent a year later. While Superintendent Louis Kishkunas had stated that, given the changing demographics, the district had expected a decrease of enrollment of 3,500 during the 1974–75 schoolyear, he was not sure that happened to the rest of the pupils.

The decline continued to 72,775 students in 1976, and 70,118 in 1977. DPS lost another 4,000 in 1978 when it was down to 66,821. By the time Judge Doyle's 1969 injunction was a decade old, DPS was at 63,225. More than three-fourths of the city's population had no direct contact with DPS by the early 1980s. Increasingly, some schools, especially on the elementary level subjected to busing, were seemingly only for those who did not have the wherewithal to provide their children with alternatives. In the process, a stark class segregation came to mark some schools in low-income areas whereby there were virtually no affluent, middle-class youngsters in the classrooms.

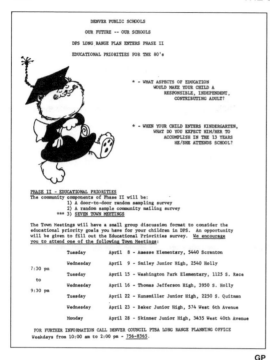

DENVER PUBLIC SCHOOLS

OUR FUTURE -- OUR SCHOOLS

DPS LONG RANGE PLAN ENTERS PHASE II

EDUCATIONAL PRIORITIES FOR THE 80's

* - WHAT ASPECTS OF EDUCATION
WOULD MAKE YOUR CHILD A
RESPONSIBLE, INDEPENDENT,
CONTRIBUTING ADULT?

* - WHEN YOUR CHILD ENTERS KINDERGARTEN,
WHAT DO YOU EXPECT HIM/HER TO
ACCOMPLISH IN THE 13 YEARS
HE/SHE ATTENDS SCHOOL?

PHASE II - EDUCATIONAL PRIORITIES
The community components of Phase II will be:
   1) A door-to-door random sampling survey
   2) A random sample community mailing survey
*** 3) SEVEN TOWN MEETINGS

The Town Meetings will have a small group discussion format to consider the
educational priority goals you have for your children in DPS. An opportunity
will be given to fill out the Educational Priorities survey. We encourage
you to attend one of the following Town Meetings:

	Tuesday	April 8 - Amesse Elementary, 5440 Scranton
	Wednesday	April 9 - Smiley Junior High, 2540 Holly
7:30 pm	Tuesday	April 15 - Washington Park Elementary, 1125 S. Race
to	Wednesday	April 16 - Thomas Jefferson High, 3950 S. Holly
9:30 pm	Tuesday	April 22 - Kunsmiller Junior High, 2250 S. Quitman
	Wednesday	April 23 - Baker Junior High, 574 West 6th Avenue
	Monday	April 28 - Skinner Junior High, 3435 West 40th Avenue

FOR FURTHER INFORMATION CALL DENVER COUNCIL PTSA LONG RANGE PLANNING OFFICE
Weekdays from 10:00 am to 2:00 pm - 756-8365.

GP

As enrollment plummeted amidst busing, DPS launched an initiative for the next decade in 1979, Our Future—Our Schools. As with all aspects of the district, the opinion of the United States District Court came first in terms of the racial composition of the student body.

The plunging membership revealed that a simple court order could not magically create equal schools or force parents to send their children to schools in a district where racial considerations more produced chaos and awkward administrative orders rather than quality education. Minority students continued to lag behind their white classmates in academic performance. Skeptics of busing became extremely tired of the hackneyed explanation that this was all due to racism. On the contrary, they argued it was necessary to look at family backgrounds and values. But the court, they complained, inflicted a highly subjective, mechanical approach on the schools. Consequently, middle-class white parents, greatly concerned with the quality of their children's education, steered clear of the ever more dysfunctional DPS. Many moved to the suburbs to escape busing.

The exodus of white students was a keynote of the collapse of enrollment. At the time of the controversial 1969 board election, the district counted 64 percent of its students as white, 21 percent Hispanic, and 14 percent black. The rest were a scattering of pupils of Asian, Pacific Island, American Indian, and mixed-race heritage. In contrast, before the start of the busing agitation, in the mid-1960s DPS had been 73 percent white, 10 percent black, and 17 percent Hispanic. By 1973, the year the Supreme Court handed down the Keyes ruling, 55 percent of DPS students were white. A year later, 54 percent of the enrollment was white, 18 percent black, and 26 percent Hispanos. In September 1975, whites were down to 50 percent of the enrollment, blacks were at 20 percent and Hispanos were at 28 percent.

In 1976, DPS became what was known as a "majority minority" district where there were more students who were minorities than there were whites. On September 24 of that year, DPS counted 28.5 percent of its pupils as Hispanic,

20.5 percent as black, 1.3 percent as Asian. Fewer than 1 percent were Indians. So-called Anglos made up 49.1 percent of the student body.

The racial disparities were greater in elementary than secondary schools. Youngsters who went to private or religious schools during the years they were slated to be bused as elementary or junior high students frequently returned to the system for tenth, 11th, and 12th grades. Additionally, there was a far greater high school dropout rate among Hispanos and African-Americans, especially from poor families, than among white pupils.

High school numbers illustrate the impact of court intervention in the 15 years following the 1969 balloting. At the time of the triumph of Jim Perrill and Frank Southworth, Abraham Lincoln High School was 85 percent white. By 1984, it was 40 percent white. The drop at George Washington was even more noticeable: 94.4 percent to 38.6 percent. John F. Kennedy declined from 97.2 percent to 49.3 percent. South went from 91.6 percent to 49.8 percent while Thomas Jefferson's numbers were 94.5 percent and 49.3 percent. West declined from 56 percent to 38.8 percent. East mostly held its own, having around 53 percent white enrollment during both years. Manual, in contrast, grew from 8.2 percent white enrollment to 48.6 percent. At that time, it was a sterling program when white students from southeastern Park Hill, Montclair, and Hilltop, who otherwise would have attended GW, made Manual shine academically.

The 1980 student census stated that 23 percent of the district's 62,026 students were black. Another 32 percent were Hispanic. It counted three percent as Asian. Together, they outnumbered the whites, 41 percent of the membership. Enrollment was down to 58,614 in 1985. By that time, whites made up but 39 percent of the student body. There were almost as many Hispanos. Blacks were around 20 percent of the enrollment. In 1988, DPS counted both Hispanos and whites as making up 36.3 percent of the student population compared to 1.2 percent Indian, 22.7 percent black, and 3.5 percent Asian. Before long, Hispanos far surpassed the number of white students, coming to encompass almost half of the school membership. By 2003, only about one-fifth of the total enrollment was white. Another fifth was black. The majority (57 percent) was Latino. Individuals described as American Indian, Asian, Pacific Islanders, or mixed race accounted for the rest of the membership.

As busing became the defining character of District #1 in the 1970s, parents frequently yanked their children out of class in the middle of the term, moving elsewhere. As enrollment plunged, DPS did not always know what happened to its pupils. In the course of 1982–83, for example, it admitted it had lost more than 3,000 students. Once more, the district was not sure how many of them were dropouts and how many had left DPS for private schools or the suburbs. From 60,433 students in 1982, DPS was down to 58,427 the next year.

The decline in confidence came out in a 1972 survey the district conducted of public opinion about the system. Compared to 1968, when 14 percent of the respondents claimed DPS was excellent, only 5 percent did four years later. In 1968, 44 percent thought the system was good, the number being 39 percent in 1972 when 46 percent labeled it simply "average." Another 6 percent called DPS "poor" compared to 4 percent in 1968. Some respondents labeled it "failing."

Photo by Phil Goodstein

In the course of the 1970s, DPS became a majority minority district whereby there were more students of color than whites in the classrooms. Included was an influx of students from Southeast Asia. Among them were those who spoke Khmer, the tongue of Cambodia. Here is the city's Khmer temple at 3455 West Ada Place.

About 14 percent stated they had no opinion. (The numbers do not add up to 100 percent. The survey observed some respondents gave more than one classification.)

The district also became poorer. An ever great portion of pupils stemmed from poverty-stricken households. As much as it had during the pre–World War I era, when the district argued Americanizing poor immigrant children was a foremost responsibility, social welfare was a prime purpose of the schools.

Nor did DPS membership reflect the population of the city as a whole. Denver continued to be a city primarily populated by individuals from Europe who were not Hispanic. By 1991, when DPS listed 60,704 students—up from 59,400 five years earlier—it stated it was 66.2 percent "minority," including American Indians, 1.4 percent, blacks, 21.6 percent, Asians, 3.6 percent, and Hispanos, 40.4 percent. White students were at 33 percent. About 55 percent of Denver was white.

The 1970s and 1980s saw a sizable influx of students from Asia, particularly those whose first language was Vietnamese, Khmer (Cambodian), or $_{Korean}$. Sixteen percent of the students, the administration explained, were from families receiving Aid to Dependent Families and Children. A total of 42 percent qualified for free or reduced-price lunches versus 18 percent in Colorado as a whole. Teachers were overwhelmingly white—DPS counted 9.5 percent of its instructors as "minority" along with 25.8 percent of its classified staff.

Eventually, backed with funds from the federal government, DPS used its free or reduced-price lunch program as something of a barometer of poverty within schools.

The district, relying on Washington guidelines, counted family size and income in determining which children it allowed to receive free or low-priced lunches. The state paid part of the cost of the meals. Not all eligible parents participated in the program. Some did not want what they believed was charity; others were so fearful of any interaction with the authorities that they did not fill in required paperwork.

A National Model

DPS was not alone. Enrollment in large school districts plunged everywhere during the 1970s. Besides the aging of the baby boomers, this reflected the growing population of the suburbs over cities across the country. School busing was a factor in numerous communities. Citing the Keyes precedent, federal courts frequently intervened in northern school districts, ordering busing to redress discriminatory practices. No place did this result in marked improvement of a school system. On the contrary, schools were in chaos across the country.

In some communities, particularly in Boston, vicious racial hatreds flared. Far from uniting the population and being the center of a common culture, schools were increasingly points of division. Politically, the country started rapidly moving away from the Great Society and the New Deal consensus. The Republican Party, with its Southern Strategy and race-baiting, made significant gains despite the Watergate scandal.

In response to the increasing polarization between urban and suburban districts, national advocates of equal educational opportunity insisted that the court purview of the schools must extend beyond a single school district; it had to encompass an entire metropolis. This was especially the case in Detroit, an area increasingly divided between a black city and white suburbs. Listening to the evidence, the United States District Court in Detroit ruled busing must include the suburbs.

Mile High foes of busing had insisted that this must also be the case in Denver. In January 1974, the unanimous school board, which included busing advocates Kay Schomp and Omar Blair, asked Judge William Doyle to include the suburbs in an remedy of District #1 segregation. It pointed to the mass white flight from DPS. Without addressing the suburban dimension, the board insisted, the busing order could only be a mockery of an integrated district. The court paid no attention to the request.

By this time, the Detroit case was highly controversial nationally. The Supreme Court recognized this. A year after it had handed down the Keyes decision, the high court rejected the Detroit proposal on July 25, 1974. In other words, city borders were the limits of desegregation. Subsequently, in response to the chaos school busing had caused in Boston, where there was massive community resistance, including violence, the United States Supreme Court grudgingly permitted what it called a "heckler's veto." This allowed a judge to craft his school integration order in response to fears of mass violence or how a busing program might destroy the integrity of the schools. Attorney General Griffith Bell, who served under Democratic President Jimmy Carter, echoed this. Busing, he declared, was not a panacea. On the contrary, it was a tool that should be kept to an absolute

Photo by Phil Goodstein

In the 1970s, Denver Christian High School, at the southwest corner of Evans Avenue and South Pearl Street, went from being a parochial school for children growing up in the Dutch Reformed and Christian Reformed churches to a wide-ranging religious school reaching out to self-avowed Christians who did not want their offspring in Denver Public Schools.

minimum in dealing with the problem of school segregation. Soon this was the national consensus.

Across the country, judges increasingly conceded that simply ordering busing in the name of abstract integration did not assure either excellent schooling or equal educational opportunity. Nor was it worth imposing orders that led to violence and increasing distrust of the courts. Consequently, the judiciary started backing away from the program and ending supervision of de facto segregated northern districts.

This was not the solution to the lack of equal educational opportunity. Or so proponents of integration asserted. A way of redressing the division between city and suburban school districts was through metropolitan cooperation. Citizens and politicians needed to treat all jurisdictions as unified entities. Through economic development programs, the government could root out pockets of poverty in both the central city and the suburbs. Ideally, this would lead to integrated neighborhoods and integrated schools everywhere.

To help make this happen, in 1989 Denver turned over its prime cultural institutions—the Zoo, Art Museum, Botanic Gardens, and what was then the Museum of Natural History—to an independent Scientific and Cultural Facilities District whereby the city no longer had a direct link with these programs treasured by many in the suburbs. Building on this gesture of cooperation, a Blue Ribbon Committee, named by DPS Superintendent Evie Dennis in February 1994, called for linking the city and suburbs in housing and development programs. Like many previous proposals, the suggestion went nowhere. Many in the suburbs made it clear they lived there because they did not trust Denver, a place they equated with poverty-stricken blacks and Latinos. For that matter, past efforts at economic uplift had failed to end endemic poverty. If anything, with the onset of busing, Denver's social and economic divisions became ever starker and more visible. Meanwhile, anti-busing forces dominated the city in the 1971 school board election.

A Note on Sources:

Pearson, "Denver Case," 177, discusses federal funds available for busing and the school board's shifting position on applying for them. GP has, in loose papers in the box dealing with the late 1960s, the suggestions of the joint committee of the PTA, the DPS Office of School–Community Relations, and the ASA about ways to welcome students bused into schools. An LWV report, "A New Look in Schools," April 1969, outlined the Gilberts Plan and urged the need for community preparation for its successful implementation. A copy is in an unnumbered folder in Box 13 of the Banks papers.

The South Alumni Association has an extensive archive about the school in its Historical Room in the basement of the schoolhouse. Included are old yearbooks, student and alumni publications, and materials on the 1970 upheavals. In the early 1990s, retired South history teacher Paul Ton gave me his take on the changing character of the school amidst the integration fights. He was generally quite negative about both the actions of the school's administration and the court intervention. The 1971 South yearbook, *Johnny Reb*, 66, reviewed the clashes in October 1970.

RMN, October 30, 1970, p. 5, reported tensions between students and Erick Holland in reviewing problems at South. *RMN*, March 19, 1997, recalled the life of Holland. CJ Backus found a picture of him, remembering him as an assistant principal at George Washington in the late 1960s when she was a student there.

Newspaper accounts of problems at South included *University Park News*, November 5, 1970, p. 1, and *DP*, October 30, 1970, p. 3, and December 7, 1970, p. 93. I touch on the troubles at South in *Washington Park*, 131. *RMN*, October 30, 1970, p. 5, mentioned the sit-in at West.

School Book, 409–13, has background on George Washington High School. In informal conversations between 2010 and 2016, the late Wally Ginn recalled his experiences as an instructor at schools on United States military bases in England and Germany during the 1960s and 1970s. He emphasized the discipline instilled in the children of many military personnel. In passing, he related the story about soldiers and airmen who found themselves transferred when their children misbehaved in the schools on military bases. Caroline Green has reflected on her experiences of being a "military brat" during the 1960s in assorted discussions since 2013. CANS, *Judicial Fiat*, 15, observes Judge Doyle rejected the plea to allow seniors to remain in and graduate from their old high schools.

In a January 23, 2018, e-mail, Doug Gerash reminisced about being a student at GW in the fall of 1970 and the chaotic events there. Charlie Salzman has also shared his memories of being at GW at the time. Shortly before his death in 2019,

Daniel Lowenstein remembered attending GW in the mid-1970s. Like Salzman, he eventually left the school for an alternative program. All emphasized what they believed was the alienating, rigid, mind-destroying, hierarchical nature of the high school. On January 24, 2020, CJ Backus remembered the school's strict dress code. *DP*, December 6, 2019, p. 1A, discussed how early school hours disrupt adolescent sleep patterns.

Interviews with Anna Jo Haynes and Lorie Young in *Our Neighborhood Schools* in Alweis, *Rebels Remembered*, emphasize the fear many children had riding the bus and the role of community volunteers who sought to alleviate tensions. *RMN*, October 20, 1970, p. 5, reported Tramway canceling service to GW. *RMN*, October 30, 1970, p. 5, observed Tramway's resumption of the bus route under pressure from the state Public Utilities Commission.

DP, September 24, 1970, p. 1, reported the problems at GW. *RMN*, September 26, 1970, p. 5, told of the second day of clashes. *DP*, October 21, 1970, p. 1, and *RMN*, October 21, 1970, p. 5, observed new violence. GW physics teacher Buel C. Robinson wrote an excellent account of what happened in *DP Empire*, January 3, 1971. *Look* reviewed the upheavals, March 9, 1971, pp. 20–29. A copy is in FF 8:78 of the DPS papers, along with an undated, unidentified letter to the editor from GW teacher Irwin Hoffman complaining that the article was unfair. The 1971 GW yearbook has a few pictures about the event, but virtually no discussion about what happened. Also see Watson, "Barricades," 195. Ibid., 195–96, touches on the problems at Hamilton. *DP*, March 20, 1970, p. 37, reported the school board debating accusations about the beating of white girls at Smiley.

On August 14, 2019, Ed Benton related the story of his sit-in at DPS headquarters over the question of filling the schools with armed patrolmen. *RMN*, September 30, 1970, p. 28, had Benton's attack on the school board's responsibility for the problems at GW. *RMN*, October 24, 1970, p. 5, and October 25, 1970, p. 5, looked at the protest at 414 14th Street. *DP*, October 24, 1970, p. 1, reported Chief George Seaton ordering the end of a police occupation of the schools.

CJ Backus has recalled Jack Beardshear who was the principal of George Washington when she graduated from the school in 1970. She traced biographical information about him. Dick Koeppe gave me his memories of Beardshear, including the story about Jim Beam, on August 26, 2019. At that time, Koeppe related how the GW faculty had been terrified and the way teachers stepped forward in assuming extra disciplinary responsibilities. *DP*, May 31, 1972, p. 4, reported Beardshear's request for a transfer from GW.

DP, October 3, 1970, p. 3, looked at the response of the GW faculty to the upheavals. FF 1:9 of the Noel papers has a list of black teachers assigned to GW for the 1970–71 schoolyear. FF 9:8 of the Herrick Roth papers at the CU Archives, COU 1395, has a DFT announcement of supporting the faculty at GW. It argued they had little say in making decisions at the school while they suffered the consequences of bad administration policies.

In the late 1990s, Ida Uchill, who taught at GW at the time of the explosion, shared her memories of the events and the "brainwashing" sessions. South High instructor Paul Ton also used the term "brainwashing" to refer to the overbearing, politically correct sessions to which he and other instructors were subjected to in response to the racial upheavals. *New Yorker*, August 19, 2019, p. 21, had reflections about the condescending nature of mandatory classes about racial sensitivity.

Uchill further complained about the reduction of George Washington's standards. In particular, she observed the administration order to remove instruction about Shakespeare and Dickens from 10th-grade English classes. In his novel, *The Human Stain* (Boston: Houghton Mifflin, 2000), 330–31, Philip Roth observes the decline of the classics nationally in the 1970s in college curricula.

RMN, February 9, 1975, p. 8, reported that black state Senator Regis Groff, a DPS instructor, had introduced a bill calling for the banning of the P&R as being unfair to minority students. *RMN*, November 2, 1981, p. 4, mentioned blacks and Hispanics seeking to have the district revise the P&R examination.

Allison, ed., *Without Consensus*, 49–78, emphasizes the ties between social class and education. Included was the lament of Jenkin Lloyd Jones, "Why Pull Education Down to the Slum Level?" 71–73. Pearson, "Denver Case," 195, reports the court order for school improvement, human relations, and inservice training. Ibid., 195–96n, looks at the court's other recommendations, which is 313 FSupp 90.

SRv, April 1962, pp. 2–3, had estimates of school population in 1967 compared to the capacity of existing classrooms. CANS, *Judicial Fiat*, 9, lists the massive drop of white enrollment in the face of the busing order in 1973–74. DPS records for enrollment in the 1970s are particularly bad. Frequently, its numbers were not consistent. It quit publishing its annual "Facts and Figures" brochure at this time about its enrollment. The district's annual reports glaringly failed to state the number of students. Nor is the list in Forrest, *Schools*, 19, reliable. *RMN*, October 12, 1974, p. 5, looked at the rapid decline in the district's membership. Catherine E. Dwyer, "Mandatory School Desegregation and Its Impact on Urban Demographics" (M.A. thesis, DU, 1993), focuses on the shift of the city's population as a result of busing.

QM, February 1996, focused on what it called the "post-Keyes" era of DPS. In the process, it reviewed the impact of busing on DPS enrollment, reviewing the court order. Lee Chungmei, *Denver Public Schools: Resegregation, Latino Style* (Cambridge: Harvard Civil Rights Project, 2006), looks at the links between busing, the end of court oversight, and how DPS became a "majority minority" district. *BN*, February 9, 2000, spelled out free and reduced-price lunch rules.

Pearson, "Denver Case," 188, mentions the role of Martha Radetsky. I observe her importance and that of her husband in *Washington Park*, 156–57. *DP*, September 28, 1970, p. 33, quotes Manny Salzman, a Hilltop Jewish parent who was highly supportive of integration efforts. During the 1990s, retired DPS teacher Ida Uchill, the pioneer historian of Jewish Colorado, and I had long discussions about whether the rise of local Jewish day schools was a product of Zionism or the result of the upheavals in DPS.

Orfield, *Must We Bus?* 59, observes the growth of private and religious schools nationally in the 1970s amidst the commotion connected to busing. *RMN*, November 30, 1986, p. 10, reviewed the rise of home schooling and the problems associated with it. Dorothy Gotlieb reflected on home schooling during a January 23, 2020, interview, recalling her experience with the Colorado Department of

Education in regulating home schooling. Karyl Klein, the archivist of the Denver Catholic Archdiocese, reflected on the closing of many parochial schools in the 1970s during a chat on October 12, 2019.

PTA Today, March 1979, pp. 4, 8, editorialized against the growth of private schools. In passing, p. 14, it attacked the myth of schools as blackboard jungles. *RMN*, October 5, 1985, p. 10, reported the increase in enrollment in private schools. The article emphasized the massive decline of membership in DPS in 1974–75, the first full year of busing. *RMN*, October 6, 1976, p. 5, looked at the changing demographics of District #1's enrollment. Fishman, "Endless Journey," 720, gives statistics about the transformation of racial membership in the high schools.

DP, May 2, 1979, p. 69, cited the loss of 80 students a week. *RMN*, June 20, 1983, mentioned the district's drop of 3,000 students in the 1982–83 schoolyear. There is a comparable, unidentified clipping on the subject in the 1982–83 PTA Historian's Notebook in GP.

Orfield, *Must We Bus?* 126–27, deals with debates about violence in schools and links to busing. I review the Columbine High School Massacre in *DIA*, 108–15. Also see Dave Cullen, *Columbine* (New York: Twelve, 2009). On August 14, 2019, Ed Benton and his daughter Margaret reflected on the Columbine Massacre as opposed to the diversity at East High. In passing, they recalled Robert Colwell's comments about Columbine in contrast with East. The publication of the AFT, *American Teacher*, September 1971, p. 27, observed the increase of violence in suburban school amidst controversies over busing.

CANS, *Judicial Fiat*, 2, 8, tells of the way the school board asked Judge Doyle to include the suburbs in the busing order. Kluger, *Simple Justice*, 771–72, looks at the Detroit case, *Milliken* v. *Bradley*, 418 US 717. There is a discussion of it in Browning, *From Brown to Bradley*, 173, 223–308, and Orfield, *Must We Bus?* 31–35. J. Anthony Lukas, *Common Ground* (New York: Vintage, 1986), 235–36, deals with how the Keyes case impacted Boston school busing debates. *Washington Post*, December 16, 2019, seemingly rediscovered the wheel, reporting how borders of school districts segregate schools.

Lukas, *Common Ground*, 650, mentions the "heckler's veto." Woodward, *Jim Crow*, 167, observes that in the late 1950s the Supreme Court refused to permit a postponement of integration orders in the face of mass white violence in the South. Howard I. Kalodner, in his introduction to Kalodner and Fishman, *Limits of Justice*, 7–8, emphasizes the way the courts had to take public opinion into account in getting the citizenry to accept school integration orders. Orfield, *Must We Bus?* 39, emphasizes the changing views of the courts on ordering busing and the opinion of Griffith Bell.

The 1995 notebook in GP has the November 16, 1994, interim report of the Blue Ribbon Committee pushing for racial and ethnic diversity between Denver and its suburbs as a means of redressing school segregation. I deal with links between Denver and suburban schools in *DIA*, 96, 99, 107–08, while analyzing wars between Denver and the suburbs, 356–57, 383–84.

Chapter Eight

An Anti-Busing Sweep

As school controversies were endless, numerous short-lived groups popped up to support or oppose busing. Among the first organizations to speak out against the measure was the Denver Neighborhood School Association. Reverend James C. Miller of Montclair Community Church formed it in May 1969. His congregation, at 1312 Uinta Street, was in a lower-middle-class white neighborhood.

The Denver Neighborhood School Association was among Miller's many political activities. Ordained in the Reformed Church of America, he claimed inspiration from Martin Luther King. The white parson agreed with the civil rights leader: clerics had actively to intervene in politics. As such, he was bringing his interpretation of the scriptures into civil life. Personally, he called himself a "fundamentalist-type of preacher."

Most of all, Miller endorsed the John Birch Society. This was a group formed in the wake of the outbreak of the Korean War. It argued the International Communist Conspiracy was all embracing. It stretched from the Kremlin to the White House—at one time, the group's leader, Robert Welch, declared President Dwight Eisenhower was a communist. Miller was the Denver head of the Birch Society. His church hosted its meetings. The house of worship was also the gathering spot of the Denver Neighborhood School Association.

Yes, Miller admitted, DPS was a thoroughly racist system. He had personal experience to prove as much. Taking advantage of open enrollment, he sought to transfer his eighth-grade daughter, Elizabeth, from Smiley Junior High to Hill Junior High. DPS rejected her because she was white. The politically correct, the preacher declared, would have raged in protest had the schools refused to admit a black girl because of her color.

Photo by Phil Goodstein

Reverend James C. Miller, the local head of the John Birch Society, made his church at 1312 Uinta Street a center of opposition to busing in the late 1960s/early 1970s.

Before long, the Denver Neighborhood School Association collapsed. Giving up on DPS, Miller sent his daughter to Denver Christian School. This was an institute evolving from a parochial academy for children of the Dutch Reformed and Christian Reformed churches to a chain offering a "biblical worldview" for those who did not want their children in public schools.

Within a few years, Miller faded from the scene. Eventually, a black congregation occupied Miller's old church at 1312 Uinta Street. The surrounding area became filled with immigrants from around the world.

Some, who found Miller was too extreme, particularly with his John Birch Society affiliation, sought to project themselves as the embodiment of common sense, neighborhoods, and the best of the traditions of DPS. Transitory groups targeting busing came and went such as United Schools Against Forced Busing and Save Our City Schools. Opponents of busing particularly targeted the three seats open in the 1971 school board election.

The Neighborhood Schools Committee

By this time, school board politics were as murky as ever. Not only did the Republican Party seek to recruit a slate, but so did ad hoc coalitions of advocates of neighborhood schools. Proponents of busing had links with civil rights organizations, the Democratic Party, what became the Greater Denver Ministerial Alliance (a group of black clerics), and Greater Park Hill Community Incorporated, the new incarnation of the Park Hill Action Committee. They worked with remnants of Speak Out on School Integration and Citizens for One Community to elect their candidates to the board.

The controversy came right when "community control" was a buzzword. Blacks had especially pushed it in New York City during a bitter strike in 1968 pitting a poor section of Brooklyn against the local branch of the American Federation of Teachers. None of the leading figures in the Mile High busing debate noted the irony that civil rights activists were now calling for the courts to override community control as defined by voters who had selected an anti-busing school board. At the most, during his successful campaign, Jim Perrill had emphasized that "power comes from people." Neither he nor other proponents of neighborhood schools hoisted the banner of community control or "power to the people," another radical phrase of the day.

Rather, as they had in 1969, opponents of forced busing simply spoke of defending the existing system of neighborhood schools as the embodiment of common sense and educational success. Once more, they were far better organized than integration advocates. Those wanting to end the coercive program ordered by the courts crafted a ticket for the May 1971 school board contest. Leo LeLauro, a dentist living and practicing in southwest Denver, chaired what anti-busing activists called the Neighborhood Schools Committee. It named Ted Hackworth, Bob Crider, and Bert Gallegos to replace James Voorhees, Rachel Noel, and John Amesse whose terms expired that month.

Neither Noel nor Amesse sought to stay on the board. Amesse, who was in failing health, died a few months after he left office. Noel announced she had accomplished all she could on the board. After the election of Perrill and Southworth in 1969, at times the majority of the board deliberately sought to make her feel most uncomfortable. Included were a couple of members who obnoxiously smoked cigars during board meetings. This did not keep Noel from speaking out, clearly making her points. "If we let the bigots have their way at successfully opposing measures to integrate Denver Public Schools, Denver will move toward an apartheid society," she declared, vowing the necessity of fighting back.

After having been a senior counselor on the city's Commission on Community Relations from 1963 to 1969, Noel moved over to a post as a professor of sociology at Metro. She drew on her master's in sociology from Fisk University where she had studied under a leading black expert on African-American life, Charles Johnson, who was the president of Fisk. In 1971, she additionally became chairwoman of Metro's new Department of Afro-American Studies. Poor health led her to retire from the college in 1980.

To salute Noel's service, Metro created an annual appointment of a Rachel B. Noel Distinguished Visiting Professor. The person receiving the honor delivers a prestigious Rachel Noel Lecture. The talk is at Shorter African Methodist Episcopal Church. (Noel was a member of Shorter Church where she taught Sunday School. The congregation has celebrated her with a stained-glass window.) The scholar receiving the Noel appointment additionally conducts a forum based on the lecture at Metro. Back in 1971, Black Educators United, a coalition of African-American teachers who worked for District #1, created a Noel Scholarship awarded to a DPS high school student.

In 1976, when Jim Carrigan, who held the at-large seat on the University of Colorado Board of Regents, quit the post on being named to the Colorado Supreme Court, Governor Richard Lamm selected Noel to succeed him. In some accounts, Carrigan had recommended her to Lamm as his successor. He was clearly pleased she was following him on the board. Back in 1969, in the wake of the triumph of anti-busing forces, those resolving to sue DPS had pondered approaching Carrigan, an outstanding trial lawyer, to handle the case. Noel kept her place on the CU Board of Regents in 1978, winning a six-year term when she staged an aggressive grassroots campaign at the same time Lamm gained re-election as governor.

In 1981, Noel won leadership of the CU Board. At the same time she headed the regents, for a while her son Edmond "Buddy" Noel Jr., was the chairman of the board of Colorado State University. They collaborated in pushing greater cooperation between the state's two major public universities and in reviving sports competitions between them. The civil rights activist did not seek re-election in 1984.

Rachel Noel additionally was on the board of the Denver Housing Authority and many other agencies. Included was membership on the United States Civil Rights Commission. Numerous colleges granted her honorary degrees. Mayor Federico Peña saw that she chaired the city's black advisory council. The American Civil Liberties Union awarded her its Carle Whitehead Award in 1985, a citation going to the individual most fighting for freedom and the Bill of Rights in the region. In 2002–03, DPS named a new middle school for her at 5290 Kittredge Street.

In looking back on the controversy, Noel conceded that busing did not achieve what she hoped it would. In part, this was because so many opposed it and made sure that it did not work. Still, she insisted it was a necessary step in increasing human interaction and understanding, so helping build a better world. The black school board pioneer passed away in February 2008.

Hackworth-Crider-Gallegos

Back in 1971, opponents of busing were glad to see Noel leave the school board. The Neighborhood Schools Committee observed its three candidates had deep roots in the community. A 1945 graduate of East High, Theodore J. "Ted" Hackworth Jr. was an Air Force veteran who had graduated from the University of Denver. Over the years, he had held numerous sales jobs, including for Continental Bakery, Sigman Meats, and Pitney Bowes, an office machine and supply firm. In the course of selling its products, he developed links with lobbyists, leading him into politics.

Back in 1952, with his wife Doris, also a DPS graduate, Hackworth moved into the newly developing Brentwood neighborhood in southwest Denver, settling at 2626 South Green Court. The couple was later in Harvey Park at 3955 West Linvale Place. On the side, he was a leader of the Boy Scouts. Eventually, Hackworth had real estate holdings.

In 1968, Ted Hackworth gained the presidency of the Harvey Park Improvement Association. For years, he had a close personal and political relationship with Robert L. "Bob" Crider. The two subsequently served together on city council. In 1971, Crider joined Hackworth as part of the neighborhood school ticket.

A Denver native, born on June 21, 1938, Crider grew up close to Ebert School, eventually winning his diploma from Manual. Besides attending the University of Denver, he also took post-high school classes at Opportunity School. For 17 years he was in the trucking business as a driver, dock worker, and a dispatcher. In the process, he became active in the International Brotherhood of Teamsters.

Author's collection

Bert Gallegos gained election to the school board in 1971 as a vehement anti-busing candidate who claimed to speak for Latino Denver.

At the time he ran for the school board in 1971, Crider lived at 4932 Bryant Street. The candidate was a member of the PTA of the nearby Beach Court School (4950 Beach Court). Back in 1969, he had unsuccessfully sought a place on the school board. The next year, he emerged as the vice president of something called Citizens for a Better Denver. He built on this to get the nod of the Neighborhood Schools Committee. Hackworth was a registered Republican; Crider was a Democrat. At one time, the third candidate on the ticket, Bert A. Gallegos, was both.

Born in Santa Fe on September 19, 1922, Gallegos grew up in Pueblo. After attending CU, he gained his bachelor's from the University of Southern California. The same school subsequently granted him a law degree. He went on to earn a master's in public administration from CU. The candidate worked for such major corporations as Colorado Fuel & Iron and Stearns Roger. Throwing himself into politics, he was active in the Young Democrats. Additionally, he was a member of numerous uplift organizations including the Latin American Educational Foundation, the Junior Chamber of Commerce, and the Urban League. For a while, he was on the board of the city's Commission on Community Relations. The aspiring politician settled in new Park Hill at 2901 Newport Street, later moving into Brooks Towers at 1020 15th Street. In 1956, he gained a place in the legislature as a foremost Latino Democrat.

In office, Gallegos fought for civil rights and fair housing. He believed the Democrats snubbed him when he failed to gain re-nomination to the House in 1962. In response, just before the general election, he switched to the Republicans. He failed in bids as the GOP candidate to win a place on the Juvenile Court in 1964 and the Denver District Court in 1966. By that time, he was a foremost conservative Republican Spanish-American. The Neighborhood Schools Committee announced Gallegos was the voice of the 100,000 Hispanos in the city.

Ted Hackworth was part of the successful anti-busing slate in the 1971 school board election.

Not all Latinos backed Gallegos. He knew this. In particular, he was a bitter opponent of Chicano nationalists and those who wanted affirmative action. Committed to school issues, he served as chairman of the district's Hispanic Education Advisory Council prior to his run for the board. Additionally, in 1971 Gallegos was a major cog in helping incumbent Mayor William McNichols win re-election in a June runoff over Dale Tooley. The challenger had allied himself with the advocates of integration. McNichols' backers had loudly whispered about this, smearing Tooley, a man who long wanted to become mayor.

Back in May 1969, Tooley had urged compromise on the busing issue even while allying himself with the ticket of Benton and Pascoe as the de facto Democratic Party slate. Typical of the mayoral contender, who frequently shifted stances while generally allying himself with the liberal wing of the Democratic Party, Tooley was among the lawyers meeting in the wake of the defeat of Benton and Pascoe to ponder a suit against DPS.

Amidst the commotion over the 1969 school busing election and the court intervention, McNichols had determinedly kept his silence on the matter. The mayor, the incumbent explained, had zero power over the schools; that was the role of the board of education. He was not going to interfere with its decisions. For that matter, during the violence and turmoil sweeping the city in the wake of the court order, McNichols provided no moral leadership of working to assure Denver was a racially diverse but united community.

Besides opposition to what supporters repeatedly branded "forced busing," the ticket of Hackworth, Crider, and Gallegos stated DPS had to emphasize vocational training. Not all jobs, the candidates pointed out, required college education. They also called for economy in the schools. Besides ripping apart the school system and the city, court-ordered busing was extremely expensive. Further, the district must operate on a pay-as-you-go basis. As such, they observed voters had been wise to reject the 1967 bond issue. It was another sign the electorate did not trust the pro-busing ideologues.

The Integration Ticket

Against the neighborhood schools slate, Citizens for One Community and champions of integration put up the ticket of incumbent James Voorhees and Warren Alexander. The latter was among the many black military veterans loudly campaigning for integration and equal educational opportunity. Born in San Antonio, Texas, on May 27, 1921, to a Methodist preacher, he followed in his father's footsteps, also gaining ordination though he never held a pulpit.

The Air Force brought Alexander to Denver. Soon he was a leader in the successful 1959 campaign for Colorado to adopt a fair housing law. In the process, he was among the black pioneers of what was then white new Park Hill, settling at 3540 Ivanhoe Street. Within a few years, he was the president of the neighborhood group, the Northeast Park Hill Civic Association. As civil rights upheavals heated up in the 1960s, Alexander emerged as the deputy director of the Colorado Civil Rights Commission. His wife, Mary, was a leader of the Denver County PTA. By the early 1970s, he had succeeded Minoru Yasui as the head of the Metro Denver Urban Coalition in promoting a peaceful community. (Rachel Noel was on the board of the Urban Coalition.)

The candidate had retired from the service as a major, a sign he had been unable to gain promotion to lieutenant colonel. Still, Alexander was loyal to the military. This especially came out in 1977 when, closely linked with the Democrats, he was the key local figure in President Jimmy Carter's reimposition of the draft. By this time, seeing that new Park Hill was overwhelmingly black, Alexander had been among the first African-American settlers in emerging parts of southeast Denver, moving to 3413 South Akron Court. The civil rights activist died on June 6, 1994, at age 73.

Alexander's move to the southeastern edge of the city was significant. It was part of a kind of black flight. In the same way whites fled cities after World War II to escape urban problems, so did some African-Americans. Part of the original black migration to Park Hill was a desire by middle-class blacks to get out of what they believed was the poor ghetto in Five Points. Then, as new Park Hill became overwhelmingly black, some African-Americans, such as Alexander, moved again. For that matter, blacks and Hispanos joined whites in exiting Denver for the suburbs during the 1970s and 1980s. They were not only dissatisfied with busing, but feared the breakdown of the city and lack of safety in it. Within a few years, some of the suburbs, particularly Aurora, had a sizable number of African-American residents.

Besides backing integration, Alexander campaigned to re-arrange the school year. Rather than having a summer break, he called for DPS to impose a growing trend known as 45–15. In this scenario, students attended classes for nine weeks or 45 days. They then had a three-week (15-day) break. It never caught on.

Desegregation advocates did not select a third candidate for the board. They feared that doing so would dissipate their vote, especially away from Alexander. It was urgent, they believed, that a black be on the school board.

Other African-Americans agreed, also running for the board. Among them was community activist and educator Jennie Rucker. She had entered West High in 1937. There she found herself blocked when she wanted to learn typing and

VOTE FOR VIVIAN DODDS — DENVER SCHOOL BOARD

Vivian Dodds, concerned and aware of school problems, is the mother of three children in the Denver Public School system. She is a participant in parent and teacher affairs at Ellis, Hallett and Merrill schools. Mrs. Dodds holds her degree in nursing from Cornell. She is active in the League of Women Voters and the Ellis Budget Advisory Committee. She lives in southeast Denver, and is the wife of a University of Denver faculty member.

Vivian Dodds Believes:

- **We must** find areas of agreement and work together for the educational growth of **All** children.

- **We must** create new channels for exchange of ideas between community and school board.

- **We must** give more attention to early childhood and elementary school programs.

- **We must** work for adequate financing and sound budgeting.

- **We must** spend considerable time in selecting a new superintendent, seeking an educator who will recommend new methods, better ways to educate our children.

- **We must** bargain fairly and in good faith with whatever group the teachers select as a bargaining agent.

- **We must** ask, in all decisions, **Is It Good For The Children?**

DEAR VOTER,

We want **every** child to ge the best possible education. The School Board can find new ways to use the thinking of interested citizens to accomplish this goal.

School Board members must seek the opinions, the thoughts, the ideas of those in the community. To operate any other way produces board action in a vacuum. School Board members should develop specialized knowledge of a program or a geographical area, using the talents of the area advisory councils.

During the next six years there will be many problems facing Denver, including the complex and difficult problem of financing. We must analyze our sources of revenue and determine if there could be a better way.

P.S. A personal note — Get involved in this important school board election. Attend meetings. Ask questions. And VOTE ON MAY 18!

Vivian Dodds

Doris Banks Papers, Auraria Archives

The Denver Post *endorsed Vivian Dodds as a candidate of unity in the 1971 school board election. She failed to win a seat.*

shorthand. Her counselor explained few jobs were available for black women as secretaries. Despite this, Rucker learned typing and shorthand, graduating from West in 1940. For a while, she was secretary at Whittier School under the district's first black principal, Jessie Maxwell. For more than 50 years, Rucker was involved in school issues. Former teacher Wendell P. Sexton was another independent black contender in the contest.

Roger Persons, a white North High graduate who was a teacher, also sought a place on the board. He was quite well informed about the issues, especially state policy on education. A friend, State Representative Dennis Gallagher, fed him with insider reports about legislative debates on the schools. Persons gained the endorsement of the Teamsters in the race. That union also backed one of its own, member Bob Crider.

Besides supporting Alexander and Voorhees, the *Denver Post* endorsed Vivian Dodds. A nurse who was the mother of three children in DPS, she had been active in the PTA at Ellis, Hallett, and Merrill. Additionally, Dodds was a proud member of the League of Women Voters. Her husband was a professor at the University of Denver. What the city needed, she stressed, was unity rather than the polarization over busing.

Besides backing Voorhees, the *News* called on the electorate to put Clarence Brisco and David Sandoval on the board. Brisco, an African-American who was an employment opportunity counselor at the University of Colorado Health Sciences Center, was a former teacher, mental health worker, and participant in Great Society programs. He ran as a team with James E. DeLine, a fellow counselor. Sandoval, an ex-DPS teacher and counselor who then taught at Metro, was a backer of the Congress of Hispanic Educators, a professional group insisting that DPS consider the Latino dimension of equal educational opportunity.

Gallegos led the balloting, 47,976. Crider came in second, 47,448. Hackworth was third, 43,790. Voorhees trailed with 39,947. Alexander was a distant fifth, 30,928. Fifteen other candidates were also on the ballot, including David Sandoval, 14,009, and Eloy Espinoza, 9,296, contenders of La Raza Unida, the effort to have a militant Chicano party. Rucker got 5,648 votes. *Post*-supported candidate Dodds was at 23,953. Many Latinos heralded the triumph of Gallegos. He was the first Hispano elected to the board. The result of the polling gave advocates of neighborhood schools all seven places on the board.

The new school board consisted exclusively of men. This was the first time there had not been a woman on the board since 1921. The hiatus lasted two years. By 1978, there were four women on the board. After the 2017 election, all seven members of the board were women. All the while, the decisions of the United States District Court rather than the elected body determined the immediate future of the district.

The Finger Plan

On April 26, 1971, right when anti-busing forces were poised to triumph in the school election, President Richard Nixon elevated Judge William Doyle to the Tenth Circuit Court of Appeals. In part, he promoted Doyle because he did not want the seemingly liberal Democrat to become the chief judge of the United States District Court of Colorado. Scuttlebutt claimed the appointment was the president's way of delivering for Colorado Senator Gordon Allott who wanted Doyle off of the busing litigation.

The move failed to remove Doyle as the judge overseeing the Keyes case. At the behest of the plaintiffs, the Circuit Court and the District Court agreed that Doyle would remain in charge of the busing suit as an acting District Court judge while the appellate courts pondered the question of Denver school integration. As such, Doyle dealt with the litigation in the wake of the 1973 Supreme Court decision.

Following the high court's ruling, Judge Doyle conducted a new hearing to review the meaning of the opinion. Not surprisingly, on December 11, 1973, he ruled that DPS was a dual rather than the required unitary district. Consequently, all of the schools in the system must be involved in a desegregation program. As such, he modified his initial findings in the Keyes case. De facto segregation in Park Hill, he announced, created the presumption of segregation in the system as a whole. The solution, consequently, must be city wide. It was not just to provide relief primarily for Park Hill as the Gilberts Plan had originally intended. Doyle called for both the plaintiffs and DPS to file integration plans to assure DPS became a desegregated, unitary district.

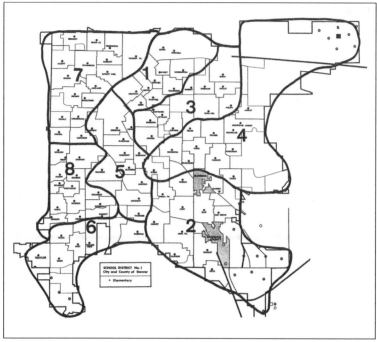

In pondering how to redress segregation in Denver Public Schools, United States District Court Judge William Doyle reviewed numerous busing plans. This map shows a proposed division of the city's schools submitted by the plaintiffs in the case.

The plaintiffs emphasized "short busing," trips between nearby schools. For example, their program combined Boulevard Elementary, 2351 Federal Boulevard, with Brown Elementary, 2550 Lowell Boulevard, while suggesting a pairing between Philips and Ashley (1914 Syracuse Street), and a link between Park Hill and Hallett. The school board submitted its proposal on January 23, 1974. To ponder the suggestions, beginning on February 19, Doyle held a lengthy hearing on precisely how to integrate the schools. On and off, he heard testimony on the matter until March 27.

The jurist did not like the district's program. The school board once more insisted that it had done as much as it could. DPS claimed it essentially offered equal educational opportunity to all. At the most, it conceded there might be busing. Though advocates of neighborhood schools had previously opposed educational parks, the board now revived the proposal, calling them "educational enrichment centers."

Superintendent Louis Kishkunas had put together a task force to draw up the proposal. It was something of a last-minute rush job. Members of the board only saw it shortly before DPS offered it to the court. Included was closing of 11 elementary schools, overwhelmingly older buildings, particularly those on Capitol Hill and in African-American neighborhoods. Students who had studied in them would travel via bus to the educational enrichment centers.

Nor did the judge favor the plaintiffs' solution. They continued to make Park Hill the center of their universe. Their suggestions primarily drew on the Gilberts Plan to assure desegregation in their neighborhood. DPS problems, Doyle repeated, were district-wide. The Supreme Court had said as much. Only through the complete integration of all Denver Public Schools was it possible to redress past injustices and end court oversight of the schools. Seeing no better solution, he stated it was necessary to employ massive busing to assure desegregation.

Ironically, Doyle's decision is what anti-busing forces had loudly feared in 1969. They had opposed the Gilberts Plan as opening the door to the destruction of neighborhood schools via busing, which, they would sure, would soon encompass the entire city. In contrast, backers of the Gilberts Plan had presented the program as a prophylactic to limit the impact of busing. Now, having lost the court case, opponents of busing saw their nightmare becoming true.

On April 24, 1974, Doyle announced his decision. The judge depended on the findings of his own expert on school integration, Dr. John A. "Jack" Finger Jr. A native of Winchester, Massachusetts, born on March 11, 1920, he earned his bachelor's at the Massachusetts Institute of Technology, going on to receive a doctorate from the Harvard School of Education. Once a teacher in New England, Finger became a principal in New Hampshire. He was subsequently an associate professor of education at Colgate University, moving to a post at the University of Rhode Island, additionally having ties to Brown University. Along the way, Finger consulted for both the Department of Health Education and Welfare and the Legal Defense Fund of the NAACP. He developed such close links with the civil rights organization that he served on the LDF board. The court ruled he was an national expert on desegregation. It rejected the defense's claim that Finger could not be an unbiased referee given his links with the LDF, an organization helping finance and giving legal assistance to the plaintiffs. About the time Finger consulted for the United States District Court of the District of Colorado, the professor also helped draw up the most dysfunctional forced-busing scheme in Boston.

Finger submitted a three-pronged desegregation proposal to Judge Doyle on April 5. First, it modified the attendance borders of 24 elementary schools. Second, the consultant rezoned the borders of an additional 23 schools, a decision primarily impacting the areas from which pupils were bused. Finally, he paired 37 minority and white schools. Altogether, his plan subjected 11,968 youngsters to busing for racial integration. The order meant pupils had to spend an average of 40 minutes a day on the bus getting to and from school. In some cases, elementary students had to get on the bus by 8:00 AM, not coming home until 5:00 PM. This might well prepare them for life as commuters who were endlessly on the road going and coming from work. For that matter, busing became a keystone of DPS at a time when sprawl was becoming a defining character of the metropolis.

The Finger Plan essentially made the temporary busing assignments of 1969–70 permanent. Drawing on the suggestions of *Denver Post* educational writer Art Branscombe, a major supporter of busing who was active in Park Hill integration efforts, Finger called for busing students between paired schools for alternating grades. Pupils from one academy, in other words, would attend the sister school for first, third, and fifth grades; second, fourth, and sixth graders would go to the other school. Before long, Finger modified this with a scheme assigning students to spend half of each day in one school, the other half in the paired academy. Included were specific homerooms. A variant of the plan, impacting some pupils, was to bus them every other day between their home school and sister school. The Finger Plan also continued busing at junior highs and high schools. All elementary schools retained neighborhood-based kindergartens.

The effort included extra buses to pick up stragglers. The district also had to provide transportation to bring children home who got ill during the schoolday. The busing schedule made no provision for students wishing to participate in after-school activities or those whom teachers ordered to after-school detention as punishment for misbehavior. To comply with the order, the school board voted on June 13, 1974, to buy 91 new buses for $1.6 million.

Prior to the Finger Plan, DPS stated it had 16,660 students eligible for busing in 1973–74. It transported 13,800 of them daily on 141 buses. (In a different statement, DPS announced it was busing 18,698 students, including where there was no nearby school.) Now, because of the court order, it had to worry about transporting about 25,000 students on buses every day. The average ridership was 22,500 on 232 buses. The additional cost to the district was $5,546,303.

Busing schedules especially interfered with extracurricular activities at junior highs and high schools. The integration order meant those living close to a school did not necessarily attend it, but were bused miles away. High school students dwelling on Hilltop, for example, mostly went to Manual rather than George

Photo by Phil Goodstein

The Finger Plan linked schools in southwest Denver with those in the northwest quadrant of the city. Gust School, 3440 West Yale Avenue, for example, was paired with Bryant-Webster, 3635 Quivas Street.

Washington. Youths whose homes were close to Manual sometimes found themselves sent to John F. Kennedy or Thomas Jefferson. In some cases, Hispanos living in what had been the attendance zone of Manual landed up attending North High with other Hispanos.

At Finger's suggestion, Doyle mandated a quota percentage of enrollments based on race at all schools. Every building had to be within 15 percent of the overall racial/ethnic division of the district as a whole. In some instances, the Finger Plan designated specific numbers. Morey, for example, had to be 50 percent white; Cole, 60 percent, and Manual 56 percent. In no time, given that whites became a minority of the district's total enrollment, it was impossible to fulfill this part of the order.

The court also addressed DPS staff segregation. For years, the district had automatically assigned black teachers to black schools. Whittier and Smiley particularly stood out for their large numbers of African-American instructors. The court paid no heed to the district's claim that such assignments helped black students learn better with African-Americans as teachers and role models. Doyle, who had previously agreed to this point, now insisted staff and teachers should reflect the racial/ethnic diversity of the district as a whole. Integrated schools, he ruled, had to have integrated faculties and office personnel. Additionally, DPS had to assure that classrooms were not internally segregated. Ideally, every classroom should mirror the overall racial composition of the district.

The court further ordered DPS to have inservice training for teachers, staff, students, and parents in preparation for the 1974–75 schoolyear when the Finger Plan was to go into effect. Doyle additionally mandated that DPS not skimp on existing programs designed to enhance the education of students such as tutorials and health services. Busing, however, often meant the end of enrichment programs of young learners at low-income schools. The judge further required the board to purchase necessary buses to implement the order while it was to pay the consulting fees of Dr. Finger and the legal costs of the plaintiffs since 1969.

As part of its efforts to comply with the court mandate, in March 1975 the school board adopted an affirmative action plan in the hiring of teachers. For some time thereafter, blacks and Hispanos were the prime people DPS offered contracts as new instructors. This naturally led to resentment among failed white applicants who were sure a racist hiring system kept them from getting posts. The court further stipulated DPS must file regular reports about its actions in making desegregation and equal educational opportunity a reality. The district could not change school attendance borders without the authorization of the court.

The Finger Plan in Action

The school board had severe problems with the Finger Plan. DPS observed that some of the consultant's attendance boundaries were most awkward. The outsider admitted that he had designed much of the scheme based on computer data—he did not know the city, the neighborhoods, traffic patterns, or the specific traditions of the schools and their attendance areas. On the contrary, he sometimes ripped apart areas whereby close friends who lived across the street from one another found themselves sent to different schools.

The plan was unclear about specific numbers and the actual means of implementation. It failed to provide a strong linkage between sister schools. They sometimes had different curriculums. In other instances, teachers in one school simply repeated the lessons the youngsters had received in the other school. At times, instructors talked about "our kids," those living near the schools, in contrast to "their kids," the students who were bused in. Doyle rejected any modifications of the Finger Plan.

The Tenth Circuit Court had problems with it. On August 11, 1975, it ordered Doyle to rewrite the effort. The appellate court found the scheme anything but a workable means to make DPS into a unitary district. On January 12, 1976, the Supreme Court refused to review the Tenth Circuit Court's decision.

This led Judge Doyle to hold another hearing on January 20, 1976. Listening to the evidence and the judgment of the Tenth Circuit Court, the jurist modified the Finger Plan on February 9. Busing, he announced, was to be all day with the beginning of the 1976–77 schoolyear. Instead of having students attend sister schools for a half day each, he divided many elementaries into primary and intermediate schools. Under his order, students in paired schools would attend primary school for grades one, two, and three; the other half went to the intermediate school, grades four, five, and six. All elementary schools retained neighborhood-based kindergartens.

In the light of the ruling by the Tenth Circuit, the court depaired some elementary schools. For example, both Johnson (1850 South Irving Street) and Lincoln (715 South Pearl Street) schools were no longer subjected to busing. Both had a natural ethnic mix of somewhere between 34 and 64 percent white. This was enough, the appellate judges decided, for them to be integrated. The Finger Plan had paired Lincoln with Fairmont (520 West Third Avenue), linking Johnson with Gilpin.

In light of the Tenth Circuit's modification of Doyle's ruling, Lincoln received minority students who were bused to it from satellite areas. These were strips defined by the court as attendance districts outside the specific borders of any defined neighborhood school. Satellites included Lowry Air Force Base, newly developing areas which yet to have schoolhouses, and some sections isolated from nearby schools. In other cases, satellites were adjacent to schoolhouses. For instance, some youths living close to Edison School, 3350 Quitman Street, found themselves assigned to Valdez School near West 29th Avenue and the equivalent of Bryant Street. (The plaintiffs' 1974 busing plan had paired Edison with Ashland School at West 29th Avenue and Firth Court, the building which Valdez School replaced.)

The court particularly used the satellite concept for junior high schools. They were not paired, but received students from across the city from satellite areas. So it was that adolescents dwelling near Cole Junior High School and in Swansea found themselves transported to Henry Junior High (3005 South Golden Way) in far southwest Denver. At other times, the court sent them to Merrill Junior High (1551 South Monroe Street).

Abstract integration, Doyle increasingly made clear, was the only way of redressing past segregation in DPS. He never took into account whether it actually improved education. Nor did his order assure school continuity, the idea that students should stay together in the same school for the duration of their education

DENVER PUBLIC SCHOOLS

STEDMAN/WASHINGTON PARK PTSA NEWS
January/February, 1980

GP

Paired elementary schools often had combined PTAs. Such was the case with Stedman and Washington Park schools. Backers called the sister academies SWAP for Stedman–Washington Park.

in elementary, junior high, and high school. On the contrary, the modifications of the busing order meant students frequently attended a different school year after year, so confusing them as to requirements while they failed to bond with the school and their fellow students.

After massive modifications of the Finger Plan, DPS had 46 paired elementary schools. The scheme generally linked schools in northeast Denver with those in southeast Denver. There was a similar connection between southwest and northwest Denver. Change was constant since neighborhood and school enrollment patterns shifted. The court and the district repeatedly modified pairings and attendance borders until end of court-ordered busing in 1995–96. In part, this reflected the continual opening and shutting of schools during these years. The United States District Court had the oversight of such decisions. Consequently, what was true about the nature of paired schools one year was not necessarily the case the next year.

A school busing constant was linking together elementary schools in the different parts of town. For example, all the paired schools in Park Hill were for the same grade level. This kept parents from moving their children about them so they could attend neighborhood schools for both primary and intermediate classes.

Those who thought busing did far more harm to children than helped them sought to get around this. From the beginning, many white parents half submitted to school busing. They sent their children to their neighborhood school for either grades one, two, and three or four, five and six. During the other years, to keep their children off the bus, they arranged for the youngsters to go to private or religious schools or home schooled them.

Typical of the changing pairings was the linkage between Centennial (4665 Raleigh Street), Remington (4735 Pecos Street), and Smedley (4250 Shoshone Street) schools. The district and court soon changed it to a connection between Centennial and Remington while it paired Smedley with Kaiser (4500 South Quitman Street). There had already been changes in the Remington ties when the district had closed Berkeley School (5025 Lowell Boulevard) in 1976 to make way for Centennial. Previously, Alcott (West 41st Avenue and Tennyson Street), which also closed for Centennial, had been paired with Smedley.

Added to the confusion of specifically defining the scope and connections of the schools, the district changed pairings and definitions when it moved sixth graders from elementary schools to middle schools in 1988. Now the old division between primary (grades one, two, and three), and intermediate (grades four, five, and six), was passé. For the most part, paired elementary schools were either first and second grades or third, fourth, and fifth grades.

Paired schools were sister schools. They issued joint publicity brochures and had combined parent-teacher associations. The administration created a paired school assistance project to encourage the smooth cooperation between sister schools. Reflecting the class and economic divisions at the heart of busing, often parents in affluent, predominantly white schools were far more active in school programs than those in poverty-stricken sections. The busing order failed to provide after-hours transportation so low-income parents lacking a vehicle could travel across town for meetings and performances at their children's schools.

Typical of the uneven workings of busing was the pairing between Crofton (2409 Arapahoe Street), a primary school, and Steele (320 South Marion Street Parkway), an intermediate school. The former was adjacent to housing projects. For decades, Crofton had been among the poorest schools in the city with predominantly a Latino enrollment. Steele, in contrast, was nestled between the Denver Country Club and Washington Park. Students bused from Steele to Crofton observed that the furniture, books, and facility were definitely of a much lower quality at Crofton compared to their home school.

To make sure busing worked, concerned parents created a combined PTA, SCOPE, the Steele–Crofton Organization of Parents and Educators. Despite the best intentions of supporters, the group often failed to involve the Crofton community. Turnout by white parents at SCOPE events was quite good; few of the poverty-stricken black and brown families living near Crofton were present. Illustrative was an annual SCOPE house tour. This was a great money-making effort. SCOPE launched in 1988. During it, backers opened their homes to the curious for a day. The tour was always in and about Washington Park. None of the homeowners who were renovating vintage manors in Curtis Park close to Crofton were visibly involved in the effort.

The split between Steele and Crofton was not an isolated incident. Another example was the pairing of Kaiser and Smedley. Kaiser opened in an isolated enclave to the south of Fort Logan in 1974, remembering veteran teacher Mary S. "May" Kaiser. Smedley saluted a pioneer dentist, William Smedley, who served for about 25 years on the school board of the old North Denver District #17. It opened in 1902, the year he stepped down from the board. The court authorized Kaiser as part of a DPS school building initiative based on the assurance it would be part of an integrated, unitary district.

The southwest Denver school was a primary, paired with Smedley, grades four, five, and six. Few Kaiser students rode the bus to Smedley. A 1993 review showed that whereas 193 youngsters from Smedley came to Kaiser, only ten students in

Photo by L. C. McClure, DPL

No school more changed its orientation from the beginning of the busing era into the 21st century than Smedley at 4250 Shoshone Street. Shown is the 1902 building shortly after a 1911 addition.

the Kaiser district commuted to Smedley. At least 200 children in the Kaiser attendance district went to schools other than those operated by DPS. Included were schools in the nearby Jefferson County and Sheridan districts. Incidentally, of the ten students who took the bus from Kaiser to Smedley, five were white, four were Hispanos, and one was black. Smedley parents rarely traveled across town to attend after-hour events at Kaiser.

The legislature made it much easier for parents, particularly middle-class whites, to avoid busing in 1990 when it passed the School Choice Act. This permitted students to attend any public school they wished, including those outside of the district in which they lived, if space was available at the school to which they applied. Suburban districts emphasized this. Wheat Ridge and Westminster high schools, for example, sought to pull in students living in North Denver who were not happy about attending North High. State school financial mechanisms were such that the more students a school enrolled, the more money it received from the commonwealth. As such, districts outside of Denver were often glad to take in students who otherwise would have attended Denver Public Schools. In most instances, students living in an attendance zone outside of the school they attended were responsible for their own transportation. This kept those with low incomes or lack of access to convenient public transportation from taking advantage of the program.

The Kaiser-Smedley split was common. At schools in southeast and southwest Denver, white parents who backed busing and were active in school issues repeatedly complained that they had reached out to parents in sister schools, inviting them to social activities. They rarely got much if any response. Those living on the other side of town seemingly lacked the means or interest to make special trips to schools that were miles away. Added to this was a longtime lack of rapport between some economically distressed families and the schools—even when the buildings were nearby, parents still did not attend school functions. The few efforts to provide transportation to parents to get to schools across town had virtually no success.

Typical of the trauma of busing is what happened at Cheltenham School at 1580 Julian Street. The Finger Plan paired it with Samuels School at 3985 South Vincennes Court in far southeast Denver. Some Samuels parents were highly supportive of the effort. They met with Cheltenham principal George Mansfield who had built a strong parent-teacher organization. The newcomers, however, failed to connect with existing parents who shunned them as colonial interlopers whereby the previous backers of the Cheltenham parent-teacher organization stayed away from the school.

Paired schools changed as the city's population patterns evolved in the 1970s and 1980s, partially as a result of busing. This especially stood out in southwest Denver. Within a few years, the section went from being primarily a white enclave to a Hispanic zone. Despite this, the court continued to insist on paired busing between schools in northwest and southwest Denver. Foes of the program observed this meant transporting Latinos from schools in northwest Denver to southwest Denver at the same time the buses took Latinos from southwest Denver to northwest Denver. At the most, a modification of the court order allowed some southwest schools, such as Sabin (3050 South Vrain Street) and Schmitt (1820 South Vallejo Street) to join Johnson as once more being neighborhood walk-in academies.

Bernie Valdez

The focus on busing of Hispanic youngsters reflected another dimension of the busing controversy. Denver was not simply a city divided between blacks and whites, but there were a large number of residents of Spanish heritage. Such individuals had started visibly moving to the city after World War I. Typical of the their uneven reception and character were the many names the media used to describe them. At times they were the Spanish Speaking or the Spanish-Surnamed. The press also called them Spanish-Americans, Latin Americans, and Mexican-Americans. A city study branded them "Denver Americans of Spanish Descent."

People of Hispanic origins who had lived in the southwestern United States since the 19th century insisted they were not Mexicans, a label for those who had come from across the border. Militants in the community branded themselves Chicanos. Others were Hispanos or Hispanics. In the early 21st century, Latino became a favored term, especially among the striving middle class. By the end of the 2010s, "Latinx" was increasingly popular.

As the Hispanic dimension of school busing became ever more visible, Bernie Valdez was the voice of Latino Denver on the school board. In 1972, he replaced Bert Gallegos on the body. The departing member stood out as a premier conservative Hispano. President Richard Nixon recognized this. Seeking to reach out to middle-class Spanish-Americans, in January 1972 Nixon nominated Gallegos as general counsel for the Office of Economic Opportunity in Washington. This was the agency officially conducting the War on Poverty. The Nixon administration aimed to kill that Great Society effort, seeing Gallegos as an executioner.

On gaining confirmation, Gallegos quit the board in early April to move to Washington. Speaking for the board, Jim Perrill stated he hated to see Gallegos go. The Spanish-American attorney subsequently returned to Denver. As feisty and as combative as ever, in 1984 he failed as the Republican candidate for district attorney against incumbent Norm Early. He later moved to Pueblo where he died on April 6, 2005.

Bromwell School Library

In 1972, Bernie Valdez gained appointment to the school board as the voice of Latino Denver.

On Gallegos' resignation, the other six members of the school board agreed it was necessary that a Spanish-Surnamed individual fill the vacancy. In June 1972, they named a highly visible community figure, Bernard "Bernie" Valdez, to join the body. Before the board did so, many groups lobbied to get it to select their nominees to replace Gallegos. Typical was United Parents of Northeast Denver. Primarily a black group, it pushed for improvements to junior high and high schools filled with African-American youngsters. The society wanted its head, Toni McCann, on the board.

The new member was the manager of the Denver Department of Welfare, the forerunner of the Department of Human Services. Born on a farm near Cleveland, New Mexico, in 1912, Valdez dropped out of school when he was quite young. With his family, he arrived in Colorado in 1926 as a migrant laborer in the sugar-beet fields. A couple of years later, after his father's death, the Valdez family settled in Limon. He went back to school. After a while, he again dropped out, taking a job with the Civilian Conservation Corps, a New Deal program. Not until 1936 did he gain his high school diploma when he was living in Fort Collins.

Soon thereafter, Valdez came to Denver. He was part of a cooperative grocery store. Additionally, he supported the unionization drives of the Congress of Industrial Organizations. At the same time, he enrolled at the forerunner of the University of Northern Colorado in Greeley, graduating with a bachelor's in sociology in 1939.

With his degree in hand, Valdez returned to New Mexico where he worked in a cooperative health venture. In 1948, he permanently made Denver home. He got positions with local, state, and federal agencies seeking to redress the problems of migrant laborers and the endemic poverty and unemployment within the Mexican-American community. In the process, he helped form such groups as the Latin American Educational Foundation and the Latin American Research and Service Agency. By the time of the launch of the latter in 1964, Valdez was a highly visible figure in all establishment programs dealing with Hispanic Colorado. Most of all, for some years he was an employee of the Denver Housing Authority, managing some of its projects.

In 1963, Mayor Tom Currigan named Valdez to his cabinet. The New Mexico native stayed with the Department of Welfare/Social Services until his retirement in 1979. Back in 1962, Valdez had been among those serving on the Special Study Committee on Equal Educational Opportunity.

As was the case with most of the Latino community, Valdez had no enthusiasm for school busing. What his people needed, he emphasized, was a discrimination-free district that addressed the cultural heritage of Hispanos, complete with recognizing language and economic problems. While establishment Denver heralded Valdez, radical Chicanos around the Crusade for Justice saw him as a token and a sellout.

The 1973 Board Election

Valdez sought to stay on the board in 1973, running for a six-year post when the terms of William Berge and Stephen J. Knight Jr. expired. Additionally, voters needed to fill the remaining four years in the term of Gallegos. The Hispano who had replaced Gallegos aligned himself with Berge and Knight as part of the "Protect Your Neighborhood Schools" ticket. Knight was the anti-busing candidate for the vacancy term. Thirteen other candidates also sought places on the bureau.

Against the neighborhood schools slate, advocates of integration lined up behind Kay Schomp and Omar Blair—Schomp ran for the four-year term. The challengers observed the fruits of the incumbents' anti-busing policies: costly litigation, community breakdown, a decline of academic achievement, and a seemingly unhinged city. It was time to put education first and accept that racial equality and the court order were here to stay.

Both the *News* and the *Post* endorsed Blair and Schomp. The *News* also urged keeping Berge on the board. The *Post* backed Valdez. In a low turnout, Schomp bested Knight, 17,977–14,499, for the vacancy spot. J. Scott Gustafson, 1,676, Antonio Archuleta, 943, and Roberta Vollacto, 626, were far behind.

Blair led the voting for the six-year terms, 17,859. Valdez came in second 17,506. Berge trailed at 15,065. PTA contender Lila Swallow received the backing of 9,615 voters. Edward Robman was at 6,370. Six other candidates gained a scattering of votes. Advocates of brotherhood saw the triumph of Schomp and Blair as a great achievement. Ideally, the new members would help heal the breakdown of the district.

Blair was the candidate of a black caucus. Then state representative Wellington Webb chaired it. The group was insistent that the way for more African-Americans to gain elective office was for blacks to vote as a bloc for candidates of their race chosen by community leaders. In reflecting on his school board career, Blair later stated Rachel Noel had been the prime figure in recruiting him to run for the agency.

As the campaign heated up, Blair's backers especially lobbied Lila Swallow, a former head of both the Denver and the Colorado PTA, to withdraw from the race. They feared her candidacy would take votes from Blair and Schomp. She ran anyway. The DCTA backed her.

Photo of painting at Blair-Caldwell Library

Omar Blair won a seat on the school board in 1973, breaking the complete hold of the anti-busing majority. He was a most forceful figure on the body until his departure in 1985.

In part, Blair's triumph was due to the heavy support he received in Park Hill. Some living there cast only one vote for the two six-year terms, not wanting anything to interfere with the return of an African-American to the school board. On the body, Blair had a commanding presence. He often clashed with others there and in the community.

Born in Houston on July 16, 1918, Blair was the son of the operator of a dry-cleaning establishment. The family moved to Denver when he was quite young. For a while, they lived above their shop near the north corner of 26th and Welton streets in the heart of Five Points. After his parents divorced when Blair was in the third grade, he moved with his father to Phoenix. Later, he and his father lived in Albuquerque where the future board member graduated from high school—he was one of six black students in a class of 600.

Six foot, four inches tall, Omar Blair was a superb athlete, gaining a scholarship to the University of California Los Angeles. In April 1941, he left school to enlist in the Tuskegee Airmen. This was a military response to the civil rights upheavals roiling the country as it prepared to enter World War II. To rally blacks for the fighting, the War Department allowed African-Americans to fly planes in the Army Air Forces. Training was at the Tuskegee Institute in Alabama, once the headquarters of Booker T. Washington, the leading advocate of black accommodation and uplift at the turn of the 20th century. Patriotic blacks literally flocked to the program. In later years, being a Tuskegee Airman was a sign of utmost prestige among the black middle class. (Warren Alexander, who had failed in his run for the board in 1971, was another Tuskegee Airman.)

For quite a while, the Army Air Forces refused to allow the black pilots to serve abroad. In response to mass lobbying, it sent some of them to North Africa in 1943. Soon it stationed many of them in Italy. Among them was Blair who left the service after the return of peace. Before long, he was back in Albuquerque, joining his father's business. He took classes at a business college.

The veteran permanently settled in Denver in 1951. He re-enlisted in the service, being assigned to a post at the Rocky Mountain Arsenal, an Army facility producing and storing deadly chemical and biological weapons adjacent to Stapleton Airport. He was subsequently an equal opportunity investigator for the Air Force at Lowry. From there, he moved up to being the assistant equal employment

officer at the Air Force Accounting and Finance Center. In 1975, after 28 years
in the service, he retired as a major, forced out of the service by his failure to gain
promotion to lieutenant colonel. After leaving the Air Force, Blair was a proud
member of the American Federation of Government Employees, a union affiliated
with the American Federation of Labor–Congress of Industrial Organizations.
Additionally, he was active in the Chamber of Commerce and a stalwart of the
East Denver YMCA. The last was the African-American branch of the club/
community organization.

Back in 1968, Blair had gained a place on the board of the Denver Urban Renewal
Authority (DURA). This was a year after it had received voter authorization to
destroy the heart of downtown along Larimer Street. It was deaf to pleas to preserve
the distinguished mid-rise Victorian landmarks in the area. Blair stayed on the
DURA board for a decade, never questioning its relentless efforts to demolish
yesterday's Denver. On the school board, he frequently clashed with preservationists
who wanted to keep old schoolhouses standing.

Back in 1973, Dana Crawford, the founder of Larimer Square and a
preservationist who was able to work with DURA, was a co-chairwoman of Blair's
school board campaign committee. Alex Holland, a former city councilman who
was a major figure in DURA, was on the board of the Blair campaign committee.
So was another former city councilman who was a downtown business leader, Phil

Photo by Phil Goodstein

*Shorter African Methodist Episcopal Church, at the southeast corner of Martin
Luther King Boulevard and Jackson Street (Richard Allen Way), includes the
Omar Blair Fellowship Hall. It recalls a church deacon who was a member of
the school board. While on the board, Blair helped the congregation acquire the
land from DPS. The school district had once proposed using the acreage to erect
a new home of Gove Junior High.*

Milstein, a founder and member of the Denver Landmark Preservation Commission. Past school board member James Voorhees joined them as did future board member Virginia Rockwell. Leaders of black Denver such as Bill Roberts, Arie Taylor, Wendell Liggins, Bernard Gipson, and James Reynolds were also prominent endorsers. So was Wayne Knox, a white school teacher who served in the legislature from southwest Denver. Radio personality Gene Amole and anti–Winter Olympics activist John Parr additionally endorsed the campaign.

After being active in Speak Out on School Integration, Blair became an inaugural member of District #1's black advisory council. Members of it served for two-year terms, nominated by members of the community, the DPS administration, and the school board. The group did not have any formal powers, but was supposed to act to assure the district was aware of the concerns of this part of the city.

Within a few years, DPS reached out to numerous constituencies, forming other advisory councils. Included were committees representing Hispanos, American Indians, and Asian-Americans. Back in 1971, the school board had created a new citizens advisory committee. It did not have the scope or the 1967 Advisory Council. From the beginning, Blair had been most active in pushing the Keyes case, helping raise money for the litigation. He was a logical choice for proponents of returning the school board to where it had been during the heyday of Rachel Noel.

Besides serving on the school board, Blair was a deacon at Shorter African Methodist Episcopal Church, a mainstay of the black religious community. In 1978, he played a key role when the church decided to relocate from its historic home at the northwest corner of 20th Avenue and Washington Street. With Blair's help, it procured 4.04 acres from DPS at the southeast corner of Jackson Street and Martin Luther King Boulevard. This was the land where the district had once planned to erect the new Gove Junior High. The congregation acquired the real estate from the system for $255,000. Blair lived nearby at 2643 Jackson Street.

On the heels of occupying its new building, in 1980 Shorter successfully lobbied the city to rename Jackson Street between 29th Avenue and Martin Luther King Boulevard "Richard Allen Court." The name memorialized the founding bishop of the African Methodist Episcopal Church. In correspondence with King Trimble, who represented the area in both the legislature and on city council, Blair described a citizen opposed to the action, and who questioned a conflict of interest between Blair's role on the school board and the sale of the property, as a "disgruntled idiot." The language was typical of Blair. At times, he was extremely outspoken. He admitted this in a *Denver Post* interview stating "they call me a cantankerous old bastard. I am." Reflecting his military background, he continually emphasized the necessity of a strict teacher dress code.

The Country Club Members

Katherine W. "Kay" Schomp joined Blair as a new board member. Born in Pueblo on August 10, 1917, she was the daughter of Roy J. Weaver, the region's commanding Oldsmobile dealer. After studying at CU, she gained her bachelor's in international relations from George Washington University in 1939. She married a promising young car salesman, Ralph Schomp, who came to take over her father's

In 1973, Kay Schomp, a PTA activist who was the wife of a leading car dealer, gained a place on the school board as an advocate of desegregation. Here she stresses the importance of books in school libraries.

firm, Weaver–Beatty Oldsmobile, turning it into Ralph Schomp Oldsmobile. Personally, she was most active in the League of Women Voters. Additionally, she was a foremost figure in the ACLU, receiving its prestigious Carle Whitehead Award in 1975. The mother of six girls, Kay Schomp was a leader of the PTA, serving as the head of the chapter at Moore School. In the early 1970s, she was involved in Denver QuEST, a coalition sponsored by the Denver Federation of Teachers which sought to bring the entire community together in supporting the schools.

Traditionally, the PTA had usually had an informal representative on the school board. A couple of men associated with the automobile business had been members during the mid-20th century: Packard dealer Charles Hanington, and LeRoy Kent Robinson who had a Buick outlet. Elite Capitol Hill or the Country Club neighborhood likewise frequently had a presence on the body. Schomp filled all three categories. The contender lived atop Quality Hill, part of distinguished Capitol Hill, at the southeast corner of Seventh Avenue and Clarkson Street. But Schomp was not a traditional conservative. On the contrary, she described herself as a rabble-rouser, promising it would no longer be business as usual if she were on the board of education.

Schomp pushed the bureau to open its meetings compared to its history of secrecy and closed committee sessions. At a time when DPS was readily destroying its historic buildings as hideous, worn-out vestiges of Denver's Victorian past, she was the only person on the board to state some of them should be saved. In particular, she was among those seeing that Moore School gained landmark protection on March 14, 1975.

Among Schomp's ventures on the board was pushing a 12-member City–School Cooperation Commission. It emerged in 1975 with six representatives each from city hall and DPS. Ideally, Schomp and other backers explained, the committee would coordinate programs, including playgrounds, parks, and public safety.

Over the years, relations between the City and County of Denver and District #1 waxed and waned. At times, the city and DPS worked together closely, including sharing schools as community and recreation centers. On other occasions, there was little communications between them. The City–School Cooperation Commission alternated between being active and somnolent during the next few years.

Between 1975 and 1981, Schomp served on the board with an associate who was also part of the Country Club crowd and had been a leader of the PTA, Virginia "Ginny" Packard Rockwell. Back in 1964–65, when Schomp was the president of the Moore PTA, Rockwell had led the Bromwell PTA. Rockwell had gone on to serve as president of the Byers Junior High PTA, being vice president of the group at East High. Like Schomp, Rockwell personified the city's tradition whereby the wealthy were on the school board as part of their community service. She identified herself as simply a homemaker.

Born in Denver on February 7, 1924, to an orthopedic surgeon, Ginny Packard attended Moore School where she met her future husband, Bruce Rockwell, when they were in kindergarten together. After attending Morey, she graduated from the elite private Kent School for Girls rather than East High. She went on to earn her bachelor's from Smith College. Back in Denver, she reconnected with Bruce Rockwell, marrying him on April 22, 1950. The couple became quite close to members of the Stephen Knight family, living in what was once a Knight manor to the south of Botanic Gardens at 815 Vine Street.

A brilliant product of DPS, born on December 18, 1922, Bruce Rockwell had been head boy at East High before attending Yale. In 1947, he became executive secretary to newly elected Mayor Quigg Newton. From there, he moved over to the advertising firm of William Kostka & Associates. The former East head boy joined Colorado National Bank in 1953. Twenty-two years later he became its head. Back in 1958, on the establishment of DURA, Rockwell emerged as a key figure on its board as the agency plotted with downtown business interests to remake the city. By the 1980s, as the head of Colorado National Bank, Bruce Rockwell was seemingly everywhere, heading countless committees and being a kingpin in the Chamber of Commerce and the Denver Partnership.

When the school busing controversies heated up in the late 1960s, Bruce Rockwell had been among the board members of Speak Out on School Integration. He went on to assist the Denver Equal Education Opportunity Fund, the group formed by Fred Thomas to finance the Keyes case. In 1973, he was co-chairman of the Omar Blair school board campaign. Additionally, he served on the executive committee of the Community Education Council, the body appointed by the court to review the success of the busing program.

Virginia Rockwell was a traditional blueblood on the school board. She gained election in 1975 as a candidate of tolerance and accepting school busing. Bob Crider, who was on the board, from 1971 to 1983, is on the left.

Ginny Rockwell launched her bid for the school board in March 1975 at her alma mater, Moore School. This was the culmination of 15 years of active involvement in school issues. Included was volunteering at her children's schools. She had an extremely assertive personality. Over the years, she had backed drives for civil rights. In many ways she was the personification of affluent liberals who were sure integration could work. Besides, without busing, people like Rockwell and Schomp feared that such traditional Capitol Hill schools as Moore and East might collapse as Denver became a racially polarized city. On the side, Ginny Rockwell was an accomplished athlete, particularly as a competitive horsewoman and a tennis player.

Neither Jim Perrill nor Frank Southworth, the two victors of 1969 whose terms were up, sought to remain on the board in 1975. Back in 1972, Southworth had gained a seat in the Colorado House of Representatives. He was a fanatical supporter of a national drive, embraced by the White House, to amend the United States Constitution to prohibit school busing for integration. With his backing, the state legislature adopted a joint House resolution in April 1974 declaring its support for such an amendment.

Southworth built on this when he ran for Congress in the fall of 1974 against incumbent Democrat Pat Schroeder. She refused to back the amendment. In November, she clobbered Southworth, 93,486–65,016. Back in 1969, her husband, Jim Schroeder, had been among the attorneys consulting about the possibly of suing DPS in the wake of the triumph of the anti-busing slate in the school board election.

In 1975, Southworth was the founding president of the National Association for Neighborhood Schools. This was a time when school busing controversies swept the nation. Seemingly, he hoped to make Denver's awkward response to the court order a national model. The former board member subsequently served on a wide variety of bureaus, including the Centennial Chamber of Commerce. He passed away on February 16, 2016. His wife of 66 years, Doris Beck, died the next year. Back on January 31, 1986, Perrill had entered the other world.

That was in the future. In 1975, Larry McLain was something of Ginny Rockwell's running mate in the contest as the pro-integration ticket. A pediatrician with three children, he was especially proud of his religiosity, being a member of the Fellowship of Christian Athletes and the coach of a little league football team. He dwelt in a manor in the heart of affluent Park Hill at 1750 Hudson Street.

Among the other challengers was Jack Marsh. A freight handler, he was the candidate of the Socialist Workers Party, a self-avowed revolutionary Trotskyist group. Despite this, Marsh heralded the United States Constitution and the ruling of Judge Doyle as virtually holy writ opposed to the "criminal nature of the Denver school board."

In the balloting, Rockwell led the field of eight with 46,762 votes. Anti-busing candidate Naomi Bradford won the second seat, 36,407. She eased out McLain, 35,363. Nolan Winsett, the leader of the anti-busing Citizens Association for Neighborhood Schools, was number four, 22,605, trailed by attorney Alan Bucholtz, 21,451, educator Everett H. Chavez, 14,098, Jack Marsh, 7,767, and West Side social gospel preacher Ramiro Cruz-Ahedo, 6,563. Among other issues, the new board members had to deal with the district's changing superintendents.

A Note on Sources:

In a letter to the editor, *DP*, March 2, 1966, p. 25, James C. Miller celebrated the police. The *Post* told of Miller's clash with the Denver Association of Evangelicals, December 1, 1966, p. 44. It painted his links to the John Birch Society, October 18, 1966, p. 12, and outlined his involvement with the Denver Neighborhood School Association, September 21, 1969, p. 27. There are clippings about him, mostly undated and unpaginated, in an unnumbered folder in box 13 of the Banks papers. Included is the *Littleton Independent*, December 2, 1966, and January 5, 1967, *RMN*, December 23, 1967, and *DP*, December 24, 1967, on his promotion of the John Birch Society. The Banks folder also has articles about Miller from the *Denver Blade*, an African-American newspaper, painting the preacher as the epitome of white racism.

Passing mention of United Schools Against Forced Busing is in Meadow, "Hard Years," pp. 23–26. I touch on the evolution of Denver Christian School in *University Park*, 190–91. An advertisement for the program, stressing its "biblical worldview," was in *Colorado Parent Education Guide 2019*, p. 37.

Lukas, *Common Ground*, 220, observes the irony of the demand for community control amidst busing. Trillin, "Doing the Right Thing," *New Yorker*, May 31, 1969, p. 87, quotes Perrill's views, and, p. 88, observes black demands for community control as opposed to busing.

Watson, "Barricades," 193, mentions Rachel Noel did not seek re-election in 1971, glancing at that year's election. Taylor, "Leadership," 165–66, outlines the 1971 school board race. Ibid., 178, tells of Bert Gallegos' role on the board. The 1958 *Who's*, 202, includes Gallegos. I touch on him in *DIA*, 402–03. FF 21:2 of the Yasui papers has the results of the 1971 contest.

Noel especially stressed her studies at Fisk on side B of tape one of OH-84 at DPL. A biographical sketch of Noel at her memorial service outlines her academic career at Metro; a copy is in the vault at DPL. FF 2:20 of the Noel papers mentions the Noel Distinguished Professorship.

DP, October 17, 1976, p. 3, and *RMN*, October 17, 1976, p. 5, told about Rachel Noel's appointment to the CU Board of Regents. *RMN*, March 12, 1978, reported her goal to gain a six-year term on it. *RMN*, June 21, 1981, p. 56, announced her selection as the head of the body. *RMN*, April 20, 1984, p. 22, chronicled that she was not seeking to stay on the board. FF 2:22 of the Noel papers is on her appointment to the CU Board of Regents. Robert Connery states that the plaintiffs had pondered asking Jim Carrigan to be their lawyer in *DU Law Review*, 90:5 (October 2013), 1104. During a September 13, 2019, interview, Buddy Noel recalled his service on the CSU board of trustees.

FF 2:14, 17, of the Noel papers highlights Noel's many achievements. Included was an award Metro gave her in 1991 at its annual ball for her exemplary service. *Colorado Statesman*, October 12, 1990, p. 1, and *DWN*, October 11, 1990, p. 10, observed Governor Roy Romer specially feting her.

The former school board member reflected on her hopes and disappointments in busing in her interview at the end of *Our Neighborhood Schools* in Alweis, *Rebels Remembered*. She reflected on the impact of the Keyes case on the 20th anniversary of the litigation in FF 1:29–30 of her papers. *DP*, February 5, 2008, reported her passing.

Kelly, *Old Gray Mayors*, 247–48, links the question of school busing to the 1971 mayoral election. Dale Tooley gave his account of the race, complete with the issue of busing, in *I'd Rather Be in Denver* (Denver: Colorado Legal Publishing, 1985), 51. An unnumbered folder in box 13 of the Banks papers has a copy of a May 6, 1969, letter from Dale Tooley to Superintendent Robert Gilberts urging compromise on the busing issue. Connery in *DU Law Review*, 90:5 (October 2013), 1104, lists Tooley as among the lawyers who met when integration forces first pondered suing DPS in the wake of the May 1969 election. *RMN*, June 11, 1969, p. 6, printed Bill McNichols' declaration of silence on school matters. CANS, *Judicial* Fiat, 13, complained about the mayor's neutrality on the busing issue.

Sharon R. Catlett, *Farmlands, Forts, and Country Life* (Boulder: Westcliffe, 2007), 175–76, heralds Ted Hackworth. I trace Bob Crider's career in DIA, 424–25. On occasion, Cathy Donohue has recalled her service on city council with the two anti-busing candidates.

There is an interview with Warren Alexander in the Branscombe papers. I outline his Park Hill and civil rights presence in *Park Hill Promise*, 46, 285, 334, 455, 494, 500–01. Orfield, *Must We Bus?* 73, stresses black flight. *Park Hill Promise*, 76, 78, 475, and *Curtis Park*, 155, 156, 160, deal with that phenomenon. *Our*

Neighborhood Schools in Alweis, *Rebels Remembered*, observes that many blacks and Latinos left the city in the 1970s at the same time whites were fleeing busing.

DP, September 21, 2018, p. 16A, reviewed the career of Jennie Rucker. *Our Neighborhood Schools* in Alweis, *Rebels Remembered*, has an interview with her where she mentions her experiences in DPS and the discrimination to which she was subjected.

On April 25, 2019, Roger Persons recalled the 1971 school board campaign. *RMN*, May 10, 1971, p. 42, had the paper's endorsements in the race. The *Post* made its recommendations, May 18, 1971, p. 22. *RMN*, May 9, 1971, pp. 5, 8, of an election supplement, looked at the school board race. So did *DP*, May 19, 1971, p. 85.

LWV, *Composite View*, 2, 4, mentions how Doyle presided in the case even while moving up to the Tenth Circuit. *RMN*, April 23, 1976, p. 15, reported the development. CANS, *Judicial* Fiat, 7, observes Doyle's appointment to the Tenth Circuit and the way the plaintiffs successfully petitioned for him to remain sitting on the Keyes case. During a wide-ranging interview on July 23, 2009, veteran attorney John McNamara reflected on Judge Doyle and how his elevation to the Circuit Court was linked to the politics of busing, the influence of Gordon Allot, and was an effort to get Doyle off the Keyes case.

The judge's December 11, 1973, ruling is 368 FSupp 207. A copy is in FF 2 of the Jane Michaels papers. Pearson, "Denver Case," 201–02, outlines it. Meadow, "Hard Years," *CJ*, May 8, 1974, pp. 23–26, tells about the way DPS drafted its integration plan, "A Plan for Equal Educational Opportunity in the DPS," at the last minute, and how the proposal aimed to close many central city schools.

FF 3 of the Michaels papers has Judge Doyle's correspondence about the Finger Plan, outlining the logic of his decision. FF 4 has additional materials on it, mostly copies of published court rulings. FF 5 is the official court endorsement of the Finger Plan. The *1975 DPS Report*, 6, outlines the Finger Plan. It tells about the ruling of the Tenth Circuit Court modifying it, 7.

CANS, *Judicial* Fiat, 2, 9, 12, mentions the Finger Plan, and observes the conflict of interest between John Finger's connections with LDF and his role as a supposedly independent court expert. Emory University has an eight-box, unprocessed collection of Finger's papers, #1031. The inventory lists boxes seven and eight as having materials on Denver. Lukas, *Common Ground*, 239, observes Finger's role in Boston. Maurice Mitchell, "The Desegregation of Denver's Public Schools," *Center Magazine*, November-December 1978, p.73, observes how teachers referred to "our kids" and "their kids."

Bardwell, *Segregation*, 35–36, 46, is typical of the many busing plans suggested to the court. *RMN*, April 18, 1974, p. 1, announced Judge Doyle's ordering of the Finger Plan. Pearson, "Denver Case," 202–03, LWV, *Composite View*, 6–8, and Bailey, "Journey Full Circle," 107, 112, look at the Finger Plan and Doyle's decision. The judge's order of April 17, 1974, is 380 FSupp 673. The Tenth Circuit modified it, 521 F.2d 465.

The 1974 *DPS Report*, no pagination, discussed the impact of the Finger Plan, listing numbers and costs. Meadow, "Hard Years," pp. 23–26, also discusses the number of students whom the district bused. *SN*, April 29, 1974, p. 37, outlined the implementation of the Finger Plan. Taylor, "Leadership," 221–22, reviews the initiative. So does a 1976 DPS pamphlet sketching the March 26, 1976, agreement between the court and the school district. DPS gave its views in "Response to Judge Doyle," *SR*, May 1974, p. 1.

SR, September 1974, amplified the district's response to Judge Doyle's order of April 17, 1974. Additionally, there is a May 1976 DPS "Special Report," listing the changing nature of paired schools in response to court decisions. FF 1:81 has an August 28, 1975, DPS packet on paired school information. Materials on the implementation of busing, complete with a school racial census, is in FF 1:84. CANS, *Judicial* Fiat, 12, estimates the costs of busing and how DPS found itself having to pay most of the court expenses of the plaintiffs.

There are clippings on the Finger Plan in both the 1973–74 PTA Notebook and the 1973–74 PTA Historian's Notebook in GP. *DP*, April 16, 1974, p. 74, stressed the unclear numbers and fuzzy specifications of the Finger Plan. Fishman, "Endless Journey," 640–43, reviews the legal dimension of the Finger Plan within the overall context of the *Keyes* case.

Evie Dennis, "Developing and Implementing a Viable Intergroup Educational Program in the Denver Public Schools" (Ed.D. dissertation, Nova University, 1976), is a glowing review of the inservice program. The very short work gives little specifics about exactly what it was or how it operated. Rather, it is simply a compilation of surveys about it by the woman who had administered them.

Fishman, "Endless Journey," 198–99, 204, 214, 215, and Pearson, "Denver Case," 204, look at the faculty integration stemming from the court order. *SN*, April 29, 1974, p. 37, and May 28, 1974, p. 43, discussed how the court order required the desegregation and reassignment of teachers and staff. *SN*, March 31, 1975, p. 33, mentioned the affirmative action hiring plan for teachers. The 1974 *DPS Report*, no pagination, already referred to the district's emphasis on hiring teachers based on race and ethnicity. *RMN*, August 8, 1983, p. 7, reviewed the continuing affirmative action program in selecting teachers.

Pearson, "Denver Case," 217, observes problems with the Finger Plan and the lack of coordination between sister schools. The article argues the effort worked much better during the 1975–76 schoolyear than it had in 1974–75.

In sporadic discussions, Dorolyn Griebenaw has recalled her son going to Valdez, its character, and the nature of Edison School. Box 4 of the Ash Grove PTA Papers, WH 923, at DPS, is filled with documents about busing controversies in the 1970s. Included are FF 4:75, on programs to expand equal educational opportunity, FF 4:77, clippings and flyers on desegregation from 1974 to 1976, and FF 4:79, the March 1979 Task Force on Integration's report. FF 21:42 of the Yasui papers is on the status of busing in 1980–81, including the use of satellite areas for junior high schools.

I review the links between Steele and Crofton schools in *Washington Park*, 176–77, and *Curtis Park*, 104–05. In 2008, Dean Nye recalled his experiences of being bused between the two schools in the 1970s.

Focus, November 1978, p. 3, mentioned the paired school assistance project. FF 5:32 of the DPS papers has an October 3, 1993, clipping from the *Denver Post* about the uneasy relationship between Kaiser and Smedley. Letters in FF 7:42 of the DPS collection on Henry Junior High discuss how problems at the school were aggravated by the way its local supporters were unable to connect with parents of students who were bused to it from Elyria and Swansea. Dorothy Gotlieb related the story about Samuels and Cheltenham schools on January 23, 2020. On September 28, 2019, Jane Lane recalled the impact of busing on her family and the way her siblings managed to get around it during their years in elementary school.

RMN, April 28, 1977, p. 5, told about the problems with paired schools and how not all white families embraced busing to minority schools. Chalkbeat, drawing on a report of Ready Colorado, "Open Doors, Open Districts," in *DP*, January 17, 2019, p. 6C YourHub, reviewed the legacy of the 1990 School Choice Act.

Vincent C. De Baca, ed., *La Gente* (Denver: CHS, 1998), is an introductory overview to Colorado's Hispanic legacy. FF 8:9 of the CCR papers has the study of "Denver Americans of Spanish Descent." FF 8:10–11 is a copy of a 1950 "exploratory survey" of the "Spanish American Population of Denver." I deal with Latino Denver in *DIA*, chap. 3, and *Soup Lines,* 228–31, 429, 431, 435, 452, 464, 504, 505, 509, 515.

RMN, April 19, 1972, p. 8, and *DP*, April 19, 1972, p. 21, reported the resignation of Bert Gallegos from the school board. *DP*, April 21, 1972, p. 88, had Perrill's farewell to Gallegos. *RMN*, May 19, 1984, p. 17, sketched the former board member's run for district attorney.

DP, April 21, 1972, p. 88, observed United Parents of Northeast Denver and the board bid of Toni McCann to take Gallegos' place. Taylor, "Leadership," 184–85, discusses how Bernie Valdez succeeded Gallegos on the school board. *RMN*, June 16, 1972, p. 5, and *DP*, June 16, 1972, p. 27, told of Valdez's appointment. Valdez shared his memories with me on December 30, 1996.

Taylor, "Leadership," 194–96, reviews the 1973 board election. Also see *DP*, May 8, 1973, p. 21. A profile of Omar Blair is in Wallace Yvonne Tollette, *Colorado Black Leadership Profiles* (Denver: Western Images, 2001), 90–91. There is a collection on him at BCL, ARL3, and a file on the man in the Branscombe papers. Art Branscombe recalled Blair in *GPHN*, April 15, 2004, p. 1. Also see Mauck, *Five Points*, 114. There was a feature on the Denver Tuskegee Airmen in *RMN*, August 20, 1995, p. 39A; compare Mauck *Five Points*, 89, and FF 50 of the Joan Reese papers at BCL, ARL11.

FF 2:28 of the Noel papers focuses on the Black Education Advisory Council, complete with some of its reports during the 1990s. FF 21:2 of the Yasui papers outlines the 1973 school board election, including the role of the black caucus. *SN*, September 27, 1971, p. 7, observed Blair's appointment to the black advisory council; cf. *Cmq*, March 1972.

In an interview in *Our Neighborhood Schools* in Alweis, *Rebels Remembered*, Blair states Rachel Noel recruited him to run for the board in 1973. *SN*, June 1977, p. 35, featured Blair's election as board president, quoting his acceptance speech, pp. 35–37.

The 1988 *DPS Facts and Figures*, 16, lists the multiple advisory councils in the district. *RMN*, January 6, 1971, p. 18, and December 20, 1971, p. 8, looked at the emergence of the Denver Education Advisory Committee.

SN, October 9, 1978, p. 15, reported DPS selling the property near Jackson Street and Martin Luther King Boulevard to Shorter Church. I touch on the history of the congregation and its move in *Curtis Park*, 268–69. There is correspondence dated January 28, 1981, between Blair and King Trimble in the Trimble papers, ARL16 at BCL, FF 31. A profile of Blair was in an unidentified article in the 1984–85 clipping notebook in GP. An unidentified March 17, 1984, clipping in the 1983–84 PTA Historian's Notebook told of Blair's push for a teacher dress code. GP has an undated article without a page number from 1985 where Blair admits that he is "a cantankerous old bastard."

I deal with Roy Weaver and the Kay Schomp family in *Civic Center*, 229–31. Taylor, "Leadership," 100, tells of her ties to the LWV. Ibid., 194, 196, looks at her election to and service on the board. *RMN*, March 13, 1977, p. 17, contained Schomp's announcement for the board. A copy of her announcement statement is in box 8 of the Banks papers. *RMN*, October 8, 1990, profiled Schomp; a copy is in FF 7:7 of the DPS papers. *DP*, November 23, 2000, p. 4B, *RMN*, November 23, 2000, p. 14B, and *BN*, December 8, 2000, mourned her passing.

A January 13, 1977, DPS PR and *SN*, January 17, 1977, p. 18, outlined Schomp's role on the City–School Cooperation Commission. *SN*, December 12, 1975, p. 20, observed Schomp's receipt of the Whitehead Award.

A copy of the 1975 LWV election guide, featuring the school board race, is in box 8 of the Banks papers. *Rocky Mountain Journal*, April 30, 1975, p. 4, profiled that year's school board race. *RMN*, April 5, 1975, observed Jim Perrill was not seeking re-election. A special June 1977 edition of *SN*, p. 37–38, quoted Rockwell's acceptance speech as vice president of the board. Connery in *DU Law Review*, 90:5 (October 2013), 1107, cites Bruce Rockwell's involvement with the Denver Equal Education Opportunity Fund. Thomas J. Noel, *Growing Through History with Colorado* (Denver: Colorado National Bank, 1987), 102–03, heralds Bruce Rockwell, and mentions his wife, 103. The book, a subsidized history of Colorado National Bank, fails to observe the problems at the financial institution that forced Rockwell to leave as its leader in 1985.

Bailey, "Journey Full Circle," 120, observes the legislature backing the national anti-busing amendment. Meadow, "Hard Years," pp. 23–26, emphasizes Southworth's policy of blocking busing and his endorsement of the anti-busing constitutional amendment. Connery, *DU Law Review*, 90:5 (October 2013), 1106, lists Jim Schroeder as among the lawyers involved in discussions in planning what became the Keyes case. I deal with Pat Schroeder's political career in *Our Time*, 466 70. Pp. 222–25, below, look at Naomi Bradford and her triumph in the 1975 school board race.

Chapter Nine

Changing Superintendents

On gaining a place on the school board in 1975, Ginny Rockwell joined with Omar Blair and Kay Schomp as a strong, three-member minority in favor of integration. They allied with Bernie Valdez whom they elected president of the board to succeed the outgoing Jim Perrill. The four members soon had severe problems with the man Perrill had made superintendent in 1973, Louis Kishkunas.

Robert D. Gilberts had never performed as expected as superintendent. Not only was he caught up in the busing maelstrom, but had failed in his drive to reorganize elementary schools and push through the 1967 bond issue. Additionally, in 1969, under his aegis, labor relations in the district became so bad that the teachers went out on strike that November.

By 1970, rather than a record of achievement, these defeats weighed down on Gilberts. Seeing more turbulence ahead, he bailed out on April 30 when he announced he was walking away from the last two years of his five-year contract. Rather than sticking with the increasingly troubled DPS, he was leaving it at the end of the schoolyear for a lower-paying job as the dean of the school of education at the University of Oregon.

The superintendent asserted the Beaver State offer was among the many job proposals he had received, including to lead districts in Milwaukee and Philadelphia. Besides, he desperately wanted out of DPS. In later reflections, he stated he knew he had to leave the Denver district since the school board was not rational on integration and he refused to be superintendent while DPS followed a suicide path.

Gilberts did not say as much on heading to Oregon. In contrast to his 1967 promises, when he eagerly signed on with DPS, the departing superintendent declared he had long wanted to be part of a college education program, ideally one where he could work with graduate students. Ignoring the problems that had swamped him during his three years as chief of Mile High education, on leaving town Gilberts confidently stated the district was in excellent shape. It was a "modern and accountable school system." Since taking charge, he claimed to have addressed the vital needs of restructuring DPS whereby the district was on the path for continued success.

At the University of Oregon, Gilberts cultivated a most informal style, even growing a beard and mustache. He shaved them off when he found himself ordered to get a suit and testify before a key state commission. The former DPS superintendent stayed at the University of Oregon until his retirement. He died in Oregon at age 93 in 2018.

Many were glad to see Gilberts go. They found him a pompous stuffed suit. In contrast, the media generally accepted the departing superintendent's claims at face value. Already in September 1969, a *Denver Post* review of DPS had concluded the system was headed in the right direction. The district now faced the challenge of finding a leader to guide it through the pitfalls of the court order.

Howard Johnson

The school board believed it had found a worthy man for the job when it named deputy superintendent, Howard Leslie Johnson, to succeed Gilberts. The new administrator was very much a DPS success story. A native of Mankato, Minnesota, born on October 22, 1908, Johnson attended Hamline University in St. Paul before gaining a bachelor's of science from the University of Nebraska. The new superintendent followed this with a master's at DU. After gaining a post with DPS in 1928, two years later he moved to South High as an instructor. There he immediately stood out as a coach. Under him, South repeatedly won baseball and football championships. Eventually, the Colorado High School Coaches Association Hall of Fame enshrined him. Personally, Johnson and his wife Bonita were childless. They often took in foster children.

In 1939, Johnson left South to become assistant principal at West. At that time, superintendents everywhere looked to coaches as ideal men to lead schools or at least become assistant principals. The coaches knew how to impose discipline and order. For decades, many of the men rising to become DPS principals had sports backgrounds. Even at that, they were educators. Men who were coaches were also expected to be in the classroom daily. They not only taught physical education, but also such topics as social studies, math, English, and science.

After five years at West, Johnson took charge of Opportunity School in 1944. In that post, he was a key player in the creation of KRMA, Channel Six. The station went on the air in 1956. It was part of the district's adult education ventures headquartered at Opportunity School, having its studio there.

The future superintendent had wide-ranging links. For a while, he was an instructor in the summer school program at Colorado State University. In 1949–50, he was a consultant for the census bureau. Between 1952 and 1964, he was a part-time arbitrator of labor-management disputes. On July 5, 1960, DPS elevated him to assistant superintendent in charge of personnel—he filled the post of the

Most Courses at Opportunity School Keyed to Industry

"A public school adult education program can not remain in an Ivory Tower . . . it must have fast and accurate communication with the public and industry . . . to us the lay advisory council has proven to be the best procedure we have yet found . . . it helps to secure over-all understanding of the program and assurance that students will get the utmost in training."

Howard L. Johnson, Principal
Emily Griffith Opportunity School

SRv

As head of Opportunity School, Howard Johnson emphasized the utilitarian nature of its programs. He went on to be superintendent from 1970 to 1973.

recently retired Peter Holm. As such, he was among the leaders of the district as it experienced the upheavals of the 1960s.

The school board passed over Johnson in 1967 when it sought a replacement for Oberholtzer. Wanting new blood, it dismissed the assistant superintendent as part of the bureaucracy that had made business as usual possible. Even at that, on June 20, 1968, the board named him deputy superintendent. In that post, Johnson was in charge of DPS negotiations when the teachers went on strike in November 1969. Back in 1963, he had conducted the inaugural "professional negotiations" between the district and the Denver Classroom Teachers Association.

The board gave Johnson a one-year contract in May 1970. Given the challenges of busing, it wanted a veteran administrator in charge of the system. In part, the governing bureau chose Johnson precisely because the new superintendent had been part of the district for many years. Ideally, he would return DPS to the good old days of Oberholtzer.

The former coach took charge right when busing for desegregation was becoming a reality. The situation, particularly the community tensions and violence in the schools, dismayed Johnson. He had never been sensitive to racial disparities in the district or the city. If anything, the superintendent denied DPS engaged in segregation. The upshot is that he was lost amidst the upheavals, providing no leadership or direction as DPS teetered on chaos. Despite this, the board gave him a two-year renewal of his contract in June 1971. Apparently, nobody else was available to lead the district at this time of troubles. In 1972, the Colorado branch of the Sons of the Revolution named Johnson its citizen of the year.

In September 1972, Johnson stated he was entering his last year with DPS. With his 65th birthday approaching, he was not going to seek an extension of his contract. In part, his announcement came when it was obvious that the board had no plans to renew the agreement. Rumors were rife that those needing to consult the superintendent, especially in the afternoon, went across the street from DPS headquarters at 414 14th Street where they sometimes found the inebriated Johnson at the bar of the St. Francis Hotel, 411 14th Street. Even so, members of the PTA heralded him. They arranged for their annual meeting on April 3, 1973, held at South High, to be Howard Johnson Day, celebrating Johnson's 45 years with the district. He passed away on July 6, 1986.

Louis Kishkunas

Just before the May 1973 school board election, the incumbents named Louis Kishkunas to replace Johnson as superintendent. Rather than selecting a senior administrator from within the district, DPS once more brought in an outsider. Its 46-year-old choice came to Denver from Pittsburgh. Born in Chicago, on March 24, 1927, Kishkunas enlisted in the Navy in 1944 fresh out of high school. After the war, he gained his bachelor's at the University of Northern Illinois followed by a master's at the University of Illinois. In 1957, Columbia Teachers College awarded him a doctorate. Physically, Kishkunas was a big man who usually towered over his companions. At times, he used his size in an effort to intimidate others.

Kishkunas returned to the Navy during the Korea War. For some years, he was in the reserves, retiring as a lieutenant commander. Back in civilian life, he taught and traveled widely, holding jobs in Rockport and Oak Park, Illinois, in addition to teaching at Joliet Junior College. The future superintendent had been an administrator in Ossining, New York, and Barrington, Illinois, before going to Pittsburgh in 1964 as an assistant superintendent. Before long, he was the Steel City deputy superintendent, taking the reins of the district in 1969. There he emphasized technical and vocational education while he worked to decentralize the school system. In 1971, teachers staged a seven-day strike against the school district while Kishkunas was in charge.

Some in Pittsburgh greatly urged Denver to hire Kishkunas. That would get him out of their city. By this time, the Pittsburgh school board was deeply divided over whether Kishkunas was the appropriate leader for its district. Like Denver, the Steel City was enmeshed in controversies over school desegregation and busing—the courts had ordered the integration of its district in 1971.

Back in 1970, Kishkunas met Jim Perrill at a national education conference. Perrill not only urged his fellow members of the Denver board of education to name Kishkunas superintendent, but he came to serve as the pedagogue's attorney. The board unanimously voted to hire Kishkunas on May 11, 1973, awarding him a three-year contract. There had been 203 other applicants for the job. Some around the administration nicknamed the superintendent "Kishyku."

The Denver Classroom Teachers Association, the teachers union, went out of its way to welcome the new superintendent. It invited members to a black-tie dinner for him at the Brown Palace at the beginning of the 1973–74 schoolyear. Leading politicians were present at the bash.

On taking charge of DPS, Kishkunas modestly stated he did not know the answers to the massive fissures dividing American society. But this did not mean DPS could not provide excellent education. Denver, he announced, was a friendly city. The district would work with the citizenry and forge ahead. Personally, the superintendent was a major aficionado of fire trucks and a collector of Model-A

Louis Kishkunas, right, arrived in Denver from Pittsburgh in 1973 as DPS superintendent. Here he presents a plaque to Bromwell principal James Manley in 1976 on the dedication of a new wing of the school.

Fords. He arranged for students at Opportunity School to restore his personal vintage fire wagon. Before long, many teachers dismissed the superintendent as a braggart.

Immediately, Kishkunas was caught in the tensions over court-ordered desegregation. He allied himself with the anti-busing board majority that had hired him. The superintendent also revealed a lingering racial fear. Kishkunas caught the attention of the *New York Times* in December 1973 when he stated he had grave concerns about forcing white students to ride school buses to black neighborhoods. Even at that, he saw that his daughter got on the bus, being transported to Cole Junior High from the family home in far southeast Denver at 8572 Oxford Drive. Integration backers cited this as a success. With the younger Kishkunas in the classroom, they claimed, Cole suddenly got new textbooks while the district repainted the building.

Tensions quickly flared between Kishkunas and Omar Blair and Kay Schomp, the two board members integration forces elected in 1973. Seeing this and wishing to keep Kishkunas in office, just before the May 1975 election, at the behest of Jim Perrill, the board voted, four-to-three, to extend the superintendent's contract from July 31, 1976, to July 31, 1978. Simultaneously, the board renewed the contracts of his three top aides. The extension of Kishkunas' contract, Perrill explained in association with his cohort Frank Southworth, who was also retiring from the board, was their parting gift to a man who had served the system well. It assured continuity in the district regardless of whom the voters selected to replace them. This proved ominous.

Bernie Valdez had joined Kay Schomp and Omar Blair in opposing the extension of Kishkunas' contract. Succeeding Perrill as board president, Valdez always projected himself as someone able to bring together different constituencies and work with everybody. He stated he did not want the job as president—his family opposed it. Given pressure from his fellows, however, he concluded it was his obligation to serve. He stepped down after two years. In the post, he increasingly wavered about the job Kishkunas was doing. (Omar Blair was vice president under Valdez.)

On the board, Ginny Rockwell also had problems with Kishkunas. She and others critics saw the superintendent as an unbending administrator who failed to redress the problems associated with the implementation of busing. While the district's chief had the firm backing of the vehemently anti-busing Naomi Bradford, neighborhood school advocates Bob Crider and Ted Hackworth were lukewarm in their support of him.

Straight Creek Journal, an alternative weekly newspaper, blasted the superintendent for his bad management and his unwillingness to admit problems. Kishkunas, it declared, was the personification of "incredible bureaucratic stupidity and insensitivity." The four-member majority of the school board—Valdez, Rockwell, Schomp, and Blair—agreed that Kishkunas was not the man for the job on December 9, 1976, when it ousted the superintendent.

Former board member Jim Perrill thereupon represented Kishkunas in settling with the board for the unexpired term of the superintendent's contract. In 1978, Kishkunas became superintendent in Hastings, Nebraska, a town of about 23,000 residents. After his retirement from the post in 1983, Kishkunas settled in Glenwood, Iowa, tending an apple orchard. On the side, he was a passionate member of the Republican Party and a Rotarian. Married in the Mennonite Church in Chicago in 1950, he was a Methodist by the time of his passing on February 29, 2008.

More Bombs

B y the time of the 1975 election, yet more upheavals had rocked DPS. Included was a new wave of bombings. Right after the 1973 balloting, a device exploded late on the evening of Saturday, May 19, at the Irving Street Center (the old Cheltenham School at the northwest corner of West Colfax Avenue and Irving Street). The building housed some DPS administrative offices, especially the district's special education program.

On the heels of the explosion, which did little damage, a bomb ripped the third floor of the DPS administration building, 414 14th Street, at around 4:00 PM on Tuesday, May 22, 1973. It cracked a cinderblock wall all the way to the basement, broke numerous windows, and injured two. The police called it a "terror bombing" in the middle of the day that was "meant to maim or kill."

There were numerous rumors about the bombings. The authorities received many false alarms, including a May 23 bomb threat at Ellsworth School—the police arrested some students there for placing a prank call. The same day, two bombs exploded in the driveway of the home of Bernie Valdez at 2109 Eliot Street. One

Photo by Phil Goodstein

From 1923 to 1975, the DPS administration building was at 414 14th Street. A bomb badly damaged the structure on May 22, 1973.

damaged his van; the other ravaged his trailer. There had been no warning. He escaped injury. On the heels of this, four flares strapped together to look like a bomb were discovered on June 9 under the hood of a bus at the Hill Top garage. A bomb exploded on Wednesday, September 2, 1973, at the offices of the DCTA at 1535 High Street. Once again, there were no arrests for the crimes.

In late October, the police found numerous unexploded bombs around the city. This was the situation on October 27, 1973, when school board member Bob Crider received a large envelope in the mail at his house at 4932 Bryant Street. It had the return address of the DCTA. Opening it, he discovered three sticks of dynamite attached to a timer. The package did not explode.

The police accused a radical Chicano attorney, Francisco "Kiko" Martinez, of sending the bomb along with two other mail devices at that time which also did not detonate. In a sensational case, lasting until 1989, the courts eventually cleared Martinez of all counts. Included was the revelation that Fred Winner, the chief judge of the United States District Court in Colorado, had colluded with the FBI, the police, and prosecutors in the effort to convict Martinez. In particular, the jurist held a secret conference with them during the first of Martinez's trials in the hope of learning the nature of the defense's case.

CANS

School board politics continued to be explosive. Following the triumph of Blair and Schomp in 1973, proponents of neighborhood schools insisted they needed a permanent organization to fight court-ordered busing. Nolan Winsett, a management consultant and real estate salesman who lived at 1570 South Milwaukee Street (he also shows up at 1500 South Bellaire Street), was the

Drawing by Gregorio Alcaro

Nolan Winsett, a former CIA operative who was a real estate broker, was the founder of the anti-busing Citizens Association of Neighborhood Schools.

driving force in creating the Citizens Association for Neighborhood Schools (CANS) in February 1974. The group was something of a consolidation of numerous efforts to have a coordinated voice opposing busing. By this time, "Preserve Our Neighborhood Schools" was a national slogan of those who were uneasy with integration and court meddling in local school districts.

Born in 1938 in Flintville, Tennessee, the CANS founder had arrived in Denver in 1949. A 1957 graduate of South High, Winsett had gone on to earn his bachelor's from DU. Between 1963 and 1968, he claimed to have worked for the CIA. The leader of CANS had links with the *Sentinel*, a chain of suburban newspapers. He had served in the past on a DPS advisory committee.

By the time he launched CANS, Winsett was a Republican activist who had connections with Bill Armstrong, elected to Congress in 1972 to the new suburban District #5 as a reactionary Republican. Winsett also had ties to Sam Zakhem, a wealthy Republican state legislator from South Denver who helped fund some of the anti-busing initiatives. Personally, Winsett described himself as a Native American, stating he was part of the Cherokee tribe. The classification, he cynically explained, meant that his children did not need to ride the bus in the name of integration since the courts judged everybody by race and exempted Indian children from the desegregation order.

Winsett was not alone in claiming to be an Indian. Many other parents also discovered a supposed Indian heritage as a way of escaping busing. There was virtually no enforcement mechanism to check this dodge. Meanwhile, CANS frequently picketed exponents of busing. The group filed for incorporation on March 21, 1974.

People, Let's Unite for Schools (PLUS) emerged in April 1974 as an effort to combat CANS. It drew on members of 50 or so civic organizations, calling for a calm community that patriotically obeyed the decisions of the court. (Many in the civil rights movement had previously been foremost proponents of civil disobedience against what they claimed were racist laws and court decisions. Now they insisted it was mandatory always to obey the law.) Stating it was not necessarily in support of busing, PLUS drew the support of numerous groups calling for a tolerant, law-abiding community such as the Denver Bar Association, League of Women Voters, and the Anti-Defamation League. Various neighborhood improvement organizations backed it. Former school board member Ed Benton was highly visible in the group.

Ann Fenton, the project director of PLUS, was a foremost backer of the Adopt-a-School Program, a DPS program emerging in the late 1970s which sought to link District #1 with the corporate community. PLUS incorporated as a non-profit. It worked closely with the PTA in various ventures. Holy Redeemer Church, 2552 Williams Street, the city's historic congregation for African-American Episcopalians, served as the office/headquarters of PLUS. The church's pastor, Richard "Rick" Kerr, had previously been an assistant at St. Thomas Episcopal in Park Hill.

The DCTA signed on with PLUS. This was the first time the teachers' association had definitely aligned itself with the busing order. Back in 1968, the assembly was deeply divided by the question of integration. When the leadership of the DCTA announced its support for the Noel Resolution that spring, threatening to call a one-day protest strike if the board did not pass the measure, the rank-and-file vehemently protested. They sought to oust the group's president and impeach a past president from the board. The controversy saw the departure of the association's executive director.

According to the DCTA's new director, Clarke Ballinger, teachers were "petrified" by integration. They feared being caught in the center of the busing controversy. Nor were they happy about court dictates transferring them in the name of integration from schools where they were well established and often close to where they lived. DCTA's endorsement of PLUS showed that teachers realized there was no escaping the court decision and they needed to make busing work for the benefit of all.

Shortly after its formation, CANS called a one-day boycott of the schools on February 22, 1974. Somewhere between 41 and 50 percent of the pupils were absent that day. Few were in the high schools. At John F. Kennedy, for example, only 161 students showed up for classes out of an enrollment of 1,457.

This was not necessarily a political statement. Many adolescents saw the boycott as an ideal excuse to ditch school. Even so, CANS argued that the boycott was a great success. The protest, it claimed, was necessary to show massive opposition to "the indoctrination of parents and students and teachers in the working of the [integration] plan rather than pure education." Building on this, CANS staged numerous other protests against busing during the spring of 1974.

Judge Doyle allowed CANS to interview in the Keyes litigation. That decision meant little. CANS was essentially an activist group, not an organization committed to legal strategies. It withdrew from the busing suit on September 11, 1974.

Still, CANS was committed to electoral politics. Toward this end, it brought in Republican leaders from Washington who were crusading to amend the United States Constitution to prohibit busing for school integration. The group drew 3,200 to such a rally. The anti-busing organization further argued that busing forces were well financed nationally, observing their funding from the NAACP Legal Defense

Fund while it presented itself as a grassroots citizen organization. It admitted that the likes of cable television magnet Bill Daniels generously contributed to the anti-busing cause.

To give the public its view of what was going on, CANS published a 20-page pamphlet, *Education by Judicial Fiat*. The work reviewed the busing wars. It emphasized that the court intervention was highly dysfunctional and a denial of the tradition of local control of the schools. Additionally, it focused on the amazing conflicts of interests between the plaintiffs and the United States District Court while it emphasized white flight as the way many concerned parents responded to

ROCKY MOUNTAIN STUDENT COALITION AGAINST RACISM

Dear Friend,

School desegregation is the number one issue facing the American people today. The papers are full of the activities of the foes of busing. The marches in Boston and Louisville and the stoning of buses carrying Black students testifies to organized nature of the racist movement today. The aim of organizations like ROAR in Boston and CANS in Denver is to prevent the busing of minority students into previously all white schools. Their campaign is designed to return us to the days of Jim Crow and "separate but equal" school segregation.

The 1954 Supreme Court decision which outlawed school segregation is 21 years old. What we need today is a revival of the civil rights movement. We say "21 years is too long. Implement the law!"

In the words of Dr. Kenneth Clark of the New York Board of Regents and longtime civil rights activist, "the Student Coalition Against Racism is one of the most important developments in the new civil rights movement of the '70s".

The second national conference of the Student Coalition Against Racism held recently in Boston was followed here in Denver by a well attended public Speak-out Against Racism and a successful student conference which mapped out a campaign of activities for the week leading up to Nov. 22nd.

Among the many activities planned are educational events including such topics as: the history of School Desegregation in Colorado; a panel discussion on Bilingual and Bicultural Education/A Right Not a Privilege. Special events will take up other questions like Indian education and other aspects of racist oppression. All of these events will culminate on Nov.22nd with a march and rally in support of desegregation, bilingual and bicultural education and affirmative action.

November 22nd is a day that has been set to coordinate support activities in every major US city. The impact of these concurrent events will be a powerful answer to the anti-busing forces and it will strengthen the movement for desegregation.

To carry-out this counter-offensive we need your support and financial help. Please fill-out the attached endorser card and send your generous contribution to us today.

JAMES REYNOLDS
Dir, Colo. Civil Rights Comm.

JOSEPHINE PEREZ
Plaintiff, Keys Case

ROBIN POWERS
Coordinator, RMSCAR

JOE EDDIE ROY, Sr.; Mrs.
Pres, Colo/Wyo. Conf. of Branches,NAACP

KEEP THE BUSES ROLLING

ROCKY MTN. STUDENT COALITION AGAINST RACISM
1739 MARION STREET
DENVER, COLORADO 80218

Doris Banks Papers, Auraria Archives

At the same time anti-busing forces mobilized, so did supporters of integration. "Keep the Buses Rolling" was the slogan of the Rocky Mountain Student Coalition Against Racism in the mid-1970s.

forced busing. The brochure repeatedly quoted the opinion of Justice Lewis Powell in the Keyes case. It argued his fears that a mechanical busing order could more harm than assist education were becoming true.

More than anything, CANS called for resistance and delay of the court order, being sure that the busing mandate was soon going to collapse. Here it followed the policy of school board president Jim Perrill. He insisted DPS do nothing to facilitate busing for integration. With opposition to busing growing across the country, ideally foes of the program might yet triumph despite the court rulings.

In a way, the comments of Perrill assisted the United States District Court. Part of the Supreme Court's order for implementation of the 1954 decision on school integration was that federal courts review local integration efforts based on "good faith implementation." The United States District Court had no problem deciding that, under the leadership of Perrill, DPS did not show any good faith.

Seeing the need to act locally, CANS' prime effort was an initiated petition to amend the Colorado Constitution in November 1974. The measure was to "prohibit the assignment or transportation of students to public education institutions in order to achieve a racial balance of pupils at such institutions." Sponsors argued they were actually the ones fully in tune with the Civil Rights Revolution: there was to be no official governmental judgment of people based on their color or ethnicity. To emphasize this, they specifically linked the amendment with an existing part of the constitution that prohibited the teaching of any religious/sectarian doctrines in the public schools. They soon gathered 94,167 signatures, more than twice the number necessary for the measure to make the ballot, filing them with the secretary of state on July 5, 1974. The measure officially became Proposition Eight.

As the election loomed, CANS announced students should boycott classes every Friday in October to protest the court interference in the local school district. Integration activists reacted with fury. CANS, they declared, was trying to destroy the public school system and cause unnecessary community strife. They even claimed that by having students stay out of classes at that time, the result would reduce state and federal funding to the district—government money to the schools was based on the number of students who showed up in class in late September/early October. Backers of busing convinced Judge Doyle to issue an injunction against CANS' call for the boycott. When it appeared this might lead the government to gain possession of the CANS' mailing and membership lists, its head, Nolan Winsett destroyed them. He stated he had more than 20,000 names on them. In different accounts, membership ranged from 1,500 to 20,000. Membership cost $45.00 per family with a $450 corporate membership. CANS had a treasury of $12,000.

The school boycott flopped. Few supported it. By this time, integration champions of the schools, who had called for boycotts in the past as part of civil rights protests, including to force the school board to adopt the Noel Resolution, insisted that every day of school was so important that it was intolerable ever to boycott the schools even for a one-day protest.

Meanwhile, CANS pushed through Proposition Eight, 485,536–220,812. Denver endorsed it, 101,654–60,681. The CANS' amendment had the most support of any issue or candidate on the ballot. By this time, both the Colorado Association of

School Boards and the Colorado Association of School Board Executives had come out against busing, complaining the court order interfered with school autonomy.

The November 1974 polling also saw voters adopt two other measures provoked by busing. Both limited the ability of Denver to annex suburban land. Until the onset of court-ordered desegregation, many living in unincorporated areas adjacent to the Mile High City were happy to become part of Denver, partially pulled in by the schools. Now, with busing in place, the suburbs sought to protect themselves from Denver. Around the time that busing controversies soared, Wheat Ridge and Lakewood incorporated to keep Denver out. Those opposed to busing and the seemingly imperial power of the Mile High City, additionally sought to limit Denver's annexation powers by amending the state constitution.

Frieda Poundstone, a suburban politician and lobbyist close to the politically charged, reactionary Coors family, was the prime player in promoting a measure prohibiting the Mile High City from annexing land without the expressed authorization of voters living in the targeted property. Her measure, Proposition One, easily passed, 409,174–292,060. Denver rejected it 61,320–95,163. Simultaneously, the electorate adopted Proposition Five, 397,442–252,256 (58,926–91,942 in Denver). It created a Denver/suburban boundary commission to review and authorize annexations. The Mile High City had three seats on it; Adams, Arapahoe, and Jefferson counties each had one representative. Since a majority was necessary for Denver to annex the land, the board killed all annexation proposals until the late 1980s when the drive to build Denver International Airport saw the entire establishment rally to permit the Mile High City to take the desired real estate.

The immediate goal of the 1974 measures was most successful in protecting suburban students from the morass of Denver Public Schools and the threat of busing. As a sign of distrust in the district, Mile High voters also rejected a request to hike the mill levy in November 1974, 38,605–61,181. In part, they said no because they believed DPS would primarily use the extra money to pay for busing.

At the same time, in the Watergate election, voters put into office such Democratic candidates as Richard Lamm for governor and Gary Hart for the United States Senate. While the Democrats gained the Colorado House of Representatives for the first time in a decade, they failed to win the Senate. Anti-busing activists in the suburbs assured those areas, particularly Arapahoe and Jefferson counties, became dominating outposts of the Republicans. Not until the early 21st century were the Democrats able to break that hold and again gain a majority in the General Assembly.

The Watergate election impacted a national anti-busing drive. As he sought to consolidate himself in office and win re-election in 1972, President Richard Nixon openly backed the campaign to amend the United States Constitution to prohibit school busing for racial integration. The matter lingered until after the 1976 election of Jimmy Carter to the presidency. By that time, the Democrats, though not at all enthusiastic about busing, at least accepted that it might be necessary to redress segregation. They had no use for the constitutional amendment, killing it.

Meanwhile, ever more people voted with their feet, leaving Denver to escape busing. At a time when the metropolitan area sprawled, growing from a population

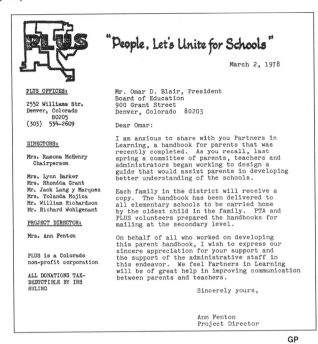

"People, Let's Unite for Schools"

March 2, 1978

PLUS OFFICES:

2552 Williams Str.
Denver, Colorado
80205
(303) 534-2609

DIRECTORS:

Mrs. Ramona McHenry
 Chairperson

Mrs. Lynn Barker
Mrs. Rhondda Grant
Mr. Jack Lang y Marquez
Mrs. Yolanda Mojica
Mr. William Richardson
Mr. Richard Wohlgenant

PROJECT DIRECTOR:

Mrs. Ann Fenton

PLUS is a Colorado
non-profit corporation

ALL DONATIONS TAX-
DEDUCTIBLE BY IRS
RULING

Mr. Omar D. Blair, President
Board of Education
900 Grant Street
Denver, Colorado 80203

Dear Omar:

I am anxious to share with you Partners in
Learning, a handbook for parents that was
recently completed. As you recall, last
spring a committee of parents, teachers and
administrators began working to design a
guide that would assist parents in developing
better understanding of the schools.

Each family in the district will receive a
copy. The handbook has been delivered to
all elementary schools to be carried home
by the oldest child in the family. PTA and
PLUS volunteers prepared the handbooks for
mailing at the secondary level.

On behalf of all who worked on developing
this parent handbook, I wish to express our
sincere appreciation for your support and
the support of the administrative staff in
this endeavor. We feel Partners in Learning
will be of great help in improving communication
between parents and teachers.

Sincerely yours,

Ann Fenton
Project Director

GP

People, Let's Unite for Schools (PLUS) was a civil rights group working
to get the community to accept court-ordered busing in the 1970s.

of 1,239,545 in 1970 to 1,620,902 in 1980, Denver's population declined from 514,678 to 492,365. A decade later, the Mile High City had shrunk to 467,610 while the greater metropolitan area was up to 1,980,140. School busing alone was not responsible for the population loss. Major cities were drastically losing population across the country during this epoch. The Mile High decline partially stemmed from urban renewal, particularly the deliberate destruction of low-income housing during those 20 years.

Not only did the total enrollment of DPS decline in the wake of busing, but the number and percentage of white students in the schools plummeted. Whereas 93.7 percent of children in the suburbs went to public schools, the number in District #1 was 85.9 percent in the 1980s. At that time, the consolidated Jefferson County School District R-1 surpassed DPS as the largest system in the state. In 1986–87, DPS had 60,252 students versus 75,613 in Jefferson County. The count in 2001 showed Jefferson County with 87,703 compared to 70,817 in DPS. Denver once more gained the lead in 2013-14 when it had 86,043 students when Jefferson County counted 85,983.

A generational pattern came to mark many middle-class white Denver neighborhoods. While young couples often settled in the city, a considerable number moved to the suburbs once their children were of school age. A gap so opened in numerous sections of town where there were few public school children in stable white middle-class areas.

A side effect of busing was the rise in visibility of the emerging homosexual community. Not only was this a period when social norms and laws against homosexuality more or less dissipated, but many gays sought to show their responsibility and support of the system. In the process, they often became proud homeowners in places such as Capitol Hill, Baker, and Curtis Park. Since, at that time, they did not have to worry about children and schools, they did not move out in the face of the increasing disconnect between the schools and parents.

Naomi Bradford

Most of these issues were beyond the scope of CANS. The group suffered turbulence in early 1975 when it sought to work with Return Our Alienated Rights (ROAR), a group physically fighting school busing in Boston where violence soared. About 375 members resigned from CANS, stating they wanted to have nothing to do with the Klan-like, neo-Nazi behavior of ROAR. The courts dismissed a suit filed in May 1975 by 10 residents demanding that the attorney general and the Colorado Department of Education enforce the provisions of the anti-busing amendment which CANS had pushed through the previous November.

As the May 1975 school board election approached, CANS leader Nolan Winsett sought a place on the agency overseeing DPS. So did the head of the group's powerful section in southwest Denver, Naomi Bradford of 2382 South Raleigh Street. The latter won a seat; Winsett came in fourth in a field of eight. For the next couple of years, members of CANS continued to squabble with the school board, the courts, and each other. Eventually, the group provoked the wrath of Superintendent Kishkunas who blasted the organization for its "ostrich" opposition to court-ordered busing.

After the 1977 school balloting, when Winsett again lost as a contender for the board, CANS essentially faded away. (Winsett died on May 4, 2013, after a long illness.) While candidates opposed to busing continued to win places on the board into the 1980s, they no longer had the ideological frenzy of those previously elected. For the most part, such contenders simply projected themselves as people advocating common sense against an ever more dysfunctional district that was under the control of the United States District Court rather than the voters or the board of education.

During her 18 years on the school board, Naomi Bradford was the dying remnant of the anti-busing passions of the late 1960s/early 1970s. Born Naomi Llewella Taylor in Los Angeles on July 1, 1940, she had a tough childhood with her poverty-stricken family constantly moving. For a while, she joined them in the fields when they were migrant farmworkers in Oregon. Constantly being in and out of different schools, the young woman did not perform well academically.

In 1960, Naomi Taylor married Ronald "Ron" Bradford, a bus driver. Soon she was the mother of three children. In some accounts, she stated she attended Concordia College in Oregon. In other versions, she asserted she had earned a teaching degree from Concordia College in Seward, Nebraska. Not disclosing at what level or what subject she taught, she recalled being an instructor for one year in a California public school before being in the classroom for three years in

Bromwell School Library

By the time she left the school board in 1993, Naomi Bradford was the last of the members who had risen based on a fierce opposition to mandatory school busing.

private and religious schools in Washington state and Colorado. Eventually, Bradford studied at the for-profit University of Phoenix and at a forerunner of Colorado Christian University. The candidate went on to teach in parochial schools and at West High, coming to be the principal of North East Charter Academy in Denver.

In many ways, Bradford was the personification of lower-middle-class whites opposed to busing. These were people who struggled to survive economically. Many were lured by demagogues who attacked the civil rights movement with the message that if blacks got more, whites would get less. People comparable to Bradford particularly feared African-Americans coming to their neighborhoods via school busing, sure that blacks would bring the problems of the so-called ghetto with them. Against this, Bradford and CANS celebrated neighborhood schools filled with children walking to the bastions of education. Besides, she insisted, schools had to be community centers. By forcing children on the bus, the courts separated residents from these vital institutions that shaped neighborhoods.

Originally, Bradford's husband had been the anti-busing activist in the family, serving as the inaugural secretary-treasurer of CANS. Once president of the Johnson School PTA, Naomi Bradford had been most active in the 1974 push to amend the Colorado Constitution to prohibit school busing for racial integration. She did so as a leader of CANS. Additionally, she was a stalwart member of the Harvey Park Improvement Association. Doris Hackworth, the wife of school board member Ted Hackworth, once headed it.

In January 1975, Bradford announced for the school board along with Winsett. Both stressed they were running as individuals, not a ticket. Then self-described as a housewife who was married to a Regional Transportation District (RTD) driver, Bradford promised she would be a fulltime board member. She observed that her children at Johnson School were not subject to busing because she had registered them as having American Indian heritage—she pointed out she was part Navajo and part Hispanic. Building on her political connections and the lingering opposition to busing, Bradford won the second seat in the 1975 balloting, trailing the pro-integration Ginny Rockwell.

No sooner was Bradford on the board than she was a loose cannon. She constantly clashed with her fellow members. Time and again, she described herself as a fighter. Given the general complacency of the board and the district, she proclaimed that she had to shake it up.

The insurgent was not always able to back her assertions. In 1976, neighborhood school advocates Bernie Valdez and Bob Crider condemned her for false information about the district's pension fund. Bradford had loudly charged a conflict of interest existed between DPS and Colorado National Bank, the manager of the system's pension fund. At that time, Ginny Rockwell's husband, Bruce Rockwell, was the foremost figure at the bank. The district explained it put the money into Colorado National because the financial institution gave it the best deal. The dispute so escalated that other members of the board voted, five to two, to censure her on August 12, 1976—Ted Hackworth joined her in saying no to the motion.

By this time, fellow anti-busing board member Crider mocked Bradford for her rambling, incoherent speeches. *Straight Creek Journal* described her as being "abusive, demeaning, and vindictive." Despite such attacks, Bradford did not shut up. She refused to join other members of the board on retreats in the mountains. At a time when DPS was suffering from severe financial shortages, she especially ripped board "junkets," including trips to out-of-state conferences. Besides, citing her childhood experiences, she knew what poverty meant. This was unlike virtually anybody else who had ever served on the school board. All, she explained, had been either middle-class or upper-class. She insisted she brought a view from the bottom to the agency.

Most of all, Bradford endlessly quarreled with Omar Blair. The two continually accused each other of unethical conduct. The CANS activist also hinted he sexually harassed her. Republican loyalists generally supported her at a time when they were increasingly losing elected posts within the city. In both 1978 and 1980, the GOP nominated Bradford to run for Congress against Pat Schroeder. Though she lost both races, she kept her position on the school board in balloting in 1981 and 1987. In both instances, Bradford had excellent name recognition and appealed to voters who wanted a fighter on the board.

From 1983 to 1985, Bradford was president of the agency. This was a great achievement. It also reflected how anti-busing forces made headway in the 1981 and 1983 board elections. Drawing on Republican Party links, Bradford gained appointment under Ronald Reagan as the regional director of ACTION. Community pursuits included serving on the board of Hispanics of Colorado. The Colorado Association of School Boards Hall of Fame and the DPS Athletic Hall of Fame honored her. The last observed her intent commitment to competitive school athletics.

(The DPS Athletic Hall of Fame emerged in 1975. It had various subsections including for coaches, athletes, and members of the community who supported school sports programs. Not surprisingly, it frequently enshrined members of the school board and the administration. The district did not have a specific academic or teachers hall of fame.)

Tensions were always extremely taut between Bradford and the DCTA. Rather than granting that the union was a legitimate voice of instructors and had full legal recognition as their bargaining agent, she urged the district to reject its demands. This was particularly the case in 1991 when the DCTA threatened to strike in response to the intransigence of management. Bradford thereupon branded teachers who were willing to stand up for themselves by a readiness to strike as "wretched human beings." When DCTA members responded by picketing her house, her son swung a baseball bat at the teachers. The DCTA called her an "embarrassment" to Denver education. The union celebrated

NSAC

Joseph Brzeinski was superintendent from 1977 to 1984. Here he meets with some of the district's students.

when she lost her bid for a fourth term in 1993. (Back in 1987, the Denver Area Labor Federation, representing unions affiliated with the AFL–CIO, including the Denver Federation of Teachers, had endorsed Bradford for re-election.)

In 1996, out of office, Bradford unsuccessfully took on corporate Democrat William "Gully" Stanford, a major advocate of charter schools, in the race for the Denver seat on the state board of education. He triumphed 90,538–79,224. The victor, once a member of the Chamber of Commerce Education Committee, had been active in the collaborative decision-making council at Smiley and had spoken favorably about vouchers. Besides being a publicist for the Denver Center for the Performing Arts, Stanford was among the backers in creating the Denver School of the Arts. In the race, Bradford described herself as a management consultant. By the time of her death on March 13, 2007, from heart disease, Bradford had relocated to Lakewood. During her years in office, she had helped hire and fire Joseph Brzeinski as superintendent.

Joseph E. Brzeinski

In January 1977, Bradford had moved to rehire Kishkunas as superintendent. She failed to convince her fellow members of the board. The bureau had ousted him after it had reviewed his performance. This proved ominous for his successor, Joseph Brzeinski. He was another stalwart of the system.

Born in Denver on January 1, 1926, the new superintendent grew up at 4767 High Street, directly to the north of Elyria School. His mother was a school librarian, encouraging him to do well in school. From Elyria he went to Cole Junior High before graduating from Manual in 1944. Brzeinski thereupon joined the military. After the war, he enrolled at the University of Denver, going on to get a master's from the school. In 1949, he signed on as a classroom teacher. As a bright young scholar and instructor, Brzeinski caught the eye of Columbia Teachers College. When he was a teacher at Smedley in 1955, it awarded him a year-long study scholarship. Eventually, he received his doctorate from the renowned New York school. His dissertation focused on how the leadership of a district can affect change. By the time he was superintendent, he lived in new southeast Denver at 3270 South Clermont Street near Bradley School.

In 1957, Brzeinski moved to the administration. During the 1960s, he steadily rose in DPS, going from the coordinator of instruction to the supervisor of general curriculum to the director of the department of research to the head of the planning department. Along the way, he emerged as the coordinator of the district's federal program, an effort to assure DPS got the most possible dollars it could from Washington initiatives nurturing education. He was among the top officials under Superintendent Gilberts. On September 13, 1973, Brzeinski emerged as an assistant superintendent. Two years later, with Roscoe Davidson, he became associate superintendent—this was a new post. In many ways, Brzeinski was the man who made the district work, particularly the front office, during the Kishkunas years.

An excellent bureaucratic fighter, Brzeinski emerged as interim superintendent on March 5, 1977, following the ouster of Kishkunas. He gained the post when he beat out three other top figures in the administration, Carle Stenmark, James O'Hara, and James Bailey, after a grueling 11-hour executive session of the board. Some members did not want to repeat the past mistake of naming a superintendent right before a board election. Not until February 17, 1978, did the governing body officially appoint Brzeinski superintendent. He was the first DPS alumnus to hold the post. In February 1983, with school board elections looming, the board extended the chief's contract until 1986. Unwittingly, it set the stage for a repeat of what happened to Kishkunas.

On taking charge of DPS, Brzeinski conducted something of a purge of insiders, seeing that his supporters had key positions over those who had backed Kishkunas or the new superintendent's rivals. As it had been for years, the administration was dominated by men. They made up 120 of the district's 130 top-paid executives. Part of his effort in reorganizing the front office, the superintendent explained, was consolidating positions given the drastic decline in enrollment.

Plummeting numbers, Brzeinski further observed, meant DPS had to close schools. The district still had the capacity to educate 100,000 children while its membership was down to 66,000. His goal, he repeatedly stated, was to restore DPS as a "Cadillac system," which he recalled as a student and a teacher. As became a repeated promise among superintendents, Brzeinski vowed the system would concentrate on reading for elementary children. He swore that art and music would be part of the general curriculum. "Great Schools Start Here" was the slogan he plastered on buildings for the start of the 1978–79 schoolyear. Another year, he ordered the schools to display numerous signs declaring "Achievement–Standards–Progress."

Photo by Phil Goodstein

Superintendent Joseph Brzeinski saw DPS place "Welcome" signs on the doors of its buildings, emphasizing they were community assets, not isolated fortresses. Most of the signs soon disappeared. This one remained at Slavens School, 3000 South Clayton Street, into the 2010s. By that time, the school had closed its main entrance in favor of an entry by its parking lot.

Additionally, on taking charge as superintendent, Brzeinski saw the schools place "Welcome" decals on the front doors. He also created the Citizen Service and Response Center. Located at the central administration headquarters, it was a new name for the public relations department. The office, the superintendent stressed, was a place where the citizenry could learn what was happening in the schools. The moves were necessary, he argued, because the schools had become extremely unfriendly, unwelcoming places. Amidst the bombings and violence during the controversies over desegregation, the schools had to increase their security. This included locking off virtually all doors to the buildings except for the main entry. In some places, there were no handles on the outside of doors.

As part of the Citizen Response Center, DPS worked closely with the PTA, the Chamber of Commerce, and the Board of Realtors. The result was a handbook for real estate agents. It outlined the location, programs, and achievements of each of the city's schools. Ideally, this way parents with school-aged children could buy homes in Denver knowing their children would be attending quality schools.

Eventually, schools locked their doors during the schoolday. Those needing to get in, including students, had to ring a bell and identify themselves via an intercom system. Many of the schools had security cameras, especially around the exterior. The cameras did not necessarily show what occurred inside the buildings. This came out after an April 24, 2018, police raid on Rise Up Community School, 2342

Broadway. A DPS alternative program, its teachers and students complained that the police entered the building with guns drawn, looking for a student wanted by Lakewood. The police denied they had pulled their weapons. No surveillance film revealed what had happened. In the wake of the incident, some students of questionable immigration status quit attending class, fearful of another police raid.

As had administrators since at least before World War I, Brzeinski also found he had to concentrate on the social-welfare role of the schools. Such assistance was so much part of DPS that the district had a Pupil Welfare Fund. Dating from the early 20th century, it provided money for students in urgent need. The federal Department of Agriculture encouraged school nutrition programs, offering steeply discounted commodities to the schools for lunch programs. Included in the 1950s was allowing the district to buy one-half pint cartons of milk for three cents each. This allowed the district to sell them to students for five cents each. Drinking milk daily, school and medical authorities agreed, was necessary for healthy bodies and healthy learning.

After initially opposing a citizen effort, Brzeinski agreed about the importance of breakfast programs in some schools, particularly those in poverty-stricken neighborhoods. All too many youngsters, he realized, were dependent on school meals—they were the most nourishing ones children ate daily. This was so much the case that in some places teachers, staff, and social workers arranged care packets for the students for days when schools were not in session. Illustrative was the weekend food program of the Greater Park Hill Community. During the schoolyear, the neighborhood group provided five meals and two snacks during weekends for students who otherwise might go hungry. In the course of 2019–20, it reached out to about 70 youngsters. By that time, the city operated a free lunch program at many schools in the summer.

Adopt-a-School

Besides the nutrition programs, under Brzeinski the district also reflected DPS's traditional close cooperation with the world of business. Though the direct link between the Chamber of Commerce and DPS faded during the 1960s and 1970s when the corporate body no longer had caucuses designed to put its supporters and members on the school board, the business syndicate continued to stress the vital role of the schools. The Chamber had an Action Force on Education. Through it, the assembly readily advised DPS as to whom to choose as superintendent and what programs the district should embrace.

As they had been for years, corporate voices were especially loud in the 1970s in criticizing the schools. Graduates, they complained, were inept, unable to perform what management believed were simple tasks that any young adult should be able to complete. Alas, this included products of both supposedly good suburban schools and those churned out by DPS. The new employees could not make change or balance a checkbook. Frequently, they were irresponsible, tardy, and had little team commitment. Employers, consequently, had to spend extra funds to train them.

There was nothing new about such laments. In part, DPS had instituted the Proficiency and Review examination in 1960 to assure that all high school graduates were literate, competent members of society. The same year, the administration beefed up its graduation requirements. As the complaints showed, the difficulties persisted. Nor were they limited to Denver—they were everywhere.

Washington agreed. In 1977, as a trailblazing means to solve the problem, the federal Department of Health Education and Welfare awarded DPS a grant to coordinate a partnership between businesses and the schools. The goal was to graduate students who valued timeliness and customer service. In response, not only did DPS once more toughen its graduation requirements, but it launched the Adopt-a-School program under the district's Department of Instructional Services.

Adopt-a-School was a partnership between 17th Street and District #1. Leading employers signed on. Under the program,

Adopt-a-School was a corporate-oriented program to increase business involvement in DPS. Launched with federal support in 1977, it suffered revenue shortages in the 1980s whereby the PTA staged fundraisers for it, including efforts to compile a cookbook.

companies embraced specific schools. Executives visited the classrooms, informing future employees of what business was really all about: obedience and a commitment to the status quo. Since the 19th century, DPS and the Chamber of Commerce had agreed that teaching students as much was a prime role of the schools.

Initially, ten businesses joined, supporting six schools as part of the Adopt-a-School initiative. Denver Brick and Pipe was among the pioneers, appropriately teaming up with Manual High School whose students had once been the Bricklayers. The United Bank of Denver embraced Baker Junior High. King Soopers and Mountain Bell (the telephone monopoly) adopted Kepner Junior High. Pepsi and Rockmont Envelopes, both in an industrial district close to Globeville, sponsored Garden Place Elementary at 45th Avenue and Lincoln Street. The Montbello-based Samsonite adopted Oakland Elementary, 4825–45–65 Oakland Street, and the emerging McGlone Elementary, 4500 Crown Boulevard. The East Denver Kiwanis Club asserted itself at Teller Elementary, 1150 Garfield Street.

Some government institutions were among those embracing Adopt-a-School. Lowry Air Force Base, for example, worked with children at Smith Elementary. Every Friday, members of its Sergeants' Association visited Smith for a reading hour. The University of Colorado Health Sciences Center, then at Ninth Avenue and Colorado Boulevard, reached out to the nearby Gove Junior High. Rocky Mountain Empire Sports, the owner of the Denver Broncos and the minor league Denver Bears baseball team, connected with Lake Junior High, a school about half-a-mile west of Mile High Stadium.

In places, the sponsoring firms often spotted promising students, offering them jobs. Rather than having a say in the matter and how dictates of businesses fit in with the curriculum, teachers sometimes found themselves told to give the businesspeople a free hand. On occasion this led to dreary classroom sessions since not all of the executives were inspiring, literate speakers. The program's requirements of time and money in adopting a school precluded all but major firms from participating in it. Even at that, Adopt-a-School often lacked manpower. The Denver Council of the PTA called for concerned parents to donate their time to assist the initiative. In part, Adopt-a-School needed to recruit volunteers because sponsoring businesses failed to provide the promised assistance.

Despite these problems, DPS celebrated Adopt-a-School as an outstanding success. Washington cited the Mile High program as a national model. The effort faded after about a decade. District #1 subsequently featured what it called "Business Connect," another effort to show the corporate orientation of the system. The DPS Foundation, a group emerging in 1992, emphasized business collaboration with the schools. It reported that, as of 2014–16, it worked with 73 firms in partnering at 42 schools. The corporations donated around $125,000 in

Photo by Phil Goodstein

In the 21st century, schools displayed banners advertising corporate backers, including liquor stores. This display was on the fence at McKinley–Thatcher School at the northwest corner of South Logan Street and Louisiana Avenue.

direct and in-kind materials to the schools they were helping. Representatives of many 17th Street firms filled the board of the DPS Foundation.

The presence of business interests naturally impacted the scope of classes. Little mention was made of trade unions and the historic clashes between labor and management. Speakers from unions rarely had the same chance as businesses to address students, introducing them to this part of the world of work. During the 1970s and 1980s, Coors Brewery, an avid participant in the Adopt-a-School initiative, was engaged in a vicious anti-union campaign. Its representatives brought the firm's anti-union perspective into the classrooms. Besides so being able to slant the nature of what the schools taught, companies found they could deduct the cost of their donations to the district from their taxes.

About the time DPS was heralding Adopt-a-School, corporations were eagerly moving into the classrooms. This included being allowed to place vending machines selling soda pop and snacks in hallways. Their installation marked the failure of a campaign of the 1970s to teach children healthy dining complete with nutritious meals in lunchrooms. At times, in the name of generating more money for the schools, the PTA collaborated with merchants, especially major national chains. Through something called School Cash, the PTA arranged for funds to go to schools based on how much parents spent at participating merchants.

Advertising was often part of materials provided to the schools, including for supposedly educational programs. In places, schools placed banners on their fences heralding sponsors of educational ventures. Among them were liquor stores. The backers of the program saw no irony about this even while the schools had programs warning youngsters about the dangers of alcohol, drugs, and tobacco. For that matter, many PTAs had fundraisers centered around liquor stores and drinking. At Lincoln Elementary, a fence display touted the advantages of chiropractic treatment for youngsters.

Even before embracing Adopt-a-School, DPS had operated Project Business in eighth-grade classrooms. Launched in 1971 with foundation money and the backing of Junior Achievement, this was an effort to educate students about the wonders of the private enterprise system. Missing was any education about what students faced as life-long wage earners.

Junior Achievement was a well-established national program recruiting high school students into the world of business. It was an effort seeking to transform adolescents into aspiring capitalists. Businesses worked with the schools in sponsoring the program where students formed miniature companies that marketed their securities and goods to supportive buyers. Back in the mid-20th century, there was a junior chamber of commerce at East and Manual. A goal was to assure boys and girls embraced the business ethic. It was not connected with the Junior Chamber of Commerce that became the Jaycees. Eventually, Denver Junior Achievement operated out of the headquarters of the Chamber of Commerce.

Promoters emphasized that Adopt-a-School and the district's business orientation helped with finances. Regardless of how much money taxpayers appropriated for the district, it was never enough. This was particularly the case at individual schools. Extra expenses were needed to pay for field trips and enhancement

Photo by Phil Goodstein

At times, the Denver Metro Chamber of Commerce has had an overwhelming presence in Denver Public Schools. On other occasions, it seems to get its wires crossed. Here is the alley side of its headquarters at the west corner of 15th and Market streets.

programs. The businesses adopting schools sometimes helped underwrite them. So did philanthropic grants.

Completely missing from such an orientation were the views of Margaret Haley, the firebrand founder of what became the American Federation of Teachers. At the 1901 convention of the National Education Association, she loudly declared the schools did not want charity. If business interests and the wealthy truly wanted to help the schools, they would agree to a tax system whereby they paid their fair share for them. A prime necessity for a free education system, Haley and her backers agreed, was that it had to be free of the charity of the rich.

That was a forbidden topic, both at the beginning of the 20th century and one hundred years later. During the heyday of the Adopt-a-School program, the Public Education & Business Coalition emerged to institutionalize corporate domination of the schools. Its board was a reflection of the area's most powerful and largest employers including Gates Rubber, Columbia Hospitals, United Bank (eventually swallowed by Wells Fargo), US West (then the area telephone company), and United Airlines. Top law firms, such as Holland & Hart, Sherman & Howard, Brownstein Hyatt Farber, and Holme Roberts & Owen, were on board. The *Denver Post*, which under owner Dean Singleton was outspokenly anti-union, was another key backer.

As much as in the day when most school board members were closely linked to the Chamber of Commerce, corporate Denver got the school system it wanted and deserved. For the most part, 17th Street also backed DPS bond issues and building programs. Even as it did so, it always had to be aware of the supervision of the United States District Court.

A Note on Sources:

Reports about Gilberts' planned departure were in *RMN*, May 1, 1970, p. 1, and *DP*, May 1, 1970, p. 1. *SB*, May 11, 1970, pp. 125–26, printed the superintendent's resignation statement. Schwartzkopf, "Collective Bargaining," 201, quotes Gilberts as leaving DPS because he believed the school board was not rational on integration and was on a destructive course. Dick Koeppe mentioned Gilberts' desperate desire to get out of Denver during an August 26, 2019, interview. At that time, Koeppe also shared stories about Gilberts in Oregon.

Art Branscombe has an erroneous story that Gilberts was fired in his interview in *Our Neighborhood Schools* in Alweis, *Rebels Remembered*. A special section of *DP*, September 22, 1969, was "Schools: Relevant Restive Remiss?" It outlined the controversies faced by the district and the continuing pressures on public education everywhere.

Taylor, "Leadership," 91, 155–57, 185, 189, touches on the career of Howard Johnson. He is in the 1958 *Who's*, 292. *SRv*, January 1957, p. 4, heralded Johnson's leadership of Opportunity School. *SB*, April 24, 1965, p. 124, mentioned his promotion to assistant superintendent. Schwartzkopf, "Collective Bargaining," 201, observes Johnson's role in the 1962 "professional negotiations" with the DCTA. *RMN*, June 19, 1970, p. 8, observed DPS naming him superintendent. *SN*, February 14, 1972, p. 29, acclaimed the Sons of the American Revolution honor. The 1972–73 PTA History Notebook in GP has the proclamation of Howard Johnson Day. *DP*, July 10, 1986, p. 28, recalled his career. Jimi O'Connor remembered Johnson and the superintendent being in the bar of the St. Francis Hotel during chats on March 5, 2011, and January 9, 2018. He also called my attention to Johnson as a foster parent.

DP, May 12, 1973, p. 1, reported the hiring of Louis Kishkunas. *SN*, September 5, 1973, p. 1, had the superintendent's greetings to the city and district. *DP*, May 10, 1975, p. 5, *SN*, May 12, 1975, p. 39, and *RMN*, May 10, 1975, p. 5, told of the extension of Kishkunas' contract. Taylor, "Leadership," 191–92, deals with his tenure. Orfield, *Must We Bus?* 356, observes the 1971 busing order in Pittsburgh, saying nothing about the role of Kishkunas. *NYT*, January 11, 1971, reported the end of the Pittsburgh teachers strike.

A copy of the invitation to the DCTA black-tie dinner for Kishkunas is in the 1973–74 PTA Historian's Notebook in GP. Dorolyn Griebenaw remembered "Kishyku" as the nickname for the superintendent during a discussion on February 27, 2018. On October 3, 2015, Jimi O'Connor shared the story about Kishkunas and fire trucks. He described the superintendent as a braggart during an interview on January 9, 2018. Schwartzkopf, "Collective Bargaining," 201, profiles the administrator as a bull in a china shop.

DP, December 3, 1976, p. 1, observed mounting tensions over Kishkunas. *DP*, December 10, 1976, p. 1, *RMN*, December 10, 1976, p. 5, and *SN*, January 31, 1977, p. 19, reported his ouster. *SCJ*, December 16, 1976, pp. 4–5, reviewed the controversy in an editorial, "Why Kishkunas Was Canned." In passing, the paper blasted the hideous coverage of the schools in the *Post* and *News*. It argued there was no liberal bloc on the school board. The supposed liberals simply wanted a functioning system within the framework of following the court order. They were as committed to the corporate domination of the schools as the outright anti-busing conservatives.

Meadow, "Hard Years," *CJ*, May 8, 1974, pp. 23–26, quotes Kishkunas' fears about white students having to ride buses to black neighborhoods. He cites *NYT* of December 28, 1973. The Evie Dennis interview in *Our Neighborhood Schools* in Alweis, *Rebels Remembered*, reports Kishkunas sent his daughter to Cole, resulting in the school getting new textbooks. *RMN*, January 24, 1977, p. 5, mentioned the settlement with Kishkunas. Kurt Johnson contributed an obituary about the former superintendent to the web site findagrave.com.

Taylor, "Leadership," 197–98, 206, mentions the bombings. *RMN*, May 21, 1973, p. 11, told of the explosion at the Irving Street Center. It reported the blast at 414 14th Street, May 22, 1973, p. 1, and observed the police's conclusion it was a "terror bombing," May 23, 1973, p. 5. *RMN*, June 10, 1974, p. 5, reported the discovery of the flares under the hood of a bus at the Hill Top garage. I discuss the wave of bombings in *DIA*, 148–57. Kiko Martinez has shared memories of his case. In 1995–96, Walter Gerash allowed me to read his file on Martinez. Taylor, "Leadership," 206–07, implies Martinez committed the crime. *CANS, Judicial Fiat*, 15, reviews the bombings.

Orfield, *Must We Bus?* 6, observes the "Preserve Our Neighborhood Schools" slogan. There was a good deal on CANS in the what was drawer 33 of the Branscombe papers. *GPHN*, July 21, 1994, pp. 8–9, recalled CANS as a primary anti-busing force. Materials on the group are in FF 1:1 of the Keyes papers, COU 931, at the CU Archives. *DP*, March 16, 1977, p. 12, observed CANS' links to the *Sentinel* and Bill Armstrong. Bailey, "Journey Full Circle," 117–18, states CANS had 1,500 members. *SCJ*, July 2, 1974, p. 6, reported it had 20,000 members. Pearson, "Denver Case," 205–06, focuses on CANS' emergence and activities. The study stresses the anti-busing amendment.

Ibid. mentions *Education by Judicial Fiat*. A copy of the pamphlet is in FF 1:1 of the Keyes papers. A September 24, 1974, statement by the Center for the Study of Education, also in FF 1:1 of the collection, outlines the national funding of advocates of school busing. *CANS, Judicial Fiat*, 15, observes that the Colorado Association of School Boards opposed the busing order. It emphasizes the necessity of a citizen mobilization to fight busing, 17.

RMN, June 14, 1974, p. 5, reported CANS' ballot initiative. Bailey, "Journey Full Circle," 119, quotes the text and observes how it was linked with the anti-sectarian clause in the state constitution. *DP*, November 6, 1974, p. 1, reported the election results. They are rather different than the official Colorado Secretary of State's abstract of the returns. Meadow, "Hard Years," pp. 23–26, observes CANS intervention in the Keyes case and its school boycotts.

There are scattered materials on PLUS in the folder "1976–77–78" in GP. Included are letters from Ann Fenton both backing that group and the Adopt-a-School program. Pearson, "Denver Case," 209, emphasizes PLUS as a community coalition for a peaceful city. Schwartzkopf, "Collective Bargaining," 187–89, observes the massive polarization of members of the DCTA about the Noel Resolution. She does not connect it with how busing impacted the everyday lives of instructors. FF 2:6 of the Keyes papers deals with the court ordering faculty integration.

Pearson, "Denver Case," 214–15, looks at Perrill's strategy of delay and resistance. Woodward, *Jim Crow*, 152, emphasizes the "good faith implementation" rule. Maurice Mitchell, "The Desegregation of Denver's Public Schools," *Center Magazine*, November-December 1978, p. 69, complains how many anti-busing parents suddenly became "Indians" to escape the court order.

Reports on CANS' boycott call include *DP*, September 20, 1974, p. 21, September 22, 1974, p. 39, September 28, 1974, p. 3, and October 3, 1974, p. 3, and *RMN*, September 20, 1974, p. 5, September 21, 1974, p. 14, October 3, 1974, p. 10, and October 27, 1974, p. 8. *RMN*, September 28, 1974, p. 1, and *DP*, September 28, 1974, p. 3, reported Winsett burning CANS' membership lists. Some of these articles are in FF 1:1 of the Keyes papers.

DP, September 24, 1974, p. 3F, argued the boycotts were a cynical means to cut state funding to DPS. *DP*, October 3, 1974, p. 3, reported the flop of the boycott. *DP*, October 10, 1974, p. 1, and *RMN*, October 10, 1974, p. 5, told of Doyle's order against the action. Also see LWV, *Composite View*, 8–9. Materials in the CANS file in the Branscombe papers observe the declaration of integration advocates in Park Hill that it was impermissible ever to boycott a day of school. Woodward, *Jim Crow*, 183, reflects on the many black boycotts of the 1960s to protest racial injustice in the schools.

A copy of CANS' filing for incorporation is in FF 1:1 of the Keyes papers. *SCJ*, July 2, 1974, p. 6, looked at Nolan Winsett amidst his effort to get the anti-school busing measure on the state ballot. *DP*, January 24, 1975, p. 4, profiled Winsett when he announced for the school board. *RMN*, January 6, 1976, p. 8, told of Kishkunas' attack on CANS. CJ Backus has pulled up biographical information on Nolan Winsett for me. Included was a brief mention of his death in *DP*, August 9. 2013.

Orfield, *Must We Bus?* 243, 280, 332, stresses Richard Nixon's anti-busing stance and efforts to exploit racial divisions and opposition to forced school integration. The study mentions the anti-busing amendment, 316, 335. Pearson, "Denver Case," 207, emphasizes the anti-busing amendment and the rejection of the mill levy hike. Ibid., 206, tells of the links between CANS and ROAR. It glances at the suit to enforce the anti-busing amendment, 207.

When I was working on my *Curtis Park* in 2014, John Hayden enlightened me on the relationship between the middle-class homosexual community, gentrification, and school busing controversies. *DP*, May 21, 1975, p. 26, reviewed the 1975 school board balloting. Virginia Rockwell discussed how Bernie Valdez was elected president of the board in *SN*, June 1977, pp. 37–38.

DP, January 24, 1975, p. 4, reported Naomi Bradford launching her run for the school board. In sporadic discussions, Rita Montero has recalled her friendship with Bradford. Taylor, "Leadership," 218, touches on CANS and Bradford's connections with it. Art Branscombe had a sympathetic look at Bradford, especially her poverty-stricken early years, *DP*, October 19, 1975, p. 24. *Denver Magazine*, December 1976, pp. 44–45, profiled her. *DP*, August 13, 1976, p. 1, and *RMN*, August 13, 1976, reported the board censuring her. *SCJ*, December 16, 1976, pp. 4–5, attacked Bradford as being semi-literate, bewailing her as a demagogue who used vicious language against her foes. *DP*, April 26, 1978, p. 3, announced her campaign for Congress against Pat Schroeder.

An unidentified article in *DP*, in the 1984–85 clipping notebook in GP, profiles Bradford when she was president of the school board. A July 9, 1976, DPS PR had a bitter attack on Bradford by Valdez and Crider. *DP*, May 26, 1986, p. 1B, looked at Bradford's stormy role on the school board. *RMN*, April 24, 1979, p. 1, quoted Bradford's criticism of board "junkets." *DP*, May 19, 1993, p. 1A, in reporting on Bradford's defeat for re-election, mentioned her clashes with the DCTA.

Focus, December 1981, pp. 4–5, featured the DPS Athletic Hall of Fame. *BN*, January 19, 1996, observed the 25th annual gathering of the DPS Coaches Hall of Fame. Also see *SN*, February 14, 1978, p. 37. *SN*, January 24, 1984, p. 37, told of Bradford's induction into the DPS Athletic Hall of Fame. Volume three will discuss teacher awards, the closest backers of schools have had to an instructor hall of fame.

DP, May 13, 1987, p. 10, and May 20, 1987, p. 5A, looked at Bradford's re-election. There were obituaries of Bradford in *RMN*, March 16, 2007, p. 11B, and *DP*, March 20, 2007, p. 4C. FF 7:8 of the DPS papers observes Gully Stanford's push for the Denver School of the Arts. I make passing mention of him in *Park Hill Promise*, 345–46. There will be a discussion of the School of the Arts in *Schools for a New Century*.

RMN, January 24, 1977, p. 5, told of Bradford's move to get DPS to rehire Kishkunas. *RMN*, March 6, 1977, p. 5, and March 8, 1977, p. 8, and *DP*, March 6, 1977, p. 1, March 10, 1977, p. 1, reported DPS naming Brzeinski superintendent. On November 24, 2018, Jimi O'Connor shared his memories of Brzeinski and how the educator rose in the system. Taylor, "Leadership," 118–19, looks at Brzeinski's role under Gilberts. *SN*, October 1, 1973, p. 7, observed Brzeinski's elevation to assistant superintendent. *SN*, May 12, 1975, p. 39, chronicled the creation of the post of associate superintendent.

RMN, March 20, 1977, p. 5, profiled Brzeinski. *RMN*, June 7, 1977, June 17, 1977, June 19, 1977, p. 6, and July 17, 1977, p. 5, focused on the factional politics within the DPS administration. Included was a discussion of the way Brzeinski purged those who had supported Kishkunas. It also outlined the top-heavy nature of the male bureaucracy in the district. A June 16, 1977, DPS PR explained Brzeinski's reorganization plan and the consolidation of the hierarchy.

SN, January 8, 1978, p. 27, stressed Brzeinski's community outreach efforts and receptions. *SN*, October 9, 1978, p. 15, announced the Citizen Service and Response Center. *Cmq*, November 1978, p. 2, told about the creation of the center.

SN, May 25, 1973, no pagination, emphasized the need for schools to be on heightened awareness of security and locking off all but one door to visitors. On

p. 9, it stressed the cooperation of the PTA, DPS, the Chamber of Commerce, and the Board of Realtors in creating the "Community–School Directory." *SN*, August 29, 1977, p. 1, stressed the welcome signs and "Great Schools Start Here" slogan; cf. *DP*, August 27, 1977, p. 2. *SN*, October 7, 1980, p. 14, had the "Achievement" slogan. *DP*, May 17, 2018, p. 1A, and May 18, 2018, p. 2A, reported the encounter at Rise Up School. *DP*, April 28, 2019, p. 4B, discussed the decline of attendance at Rise Up School in the wake of the incident.

CI, December 1925, emphasized the social-welfare activities of the schools, particularly volunteer efforts by teachers. *SB*, September 26, 1955, p. 13, told of the milk program. *SB*, December 6, 1965, p. 55, November 8, 1971, p. 14, and *SN*, September 20, 1976, p. 5, mentioned the Pupil Welfare Fund. *RMN*, September 17, 1978, p. 8, observed the campaign for a breakfast program in the schools. *RMN*, June 28, 1982, p. 7, reported the summer lunch program. *SN*, October 25, 1978, p. 18, stressed the effort. Also see *PTA Today*, October 1978, p. 12. The October 2019 meeting of Greater Park Hill Community Incorporated heralded the group's weekend food program.

An undated article in the 1960–61 PTA Historian's Notebook in GP discusses DPS imposing tougher graduation requirements. *SN*, May 9, 1977, p. 31, and an April 5, 1977, DPS PR once more emphasized stricter graduation requirements.

Focus, November 1978, p. 4, extolled the Adopt-a-School project. Also see the June 16, 1977, school board minutes, p. 24, and the 1980–81 *DPS Report*, 15. *SN*, January 24, 1979, p. 46, and March 5, 1979, p. 52, touched on some of the Adopt-a-School partnerships. There was also praise for Adopt-a-School program in the 1980–81 *DPS Report*, 15, the 1982–83 *DPS Report*, 18, and the 1985 *DPS Report*, 5.

Cmq, October 1977, and March 1978, heralded the creation of the Adopt-a-School program, outlining sponsors. There was comparable celebration of the effort, March 1979, p. 7, and December 1980, p. 5. *Cmq* hailed ten years of the initiative, April 1987, p. 7. *Cmq*, March 1982, p. 3, called for volunteers for Adopt-a-School. DPS PR, November 2, 1989, told of the Lowry Sergeants' Association and its activities at Smith School. *The Nation*, September 19, 1981, had an article "Schooldays for Big Business," ripping the values at the heart of Adopt-a-School.

Undated clippings in the 1973–74 PTA Historian's Notebook in GP emphasize the Chamber of Commerce's continuing vigor in school decisions. *DP*, April 26, 1998, had a special section, "Public Schools, Public Interest," a report championing the work of the Public Education & Business Coalition. The piece saluted the corporate domination of the schools. *DP*, July 2, 2000, p. 1B, extolled DPS's commercial deals. *SN*, March 10, 1982, p. 49, celebrated Project Business.

PTA Today, October 1978, focused on school nutrition, esp. see pp. 3, 6. It attacked junk food, p. 8. On occasion, the late Dr. Manny Salzman discussed his crusade against schools selling soda pop.

Upton Sinclair, *The Goslings: A Study of the American Schools* (Pasadena, CA: Upton Sinclair, 1924), 241, quotes Margaret Haley while outlining the way the wealthy dodged school tax commitments. He emphasizes the need for schools to be free of dependence of the charity of the rich, 440. Also see Marjorie Murphy, *Blackboard Unions* (Ithaca: Cornell University Press, 1990), 54–55. *Schools for a New Century* will look at the rise and functioning of the DPS Foundation.

Chapter Ten

Judge Matsch

By the time Joseph Brzeinski became superintendent, Judge Richard P. Matsch oversaw the Keyes case. While members of the school board and superintendents changed, court oversight remained. The jurist took charge of the litigation on March 26, 1976.

This was just after Judge William Doyle had completed the final modifications of the Finger Plan, getting all sides to agree to its implementation in the fall. His order, the jurist declared, essentially marked the end of the litigation. The court had addressed all of the substantive issues stemming from the original hearing for an injunction in the summer of 1969. Besides, Doyle needed to turn his full attention to his duties on the Tenth Circuit Court of Appeals. Doyle took senior status as a judge in December 1984. He died on May 2, 1986, at age 75 after a long illness. Among those praising him at his funeral was Gordon Greiner, the plaintiffs' chief attorney. He called Doyle an old friend who was "a courageous judge who had tried to make integration work."

On Doyle's exit from the Keyes case, by lottery, the District Court assigned the busing case to Matsch. He was born in Burlington, Iowa, on June 8, 1930, to German Lutheran parents. The judge received his bachelor's from the University of Michigan in 1951. Two years later, the school awarded him a law degree. Soon thereafter, he passed the Iowa bar. Between 1953 and 1955, he was in the Army, working in counterintelligence in Korea. The aspiring attorney came to Colorado in 1956, going to work for the 17th Street firm of Holme Roberts & Owen. Originally settling in southwest Denver, he carpooled to the law office with future school board member Ed Benton who lived nearby and also worked for the firm.

In 1959, Matsch became an assistant United States attorney. The lawyer left that post in 1961 when he signed on as a deputy Denver city attorney. Once more in private practice from 1963 to 1965, Matsch thereupon worked for the United States District Court as a bankruptcy referee until President Richard Nixon named him to the federal bench in 1974.

The judge was renowned for wearing cowboy boots under his judicial robes. Personally, he dwelt on a ranch outside of Louisville. There he was up daily at 5:30 AM. The first task of the morning was cleaning up after his horses. George Patton was a personal hero—the judge had a portrait of the general in his office. He also heralded Atticus Finch, the attorney in *To Kill a Mockingbird*.

In the courtroom, Matsch was most decisive. On starting a trial at 9:00 AM daily, he ordered the bailiff to lock the courtroom door, not allowing in any latecomers. At times, he exploded at

Drawing by Gregorio Alcaro

From 1976 to 1995, United States District Court Judge Richard Matsch oversaw Denver Public Schools, ruling on whether it was finally a unitary district and had obliterated all traces of racism in it.

attorneys whom he thought were ill prepared or ignoring the rules of the court. His best known case was presiding at the trials of Timothy McVeigh and Terry Nichols, the men found guilty of blowing up the Alfred P. Murrah Federal Building in Oklahoma City in 1995. Murrah, incidentally, had been on the three-judge panel of the Tenth Circuit Court of Appeals in 1969 that had ordered a revision of Judge Doyle's original injunction in the Keyes case.

From the time he took charge of the Keyes case, Matsch followed in Doyle's footsteps. The jurist showed himself extremely skeptical of the district's claims. Like Doyle, Matsch reviewed DPS administrative decisions, ordering the reassignment of some pupils. He had to act. DPS repeatedly returned to court. Time and again, it argued that its latest tweak of the busing order showed that it had indeed become a unitary district whereby court oversight was no longer necessary. Such was the plea of pro-integration forces who took control of the school board following the 1977 elections. As much as the previous neighborhood school majority, they did not want DPS under the leash of the federal court.

Initially, Matsch was receptive to DPS. On assuming jurisdiction in the case in 1976, he granted the district something of an informal three-year moratorium on tinkering with the recently issued order by Judge Doyle instituting full-day busing. By 1979, he realized this had not allowed for the stabilization of the system, the end of white flight, or stemmed the decline in enrollment. Taking an active interest in the litigation, that year Matsch ordered DPS to speed up the creation of a "unitary, non-racial school system." His decision came after he had held extensive hearings about the status of compliance and the court order. DPS argued conditions had changed since the 1976 implementation of all-day busing. It needed freedom from the court to close some schools and open others.

As he began the hearings in 1979, Matsch expressed hope that it was time to put an end to ten years of litigation. He believed the parties could reach a compromise. Before long, however, he concluded that DPS was obstinate. In an exasperated tone, the judge observed it was 25 years since the initial Supreme Court ruling in 1954 outlawing segregation in schools. The DPS case had been before the judiciary for a decade. During this period, the district still had not accepted the essence of the Supreme Court decision: racial discrimination in public schools was illegal. There was no specific constitutional right to neighborhood schools. Quotas and busing were necessary to redress discrimination. Racial ratios were only the beginning of the remedy. As such, DPS remained under court order.

Listening to the plaintiffs, the jurist was also concerned about evidence that despite the busing edict, many schools remained internally segregated. Black students were overwhelmingly in modified classes while whites filled accelerated sessions. He ordered DPS to investigate whether this was a deliberate ploy to keep races apart. In the process, advocates of integration blasted the district's tracking program. In doing so, they failed to address whether there should be such a complete mixing of youngsters that tone-deaf students must be part of choruses next to highly talented singers.

On July 30, 1979, Judge Matsch went along with the district's request to close Elyria, Belmont, Ellsworth, and Emerson schools. Additionally, he allowed DPS to modify the attendance borders of some schools while giving the district permission to open new schools in Montbello. He ended on an optimistic note: with further progress and the cooperation of the district, it finally would be time to start discussions about the end of court supervision of DPS.

The jurist once more said no to the district's plea for relief in 1980. DPS lamented that, in the face of busing, its enrollment had collapsed from 95,000 in 1970 to 60,000 a decade later. Neither Matsch nor Doyle ever bothered themselves with the specifics about how busing actually impacted the learning process and community relations. The court never gave any consideration to whether busing caused severe problems for students who found themselves constantly riding the bus while frequently having to adjust to new schools in the name of abstract integration. On the contrary, echoing the Supreme Court, Doyle and Matsch alike emphasized that the role of the courts was to assure that there was no trace of racial discrimination in the way District #1 dealt with its pupils. Busing, they insisted, was a way to achieve this. Besides, they did not have any other tool as effective as busing to mix black and white students.

The Community Education Council

Matsch repeatedly stated he was ready to end court oversight of DPS once the system proved it was a unitary district. Neither he nor the school board had any precise idea of how to achieve this. All of this came out when the school board filed the Ad Hoc Plan with Judge Matsch in 1981. By this time, the court claimed

Center Magazine

In 1974, Judge William Doyle named DU Chancellor Maurice Mitchell the head of the Community Education Council, a body the United States District Court charged with seeing that DPS indeed integrated its schools.

it was listening to the community. Such was an ostensible role of the Community Education Council (CEC). As part of his order implementing the Finger Plan, Judge Doyle had created the panel on April 8, 1974, as a way of receiving public input about how well the school integration order was working. DPS, he stated, was to pay for the cost of the commission.

Doyle appointed DU chancellor Maurice Mitchell as the inaugural head of the CEC. Lacking an academic degree, Mitchell had close ties with the national business and political elite. Starting out as a classified ad salesman for the *New York Times* in 1935, he rose in journalism and broadcasting. After World War II, he briefly taught summer seminars at DU as part of the school's efforts to develop professional standards for broadcast journalists. Before long, he was the head of the film division of Encyclopedia Britannica. A goal was to supplant the classroom teacher as the primary conveyor of information. Mitchell admitted there were problems with this approach while he went on to serve as the president of Encyclopedia Britannica from 1962 to 1967 when it was at the peak of its influence. DU recognized Mitchell in 1958 when it awarded him an honorary doctorate of law.

As an avid salesman with an excellent gift of gab, Mitchell took charge of the school in 1967. Three years later, he arranged for the governor to send the National Guard to the DU campus in May 1970 to crush a student protest against the Vietnam War in the wake of the murders at Kent State and the United States invasion of Cambodia. Conservatives hailed Mitchell for such a repressive stance.

Those celebrating Mitchell soon had qualms about the chancellor when he spoke out in favor of integration when he served on the prestigious, six-member United States Civil Rights Commission. The chancellor was on the federal agency for six years, overseeing investigations across the country. He quit in early 1973, protesting the way President Richard Nixon had purged the chairman of the body, Theodore Hesburgh, the head of Notre Dame University, for being too favorable to civil rights campaigns. Mitchell, in turn, claimed that under his leadership, DU had not experienced any student upheavals, especially after Kent State. For somebody who dealt most arbitrarily with student protestors, he also asserted that he had made sure the school had a student bill of rights and due process in disciplining students.

From the beginning, foes of busing were not happy about the Council. They mocked Mitchell, observing he had been so unconcerned about the busing controversy in 1969 that he had not voted in that year's pivotal school board election. His presence on the CEC showed it was not the voice of everyday people, but rather represented the Mile High elite. CANS was particularly loud on this point. In July 1975, it demanded the court oust Mitchell from the body since it saw the DU head as overwhelmingly supportive of busing. Mitchell, who often spent two days a week on CEC business, exited Denver in 1978 when he quit as DU chancellor. He proceeded to lead a think tank, the Center for the Study of Democratic Institutions in Santa Barbara, California. That program was seeking to continue its autonomous existence after the death of its founder, Robert M. Hutchins in 1977. Mitchell had been a close friend of Hutchins dating from the DU chief's days with Encyclopedia Britannica. The former CEC chief stayed at the Center for two years when the program collapsed as an independent entity. The retired DU chancellor died in Santa Barbara in December 1996 at age 81.

The Community Education Council started out with 41 members. They were supposed to represent all parts of the community. Included were the presidents of the DCTA and the Chamber of Commerce. There were members of the legislature, clerics, academics, people from the Colorado Department of Education, and a few high school students. Before long, the body grew to 61 members.

The prime purpose of the Council was to monitor the schools to see that they were implementing the desegregation order. The group relied on volunteers. Such concerned citizens visited all of the district's schools at least once a week, reporting on how well they were complying with the court's ruling. In training the 210 who stepped forward to take the posts, the Council emphasized the volunteers had to act as referees, not as advocates. Nonetheless, many principals and teachers found the representatives of the Council to be busybodies and nuisances who found fault with all parts of the schools. The Council repeatedly and successfully asked the court to order DPS to cooperate with CEC monitors. Teachers particularly resented repeated requirements, imposed by the court and the Council, that they stay after school when they were forced to listen to morally righteous lecturers tell them about their need to be more sensitive to the educational needs of blacks and Hispanos.

Reflecting community divisions, members of the Council greatly differed about the wisdom of the busing order. To prevent squabbling, Mitchell ran the body with an iron hand. He announced that he alone spoke for the Council. The chancellor often dictated policy rather than having democratic meetings where those serving on the board determined the body's stances.

In October 1977, the court reorganized the Council with 19 members. About that time, Mitchell stepped down from it. Those serving on the board included past warriors in school busing fights such as Ed Benton, Rachel Noel, and Jim Perrill. Pro-integration community activist Martha Radetsky served as its secretary. For a while, former state legislator Jean Bain chaired the commission—she was the wife of retired school board member Francis Bain. Gerald Phipps, the owner of the Denver Broncos, and Earl Stone, the rabbi of Temple Emanuel, were among the community figures on the board. Robert Yegge, the dean of the DU College of Law, was its legal liaison.

Francisco A. Rios, a professor at the University of Colorado Denver, succeeded Bain as the chair of the body. The Council continued to tell the court where it believed the district was failing to make desegregation a reality. At times, it requested meetings with Judge Matsch, informing him of problems and how the jurist needed to modify the order outlining the group's powers. Non-members found the Council utterly arrogant. They griped that it frequently met in private or kept others from listening to its deliberations via going into executive session. The PTA particularly bemoaned such conduct. Previously, Maurice Mitchell had banned closed CEC meetings.

The Council criticized the school board, including Omar Blair who had gained the presidency of the body in 1977. The attacks wounded him. It was, he asserted, a "disquieting experience" to find himself, a veteran advocate of equal educational opportunity and desegregation, accused of being more part of the problem than the solution.

Simultaneously, Superintendent Joseph Brzeinski explained it was impossible to have a completely unitary school system: students learn at different paces and there is no one common curriculum applicable to every child. The court ignored this, continuing its oversight. Complete equal education opportunity via busing, it repeatedly insisted, trumped all other considerations in determining district policy.

The PTA Dimension

By the time Blair emerged as president of the school board, serving from 1977 to 1981, DPS repeatedly insisted that it was a unitary district. Pro-integration voices on the school board, notably Kay Schomp and Ginny Rockwell, echoed him. The Denver Council of the PTA readily agreed. The parent-teacher group lobbied Judge Matsch to end the busing order.

Even at that, the PTA sometimes criticized the school board. It observed that Matsch was correct: the solution to the problem was not the continual manipulation of figures, but action to show that DPS actually provided equal educational opportunity for all. Neither the PTA nor the court was able to define precisely how

GP

For years, the PTA stressed vocal music at its meetings. Included was a city-wide Mothers Chorus. Here it performs a 1954 Christmas concert.

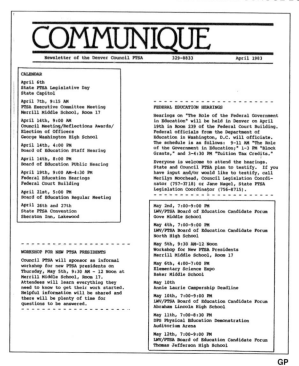

COMMUNIQUE

Newsletter of the Denver Council PTSA   329-8833   April 1983

CALENDAR

April 6th
State PTSA Legislative Day
State Capitol

April 7th, 9:15 AM
PTSA Executive Committee Meeting
Merrill Middle School, Room 17

April 14th, 9:00 AM
Council Meeting/Reflections Awards/
Election of Officers
George Washington High School

April 14th, 4:00 PM
Board of Education Staff Hearing

April 14th, 8:00 PM
Board of Education Public Hearing

April 19th, 9:00 AM-4:30 PM
Federal Education Hearings
Federal Court Building

April 21st, 5:00 PM
Board of Education Regular Meeting

April 26th and 27th
State PTSA Convention
Sheraton Inn, Lakewood

- - - - - - - - - - - - - - - - - - -

WORKSHOP FOR NEW PTSA PRESIDENTS

Council PTSA will sponsor an informal
workshop for new PTSA presidents on
Thursday, May 5th, 9:30 AM - 12 Noon at
Merrill Middle School, Room 17.
Attendees will learn everything they
need to know to get their work started.
Helpful information will be shared and
there will be plenty of time for
questions to be answered.

- - - - - - - - - - - - - - - - - - -

FEDERAL EDUCATION HEARINGS

Hearings on "The Role of the Federal Government
in Education" will be held in Denver on April
19th in Room 239 of the Federal Court Building.
Federal officials from the Department of
Education in Washington, D.C. will officiate.
The schedule is as follows: 9-11 AM "The Role
of the Government in Education;" 1-3 PM "Block
Grants," and 3-4:30 PM "Tuition Tax Credits."

Everyone is welcome to attend the hearings.
State and Council PTSA plan to testify. If you
have input and/or would like to testify, call
Merilyn Moorhead, Council Legislation Coordi-
nator (757-3718) or Jane Nagel, State PTSA
Legislation Coordinator (756-8715).

- - - - - - - - - - - - - - - - - - -

May 2nd, 7:00-9:00 PM
LWV/PTSA Board of Education Candidate Forum
Gove Middle School

May 4th, 7:00-9:00 PM
LWV/PTSA Board of Education Candidate Forum
North High School

May 5th, 9:30 AM-12 Noon
Workshop for New PTSA Presidents
Merrill Middle School, Room 17

May 6th, 4:00-7:00 PM
Elementary Science Expo
Baker Middle School

May 10th
Annie Laurie Campership Deadline

May 10th, 7:00-9:00 PM
LWV/PTSA Board of Education Candidate Forum
Abraham Lincoln High School

May 11th, 7:00-8:30 PM
DPS Physical Education Demonstration
Auditorium Arena

May 12th, 7:00-9:00 PM
LWV/PTSA Board of Education Candidate Forum
Thomas Jefferson High School

GP

*The Denver Council of the PTA expressed its views in
a monthly newsletter,* Communiqué. *The publication
frequently mentioned developments in the busing case.*

this was to be done. At the best, working with the district, the PTA launched an
aggressive program during 1979–80, "Our Future—Our Schools." It included a
detailed survey of residents about how to redress popular complaints concerning
the schools while enhancing the image of the system. The initiative failed to have
virtually any impact on Matsch or those who were highly skeptical about busing
and the direction of the schools.

The PTA's position was a change. Back in the early 1970s, when busing was
ripping apart the city and the district, the PTA had been virtually silent on the
controversy. The group suffered a severe decline in numbers at that time. Not only
did membership drop in DPS, but so did parental involvement. From an enrollment
of 59,956 in the early 1960s, the PTA was down to 40,000 by end of the decade. It
had but 20,000 members in the mid-1970s. After ten years of busing, it had fewer
than 10,000 members.

At times, the group had an unclear identity. In 1972, it officially became the
Parents, Teachers, Students, Administrators (PTSA). Some chapters were "PTO,"
the Parents–Teachers Organization. Others were simply the "Family Association."
Not all school parent-teacher organizations affiliated with the Denver County PTA.

The PTA also struggled with the changes of the day. Indicative of its failure to
reach out to working women, its board usually met at 1:00 PM on weekdays. The

group experienced a good deal of turbulence during the first decade of busing. Illustrative was the lack of an affiliated PTA at Park Hill School in the early 1970s. In some cases, loyal backers of the organization, including elected officers, suddenly announced their resignations in the middle of the schoolyear, explaining, they had moved outside of District #1 in the best interests of their families. Around 1978, the organization ceased primarily referring to women by their husband's names such as Mrs. Joe Smith or Mrs. James Jones. From being overwhelmingly a woman's group, it conceded that fathers were parents too who were most welcome to be part of its activities.

The social component of the PTA, which had once included a lot of group singing with what it called Mothers Choruses, increasingly disappeared. By the late 1970s, the PTA leadership was so assertive that newspapers even called the group "uppity." In 1978–79 the PTA was particularly active in demanding a role in negotiations between the school district and the DCTA on a new teachers contract. Working with the state PTA, it declared "Every Child. One Voice."

Back in the early and mid-1970s, the PTA had argued it was the obligation of one and all to obey the law to assure the smooth functioning of the schools. Opposed to its effort to make desegregation work, the PTA complained that the administration was incredibly remiss in informing parents about the specific busing decisions and how they impacted students. As busing convulsions continued to rip the city, the group worked with the city's Commission on Community Relations to prepare an information pamphlet outlining the court order while promoting the quality of DPS programs. The League of Women Voters was also active in efforts to explain exactly what busing meant, publishing brochures about the topic.

Judge Matsch no more listened to the PTA than he did to the school board. In 1981, he ordered each school to have an inservice committee on human relations. It was to consist of the principal, six staff members/teachers, six parents, and two students in the high schools. The purpose was to see that faculty and staff members attended mandatory sessions about the need to be aware of racial issues. At another time, the court arranged for a school assistance review advisory committee consisting of 12 adults and nine students. In the meanwhile, the PTA was part of another DPS venture, the Ad Hoc Committee.

The Ad Hoc Committee

On May 15, 1980, believing that Judge Matsch was open to ending court oversight, the board adopted Resolution 2019. Among other provisions, at the urging of board members Kay Schomp and Marion Hammond, it created the Ad Hoc Committee for a Unitary School System. The motion declared it was time for the United States District Court to step down from its oversight of the district. The pro-integration majority of the board vowed it was committed to carrying out the busing order. The court, the Ad Hoc Committee complained, actually caused more trouble than solved DPS problems. This was the board consensus.

Busing, advocates of integration argued, was not the only way to assure desegregation and equal educational opportunity. The district needed freedom from court oversight to employ creative tactics to assure DPS was a unitary district. The 1980 annual DPS report, for example, urged open enrollment and the creation of magnet schools and middle schools as ways of showing DPS was resolving racial disparities. Judge Matsch rejected the suggestions, ruling the proposals did not assure desegregation.

Besides backers of the PTA, the Ad Hoc Committee included representatives from the League of Women Voters, and members of the African-American and Hispanic DPS advisory councils. Concerned citizens joined them along with top-ranking administrators. After numerous public meetings, the committee presented its report to the community on June 5, 1981.

To get the court to end oversight of DPS, the Ad Hoc Committee asked Judge Matsch to allow DPS to form magnet schools that drew in learners from all parts of the city regardless of specific attendance borders. The board called the proposal the "Ad Hoc Plan." As much as anything, it aimed to curb mandatory busing while promoting walk-in schools. The initiative tinkered with attendance zones, promising to reduce by 2,600 the number of children who had to ride the bus for integration. Ideally, these changes would allow all students to attend the school of their choice.

Backers of the Ad Hoc Plan campaigned for the measure. Against the unbending attitude of the court, they insisted District #1 had to be a flexible system. There were better ways of assuring quality education for all than simply forcing students

Photo by Phil Goodstein

In 1902, Byers School occupied its new home at the southwest corner of West Byers Place and South Bannock Street. It became Alameda School in 1921 after Byers Junior High School had its first classes that year. DPS closed Alameda School in 1974, citing the low membership and the plunging enrollment of DPS as a whole. The building subsequently became condominiums.

to ride halfway across town on buses while enrollment declined and academic performance stagnated.

Critics also observed a massive gap in studies about busing. Amidst all the concerns about integration and problematic test scores, there were no specific breakdowns of the results of the tests based on race, ethnicity, or family educational background and income. Apparently, a concern about the privacy of the students kept the district or federal education authorities from probing such linkages. The absence of such data, critics of busing insisted, might be to cloak that the integration program failed to address some of the most fundamental problems with unequal school achievements in an unequal society.

The Community Education Council opposed the Ad Hoc Plan, not believing it redressed segregation. School board member William Schroeder also voted against it. Reverting to the views of the early 1970s, he called for junking the busing system in favor of neighborhood schools and open enrollment. The divided school board sent the two proposals to Matsch. The judge rejected both of them on October 30, 1981. He once more stated that DPS was still not committed to becoming a unitary district. But, he emphasized, he was not a school administrator. It was up to the district, not the court, to come up with the proper measures to make the system a truly integrated system.

In response to the latest setback, the board drafted the Total Access Plan. It was an instant product of the staff, drawn up in two weeks in the fall of 1981. The proposal once more emphasized open enrollment and magnet schools. In the hope of selling it to the court and the community, the board hired new lawyers and a publicity firm to tout the initiative.

The board so acted because the Total Access Plan immediately encountered resistance. About 20 teachers signed a letter to Matsch, urging him to say no to it. After another hearing, Judge Matsch rejected the Total Access Plan on March 15, 1982, since it failed to remove the vestiges of racial discrimination from the district. He ordered a new plan within 30 days.

The board quickly responded, submitting what it called the Consensus Plan. It was a hodgepodge of the Ad Hoc Plan and Total Access Plan. Included were modifying school attendance districts to provide for 11 more walk-in elementary and six junior high schools. The initiative also asked the court to allow DPS to open two magnet schools in the fall of 1982. On May 12, 1982, Judge Matsch accepted a good deal of the Consensus Plan as an interim measure. Even while permitting some of the proposed changes to reduce busing, he insisted busing must remain a crucial part of District #1's quest to become a unitary system.

As it was, the Consensus Plan shaped DPS's integration polices for the next six years. At the same time Judge Matsch continued his oversight of District #1, the federal Department of Justice intervened in the litigation on February 8, 1984. That day it filed a brief asking to be added as a friend of the court.

This was the first time the Department of Justice had sought to join an integration case that had been filed by citizens. It did so at the behest of school board president Naomi Bradford. Without consulting others on the board, she approached the federal agency. Given the Republican control in Washington and how the Ronald

Reagan administration had no use for school busing and the idealistic programs of the 1960s, she hoped the brief from the Department of Justice would convince Judge Matsch that it was time to end court oversight of DPS. Nothing of substance resulted from this. Meanwhile, the Consensus Plan opened the door for a new part of the district, magnet schools.

Magnet Schools

Magnet schools were a national rage in the 1980s. They were distinctive programs open to all students in the district. Ideally, magnet schools would have such an allure that pupils, especially whites, would travel across town to them, particularly to such places as Manual High and Cole Junior High.

Manual, opened in 1893, had been the city's first magnet school. Besides vocational education, it had an advanced program for students desiring to learn art and architecture. Youngsters wanting a high-quality technical, scientific education also enrolled at Manual compared to the classics/college preparatory curriculum that was the keynote of East High School.

After the 1902 consolidation of District #1 of the City and County of Denver, Manual increasingly became a regular high school while East, West, North, and South added vocational education. As such, magnet schools were something of a novelty when the 1966 Advisory Council on Equal Educational Opportunity suggested them as a way DPS could emerge as a naturally integrated district.

The 1969 Gilberts Plan stressed magnet schools along with its push for educational parks. The assumption was that all students, including African-Americans and Hispanos, were equal consumers with middle-class white learners. As such, they would enroll in equal numbers in the magnet schools. Before anything happened, the 1969 school board election and the court order kept DPS from making magnet schools an immediate reality.

As DPS declined in the 1970s, concerned parents and administrators were sure magnet schools were a much better option than continued busing. Superintendent

Photo by Phil Goodstein

Gilpin School was the city's pioneer magnet school. Here is its 1951 building seen from the west corner of 30th and California streets.

Howard Johnson had already made them a central part of the program he presented to Judge William Doyle in early 1971. The jurist rejected them.

DPS kept trying. In court hearing after court hearing during the next decade, the district insisted that magnet schools were a superior alternative to busing. By the early 1980s, even integration advocates admitted busing had not delivered as promised. Proponents of desegregation could no longer blame the resistance of the board—it no longer systematically opposed the court order. White flight continued, particularly of families with school-aged children. The solution, desegregation champions agreed, were innovative programs to pull white youngsters into what had been minority schools.

With the authorization of the court, this led to the launch of two magnet programs in 1982. These were places where, with the approval of Judge Matsch, the district could bend the busing order. In permitting them, he required DPS to make racial ratios a prime part of the shaping of such schools. The magnet programs were to illustrate the wonders of school choice whereby parents were no longer be trapped by the district's unbending attendance districts and the court busing requirements.

Gilpin School was in the vanguard. It dated from 1881, honoring Colorado's first territorial governor, William P. Gilpin (1861–62). During the late 19th century, Gilpin was a premier school when it served the elite Curtis Park neighborhood. As that section became increasingly diverse in the early 20th century, Gilpin was an ideal integrated school pulling in whites, blacks, Hispanos, and people of East Asian heritage. Before long, virtually all students came from working-class families after the exit of the wealthy from the neighborhood.

The school had never performed well after it occupied a new $912,717 building at 30th and California streets in September 1951. Essentially, the 30-classroom building, occupying a 4.03-acre plot, was the neighborhood school of Curtis Park and Five Points. Some of its students lived in nearby housing projects. Few Gilpin students came from families where college education was a tradition.

Busing paired Gilpin with Doull School at 2520 South Utica Street. While the boys and girls from Curtis Park and Five Points dutifully rode the bus to Doull for fourth, fifth, and sixth grades, few Doull children arrived at Gilpin for grades one, two, and three—both schools had kindergartens. Gilpin additionally featured an early childhood education program. From upwards of a thousand students during the peak of the baby boom era, Gilpin was down to 390 in 1978. During hearings over desegregation at that time, the plaintiffs had pointed to the low number of whites at Gilpin given the lack of the participation in busing of many parents who lived in the Doull attendance area.

To get more whites to the Five Points building, board member Kay Schomp suggested transforming Gilpin into an extended-day school. This was a program that would open as early as 6:00 AM and stay open to at least 6:00 PM. Both before and after regular school hours, it would provide nutrition and supervised programs for the children of downtown office workers. It imposed a tuition charge to pay for this form of child care.

The initiative, Schomp and backers believed, would bring in middle-class white students. These sons and daughters of office workers and professionals would both naturally integrate Gilpin and raise achievement levels. Parents and students were on their own in getting to the building. In other words, it was not available to low-income parents lacking cars or a means to send their children across town to Gilpin.

Prior to the launch of the extended-day school, DPS had implemented what it called the Latch-Key Program in 1979. In association with the private Mile High Child Care, a coalition of area preschools and childcare programs, this initiative provided safe places at schools where children, who had nobody at home, could stay from 6:00 AM to 6:00 PM. As they had for years, many schools had after-hour recreation programs where youngsters could remain in the buildings till around 5:00 PM.

On its launch in 1982, the extended-day school at Gilpin reaped most favorable publicity. Champions of children heralded it. Drawing on her excellent business ties, Schomp connected with the Chamber of Commerce and Downtown Denver Incorporated to extol the program. The Piton Foundation provided funds to launch the effort. The Rockefeller Brothers Fund granted it additional money as a way of letting Denver escape from the rigid character of court-ordered busing. Gilpin, publicists proclaimed, was "the school that works for people who work."

Low-income mothers and fathers, not just members of the middle class, agreed that the extended-day program was an excellent idea. They wanted to enroll their children, but could not afford the tuition costs. Such applications surprised many Gilpin advocates—they had bluntly geared the extended-day program to white families who were able pay the charge. In the face of demand from poverty-stricken families, DPS saw Gilpin needed a scholarship program and tuition waivers. The federal government assisted with grants to low-income families wanting to participate in the extended schoolday. Such families were still on their own getting their children to and from Gilpin.

The addition of the tuition waivers enhanced the extended-day program. The Gilpin model was such a success that it quickly became the template for numerous other schools in the district that added extended-day programs. Once more, a tuition charge loomed. It especially hit economically stressed families that were above the poverty line, but which could not easily pay the costs.

For a while, so many students flocked to Gilpin that it limited itself to early childhood education through third grade at its California Street building. It sent those in fourth and fifth grades to Crofton School at 24th and Arapahoe streets, a place the district had shuttered in 1992 when it had transferred Crofton students to Ebert School near 23rd Street and Glenarm Place. (DPS had moved sixth graders to middle schools in 1988.)

Academically, however, Gilpin failed to flourish. The élan of the extended-day program especially faded after the end of the busing order in 1995–96. Besides, parents could then send their children to extended-day programs closer to their homes. The central administration concluded that Gilpin needed a complete reorganization in 2007–08 when it branded it a failing school. The solution was transforming it into the Gilpin Community Montessori School. It offered classes from preschool through eighth grade. Other programs soon supplanted that effort.

Mitchell Montessori School

By the time Gilpin became the Community Montessori School, many champions of children heralded Montessori programs as on the cutting edge of educational excellence. This was a change. Critics had long dismissed the doctrines of Maria Montessori (1870–1952) as an esoteric effort for youngsters with learning difficulties. An Italian psychiatrist, she had focused on educating students with mental deficiencies. She had created her first children's house in Italy in 1907, focusing on those between three and six years of age. In it, the educator combined freedom of movement with detailed instruction and supervision. Eventually, Montessori presented herself as something of a wonderworker, declaring she had developed "education capable of saving humanity."

Those who did not believe this dismissed Maria Montessori's writings as virtually unreadable. The pedagogue, they argued, combined a strong authoritarian streak under the cloak of freedom of play. The program required students to enroll at a young age. In consequence, those who had not been in a Montessori program since age three often found it hard to grasp how they were supposed to behave and learn. In contrast, advocates believed the combination of direction and autonomy was the ideal course of education.

The Montessori program was still something of a novelty when the first modern Mile High children's house opened in 1965 as a private venture. Charging tuition, it pulled in the offspring of affluent families, particularly of parents who were

Photo by Phil Goodstein

In 1991, working with Mitchell students, Carlota Espinoza painted Mother Earth/ Soul of the World *along the north side of Mitchell School near 33rd Avenue and Lafayette Street.*

dissatisfied with the rigidity and routine of the public school system. (Back in the 1910s, there had been a short-lived Froebel Montessori School in Denver. Besides honoring the founder of the Montessori Method, it also recalled Friedrich Fröbel [Froebel], the man who shaped the kindergarten ideal.)

As the regular schools failed, both in Denver and the suburbs, Montessori efforts became increasingly popular. Part of the push for magnet schools saw Mitchell School, 1350 33rd Avenue, emerge in 1986–87 as the district's first Montessori effort. It was for children from ages three to six, essentially covering preschool, kindergarten, and first grade.

Mitchell School stemmed from an 1883 Fourth Avenue School at the corner of Lafayette Street and one of the city's many Fourth Avenues. With a renaming and renumbering of the streets, the building became 32nd Avenue School. The district dubbed it Lafayette School in 1897. The next year, when students occupied a large new building, the place became Maria Mitchell School, celebrating the most famous woman astronomer of the day.

Additions and modifications of the building followed during the 20th century. In 1920, DPS stated Mitchell had an enrollment of 1,028. It hovered near that number into the 1960s. A 1965 listing stated the expanded building had 1,050 seats in 37 classrooms. After World War II, the school filled with black students.

Enrollment at Mitchell steadily declined during the late 1960s with the aging of the baby boomers. Even at that, it had an attendance of 886 in 1970. The firm of DMJM–Phillips–Reiser redesigned the building in 1973–74. At that time, DPS stated Mitchell had a capacity of either 720 or 850 seats after the demolition of the 1898–99 structure and a 1902 wing. By then the schoolhouse extended to Marion Street on the west with the main entry near 33rd Avenue and Lafayette Street. Students were the Thunderbirds.

Busing paired Mitchell with Denison School at 1821 South Yates Street when Mitchell offered early childhood education, kindergarten, and grades one, two, and three. It especially emphasized a reading program, working with students aides from the nearby Cole Junior High School. Mitchell had 600 students by 1978. For a while, Mitchell was additionally paired with Force School, 1550 South Wolfe Street.

In addition to adding a Montessori magnet to Mitchell, the school also had regular classes. In 1986–87, it counted 171 learners in the Montessori program from age three through kindergarten. Additionally there were 91 students in first, second, and third grades. For a while, Mitchell was paired in enrichment efforts with Barrett and Harrington. Included was a whole language program at Barrett.

In 1996, DPS closed the Montessori magnet at Mitchell. With the end of busing, it feared the old Lafayette Street School would be overcrowded with neighborhood children. The previous year the superintendent's office had listed the building as having room for 600 youngsters in 20 classrooms when it had an enrollment of 553. Now that DPS was no longer under the court order, DPS revised its numbers, stating the building had room for but 550 students compared to 669 in the attendance zone. (The changing numbers about Mitchell were reflective. In different surveys, DPS frequently listed widely contrasting numbers about the capacity of its schools.) Besides, by this time the district had Montessori programs in other buildings.

Knight Fundamental Academy

Besides the seeming openness of Montessori programs, magnet schools offered strict discipline. This was the case at Knight School, 3245 Exposition Avenue. The building became a magnet, Knight Fundamental Academy, in 1982 at the same time the Gilpin Extended-Day School program opened. DPS had planned a schoolhouse close to the Polo Club since the 1920s. Initially, it was going to be Bonnie Brae School for the name of a nearby neighborhood. At that time, DPS acquired land for the facility near South Steele Street and Kentucky Avenue.

With money from the 1948 bond issue, work got underway on the $698,391 schoolhouse across the street from the super elite Belcaro neighborhood. The district christened the schoolhouse for the father-and-son team of Stephen Knight Sr. and Jr., both of whom had served multiple terms on the school board. Temple Buell designed the building. The influential Platt Rogers Construction built it, a firm which was eventually Gerald Phipps Construction. Its new namesake was the son of United States Senator Lawrence Phipps who had grown up nearby in the exclusive Belcaro palace of his father—Gerald Phipps had married the daughter of Platt Rogers.

Knight School included 13 classrooms, three rooms for joint art and social studies programs, two kindergartens, an auditorium, a playroom, lunchroom,

Photo by Phil Goodstein

Most DPS elementary schools have come to have ceremonial arches. The one at Knight School, 3245 Exposition Avenue, stands out. In 1982, Knight became a fundamental academy, a magnet school pulling in children whose parents wanted a highly controlled environment emphasizing traditional basic subjects.

office, community room, music room, and a library on an eight-acre campus. In a word, it was the latest and most fashionable expression of postwar school design.

Students took their first classes at Knight in September 1951. Before long, the school was past its capacity of 570. For a while, it was on double sessions. A 1965 inventory listed it as having 19 classrooms. During that decade, membership fluctuated from 525 to 645. Enrollment plunged with the coming of busing and the aging of residents in the Belcaro and Bonnie Brae neighborhoods.

Busing paired Knight School with Barrett School at 29th Avenue and Jackson Street when Knight had a kindergarten and grades four through six. Included were students bused in from Lowry Air Force Base—all Lowry kindergartners went to Knight. From 443 students in 1978, the Bonnie Brae building was down to 274 two years later. Most of its students came from the Barrett district; very few Knight children rode the bus to Barrett. Many of the parents of school-aged children living close to Knight School sent them to private academies. Even at that, Knight emphasized it had a large number of parent volunteers.

The plummeting membership at a time of austerity led DPS to ponder shuttering the schoolhouse. Instead of doing so, the district stated Knight was to become a learning space stressing discipline, order, and routine. To get their children into Knight Fundamental Academy, parents had to agree to participate in school programs. They signed contracts stating their children would behave and do the assigned lessons. The school informed parents it would not retain students who misbehaved or failed to fulfill their potential.

Knight emphasized drill-oriented instruction. Included were the students orderly walking in the hallways, with arms folded. This was part of the emphasis on "traditional American values of patriotism, good citizenship, work, honesty, pride, courtesy, and respect for self, others, and authority." Flag worship was part of the daily lessons. None of the school's promotional materials talked about the necessity of students questioning the world or engaging in self-directed learning.

Those who decried the seeming permissiveness of modern education heralded Knight, especially when its students scored near the top on standardized tests. Many African-Americans embraced the program, seeing their children were bused into it. So many applied that the school had a waiting list. Even at that, it failed to bond with the parents of elementary students who lived in walking distance of the school.

The demand for places at Knight Fundamental Academy led DPS to create a second fundamental academy at Traylor School, 2900 South Ivan Way, for the 1991–92 schoolyear. During most of the busing era, Traylor had been linked with Greenlee and Fairview schools, having a kindergarten and grades four through six. The building featured a glassed-in courtyard that separated the auditorium, lunchroom, and gymnasium from the classrooms. During the first part of the busing era, enrollment at Traylor had drastically declined as parents did everything they could to keep their children from riding the bus—generally, neighborhood children attended it for three years and went to private or parochial schools for the years the district wanted to bus them. Traylor's enrollment in 1978 was 465. By 1990, the school board, with the authorization of the court, realized that the paired busing with Greenlee was not working. It ended the connection for the 1991–92 schoolyear when the district transformed Greenlee into an extended-day program.

On the conversion of Traylor into a fundamental school, DPS gave youngsters living in the school's attendance area the first right to enroll. Minority youths who did not wish to attend the fundamental program went to Sabin School. The district channeled whites into the paired Smedley and Kaiser schools.

After students started attending Traylor Fundamental, Knight took in those who dwelt east of the Platte River. Before long, demand for spots at Knight was so great that the fundamental academy took in only those living east of South University

Author's collection

Traylor School, 2900 South Ivan Way, was the city's second fundamental academy after Knight School. Students are the Tigers.

Boulevard, a road a half-mile west of the school. Traylor Fundamental claimed to be "loosely" modeled on Knight, being an independent program.

When it was paired with Greenlee and Fairview, Traylor had been about 25 percent white and 75 percent minority. By the mid-1990s, as it blossomed as a fundamental academy, Traylor had an enrollment of 583. The school was an integration success. A census in 1995–96 listed it as 47.9 percent white, 41.8 percent Hispanic, 4.7 percent black and 1 percent Native American. That year, it was able to accept only 40 first graders outside of its borders out of 110 who applied. While Traylor had outstanding attendance, complete with parental participation, its test scores were mediocre. Traylor students were the Tigers.

By the early 1990s, DPS had many other magnet programs. Because of the court order, it limited voluntary choice into some of them based on race. For example, whites attending such "minority" schools as Amesse, Bryant-Webster (3635 Quivas Street), McGlone, Remington, Munroe, and Valdez (2525 West 29th Avenue), could not escape busing by enrolling in a magnet school.

A count in the mid-1990s showed that both Traylor and Knight students mostly came from middle-class families. Compared to an official 36 percent poverty rate within DPS, the district counted 15 percent of such students at Traylor and 16 percent at Knight. At that time, the district stated it had a total of 63 schools—54 elementaries, eight middle schools, and one high school—in which the poverty rate greater than 36 percent. Within a few years, particularly after the end of court-ordered busing, some schools showed upwards of 90 percent of their students qualifying for free or low-priced lunches, a commonly used measure of the poverty rate. The last was a formula based on family income. Some students, whose families did not qualify for free lunches, often struggled to pay for lunches.

This was in the future. In the interim, DPS saw magnet schools as a great success. Such programs hinted at a wave of choice that dominated the system in the early

21st century. Meanwhile, another 1982 reform authorized by Judge Matsch as part of the Consensus Plan, middle schools, was much more problematic.

Middle Schools

A major change in the organization of DPS during the busing era was replacing junior highs with middle schools in 1982. By that time, educators everywhere agreed that the junior high system had failed. Junior high youngsters were caught between elementaries and high schools. They were in the pangs of puberty. The youths sometimes reacted to a confused life and world by rebelling. Added to this were learning problems. Pupils who were already academically struggling frequently fell hopelessly behind their peers in junior high. Failing students, unable to grasp lessons, were often among those suffering the worst disciplinary problems. Many soon dropped out. Promoters of middle schools stated there had to be a better way.

Middle schools were the trend everywhere by the late 1970s. In part, this stemmed from the changing nature of school enrollment. Not only in Denver, but nationally the number of students declined in the 1970s and 1980s after baby boomers had made their way through high schools. High school buildings, which had been extremely packed a few years earlier, now had plenty of extra space. In places, the number of students in high school so sagged that administrators feared the programs could not keep up with rival suburban schools, especially in sports.

The state high school athletic association divided high school athletics by the size of the enrollment of schools. Denver had always been at the top of the rankings. Prior to World War II, DPS teams had played in a six-member league with Boulder High School. The university town's program was the only local high school with a comparable enrollment to DPS high schools at that time. In the course of the 1950s, and 1960s, suburban schools soared. Wheat Ridge High School had an outstanding basketball team. Cherry Creek High, which peaked with more than 4,000 students, excelled in all competitions.

To solve both the problems of junior high schools and fill empty high school buildings, educators increasingly moved ninth graders, technically high school freshmen, back to high school. Middle schools, focusing on students in seventh and eighth grade, thereupon replaced the junior highs. Back in the 1960s, "middle school" was sometimes used to refer to proposed intermediate schools for grades four, five, and six. During the 1967 bond issue campaign, for example, opponents urged a no vote on the matter because they did not believe what they termed "middle schools" was a good idea.

Back in February 1967, shortly before leaving office as superintendent, Kenneth Oberholtzer reorganized the junior high curriculum. Previously, it offered students numerous different subjects, being something of a sampler of the liberal arts and sciences. Now, he insisted, DPS had to cut back on art and music while gearing junior highs pupils more to the demands of high schools and colleges. Though DPS changed junior high requirements, the schools remained extremely troubled. Sometimes they were violent. Usually, they had the worst discipline problems in the district.

During the 1970s, DPS conducted numerous studies about the future of junior highs and high schools. On August 16, 1979, the board adopted Resolution 2079. It ordered the superintendent to draw up what it called the Long-Range Plan. This was an effort to craft the character of the district for the next decade. Included was probing the nature of education for those aged 12 to 14, i.e., those attending junior high schools. In particular, it called for substituting middle schools for junior highs.

The conversion was not as simple as it seemed. As with every other important district decision at the time, it first had to clear the United States District Court. Other obstacles popped up. Consequently, while DPS initially announced it was implementing the middle school program as of the beginning of the 1980–81 schoolyear, it did not launch middle schools until two years later.

No sooner had ninth graders moved to high school in the fall of 1982 than new difficulties emerged. Much to the surprise of pedagogues, many of the freshmen were lost in high schools. The places had quite a different complexion than junior high schools. There was nothing new about the disorientation of freshmen. The creation of junior highs around the time of World War I partially stemmed from the observation that ninth graders often did not fit into high schools.

At first, DPS kept ninth graders in the old junior high schoolhouses, separating them from those in seventh and eighth grades. Once the ninth graders moved into the high school buildings, middle schools had many empty classrooms. The solution, the school board declared by a five-to-two vote on January 7, 1988, was to

Photo by Phil Goodstein

In the 1920s, DPS took immense pride in its new junior high schools, including Skinner, opened in 1922 at 3435 West 40th Avenue. By 1979, the district had committed itself to transforming junior highs into middle schools. It did so for the 1982–83 schoolyear.

transfer sixth graders to middle schools for classes beginning in the fall. It explained sixth graders were too old to mix with children in preschools, kindergartens, and the lower grades.

The reorganization of middle schools saw a major expansion of the school administration. This came amidst the endless budget crunch and the cutback in art and music programs. Besides a principal, most middle schools had a vice principal. Next came an assistant principal in charge of imposing discipline. Additionally, there was an advisor for boys and an advisor for girls. Counselors for boys and girls joined them.

An instruction coordinator was part of the oversight of junior highs/middle schools. Some teachers branded him the "straw boss." Eventually, the post blended in with that of the multiple assistant principals at middle schools. At times, the schools listed people such as the counselors and advisors as faculty members. This had the advantage of making the schools appear to have a lower student-teacher ratio, supposedly a sign of a quality school.

Middle schools failed to produce the promised wonders. While some teachers especially reached out to students in the sixth, seventh, and eighth grades, others sought to flee middle schools as soon as possible. Discipline problems remained endless. Many parents did not want their children enrolled in middle schools, pointing to the vicious playground life and bullying they entailed. The "mean girls of middle school" became something of a cliché about the extreme snobbish divisions among students.

Grammar Schools

A solution was transforming elementaries back into grammar schools with classes from kindergarten through eighth grade. Moore School, at Ninth Avenue and Corona Street, was in the vanguard in the fall of 1994. In part, this reflected extreme unease among many parents about having their children go to Morey Middle School, a place suffering turbulence during the period. DPS pointed to the Moore effort as a magnet and part of its school choice options.

Slavens School, 3000 South Clayton Street, added a middle school program in 1998. This was two years after DPS had reopened and remodeled the building. The school's fate illustrated the evolution of the Southern Hills neighborhood. Denver annexed the spread south of Yale Avenue and east of South University Boulevard after World War II. The newly developed section quickly filled with upper-middle-class homes. In 1957, the district opened the school, honoring Leon E. Slavens (1894–1954), a man who spent much of his life as a District #1 principal. Students were often the sons and daughters of people associated with the nearby University of Denver.

Initially, the schoolhouse lacked space for the 600 youngsters who showed up on opening day. No sooner had the district completed an addition with four classrooms in 1961, giving the 21-classroom building an L shape on a 6.39-acre campus, than the schoolhouse was again past capacity. Within a few years, the numbers declined when baby boomers moved on to junior highs.

Banners are frequent at elementary schools. Shown are some on the playground at Slavens School, 3000 South Clayton Street. It was a highly successful program in the 21st century with classes stretching from kindergarten through eighth grade.

With the coming of court-ordered busing, ever fewer residents sent their children to Slavens. From 528 students in 1974, it was down to 269 four years later. Most of them were bused in from the attendance district of Columbine School at 29th Avenue and Columbine Street. Slavens, with kindergarten through third grade, was later paired with Wyatt School at 3620 Franklin Street.

The school pairings greatly frightened some parents who lived close to Slavens. They had moved to Southern Hills since they were among those who believed everything old was bad. As such, they automatically viewed Victorian structures such as Wyatt as a 19th-century monstrosity that could not produce modern education. This was among the factors leading them to withdraw their children from the public school system.

Citing the lack of students, DPS closed Slavens in 1982 when enrollment was around 270. It used the building for auxiliary offices, including for its department of curriculum development. For a while, the district leased part of the space to preschool and daycare programs. The Greek Orthodox Church was among the tenants. In 1984, DPS was ready to sell Slavens to the congregation. That proposal fell through and Slavens remained DPS offices.

As the original settlers of the area near Slavens moved out or died, young couples once more started to populate the area close to the school in the late 20th century. With the end of court-ordered busing, they wished to send their children

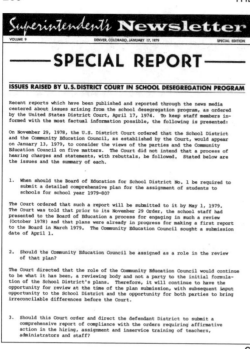

Superintendent's **Newsletter**

VOLUME 9   DENVER, COLORADO, JANUARY 17, 1979   SPECIAL EDITION

——SPECIAL REPORT——

ISSUES RAISED BY U.S. DISTRICT COURT IN SCHOOL DESEGREGATION PROGRAM

Recent reports which have been published and reported through the news media centered about issues arising from the school desegregation program, as ordered by the United States District Court, April 17, 1974. To keep staff members informed with the most factual information possible, the following is presented:

On November 29, 1978, the U.S. District Court ordered that the School District and the Community Education Council, as established by the Court, would appear on January 13, 1979, to consider the views of the parties and the Community Education Council on five matters. The Court did not intend that a process of hearing charges and statements, with rebuttals, be followed. Stated below are the issues and the summary of each.

1. When should the Board of Education for School District No. 1 be required to submit a detailed comprehensive plan for the assignment of students to schools for school year 1979-80?

The Court ordered that such a report will be submitted to it by May 1, 1979. The Court was told that prior to its November 29 Order, the school staff had presented to the Board of Education a process for engaging in such a review (October 1978) and that plans were already in progress for making a first report to the Board in March 1979. The Community Education Council sought a submission date of April 1.

2. Should the Community Education Council be assigned as a role in the review of that plan?

The Court directed that the role of the Community Education Council would continue to be what it has been, a reviewing body and not a party to the initial formulation of the School District's plans. Therefore, it will continue to have the opportunity for review at the time of the plan submission, with subsequent input opportunity to the School District and the opportunity for both parties to bring irreconcilable differences before the Court.

3. Should this Court order and direct the defendant District to submit a comprehensive report of compliance with the orders requiring affirmative action in the hiring, assignment and inservice training of teachers, administrators and staff?

GP

Reports about the status of court-ordered busing were endless from 1969 to 1995.

to a neighborhood school. This led to the reopening of Slavens for the 1996–97 schoolyear. It immediately stood out for impressive test scores. In response to the problems at middle schools, parents convinced DPS to extend classes at Slavens from kindergarten through eighth grade.

Slavens' enrollment averaged between 450 and 500. Eventually, the building was packed with a waiting list. An expansion followed near the end of the second decade of the 21st century. Parents readily participated in school programs.

Ratings in the late 2010s listed Slavens as the number-one district-run elementary in Colorado. The federal Department of Education declared it a Blue Ribbon School, heralding its achievements. By 2019, 82 percent of its 700-plus students were white, 8 percent of mixed race, 6 percent Hispanic, 2 percent Asia, 1 percent black, and 1 percent other. But 5 percent of the membership qualified for free or reduced-price lunches. Students were the Storm.

Originally, some of the middle school students at Slavens arrived via bus from the attendance area of Cole. Despite the promises of middle schools and endless enrichment programs at Cole, nothing worked at that school in a low-income area populated by people of color. The district closed Cole as a traditional middle school in 2004. By this time, numerous other elementaries also included students in sixth, seventh, and eighth grades.

Back in 1999, the district had re-introduced sixth grade at Bradley, Denison, and Ebert. A 2007 school listing observed there were programs stretching from at least kindergarten through eighth grade at such places as Bryant-Webster, Centennial, Fairmont, Howell (14250 Albrook Drive), Grant Ranch (5400 South Jay Circle), Greenlee, Greenwood, Harrington, Roberts (2100 Akron Way), and Waller (21601 51st Place). Force, Kaiser, Steck, Green Valley (4100 Jericho Street), and Whittier, were among places including sixth grade. The district insisted the program was necessary since not all sixth graders were ready for middle school. Many parents continued to insist on the sixth grade in elementary schools as a way of keeping their children out of problem-filled middle schools.

As had been the case of the old pre-junior high grammar schools, academies with students ranging from preschool to eighth grade often suffered tensions since the older students did not relate well to the younger learners. In some cases, such as at Park Hill School, after a few years, the program returned to early childhood education through fifth grade after having had classes for those in sixth, seventh, and eighth grades.

Nor were the high schools always successful in pulling in ninth graders. For a while, North High School used the empty Smedley School to teach freshmen whom it separated from the older students. (Part of the high school curriculum included mixing students of different classes and ages.) In a word, the middle school transformation bred new challenges. None of the reforms ever quite delivered the way proponents were sure they would.

Continuing Oversight

All the while, court oversight and busing continued. By the 1980s, desegregation controversies had mostly faded in other northern cities. Judge Matsch would not let go of Denver. Year after year, the story was the same. DPS came up with numerous proposals to meet the court mandates. At times the jurist expressed optimism that the district had almost fulfilled the court's orders. On other occasions, even supporters of desegregation voiced frustration with the judge's continual rejection of the district's efforts. Seemingly, no sooner had it complied with the existing court order than the court changed the requirements of what it had to do to become a unitary district.

Given these factors, Matsch continued to reject citizen proposals to end court oversight. For example, he did not listen to the Denver Coalition for Educational Priorities. It emerged in 1983–84 when the district pushed for a hike in the mill levy. The body was a partnership of 11 citizen and parent groups. The PTA, which had a falling out with the central administration over district finances, pushed the Coalition along with the Chamber of Commerce. Backers included the League of Women Voters, the Junior League, the American Jewish Committee, and the Urban League. A Denver Desegregation Project signed onto its efforts. None of its suggestions met Matsch's criteria for the end of busing. The group soon faded from the scene.

As DPS enrollment continued to decline and racial quotas remained the court's defining measure of the district, Matsch acted to impose an even more severe busing regimen. This resulted after he announced in December 1981 that he was disbanding the Community Education Council as of the end of the 1981–82 schoolyear. In its place, in December 1982 the jurist appointed a three-member Compliance Assistance Panel to advise the court. It consisted of three experts, all of whom taught in out-of-state college education programs: Willis Hawley of Vanderbilt, Beatriz Arias of Stanford, and Charles Willie of Harvard. None of them knew much about Denver. Matsch ordered DPS to pay for their advice.

The recommendations of the Panel caused new turbulence. From the beginning, DPS opposed the Panel. The board ordered the staff not to assist the outsiders. It was soon obvious that the professors had a completely different take on what was happening in the district than did DPS or members of the community.

The three members lamented that District #1 was still not well enough integrated. Population changes and dropping enrollment since the imposition of the Finger Plan, the experts observed, led to an ever greater percentage of minority students in classrooms. DPS, they suggested, had to readjust its attendance boundaries annually to redress this. Translated, their proposal meant that DPS would endlessly shift students around whereby every year youngsters would have to adjust to new school settings. The proposal undermined the principle of educational continuity: that students should stay together in the same school and program whereby they and the teachers got to know each other and there was a consensus about requirements and expectations.

At the best, the Compliance Assistance Panel stated no school should have more than 65 percent white students. Each facility had to have a minimum of 15 percent blacks and 15 percent Latinos. If the numbers of a minority group fell to fewer than 10 percent, a new busing scheme was necessary. DPS, it insisted, also needed more training programs, actions to redress the imbalance in discipline between races. Additionally, the district must restrict hardship transfers. These were where parents convinced DPS to allow waivers from busing because of family and work problems. Henceforth, the system was to grant them only under the direst circumstances unless the applicants showed that such transfers actually enhanced the integrated nature of the schools.

Besides, busing was not responsible for the massive collapse of DPS enrollment. At least that was the claim of Panel member Charles Willie. There was no connection, he declared, between white flight and school busing. An African-American, Willie had previously been a prime proponent of the highly dysfunctional busing plan in Boston that had brought community chaos rather than educational advancement.

Though Willie denied a link between busing and white flight, everybody else recognized it. Some called it "bus flight" with the school buses chasing families from the city. Among those who fled Denver to get away from mandatory busing were DPS teachers who did not want to send their children to a district where the schools were in turmoil amidst the mechanical court order.

For the most part, instructors moving out of the city kept their posts with DPS. The district had a low teacher turnover rate during the 1970s. This both reflected the contract stemming from a successful 1969 strike and a hiring freeze DPS imposed during the 1970s when enrollment plummeted while severe budget problems were endless.

To assure employees were loyal Denver citizens, in 1978 the school board imposed a residency requirement. As of January 1, 1979, all new personnel had to live in the City and County of Denver. Soon thereafter, the legislature outlawed the imposition of such school district residency requirements. Even at that, not until April 1985 did the board officially rescind the residency requirement which it had never thoroughly enforced. (A City and County of Denver residency requirement, adopted in 1978, remained in effect until 1998.)

Nor were the suggestions of Willie and cohorts well received by the populace. Backers of DPS complained that the Harvard professor and the other members of the Panel were nothing but ultra-manipulators whose proposals would make dysfunctional busing even worse. Popular protests forced the experts to modify their program. In reviewing the suggestions, Matsch did not order the implementation of much of their "compliance assistance plan." DPS continued to force about 12,000 of its 60,000 students on buses in the name of abstract integration.

A Lack of White Pupils

By 1985, nothing had changed. Once more, DPS asked the United States District Court to release it from the busing order. The plaintiffs opposed the request. They argued there were still severe racial gaps in DPS. Despite 15 years of busing, they pointed out that Harrington, Barrett, and Mitchell were still mostly black. As much as they had in 1969, these schools reflected the racial composition of the neighborhoods in which they were located rather than being representative of the total student mix of the district.

Judge Matsch agreed with the plaintiffs. He ordered DPS to take new efforts to assure the desegregation of the three elementary schools in black areas. The Mitchell attendance area, for example, was 96 percent minority. Many of the children lived in public housing where 99 percent of the residents were black,

Photo by Phil Goodstein

Cory School opened in 1952 at 1550 South Steele Street. By the mid-1980s, there were few elementary school-aged residents living within its attendance zone whereby DPS seemingly could not find enough white pupils to bus to fulfill the court integration order.

Hispanos, or Native Americans. Additionally, part of the problem DPS explained, was the lack of white pupils. This was particularly the case at Cory at 1550 South Steele Street. It had recently canceled its kindergarten program since there were so few youngsters who were four and five years old in the school's attendance district. Then, rather than enrolling them in DPS, parents opted to send their children to private or religious schools for grades one through three instead of having them bused across town.

Cory had opened in 1952, remembering John Cory who had served as a high school principal before becoming assistant superintendent for secondary education. During the busing epoch, DPS paired Cory with Barrett and Hallett schools. Neighborhood children entered Cory for fourth, fifth, and six grades. (Amidst a wave of closing schools in 1978–81 in the face of the drastic decline of enrollment, Cory was on the chopping block. It managed to stay open. After the end of busing in 1995–96, it gained a reputation as among the top schools in the district.)

Parental choice also kept parents of white Ellis School children from sending them to Harrington for fourth, fifth, and sixth grades. Though the court ordered DPS to invest more than a $1 million to redress the segregation at Barrett, Harrington, and Mitchell, nothing worked. Before long, there were also complaints that Gilpin School was hopelessly segregated. Both foes and friends of busing lamented that frequently the court-ordered scheme did little more than transport children across town from one segregated school to another segregated school.

The 1985 survey of Harrington, Mitchell, and Barrett came after Community Education Council reviews in 1977 and 1978 had decried eight schools as not being truly integrated. At that time, the oversight body stated that Valdez, Mitchell, Eagleton, Fairview, Oakland, and Gilpin schools suffered unacceptable racial disparities. The 1978 analysis also complained that Lake Junior High and West High were "virtually unchanged" in their ethnic/racial enrollments despite busing.

Part of the problem, the district observed, was the paucity of white students. The rapidly plunging enrollment was overwhelmingly the result of the massive exit of white pupils. As such, there were simply not enough "Anglos" to fill the classrooms with the court-mandated numbers to assure desegregation. As the 1985 complaint revealed, conditions had not changed during the intervening years despite repeated orders from the court that DPS must have busing.

In some places, the lack of school integration reflected the way parents went out of their way to assure their children attended some schools and not others. Once more, Park Hill School was the exemplar. By 1979, it was among the healthiest integrated schools in the district. It counted 470 of its 730 pupils as white, making it a showcase for desegregation. The number was considerably down from 1970 when DPS stated Park Hill had space for 1,050 students when it had an enrollment of 1,115. For a while, the school had been on double sessions. It was not subjected to busing.

In contrast, Stedman School, about a mile and one-quarter to the north, was down to 167 students in a building DPS now stated had room for 400. (In the mid-1960s, DPS had counted more than 700 pupils at Stedman. A 1970 survey reported 601 students at the school, a place with 600 seats.) By the time of the

Photo by Phil Goodstein

Harrington School opened in 1926 at 3230 38th Avenue as Adams Street School.
Advocates of integration complained that it suffered from a lack of white students
in the 1970s and 1980s.

1979 report, DPS counted 32.3 percent of Stedman students as white. In part, both
the 1982 creation of the extended-day school at Gilpin and the 1986 launch of a
Montessori magnet program at Mitchell were a means of redressing the district's
inability to find white children to fill the classrooms in those schools.

During the 1985 court hearing, advocates of busing also wanted Judge Matsch
to order DPS to undertake more aggressive efforts to integrate its staff. Even while
stating DPS had still failed to show itself a unitary district, Matsch gave DPS greater
autonomy, particularly in adjusting school boundaries.

In November 1985, DPS appealed Judge Matsch's ruling to the Tenth Circuit.
This led to a hearing before the appellate court in March 1986. A three-judge
panel upheld the District Court. Not only was Matsch reluctant to let go of his
oversight of District #1, but Rachel Noel and some of the original plaintiffs in the
Keyes case wanted the court to remain the final arbiter of school decisions. Their
lawyer Gordon Greiner continually challenged any and all DPS suggestions of
ending court oversight.

Greiner constantly mocked the school board and the DPS administration. They
were in a state of "self-induced helplessness." The district's leadership was so
eager to defeat integration that it claimed it had no power to make sure that busing
worked. For that matter, busing was a "phony issue." To prove this, Greiner pointed
to the massive employment of busing in the suburbs. The real issue was busing
for integration. Given this stance, he and Noel made it clear they simply did not
trust the district. Without the heavy hand of the United States District Court, the
plaintiffs feared DPS would return to its old racist practices.

From the beginning, Noel had been convinced DPS was an outstanding system for white students. The end of busing, she feared, would so deprive black students of their right to receive an education equal to what DPS delivered to whites. Nationally, Roy Wilkins, the head of the NAACP, admitted that while there were severe problems with busing, they were worth the trouble in assuring equal educational opportunity.

Not all of those who sued the district in 1969 agreed with Noel and Wilkins. For example, plaintiffs Edward J. Starks, Jr. and Josephine Perez expressed qualms about busing and its impact. Starks stated he had joined the suit to assure quality education. Against this, integration proponents, with the help of the courts, had turned busing into a panacea. Perez stated she was an advocate of integration and equal educational opportunity. Busing had not achieved it. Miller Hudson, who had political ambitions in the 1970s, passed on a run for the school board during the middle of the decade after he encountered turbulence from busing advocates who branded him a racist when he claimed the question was not busing, but what happened at the school at the end of the bus ride.

Eventually, lead plaintiff Wilfred Keyes also questioned what the case had wrought. At first, he was highly supportive of busing, stating that if busing was necessary for equal educational opportunity, then "let's get on with it." In looking back at the suit, Keyes stated he neither expected nor wanted court-ordered school busing for desegregation. All he desired was open enrollment whereby his children had a fair chance in a nondiscriminatory school system. The chiropractor, a member of Jehovah's Witnesses, died at age 74 on April 14, 1999. In the meanwhile, the city's largest ethnic group, people of Latin American heritage, had become ever more part of DPS and the busing order.

A Note on Sources:

Reports of the death of William Doyle include *RMN*, May 3, 1986, p. 8, *NYT*, May 4, 1986, p. 44, *DP*, May 3, 1986, p. 1C, and *Denver Catholic Register*, May 14, 1986, p. 7. Logan, *Tenth Circuit*, 516, outlines the early career of Judge Richard Matsch. During an August 14, 2019, interview, Ed Benton recalled his initial acquaintance with Matsch and how they carpooled from southwest Denver to downtown in the late 1950s when both worked for Holme Roberts & Owen. *New Yorker*, May 21, 2018, pp. 48, 50, profiled Matsch, particularly his role in the Timothy McVeigh case. *NYT*, May 29, 2019, reviewed the jurist's career on his passing. Fishman, "Endless Journey," 190–91 traces Matsch's background and intervention into the Keyes case. Crucial rulings by Judge Matsch on the litigation include 474 FSupp 1265, 609 FSupp 1491, 653 FSupp 1536, and 670 FSupp 1513.

Bailey, "Journey Full Circle," 124–25, tells of the 1979 probe of whether DPS was internally segregated despite the busing order. Fishman, "Endless Journey," 199–200, ponders the continuing problem of the internal segregation of classrooms. *RMN*, January 10, 1979, p. 8, contained charges about segregated reading programs. In an interview in *Our Neighborhood Schools* in Alweis, *Rebels Remembered*, Evie Dennis claimed DPS desegregated the schools, but did not integrate them, pointing out the internal segregation of classrooms. *GPHN*, June 2019, p. 10, recalled internal segregation in the schools.

DP, July 31, 1979, p. 3, told of Matsch's order. So did *Cmq*, September 1979, p. 3. *RMN*, December 2, 1980, p. 4, reported DPS's appeal for relief from the court ruling and the district's drastically shrinking enrollment.

A folder simply identified as "1980s" in GP contains a good deal on the clashes over busing and Judge Matsch's opinions in 1980. Included is a *Post* editorial, April 13, 1980, p. 20, observing that obstinacy on both sides led to "short-range chaos." There is also a May 12, 1980, PTA letter to the board of education in the folder that criticizes the board for failing to address Judge Matsch's concerns on how to make DPS into a unitary district. Additionally, the folder has materials about the "Our Future—Our Schools" campaign. Bailey, "Journey Full Circle," 136–37, looks at Matsch's efforts to define a "unitary district."

RMN, May 11, 1974, p. 8, and *DP*, May 12, 1974, p. 47, reported the creation of the CEC. Materials on it are in FF 1:18–22, 24, of the Noel papers and FF 1:3 of the Keyes papers. FF 9:90 of the DPS papers has the court appointment of the Council. *RMN*, May 18, 1975, p. 13, told of the reappointment of the panel. *RMN*, February 15, 1975, p. 5, and *DP*, February 14, 1975, p. 20, observed the group's first report. *DP*, November 1, 1975, p. 2, analyzed the Council's role as the court monitor over how well desegregation was working. *Cmq*, April 1978, looked at the members of the group. Judge Matsch discussed the body's powers, modifying its size in 474 FSupp 1265.

On May 30, 1975, p. 18, the *News* mentioned Maurice Mitchell's re-appointment as the head of the Council. My *University Park*, 60–62, 64, outlines Mitchell's background and role at DU. Also see Steve Fisher, *The University of Denver* (Charleston: History Press, 2014), 86, 129, and Allen duPont, *From Denver to the World* (Denver: DU, 1989), 161–73.

Center Magazine, the publication of the Center for the Study of Democratic Institutions, January-February 1978, p. 1, heralded Mitchell becoming the head of the think tank. The chancellor traced his career in a wide-ranging interview in the March-April 1978 issue, pp. 7–16. Included were his remarks there had been no drastic and dramatic conflicts over the Vietnam War at DU, p. 10. He further talked about his experiences in the July-August 1978 issue, pp. 2–7, while writing about his involvement with CEC in "The Desegregation of Denver's Public Schools," November-December 1978, pp. 67–76.

Based on an interview with Mitchell, Pearson, "Denver Case," 204–06, 210–15, 221–22, is overwhelmingly positive about the achievements of the CEC. *RMN*, July 31, 1975, p. 8, and *DP*, July 31, 1975, p. 14, reported CANS' blast against Mitchell.

RMN, May 11, 1976, p. 14, observed Jean Bain taking charge of the CEC. Francisco Rios outlined the origins and purpose of the group in a February 14, 1978, memo in the folder "1976–77–78" in GP. *DP*, June 29, 1978, p. 47, mentioned a report from the Council about the failure of DPS to make desegregation a reality in some schools. *Cmq*, August 1980, pp. 3, 5, 7, had PTA complaints about the executive sessions of the CEC. Also see *RMN*, January 11, 1979, p, 5.

A special issue of *SN*, January 17, 1979, pp. 39–42, looked at the status of the district's compliance with the court desegregation order. Included was a discussion of the scope of the CEC, Omar Blair's remarks about it, p. 41, and Joseph Brzeinski's views, p. 42. *SN*, June 4, 1979, pp. 72–73, quoted Judge Matsch's ruling about the status of the court order. FF 1:20 of the Noel papers has a copy of Resolution 2060 in which DPS had petitioned the court for a release from supervision.

Cmq, June 1980, p. 1, reported the creation of the Ad Hoc Committee, listing its members. *PPV*, 1:1 (1981), p. 7, outlined the effort. Ibid., pp. 13–14, gave the inside view of the Ad Hoc Committee by school board member Kay Schomp. An undated *DP* editorial in the 1982–83 PTA Historian's Notebook in GP observed the roles of Marion Hammond and Kay Schomp in the Ad Hoc Committee and their calling for the end of court oversight of DPS. *Cmq*, September 1980, p. 1, November 1980, p. 2, December 1980, p. 2, January 1981, p. 2, March 1981, p. 2, and June 1981, p. 2, stressed the Ad Hoc Committee. FF 21:42 of the Yasui papers has the 1981 report of the Ad Hoc Committee for a Unitary School System. There is also a report on the subject in FF 1:24 of the Noel papers which additionally has material on the Total Access and Consensus plans. *DP*, December 15, 1981, p. 1B, discussed the Ad Hoc Plan. *RMN*, June 6, 1981, p. 7, told of the report of the Ad Hoc Committee, observing Judge Matsch's rejection of it, November 13, 1981, p. 4. Fishman, "Endless Journey," 649, mentions the court ruling on it. Bailey, "Journey Full Circle," 126–28, reviews the effort. Her work, 142–46, looks at the hearings before Judge Match in 1984 and 1985 and the appeal to the Tenth Circuit Court.

Cmq, March 1974, and September 1975, includes the PTA call for calm and the acceptance of school busing. An April 26, 1974, letter in the 1973–74 PTA Notebook in GP criticized the school board/administration for the district's failure to collaborate with the PTA to make busing work. The 1974–75 PTA Notebook in GP traces the declining membership of the PTA from the late 1960s through the mid-1970s. There are letters of resignation and disaffiliation from the PTA in the folder "1976–77–78" in GP.

The correspondence file of the 1975–76 PTA papers in GP includes the tendered resignation of PTA president Cathy Crandell in 1975 on her moving out of Denver at the beginning of the school year in the best interests of her family. It also observes that Mrs. Ricky Marquez, who had been on the ballot to become PTA president, dropped out of the race because she and her family suddenly moved out of town. The 1978–79 PTA notebook in GP has newspaper clippings about the organization, mostly undated, that mention the PTA's role and question whether it was an "uppity" group. The notebook has a great deal about the club's efforts to involve itself in negotiations on the new teachers contract. *Cmq*, September 1978, p. 2, stressed the PTA's interest in the talks between the DCTA and DPS. The folder "1976–77–78" in GP has an April 16, 1976, memo discussing links between the CCR, DPS, and the PTA.

SN, September 16, 1981, p. 6, outlined the court order for inservice school committees. Also see Fishman, "Endless Journey," 197. *SN*, May 26, 1982, p. 69, discussed Judge Matsch's May 12, 1982, ruling and the end of the CEC. *RMN*, May 10, 1981, p. 24A, May 11, 1981, p. 6, and May 12, 1981, p. 6, was a retrospection on the first decade of busing, asking if minority students actually received any help from it. *PPV*, 1:1 (1981), also had a review of the first decade of busing. It was a magazine published by the Western Resource Institute, receiving federal funds, to help inform minority parents of the school desegregation efforts. The journal outlined the chronology of the effort, pp. 3–4. *PPV*, May 1981, pp. 5, 9, 12, raised the point about the lack of test scores based on race and ethnicity in questioning the candidates in that year's school board contest.

Fishman, "Endless Journey," 192–94, Flicker, *Justice and School Systems*, 11–12, and Bailey, "Journey Full Circle," 126–31, observe the debates over the Ad Hoc Plan, Total Access Plan, and Consensus Plan. *RMN*, October 7, 1981, p. 4, mentioned Bill Schroeder's anti-busing proposal. *RMN*, November 13, 1981, p. 4, reported Judge Matsch rejecting it and the Ad Hoc Plan. It further reported his other decisions, including the Consensus Plan, March 19, 1982, p. 6. A copy of the jurist's May 10, 1982, ruling, 540 FSupp 399, is in the 1983–84 PTA Notebook in GP.

The text of the Total Access Plan is in FF 4:89 of the Ash Grove PTA Papers. *Focus*, January 1982, outlined the effort. *SN*, January 13, 1982, p. 33, January 27, 1982, p. 37, February 10, 1982, p. 41, and March 25, 1982, p. 53, emphasized the initiative, featuring choice. *RMN*, December 1, 1981, p. 1, stressed the open enrollment dimension of the Total Access Plan. It highlighted the magnet proposal, December 11, 1981, p. 6. *DP*, May 16, 1982, p. 1A, and *SN*, May 26, 1982, p. 69, reported Matsch's decision insisting busing was necessary for DPS.

In passing, Fishman, "Endless Journey," mentions magnet schools and the court's authorization of them. Ibid., 198, 214, deals with hardship transfers. Matsch commented on DPS integration plans, authorizing the Consensus Plan, in 609 FSupp 1905. *RMN*, December 16, 1983, p. 1, observed a new DPS request for the court to end the busing order. Fishman, "Endless Journey," 203, discusses the intervention of the Department of Justice in the Keyes case. Also see *RMN*, February 9, 1984, p. 6.

SR, January 21, 1971, and March 17, 1971, esp. p. 8, outlined Superintendent Howard Johnson's magnet school proposals. *DP*, February 24, 1982, p. 10A, profiled the hopes of backers of magnet schools. The 1983–84 PTA Notebook in GP includes promotional materials for the extended day program at Gilpin. There is a review of the district's first modern magnet schools in an October 1982 DPS study "Planning and Development: A Progress Report." The document specially deals with Gilpin, pp. 8–10, and Knight, pp. 7–8. *RMN*, December 26, 1986, p. 10, exuberantly praised the Knight program. *Focus*, April 1983, p. 2, outlined the extended-day program at Gilpin.

The November 1993 and November 1994 enrollment guidelines reports for elementary magnet schools, in the 1995 notebook in GP, spell out the district's commitment to magnet schools, referring to Resolution 2233 of April 10, 1984. *BN*, February 9, 1996, recalled the measure. Also see Evie Dennis, *Report to the Board on Resolutions 2233 and 2314* (Denver: DPS, [1988]), 30, 32. The 1992–93 notebook in GP includes a discussion of Resolution 2233 and magnet schools. The DPS pupil assignment rules, as amended on February 20, 1996, outlined how magnets allowed parents choice, specifically looking at Gilpin and other programs. A copy of the district's rules on "Choice and Pupil Transfers" for 1996–97 is in the 1997 Policy Updates Notebook in GP.

FF 4:105–07 of the DPS papers focus on the 1951 Gilpin building. FF 4:112–29 are on the extended day program at Gilpin. Also see my *Curtis Park*, 53, 90. *Cmq*, December 1979, p. 5, reported the Latch-Key program.

A listing in the membership directory of the Denver Teachers' Club, ca. 1912, observes a member was affiliated with the Froebel Montessori School. I have not been able to find any details about it. *DP*, October 11, 1964, p. 26, announced plans to open a Denver Montessori House. *RMN*, March 6, 1968, p. 50, reported the city had two Montessori programs.

The 1986–87 *DPS Report*, p. 9, glances at the emergence of the Mitchell Montessori program. Also see the "Elementary Magnet Enrollment Guidelines" of November 1994, p. 8, in the 1995 notebook in GP. *GPHN*, October 2013, p. 5, spelled out the Montessori curriculum. McGoey, *No Free Gift*, 72, observes the ideological debates about Maria Montessori. *Schools for a New Century* will focus on subsequent Montessori debates, especially concerning Ana Marie Sandoval School and the fate of the Montessori program at Gilpin.

FF 5:89–96 of the DPS papers are on Mitchell. *School Book*, 64, 65, deals with the origins of the school. DPS PR, October 24, 1991, told of the mural by Carlota Espinoza. Mary Motian-Meadows and Georgia Garnsey, *The Murals of Colorado* (Boulder: Johnson, 2012), 135, 136, celebrates Espinoza's work.

Dennis, *Report on Resolutions*, 33–34, looks at the Montessori program at Mitchell and the school's ties to Barrett and Harrington. FF 5:94 of the DPS papers has a pamphlet on the Montessori program.

SB, November 14, 1949, p. 1, celebrated the construction of Knight School. Files on it are FF 5:42–50 of the district's papers at DPL. I review its links to the Belcaro and Bonnie Brae neighborhoods in *Washington Park*, 219–20, and *School Book*, 391. *WPP*, March 1997, p. 4, highlighted Knight Fundamental Academy. A November 1994 DPS report analyzed the character of Knight Fundamental, dealing with the possibility of allowing nearby students to enroll in it; a copy is in the 1994–95 notebook in GP. FF 5:46–50 of the DPS papers review the program. Volume three will deal with the subsequent development of Knight School.

Cmq, June 1979, p. 3, had a PTA discussion of the impact of busing on Traylor. *RMN*, October 3, 1990, p. 7, November 1, 1990, p. 6, December 14, 1990, p. 22, and September 10, 1991, p. 20, reviewed the problems of busing between Traylor and Greenlee and the reorientation of the academies.

A March 1996 program evaluation of Traylor Fundamental Academy, in the 1996–97 notebook of the GP, outlines the origins of the effort. It also looks at Greenlee. "Report on Elementary Magnets" for 1995–96, in the 1994–95 notebook in GP, p. 4, observes that whites were ineligible to apply in some cases for magnet schools. A 1995 DPS count of poverty in the schools is in the 1995 BSC Notebook in GP.

GP includes a 1979–80 scrapbook filled with clippings about plans to introduce middle schools. A January 23, 1981, letter from an unidentified assistant superintendent, in loose papers in GP, has answers to questions about plans for the middle schools concerned citizens asked at public meetings on October 31 and November 1, 1980. *Cmq*, June 1981, p. 6, outlined plans for the middle schools. FF

1:47 of the Ash Grove PTA Papers has the DPS middle school handbook for parents of 1982. GP also has a copy of the October 1982 report of the DPS Department of Planning and Development about how middle schools were to shape the future of the district.

RMN, March 14, 1980, mentioned suggestions of returning ninth graders to high schools. *SN*, October 21, 1980, p. 18, featured the transfer as part of the district's plan for the 1980s, "Schools of the Future." The 1982–83 *DPS Report*, 10, emphasized the shift of ninth graders back to high school.

RMN, January 23, 1967, p. 5, observed Oberholtzer's revision of the junior high curriculum. On December 7, 2018, retired DPS junior high/middle school teacher and counselor Jimi O'Connor reflected on the cynical studies about middle schools. He stated the need for greater high school enrollments for sports competitions was a prime factor behind the shift of ninth graders back to high schools.

Cmq, May 1980, reviewed the origins of the Long-Range Plan and its links to middle schools. It had already emphasized the initiative, December 1979, p. 1. *Cmq*, June 1980, p. 1, observed the board delaying the planned implementation of middle schools.

Middle Schools: How They Work is an undated DPS brochure touting middle schools as a sure-fire solution to the problems which had plagued junior highs. A copy is in FF 2:19 of the DPS papers. *Focus*, December 1980, pp. 1–3, insisted middle schools were "a step forward." The December 1981 *Focus*, p. 7, emphasized preparations to make them a reality. The publication declared 1982–83 "The Year of the Middle School," September 1982, p. 1.

There are numerous undated articles in the 1986–87 Clipping Notebook in GP dealing with the push to transfer sixth graders to middle schools. *Cmq*, February 1988, p. 10, reported the board's January 7, 1988, decision sending sixth graders to middle schools. The red 1996–97 BAC notebook in GP includes a February 1997 programmatic explanation of "Middle School Model — History and Present Status."

On January 9, 2018, veteran junior high/middle school teacher Jimi O'Connor explained the crucial importance of the programs, especially for struggling students. On November 17, 2018, he recalled the nature of the administration of the middle schools, the role of the straw boss, and the way the schools counted the student-teacher ratio.

The 1995 BSC Notebook in GP includes a June 1995 review of the effort to expand Moore to eighth grade. On occasion, Delia Armstrong, principal of Moore in the 1990s, has shared her memories. Back in the mid-1990s, K. Ely Tannenbaum, a member of the Morey collaborative decision-making committee, gave me his views of the middle school and how accounts unfairly defamed it. *BN*, November 20, 1998, observed the adding of middle school programs to Moore and Slavens. *Cmq*, April 1984, p. 2, mentioned leasing parts of Slavens to the Greek Orthodox Church. FF 6:39 of the DPS papers deals with leases of the empty Slavens to preschools.

An unidentified March 17, 1984, clipping in the 1983–84 PTA Historian's Notebook in GP reported plans to sell Slavens. *School Book*, 391, sketches the contributions of Leon Slavens and the opening of the school named in his memory. *BN*, January 12, January 19, and January 26, 1996, mentioned plans to reopen

Slavens. *BN*, January 28, 1998, stressed the links between Slavens and those living in the attendance district of Cole.

Back in the early 1990s, Stephanie Miles recalled being ordered on the bus from Slavens and how she and her family feared the ancient quality of Wyatt School. On October 6, 2018, Kelly Waters shared her experiences as a teacher at Slavens, discussing parental involvement and the waiting list at the academy. Chalkbeat, September 27, 2019, celebrated Slavens as a National Blue Ribbon School.

FF 1:24 of the DPS papers is a March 12, 2007, listing of the district's schools, observing programs stretching through eighth grade. *BN*, February 18, 1999, reported adding sixth grade back to Bradley. *BN*, February 16, 2001, mentioned the reintroduction of sixth grade at Sabin School. It also commented on the increasing popularity of that effort.

Cmq, February 1983, p. 2, reviewed Judge Matsch's latest decision on the busing case and the appointment of the Compliance Assistance Panel. Articles on this include *RMN*, December 17, 1982, p. 7, and *DP*, December 17, 1982, p. 4B. There are many clippings, mostly undated and unidentified, in the 1982–83 PTA News Notebook in GP about Matsch's panel of outside experts. Specifically identified pieces include *RMN*, March 15, 1983, p. 8, and March 19, 1983, p. 16, and *DP*, March 12, 1983, and April 16, 1983.

Lukas, *Common Ground*, 244, observes Charles Willie's role in Boston. Ibid., 649–50, lists the massive drop in enrollment in Boston schools in response to busing despite Willie's assertion there was no link between busing and white flight. In contrast, Fishman, "Endless Journey," 658, is most aware of the connection between the Keyes case and white flight. So is Orfield, *Must We Bus?* 36, 71. CANS, *Judicial Fiat*, inside back cover, has detailed statistics about the decline of white enrollment in response to the busing order. The 1983–84 PTA Notebook in GP includes a discussion of the views of Willie.

Fishman, "Endless Journey," 197–98, 210, observes clashes between the Compliance Assistance Panel and DPS. Also see FF 1:16 of the Keyes papers, *DP*, March 12, 1983, and April 8, 1983, and *RMN*, March 15, 1983, p. 8, and March 19, 1983, p. 16, on the Compliance Assistance Panel.

RMN, February 9, 1984, p. 6, emphasized the Department of Justice's continuing interest in DPS as the national exemplar of court control in forcing a big city system to be a "unitary district." *DP*, February 10, 1984, and *RMN*, May 24, 1984, reported Gordon Greiner's insistence on continued court oversight.

There is a glance at the Denver Coalition on Educational Priorities in FF 21:33 of the Yasui papers. I have a copy of *Citizen's Guide to the Denver Public School Budget*, a brochure issued by the Coalition in 1984. The inside cover spells out membership in the group and its goals.

On November 17, 2018, Jimi O'Connor recalled "bus flight." He also reflected on the exodus of many DPS teachers, especially those with school-aged children, from Denver. Pearson, "Denver Case," 180, mentions the low teacher turnover rate in DPS during the 1970s. *RMN*, June 15, 1978, p. 6, reported the push for a residency requirement. *Cmq*, December 1978, p. 4, told of the board adopting such a policy. *Cmq*, June 1979, p. 2, chronicled the legislature killing a bill for residency requirements. *RMN*, April 26, 1985, p. 8, observed the board rescinding the residency requirement.

General articles on busing and court oversight are also in the 1983–84 PTA Historian's Notebook. Other PTA notebooks contain numerous PTA letters and resolutions urging the court to end its oversight. They also include Matsch's decisions of November 12, 1981, and May 12, 1982, both of which ripped the district's continual failure to meet the judge's mandates. The 1982–83 PTA Historian's Notebook in GP additionally has many newspaper articles about clashes between the board and the Compliance Assistance Panel.

DP, April 9, 1983, told of the frustration of pro-integration board member Marion Hammond about Matsch's continual rejection of DPS efforts. Also see *DP*, April 9, 1983. An op-ed piece in *RMN*, April 28, 1983, mocked how the court kept changing its definition of a unitary district. Matsch's 1985 ruling is 609 FSupp 1491.

Undated articles in the 1985–86 PTA Clipping Notebook in GP discuss the problems with the racial disparities at Harrington, Mitchell, and Barrett. They additionally talk about the lack of kindergartners at Cory and the way many white parents did not allow their children to get on school buses. Fishman, "Endless Journey," 200, observes the racial census of the Mitchell attendance area. The Evie Dennis interview in *Our Neighborhood Schools* in Alweis, *Rebels Remembered*, observes that busing often simply hauled children from one segregated school to another one.

DP, June 29, 1978, p. 47, bemoaned the lack of desegregation success at some schools and the report of the CEC. *RMN*, April 28, 1977, p. 5, had reported the resegregation of some of the schools stemming from the massive loss of white pupils. *RMN*, January 15, 1989, p. 1, repeated the refrain that integration was lagging and busing had not achieved the promised results. On January 18, 1989, p. 8, the *News* reported how the school board mentioned this when again asking the federal District Court for relief from the busing order.

DP, May 22, 1979, p. 16, observed the contrasting enrollments and racial compositions of Park Hill and Stedman schools. There are undated articles from the *News* and the *Post* about the 1985 busing hearings in the 1985–86 PTA Clipping Notebook in GP.

American Teacher, September 1971, p. 10, reported Roy Wilkins' views on busing. CANS, *Judicial Fiat*, 11, quoted the perspectives of Edward J. Starks and Josephine Perez. On December 17, 2019, Miller Hudson shared the story about his pondering a run for the school board in the mid-1970s. *RMN*, February 18, 1985, p. 10, reflected on Wilfred Keyes' changing views on busing. *GPHN*, June 17, 1999, p. 12, reviewed his life.

Chapter Eleven

Bilingual Education

I n addition to the order mandating DPS must bus children in the name of abstract racial equality, the Keyes case saw the United States District Court require DPS to be highly conscious of ethnic divisions. This not only included defining people of Spanish heritage as a distinct group who had to be integrated with black and white pupils, but it also mandated that the system be aware of the backgrounds of students whereby, as necessary, it provided bilingual education. Here it listened to Hispanic civil rights groups that argued problems in the schools and unequal educational opportunity stemmed as much from ethnicity as they did from race.

In the decades after World War II, when the city's Hispanic population rapidly grew, DPS sporadically reached out to Latinos. Among other programs, it promoted Spanish language classes. In October 1953, at the behest of the city's Commission on Community Relations, DPS worked with city hall to form the City–School Project. This was an effort to redress the specific reasons people of Spanish heritage faced severe problems in the schools. The program, which lasted into the mid-1960s, included sponsoring a Latin American Student Council for students at West, North, and Manual. Most of all, the City–School Project emphasized the need to keep Hispanic youngsters in school. Not only did many of them drop out of DPS, but they also left the city's parochial schools in large numbers before graduating.

Lino Lopez was a key figure in the City–School Project, serving as a consultant to the Commission on Community Relations. He subsequently worked for DPS in dealing with the district's cultural relations. Mildred Biddick, a former principal who coordinated the Special Study Committee of 1962–64, was the director of the City–School Project from 1961 to 1966. Lena Archuleta went from the program to helping coordinate the district's Office of School–Community Relations.

Photo by Phil Goodstein

DPS has recognized the large number of students whose first language is Spanish. In places, such as Colfax School near West Colfax Avenue and Tennyson Street, signs are often in Spanish.

The Keyes case also impacted local terminology. Amidst the litigation, the courts and the media adopted the term "Anglo" for all students of European descent other than those of Spanish origins. In the process, the historic enemies of the English, the Irish, became Anglos. So did Italians, Poles, and East European Jews. It was never clear if Basques or people from Portugal or Catatonia were Hispanos or Anglos. A discussion of this irony was completely beyond the integration debate.

Back in 1962, DPS launched Operation Amigo, an effort to give schoolchildren a better understanding of Latin America. The assumption was that those studying the subject were of non-Hispanic backgrounds. Here and there, the district placed Spanish-speaking youngsters in classes designed to teach the tongue to those who grew up speaking English. The whole issue of the way DPS treated youngsters who spoke a first language other than English was initially absent from the intense busing debates of the late 1960s/early 1970s.

This was a change. As immigrants had poured into Denver in the 19th century, DPS stated Americanizing them was a prime purpose. This included emphasizing the ideals of American democracy in classrooms filled with youngsters whose families stemmed from different lands. Ideally, schools taught the sons and daughters of immigrants the habits, values, and customs of the United States whereby the melting pot was predominantly filled with the traditions of the English-speaking peoples.

Photo by Phil Goodstein

People of Spanish-language background have often been invisible to white, ruling Denver. Nearly 100,000 Latinos marched on May Day 2010, asserting their identity and pride. Pictured is part of the lengthy procession near 12th Avenue and Lincoln Street.

DPS bluntly hoped that youngsters, so exposed to White Anglo-Saxon Protestant society in school, would take the lessons home with them, helping Americanize their parents. Every now and then, some schools, particularly those filled with immigrants, had international programs designed to acquaint so-called old-line Americans about the contributions of peoples from around the world.

Virtually from the time Denver started to fill with people of Latin American backgrounds in the 1920s, such individuals banded together in civil rights groups and self-help organizations. They did not, however, focus on the schools. Most newcomers dutifully sent their children to the assigned neighborhood schools. Frequently, they did not participate in them. In part, this stemmed from a fear of authority—some had fled from coercive governments elsewhere. Others found themselves intimidated by teachers and principals. When confronted, they were usually quite deferential to the school authorities. Nobody in Latino Denver was a prime advocate of busing during the late 1960s.

In the face of the Keyes litigation, Latinos found their children bused across town in the abstract name of integration. In the process, the students lost a home base in a school where teachers understood their culture. Appalled that the court intervention had actually made conditions worse, Spanish-Americans increasingly insisted their children needed classes relating to their culture. Given that the city was increasingly becoming home of people from south of the border who spoke Spanish as their first language, it was also necessary to provide instruction in Spanish in schools with a predominantly Latino student body. This, backers hoped, was the first step to help the youngsters gain a mastery of English whereby they had an equal opportunity for educational and business success in an English-speaking world.

The Congress of Hispanic Educators

Virtually from the time school busing controversies first pulsated in the 1960s, members of the Latino community were concerned the district was failing their children. Many of the Spanish-Surnamed wanted the system to address itself to the inferior performance of people of Latino heritage. Amidst the busing controversies, the district reached out to Mexican-American Denver around 1970 when the school board named 12 community figures to a Hispanic Education Advisory Council. Members included West Side political boss Waldo Benavidez, broadcaster Levi Beall, Eloy Mares, a senior figure in the Juvenile Court, and attorney and future school board member Bert Gallegos. Ideally, the body made sure the board of education was aware of Latino concerns.

Near the end of the 20th century, Mexican-American educational advocates urged DPS to adopt El Alma de Raza as a program emphasizing the culture of Hispanos—it meant the soul of the people. By that time, numerous Latin American educational advocacy groups had come and gone. Back in the late 1980s, for example, school board member Rich Castro was linked with a Hispanic Citizens Committee. No group had a greater influence on DPS policies dealing with Latinos during the Keyes era than the Congress of Hispanic Educators.

A profession group, the Congress asserted itself as busing controversies roiled the city in the late 1960s/early 1970s. Primarily, it consisted of Latino DPS teachers who insisted on recognition and respect. Back in 1969, it was greatly concerned that the whole debate over busing ignored the city's many Spanish-Surnamed children. Then about 20 percent of the total DPS enrollment, Hispanos had the worst achievement level and the highest dropout rate. That the status of such children was not an issue in the raging school controversies, the organization realized, reflected how black civil rights groups were well organized and had a specific program of action. The Spanish-Surnamed, the Congress of Hispanic Educators lamented, did not have the vision and unity of African-American Denver.

Corky Gonzales of the Crusade for Justice agreed. As the crucial 1969 balloting neared, he attacked busing as a wrong solution to the problems of a "faulty and regressive education system." The Gilberts Plan, Gonzales continued, was "misleading, false, facetious, and pretentious." Voters of Spanish heritage overwhelming favored exponents of neighborhood schools in the May 1969 balloting.

As the triumph of Bert Gallegos in the 1971 school polling showed, there was an extremely conservative side of Spanish-American Denver. No more than among whites who were extremely fearful of busing did Hispanos endorse the program. In 1972, right as busing controversies ripped the city, a poll showed that while two-thirds of blacks thought busing was a good idea, only one-fourth of the Latinos supported the program.

In January 1974, the Congress of Hispanic Educators convinced the United States District Court that the resolution to the Keyes case had to be more than a question of black and white. That month, Judge William Doyle gave the Congress the right to intervene in the litigation as a co-plaintiff. In part, this reflected the Supreme Court decision, a ruling ordering the district to be fully aware of the concerns of Latinos.

The Mexican-American Legal Defense and Educational Fund (MALDEF) provided the Congress with legal assistance. The group had emerged in 1968. It sought to serve Chicanos comparable to the way the NAACP Legal Defense Fund helped blacks. Back when they were first pondering the suit against DPS, advocates of integration had discussions with MALDEF as well as the Legal Defense Fund.

At the time of the original busing order, there were around 5,000 students in the system who came from homes where English was not the first language. Within a few years, the number was up to 13,600. Concerned voices in Hispanic Denver, virtually all of whom spoke English, were no more happy with the performance of the district in educating their children than the way African-Americans bemoaned the poor performance of black children.

Busing, however, Latinos agreed, was not the solution. What DPS needed were programs that touched their children's ethnicity. Insofar as some lacked a grasp of English, DPS must help them acquire a command of the language. On this basis, some schools in predominantly Latino neighborhoods launched what was known as TESOL, Teaching English to Speakers of Other Languages. At times, educational and legal jargon called students who lacked a command of English "LEP," those with Limited English Proficiency.

Nobody more embraced the effort than Fred Manzanares. In 1971, he became principal of Greenlee School along the east side of the 1100 block of Lipan Street in a Latino neighborhood. Besides being a veteran educator, he was an actor. In the 1960s, he was a Spanish-language instructor on Channel Six. At that time, elementary students in fifth and sixth grades were expected to take Spanish or French. Often the schools lacked instructors fluent in the tongues. The district's solution was to have teachers oversee the classes while students watched broadcasts teaching them French or Spanish during the day on KRMA. Manzanares was a prime figure in the Spanish show, a program where the teachers often enacted skits. Already in the early 1950s, the district had started to emphasize foreign language classes at the elementary level. The effort accelerated once Channel Six went on the air in 1956.

Efforts at District #1 language instruction to those exclusively speaking Spanish also dated back to at least the early 1950s. At that time, Denver Boys, a DPS-sponsored organization reaching out to poor young men, arranged for members to perform a ten-part radio series in Spanish. It was so well received that KLMO, 1080 AM in Longmont, started broadcasting educational Spanish-language shows. In many ways, the TESOL program was fully in tune with the classes DPS had offered immigrants before World War II to help them acquire English.

The bilingual controversy touched numerous nerves. Opponents of the effort decried it as official racism. As had Americanization advocates before World

Photo by Phil Goodstein

Valdez School, near the northeast corner of the equivalent of West 29th Avenue and Bryant Street, was the epitome of Denver Public Schools amidst the city's busing wars. It opened in 1975. DPS named it for Jose Valdez, who won the Congressional Medal of Honor during World War II. The name, ideally, showed the district appreciated the district's Hispanic dimension. Shown is the building after the completion of a massive renovation in 2015.

War II, they argued a prime purpose of the schools was to create a common culture. Insofar as standard texts had written blacks and Hispanos out of the country's story, it was necessary to revise them to include everybody. Those who wanted specific education for their children as to the history of their ethnic, racial, religious, and language traditions needed to provide them for themselves. That is what Catholics had long done with their separate school system. Many Jewish parents sent their children to Hebrew schools, programs usually running after the end of the school-day. The Greek community likewise had after-school classes for its children in the history and language of their nationality. So did people of Japanese heritage. It was not the role of the public school district to have such exclusive programs.

In many ways, Corky Gonzales loudly agreed with this stance. In 1969, his Crusade for Justice formed Escuela Tlatelolco as a school stretching from kindergarten through the college level. Enrollment peaked at about 300. It gained accreditation from Goddard College in Vermont.

A prime purpose of Escuela Tlatelolco was to provide ethnic education to Chicano youths. Gonzales did not believe his people could depend on a racist school system to provide such lessons. If anything, begging the district to undertake ethnic education meant allowing bureaucrats to dictate supposed cultural diversity. Were the Spanish-American community to depend on DPS, it would admit it was unable to build an independent Chicano nation within the shell of existing Denver, a prime goal of the Crusade.

All of these factors loomed in the background when the Congress of Hispanic Educators joined the Keyes case. It recruited 13 Latino families as plaintiffs, asking the court to consider the interests of their children and whether busing in the name of abstract racial integration did anything to enhance the quality of schools attended by Hispanic youngsters. (Most of the plaintiffs spoke English as a first language. They included professionals and DPS employees.)

The intervention of the Congress of Hispanic Educators in the Keyes case was vital. The Latino dimension of DPS had been before the Supreme Court when it pondered whether Denver was an illegally segregated district. In its ruling, the court decided that Latinos, as a distinct ethnicity, had to be recognized and protected against discrimination. As such, the litigation defined the legal status of Spanish-Americans in the eyes of the courts.

Denver, Justice William Brennan declared, was a "tri-ethnic city." Consequently, a redress of school segregation required recognizing the city's large Latino population. About the same time, both the Supreme Court and Congress mandated that school districts were responsible for the needs, language requirements, and special educational challenges of Chinese-Americans, Native Americans, and children suffering from learning and physical disabilities.

The Cardenas Plan

The Congress of Hispanic Educators had intently lobbied DPS. Now and then, it targeted non-Hispanic instructors whom the system selected to teach courses on Spanish-American history, heritage, and languages—Latinos, it insisted, must be the instructors on the topics. The group also showed itself deeply concerned about racial and ethnic discrepancies in the disciplining of students, particularly in elementary schools. It observed that while some elementaries had no suspensions in the mid-1970s, at other schools they were extremely numerous and severe. Alas, the Congress complained, far more Hispanic students suffered such punishment compared to their percentage of the enrollment. Additionally, it moaned, DPS had the most suspensions of Latinos attending elementary school of any district in the country. Compounding the problem were arrogant principals who refused to meet with parents and listen to community concerns.

Building on this record, the civil rights group convinced Judge Doyle that DPS must adopt policies assuring equal educational opportunity for youngsters of Spanish background as part of the Keyes case. This included the abolition of English-only policies. The schools also had to expand the curriculum to provide Latino students with instruction about the history of Hispanos. This would best be accomplished, the Congress told the United States District Court, by exempting five elementary schools with predominantly Mexican-American enrollments from the busing order. The Montbello Citizens Committee intervened in the case, supporting the Congress of Hispanic Educators—Montbello was then a primarily black area which, within a few decades, was largely Hispanic. The NAACP LDF also backed MALDEF and the Congress of Hispanic Educators. The case also saw the court recognize the Moore School Community Association, the United Parents of Northeast Denver, the Concerned Citizens for Quality Education, and the Citizens Association for Neighborhood Schools as interveners in the litigation. On gaining court recognition, the Congress of Hispanic Educators consulted with Dr. Jose A. Cardenas of Texas. Judge Doyle recognized him as an expert on the topic of Latino education and the spokesman of the new plaintiffs. The professor devised a program whereby, rather than being bused as part of the integration order, Hispanic children would receive a vigorous bilingual/bicultural education at neighborhood schools where they made up the bulk of the enrollment.

Stating that the Cardenas Plan was "well balanced, most equitable, and most feasible," Judge Doyle incorporated it into the Finger Plan. Specifically, he exempted the five elementary schools with heavy Hispanic enrollments— Boulevard, Cheltenham (1580 Julian Street), Del Pueblo (750 Galapago Street), Garden Place, and the joint Swansea-Elyria—from busing based on the premise they would provide meaningful bilingual programs for students with Limited English

VOTE SOCIALIST
JACK MARSH
Denver School Board

For Equal Education

In 1968, a court order instructed that Denver public schools be desegrated, "root and branch," to achieve equal education for the thousands of minority students who attend school in Denver. In the seven years since that original court order, the Denver School Board has spent hundreds of thousands of dollars in continual litigation and court maneuvers with the sole and racist aim of preventing Black, Chicano and Indian students from receiving an equal education with whites and attending the schools they wish to attend. It is these oppressed minorities who have been denied an equal education, and it is they who must have the power to decide how to attain that equality. Whether it be through desegregation using busing as the practical vehicle for achieving it or through community control of schools with sufficient funds to operate them in a first-class manner supplied by the government, the decision on method should be made by the oppressed communities themselves.

For Affirmative Action

The same court order mentioned above directed the School Board and school administration to implement an affirmative action program in hiring of school personnel to correct the current racist and sexist underrepresentation of minorities and women in the work force of the Denver Public Schools. Both the Board and the administration have denied past racist hiring policies and attempted to avoid implementing the court order. I demand the immediate preferential hiring and upgrading of Blacks, Chicanos, Indians and women until the proportions, at all levels, are equivalent to the ratios of these sectors in the school population.

For Bilingual-Bicultural Education

For many students of the oppressed minorities, the English language and the American culture are alien to their heritage. They must have the right to receive an education in the language of their choice, taught in a manner that is related to their own heritage and culture. Bilingual-bicultural programs currently in operation must be expanded and adequate funding guaranteed.

For Collective Bargaining

Public education is one of the areas hardest hit by the economic crisis. Both students and teachers suffer from cutbacks and increased class size. Teachers, like other workers, must have the means to defend their economic and occupational interests. The first step would be the right to collective bargaining, including the right to strike.

Doris Banks Papers, Auraria Archives

The Socialist Workers Party regularly had a candidate in school board contests in the 1960s and 1970s. The group primarily pushed such reforms as bilingual/bicultural education when Jack Marsh was its contender in 1975.

Proficiency. In consequence, as of September 1974, DPS was to have bilingual programs in place at these schools in addition to Baker Junior High and West High. The jurist optimistically stated he hoped his ruling was the final order in the case.

The Cardenas Plan was a major modification of the Keyes litigation. While the black proponents of equal educational opportunity had simply wanted their children to share the perceived superior nature of white middle-class schools, the suit by the Congress of Hispanic Educators went much deeper. Involved were "incompatibilities." This meant that Latino youngsters who did not have a mastery of English needed programs addressing their culture. As such, it was necessary to overhaul the entire system, especially the administration of the schools and their educational philosophy.

In reviewing Judge Doyle's order, particularly his emphasis on bilingual education, the Tenth Circuit Court overturned him. In its August 11, 1975, decision that mandated fulltime busing over the half-day scheme Doyle had accepted as part of the Finger Plan, the appellate court also said no to the bilingual program. Schools with a predominantly Hispanic enrollment could no more be separate and equal from the rest of the system than any of the other schools. Bilingual education was no substitute for integration.

Besides, the Tenth Circuit concluded, there was no legal basis for the Cardenas Plan. The proposal went beyond equal educational opportunity. The courts had no business in defining educational philosophy and the specific nature of instruction. Adding to the problem was that, unlike the mechanical remedy of busing, other than Spanish-language courses and classes in cultural enrichment, the courts were unable to order districts to adopt specific programs to remedy the perceived lack of equal educational opportunity stemming from a failure to provide adequate instruction to students with Limited English Proficiency.

The decision reflected how the courts were grappling with the subject. In 1974, in *Lau* v. *Nichols*, the Supreme Court had ruled that school districts had to be aware of the linguistic needs of children in minority groups. As such, schools had to rectify perceived language discrimination. The Supreme Court, however, refused to review the Tenth Circuit's modification of Judge Doyle's order. Eventually, the District Court decided that bilingual education was necessary within the context of busing for integration.

After the Tenth Circuit Court's decision, there was a marked separation between the LDF of the NAACP and MALDEF. As much as ever, the NAACP emphasized integration; MALDEF focused on bilingual/bicultural education. While the LDF initially announced it hoped to build on the Keyes ruling to increase litigation to force the desegregation of school systems nationally, faced with financial shortages, it soon retreated. In part, it backed off of aggressive court intervention in the face of mass resistance to overbearing court busing orders across the country.

The Congress of Hispanic Educators stressed that DPS must have special sensitivity about the plight of Latino learners. The Office of Civil Rights of the federal Department of Health Education and Welfare agreed, intervening in the case on the side of the Congress of Hispanic Educators. In 1977, in response to the complaints by local Hispanos that their children were not getting equal educational opportunity in DPS, the federal agency ordered more government oversight of the district based on the federal Equal Educational Opportunities Act of 1974. Far from producing wonders, Washington interference often alienated teachers who complained about the heavy-handed supervision by those who knew nothing about the daily instruction of students. They further protested that the order placed all the burden of school failure on them, completely ignoring the vital role of the home and the larger society in academic success.

Back on June 30, 1975, Governor Richard Lamm had

A HANDBOOK FOR VIETNAMESE SPEAKING STUDENTS
PHYSICAL SCIENCE

Colorado Department of Education
National Origin Desegregation Project (LAU)
English Language Proficiency Unit
Denver, Colorado
1983

Besides teaching some students in Spanish, DPS bilingual efforts expanded in the 1980s to those who spoke Vietnamese as their mother tongue.

signed House Bill 1295. It mandated bilingual programs in Colorado public schools. A review of the district showed DPS had failed to do so for both children who spoke Spanish as their first language and speakers of four Indochinese languages. The last were among recent newcomers, brought to Denver in the wake of the Vietnam War.

For a while, DPS emphasized what it called the "transitional bilingual approach." It did so only for children speaking Spanish since it lacked both the resources and funds for bilingual education in Indochinese languages. The district tied the transitional bilingual approach to English as a Second Language instruction.

The Congress of Hispanic Educators argued this was not enough. Parents, it observed, frequently overstated their children's proficiency in English. This included parents who did not speak English and had no idea about how fluent their offspring were in the tongue. Still, the schools listened to the parents, placing students with a marginal command of English in English language programs. DPS, the Congress convinced the court, had to make sure such students indeed spoke English. As such, the district needed considerably to increase its programs for non-English speaking students. Invariably this meant Latinos. Parents speaking Indochinese languages were not nearly as well organized as the plaintiffs associated with the Congress of Hispanic Educators. Besides, many of them, new to America, were in awe of the system. Most of them wanted their children to learn English.

Initially, no one was happy with bilingual education, especially through the lens of the court order and DPS's implementation of it. Not all whom the district hired to instruct students in Spanish were fluent in the tongue. Often they were people, overwhelmingly Latinos, who grew up speaking English. Seeing the demand for bilingual educators, they returned to school to study Spanish. Not having a complete mastery of the language, they did a poor job of teaching students whose first language was Spanish.

During the 1970s, faced with plummeting enrollment and escalating costs, DPS more or less imposed a hiring freeze. About the only people it offered teaching positions were individuals with bilingual skills. This reflected the rapid growth of the size and scope of bilingual education. At times, principals automatically assigned Hispanic youngsters admitted to the schools to the bilingual programs. Latino parents who spoke English often had intensely to lobby to make sure their children were placed in classes in English. Likewise, the schools sometimes placed English-speaking youngsters of Latino heritage, who were shy about speaking out, in Spanish-language classes. This resulted in yet more confusion and a lack of academic accomplishment.

The Congress of Hispanic Educators attacked the existing bilingual programs when it returned to court in 1980. Numerous hearings ensued. On January 20, 1984, Judge Matsch ruled DPS had indeed engaged in discriminatory treatment of non-English speakers. As such, the district had to connect with them in the name

Courtesy Walter Gerash

Amidst the school busing upheavals, violence flared between the Chicano Crusade for Justice and the police. Shown are remnants of a Crusade apartment house along the west side of the 1500 block of Downing Street after an explosion ripped the building during a police shootout shortly after midnight on March 17, 1973. The authorities ordered the demolition of crucial parts of the structure before investigators could determine the cause of the blast. In the wake of this, the city paid the Crusade a considerable out-of-court settlement for the damage.

of equal educational opportunity. His ruling emphasized that the language issue was a basic part of the Keyes case.

In the wake of Matsch's decision, on August 17, 1984, the district reached an out-of-court settlement with the Congress of Hispanic Educators. Following a consent decree, the court authorized DPS to launch a program assisting students with Limited English Proficiency. At least that was the surface appearance. Once more, nobody was particularly satisfied with the agreement. If anything, there was a cynical consensus between the plaintiffs and the district that many of the bilingual programs were "mostly fluff." At times, they were nothing more than having children sing songs in Spanish and study the Mexican hat dance. The efforts failed to assure that those with Limited English Proficiency gained a fluency in the tongue. By this time, pedagogues frequently described those struggling to learn English as English-Language Learners (ELL).

The quest for equal educational opportunity for those who did not speak English as a first tongue lingered. The district reached a second settlement with the Congress of Hispanic Educators in 1999. It revised the oversight in April 2016. Judge Matsch signed another order on September 12, 2018, naming a new monitor to assure that the court retained a supervisory role over the way the district treated students who were not proficient in English. At that time, there was still a huge performance gap between youngsters who primarily spoke Spanish and the sons and daughters of affluent, white middle-class parents who had English as their first tongue. There was often minimal involvement of the parents of students with Limited English Proficiency in the schools and their children's education.

As much as ever, this reflected the huge class division in the schools and society: youngsters struggling to learn Spanish were frequently from low-income families that moved frequently and where nobody had previously graduated from high school. In a word, they lacked the academic traditions of middle-class, English-speaking youngsters where high school and college were considered part and parcel of everyday life. This issue was amazingly ignored whereby newspaper articles and academic reports kept rediscovering it.

As DPS became ever more filled with students from different races, language groups, and cultures during the 1970s, the court continued to make racial and ethnic considerations the prime determinants in reviewing district policies. This was the case across the country. In many instances, jurists realized they had neither the ability nor the wisdom to order special programs that would unfailingly nurture learning. Consequently, something of a bean-counting was the essence of court oversight.

All the while, DPS reached out to different constituencies. Besides advisory councils for black, Latino, Native American, and Asian-American communities, it had both a Denver Association for Gifted/Talented and the Gifted and Talented Advisory Council. The district listened to a Special Education Advisory Council, a Bilingual Parents Advisory Council, a Design Advisory Council, a Vocational Education Advisory Council, and a Health Education Advisory Council. Around the beginning of the new millennium, a Gay and Lesbian Education Advisory Council emerged. The bodies seemed endless. The district even used the term

"Noah's Ark" to refer to the gathering of advisory committees' representatives as the superintendent's council.

There was also a student board of education. It emerged in the 1970s as an appointed bureau with a representative from each of the city's high schools. The body gathered three times a month. Besides a business meeting, it had two sessions where it listened to fellow students and members of the school community. The group rotated its assemblies between the different schools. A prime responsibility was informing the school board of student concerns and slants on controversial issues. All the while, no group had greater influence on the board than the Denver Classroom Teachers Association, the teachers union.

A Note on Sources:

FF 4:1–9 of the CCR papers at DPL focus on the City–School Project. FF 4:9 particularly deals with the Latin American Student Council. There is a smidgen on the City–School Project in loose clippings in the Mildred Biddick papers at DPL, WH, 695. *RMN*, February 5, 1954, p. 22, stressed the problems of Hispanic students, especially their high dropout rates in both DPS and parochial schools. Volume three will look at how the district came to name a school in honor of Lena Archuleta.

School Book, 3, 70, 163, 164, 165, 203, 333, 390, 441, 457, emphasizes DPS's outreach to immigrants and Americanization programs. Hector Farias Jr., "Mexican-American Values and Attitudes toward Education," 83–89, in Allison, ed., *Without Consensus*, is an introduction to the presence of the Spanish-Surnamed in schools.

SB, January 5, 1970, p. 57, reported the creation of the Advisory Committee on Hispanic Education. It listed the membership, January 19, 1970, p. 65; cf. *DP*, February 20, 1972, p. 89. There is likewise reference to the Hispanic Advisory Council in FF 21:18 of the Yasui papers. Also see *Cmq*, March 1972. *BN*, March 5, 1998, stressed El Alma de Raza. Box 17 of the Rich Castro papers at Auraria includes a folder on the Hispanic Citizens Committee.

A statement by Gene Gallegos, the president of the Congress of Hispanic Educators, decrying the way the busing controversy was ignoring Latino youngsters, is in an unnumbered folder in box 13 of the Banks papers. The same folder also contains a declaration by Corky Gonzales attacking busing. The LWV report, "A New Look in Schools," April 1969, in a different unnumbered folder in box 13, urged integration advocates to incorporate the Hispanic dimension of DPS into their campaign for equal educational opportunity. *RMN*, March 19, 1971, p. 6, and May 3, 1971, p. 105, and *DP*, May 3, 1971, p. 1, reported Latino opposition to busing. Orfield, *Must We Bus?* 201, analyzes the results of the poll, comparing black and Hispanic views of busing.

Oxford Encyclopedia of Latinos, 3:117–21, outlines the origins and operations of MALDEF. Richard R. Valencio, *Chicano Students and the Courts: The Mexican American Legal Struggle for Educational Equality* (New York: New York University Press, 2008), 176–80, links MALDEF to the Keyes case. This is also the subject of Michael A. Olivas, "From a 'Legal Organization of Militants' into a 'Law Firm of the Latino Community,'" *DU Law Review*, 90:5 (October 2013), 1151–1208. It traces the origins and evolution of MALDEF in the 1970s, stressing the importance of the Keyes case to its development, 1153, 1156, 1158. *DU Law Review*, 90:5 (October 2013), 1256–57, includes the remarks of Phoebe A. Haddon about how the Keyes case was the first time the Supreme Court ordered a specific Latino remedy to the lack of equal educational opportunity. Also apropos is the introduction to ibid., 1027, by Tom Romero, comparing the Keyes case to *Brown* in its impact on the Spanish-Surnamed. Kevin R. Johnson, "The Keyes Case and the Nation's Educational Future: The Latina/o Struggle for Educational Equity," in ibid., 1231–49, makes the same point, esp. 1231–32.

    SB, November 19, 1962, p. 45, mentioned Operation Amigo. *SB*, November 5, 1951, p. 36, and December 3, 1951, p. 52, referred to the Denver Boys' Spanish-language broadcasts on KLMO; cf. October 13, 1952, p. 23. *School Book*, 450–51, mentions the formation of Denver Boys and its links to DPS. I touch on Fred Manzanares and TESOL at Greenlee in *West Side*, 293. Also see *West Side Recorder*, November 1971, p. 7. *SRv*, February 1964, p. 3, outlined the nature of the district's Spanish language instruction classes, particularly those on Channel Six.

    DP, September 11, 1960, p. 30C, and December 18, 1966, p. 5, reviewed the district's commitment to foreign language courses and the use of television instruction for them. I was among those taking Spanish in fifth and six grades at Park Hill Elementary from a teacher who did not know the tongue in 1962–64. *SB*, January 12, 1953, pp. 69–70, discussed DPS issuing a brochure on the district's 12-year language program.

    Vigil, *Crusade*, 160–62, deals with the origins of Escuela Tlatelolco. I give my take on in it *DIA*, 165, 166, and *North Side Story*, 195–96. Arturo E. Escobedo, *Chicano Counselor* (Lubbock, TX: Trucha Publications, 1974), 185–86, is a glowing portrait of Escuela Tlatelolco by a man who taught and served as counselor in DPS. The discussion of Nita Gonzales below, 429–30, observes the fate of the Crusade's school.

    Orfield, *Must We Bus?* xvi, 27–30, 202–05, 448, stresses the pathbreaking Hispanic dimension of the Keyes case. He expands on it in dealing with the "Rights of Hispanic Children," chap. 7, in which he also mentions Supreme Court rulings about Chinese-Americans, 207–10. The study emphasizes the division between the LDF and MALDEF, 213. Ibid., 213, discusses the impact of the Keyes case on LDF and the group's financial problems.

    Doyle's opinion about bilingual education, addressing the concerns of the Congress of Hispanic Educators, is 380 FSupp 673. The Tenth Circuit's ruling is 521 F2d 465. Also see Valencio, *Chicano Students*, 178. Moran, "Untoward Consequences," *DU Law Review*, 90:5 (October 2013), 1216, 1219, emphasizes the Hispanic dimension of the Keyes Case, arguing bilingual education was a foremost legacy of the litigation. Pearson, "Denver Case," 210, observes House Bill 1295. The *1975 DPS Report*, 7, observes the special treatment of schools with many Spanish-speaking students.

    A copy of Jose Cardenas, "An Education Plan for Denver Public Schools," dated January 21, 1974, is in the Branscombe papers. Judge Doyle's discussion of it within the context of the Finger Plan is in FF 4 of the Jane Michaels papers. *SN*, October 6, 1975, p. 9, mentions the appeals of Judge Doyle's order and the Cardenas Plan. FF 1:13 of the Noel papers includes the order implementing bilingual education in September 1974. FF 1:12 of the Keyes papers deals with students with Limited English Proficiency.

On January 9, 2018, Jimi O'Connor recalled how the Congress of Hispanic Educators got DPS to revoke his appointment to teach Spanish during a session of summer school at South around 1970. Materials on the Congress, particularly its complaints about discriminatory school discipline, are in FF 21:31 and 40 of the Yasui papers, and box three of the Keyes papers.

Fishman, "Endless Journey," 204, deals with the "incompatibilities" and the far-ranging nature of the Cardenas Plan. On 190, he emphasizes the Tenth Circuit Court's reversal of Judge Doyle's decision on bilingual education. The study pays great heed to the intervention by the Congress of Hispanic Educators in the Keyes case, 190, 203–09, 211–13, 216–18. In passing, it argues the debate over bilingual/bicultural education was a "sideshow," and a "suit within a suit." The article quotes the "mostly fluff" description, 212. Mitchell, "Desegregation," p. 73, describes the empty nature of many bicultural educational programs, particularly those which he mocked for teaching of the Mexican hat dance. Also see Orfield, *Must We Bus?* 29–30, 213–14. Peter Roos, the attorney for the Congress of Hispanic Educators, gave his take on what was occurring in *PPV*, 1:1 (1981), pp. 9–10.

RMN, December 31, 1983, p. 1, reported the legal problems with the court bilingual order. *RMN*, August 18, 1984, p. 6, stated the court had resolved the bilingual controversy. Also see Valencio, *Chicano Students*, 179–80, about the difficulties of implementing bilingual education and Judge Matsch's ruling. Julia A. McWilliams, *Compete or Close: Traditional Neighborhood Schools Under Pressure* (Cambridge: Harvard Education Press, 2019), 31, 35, 37–38, 42, 65, emphasizes the politics and educational challenges of English Language Learners, along with English as a Second Language programs, 65–79.

The unpaginated 1974 *DPS Report* emphasizes how the courts had made ethnic and racial considerations the prime determinant in their oversight of the district. The 1986–87 *DPS Report*, 24, lists some of the district's many education advisory councils. *DP*, June 8, 1977, p. 51, mentioned the emergence of the student board of education. It followed the June 6, 1977, DPS PR about the formation of the body. *SN*, September 25, 1981, p. 10, outlined the operations of the student board.

Chapter Twelve

The Teachers Union

At the same time busing controversies roiled DPS, so did labor troubles. The 1969 school board election not only assured litigation about the district's racial policies, but it helped trigger a teachers' strike. This stemmed from both the intransigent, business-oriented nature of the school board and the changing character of the Denver Classroom Teachers Association, the group representing most of the instructors.

Under Superintendent Kenneth K. Oberholtzer, numerous employee organizations surged within DPS. The same year he retired in 1967, the DCTA won a recognition election designating it as the group authorized to negotiate on behalf of teachers. The association stemmed from a 1911 effort at possible teacher unionization. Classroom educators were frustrated by low pay, the lack of tenure, and arbitrary assignments. To do something about them, as well as to enhance camaraderie and professional standards, on April 7 of that year, elementary instructors formed the Grade School Teachers Assembly at a gathering at East High.

Cora B. Morris, Jessie Hamilton, Lelia Peterson, and Amelia Webber took the lead in making it a reality. They pulled in 24 of their fellows to the organizing session. More than anything, members wanted respect. Those present were outraged by the way men received higher salaries than women instructors. The founders additionally lobbied for a teacher tenure law.

The school board rejected the Grade School Teachers' immediate demand for a hike in pay. Even so, the group's entreaty resonated. In 1914, the board announced it was increasing salaries in the hope of recruiting "abler" teachers.

By this time, the Grade School Teachers Association was affiliated with the League of Teachers' Associations, the branch of the National Education Association (NEA) for classroom instructors. "Classroom teachers association" was an increasingly common term, denoting public school instructors within the rubric of the NEA, a group then primarily a professional association dominated by superintendents and college officials even while classroom teachers made up the bulk of its membership. A purpose of the Grade School Teachers Association was to assure everyday instructors had a voice of their own.

The Colorado affiliate of the NEA, the Colorado Education Association (CEA), dated from 1875. Until 1927, it was known as the Colorado State Teachers' Association. Among its ventures was an Arapahoe County Teachers' Association in the 19th century when Denver was the county seat of Arapahoe County, an entity also including modern Adams County. (The City and County of Denver emerged as a separate jurisdiction on December 1, 1902.)

Instructors increasingly joined the CEA during the first part of the 20th century. Even at that, high-ranking administrators usually were the leaders of the CEA. DPS superintendent Aaron Gove had been the first head of the group. Superintendents Lewis C. Greenlee (1905) and Charles Chadsey (1909) likewise served terms as president. So did such veteran principals as Dora Moore, Harry Barrett, Harry Kepner, Anna Laura Force, and Emily Griffith.

In late 1922, the Grade School Teachers merged with the High School Teachers Association to form the DCTA. The High School Teachers Association dated from

Photo by Phil Goodstein

Schools sometimes consisted of more than one building. Here is the 1906 home of Berkeley School near the southwest corner of West 51st Avenue and Lowell Boulevard. A tunnel connected it with a 1923 structure to the south. On occasion, the administration isolated teachers in different buildings, separating them from instructors on other parts of the campus. Against this, stressing teacher unity, instructors formed the Denver Classroom Teachers Association in 1922.

1915. It stemmed from the Committee of Ten, formed on October 22, 1907. The inaugural organization consisted of two representatives from each of the city's five high schools. Backers complained that instructors had no job protection. The board of education frequently intervened in the schools, arbitrarily firing and transferring teachers. There were mass disparities in instructor salaries. Generally, the district automatically paid men more than women teachers.

The administration had blessed the formation of the Committee of Ten. It wanted to hear the views of teachers about salaries. In 1909, the body grew into the Committee of 15 with three representatives each from North, West, East, South, and Manual. The group evolved into the High School Council in 1912. It was then up to 18 members, including two delegates from the Evening Vocational High School and one from Longfellow High School (a program at 13th and Welton streets that was both something an annex of Manual and a forerunner of Opportunity School.) On April 20, 1915, the organization changed its name to the High School Teachers Association. Five years later, after the emergence of junior high schools, it officially became the Senior High School Teachers Association.

In 1921, Superintendent Jesse Newlon worked with the Grade School Teachers Assembly and the High School Teachers Association in getting the district to adopt a nondiscriminatory salary schedule. It paid all instructors alike based on experience and professional degrees. On the heels of this, Newlon pushed a merger between the Grade School Teachers and High School Teachers. He additionally pressured DPS instructors to affiliate with the NEA. All District #1 teachers, he asserted in 1921, belonged to the national group. As such, DPS was the only large district in the country with 100-percent membership. The superintendent played on this, annually leading a large Denver delegation to the NEA's summer convention. Newlon served as president of the NEA in 1924–25. Until his death in 1941, he was actively involved in NEA politics, arranging for colleagues to succeed him as president of the group.

Even with Newlon's goading, it took quite a while for the Grade School Teachers and High School Teachers to merge. At times, they acted as if they inhabited different worlds. High school instructors, most of whom had college degrees and were better paid, tended to look down on primary school teachers. The Grade School Teachers Assembly pointed out it had a healthy treasury whereas the high school organization was virtually broke.

Elements of unionism were present in both groups. The Grade School Teachers and High School Teachers alike saw they had to stand up for themselves against arbitrary administrators. They also needed to speak out to protect their salaries and status. Far from seeing the new bungalow schools under Superintendent Carlos Cole (1915–20) as an educational advancement, some instructors feared they were ways of destroying teacher solidarity. These were house-like buildings. Usually, these were annexes to standing, overcrowded schoolhouses.

All of this added up to unity in 1922. On April 17, Amelie Irving, a former instructor at Lincoln School who then taught at Byers Junior High, took the lead in calling for a merger. A board of three members of the Grade School Teachers met with three from the High School Teachers. William C. Shute chaired the committee.

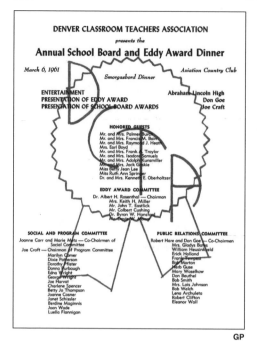

For years, the Denver Classroom Teachers Association stressed it was a professional organization. In 1960, it launched an annual banquet at which it bestowed its Eddy Award on a leading friend of education.

Born in Massachusetts on January 11, 1877, he was a graduate of Worcester Polytechnical Institute. After arriving in Denver in 1903, he joined the Manual faculty in 1907. Members elected him the DCTA's first president on October 17, 1922. He soon stepped down when he gained appointment as the principal of Wyman. The former head of the DCTA was subsequently the president of the association representing DPS principals in the 1930s when he was the head of Cheltenham School. The pedagogue retired from DPS in 1947. He died on February 3, 1954, after a long illness.

The DCTA filed for incorporation on October 17, 1922. Minnie Addleman, a leader of the Grade School Teachers Assembly who had helped make a teacher tenure law a reality, succeeded Shute as the organization's president. An instructor at Lincoln School, as much as anybody, she had been a key player in making unity happen. As head of the new group, she pushed for DPS to create a sabbatical program and a pension system. Addleman was subsequently a prime figure in forging a retired teachers division of the DCTA. Born in Illinois on September 28, 1868, she died in Denver in 1946.

Originally, Newlon suggested that the DCTA encompass all DPS employee organizations. Among them were social clubs. Members demurred. So did the Principals Association. Even at that, there was a principals' division in the early DCTA led by John Cory, head of South High from 1919 to 1939 before emerging as an assistant superintendent. Another future assistant superintendent, Claud Pendleton, was vice president of the DCTA in 1927. Douglas Ellis, a veteran principal, was vice president of the DCTA in 1936.

In January 1923, the DCTA started issuing *Classroom Interests*. A magazine coming out three to four times a year, it supplanted the Grade School Teachers Assembly's *Grade Interests*. The palm-sized *Grade Interests* had greetings from members of the school board and superintendent along with news of the organization. *Classroom Interests*, generally published in a five-inch by seven-inch format, was a combination of a gossip sheet, a celebration of a partnership between the DCTA and DPS, and a journal filled with teaching suggestions. *Classroom Interests* usually had "The Superintendent's Page" with an article by the leader of the district. It further included greetings from members of the school board.

A sign of the close working partnership between the DCTA and the administration is that the teachers' group received space at the DPS headquarters in the Commonwealth Building. When the district occupied its new home at 414 14th Street in 1923, the DCTA moved there. The relationship between the DCTA and the administration, declared Estelle Boggess, the group's president in 1926–29, was an "entente cordiale." The organization emphasized this in its slogan, "For Denver and Its Schools." The administration granted the DCTA the right to hold faculty meetings four times a year in each school to deal with the syndicate's business. In a word, the DCTA was anything but an independent union standing up for members against management. Even so, it had a strong consciousness that teachers had to assert themselves. Toward this end, in 1925 it asked the parent CEA to create a separate department for classroom teachers to assure that the state group was not completely under the thumb of administrators.

By the time it was about six months old in March 1923, the DCTA reported 1,049 members. During the 1930s, its numbers hovered from 1,335 to 1,406, about 90 percent of all fulltime instructors. The association claimed 100-percent membership in 1936–37 when it counted all 1,589 instructors in its ranks. Through membership in the DCTA, teachers were part of the CEA and the NEA—the DCTA affiliated with both groups. In 1935 and 1942, the DCTA was the official host when the NEA held its convention in the Mile High City.

During much of this epoch, the parent CEA was something of a semi-official part of the Colorado school establishment. In 1925, working with state education officials, the group thoroughly reorganized itself. In the process, the CEA carved itself into various units. Included were having annual conventions for members in western Colorado in Grand Junction and for those in southern Colorado in Pueblo. A yearly gathering in Denver in late October brought in instructors from the rest of the state. As much as ever, administrators were high-ranking figures in the state association.

At the same time the CEA formed the new organization structure, it hired its first full-time executive secretary, William B. Mooney. He was a confidant and companion of Superintendent Newlon. Additionally, Mooney had close ties with the Colorado Department of Public Instruction, the forerunner of the Colorado Department of Education. At times, Mooney was the CEA lobbyist at the Capitol.

Other Teacher Organizations

Other efforts at organization came and went among DPS employees. For a while there was a School Masters' Guild. The Denver Teachers' Club was more a social organization than a voice for those who worked in the classrooms. It had emerged in 1897 at the behest of Superintendent Aaron Gove and DPS secretary John Cotton Dana who also headed the Denver Public Library.

The Teachers' Club started out as a professional organization, helping teachers with continuing education. It soon had a social dimension. Before long, it also had a mutual assistance division, paying benefits to teachers forced to take unexpected leaves of absence because of illness and family problems. Originally, the Teachers' Club was open to all full-time employees in the district. For a while, it limited itself to full-time instructors and administrators. Then it expanded, taking in associate members who were friends of education and teachers outside of the district, including in the suburbs and members of the faculties of the University of Denver and Colorado Woman's College. The Teachers' Club additionally accepted as members people teaching at and operating private and proprietary institutions such as Barnes Commerce School, the Modern School of Business, and the College of Speech Arts. There were also members who taught at private orphanages. Such storied DPS principals as Anna Laura Force, Walter W. Remington, Warren Knapp, George W. Wyatt, Homer Philips, and William H. Eagleton were among those who created its insurance program in 1911.

At times, the Teachers' Club took political stances. Such was the case in 1917 when it was a firm supporter of keeping Carlos Cole as superintendent when the school board fired him. This, it declared, was an intolerable meddling of the board of education in the daily operations of the schools. A new board majority soon affirmed that Cole had been improperly dismissed, keeping him as superintendent.

For decades, the Teachers' Club held an annual concert where members, particularly music instructors, performed. At one time, branches included the Denver Women Teachers' Chorus, and the Denver Teachers' Orchestra. Wilberforce Whiteman, the head of the DPS music program during the first quarter of the 20th century, was the initial director of the Teachers' Chorus.

Early on, the Teachers' Chorus gave an annual recital in the spring. Beginning in 1926, the Teachers' Club concert became a grand social occasion and the main fundraiser for the organization's welfare fund. By the late 1950s, DPS also had a Music Educators Club. It was separate from the Denver Area Music Teachers Association, a group primarily composed of independent instructors who gave home lessons.

The Papyrus Club was another teacher social organization. It stemmed from a 1910 effort to involve teachers in curriculum decisions. Before long, members met informally at homes. Around 1924, they found a regular gathering spot at the Shirley–Savoy Hotel at the southeast corner of 17th Avenue and Broadway. After World War II, members assembled at the Tea Room of the Daniels & Fisher Tower. Growing old and lacking new blood, the group disbanded in June 1974.

The Denver Federation of Teachers

Labor problems convulsed DPS shortly after World War I. In February 1919, school engineers, the personnel overseeing steam-heating systems, went out on strike for higher pay in response to postwar inflation. They were part of a Steam Engineers Union. Their action forced the system to shutter 25 buildings, educating 16,800 pupils, for a week, until the workers returned pending arbitration. The

Cartoon by Doc Finch Bird

In February 1919, engineers, the men responsible for overseeing steam-heating systems in schools, went out on strike against DPS, forcing the district to close about half of its schools for more than a week.

closure came shortly after DPS had lost six weeks of instruction in the fall of 1918 because of the terrible flu pandemic. (Eventually, DPS eliminated the position of engineer. With modern technology, the position was no longer necessary to oversee boilers.)

Then, right about the end of the schoolyear, instructors, grumbling about poor pay and the tyrannical power of principals, discussed forming a union affiliated with the American Federation of Labor (AFL). More than 100 instructors attended a session pondering the topic on June 23 at East High. In exchange for allowing them to use the building, the administration insisted the teachers also listen to a representative of the NEA, then a professional organization which looked down on unions, about why instructors should reject the proposal and rather specifically affiliate with the NEA. Simultaneously, the school board hiked the pay for teachers. Efforts at unionization faded, particularly after Superintendent Newlon established uniform pay policies while the legislature strengthened tenure protection of instructors. Simultaneously, Newlon created professional requirements for teachers and worked to involve them in shaping the district's curriculum.

Unionization was again in the air during the 1930s as part of the explosion of the labor movement amidst the New Deal and the formation of the Congress of Industrial Organizations (CIO). Though there were rumblings about a DPS teachers union, not until October 26, 1946, did the American Federation of Teachers (AFT), part of the American Federation of Labor, charter local #858, the Denver Federation of Teachers (DFT). "Democracy in Education. Education for Democracy," the Mile High labor organization declared on the masthead of its newsletter, *The Denver Teacher*, echoing the slogan of the AFT and its *American Teacher*.

For years, instructors had realized that they were often held in contempt. Their poor salaries said as much. Despite their college degrees, society did not respect them as members of an honored profession who had the crucial responsibility of educating the next generation. On the contrary, it generally mocked instructors as individuals who returned to the classroom because they were unable to hold any more meaningful or economically rewarding positions. There were numerous variations on Oscar Wilde's aphorism "Everybody who is incapable of learning has taken to teaching."

Teachers, backers of the AFT asserted, had to combat such disrespect. A first step was realizing they were essentially white-collar workers who had to organize to defend themselves. This was a factor leading to the formation of teacher unions across the country in the generation after World War II.

By the time it chartered the Denver local, the AFT was a proud union. Yes, it admitted, teachers were professionals, but they needed to stand up for themselves

Photo by Karen Freml

In 1948, members of the American Federation of Teachers held their national convention in Glenwood Springs. There they selected DPS teacher John M. Eklund as president. Shown is the famous hot springs pool in Glenwood Springs.

and practice solidarity. The group stemmed from a Chicago teachers union at the turn of the 20th century. Branches of the AFT often emerged in response to the refusal of superintendents and school boards to treat teachers with honor.

The DFT quickly grew, gaining support of 440 of the district's 1,700 instructors. In 1949, the local successfully lobbied the legislature to strengthen the state's teacher tenure act. Additionally, it urged the necessity of equal educational funding through the commonwealth. As much as the school board and advocates of education, the DFT argued that DPS desperately needed a building program to relieve overcrowded classrooms. In the process, it projected itself as a partner in education.

In May 1946, the Colorado Federation of Teachers (CFT) emerged as the state affiliate of the AFT. Included were locals in Pueblo and at the University of Colorado, both of which dated from 1937. There were also representatives from Adams City, Boulder, Colorado Springs, Loveland, Fort Morgan, Holly, and Opportunity School.

The state federation hosted the national convention of the AFT in July 1948 in Glenwood Springs. By this time, Cole Junior High teacher John M. Eklund stood out as the leader of the union in Colorado. A native of Burlington, Iowa, born on September 14, 1909, Eklund attended public schools in Kansas, before graduating as an English major from Bethany College in the Sunflower State. From there he headed to the Iliff School of Theology. Following in his father's footsteps, he gained ordination as a Methodist preacher. Additionally, he earned a master's in education from DU. Eventually, Eklund gained a doctorate of education from Teachers College at Columbia University. A relative, Donald Eklund, taught at Smiley.

The pedagogue joined DPS in 1936, initially being an English teacher. After the return of peace, John Eklund was among those insisting DPS treat its teachers with dignity. He was outspoken when he attended the October 1945 state convention of the CEA. There he delivered stinging remarks from the floor about the group's failure to stand up for classroom teachers.

Many in the group agreed with Eklund. They marched from the meeting at the Denver Auditorium to the Capitol, requesting higher pay. By this time, DPS wages had been frozen since 1938. That year, the district had rescinded half of a "voluntary" 20-percent reduction in pay it had imposed in 1934–35. Other than the rally, CEA did nothing to see that teachers gained better compensation in dealing with the soaring postwar cost of living.

Dismissing both the CEA and the DCTA as do-nothing organizations afraid to stand up for teachers, Eklund and four other instructors pondered affiliating with the AFT. They had about 50 backers when they applied for a charter from the national teachers federation. The Mile High affiliate drafted a 16-point program. Besides better pay, it emphasized that teachers should have a say in shaping the direction of the schools.

Fifty-four of the 55 teachers who signed the March 1946 charter application were men. This was indicative. The overwhelming bulk of those lining up behind the DFT were men, including returned veterans who worked in secondary schools. The group had a tough time gaining the backing of women who taught in elementary schools. The female instructors, Eklund complained, were "compliant, submissive, and conservative." Generally, women teachers in elementary schools were automatically anti-union, seeing themselves as professionals. In part, in the hope of getting them to reconsider, Eklund and associates named their group the Denver Federation of Teachers as opposed to the suggestion it be the Denver Teachers Union.

Initially, backers of the DFT met in bars, restaurants, and hotels. When they found the administration receptive to their drive, they had sessions in the board room of DPS headquarters at 414 14th Street. Not all backers liked that location. Meeting there, Smiley teacher Herrick Roth argued, hinted the group might be a company union. At the most, about 50 instructors gathered at any one DFT session. Initially, the group did not aim at union recognition and collective bargaining; it simply wanted to be a powerful voice that made sure teachers were heard while they received better pay and more respect.

In no time, the administration recognized that the DFT was anything but a company union. Top officials called in leaders of the group to give them "proper advice," i.e., they should steer clear of militant unionism. Besides speaking for teachers, the DFT reached beyond instructors, seeking to represent school secretaries, nurses, janitors, and others who worked in schoolhouses. It soon dropped such aspirations.

The school board, in turn, realized it had to hike the pay of instructors. In 1946, the district announced it was increasing annual teacher salaries by $150 a year over the course of the next four years. Before long, a starting teacher's salary was $2,200, up from $1,000 annually for an instructor without a bachelor's degree. Around the end of the war, DPS required all new instructors to have a bachelor's degree.

Under the impact of DFT lobbying, postwar inflation, and the way the district saw it had to recruit more teachers to fill the classrooms of the ever-growing system, by 1957 the starting salary was $3,900. The highest pay was $6,525 for a senior instructor with advanced degrees, up from $5,000 in the late 1940s.

As he asserted himself in the DFT, Eklund transferred to Opportunity School where he worked as a counselor for the Veterans Administration. This was apropos. Early on, teachers at Opportunity School were among the foremost backers of the AFT. Nationally, the union gained the alliance of vocational teachers while it opposed the isolation of vocational programs from the regular school curriculum. Back in 1928, local #203 of the AFT emerged at Opportunity School for vocational teachers. Eventually, DPS reached terms with local #203. This was the first collective bargaining agreement the AFT signed west of the Mississippi.

During the 1930s, the AFT also had strong links with adult education instructors. At that time, the Works Progress Administration of the New Deal collaborated with Opportunity School in offering classes for adults. Additionally, the union had a noted political slant. In particular, it opposed the presence of militarism in the schools, especially Junior Reserve Officer Training Corps programs and what it branded chauvinist education. The AFT was ambivalent about federal aid to education while the NEA was a firm advocate of that measure. In part, the AFT questioned it since it had many members who taught at Catholic schools—the hierarchy long opposed federal aid as undermining parochial schools.

In 1928, instructors at Opportunity School, at 13th and Welton streets, formed local #203 of the American Federation of Teachers. They subsequently won the first collective bargaining agreement between a union and DPS. Shown is the proposed new home of Opportunity School, a building going up in 1926.

Eklund rapidly rose in the teachers union. Besides being the founding chairman of the DFT, he was soon the national representative of the AFT for the Rocky Mountain region and California. In the highly factionalized national union, he was the candidate of the "liberal" caucus when he won the presidency of the AFT in 1948 during the union's national convention in Glenwood Springs. He ousted incumbent John Landis.

The AFT's new head remained an Opportunity School counselor while serving as the leader of the union. He traveled widely on group's business, remaining in office until 1952. The preacher served the union at the peak of the Cold War. In the process, Eklund found himself constantly defending academic freedom against the endless efforts of anti-communists to undermine and red bait teachers. This was a period when super-patriots showed their scorn for the Bill of Rights. All instructors, they demanded, had to sign oaths swearing their obedience to the existing order. Those pushing the mandatory vows did not observe that the constitution included the right of free speech and association. Nor did they pay any heed to the country's revolutionary foundations.

The Opportunity School counselor was a supporter of the Cold War. The State Department collaborated with the AFT, seeing that Eklund traveled to Paris as an official State Department representative of organized labor at a congress of the United Nations Educational Scientific and Cultural Organization. Eklund also served as the president of the Colorado chapter of the Americans for Democratic Action, a liberal group backing the Cold War. Under his leadership, the AFT acted to eliminate its Jim Crow locals in the South.

As president of the union, Eklund contributed a chapter, "Let's Weigh the Criticisms of Modern Education," to a 1953 anthology, *Freedom and Public Education*. This was a reprint of an article he had contributed to the AFT's *American Teacher* in December 1951. There he stated the obvious: schools have problems. Rather than directly addressing them, however, administrators often cloaked them while nefarious tax-cutters targeted the schools as part of a general attack on the social safety net of the welfare state.

About the time the book came out, Eklund left DPS to manage the education department of the National Farmers Union, a liberal group of small farmers pushing cooperation. The educator was also very active in the National Council of Churches. Eventually, he left town, working for the Agency for International Development, part of the foreign policy establishment widely suspected of having links to the CIA. In that position, the former AFT president promoted agricultural cooperatives in Asia and Africa. Eklund retired to Florida where he died at age 87 in January 1997.

Herrick Roth

Nobody more impacted the DFT during the 1950s than its executive director, Herrick Roth. Born in Omaha, on March 19, 1916, to a small-town banker, his family moved to Warm Springs, South Dakota, in the Black Hills when he was two years old. After growing up there, he proceeded to the University of Denver in 1933, standing out on campus as the editor of the student newspaper, the *Clarion* in 1937–38. A colleague on the sheet was future Colorado Governor John Love. At that time, Roth was unsuccessful in a bid to gain the presidency of the DU student body.

After graduating from DU, Roth went on to get a master's from the University of California. He joined DPS as an instructor in 1938. During World War II, Roth served in the Army, spending 55 months in the Signal Corps. For the most part, he wrote radar manuals. After the fighting, he returned to DPS in January 1946, teaching first at Morey and then at Smiley.

On regaining his place in DPS, Roth immediately learned he was expected to pay annual dues of $1.00 to the DCTA, $5.00 to the CEA, and $8.00 to the NEA. He considered this a most unfair assessment, considering that the groups did not do anything for him as an instructor. In response, he became a charter member of the DFT. Not only was he its first secretary, but, on the emergence of Colorado Federation of Teachers, he became its executive secretary, holding the post until 1959. After taking charge in 1951 as the executive director of the new Mile High branch of what became the American Federation of State, County, and Municipal Employees, he left the classroom to become a fulltime union functionary. Redbaiters taunted Roth as a communist when he pointed out the Wall Street domination of Colorado.

A most articulate, aggressive individual, Roth dominated all of those around him. Many found it impossible to have a discussion with him. As soon as others said anything, he was apt to reply with a lecture, deflecting direct questions. Simultaneously, he threw himself into politics. In 1947, he was most unsuccessful in trying to elect a pro-union ticket in that year's school board contest. Affiliating with the Democrats, Roth won election to the Colorado House of Representatives in 1948. In 1956, he gained a seat in the state Senate. There he became friends with a dynamic Republican leader of the House of Representatives, Palmer Burch. Both were committed to education. Over the next decade, the two constantly clashed and collaborated. Roth's political ambitions suffered a setback in 1960 when he failed in his re-election bid to the Senate.

Simultaneously, Roth was committed to the union movement. In 1953, he gained election as a vice president of the AFT, serving until 1958 before regaining the post in 1962. Back in 1952, the union leader had rallied members of both the AFL and CIO to form a joint committee backing DPS and that year's bond election. Labor's involvement in the schools, he argued, was urgent. DPS was on the verge of capitulating to book-burners and censors. It had recently pulled "worthwhile reference material" from high school libraries since the publications forced students to think and challenge accepted wisdom.

As a vice president of the AFT, Roth was frequently a delegate to national conventions of the American Federation of

Author's collection

George Cavender went from teaching school at East High to a place on city council to the leadership of the Colorado AFL–CIO.

Labor. Back in Denver, he regularly attended school board meetings, addressing the body. Not only did he call for better pay and working conditions for teachers, but he backed countless worthy causes. Personally, he was a Cub Scoutmaster who was an enthusiast of the Boy Scouts. He joined the ACLU, the United World Federalists, and the Colorado Children's Aid Society while he championed the Histadrut, the Israeli labor federation. Additionally, he was a backer of militarism. This included both urging DPS to collaborate with the service in cutting dropout rates in preparing boys for the military, and lobbying for DFT president Gene Schipman, a colonel in the Marine Reserves, to gain appointment as a brigadier general. At times, Roth was most critical of Kenneth Oberholtzer, especially charging the superintendent with trying to make DPS employees part of the administration's election machine.

George Cavender was Roth's mentor. A native of Des Moines, born on April 24, 1910, he grew up in Denver and Englewood. He received both his bachelor's and master's from the forerunner of UNC. After four years as an instructor at his alma mater, Englewood High School, Cavender started teaching in District #1 in 1938, being among the founders of the DFT. From Smiley, he moved to East High.

Back in 1945–46, Cavender had been a close associate of John Eklund in forging the DFT. Even at that, he had been hesitant about joining with a group affiliated with the American Federation of Labor. In no time, he became a foremost champion of the AFL. He left the school system in 1948 when he became education director of the Colorado State Federation of Labor, the state affiliate of the AFL. He succeed Robert Ozanne in that post. His predecessor was another East teacher who had been among the five founders of the DFT.

During the 1950s, Herrick Roth was the exec-
utive director of the Colorado Federation of
Teachers. He went on to head the Colorado
Labor Council. Here he participates in the
dedication of a new wing of Bromwell School
on the Colorado Centennial in 1976.

Cavender went on to win election as the president of the state union alliance in 1949. After serving on the Englewood city council from 1938 to 1943, Cavender relocated to Denver, being on city council from 1948 to 1959 when he represented the northwest quadrant of the community. Republican Richard Batterton, the candidate backed by business interests and labor haters, narrowly defeated Cavender in 1959 when the former teacher ran for mayor.

By this time, Cavender was the president of the Colorado Labor Council. This was the coalition of state unions formed in 1956 following the merger of the AFL with the Congress of Industrial Organizations (AFL–CIO). He left the position in early 1962 to become Denver postmaster general. The instructor was always, first and foremost, a Democrat.

In later years, Cavender proudly reminisced about how labor had rallied to the Democrats and helped finance elections while turning out the vote. He retired in 1974, dying in October 1992.

Roth succeeded Cavender as the president of the Colorado Labor Council. He used the post to host "Labor's Language," a Sunday television show going on the air in 1963. On it, he interviewed fellow unionists, celebrities, and politicians. In 1972, Roth lobbied the legislature to give judges greater power to punish and imprison juvenile offenders. The PTA and the Denver Juvenile Court successfully rallied against the bill as a vicious measure that could well cause more problems than it redressed. Giving teachers greater disciplinary powers over students was a prime goal of the Denver Federation of Teachers.

Most of all, in 1972, Roth bid for national attention and influence. That year he bucked George Meany, the president of the AFL–CIO, when he saw the Colorado Labor Council endorse George McGovern for president. In response, Meany, who hated McGovern and the anti-Vietnam War movement which had helped McGovern gain the Democratic nomination, purged Roth as president of the Colorado Labor Council, placing the state labor federation in trusteeship. Back in 1965, in a quixotic attempt, Roth had run against Meany for the presidency of the AFL–CIO. The 1973 AFL–CIO convention upheld Meany against Roth's appeal of his ouster.

The same year he lost leadership of the Colorado Labor Council, Roth did not seek to retain his post as a vice president of the AFT given his clash with George Meany. That year, a pro-war caucus dominated by Albert Shanker, soon to be president of the AFT, overwhelmingly defeated opposition factions, including the Unity Caucus of which the former Smiley teacher was a leader. Roth's effort to project himself as a political martyr was to no avail in 1974 when he unsuccessfully sought the Democratic nomination for the United States Senate. Though a poll early that year showed him holding a two-to-one lead over others seeking the post, he lost the September primary to Gary Hart, the man who had been the manager of the 1972 McGovern presidential campaign.

Roth went on to serve as the head of the Colorado Department of Labor and Employment under Governor Richard Lamm in 1975–76. He also was in charge of the 1976 Colorado Centennial celebration. For a while, Roth was an adjunct faculty member of the DU College of Business. He additionally formed the Colorado Forum as his way of shaping public policy. On it, he collaborated with leading voices of business. During his later years, Roth was a consultant who loudly advocated a highly controversial, environmentally damaging water project in southwestern Colorado. DPS came to have a Herrick Roth Public Policy Lecture in the summer. The former DFT leader died in January 2008.

Amidst the political commitment of the union, the DFT also had a social side. Indicative is that during the seventh annual state conference of the Colorado Federation of Teachers in October 1952 at the Albany Hotel at 17th and Stout streets, the DFT invited all school teachers to a bingo party. (At times, the parent AFT featured a "Miss Union Teacher" beauty contest.)

The Mile High local held the bingo party at the same time the CEA was holding its annual meeting at the Auditorium. Since the late 19th century, the last week of October had been a popular time for meetings of school employees. Their sessions were simultaneous with the fourth annual conference of the district's Clerks and Secretaries Association. Until 1967, when the CEA ended its October convention, the district gave workers two days off to attend the gatherings of employee organizations.

The Colorado Federation of Teachers, incidentally, had to fight to have its convention at the same time the CEA was holding its conclave. After the emergence of the union, Superintendent Charles Greene stated that if members of the DFT did not attend the CEA gathering, he would dock their pay. The labor organization fought back, claiming the two-day break was a paid school holiday. When it threatened to go to court on the matter, the administration backed down. Speakers at the founding DFT convention in October 1946 included future Secretary of Agriculture Charles Brannan of the National Farmers Union and acclaimed journalist Norman Cousins who was in town to address the CEA gathering. Though the DFT never came close to representing a majority of DPS teachers, its presence forced the administration and the DCTA to respond to the call for unionism.

The Employees Council

Since the days of Jesse Newlon as superintendent, the administration had had sporadic programs to reach out to teachers. Nobody more sought to collaborate with instructors than Superintendent Alexander Stoddard (1937–39). A prime initiative was the School Policies Council. It was, he announced, the embodiment of democracy. He designed the body to bring together all who received a DPS paycheck. Before long, there were 175 members on the board of the Council. Some were ex officio from the central office. Most were elected by their fellows. The group met monthly at Morey Junior High. Anybody could promote new policies and initiatives. A wide variety of committees pondered them. As superintendent, Stoddard had only his one vote in the Council's policies. The school board, which tended to listen to Stoddard, had a veto power. No school board members were on the Council.

The employee organization received great national publicity. Educational advocates saw it as opening new vistas of citizen participation in the school system. The Rockefeller Foundation's General Education Board helped pay for it with a $5,000 grant. Ideally, members of the everyday public could approach the Council and be heard.

Stoddard was ecstatic about the effort. "We are witnessing a revolution," he declared. It showed that the answer to fascism was not communism, but the "philosophy of democracy" as embodied in the Council. He pushed the American Association of School Administrators, the branch of the NEA representing superintendents, to make the Council a national model.

Despite Stoddard's hopes, before long the Council essentially became something of a company union. Simultaneously, the superintendent pushed to make sure teachers played an active role in forging and overseeing the DPS pension program. At an early date, District #1 had had a teacher retirement fund. During the 1930s,

Photo by Phil Goodstein

Faculty Row *is the name sculptor William Garrison gave to this bas relief above the main entrance of South High. The frieze at the bottom depicts the endless clashes at teacher meetings. The Employees Council was a post–World War II association designed to bring harmony among them and all who worked for the district.*

teachers gained a significant role in promoting and managing it. Eventually, an elected teachers' board oversaw the Employees' Pension and Benefit Association.

In the spring of 1934, eight teachers established the DPS Credit Union. The district looked favorably upon it, providing it with office space at administration headquarters at 414 14th Street. The quasi-bank relocated in 1956. For a while, it shared an old house at 1535 High Street with the Denver Classroom Teachers Association. Over the years, the credit union continually increased its outreach, including to DPS students and their families. In 2006, the organization, after a series of mergers and ever expanding operations, became the Westerra Credit Union.

The School Policies Council did not last long after Stoddard left the district in 1939 to take charge of the Philadelphia school system. Kenneth Oberholtzer undertook an initiative comparable to the School Policies Council, the Employees Council, after he emerged as DPS head in 1947. The new superintendent forged the Employees Council as a voice of those working for the district. When he took charge of DPS, upwards of 20 different groups claimed to speak in behalf of employees. By collaborating together, Oberholtzer insisted, all who labored for DPS would benefit in a flourishing system. Through working with employee organizations and listening to their concerns, the superintendent knew he would have a better feel of what was going on inside of the district.

Workers at different schools elected representatives to the Employees Council. Besides instructors, there were bus drivers, food service workers, janitors, and secretaries. Administrators were also part of the mix. The *Superintendent's Bulletin*, a four-page weekly issued by the district headquarters, frequently listed meetings of the Employees Council as it reported developments and told about the officers of the association. The sheet never gave comparable coverage to sessions of the DCTA or DFT. The Employees Council usually met at the centrally located Evans School at West 11th Avenue and Acoma Street. This was especially the case after Evans opened a new auditorium in 1951. Other school groups also frequently gathered at the school.

In many ways, the Employees Council was a traditional uplift group. It was in charge of a DPS blood bank. Its Committee on Drives and Campaigns oversaw annual fundraisers within DPS, especially for the Red Cross and the Community Chest/United Way. Banner headlines in the weekly *Superintendent's Bulletin* told employees it was their "civic responsibility" to donate generously to these causes.

Besides promoting such charitable drives, the district used the Employees Council to endorse DPS's strong ideological agenda. As part of a Cold War mobilization, the system brought programs of the Crusade for Freedom into classrooms. Superintendent Oberholtzer additionally invited members of the Employees Council to join curriculum committees and efforts to study the district's salary schedule. A concerned teacher could always find a post on some DPS advisory committee or uplift effort.

Retired employees banded together into the DPS Retired Employees Association. They formed Denver School Employees Senior Citizens Incorporated (DESCI). It stemmed from a grassroots effort to provide housing for retired DPS employees, mostly single women. With a 40-year mortgage from the Federal Housing

Photo by Phil Goodstein

Utility lines surround the apartment house Denver School
Employees Senior Citizens Incorporated (DESCI) opened in 1963
at 13th Avenue and High Street for retired educators.

Administration, in 1963 the organization opened DESCI, a 12-story apartment
house for retired school employees at 1910 13th Avenue (the northeast corner of
High Street). For a while, the building included a gift shop filled with craft works
by people associated with DPS.

DESCI kept the rents quite low. This came at the cost of failing to have an
adequate maintenance budget. By the early 21st century, the highrise faced
expensive repairs. Nor was the building up to modern codes to treat people with
medical emergencies. Additionally, it was no longer the home of that many retired
teachers—they made up about 40 percent of the tenants. A new generation of DPS
had failed to develop the close, intimate links which had once been part of the
district. The upshot was the sale of the building in 2012.

The deal required the new owner to allow tenants to remain there for at least
ten years. DESCI used part of the proceeds from the sale to subsidize the rent
of such tenants. It spent another part of the sum to help active school employees
find affordable housing elsewhere in the city. The new owner relabeled DESCI
"The Metropolitan."

The Denver Retired Teachers' Club kept going. It had something of a social-
welfare mission. Besides helping deliver meals on wheels, it lent medical

equipment, such as walkers, to active and retired school teachers and their immediate families. It operated out the district's Acoma Campus, 1617 South Acoma Street.

In 1995, the Retired Teachers' Club created a scholarship foundation. At that time, the DPS Retired Employees Association took some money out of its treasury, allowing the group to award two $1,000 scholarships annually. Gifts and bequests saw the foundation grow to where, by 2019, it was able to grant eleven $10,000 scholarships each year when the foundation reported assets of $7,721,587. The Denver Teachers' Club, in turn, continued to emphasize supplemental benefits for active instructors. In particular, it helped them in case of prolonged illness or family crises.

While the DFT had no problem with the ventures of DESCI and the Retired Teachers' Club, it questioned whether instructors improved education or their working conditions by collaborating with management and backing the Employees Council. It charged the Employees Council was nothing but an old-fashioned company union that more represented management than it was an autonomous voice for those selling their labor power to District #1. Federal labor statutes, it observed, had outlawed company unions in the 1930s. On this basis, in the mid-1950s the union sued the district for its illegal endorsement of the Employees Council. In May 1956, Denver District Court Judge Edward Day, ruled the Employees Council was a legitimate group representing those who worked for District #1.

Even so, the Employees Council struggled for the loyalty of workers by the 1960s. Not only was unionism increasingly part of school districts, but personnel disputes grew in the system. Teachers found themselves forever trying to keep up with the cost of living. The DCTA stepped forward, coming to represent teachers as a de facto union.

The Recognition of the DCTA

In part, the DCTA surged through being something of a mutual aid organization. In 1936, in collaboration with the CEA, it started offering members hospitalization insurance. General health insurance followed. Teachers found they received other rewards, including a retirement plan, by paying DCTA dues. For some years, the parent NEA sold itself to teachers through offering numerous membership benefits.

The DCTA forged ahead of the Employees Council in February 1963 when it gained school board recognition as the official bargaining agent for teachers. The declaration came amidst sporadic picketing of board headquarters by the DFT. Since 1961, members of the latter group had been inspired by the success of the United Federation of Teachers. This was the branch of the AFT in New York City that had recently gained recognition to represent instructors. The DFT hoped to follow in its footsteps. At that time, it included about than 10 percent of all DPS teachers. To show it represented all instructors, in 1962 it launched a petition drive for a union recognition election. About one-third of all teachers signed the document.

In response, the school board turned to the DCTA, officially stating that if any outside group was to represent teachers, it was to be this branch of the Colorado Education Association. The Employees Council decried the recognition of the DCTA. The board's action, it complained, had given it "second-class status." By this time, the DCTA claimed membership of about 2,800 of the district's 3,700 instructors. The group immediately asked for negotiations for a contract. The board refused to go along.

The DCTA was increasingly estranged from the parent CEA. The state group, the Denver organization complained, was filled with old fogeys who always sided with the administration as opposed to classroom teachers. As a sign of its new orientation, the DCTA hiked its dues from $3.00 to $5.00 a year in 1961. Some of the money went to hire its first executive director, Betty Jean Lee, who had been the education reporter for the *Denver Post*.

The board's recognition of the DCTA reflected an increasing consensus that DPS had to create a negotiation policy with an organization representing teachers. By this time, in tune with the National Education Association, the DCTA insisted it was committed to "professional negotiations" in contrast to trade union-oriented collective bargaining. The NEA had made this point when it had assembled in Denver in early July 1962 for its 100th annual convention.

Superintendent Oberholtzer recognized the growing clout of the DCTA. That fall, he saw the administration engage in professional negotiations with the DCTA in the hope of drawing up "principles and procedures relating to teachers and teacher organizations." This was the first time a large urban unit of the NEA had engaged in professional negotiations with a school district.

The board of education was deeply divided about professional negotiations. Despite this, the DCTA forged ahead. In 1963 the proto-union convinced the board to overrule Oberholtzer in terms of specific salary suggestions. Two years later, the DCTA threatened to strike over personnel problems at Fairmont School and Thomas Jefferson High School.

The clash at the high school was particularly bitter. It centered over whether coach Myron "Mike" Willett had the right to dismiss a boy, who had been drinking, from the baseball team. Principal Milton Rebell stated he did not after the youth's parents complained. Oberholtzer upheld the principal over the coach. In response, the DCTA used all of its power to back Willett. It called a meeting of the Denver Coaches Association, a unit of the DCTA. The organization voted 69–4 that it was ready to strike over the matter. At the behest of the DCTA, the NEA sent Stephen B. Reichert, a Los Angeles labor specialist, to Mile High City to assist the local.

The result was a tumultuous school board meeting on March 15, 1965. Oberholtzer sought to browbeat the head of the coaches' association, East High basketball coach Paul Coleman. The superintendent conceded Thomas Jefferson had a rule against athletes drinking and smoking. Students had agreed to it. But since DPS did not have such a prohibition, Willett could not discipline those who broke the stipulation. Amidst escalating tensions, the father of the disciplined boy announced his son had quit the baseball squad. Given community support of Willett and the union's militancy, Oberholtzer backed down. The school board specified that coaches had the disciplinary power claimed by Willett.

In part, tensions over Willett reflected teachers' complaints that Oberholtzer was a distant figure. While he readily mingled with leaders of the PTA and members

In 1965, tensions over the way the administration dealt with faculty members at Fairmont School, 520 West Third Avenue, helped transform the Denver Classroom Teachers Association into a union. The group threatened to strike if the administration did not listen to its account of what was happening there.

of the business community, he had no regular contact with classroom instructors. Teachers lamented the blunt and seemingly callous way they were treated by the likes of deputy superintendent Roy Hindermann.

The events at Thomas Jefferson also revealed extreme fissures in the Colorado Education Association. The Administrators and Supervisors Association (ASA), the group representing principals, blasted the DCTA in the dispute. The Denver Coaches Association and the DCTA, it argued, did not have the slightest right to tell principals and the superintendent how to behave. In the process, it complained to the state and national associations about the conduct of NEA representative Reichert who was anything but polite to Oberholtzer during the clash. On the contrary, Reichert behaved as a militant trade union negotiator battling management.

Instead of backing the teachers, the CEA stated it was neutral on the dispute between the DCTA and the ASA. It was obvious this was an untenable stance. The CEA either had to represent teachers or management; it was no longer able to speak for both. The result was that the ASA went its separate way from the CEA.

The principals' group, incidentally, had ratified its new constitution in November 1962. This was a time when other groups representing management increasingly left the NEA. The forerunner of the ASA, the Principals Association, had emerged at a January 18, 1906, meeting. Stalwarts of the district who are remembered by schools, including Homer Philips, Elizabeth Skinner, Jessie Hamilton, and Eugene Stevens, were among the founders. Charles M. Osenbaugh (1877–1930) was the first president. Born in Missouri, he emerged as the inaugural principal of Swansea School in 1891. He went on to lead Wyman School from 1897 to 1902. He later was the joint principal of South High, Grant Elementary (South Pearl Street and Colorado Avenue, a building it shared with early South High), and Fleming Elementary (South Grant Street and Colorado Avenue, the forerunner of Thatcher School). In 1912, Osenbaugh left Denver to serve as the principal of the high school in San Jose, California. At the time of his death at age 62, he was the head of the Northern State Teachers College of California.

Dora Moore, Edward L. Brown, Anna Louisa Johnson, Harry Kepner, Louisa Merrill, George McMeen, Anna Force, Leon Slavens, Peter Holm, Margaret M. Smith, Rufus Palmer, Mary Carson, Frances Doull, Roscoe Hill, and John Cory were subsequent well-known figures in the Principals Association. Not surprisingly, the association requested better pay and working conditions for its members. Around 1927, the group became the Denver Principals and Directors Association, using the initials DP&DA. At times, it had separate departments for elementary, junior high, and high school principals. Besides principals, the ASA represented high-ranking figures at DPS headquarters.

For a while, the Administrators and Supervisors had close ties with DACS: Deans, Assistant Principals, Coordinators, and Supervising Teachers. That group had once been the Assistant Principals Association. Along with the ASA, it often functioned more as a professional group than a union representing members. During the 1960s, DPS employee groups included chapters of Administrative Women in Education, Teachers in Elementary Education, and the High School Women's League. Many such organizations were highly transitory.

After World War II, groups surged claiming to speak for non-teachers. Included was the Denver Association of Educational Office Personnel. It emerged in late 1963/early 1964. The organization stemmed from 1932 as the Clerks and Secretaries Association. North High secretary Florence Stubbs was the moving force in establishing it. That year, DPS had recruited her for a committee about pending salary cuts caused by the Depression. She realized she would have more clout as the representative of her fellow workers than simply as an individual. Under her goading, 84 school secretaries and office workers gathered that fall at Morey. For some years, as the Association of Educational Office Personnel (DAEOP, subsequently the Denver Association of Educational Office Professionals), the group staged a candy sale in the schools prior to Christmas. The club gave back to their fellow workers by hosting an annual Christmas tea and awarding scholarships. The group became part of the Colorado Association of Educational Office Professionals.

School nurses, psychologists, and social workers, finding themselves excluded from the DCTA, organized in the Denver Association of Specialized Services for Children. At times, it was the Association of School Nurses, Social Workers, and Psychologists. Eventually, the organization became a unit within the DCTA when the Teachers Association expanded to include what it called "specialized service providers."

In 1974, the DCTA granted seats on its board to both the Congress of Hispanic Educators and Black Educators United. The latter was a caucus of African-American teachers. Paul Hamilton, who once taught at Lake Junior High, led it in the 1970s. Politically involved with the Democrats, Hamilton served in the

In 1959, DPS opened George McMeen School at 1000 South Holly Street, honoring a recently deceased principal who had led the district's Principals Association. The banner on the left, incidentally, shows McMeen had earned the status of being a "distinguished school."

Colorado House of Representatives during the 1970s. For a while, he affiliated with the DFT. This was at the same time that Wayne Knox headed the CFT in the late 1960s/early 1970s. A teacher in Adams City, Knox, a committed New Deal Democrat, won election to General Assembly in 1970. He remained in office until his retirement from the statehouse in 1996.

Until the DCTA opened its board to the two groups, the union had been officially neutral on the Keyes case. It had stressed the non-discriminatory provision of the 1969 contract it had signed with DPS: the district was not to single out teachers because of race, religion, or ethnicity. As such, it feared court orders demanding the integration of faculty endangered the working conditions of its members. The court intervention, it observed, meant that the administration, following the busing order about the necessity of integrating the district's faculty, could arbitrarily switch teachers between schools. With the Supreme Court decision and Judge Doyle's issuing of the Finger Plan in 1974, the union officially declared its commitment to making integration work. (Back in 1962, the Denver Federation of Teachers had suggested busing for integration.)

Within DPS, there was also a branch of the Colorado Association of Women Deans and Counselors. Additionally, there was the Denver Counselors Association. The Central Administration Personnel Association was another employee group. The Black Administrators and Supervisors Association emerged to represent African-Americans in the district's hierarchy.

DPS also had branches of the Council of Exceptional Children, and the International Reading Association. Those seeking fraternal life could join the Alpha Lambda branch of Kappa Delta Pi, an honor society for teachers. School Dames, Denver Schoolmasters' Guild, and the DENSKOMEN were something of social clubs by and for teachers and administrators.

Already after World War II, there was the Association of Operating and Maintenance Employees. It grew into the Operation, Maintenance, and Transportation Association by the 1960s, representing custodians. For years, a DPS Custodians Association had its office at the main administration building, working closely with the district. In 1963, in the wake of the school board's recognition of the DCTA as the official bargaining agency for teachers, the Custodians Association applied to be the recognized union/bargaining agent for those working in maintenance and school transportation. The group evolved into the Association of Building Operations Employees. The Association of Building and Grounds Service Personnel spoke for mechanics. Eventually, the groups combined as the Association of Buildings, Grounds, & Warehouses. Together, they became the Operations, Transportation, and Maintenance Association. The district also had a Facility Managers Association. Eventually, the Communications Workers of America represented custodians.

Other organizations included a group representing Professional–Technical Employees. DPS even had a category for "classified non-affiliated" workers. Local #1563 of the Amalgamated Transit Union (ATU) emerged as the representative of bus drivers and mechanics. It was a spinoff from ATU #1001, the branch representing workers at RTD.

Photo by Phil Goodstein

The DPS Service Building opened in 1958 at 2800 West Seventh Avenue. The Association of Buildings, Grounds, & Warehouses has represented some of those working there and employees maintaining the physical plant of the district.

The Recognition Campaign

During the first half of the 1960s, the DCTA and DFT constantly clashed, both claiming the right to represent teachers. The DFT was particularly outspoken in suggestions about how to improve the schools and teaching conditions. Under the leadership of Robert Rothstein, an instructor at George Washington, the DFT presented plans whereby teachers could collaborate better with administrative personnel to enhance the learning climate. The union frequently complained about how bureaucratic dictates from above interfered with effective instruction. To improve learning, it called for sending teacher aides into classrooms.

In 1965, the PTA blasted the DFT when the union drew up a list of "problem schools." This, the PTA complained, gave the district and its students negative publicity. The effort was necessary, Rothstein replied, to highlight where the district required improvement. By focusing on schools suffering turbulence, the teachers could work with the administration to redress difficulties. Such attention was needed rather than the way union haters automatically blamed teachers for failures in the classrooms. Eventually, the Mile High PTA Congress accepted teachers unions as a fact of life. Following national policy, the Denver council stated its goal was to be a "neutral forum" to advance education when labor and management clashed on school issues.

During the 1960s, the DFT held an annual scholarship achievement banquet where it presented awards to outstanding students. Drawing on the support of the AFT, it drew up "The Effective Schools Program in Denver." The local modeled it based on the achievements of the United Federation of Teachers, the New York City branch of the AFT. The way the United Federation of Teachers forged ahead shaped the DFT's goals.

When it originally sought recognition in the 1950s, complete with the right to engage in collective bargaining on behalf of teachers, the DFT stated that, as public employees, teachers would not go out on strike. Rather, the group wanted the impartial arbitration of disputes. (Historically, unions have opposed binding arbitration. Such a procedure kills the militancy of rank-and-file workers while it delays the resolution of pressing grievances. It also assumes that the system is essentially permanent and that arbitrators are completely neutral referees.) Now, citing the national successes of the AFT, the DFT stated it was a full-fledged union, being ready to do everything legally possible to benefit teachers and education.

Jarrell Ward "Jerry" McCracken emerged as the head of the DFT around 1966—he had previously held the one-year post in the early 1960s. Born in Lincoln, Nebraska, in 1933, he arrived in the Mile High City after getting out of the military. In 1956, he signed on as a Latin teacher at Smiley Junior High. A man of immense knowledge, his classroom lectures often ranged into arcane subjects as he connected a seemingly dead language with the present. Deeply caring about his students, he made them want to learn. On a couple of occasions, he won the award as the district's most outstanding instructor. McCracken took a leave of absence from his teaching duties in the spring of 1967 to campaign for recognition of the DFT.

Ronald Carlson, left, a Gove social studies teacher, emerged as the president of the Colorado Education Association in 1967, when the group was moving from being a professional association to a teachers union. Back in 1962, Carlson had been president of the DCTA when he was the first head of the group to get time off from his job to serve as the leader of the teachers association.

By this time, the DCTA was increasingly behaving as a union even while it insisted it was still simply a professional organization. The DCTA leader during the balloting for recognition was Allerton H. "Al" Barnes Jr., who had previously taught Latin at Gove. A flamboyant, short, plump man, Barnes had a flair for outlandish clothes. Born in Denver on May 25, 1924, he was a product of DPS. On graduating from high school, he headed to Wheaton College in Illinois, a conservative Christian school where he hoped to study for the ministry. A crisis of faith, when Barnes came to reject the trinity, led him to return to Colorado where he graduated from CU in 1947. In 1952, he received a master's in education from DU. For a while, Barnes still aspired to the ministry, becoming the choral director of First Universalist Church. He signed on with DPS in 1953. Seven years later, he left Gove for a spot at the new Thomas Jefferson Junior High/High School.

After stepping down as president of the DCTA, in 1968 Barnes left DPS to become the executive director of the Fairfax, Virginia, Education Association. He was on the job when a heart attack killed him at age 49 on March 7, 1974. Back when Barnes was the head of the DCTA, another Gove teacher, Ronald Carlson, emerged as the president of the parent CEA in 1967. Within a few years, Carlson was the DPS director of administration and personnel. When the DCTA voted to strike the district in 1969, Gove instructors narrowly went along, 23–16; in contrast, teachers at Smiley backed it 67–8. Confrontations at Gove during the strike were particularly intense, reflecting a deeply divided faculty.

In part, the DFT campaigned for recognition based on the need for greater physical protection of teachers. It demanded a "professional discipline clause" in a contract between the teachers and District #1. Ideally, this would prevent instructors from being assaulted, an increasingly frequent problem. As it campaigned for the measure, it failed to mention how instructors were able to impose arbitrary corporal punishment on students. Men gym teachers were notorious for impromptu spankings of boys or rapping them on the head with their knuckles, an appropriate punishment, they declared, for "knuckleheads." Now the teachers appeared shocked that students fought back, rebelling against tyrannical instructors.

The Evolution of the DCTA

At times, clashes between the DFT and DCTA verged on violence. The evolution of the DCTA reflected the changes in teacher organizations everywhere during the 1960s. The NEA and CEA were no longer the voice of administrators, but ever more of salaried instructors.

The NEA had gone from an elite group, with about 10,000 members in 1918, to more than 210,000 by the time the United States entered World War II. Most were classroom teachers. After the return of peace, rank-and-file members increasingly insisted the NEA reflect their concerns. If it did not, they threatened to break away and affiliate with the American Federation of Teachers. The CEA reflected the change, slowly evolving from a self-avowed professional organization, opposed to collective bargaining, into a de facto union which engaged in collective bargaining.

From the origins of the AFT, militant instructors had mocked the way administrators had demanded teachers be "professionals." This, union advocates argued, was nothing but an empty term that actually meant instructors had to be subservient to the administration. Indeed, superintendents not only ordered teachers about, but they even once had the right to dictate their personal lives and living quarters. Such condescending discipline showed the instructors were anything but professionals with the autonomy over their classrooms where they were able to work with their students to the best of their ability.

Nobody had more personified the DCTA during the post–World War II epoch than Ruth G. Menghin. The daughter of Italian immigrants who was born on July 29, 1908, she was a product of DPS who received her diploma from the forerunner of UNC followed by a master's from Teachers College at Columbia University. Once a classroom instructor at Emerson School, Menghin had been a close collaborator with Mary Harrington in pushing the DCTA in the 1930s and 1940s. By the time of Harrington's death in 1945, Menghin was president of the DCTA. In the early 1950s, she gained election as the head of the CEA. At the same time, she was most active in the Employees Council, serving as its chairwoman in 1952. Menghin went on to be principal of Gilpin School, Washington Park School, and Force School. Under her, the DCTA did not question the dictates of management. The educator retired after 30 years with the district in 1961. Menghin died in late June 1983. For decades, she lived at 2734 West 35th Avenue, across the street from Carl Ginn, 2729 West 35th Avenue, who served as principal of Smiley from

1937 to 1953 before emerging as the inaugural principal of Merrill Junior High, a post he held till his retirement in 1968.

As the DFT increasingly sought to assert itself in the 1950s and 1960s, principals often suggested young teachers affiliate with the DCTA as opposed to the DFT. The school board especially started to look fondly upon the DCTA as an alternative to the DFT. In 1962, after declaring it would not enter into negotiations with either the DCTA or the DFT, the board noted it was ready to engage in informal discussions with the larger group, i.e., the DCTA. It did not make any provision for a recognition election. Even so, the board's decision, including its 1963 acknowledgment that the DCTA was the official voice of the district's instructors, was a nod toward the possibility of collective bargaining between a teachers' association and DPS.

Seeing this, with the encouragement of the school board, the DCTA polled its members about the proposal. It excluded those holding a DFT card and non-affiliated teachers when it quizzed instructors about whether and how teachers should relate to management. By this time, the parent NEA also hesitatingly moved toward unionism, challenged across the country by the AFT while teacher strikes became more common. Increasingly, the DCTA represented members in grievance procedures.

Despite its vacillation about admitting it was a forthright union, the DCTA benefited from the national strength of organized labor during the 1960s. Additionally, it gained clout through the continual growth of the district. Since the end of World War II, as baby boomers flooded the classrooms, there had been a teacher shortage. By 1965, Superintendent Oberholtzer stated he would not reject DCTA requests for negotiation, but it must take the initiative. Even at that, he would not negotiate on personnel matters covered by existing regulations. The board upheld him.

Salary disputes stoked the fire of labor unrest. In the fall of 1965, the DFT launched a new petition to force a union recognition election. The board replied with delay and obfuscation. If anything, it called for teachers to work more closely with the administration and the board, particularly in imposing discipline. Additionally, the district raised teacher salaries as of September 1966. Back in 1963, starting pay for an instructor with a bachelor's degree had been $4,900. This was up from $3,775 in 1958–59. From a minimum of $5,100 a year for a beginning instructor, the district promised $5,400 annually for a first-year teacher in 1965. The salary was up to $5,500 by 1967. The highest teacher grade was for someone with an advanced degree who had been in the district for at least 17 years. The pay for such personnel went from $8,650 to $9,075. The school board pointed to the increase in compensation in justifying asking for a budget of $67,942,979 in 1965. Back in 1960, its budget had been $50,335,600. Every year since World War II, the district had required more funds. The number escalated to $76,665,201 for 1967. By 1969, the budget was $91,372,922 amidst the massive inflation of the Vietnam War era.

Increased pay was not enough. Both the DCTA and the DFT clamored for official recognition. To achieve it, on November 21, 1966, the DCTA officially presented its demand for bargaining status to the school board. By this time, it had 2,971 members out of 4,235 eligible faculty members. The DFT replied by once more calling for a

Photo by Phil Goodstein

From its origins in 1922, the Denver Classroom Teachers Association has stressed it prefers to collaborate with management. Alas, members have lamented when they have had to go out on strike, they have not been able to do so because of the district's core values. This is from a 2019 march down Colfax from East High to the Capitol during a teachers strike.

union recognition election. The board granted the DCTA's request at its session on December 15. At that time, the board also recognized the Food Service Association, Operations, Transportation, and Maintenance Association, and the Educational Secretaries and Classified Office Personnel as official bargaining agents.

Given the controversy over whether the DCTA was indeed about to emerge as a legitimate teachers union, at the December 15 session, the school board reviewed its 1962 policy of not engaging in collective bargaining with the DCTA. That day, it resolved teachers had the right to a recognition election by April 30, 1967, to decide if they wanted to be represented by the DCTA, DFT, some other group, or simply say no to all of them.

Right as the DCTA verged on becoming a union, the Employees Council saw it no longer served a useful purpose, voting to dissolve on December 12, 1966. This was the end of a long death spiral. Already back on February 13, 1963, DPS general counsel S. Arthur Henry had ruled that the Employees Council was not qualified to be a negotiating agent of the teachers under federal labor regulations.

As the election approached, the DFT realized it would likely lose the race. It sought to engage in negotiations with the DCTA to head off outright defeat. The Classroom Teachers Association refused any deal. Meanwhile, after many delays and much controversy, on February 8, 1967, the board set March 29 as the date of the recognition election.

In the month before the balloting, representatives of the DCTA and DFT staged feisty debates during after-school faculty meetings. For the most part, the DFT was on the defensive. It realized that many teachers still feared being members of a union, whereby it downplayed its identity as part of the AFL–CIO. The effort failed.

Most schools closed at 2:00 PM on election day to allow teachers to decide the issue. The DCTA easily won with 2,361 endorsements. The DFT received the backing of 1,355 teachers. There were 81 voters who did not want to be represented by either organization. Women teachers overwhelmingly backed the DCTA as their way of saying no to the unionism of the DFT. At its April 6 meeting, the board certified the results and recognized the DCTA as the bargaining agent until 1969.

After months of negotiations, the DCTA signed the district's first teacher-administration master contract in November 1967. It left many controversial points unresolved. Despite the gaps, the proto-union hailed it as a milestone, being sure it could soon settle disputed issues. As it had in the past, the DCTA urged teachers to join it, pointing to the numerous insurance and welfare benefits it offered members.

In the wake of the recognition election, Superintendent Oberholtzer led DPS's bargaining with the DCTA. Negotiations proceeded smoothly. They were not completed until after Oberholtzer's retirement. The new superintendent, Robert Gilberts, signed the deal. He was from a union family and supported collective bargaining. To facilitate negotiations with the DCTA, he named James Bailey, a future assistant superintendent, to head a new post of staff relations. The professional association's first contract went into effect on November 21, 1967, expiring on April 6, 1969.

On signing the agreement, the DCTA constantly found itself dealing with personnel issues, including what it believed were unwarranted transfers of teachers. The last particularly centered around Joy Boyd, a special education teacher at Cole Junior High. In January 1969, she found herself exiled to southwest Denver. She claimed this was the district's punishment because she was black and associated with African-American militants. The DFT seized on her case, ripping the DCTA for agreeing to a contract full of loopholes. Besides, it hinted the DCTA's parent NEA still had a racist tint, allowing for segregated affiliates in the South.

The DCTA replied that, as usual, the DFT had completely distorted what had happened. In part, it blamed this on Eugene Schipman. A veteran elementary school teacher, he had led the DCTA at the time of the 1967 contract negotiations. Before long, he had such differences with others in the DCTA that he quit the group, moving over to become first vice president of the DFT, soon emerging as the union's president. The clash illustrated that the DFT and DCTA frequently squabbled more with each other than they did with the administration.

On February 12, 1969, at the behest of the DFT, the school board ordered a new recognition election on March 5. It was necessary given the pending expiration of the 1967 contract on April 6. By this time, the DFT had around 440 members compared to 3,120 in the DCTA. Once more the two groups quarreled. The DCTA easily won the contest, 2,653–1,424 with 45 casting a ballot for neither organization.

During the campaign, the DCTA played on anti-union sentiments among teachers who had no experience in the labor movement. "DCTA remains professional" it declared, observing its affiliation with the highly respectable NEA. In contrast, it sought to smear the DFT as part of militant blue-collar unions in the AFL–CIO. Observing a prolonged, bitter teachers' strike in New York City led by the AFT in the fall of 1968, it asked instructors "Do You Want a New York in Denver?" The implication was that it would never lead Mile High teachers to walk out. A few months after it retained its post as the exclusive bargaining agent for DPS instructors, the DCTA called the teachers out on strike.

The 1969 Teachers Strike

Not only did racial tensions rack the city and DPS in the wake of the tumultuous May 1969 school board election and the litigation over integration, but the new, anti-busing, pro-business board showed it had little place for teachers or respect for the DCTA. The old board had failed to sign an agreement with the teachers association on the expiration of the contract in April. Nor did the new body reach an accommodation. It was deaf to the proto-union's pleas for more specific rules compared to the vagueness of the existing document. As the cost of living continued to soar, instructors also demanded higher pay.

The DFT continued to snipe at the DCTA. It branded the majority group as essentially a sell-out organization that was afraid to confront management and admit that it was a union. To get the pro-corporate school board to grant teachers better pay and working conditions, it insisted that teacher militancy was necessary. In response, the DCTA once more stressed it was not a union, but a

Author's collection

Teachers marched down 14th Street by the main DPS administration building during the November 1969 strike.

professional association. Unlike the DFT, which was ready to strike if necessary, it had previously vowed it would never countenance such a union tactic that would harm students.

Even so, national developments impacted the DCTA. Not only did the 1968 New York teachers strike show the growing chasm between instructors and administrators, but walkouts by public employees were becoming ever more common. Given the rising cost of living, teachers increasingly realized they had far more in common with wage workers than with such professionals as lawyers and doctors or even high-ranking school administrators. Governments treated public employees just as arbitrarily as management dealt with workers in private industry. The nature of class relations forced many professional organizations to behave as unions. Such was the case with the DCTA.

With its hard-line, pro-business attitude, the school board failed to reach a contract with the DCTA by the time the 1969–70 schoolyear started. It particularly rejected the DCTA's demand for a salary indexed to the cost of living. "Two point oh or out we go" members of the DCTA chanted, pointing to the group's salary demand and the pay index. The syndicate further protested DPS suggestions of extending the schoolday by 75 minutes with no increased pay—this was equivalent to an extra 20 schooldays a year. The district, the union argued, needed to pay teachers a minimum annual salary of $7,500, nearly $2,000 above the existing beginning wage rate. The DPS offer was around $6,700–$6,800. Under the DCTA proposal, maximum pay would rise to $14,000.

As negotiations stalemated, the administration failed to submit counteroffers. It repeatedly claimed it simply did not have the money to pay the requested salary hike. When it realized it had to respond to the DCTA's demands, the board promised it would pay the offered salaries beginning in 1971 if voters authorized a tax hike while the teachers agreed to waive many of their seniority rights. It further called for expanding the teacher's year from 180 to 210 days.

By October, the talks were deadlocked. Efforts at mediation failed. An independent fact-finder was so biased against the DCTA, complete with a condescending paternalist role, that he more alienated the teachers than encouraged settlement. In the face of the seemingly hopeless morass, the DCTA leadership saw it needed to make a drastic gesture to nudge the school board. Toward this end, it increasingly threatened to strike. To show that it meant business, on Friday, November 14, 1969, it held a strike vote. All teachers received ballots. They backed the action, 2,615–1,577.

To decide where to head next, the DCTA had a mass meeting the next day at Abraham Lincoln High School. While the leadership simply hoped to use the strike vote as a way of letting the board know how unhappy the teachers were, those at the gathering showed their total frustration with the way DPS had treated them. Essentially, the rank-and-file took over the session, using it to express their displeasure with business as usual. This culminated when, despite the suggestions of the leadership, those in attendance voted to walk out on Monday, November 17. The DFT, while endlessly murmuring that the DCTA was a poorly run, class-collaborationist sell-out organization that did not know what it was doing, endorsed the strike in the name of solidarity.

The teachers left the classrooms during a cold spell. Altogether, 3,100 of the system's 4,525 teachers joined the protest. About one-third crossed the picket lines. Among them were many members of the DCTA. About 60 to 70 percent of DCTA members walked out. In contrast, the DFT claimed that 97 to 99 percent of its members left the classrooms.

The administration was not prepared for the strike. At the most, the Friday before the walkout, it had asked principals to canvass faculty members to gauge whether they would be in class on Monday should the DCTA declare the strike. Not surprisingly, the poll was extremely unreliable. Many teachers who said they would be in school were on the picket lines on Monday. To assure that substitutes had a hard time

DPL

When teachers walked out against DPS in November 1969, they mobilized student teachers to support their action. Here aspiring instructors affiliated with the student branch of the CEA picket the DPS headquarters at 414 14th Street.

taking over from them, striking teachers made off with lesson plans and seating charts. Some provided replacement workers with bogus seating charts.

Superintendent Robert D. Gilberts sought to keep the schools open, concentrating on elementaries. With the help of unorganized substitutes and those refusing to honor the strike, DPS opened 48 of its elementaries—about half—on November 17, 1969. Often administrators herded the students into the auditorium. The labor action shut all of the high schools and most of the junior highs.

Members of the DCTA engaged in an old union tactic of constantly calling the main DPS switchboard during the beginning of the strike and not hanging up—they especially did this from pay phones. The result was hopelessly clogging up the phone system. As such, the central administration could not directly communicate with the schools. It had to get the phone company to rush to install an alternative phone system.

Not until the fourth day of the strike did the DCTA call for a solidarity boycott of the schools by students and their families. By that time, some of its members were returning to the classrooms. At the end of the week, 58 elementary and two junior high schools were open. The overall attendance rate was 27 percent.

When the strike loomed, DPS turned to the courts, demanding an injunction against the walkout. On November 18, Denver District Court Judge Saul Pinchick ruled that while the labor action was legal, strikers could not do anything to interfere with others entering schoolhouses. Consequently, the DCTA organized but token picket lines with five to ten teachers at each of the buildings. Altogether, it counted 600 members on the picket lines in front of 118 schoolhouses. Some bitter encounters and name-calling ensued between strikers and those opposing the walkout.

As part of launching the strike, the union held a mass rally in the Civic Center on the first day of the action, November 17. The afternoon event drew about 7,000 backers. After speeches, participants marched to the nearby administration building at 414 14th Street. They noted the school board was on the verge of adopting a $91.4 million budget. Out of that sum, they insisted, it could surely find enough funds to assure teachers got higher salaries.

As they struck and marched, many instructors were caught up in the militancy of the 1960s, asserting themselves as the true educators versus a parasite bureaucracy that limited their pay, initiative, and ability to help children learn. Calls included both "Teacher Power!" and "Little Old Lady Power!" Many young women teachers asserted themselves. Some waved signs, "At our price, we're still a bargain."

To counter growing defections, the DCTA turned to the Student Colorado Education Association. This was the section of the parent group on college campuses composed of aspiring instructors. The union appealed for such students not to cross the picket lines. The Classroom Teachers Association issued bulletins, trying to keep up morale. To inform strikers of breaking developments, it set up a hotline telephone which members called frequently.

The DFT saw the walkout as crucial to the area's labor climate. The body complained the DCTA had not reached out to it as part of a unity strike committee, calling on non-teacher organizations of clerks, custodians, and bus drivers to join the walkout. The DCTA replied that the DFT was a "most disruptive element." Despite the backbiting, the DFT mobilized

Echoing the rhetoric of the day, in 1969 the Colorado Education Association asserted teachers power.

for the strike. It convinced the Denver Area Labor Federation, the local coalition of unions affiliated with the AFL–CIO, to back the action. It additionally got members of the Teamsters to honor the teachers' picket line. As such, the Teamsters quit delivering supplies to the schools, including for lunch programs. This added pressure on the board to settle.

From the beginning, many teachers wavered. While some were lifelong residents, who had proudly made their way through DPS and were glad to return to the system, others were newcomers. Among them were individuals who had been allured to Colorado by the ski mystique. Neither they nor many of the Denver natives had a solid, strong background in unionism. Despite the way DPS treated them, some instructors were insistent they were professionals not grubby wage workers in need of union protection. Others committed themselves to the effort, embracing the idealism and the rhetoric of the times. In the process, they had loudly shouted during their protest march by DPS headquarters. This greatly upset the pious editors at the *Rocky Mountain News* who damned the underpaid instructors for their "pitiable, unprofessional display."

Seeing the strike was a city-wide issue, on Sunday, November 23, nearly a week into the walkout, Mayor William McNichols offered to help resolve it. DPS said no, being sure that the walkout was on the verge of collapse. Even at that, it stated it wanted a settlement. After five days, both sides were relatively close in pay demands. By Wednesday, November 26, DPS had opened 78 of its buildings. Attendance was still around 27 percent. Two-thirds of the teachers remained on the picket lines.

On November 28, the day after Thanksgiving, the district and the DCTA reached an agreement. The district conceded many of the union's demands. The DCTA called a mass meeting of all teachers at the Auditorium Arena on Saturday, November 29. The instructors agreed to the pact, 1,782–527.

The deal promised serious negotiations in the new year. Included was a new minimum salary. There was also an amnesty clause. Additionally, the settlement allowed teachers to recover up to 90 percent of the pay they had lost during the strike by working extra hours in the classroom until the end of the schoolyear. For the most part, this simply meant they stayed each evening for quite a while after the schoolday. Often they used the time to grade papers, work they otherwise might have done at home. This clause was crucial. The union had rejected a similar pay deal without the amnesty and make-up pay on November 24.

The Aftermath

All the while, clashes continued between the DFT and the DCTA. The group affiliated with the AFL–CIO complained the settlement was a sellout. It criticized the deal for failing to address the size of classes or teaching conditions. For that matter, it claimed DPS paid for the contract by cutting 125 teaching positions, so imposing larger classes on instructors. The DFT also snarled that there was no outreach to substitutes. The agreement promised only $7,000 as a minimum salary in contrast to the demand for $7,500. The DCTA claimed it had gained 155

SN

Clarke Ballinger, left, took charge as the executive director of the Denver Classroom Teachers Association in 1968, holding the post until 1988. In office, he oversaw the group consolidate itself as a union. Here he receives an award from Gordon Heaton of Regis, heralding the DCTA's collaboration with the DPS administration.

members during the action while 47 had quit the group. The Denver Federation of Teachers did not make a comparable report. Classes resumed on Monday, December 1, 1969. The DCTA and the district officially signed the contract on December 18. The new salary schedule went into effect in January 1970.

There was an extremely frosty climate in the schools between returning strikers and those who had crossed the picket lines. In some cases, former friends never spoke to each other again as a result of their differences during the walkout. Not surprisingly, many students heartily backed the teachers. If nothing else, the strike gave them an opportunity to skip classes. Some later recalled the eight-day strike as the best time they had during their schooldays.

In the wake of the strike, the DCTA was increasingly a labor association. Before long, pro-corporate advocates of children painted it as the evil teachers union. They claimed the unionized teachers did not care about education, but only about themselves. They never mentioned management policies assuring bad morale and poor working conditions.

The DFT continued to brand the DCTA as a sell-out pseudo-union. Had it been the negotiating agent, the DFT insisted, the strike never would have occurred. The incompetence of the DCTA and its failure to be a forthright union, the Mile High affiliate of the AFT argued, had encouraged the arrogance of the school board, leading to the walkout.

Opposed to the DCTA, the DFT loudly broadcast its commitment to class collaboration with management. This came out when, in the wake of the strike, it worked with the League of Women Voters to create Denver QuEST. This was a commission of 11 to 15 "leading citizens" working to resolve tensions between the teachers, administration, and the community. The DFT not only invited the Denver Area Labor Federation to be part of Denver QuEST, but it also reached out to the Chamber of Commerce, and the official organizations of the Democratic and Republican parties. The Council of Churches and the city's Commission on Community Relations joined the effort. The other groups insisted that the DCTA also be part of Denver QuEST. Standing for Quality Educational Standards in Teaching, QuEST was a national program of the AFT. The Denver chapter issued a few reports before fading away. For a while, future school board member Kay Schomp was among its supporters.

Instructors at Opportunity School retained recognition as local #203 of the Vocational Teachers Federation of the AFT. The Federation of Teachers came to represent pockets of instructors outside of District #1, especially in Mapleton, Adams County District #1, and in Douglas County. Additionally, there was the Denver Federation for Paraprofessionals, local #4463 of the AFT, the organization composed of DPS teacher aides. The union additionally asserted itself in the Nutrition Service Employees, a new identity of the DPS Lunchroom Employees Association, also known as the Association of Food Services Workers. It merged with the Paraprofessionals as the Denver Federation for Paraprofessionals & Nutrition Service Employees. Back in the late 1960s/early 1970s, local #1611 of the AFT represented workers at Denver Opportunity, the agency overseeing the Mile High War on Poverty. The union had less than sterling success in seeking to organize local college professors. The AFT also represented the Colorado Federation of School Safety Professionals, essentially members of the district's police force.

In 1972, the DFT again sought a recognition election. It failed to gather the prerequisite number of signatures. The group did not try too hard because, at that period, loud voices in the AFT were pushing for an amalgamation of the union with the NEA. This led to unity negotiations between the DFT and the DCTA. Like the national push for merger, nothing came of them. Meanwhile, a close relationship between DCTA executive director Clarke Ballinger and DPS staff director James Bailey saw the professional group and the district easily renew the teachers' contract that year. In the wake of this, the DFT became ever less visible in claiming to speak for classroom instructors. Usually, it had but a few hundred members. Meanwhile, the DCTA and district forged a workable grievance procedure.

There was a constant turnover in the leadership of both the DCTA and DFT. Appointed executive directors more oversaw the groups than elected officials. Often those who started out as backers of the teachers union landed up in the administration. Typical was Royce D. Forsyth. Born in Denver in 1927 as part of a close-knit family, he grew up just to the west of the University of Denver campus. After graduating from South High, he earned both his bachelor's and master's from that university. Fresh out of college, he signed on as a teacher at Smiley in 1949, later moving over to Merrill Junior High. As the DFT struggled for recognition, he served as its president in the 1950s, going on to be president of the CFT. In 1965, he was among the political activists working for the election of Rachel Noel to the school board.

Eventually, Forsyth held numerous posts in the DPS administration. Among them was being a founder and the supervisor of the Balarat Outdoor Education program near Jamestown and the head of the district's office of federal, state, and local governmental affairs. For a while, Forsyth was the administration's liaison with the District School Improvement and Accountability Council. This was a citizen body charged with advising the school board in the name of seeing that education was the district's primary concern. Additionally, Forsyth was the

Drawing by Gregorio Alcaro

Royce Forsyth moved from being president of the Denver Federation of Teachers to a post in the DPS administration.

superintendent's representative to the board of the Denver County PTA. Most of all, for some years the educator was the system's top legislative lobbyist. He retired from DPS at the end of 1983.

Besides his school pursuits, Forsyth, a devout Quaker, was involved in numerous community activities. He served a term as president of the Colorado branch of the American Civil Liberties Union and was a supporter of the Center for Labor Education and Research, a joint product between the state's unions and the University of Colorado. Additionally, he was a cog in the Democratic Party, including being a precinct leader/committeeman for 18 years. In 1988, he chaired the successful election campaign of Pat Pascoe for the state Senate. She was the wife of Monte Pascoe who had run for the school board in the controversial 1969 election. Forsyth went on to gain election as Denver's representative on the state board of education in 1990. The educator passed away on February 13, 2007.

Regis Groff was still another Smiley teacher who had been active in the DFT— he emerged as the group's second vice president around 1968–69 when he was at Lake Junior High. This was just before he moved over to East. Additionally, Groff was active in Park Hill integration efforts and the Democratic Party. Though he lost a primary race for the Democratic nomination to the Colorado House of Representatives in 1974, he gained appointment the next year to fill a vacancy in the state Senate. Eventually, he was also in the school administration, heading the district's human relations department. DPS came to have a Regis Groff Campus at 18250 51st Avenue in Green Valley Ranch, the location of Florida Pitt Waller School. The way Forsyth and Groff drifted away from the union was not unusual. At times, DPS consciously reached out to labor activists, including those in the DCTA, offering them administrative posts, jobs with greater pay which took such firebrands out of the sometimes hectic classroom scene.

As much as anything, the 1969 strike made the DCTA. It could not turn back from the walkout, claiming exclusively to be a professional organization. Even at that, it remained a partner of the administration, collaborating in the everyday functioning of the system. This particularly came out in the Professional Council. To resolve disputes and give the superintendent direction about the nature of professional standards while promoting "employee harmony," the contract between the DCTA and DPS created a Professional Council. For the most part, it consisted of 12 to 16 members, half drawn from the DCTA; the others were from the administration. Included were the executive director of the union and the superintendent. The group usually met monthly during the schoolyear at the board room of DPS headquarters. It had numerous subcommittees providing opportunities for rank-and-file teachers to have an input to the decisions of the council. The DCTA forged itself as superintendents Robert D. Gilberts, Louis Kishkunas, and Joseph Brzeinski came and went while DPS suffered dropping enrollment during the tumultuous 1970s. All the while, the district constantly added programs, approaches, and new buildings.

A Note on Sources:

An outline of the Arapahoe County Teachers' Association is in *CSJ*, May 1891, p. 8. Mazie L. Dolphin, "A History of the Denver Classroom Teachers' Association" (M.A. thesis, DU, 1936), 13–15, 58, touches on the Grade School Teachers Assembly. Ketchum, "CEA," paints the organizational shell of the CEA, its programs, and its leaders. Included is a list of its presidents, 77. DPL has one issue of *Grade Interests* and scattered copies of *Classroom Interests*.

Schwartzkopf, "Collective Bargaining," 74, mentions the Colorado State Teachers' Association becoming the CEA. Ibid., 72, looks at the early Classroom Teachers Association and the board's reaction to it. Harry M. Barrett, "Education in Colorado," in Junius Henderson et al., *Colorado Short Studies of Its Past and Present* (Boulder: University of Colorado, 1927), 132, stresses the reorganization of the CEA and its role in the state's educational system. There are passing materials on the nature of the CEA during the interwar era in FF 2:19–20 of the Jesse Newlon papers at DU. This is in correspondence between Newlon and William Mooney, the executive secretary of the CEA.

Dolphin, "DCTA," 7–10, outlines the origins and evolution of the Committee of Ten. She glances at the Senior High School Teachers Association, 57. The study, 12, 19–22, 57, tells of the unity of the Grade School and High School teachers and the emergence of the DCTA. It mentions the slogan, 20.

DP, February 4, 1954, p. 38, and *RMN*, February 5, 1954, remembered William Shute. *DP*, November 29, 1930, p. 3, and *RMN*, November 29, 1930, p. 3, recalled Charles Osenbaugh. *RMN*, July 1, 1983, p. 167, mourned the passing of Ruth Menghin.

Schwartzkopf, "Collective Bargaining," 74, tells of Newlon's push to combine all DPS employee organizations into a united group. Gary Lee Peltier, "Jesse H. Newlon as Superintendent of Denver Public Schools, 1920–27" (Ph.D. dissertation,

DU, 1965), 65, 242–43, emphasizes the 100-percent membership of DPS teachers in the NEA. Ketchum, "CEA," 19, 23, also reports the 100-percent enrollment. Schwartzkopf, "Collective Bargaining," 77, focuses on the DCTA's push for a separate CEA department for classroom teachers.

CI, March 1923, p. 6, listed DCTA membership, and the proposed bylaws, p. 10. On p. 15, it told about the DCTA having space in the administration building and the group's goal of collaborating with management. *CI*, June 1927, pp. 23, expressed the cordial relations between Jesse Newlon and the DCTA. The Spring 1943 *CI* celebrated the group's 21st birthday. It included a history of the organization, listing the names of its many leaders and activists. Indicative of its close ties with the administration was a letter of greetings from Superintendent Charles Greene, p. 8. The magazine looked at the emergence of the DCTA, pp. 9–15.

There are marginal notes by Jesse Newlon in FF 1:11 of his papers to an article in *Classroom Interests* in which he talks about the origins of the Teachers' Club. Dolphin, "DCTA," 9–11, outlines the emergence of the Teachers' Club and its insurance program. DPL has copies of the annual yearbook of the Teachers' Club for the period before World War I. It also has yearbooks from the 1960s and 1970s of the Denver Area Music Teachers Association. Shikes, "Three Superintendents," 160–64, looks at the rise of teacher organizations, including the School Masters Guild in the 1910s and 1920s, and their impact on the forging of the DCTA. FF 1:6 of the DPS papers glances at the Papyrus Club.

SB, February 21, 1949, p. 1, January 9, 1950, p. 1, March 27, 1950, p. 3, January 14, 1952, p. 69, March 10, 1952, p. 101, March 16, 1953, p. 107, *SB*, January 11, 1954, p. 69, March 1, 1954, p. 100, March 8, 1954, p. 101, January 20, 1964, p. 75, March 1, 1965, p. 93, and February 28, 1966, p. 99, were among its many notices about the Teachers' Club and its annual concert. *Denver Express*, May 9, 1917, had observed the group's support of Carlos Cole as superintendent. FF 9:70 of the DPS papers has the 1964 bylaws of the Teachers' Club, listing insurance benefits available to members.

DP February 10, 1919, p. 1, reported the school engineers going out on strike. It noted the end of the dispute, February 17, 1919, p. 1. On October 24, 2019, Ray McAllister discussed the tradition of building engineers and the changing nature of heating systems in the schools.

RMN, June 24, 1919, p. 3, reported the meeting at East where teachers pondered affiliation with the AFL. Also see Sinclair, *Goslings*, 158. Newlon discussed his efforts at a single salary schedule for teachers and the imposition of professional requirements in the 1923 *DPS Report*, 7, 15–17. Background on the rise and transformation of the DCTA and DFT is in Schwartzkopf, "Collective Bargaining." Allison, ed., *Without Consensus*, 187–93, includes a reactionary rant about the dangers of NEA militancy within a larger discussion of the changing nature of the teaching profession, 187–221. *American Teacher*, December 1962, p. 2, attacked the myth that, as professionals, teachers were too elevated to form unions and strike.

Sinclair, *Goslings*, 390, 403, links the moral control over teachers with their status as white-collar workers and the need for unionism. Richard Hofstadter,

Anti-Intellectualism in American Life (New York: Vintage, 1962), 310, observes the way society has generally failed to respect teaching as a highly honored profession, while stressing the low pay teachers have received, 319.

Dana Goldstein, *The Teacher Wars* (New York: Doubleday, 2014), 84, emphasizes the rise of the AFT. Marjorie Murphy, *Blackboard Unions* (Ithaca: Cornell University Press, 1990), is an overview of the emergence of the AFT and how the NEA evolved from a professional association into a labor organization.

Schwartzkopf, "Collective Bargaining," 100–01, reports on the Glenwood Springs convention of the AFT. The work, chap. 3, focuses on the rise of the DFT. There are generally critical materials on the DFT in scattered folders in boxes one and two of the poorly organized DCTA papers, WH 2125, at DPL. The collection was disposed of by the Auraria Archives. Box two has a few copies of *The Denver Teacher* for 1969. There are also scattered copies of the AFT's *Colorado Teacher* in FF 8:19 of the Herrick Roth papers at the CU Archives, COU 1395. The holding has materials on the DFT, especially for 1967–73, in FF 3:8–9.

Schwartzkopf, "Collective Bargaining," 83–84, looks at the activism of John Eklund and the 1945 CEA convention. As is typical of a sloppiness permeating her study, Schwartzkopf states the teachers lobbied Governor Ralph Carr for the pay hike. He had left the office in January 1943.

Ibid., 85–86, tells of the original push for the Denver Teachers Union and its 16-point plan. The dissertation mentions gatherings at 414 14th Street, 85, quotes Herrick Roth's problems with that location, 89, and emphasizes why the group became the DFT rather than the Denver Teachers Union, 89. The work tells about the chartering of the local, 90. It cites *RMN*, February 23, 1946, about the union campaign. On 94–95, the study observes the administration's "proper advice," and the way the school board reacted to the DFT campaign by increasing salaries. *Denver Teacher*, October 1963, p. 1, optimistically observed that women membership in the DFT was up to 44 percent of the total.

SRv, October 1957, p. 1, listed salary schedules and how DPS compared nationally in its pay rates. Shikes, "Three Superintendents," 239, looks at teacher salaries. So does Schwartzkopf, "Collective Bargaining," 93–94, 99. *RMN*, April 30, 1939, heralded the School Policies Council. *Time*, December 12, 1938, p. 8, painted it as a national model.

On August 7, 2019, Bill Himmelmann, the retired head of the Denver Area Labor Federation, recalled the DFT and the agreement at Opportunity School. He mentions the Opportunity School contract in his memoirs, *A Train Runs Through It*, 42. A copy of the CFT constitution is in FF 8:16 of the Roth papers.

SB, January 9, 1950, p. 3, announced the DFT hosting John M. Eklund at a public forum. It briefly mentioned his background and service as president of the AFT. The sheet, September 24, 1951, p. 12, observed his re-election as head of the AFT. It told of his contribution to Ernest O. Melby, ed., *Freedom and Public Education* (New York: Praeger, 1953). The article is 261–67. Eklund is in the 1958 *Who's*, 167. Murphy, *Blackboard Unions*, 195, briefly refers to his role as the head of the AFT amidst the Cold War. She observes the impact of the Cold War in the classroom, 175–76, 182, and the links between vocational teachers and the AFT,

146. *NYT*, January 26, 1997, reviewed Eklund's life. The Walter Reuther Library at Wayne State University has a small holding on him, MS 416.

The 1958 *Who's*, 477–78, features Herrick Roth, and George Cavender, 99. There is an unidentified clipping about Roth and the labor committee supporting DPS in FF 3 of the Helen Anderson papers at DU. It mentions Roth's lament about the banning of reference materials in high school libraries. The CFT backed the military in working to cut dropout rates in *CT*, April 1973, p. 1. FF 9:8 of the Roth papers is filled with letters of recommendation Roth wrote to urge the Marines to promote Gene Schipman to brigadier general.

Roth says nothing about his specific career or the dynamics of the teachers union in his rather vacuous book, *Labor: America's Two-Faced Movement* (New York: Petrocelli/Charter, 1975). The Roth papers at CU include tapes of "Labor's Language." Schwartzkopf, "Collective Bargaining," profiles Roth, 87–89, 101. She claims he was drafted rather than enlisted in World War II. The study states that the *Denver Post* was among those who branded him a communist, 114, reporting he successfully sued the paper for "slander." (Slander is a verbal attack; a libel is a defamation in print.) Harold Knight, *Working in Colorado* (Boulder: Colorado Labor Education and Research, 1971), 151, observes the libel was not in the *Post*, but in an anti-communist publication that soon folded.

Schwartzkopf, "Collective Bargaining," 115–16, observes the links between Roth and Palmer Burch. On August 7, 2019, Bill Himmelmann recalled Roth and controversies about him in the Denver labor movement during the 1970s. *Cmq*, March 1972, p. 2, told of Roth supporting a bill in the legislature allowing for increased incarceration for juvenile offenders. It observed the opposition to the proposal by the PTA and the Juvenile Court.

I deal with Roth's political career in *Our Time*, 422–23, and the *Naysayer*, March 2008. Over the years, I had sporadic interactions with Cavender and Roth. The former gladly shared his memories. The latter, who essentially introduced me to unionism during an off-campus forum when I was at East, lectured me when not denouncing my politics since I questioned labor's fealty to the Democratic Party. Knight, *Working*, 150–51, 165–66, 178–79, includes an overview of the rise of the DFT, Cavender, and Roth. Schwartzkopf, "Collective Bargaining," 83–85, 101, glances at Cavender and Robert Ozanne. On August 26, 2019, Dick Koeppe shared his memories of Herrick Roth, Jerry McCracken, Royce Forsyth, and others active in the DFT.

Shikes, "Three Superintendents," 237–38, 240–42, 247, traces the rise of the DFT, the Employees Council, and the DCTA. *SB*, February 4, 1963, p. 86, mentioned the DCTA challenging the Employees Council as the voice of DPS teachers. *DP*, May 4, 1949, p. 3, told of Roth's attack on Oberholtzer for using DPS employees to enhance the election of the administration's candidates to the school board. DPS PR, June 15, 1989, mentioned the Roth Public Policy Lecture.

FF 8:1, 7, of the Roth papers have materials on factional divisions with the AFT and the views of the Unity Caucus. *CJ*, December 7, 1972, p. 3, profiled Roth and his political ambitions. *RMN*, May 8, 1974, p. 5, reported the poll favoring Roth for the United States Senate. *DP*, April 27, 1975, p. 1, looked at upheavals at the Colorado Department of Labor under the leadership of Roth. *DP*, February 6, 1976, p. 3, mentioned Roth stepping down from the agency.

SB, December 5, 1966, pp. 53–54, reported the board of education pondering the recognition of the DCTA and the DFT's objections. *SB*, October 13, 1952, p. 23, chronicled the conferences of the CEA and CFT. It additionally observed the DFT bingo party. *American Teacher*, the journal of the AFT, December 1962, p. 1, highlighted the Miss Union Teacher contest.

SB, October 20, 1952, p. 27, listed the meeting of the Clerks and Secretaries Association. *RMN*, June 2, 1967, p. 53, reported the end of the CEA having its convention in October. I review that development in *School Book*, 445. Schwartzkopf, "Collective Bargaining," 98–99, looks at the inaugural convention of the DFT and the presence of Charles Brannan and Norman Cousins.

I have relied on the Westerra web page in tracing the evolution of the DPS Employees' Credit Union. There are mentions of the credit union in *SB*, January 24, 1949, p. 4, May 2, 1949, p. 1, and October 1, 1951, p. 14. *SB*, January 9, 1950, p. 1, reflected on the origins and operations of the credit union. Wesley, *NEA*, 338, touches on the rise of credit unions in school districts.

Schwartzkopf, "Collective Bargaining," 105–07, outlines the rise of the Employees Council as a pet project of Oberholtzer. She observes opposition to it from the DCTA and the DFT, including that members of the latter group called it a sham organization, 111. Her work reports Judge Edward Day's decision about the Employees Council, 114. *SB*, September 10, 1951, p. 1, stressed the Committee on Drives and Campaigns of the Employees Council, including the endorsement of the Crusade for Freedom. There is a portrait of the Employees Council in Shikes, "Three Superintendents," 237–38, 240–44, with a passing mention of the DFT. *SB*, January 19, 1953, p. 73, tells about the formation of a committee to study the nature of the Employees Council.

DP, September 11, 1960, p. 30C, recalled the DFT's 1956 suit over the status of the Employees Council. *DP*, December 18, 1966, p. 5, reviewed the role of Oberholtzer in forming the Employees Council. On October 3, 2015, and January 9, 2018, Jimi O'Connor recalled his activism in the Employees Council in the 1950s and 1960s.

SB, October 25, 1948, p. 1, April 25, 1949, p. 1, May 16, 1949, p. 1, March 13, 1950, p. 1, May 19, 1952, p. 138, October 27, 1952, p. 30, January 18, 1954, p. 74, March 15, 1954, p. 106, March 29, 1954, pp. 113, 116, January 25, 1965, pp. 74–75, and February 1, 1965, p. 78, reported on the Council's doings.

SB, January 27, 1969, p. 79, and December 15, 1969, p. 56, referred to DESCI. DPS PR on March 6, 1989, May 11 and May 24, 1990, outlined the changing character of the DESCI apartment house. *DP*, November 5, 2012, p. 1A, reported that the building was for sale. On September 6, 2019, Cindy Rundstrom, who had been on the DESCI board, recalled what had happened with the structure. She further discussed the Retired Teachers' Club, a group also known as the DPS Retired Employees Association. On August 28, 2019, Bernadette Seick chatted about the organization, emphasizing its scholarship foundation. Rita Montero and Dorolyn Griebenaw also informed me about the Retired Teachers' Club and its lending of medical equipment during a luncheon on February 27, 2018. That point comes out on the rather insubstantial web page of the Teachers' Club.

SB, September 24, 1951, p. 11, reported the CEA offering teachers hospital insurance. Murphy, *Blackboard Unions*, 223, stresses NEA's insurance program. A copy of the pre–World War II CEA hospital benefit plan is in FF 2:20 of the Newlon papers.

Ketchum, "CEA," 65–67, observes the origins of the CEA hospitalization insurance program and some of the group's other benefits. Dorothy E. Monninger, "The Role of the Colorado Education Association in Influencing Educational Legislation in Selected Areas, 1941–1970" (Ed.D. dissertation, CU, 1971), overviews the political achievements of the CEA, including its ties with retired teachers and the Public Employees Retirement Association.

Schwartzkopf, "Collective Bargaining," 2–3, traces the 1961 drive of the DFT and how the school board came to recognize the DCTA as the representative of DPS teachers. *RMN*, February 11–14, 1963, observed the push for teacher unionization and the recognition of the DCTA. On February 15, 1963, it reported the Employees Council's lament about its "second-class status." *DP*, March 15, 1964, p. 2, told that the school board had rejected the immediate beginning of negotiations with the DCTA. *RMN*, March 19, 1963, glanced at the DFT picket lines.

Schwartzkopf, "Collective Bargaining," 124, 155, 176, 233, emphasizes the changing character of the DCTA, and its clashes with the CEA. The study also profiles Betty Jean Lee, 128, 162. The work 126, 128, 136, stresses the DCTA's commitment to "professional negotiations," and, 133–36, looks at the 1962 NEA convention in Denver. *Denver Teacher*, October 1963, p. 2, gave the DFT's take on the difference between collective bargaining and professional negotiations.

SB, January 2, 1963, pp. 65–68, spelled out the school board's policy on negotiating with teachers. Schwartzkopf, "Collective Bargaining," 138–41, 145–48, looks at 1962 dealings between the DCTA and the administration, mentioning board divisions over them. The dissertation emphasizes this was the first time a large urban unit of the NEA had engaged in professional negotiations, 220.

On April 24, 2018, Dan Goe, president of the DCTA in 1961, recalled the status of the organization then and its transformation during the next few years. *DP*, December 18, 1966, p. 5, reviewed DCTA's growth and clashes with Oberholtzer.

There is reference to differences on personnel issues at Fairmont in *SB*, October 4, 1965, p. 17. Also see Shikes, "Three Superintendents," 242–45. Ibid., 248, stresses teachers' complaints that Oberholtzer was a distant figure.

FF 9:72 of the DPS papers has copies of Oberholtzer's statements on the Thomas Jefferson affair, minutes of the board meeting of March 15, 1965, and newspaper clippings about the development. *RMN*, March 10, 1965, and March 16, 1965, p. 5, reported the showdown. *DP*, May 18, 1965, p. 3, observed the board giving teachers the disciplinary power claimed by Thomas Jefferson coach Mike Willett. *SB*, March 29, 1965, p. 109, vaguely mentioned the problems with the coach and the DCTA's opposition to Oberholtzer's stance. Schwartzkopf, "Collective Bargaining," 156–59, reviews the dispute.

FF 9:72, 82–83 in the DPS papers have the complaints of the Administrators and Supervisors Association about the DCTA's stance at Thomas Jefferson. FF 1:9, 9:72, 77–82 in the DPS papers outline the history of the Principals Association and the ASA. There is mention of the Deans, Assistant Principals, Coordinators, and Supervising Teachers in FF 9:82. *SB*, May 3, 1965, p. 127, mentioned the Denver Elementary Principals Association.

A posting of some of the school-related professional and union associations, with a listing of their officers, is in *SB*, May 23, 1949, p. 4, May 30, 1949, pp. 2–3, and June 6, 1949, p. 4. *SN*, October 8, 1982, p. 15, spelled out the history of the Association of Educational Office Professionals. *SB*, November 12, 1951, p. 37, announced the Clerks and Secretaries Association's annual Christmas candy sale. Ibid., December 15, 1952, p. 59, told of the group's yearly holiday tea. *SB*, November 18, 1963, p. 46, observed the call to form the Denver Association of Educational Secretaries. Ibid., January 4, 1965, p. 61, listed the semi-official recognition of the DCTA, Association of Educational Secretaries, the Lunchroom Employees Association, and the Operation, Maintenance, and Transportation Association. On January 3, 1967, p. 65, *SB* observed the board's recognition of the Food Service Association and the Educational Secretaries and Classified Office Personnel.

On January 11, 1965, p. 66, *SB* reported a vote to reorganize the Employees Council. *SB*, October 25, 1965, p. 32, glances at the Administrative Women in Education. On November 21, 1966, p. 47, it highlighted Kappa Delta Pi.

SRv, January 1965, pp. 2, outlined the role of school social workers. *SB*, December 5, 1966, p. 53, and April 3, 1967, p. 113, mentioned the Association of Specialized Services. *SN*, September 7, 1976, p. 2, noted a DPS contract with it under the aegis of the DCTA. *DP*, May 23, 2019, p. 14C YourHub, observed the role of specialized service providers within the ranks of the DCTA. *RMN*, April 18, 1963, reported the application of school employees who worked in transportation and maintenance for union recognition.

Tollette, *CBLP*, 293, profiles Paul Hamilton. *CT*, October, 1970, p. 1, touted the campaigns of Paul Hamilton and Wayne Knox. *WPP*, February 1996, p. 4, observed Knox's tenure in the legislature. *DP*, July 23, 2019, p. 7A, tolled his passing. On occasion, Knox shared his memories with me.

Pearson, "Denver Case," 175, 179, discusses the DCTA's slant on the Keyes case. *RMN*, April 4, 1962, p. 5, told about the DFT's support of busing for integration. *SN*, January 4, 1972, p. 21, listed the DPS agreements with some of the unions representing teachers and classified employees. There is a 1988 list of DPS labor organization in box one of the DCTA papers. *BN*, October 16, 1998, observed recognition of the DFT as the voice of the Paraprofessionals Association.

SB, November 9, 1964, p. 40, quoted Robert Rothstein's views about a better relationship between teachers and administrative personnel. *SB*, January 31, 1966, p. 82, told of the DFT's call for teacher aides. *SB*, April 24, 1965, p. 122, reported the clash between the DFT and PTA about "problem schools." The publication noted the DFT achievement awards dinner, May 10, 1965, p. 131, and May 9, 1966, p. 135. On March 6, 1967, p. 101, *SB* told of the "Effective Schools Program" of

DFT. *PTA Today*, January 1979, p. 12, mentioned the role of the PTA in collective bargaining disputes. *Cmq*, May-June 1988, p. 8, was the PTA's self-portrait as a neutral forum on teacher-management clashes.

Schwartzkopf, "Collective Bargaining,"116, emphasizes the DFT's opposition to teacher strikes and support of binding arbitration. Ibid., 121–22, tells of the union's changing views in the light of New York developments.

In 1999 and 2001 Jerry McCracken, my Latin teacher at Smiley, shared his memories of his career in DPS and his role in the DFT. Jim McNally has fondly remembered McCracken, mentioning him in *Manual High*, 88, 97, 106. *SN*, May 5, 1980, p. 55, observed McCracken winning the teaching award. *DP*, June 21, 2002, p. 4B, mourned his passing.

Dan Goe recalled Al Barnes in an interview on April 24, 2018. Bill Robinson, who had been pastor of First Universalist when Barnes had been choir director, remembered the educator during a phone conversation on November 16, 2019. Schwartzkopf, "Collective Bargaining," 165–65, emphasizes Barnes' flamboyance. *DP*, March 11, 1974, p. 31, tolled his death.

CSJ, January 3, 1967, pp. 6–10, looked at Ronald Carlson. Schwartzkopf, "Collective Bargaining," 113, touches on his importance in the DCTA, and how Carlson was the first DCTA president who got time off from his teaching duties, 156. Ibid., 235, links the evolution of the DCTA to changes in the NEA nationally during the 1960s.

The DFT's call for a "professional discipline clause" is in box 12 of the DCTA papers. The stories about arbitrary, spontaneous corporal punishment in the schools are based on personal memories. I recall teachers suddenly punching me. As with many students, I had no recourse. Any complaints would have led to more beatings and punishment.

Murphy, *Blackboard Unions*, 34, observes early clashes between the forerunner of the AFT and administrators and the demands for "professionalism." The book deals with the anti-unionism at the core of the NEA's "professionalism," 81, 92.

SB, November 25, 1963, p. 51, mentioned the rivalry between the DFT and the DCTA and the demand for a recognition election. *SB*, November 29, 1965, p. 49, observed that the DFT was circulating a petition for a recognition election. Also see *SB*, January 3, 1966, pp. 66, 68. *SB*, May 2, 1966, p. 130, glanced at the DCTA lobbying for recognition.

A discussion of the dynamic growth of teacher unionism in the 1960s is in Murphy, *Blackboard Unions*, 226–31. Ibid., 179, observes the impact of the teacher shortage. *SN*, October 12, 1970, p. 14, reflected on that development.

SRv, January 1965, p. 1, reported on the district's teacher salary schedule. It mentioned the hike in pay, October 1965, p. 1. *SB*, March 22, 1965, pp. 105, 107, observed tensions between the DCTA and Oberholtzer and personnel grievances. The bulletin outlined the DCTA's salary proposal and request for negotiations over pupil conduct, May 17, 1965, pp. 133, 136. Also see *SB*, September 7, 1965, p. 2, on clashes between the board and the DCTA over the administration's disciplining of teachers; cf. *SB*, September 27, 1965, p. 13, on the DFT and DCTA and DPS salaries.

Schwartzkopf, "Collective Bargaining," 144, observes the decline of the

Employees Council vis-à-vis the DCTA. *SB*, January 3, 1967, p. 67, reported the end of the Employees Council. *SB*, March 13, 1967, p. 105, mentioned the early closing of the schools for the recognition election. *SB*, April 17, 1967, p. 121, listed the returns. *DP*, March 6, 1969, p. 26, reported the DCTA's triumph in that year's recognition election. Also see Schwartzkopf, "Collective Bargaining," 3–4, 166–74, on the DCTA's triumph in the recognition election. Ibid., 175–82, stresses the cooperative attitude of Oberholtzer in describing the original negotiations and contract between the DCTA and the district. Box 12 of the DCTA papers has files on the 1967 and 1969 recognition elections, including a few scattered DFT flyers denouncing the DCTA. *Denver Blade*, January 28, 1969, highlighted the Joy Boyd case, presenting the DFT's account of the affair.

Boxes 1 and 2 of the DCTA papers have numerous files on the 1969 strike, including publicity, clippings, flyers, correspondence, and an overview of the amnesty proceedings. There is also a file on legal proceedings and Judge Pinchuk's injunction in box one. Box two has the strike vote. There are also copies of the *Denver Teacher* with its criticism of the DCTA's conduct of the strike.

Schwartzkopf, "Collective Bargaining," 190–94, gives a version of the 1969 strike favorable to the DCTA leadership. She observes that it did not plan a strike and the way the November 15 meeting escaped the control of the group's officers. Ibid., 195, emphasizes the district's lack of a strike plan and problems with the phone system. The study mentions the signs of women teachers, 195, and the course of the walkout, 196–98.

On August 26, 2019, Richard Koeppe, who had been the right-hand man to Superintendent Gilberts, remembered the November 1969 strike. He specifically recalled the canvass of principals, the clogging of the central administration's switchboard, and the bogus seating charts.

CSJ, November 25, 1969, p. 1, reported the CEA version of the walkout. It analyzed the settlement, December 9, 1969, p. 1. In a review supplement, January 6, 1970, p. 7, it outlined why the teachers struck. A statement by two members explaining their reasons for staying in the classrooms was on p. 8. The November-December 1969 issue of *Slate*, the newspaper of the DCTA, gave its retrospection on the walkout. Knight, *Working*, 177–80, is favorable to the DFT. *CT*, October 1970, p. 2, complained that the DCTA contract saw the loss of 125 teaching positions.

A copy of the December 18, 1969, contract between the DCTA and DPS is in box 12 of the DCTA papers. In a January 3, 2018, interview, Ed Augden recalled the 1969 strike. He reviewed his participation in the DFT, including serving as its president from 1976 to 1980. McNally, *Manual High*, 82, is an anti-strike account of the 1969 dispute—in 1969, he reluctantly participated in the strike when he was a teacher at Smiley. On November 5, 2019, he recalled the event. *RMN*, November 22, 1969, p. 46, condemned the conduct of the teachers during the walkout.

The call for Denver QuEST is in FF 21:33 of the Yasui papers. Materials on the effort are in FF 8:2 of the Roth papers. FF 9:1 of the collection links Kay Schomp to QuEST. *CT*, October 1970, p. 3, looked at QuEST and its report on DPS. *CT*, May 1972, p. 1, and December 1973, p. 11, placed QuEST in the context of national AFT policy. FF 21:21 of the Yasui papers has a statement of DFT local #1611 about its representation of workers at Denver Opportunity. Also see FF 9:3 of the Roth papers.

Schwartzkopf, "Collective Bargaining," 204, mentions the DFT's failure to gather enough signatures to force a recognition election in 1972. In passing, 218, the dissertation states the DFT had peaked in membership in 1946 when it had about 400 members. The study celebrates the collaboration between James Bailey and Clarke Ballinger, 204–06, while stressing the successful grievance procedure, 206. FF 8:1–2 of the Roth papers, and *CT*, November 1972, p. 1, December 1972, p. 1, and February 1973, p. 1, mention the push for unity between the DCTA and the DFT. *CT*, September 1973, p. 1, observed its collapse.

Box one of the DCTA papers has a file on the AFT, outlining the evolution of that group and what the DCTA considered its objectionable policies under the leadership of Albert Shanker in the 1970s. There is passing mention of the AFT and materials about a possible merger of the DCTA and DFT in box three.

Materials on the AFT in the Mapleton District are in FF 9:9–10 of the Roth papers. *CT*, November 1970, p. 1, December 1970, p. 1, February 1972, p. 1, May 1972, p. 1, September 1972, p. 2, and February 1973, p. 1, dealt with conditions at Mapleton schools and the triumph of the AFT there. FF 9:3 of the Roth papers has the charter application for the Douglas County Federation of Teachers.

SN, August 28, 1979, p. 2, mentioned Royce Forsyth's posts in the administration. *Cmq*, February 1984, p. 3, observed the board honoring him on his retirement. *WPP*, November 2001, p. 6, looked at Forsyth's countless activities. *DP*, February 23, 2007, p. 4C, and *RMN*, March 2, 2007, p. 11B, reviewed his life. Pat Pascoe remembered him during a chat on January 21, 2020. Volume three will deal with the Balarat Outdoor Education Center. Ed Augden recalled Regis Groff as a DFT activist in a January 3, 2018, interview. I glance at Groff's wide-ranging career in *Park Hill Promise*, 181–82, 341, 410.

SB, February 9, 1970, p. 77, and March 30, 1970, p. 102, touched on the Professional Council. The 1974 *DPS Report*, no pagination, outlined its purpose. *SN*, October 27, 1982, p. 19, linked it to DCTA negotiations while describing its changing shape. DPS PR, October 24, 1990, observed the Council's makeup was a matter of bitter controversy between the DCTA and the district in contract negotiations.

Chapter Thirteen

We're On Our Way

Even while the number of students plummeted in the 1970s, DPS kept building schools. It simultaneously closed and destroyed some of its landmark structures. At first, anti-busing members of the board did not conceive that the impact of the court order would be as severe as they had predicted. In particular, they did not see the massive collapse of enrollment during the first decade of forced busing. On the contrary, they were convinced the system would continue to grow and need ever more schoolhouses.

In October 1970, the board adopted a five-year building program. To make it a reality, including both new buildings in developing parts of the city and the replacement of schoolhouses dating from before World War I, the board convinced voters to authorize a $29.8 million bond on October 25, 1971, "We're On Our Way."

The measure came just months after Bert Gallegos, Ted Hackworth, and Bob Crider had gained election to the board. Their platform in the May 1971 balloting included a commitment to "pay-as-you-go" financing whereby the district would not engage in expensive new borrowing. In office, they changed their position. Even at that, some of the construction undertaken by the board during the 1970s, such as Henry Junior High at 3005 South Golden Way in the West Bear Valley neighborhood in 1973–74, was undertaken on a pay-as-you-go basis. At least DPS announced that is how the district had paid for it in some press releases. At other times, it attributed Henry to the bond issue.

We're On Our Way included many of the specific suggestions from the failed 1967 bond issue. Included was the replacement of historic schoolhouses. Missing was any mention of educational parks. In part, the district pushed through the measure by emphasizing it would not impose any new taxes: the 19-year bonds from 1952 were on the verge of being paid off. The money set aside annually to finance them would be used for the new bond issue.

337

The building program included a disharmonious new gymnasium at West High. The bond also paid for Kaiser School, 3400 South Quitman Way in southwest Denver, Southmoor School, 3755 South Magnolia Way in southeast Denver, and a school for the emerging Montbello neighborhood—it opened as Barney Ford School, 14500 Maxwell Place, in 1973. Funds provided for, among other projects, remodelings and additions to Fairmont, Whittier, and Skinner. Money allowed the district to replace Gove, Elmwood, and Ashland (West 29th Avenue and Firth Court.) Revenue further went to a complete reconstruction of Bromwell School, and to acquire land for a promised new North High near West 32nd Avenue and Decatur Street.

In 1975, DPS built a replacement structure for the three-story Villa Park School at 845 Hazel Court. The schoolhouse dated from 1891. The district had renamed it in 1929 for the academy's veteran principal William H. Eagleton. DPS emphasized that the new one-story Eagleton was a pioneering effort to provide universal access to the handicapped. The schoolhouse came in at $1,363,400. Richard Paulin of the partnership of Childress & Paulin designed it. Revenue from a 1998 bond led to a remodeling of Eagleton in the early 21st century.

A new Wyman School at 17th Avenue and Williams Street was part of We're On Our Way. In the 1880s, the section to the east of Franklin Street between 13th and 17th avenues to York Street, Wyman's Addition, started to fill in with upper-class houses. This led DPS in 1888 to commemorate the man who had staked the land, John Wyman, when it bought lots at the northeast corner of 16th Avenue and Williams Street for a schoolhouse. Robert Roeschlaub, the house architect of East Denver District #1, designed the building. Craftsmen filled it with ornate woodwork. Students took their first classes in 1891.

Pupils quickly packed the building. By 1900, Wyman counted an enrollment of 739 in ten classrooms instructed by 19 teachers. To make room for everybody, the school installed glassed-in sections in hallways, using them as teaching spaces. During this epoch, Wyman was among the city's premier schools. Or so it projected itself, emphasizing the sons and daughters of the city's elite were among the student body. Even at that, it also had many pupils of modest circumstances who lived with their families in nearby rowhouses. A fire in early December 1916 caused $18,829 in damages. While repairs were underway, students took classes at St. Barnabas Church at 13th Avenue and Vine Street and a store building adjacent to the schoolhouse.

By the 1930s, the neighborhood adjacent to Wyman was increasingly a blue-collar enclave. Landlords divided old manors into multiple units. Poverty was ever more present in the classrooms in the 1960s while performance lagged. Already in 1938, the district had slated the schoolhouse for replacement as part of a failed bond issue.

By the time of the 1971 bond election, the district and many parents branded Wyman a disgraceful remnant of yesterday's Denver. Only a modern edifice, they argued, could provide modern education. With the funds from We're On Our Way, DPS opened a relatively windowless new structure in January 1975 along the south side of 17th Avenue between Williams and High streets. The firm of Maxwell

Photo by Phil Goodstein

An utterly bland, seemingly windowless new Wyman School opened in January 1975 at the southeast corner of 17th Avenue and Williams Street. It was typical of the schoolhouses of the day, financed by the 1971 We're On Our Way bond issue.

Saul and Associates was the architect. Citing a recently passed state law requiring handicapped accessibility, DPS specified the replacement building not have any steps. The district heralded the groundbreaking in September 1973. James Tracy, who was principal at East High from 1985 to 1990, was the principal in charge of this showcase of the building program.

New Wyman went up during the energy crisis. Ideally, few windows meant better insulation. During warm weather, this required a cooling system. Others claimed the lack of desktop windows was ominous. Students were apt to daydream by looking out the windows. A lack of windows, ideally, meant they could not daydream and so had to concentrate on schoolwork. Where classrooms had windows, they were often near the ceiling. Many suburban schools of the day also lacked windows. No windows additionally meant vandals could not break them. That was a severe problem of the day. In response, maintenance crews often placed heavy grates over the windows of some schools in poverty-stricken areas.

As with most of the elementaries arising as part of We're On Our Way, the replacement Wyman did not have classrooms per se, but "learning pods." These were adjustable areas with partitions allowing instructors to expand or contract space for the best teaching environment. Included were combining different classes or breaking students into small, isolated groups.

The effort embodied the open classroom, a fad of the day. Teachers found the lack of walls a nuisance. The pods were extremely noisy where different activities destroyed a quality learning experience. Within a few years, remodelings saw the erection of traditional walls at Wyman and other buildings that had gone up in the name of fostering the open classroom.

Photo by Phil Goodstein

New Gove Junior High, along the east side of the 1300 block of Colorado Boulevard, was an architectural showpiece of the DPS building program of the 1970s. This shot shows the east side of the building, which included the main entrance, adjacent to the parking lot. A cupola from the old building is on the right.

Soon after new Wyman opened, DPS ordered the demolition of the 1891 building. The district stated the replacement structure had room for 570 students in contrast to 420 seats in the old building. By 1975, enrollment was at 382 compared to around 600 in 1965 and 343 in 1970. New Wyman had severe disciplinary policies. The school was usually among the leaders of elementaries in suspending errant students. A census at the end of busing in 1996 stated Wyman had 298 students, 27 of whom were Native Americans, 155 blacks, three Asian-Americans, 80 Hispanos, and 33 whites. The district used money from a 2003 bond issue to modernize the 1975 structure. As was the case with many schools in the early 21st century, the administration eventually turned Wyman over to a charter school, the Denver Center for 21st Century Learning.

The building boom of the 1970s also saw the opening of a new home of Gove Junior High on the east side of the 1300 block of Colorado Boulevard. The district had repeatedly promised a new home for Gove, including Superintendent Kenneth Oberholtzer's 1962 proposal to erect it near Martin Luther King and Colorado boulevards as something of a Jim Crow building. Finally, with busing underway and funds in hand, DPS made new Gove a reality.

By the time new Gove opened, Colorado Boulevard had evolved from being a fine parkway into a busy arterial. Prior to the erection of the new building, students had to cross the street during gym class to get to the playing fields on the east side of the speedway. This resulted in a tragedy on Friday, March 25, 1965, when a motorist ran a red light and hit and killed two Gove students. In the wake of the accident, DPS worked with the city and state to place a bridge over Colorado Boulevard to connect the Gove gym with the playing fields. At the same time, citing the dangers faced by Morey students crossing 13th Avenue to playing fields, a bridge also went up over that one-way street at Emerson Street. Morey called it the "Learning Bridge."

Students took the first classes in the new Gove, designed by the firm of Rogers Nagel & Langhart, on February 2, 1976. John Rogers of the partnership was the lead architect. After fire tore through the old Gove in June 1976, DPS called in the wreckers that summer to level the 1911 erection.

Surplus Buildings

In 1979, three years after the completion of We're On Our Way, DPS concluded it had massive surplus space and more schoolhouses than it needed. That year, it counted a capacity for 58,000 students in elementary classrooms compared to an enrollment of 36,000. Superintendent Joseph Brzeinski complained DPS had "too many buildings and too few students" when he slated 12 schools for closure.

This provoked extreme neighborhood reactions. Not only did parents want to keep nearby schools open, but others, including those who did not have children in the district, argued the schoolhouses were part of distinctive residential sections. Getting rid of the buildings threatened the fabric and identity of enclaves. Fights to keep schools open were part and parcel of school board politics during the 1970s and 1980s.

Beginning in the early 1970s, DPS starting shuttering schools. At the end of the 1973–74 schoolyear, it closed Alameda School, at the southwest corner of West Byers Place and South Bannock Street, and Evans Schools, at the northwest corner of West 11th Avenue and Acoma Street. It rearranged attendance zones to fill the new Del Pueblo School near the northeast corner of West Seventh Avenue and Galapago Street. That building replaced the adjacent Elmwood School, a structure coming down in 1974. At that time, DPS targeted other buildings, usually in old, low-income sections.

Back at the semester break in January 1972, the district closed Perry School at 75 Perry Street, a program dating from 1911. All students in the area were assigned to Barnum School, about half-a-mile to the east at West First Avenue and Hooker Street, a building which had gone up in 1921. Originally Barnum School was the Hooker Annex to Perry School. There had been a previous Barnum School at West Third Avenue and King Street, land the district sold in 1919. This was five years before the Hooker Annex became the new Barnum School. When Newlon School opened in 1951 at 361 Vrain Street, its principal came to oversee Perry. DPS called in the wreckers to take down Perry School in late 1972. The district disposed of the vacant land in 1979. Eventually housing went up on the location.

Back in the mid-1960s, Perry had had about 150 students; Barnum peaked during that decade at more than 800. At the end of court-ordered busing in 1995–96, DPS counted 551 pupils at Barnum. With 20 regular classrooms, it stated the building had room for 536 learners. The district set aside $2,791,009 from a 1998 bond issue for the addition of six Barnum classrooms. Students were the Bears. Near the beginning of the third decade of the 21st century, Barnum counted about 640 students; more than 90 percent of whom were Hispanos. Virtually all qualified for free or reduced-price lunches.

While Barnum School survived, Belmont School did not at 4407 Morrison Road. The federal government paid for its erection in 1945 at 4407 Morrison Road. Washington did so since many of the parents of the children in the area, which was part of Arapahoe County School District #18, worked at the Remington Small Arms Plant at West Sixth Avenue and Kipling Street. The future location of the Federal Center, it was the area's largest employer during World War II, churning out weapons for the military. DPS swallowed Belmont School on March 27, 1947, at the time Denver annexed the property.

During the mid-1960s, Belmont had around 320 to 350 students. One hundred-percent faculty membership in the school's PTA reflected the teachers' support of the school. Without consulting residents, in early 1973 DPS announced it was going to close Belmont at the end of the schoolyear. This provoked a firestorm of protest. More than 700 residents signed a petition to keep the school open. Belmont was not subjected to the busing order.

Kay Schomp and Omar Blair, both of whom joined the board in May 1973, insisted DPS needed a better policy of consulting with the community before closing schools. The result was to keep Belmont going. It was to no avail. In April 1979, the board again voted to close Belmont at the end of the schoolyear

Photo by Phil Goodstein

In 1945, the federal government financed the construction of Belmont School, 4407 Morrison Road. DPS shuttered the building in 1979. The schoolhouse subsequently became the quarters of the Denver Indian Center.

when enrollment was 200. The district had to shutter Belmont, the administration explained, because DPS had more than 20,000 empty seats while budget pressures were unending. After negotiating an agreement for the city to buy the schoolhouse for $387,500 in November 1979, the board disposed of the property in February 1980. The Denver Indian Center, a social-welfare organization reaching out to Native Americans, obtained the structure, using it for a wide array of social services and educational programs.

In some ways, the fate of Emerson School, at the northeast corner of 14th Avenue and Ogden Street, paralleled that of Belmont. DPS retreated from its decision to close it in 1974 in response to loud community protests. In April 1979, however, the district announced the end of classes at Emerson at the end of the schoolyear. At that time, the building educated 325 youngsters from kindergarten through sixth grade in a building the district listed as having 360 seats. None of the pupils attending it rode buses elsewhere. The school received children who were bused in from Lowry Air Force Base and a satellite area near Greenlee School.

DPS sold Emerson School in November 1979 to the Capitol Hill Senior Resources. The building subsequently included community offices and a small theater. In the early 2010s, workers thoroughly renovated the 1885-vintage schoolhouse into the Ralph Waldo Emerson Center as the home of Historic Denver. By then, the building at 14th Avenue and Ogden Street was the oldest surviving structure erected as a schoolhouse in the city. For years, the bungalow annex of Emerson, dating from 1917 and known as the Emerson Cottages, was a daycare facility.

Moore School

Moore School survived at the southeast corner of Ninth Avenue and Corona Street. The building hosted its first classes in 1889 when it was known as Corona School. Twenty years later a second schoolhouse went up at the southwest corner of Ninth Avenue and Downing Street. In 1929, DPS renamed the complex in honor of its veteran principal, Dora Moore, who retired around that time.

The school had an extremely diverse socioeconomic base. Besides the offspring of the wealthy who dwelt in the nearby Seventh Avenue Parkway, Country Club, and Quality Hill districts, Moore included youngsters living in the heart of Capitol Hill when that section was something of a blue-collar neighborhood and a hippie enclave. For a while, there were a number of sons and daughters of Greek immigrants at the school. Boys and girls whose homes were in the Lincoln Park housing projects near Mariposa Street and West 13th Avenue arrived at the school via bus. They gave Moore an international complexion—often the students from Lincoln Park or their parents were immigrants. No Moore students were bused out of the attendance district in the name of desegregation.

As was the case with Wyman, DPS had already wanted to destroy the 1889 Corona building as part of the 1938 bond issue. In 1974, the district's integration plan targeted Moore School for closure. This was part of the district's systematic attack on all old buildings. The proposal also suggested shuttering Emerson. In some scenarios, the district would bus neighborhood children elsewhere, not planning any new schoolhouse in the heart of Capitol Hill.

The court rejected the DPS proposal since it failed to offer a viable desegregation program. Simultaneously, the suggestion of ending the program at Moore inflamed affluent neighbors. They formed the Moore School Community Association, intervening in the Keyes case. Republican state Senator Dick Plock, who hoped to win election as governor, was among the group's attorneys.

Backers of the growing preservationist movement joined Moore parents and neighbors in pushing to keep the school open. Those treasuring Denver's architectural heritage bewailed the constant destruction of the city's Victorian heritage. Parents of Moore students likewise worked to convince the board of education to keep the school open. On March 14, 1975, the coalition got the city officially to declare the 1889 edifice a landmark. Backers went on to create the Friends of Dora Moore in 1977, getting the building placed in the National Register of Historic Places the next year. The group raised funds to enhance programs at the school. Enrollment was 570 in the late 1970s.

A May 1990 bond issue reserved $2.9 million for a major renovation of Moore, linking the 1889 and 1909 buildings. Right when work was underway, the east side of the 1889 wing collapsed on July 22, 1992. The contractor had dug out the foundation and the support under the wall as part of the effort to install an elevator. Heavy rains weakened the surviving supports, leading to the accident. Nobody was injured. An inspection showed the structure would have remained standing without the construction. The result was a rebuilding of the damaged area. Students rode the bus to the empty Southmoor School until workers finally completed the renovation in February 1993 at the cost of $3 million. At that time, Moore had around 450 students. By the end of busing in 1996, the count was 438: 16 American Indians, 69 African-Americans, eight of Asian heritage, 165 Hispanos, and 180 whites. This made it among the most integrated schools in the district.

The school retained strong community support. The PTA hosted an annual house tour in the fall, raising money for countless auxiliary school expenses. Moore retained connections with wealthy residents living near the Country Club. School board members Kay Schomp (1973–83) and Carole McCotter (1985–95) lived in the Moore attendance area and had close connections with the school. The same was true with Sherry Eastlund who was the head of the District School Improvement and Accountability Council in the 1990s—she first became involved in DPS when her children attended Moore.

In other places, DPS paid little attention to neighbors who wanted to keep schools open as vibrant institutions. The late 1970s/early 1980s saw the shuttering of such places as Wyatt, Boulevard, Ash Grove, Sherman, Ellsworth, and Pitts. Numbers illustrated DPS's excess capacity. Following a 1969 expansion, the superintendent's office stated Park Hill School had enough room for a 1,000 pupils. By 1983, enrollment was 459. At that time, Kaiser had 347 students in a building with 808 seats. Sabin, officially with 1214 desks, had 570 members. The respective numbers at Steele were 494 and 212 and 706 and 242 at Traylor. The gap was also glaring at junior high/middle schools. Baker had a membership of 313 out of 1,062 seats;

In 1909, a new wing of Corona School went up at the southwest corner of Ninth Avenue and Downing Street. The building became Moore School in 1929. In 1993 workers completed a bridge linking it with the original 1889 structure.

Cole was at 646 in a building with 1,393 desks. Kunsmiller was down to 618 in a structure capable of educating 1,474 youngsters—at the peak of its enrollment in the 1960s, when it was on split sessions, Kunsmiller had a membership of 2,644. The numbers at Merrill were 472 out of 1,234, 512 out of 1,103 at Place, and 510 students with 1,422 seats at Smiley.

DPS was not alone in closing schools at this time. The decline of enrollment also hit suburban districts as baby boomers left high school. Nationally, a debate raged over "books versus bricks" about whether it was better to have fewer, but better large schools or smaller, neighborhood-oriented academies. As was the case with DPS, generally districts argued books in larger schools were more important than the bricks of neighborhood buildings.

For the most part, the district razed standing buildings when replacement schools opened. Such was the case at Ashland, Columbian, and Elmwood. Time and again, the board of education resolved the abandoned schoolhouses were "no longer used or useful." Preservationists decried such vandalism. They particularly clashed with board member Omar Blair. He, along with others on the board, generally reflected the ethos of post–World War II Denver that anything old was obsolete. Besides, the old buildings had severe maintenance problems and were not designed for modern technologies. Kay Schomp was a voice of dissent, urging preservation. Ginny Rockwell sometimes supported saving vintage buildings. At other times, she sided with Blair—her husband had once been chairman of the board of the Denver Urban Renewal Authority. Blair was on the board of that bureau, an agency notorious for leveling yesterday's landmarks.

No place did the school board show a greater contempt for its historic buildings than at Ashland School at West 29th Avenue at Firth Court. This had been the standout structure of the North Denver District #17, dating from 1888. Since the 1940s, the district had targeted Ashland for replacement with a modern structure. Back in 1949, for example, the board ordered the remodeling of the school's distinctive, eye-catching tower. The spire survived until the opening of the replacement Valdez School at 2525 West 29th Avenue in early 1975. Preservationists launched a campaign to keep old Ashland standing. Right when their drive was gaining steam, they discovered the DPS had sent in a wrecking crew at 4:00 AM in February 1975 to take down the tower. Once this central part of the schoolhouse was gone, the building was not worth saving.

In contrast to the Victorian majesty of Ashland School, Valdez School exemplified both the architecture of the 1970s and the politics of the school board. The firm of Haller & Larson designed Valdez, mostly with blank walls and limited windows. The replacement building cost $1.955 million with a capacity to educate 855 youngsters. Like Wyman, the interior lacked specific classrooms in favor of "instruction units" or "pods." As such, rather than having a fourth-grade class, Valdez had a fourth-grade pod. The concept never delivered as promised. Before long, a remodeling saw the installation of walls to demarcate the instruction units. Besides the pods, Valdez included two kindergartens and two rooms for special education.

Photo by Phil Goodstein

To add some charm to the charmless Valdez School, artist Barry Rose collaborated with students at the school to decorate the retaining wall of the playground along West Dunkfeld Place with mosaic tiles. Rose worked with other schools in installing such murals, including at the main administration building at 900 Grant Street.

NSAC

DPS called in wreckers at 4:00 AM in February 1975 to take down Ashland School, a building dating from 1888 at West 29th Avenue and Firth Court, to block preservationists' efforts to save the landmark.

DPS named the new building at the behest of school board member Bernie Valdez. He observed the utmost necessity of branding a school for a Mexican-American. This would help instill Latino students with pride and patriotism. In 1974, the board so announced the replacement for Ashland would celebrate Jose Valdez (1925–1945). DPS saluted him as "American soldier of Spanish descent," heralding him as the first Hispano to win the Congressional Medal of Honor. A native of New Mexico, he gave his life during World War II to save others. The christening of the building came near the end of the Vietnam War when militarism was in an extremely bad odor. The War Department had posthumously awarded Valdez the Medal of Honor on February 8, 1946.

(A resident of Ault, Colorado, Joe P. Martinez, had already received the Congressional Medal of Honor on October 27, 1943. Born into a Latino family in Taos, New Mexico, on July 27, 1920, he died on May 26, 1943, from wounds suffered during a battle to retake some of the westernmost Aleutian Islands. Back in 1958, DPS had joined with the city and the Juvenile Court in unveiling a portrait of Joe P. Martinez as role model in Juvenile Hall. The state unveiled a larger-than-life-sized bronze statue of Martinez in the Capitol Park in July 1988. Additionally, the city has named a small park off of West Eighth Avenue and Raleigh Street along Dry Gulch for Joe Martinez.)

Not all were happy with the designation of the new building for Jose Valdez. They observed the extremely problematic military connection. Latino students must have a better future than being soldiers. If the school needed a Latino-oriented name it should salute a revolutionary, civil rights activist, writer, or school teacher. The board paid no heed to such a suggestion.

Pitts School opened in 1959 at the southwest corner of Hampden Avenue and South Glencoe Street. DPS closed it in 1982, selling it two years later to a Jewish congregation, Temple Sinai. The religious organization subsequently built its new sanctuary next to the school. The original structure is on the right.

By 2012, Valdez School was showing its age. An independent building evaluation estimated the district needed to invest $9 million to "correct major deficiencies in the building." DPS found $6.3 million from a bond issue to rehabilitate the interior and bring the building up to code. It broke ground for the effort on June 5, 2014. Included was moving the main entrance away from West 29th Avenue to the middle of the parking lot. Additionally, workers touched up the exterior of the building, giving it more charm than had ever been the case with the replacement of Ashland.

Valdez students are the Panthers. Reflecting the rapid gentrification of the nearby residential section, by the end of the 2010s Valdez School was becoming increasingly integrated. Enrollment varied between 360 to more than 400. The academy counted about 62 percent of its students as Hispanos; 35 percent were white, 2 percent of multiple races, and 1 percent black. About half qualified for free or reduced-price lunches. A dual-language school, Valdez greatly improved in academic achievement in the remodeled building.

Back on September 21, 1972, also at the behest of Bernie Valdez, the school board had named another new school to honor the Hispanic community, Del Pueblo or Escuela del Pueblo, the school of the people, at West Seventh Avenue and Galapago Street. It replaced the adjacent Elmwood School, a building dating from 1885.

As with Valdez and numerous other schoolhouses of the 1970s, Del Pueblo had mostly blank walls. W. C. Muchow Associates designed the structure. The firm stated it crafted the building to emulate southwestern design, a seemingly modern pueblo-style edifice for the heavily Latino West Side near Santa Fe Drive. DPS commissioned artists to paint geometric themes on the exterior of Del Pueblo in emulation of designs on Navajo blankets. The building opened in 1973 on a 4.74-acre lot with a capacity of 480. The bill was $1,117,136.25. Wreckers brought down Elmwood School the next year.

Originally, busing paired Del Pueblo with Pitts School at 3509 South Glencoe Street. Opened in 1959, that academy recalled Ralph L. Pitts who was a teacher at

East High from 1896 to 1943. After surging in enrollment in the early 1960s when it had nearly 500 students, Pitts' numbers collapsed in the 1970s. A 1978 report stated the school had 239 pupils in kindergarten and grades four, five, and six. This not only reflected the impact of busing, but also the aging of the neighborhood: few elementary-aged children lived close to Pitts School by that time. Enrollment slipped to under 200 students in the early 1980s, including boys and girls brought in from Del Pueblo.

Even so, people living close to Pitts urged the school should remain open when DPS targeted it as a redundant facility. They pointed to its excellent academic achievement and rapport with the neighborhood. Parents emphasized this, printing a brochure, *Look! It's Working* about Pitts' success. Nonetheless, the administration closed the school in 1982. The district thereupon leased parts of the structure to the Colorado Association of School Board Executives.

The new tenant did not stay long at Pitts. The next year, DPS leased the schoolhouse to Temple Sinai, a surging Reform Jewish congregation seeking a permanent home. The board of education sold the schoolhouse to the synagogue in May 1984 for $1.75 million, crediting it with the rent it had previously paid.

A covenant stated the building was not to be used as a private or religious school. This was district policy. It refused to sell empty schoolhouses to operators of private or religious academies. Despite this, Temple Sinai used the old Pitts School for its religious school. This was a synagogue-based effort, not a day school rival to public schools. The congregation incorporated the schoolhouse into a 1986 construction project adding the synagogue's new sanctuary and social hall directly to the west of

Photo by Phil Goodstein

Del Pueblo School opened in 1973. Architects claimed it emulated the design of the southwestern United States. Here it is seen from the southwest corner of West Eighth Avenue and Fox Street.

Pitts School. In 1987, Dorothy Gotlieb, who had been program director of Temple Sinai, gained election to the school board.

After the closing of Pitts, Del Pueblo had links with Kaiser School. Eventually, it was the sister school of Bradley, a school opening in 1955 at 3051 South Elm Street. By 1980, Del Pueblo had 210 students in 16 classrooms—the district stated it had space for 486 youngsters. Enrollment was up to 321 by the end of busing in 1996 when there were two American Indians, seven blacks, eight Asian-Americans, 294 Hispanos, and 12 whites in the school. The number slipped to 154 in 2006. No program at Del Pueblo ever worked to the district's satisfaction. Besides, by the early 21st century, the administration claimed it lacked enough teachers to staff Del Pueblo. To assure no more Del Pueblo failures, the central office shuttered the school at the end of the 2006–07 schoolyear. The superintendent's office subsequently gave the building to a charter school, the Girls Academic Leadership School. To assist the program, DPS saw a massive expansion of the Del Pueblo plant in the late 2010s.

The Next Six Years

By the time Del Pueblo was three years old in 1976, DPS had gone through the funds from the five-year We're On Our Way bond issue. Though enrollment was plummeting and the administration had begun closing schools, the district's solution was erecting more schoolhouses. In January 1976, the board announced a six-year program to replace more old structures on a pay-as-you-go basis. (Historically, the district oscillated between bond issues and using existing funds to finance construction programs.)

DPS called the new initiative "The Next Six Years." In an optimistic statement, being sure enrollment was still growing and funds were unlimited, the construction program called for replacing virtually all of the city's historic junior high buildings at the same time it poured money into renovations and expansions at such junior highs as Morey, Smiley, Lake, Horace Mann, Cole, and Grant. Additional funds went to improvements and enhancements at Moore, East, and West. In outlining the goals of the Next Six Years, the administration conceded, the district no longer suffered from the acute overcrowding of previous decades.

In adopting the Next Six Years, the board repeated the mantra that old is automatically bad. Within the next decade or so, it announced, it would be necessary to replace more than 20 buildings that were at least 55 years old. Among them were seven dating from the 19th century. It aimed to start on that effort by constructing a new Columbian School at West 41st Avenue and Eliot Street. On the heels of this, it might demolish the 1911-vintage North High.

Even as it committed itself to pay-as-you-go financing, the district was increasingly pressed for funds. Struggling to contain costs in the face of soaring inflation, the superintendent annually had to request a considerably larger budget. From $91,372,922 in 1969, the district's annual expenses were up to $129,407,665 by 1973. State laws restrained the system's ability to exceed defined spending limits. If it needed more money, DPS had to appeal to the

Photo by Phil Goodstein

In the mid-1970s, in the name of modernizing the physical stock of its buildings, DPS wanted to destroy the vintage 1911 beaux-arts North High. A community effort forced the district to save the building even as it commissioned workers in 1983–84 to erect a bland new addition, bottom, onto the north side of the landmark.

state school district budget review board. Then, to increase its mill levy, it must approach the voters.

Prior to a drastic revision in the nature of imposing mill levies in 1959, a state tax commission reviewed school taxes. To hike its mill levy, a school district needed to receive the permission of that body. Taxpayers were not always willing to open up their purses. On November 5, 1974, for example, in reaction to the upheavals surrounding busing and raging cost of living, the electorate said no to a proposed hike in the mill levy.

The new buildings, the district emphasized were a wise, economical investment. They would be far less expensive to heat and maintain than its supposedly ancient schoolhouses. Additionally, new buildings were necessary to redress overcrowding. DPS emphasized this point in a new three-year contract with the DCTA in May 1976. This was at the same time the enrollment of the district was in steady decline.

Southeast Schools

The 1970s building boom saw the district add Holm School at 3185 South Willow Court and Samuels School at 3985 South Vincennes Court (near South Tamarac Drive and Mansfield Avenue). The firm of Wheeler and Lewis designed both schoolhouses on comparable plans. The district held joint groundbreakings in June 1972 for this rapidly growing part of the community as part of the We're on Our Way program.

Samuels School recalled school board member Isadore Samuels (1947–65). Holm remembered Pete Holm. A veteran principal, he had become an assistant superintendent in 1950. During the next decade, he had been a right-hand man of Superintendent Kenneth Oberholtzer, especially in dealing with school personnel. He died in July 1960 right after his retirement at age 65.

Photo by Phil Goodstein

Holm School opened in 1973 at 3185 South Willow Court. It went up directly to the south of Hamilton Junior High, right.

Both schools opened amidst busing. Holm had a kindergarten and grades four, five, and six. Initially, it was paired with Swansea at 4650 Columbine Street. At the end of the 1981–82 schoolyear, Holm became the sister school of Hallett. The southeast academy once had a newsletter, *Holm to Home.* The schoolhouse was directly south of Hamilton Junior High whose students were the Huskies. Those at Holm became the "Lil" Huskies. Enrollment was around 500 by the end of the 2010s when it offered classes from preschool through fifth grade. A survey stated around 82 to 84 percent of the pupils were from low-income families. More than half of them were Hispanos. Blacks made up 19 percent of the enrollment. Whites were 17 percent. The rest were of mixed race, Asian, or American Indian heritage.

Samuels School also opened in 1973. The school board had authorized it in the summer of 1971 on what the district simply numbered Site 148. Students adopted the Eagle as their mascot. During part of the busing era, Samuels was paired with Oakland School in Montbello. Subsequently, Cheltenham was its sister school. In the mid-1970s, with 954 students, Samuels had the largest enrollment of any elementary in the district. DPS later stated Samuels had room enough for only 500 learners. For a while Samuels, was a bilingual school for kindergarten and grades three, four, and five. Besides English and Spanish, students spoke 11 other languages. At the end of busing in 1996, it had a membership of 529. By 2019, Samuels had about 500 students, nearly half of whom were Hispanos; another 20 percent were black. Besides 20 percent whites, it had 6 percent of its students who were of Asian heritage, along with 4 percent defined as being of multiple races. More than three-fourths of the students qualified for free or reduced-price lunches.

No sooner were Holm and Samuels open than they were seemingly at capacity. In 1974, DPS authorized the construction of another southeast elementary on Site

146, 3755 South Magnolia Way. The building opened in 1976 as Southmoor School, the name denoting the neighborhood it served—the developer had donated the real estate when Denver annexed the subdivision based on DPS putting up a schoolhouse. The team of Childress & Paulin was the architect in a building with a capacity of 570.

Following the trend of the day, rather than classrooms Southmoor had "instruction areas." Instead of a library, it had an "instruction materials center." The building, initially an intermediate school for grades four through six in addition to having two kindergartens, was paired with Fairmont School at West Third Avenue and Elati Street. Southmoor later had connections with Smedley School, 4250 Shoshone Street. The school had 382 children in its classrooms in 1978.

The academy reflected the ups and downs of the area's school population. DPS closed Southmoor after the end of the 1992–93 schoolyear, claiming there were not enough children in the attendance zone to justify keeping it open. For a while, the district had some of its overflow offices there.

In 1993, the Rocky Mountain School of Expeditionary Learning occupied Southmoor. This was a program run by DPS in conjunction with suburban districts for those wanting numerous fieldtrips. After the end of busing in 1995–96, a new generation of children popped up by Southmoor School. The district responded in 1998 when it reopened Southmoor as a neighborhood elementary, relocating the School of Expeditionary Learning to Ash Grove. Southmoor students were the Moose. By the 21st century, with a gifted and talented program, Southmoor offered classes from preschool through fifth grade. Enrollment was around 450 to 500. The campus included a couple of portable units.

The Transformation of Schoolhouses

Centennial School, 4665 Raleigh Street, was another of the schools stemming from the We're On Our Way building program. It replaced both Alcott School at West 41st Avenue and Tennyson Street, and Berkeley School at 5025 Lowell Boulevard. Since the 1890s, they had been the two academies for far northwest Denver. Both programs shut when students moved into Centennial School on February 9, 1976. The new building's moniker denoted Colorado was then observing the centennial of statehood. The appropriately numbered board Resolution 1876 declared the new facility Centennial School.

The structure was a generic schoolhouse. The architectural team of Haller & Larson, which had recently completed Kaiser School, crafted Centennial with a comparable design. Haller & Larson subsequently used the same model for McGlone School in Montbello. Classrooms/pods were "teaching stations." Many of the teaching stations had doors going to the outside, another schoolhouse architectural trend of the day.

In the wake of the opening of Centennial School, DPS had no use for the Berkeley or Alcott buildings. It sold the former in 1978. A new owner remodeled the long vacant schoolhouse into residences in 1997. Dismissing Alcott School as totally obsolete, the district made little effort to sell it; rather, it targeted it for demolition.

Preservationists explored the possibility of saving Alcott School, a facility dating from 1892 which celebrated Louisa May Alcott. Before they could act, vagrants occupied the abandoned structure. Being cold, they set fires. The result was a severe, three-alarm blaze on the night of March 25–26, 1976. For a while, the conflagration was out of control in extremely windy weather. It took about 100 firefighters, using 12 pieces of equipment, hours to quench the flames. At least this was the official account of the end of Alcott School. Cynics suspected DPS might have arranged the fire as a way of blocking the drive to save the building.

The fate of Berkeley School as residences reflected another trend of the day. Original efforts to reuse the schoolhouse were of no avail. After the initial purchaser failed to redevelop the land, DPS found itself forced to resume ownership of the abandoned complex. Other efforts to sell and transform the 1.53-acre campus did not work out prior to the 1997 conversion into condos.

The first such modern metamorphosis of a schoolhouse into condos was at Thatcher School at the northeast corner of South Grant Street and Colorado Avenue. In 1979, DPS shuttered both Thatcher School and McKinley School, 1275 South Logan Street, replacing them with a combined McKinley-Thatcher adjacent to the old McKinley. Thatcher had opened in 1920, recalling banker Joseph Addison Thatcher (1838–1918) who had bequeathed funds for *The Statue of the State*, a most ornate fountain in City Park. McKinley dated from 1902, remembering President William McKinley who had been assassinated the previous year. Architect James Sudler designed McKinley-Thatcher with solar panels. Ideally, DPS hoped, they would provide for 87 percent of the school's heating needs. The schoolhouse

Photo by Phil Goodstein

In the face of the energy crisis of the 1970s, DPS commissioned architect James Sudler to design the new McKinley–Thatcher School, 1230 South Grant Street, with solar panels.

In the 2010s, schools placed glitzy banners along their fences, spelling out the buildings' names. Such is the case along West 46th Avenue to the west of Raleigh Street for Centennial School, an edifice opened during the centennial of Colorado statehood in 1976.

was something of a return to traditional school architecture with big windows to provide for natural lighting.

Busing had paired McKinley with Boulevard School, 2351 Federal Boulevard. Boulevard was a primary with grades kindergarten through third; McKinley also had a kindergarten and grades four, five, and six. In 1978, McKinley had 140 students when Boulevard had a membership of 143.

For a while, Thatcher had also been an intermediate school paired with Fairview School, 2715 West 11th Avenue. By the late 1970s, when it had 180 students, Thatcher was kindergarten through sixth grade where neighborhood children were not bused elsewhere. It received some students from two satellite areas. The school included tutors helping students whose first language was Vietnamese or Spanish.

The new McKinley-Thatcher, with a listed capacity of 360, had a kindergarten and first through sixth grades. Its students, the Bald Eagles, were not bused elsewhere. After Boulevard School closed in 1982, some living close to it continued to ride the bus to McKinley-Thatcher. The ecologically friendly building also received some youngsters from the attendance district of Ebert School near Tremont Place and 23rd Street (Park Avenue West). By the end of busing in 1996, McKinley-Thatcher had 189 pupils.

In 2019, DPS completed a $5 million renovation of the building that included six new classrooms, an art studio, and a science lab. At that time, enrollment was around 172 to 182 students. A census counted about 47 to 48 percent as white, 38 to 40 percent as Hispano, 7 to 8 percent as mixed race, 3 percent black, 2 percent Asian-American, and 1 percent American Indians. Around 45 percent qualified for free or reduced-price lunches in a rapidly gentrifying neighborhood. By the time the addition was open, the solar panels had disappeared from the school.

On the opening of the new school, DPS razed the old McKinley. It sold Thatcher in 1980. Architect/developer Bob Shopneck bought it. He transformed the building into condominiums. In ensuing decades, other closed schools such as Alameda, Boulevard, and Stevens became residences.

In 1945, amidst the housing shortage during World War II, DPS had converted Globeville School, a 1925 building at the northeast corner of 51st Avenue and

Lincoln Street, into dwellings for school employees. The district, pointing to a severe decline in enrollment, had shuttered the schoolhouse two years earlier, sending its students to Garden Place School near 44th Avenue and Lincoln Street.

In 1946, DPS transformed Albion School, a facility at the northeast corner of Colfax Avenue and Albion Street primarily educating children in the lower grades who lived at the adjacent Denver Orphans Home, into two residential units. It soon reopened Albion School for classes until permanently closing the building in 1962. A new owner demolished the rather insubstantial structure.

DPS sold Globeville School in 1949. Two years later, Laradon Hall occupied it. This was a private program for youngsters with severe developmental disabilities. "Providing Life without Limits" was its motto. Preservationists got the city to declare the building a landmark in 2004. Over the years, Laradon expanded its campus considerably to the north. It opened a school of its own in 2018. The next year, working with the United Way, it launched a public preschool program to redress the lack of early childhood education programs in the neighborhood. In part, they were missing because, amidst a drive for preschools, DPS did not offer a free universal preschool program.

At the same time DPS committed itself to McKinley-Thatcher in 1976, it targeted the nearby Lincoln School, 715 South Pearl Street, and Washington Park School, 1125 South Race Street, for replacement. It ran out of money before it was able to carry out this agenda. On June 19, 1998, the city dubbed Lincoln a landmark.

After initially being paired with Fairmont School, beginning in the mid-1970s Lincoln generally escaped court-ordered busing. To achieve racial balance, the district brought students to it from elsewhere; the court did not order those in Lincoln's attendance district to travel to other academies. During the 1980s, enrollment was about 475. Included were 350 students living close to the edifice which had served South Denver since 1890. They were joined by Hispanos from the attendance district of Fairmont School and African-Americans who dwelt close to Stapleton Airport. The Lynx was the school's mascot. Students had previously been the Pandas. Lincoln added a Montessori program near the end of the 2010s.

Washington Park School, 1125 South Race Street, did not survive. It stemmed from the 1893 Myrtle Hill School at South Race Street and Tennessee Avenue. A new structure replaced it at the southwest corner of South Race Street and Mississippi Avenue in 1906, followed by major additions in 1922 and 1928. On September 1, 1923, the district renamed Myrtle Hill School "Washington Park School." It served the neighborhood east of Washington Park while Lincoln School educated those living west of the open space. Prior to World War I, the land east of Washington Park was generally known as Myrtle Hill.

Busing paired Washington Park School with Stedman School. The South Denver program had kindergarten and grades four, five, and six. Enrollment plunged in consequence of court intervention and the maturing of baby boomers whereby there were few elementary-school aged children dwelling in the increasingly popular neighborhood. From 215 students in 1978, enrollment was fewer than 150 by 1982. The district closed the school when classes let out in June of that year. Back in the early 1960s, membership had fluctuated between

Photo by Phil Goodstein

In 1925, DPS opened a new Globeville School along the north side of 51st Avenue between Lincoln and Sherman streets. After the district closed the building in 1943, for a while the former schoolhouse was apartments. Later it became the home of Laradon Hall, a program serving children with extreme physical and mental impairments.

415 and 570. (Lincoln ranged from 570 to 635.) Steele School, 320 South Marion Street Parkway, took in neighborhood children previously assigned to Washington Park School. It also was the neighborhood school for some students living directly west of Washington Park.

In 1983, the district leased Washington Park School to Denver Academy. This was a private program dating from 1972 for the "learning impaired." Specifically, this meant troubled students, particularly those from affluent families who had had legal and behavioral difficulties. Those not liking the youngsters at Denver Academy dismissed them as nothing more than rich, spoiled brats. Had the students been from poor families, they likely would have landed up in Juvenile Hall.

DPS explained that the purpose of Denver Academy allowed it to lease Washington Park School to the program despite its rule of not selling schoolhouses to private or religious schools. Denver Academy bought Washington Park School in 1984 for around $850,000. The new owner steadily grew at its new home. The alternative school continually modified and expanded the building. Needing more space, it exited in the course of 2001–02 for the campus of the old Bethesda Sanatorium at 4400 Iliff Avenue, a place which had once been an asylum for people suffering from tuberculosis before becoming a mental health facility.

After Denver Academy left the old Washington Park School, other private schools came and went from the building. None succeeded as they hoped. There

Myrtle Hill School occupied its new home at 1125 South Race Street in 1906. It became Washington Park School in 1923, a year after the completion of a substantial addition. Another wing followed in 1928. The picture shows the surviving 1928 wing which became condominiums in the first decade of the 21st century.

was no covenant in the DPS sale of Washington Park School preventing private or religious schools from purchasing the former public school.

Meanwhile, real estate values soared by the old Myrtle Hill School. In 2005, investor Jonathan Miller acquired the complex. Neighborhood activists and preservationists vetoed his plan to level it for elite new single-family houses. The result was saving the 1928 wing of the building as condominiums surrounded by new residences.

After DPS closed Boulevard School, 2351 Federal Boulevard, in 1982, it sold the campus to a developer who promised to transform the schoolhouse into a home for senior citizens. When the new owner failed to make the project a reality, Charles Nash of Alternatives Ltd., who had been an unsuccessful bidder for Boulevard in 1982, got possession of the building. He saw workers renovate it as condominiums. Here and there, blackboards remained on the walls while some units retained teacher closets and staircase handrails. For the most part, the interior of the building looked like a modern apartment house.

Nash also transformed Alameda School into condominiums. Its home went up in 1902 at 104 West Byers Place as Byers School. The district renamed it "Alameda School" in 1921 upon the construction of the nearby Byers Junior High School. For years, Alameda was a small school, connecting with the people living in the area.

Amidst declining enrollment, DPS closed Alameda School at the end of the 1973–74 schoolyear. At first, the district aimed to demolish the structure since it was "no longer used or useful." Before anything happened, DPS announced plans to sell the schoolhouse to help pay for the acquisition of the new district headquarters at 900 Grant Street. In the interim, a preservationist outcry saved Alameda School. Until October 1981, the city used the schoolhouse as a food stamp office. Charles Nash purchased it for $182,000 on December 16, 1982. His profitable transformation of the building into condominiums allowed him to repeat his success at Boulevard School. He subsequently converted Stevens School, 1140 Columbine Street, into condos.

For years, the same principal oversaw Alameda and Sherman schools. Located at the northeast corner of Second Avenue and Grant Street, Sherman School dated from 1892, recalling Civil War General William T. Sherman. Enrollment was about 200 in the late 1970s. During the busing era, the courts decided Sherman was a naturally integrated academy.

In 1982, DPS closed Sherman as a redundant facility. Working with the Colorado Council on the Arts and Humanities, the district turned the space into the Grant Street Art Center in February 1983 with studios for 24 artists. The Sherman School annex, dating from 1920, became home of dance companies. In 1991, citing high maintenance costs, DPS sold the schoolhouse to a private adult education program, the Art Students League.

Photo by Phil Goodstein

In 1982, DPS shuttered Sherman School at the northeast corner of Second Avenue and Grant Street. The Art Students League subsequently totally revamped the building as its home and the location of artist studios.

Preservation and Destruction

In a roundabout way, Elyria School at 4725 High Street emerged as residences. DPS opened the $40,000–$45,000 building in 1924, announcing it had space for somewhere between 210 and 250 students. (In different annual reports, the administration listed different numbers and costs.) The schoolhouse replaced a facility dating from 1884–85 near Williams Street and 47th Avenue. The name derived from the community it served. The architectural team of Arthur S. Wilson and Joseph Wilson designed the new Elyria in the Mediterranean revival style. The school had six instructors, one for each grade. There was no kindergarten. A 1970 listing stated Elyria had space for 150 learners when it had a membership of 134. Elyria had a joint PTA with Swansea School. For years, the same administrator was the principal of Swansea and Elyria. For a while, he also was in charge of Harrington School at 3230 38th Avenue.

In 1975, as part of We're On Our Way, DPS opened a new home for Swansea, 4650 Columbine Street. Soon thereafter, wreckers razed the old Swansea which dated from 1891. With declining enrollment, after the 1978–79 schoolyear, DPS closed Elyria, transferring its students to Swansea. (Back in 1976, DPS had complained that new Swansea was overcrowded, sending some of its pupils to Elyria.)

During the first part of the busing era, Swansea was kindergarten through third grade, paired with Whiteman School, 451 Newport Street. For a while, Holm was Swansea's sister school. For the most part, Elyria mirrored Swansea busing patterns. Swansea was among the first schools in DPS to have a bilingual/multicultural program. In addition to a preschool, the academy was the home of an initiative DPS

Photo by Phil Goodstein

Blank walls dominate the 1975 Swansea School at 4650 Columbine Street.

elementary schools stressed in the 1970s, Identifiable Perceptual Communicative Disorders. At times, the school placed slow or uncommunicative students in it.

The new Swansea School had few windows, being the embodiment of the architectural blandness of the day. The team of Childress & Paulin designed it. As students continued to flock to Swansea, workers completed an addition in 1996. That year, at the end of busing, the school counted four American Indian students, 16 blacks, two youngsters of Asian heritage, 483 Hispanos, and 15 whites. By the last year of the 2010s, a school census reported between 486 and 526 students. It stated 91.4 percent to 93 percent of them were Hispanos. Four to 4.5 percent were black, 2 percent were white, and 1 percent of mixed heritage. Almost all qualified for free or reduced-price lunches.

Public health officials and neighborhood residents were concerned that Swansea School was directly to the north of Interstate 70 whereby children on the playground were subjected to the massive fumes, dust, and noise from the highway. At one point, the school further discovered pupils were endangered by lead in the playground dirt, a legacy of the pollution from the smelters that had once dominated the area. In the early 21st century, DPS authorized a new wing of Swansea, designed by Anderson Mason Dale, near the southwest corner of 47th Avenue and Elizabeth Street. It included traditional windows. The school was additionally the home of the Swansea Recreation Center, a program operated by the city.

Claiming it had no use for the abandoned Elyria School, the board of education authorized selling the shuttered edifice on October 20, 1979, at the same time it decided to dispose of Thatcher. The city bought the High Street schoolhouse the next year, promising to convert the edifice into a daycare center. When nothing came of that, it vowed it would transform the former Elyria School into a youth treatment center. Once more, it failed to carry out its promise. In 1988, Su Teatro bought the abandoned landmark for $142,000.

The new owner was an innovative, community-based theater stemming from the Chicano upheavals of the 1960s and 1970s. Founder and director Tony Garcia launched Su Teatro (Your Theater) in 1971 out of a theater class at the University of Colorado Denver. Initially, Su Teatro performed in parks, churches, and community centers. It had a strong social and political mission, seeking to connect audiences with controversial issues. Bilingual, its plays were usually understandable in both Spanish and English. Before long, it had a loyal group of supporters.

Garcia drew on them, getting 250 backers to contribute $20 each for the downpayment on Elyria School. A major renovation followed in 1992. Included was some city money through a federal community development block grant. Besides the theater proper, the former Elyria School included an art gallery and reached out to the community with classes. Su Teatro hosted a Chicano music festival and a Spanish-language film festival.

By the 21st century, Su Teatro had outgrown the space. Garcia developed ties with John Hickenlooper when the future mayor was still a businessman who projected himself as a patron of the arts. In office, Hickenlooper saw that the city assisted Su Teatro in obtaining property along Santa Fe Drive in the heart of West Denver. A native who had grown up in Auraria, Garcia claimed he always wanted

In 1984, DPS opened a new home for Columbian School at the northeast corner of West 40th Avenue and Federal Boulevard. Soon thereafter, it demolished the original 1892 building.

to return Su Teatro to the West Side. After some convoluted business deals and many problems and delays, Su Teatro moved to the old Cameron Theater at 721 Santa Fe Drive around 2010.

After Su Teatro left Elyria School, Jim Mercado, of J. Mercado & Associates, partnered with Empowerment Program and Community Capital Corporation to transform the building into the Odyssey Family Residence. Included was a new building south of the school where the playground/Su Teatro parking lot had been. The developer stated the $7 million venture, with 36 residential units, was a "reinvestment" in the area. Ideally, it would spark others to pour funds into the section as it thrived as a gentrifying area. Simultaneously, the city committed itself to completely rebuilding the nearby I-70 as a road with greater traffic capacity.

Proponents of saving historic schoolhouses failed to keep the old Columbian School standing at West 40th Avenue and Federal Boulevard. It dated from 1892, the 400th anniversary of Columbus' voyage of discovery. Additions considerably enhanced the schoolhouse in 1905 and 1923. In 1982, after many delays, DPS authorized a replacement building. MCB Architects designed a schoolhouse for 450 students on an expanded campus stretching to West 41st Avenue to Eliot Street. By the time all members of the school board turned out for the dedication of the new Columbian on March 19, 1985, wreckers had brought down the old building. No sooner was replacement Columbian holding classes than parents complained it was overcrowded. Though it had space for 450 pupils while 426 were enrolled, some classrooms were packed beyond capacity given the large number of young learners who were entering the system. (In the early 1960s, Columbian had between 570 and 590 students. By the late 1970s, the number was around 380. The 1996 census counted 459 pupils, 403 of whom were Hispanic.)

The school escaped busing, offering classes from early childhood education through sixth grade. It channeled some of its students into special education programs for youngsters with "Significant Limited Intellectual Capacity" and "Identifiable Perceptual Communicative Disorders." DPS oversaw a remodeling of the new Columbian in 1996 followed by replacing the roof in 1999. Students were the Cougars.

The destruction of old Columbian was among the last of the district's decisions to raze historic buildings. Responding to increasingly loud preservationist voices, DPS officially recognized and celebrated its architectural heritage in 1991. That year, in cooperation with Historic Denver and the Colorado Historical Society, the district launched a preservation project. Until then, Moore was the only functioning schoolhouse officially designated a Denver landmark. Working with the Denver Landmark Preservation Commission, DPS convinced city council to declare such academies as East, South, West, North, Park Hill, Wyatt, Ashley (1914 Syracuse Street), Ebert, Skinner, Morey, Horace Mann, and Asbury (1320 Asbury Avenue) as landmarks.

Even so, DPS still wanted to replace Smedley, 4250 Shoshone Street, a building dating from 1902. Additions had followed in 1911, 1952, and 1955. Smedley was a primary school during busing, with classes from kindergarten through third grade. For a while, students went to Centennial for fourth, fifth, and sixth grades. Later the courts paired Smedley with Kaiser. It also had some links with Southmoor.

In the early 1990s, DPS announced it was going to tear down the 1902 and 1911 wings of Smedley as part of a massive rebuilding and remodeling. This provoked the wrath of neighbors, alumni, and preservationists. They formed Save Old Smedley (SOS). The group convinced city council to declare Smedley a landmark on June 23, 1992. The building so survived as the oldest standing DPS structure in North Denver. The district thereupon constructed a free-standing annex along West 42nd Avenue.

By 1996, the city had declared 16 DPS buildings official landmarks. Included were some post–World War II schoolhouses, notably Grant, Cory, and Merrill. Exponents of mid-century modernism heralded these structures. In places, the designations came after students, parents, and teachers collaborated to campaign for landmark status. In pushing for the preservation of its buildings, the district observed that, until 1953, no two schools were designed precisely alike. That year, faced with the need to educate ever more baby boomers, it arranged for architects to craft multiple buildings on the same plan.

Some former schools also became landmarks such as Elyria, Stevens, Globeville, and Sherman. Evans School received Denver landmark status in 2001. In many ways, this building at West 11th Avenue and Acoma Street illustrated the problematic efforts to save and restore old schoolhouses. When the district closed Evans School in 1974, the edifice had no clear future. It was located in what came to be known as the Golden Triangle, once a premier residential

The owner of Evans School, at the northwest corner of West 11th Avenue and Acoma Street, thoroughly renovated the building around 2015—it had sat empty since DPS closed the school in 1974.

section which had come to be filled with public facilities, museums, apartments, factories, and many parking lots.

DPS put the Evans building on the market in April 1974. To save the schoolhouse, investors Alan and Richard Eber purchased it. They sealed it up tight, announcing they hoped to renovate it. Nothing happened. While the owners saw that the schoolhouse was well policed and protected, they let weeds grow around it. Even at that, they had it placed in the National Register of Historic Places in 1980. Not until 2014–15 did the Eber family commission workers thoroughly to rehabilitate the building. The structure continued to be mostly empty space recalling the educational glory of the area.

In 2018, former state treasurer Cary Kennedy had office space in Evans School when, with the backing of the CEA, she unsuccessfully sought the Democratic nomination for governor. The next year, former United States Attorney John Walsh had his campaign headquarters there as he sought the 2020 Democratic nomination for governor—he dropped out of the race in September 2019. (Back in the early 21st century, a building directly west of Evans School at 1100 Bannock Street had been a premier campaign headquarters for such Democrats as Ken Salazar, Bill Ritter, Mark Udall, and Michael Hancock.

On December 6, 2019, the Eber family sold Evans School in a two-part deal. One purchaser focused on the parking lots adjacent to the building, eyeing the land for residential highrises. City Street Investors, which was also a developer of highrises, acquired the schoolhouse. It talked about turning the first floor into restaurants and bars while the second and third floors became offices. This, it hoped, would assure that the old academy would become "something really useful" for the adjacent neighborhood. Nobody pondered restoring the landmark as a school.

A Classroom Shortage

By the mid-1980s, after closing and selling many buildings, DPS suddenly declared that its schoolhouses were overcrowded. Though enrollment in 1985 was at 58,614, the district insisted it did not have enough space for all learners. This was especially the case among elementary schools in the northwest sector. The district claimed it was not only out of room at Beach Court, Centennial, Cheltenham, Colfax, and Bryant-Webster, but there were also severe space problems at Brown, Columbian, Remington, Smedley, and Fairview. A lack of classrooms also plagued Cowell (4540 West 10th Avenue) and Eagleton. Cowell students met in hallways for classes.

As had long been the case, DPS numbers were highly suspect. For example, it claimed that Bryant-Webster, with an enrollment of 623, was designed for 475. In contrast, a 1962 survey stated the school's ideal capacity was 690 while it could handle 778 pupils. Back in 1978, the district did not call the school overcrowded when it counted 486 pupils. Cowell, according to DPS in 1985–86, had an enrollment of 414 in a building designed for 373. The 1962 analysis had given it space for 480 students with a maximum capacity of 555.

The reports about overcrowding came after years of declining membership and systemic reductions in teaching staffs. By 1985, the district asserted it had stabilized itself. That year, it counted 58,614 students, up from 58,271 in 1984. This was the first time the district's enrollment had gone up since the 1967–68 schoolyear. Seemingly, young families were increasingly moving to older neighborhoods, especially Hispanic sections of North Denver. Even at that, the number of white pupils continued to decline. They then made up 37.4 percent of the student body. Hispanos were 35.5 percent. Blacks came in at 22.3 percent. People of Asian heritage were 3.6 percent. The district counted 1.2 percent of its students as Native Americans.

School champions were exuberant about the increase in numbers. The district stated it was necessary to add 218 teachers while hiking taxes. In part, the additional money was to pay for increasing the scope of bilingual education. The funds further helped place ever more supervisors in school buildings. Many teachers complained that such personnel were "super-snitches" who were endlessly looking over their shoulders. The DCTA filed a grievance against the district, claiming the unwanted imposition of a supervisor at each of the city's high schools for the 1985–86 schoolyear was a violation of the contract.

In response to overcrowding, the administration leased part of the North Side Community Center at West 36th Avenue and Pecos Street, the former Mount Carmel Catholic School, to hold classes for the nearby Bryant-Webster. It hauled in a couple of portables to provide extra space at Valdez where, parents complained, kindergartens were on triple sessions. There was no talk of asking the United States

District Court to modify the busing order so students in crowded schools could be bused to virtually empty facilities in the southeast and southwest quadrants of the city. On the contrary, DPS campaigned to ask voters for funds to expand northwest schools. Additionally, a purpose of sending sixth graders to middle schools, a transfer the district implemented in 1988, was to help relieve overcrowding. The district did not link the problem of overcrowding to the way it had been shutting schools in recent years and selling off the properties. Nor did the increase in enrollment hold. By 1986, DPS was down to 58,400, falling to 57,503 the next year.

900 Grant Street

The district applied part of the proceeds from the 1974 sales of Alameda and Evans schools to procure a new administrative headquarters at 900 Grant Street. For years, DPS had been overcrowded at 414 14th Street, its office building since 1923. With the steady increase of enrollment after World War II, the number of front-office staff naturally grew. Compared to 145 administrators in 1950 when DPS had 51,780 students taught by 2,047 teachers, by 1960 there were 214 in the front office when enrollment was 90,518 with 3,409 teachers. The increase in the size of the front office, the superintendent's office emphasized, was far less than the expansion of the system.

As the district grew, DPS rented space near 414 14th Street for auxiliary offices. At times, it had offices in different schoolhouses. In 1958–59, the district erected what it called the Service Building at 2800 West Seventh Avenue. Also known as the Maintenance Building and the Warehouse, the complex included shops, especially for the maintenance, landscaping, and the enhancement of buildings. At times, the initials ABGW appeared, standing for "Association Building Grounds Warehouse." The complex was home of the district's carpenters, electricians, and plumbers. It was also the quarters of the DPS Press on which the district printed its many newsletters and brochures. Previously, the DPS Press had been at Opportunity School. The system additionally placed its testing center at 2800 West Seventh Avenue, the facility where it scored tests and stashed away the examinations.

Before occupying the Service Building, DPS had had its main warehouse at 1278 Fox Street (the southeast corner of West 13th Avenue and Speer Boulevard). As much as anything, it was where the district kept its textbooks. That edifice had gone up in 1904. An addition had followed in 1924. When the district occupied the Service Building, the administration converted its old warehouse into offices. DPS put the Speer Boulevard building on the market in 1974, not selling it until December 15, 1978. Wreckers brought it down five years later.

Directly to the west of the Service Building was the district's main bus garage, known as Hill Top, 2920 West Seventh Avenue. It was atop a steep hill close to the interchange of Federal Boulevard and West Sixth Avenue. Previously, DPS had lacked a specific location to store its buses. Inventories of the district's assets simply stated it parked its buses at "various schools." Between 1974 and 1976, DPS also operated what it branded Riverfront, a bus maintenance facility at West Sixth Avenue and Alcott Street. Between 1950 and 1960–61, DPS additionally

After DPS left its administrative headquarters at 414 14th Street in 1975, the building became city offices. It was subsequently the headquarters of the Denver Art Museum. In the mid-2010s, a new owner remodeled the building into residences. As part of the process, students and teachers at DPS's School of the Arts added artwork to the chain-link fence on the Tremont Place side of the landmark.

had the Denargo Garage at 29th Street and Broadway for some of its buses. The Northeast Terminal opened in Elyria in 1976 at 1805 48th Avenue as a place to store buses. DPS also had a major bus operation along the east side of Federal Boulevard between West Severn Place and West Eighth Avenue, a block away from the Hill Top garage.

The district's routing office, 2929 West Seventh Avenue, was across the street from the main bus terminal. What DPS once called the Green Building, 2915 West Seventh Avenue, was another part of the complex as was the Blue Building, 2909 West Seventh Avenue. Included were the training and safety divisions of the district's transportation department.

In 1968, DPS acquired the Bryant Street Center at 2525 West Sixth Avenue (at Bryant Street), close to the Service Building/Hill Top complex. An annex to the Bryant Street Center followed the next year. The district sold both properties on January 31, 1979. By the late 1960s, DPS also had the nearby Yuma Street Center at 2320–40 West Fourth Avenue. That was where the administration placed the district's federal projects program and had its office of food and nutrition. Officially, it was Enterprise Management. A sign declared "Food & Nutrition Services. Warehouse & distribution. School Supply store. Vending." In 2000, DPS purchased properties at 2600, 2700, and 2790 West Seventh Avenue for $909,300 for what it then called the "Hilltop Service Center."

In 1974, DPS purchased 900 Grant Street as its new headquarters.

By the 1960s, the district argued a new administration building was urgent. The failed 1967 bond issue included funds for such an undertaking. After that defeat, the superintendent's office revived an old scheme to convert Cole Junior High into the system's headquarters once it had arranged a new building for the students.

The We're On Our Way program did not include a replacement structure for Cole. Rather, after years of debate, on March 28, 1974, DPS acquired a seven-story structure at 900 Grant Street for $3.75 million. In 1964–65, William Muchow, a foremost modern architect who designed some schools and many office buildings, received a commission from Financial Programs Incorporated to craft the building as the company's headquarters. With Bob Crider and Frank Southworth voting no, the board approved the purchase during its February 28, 1974, meeting. After closing on the edifice, the district drastically remodeled the midrise.

The building, which included both a full basement and a subbasement, seemed adequate for all district offices, allowing DPS to consolidate them and dispose of excess properties. Insofar as it needed additional office space, the administration found it in empty rooms of schoolhouses as the district's attendance plummeted. The district officially moved out of 414 14th Street on February 1, 1975, occupying its new home two days later. Around the same time, the district undertook an aggressive school building program in the newly developing Montbello neighborhood.

Montbello Schools

Even as DPS shut and sold schoolhouses during the busing era, it added buildings in the newly developing northeastern section of the city. Beginning in the 1970s, construction was unending in Montbello and at the adjacent Green Valley Ranch. Both were something of instant, planned neighborhoods. They especially soared with the opening of Denver International Airport in 1995. A prime purpose of the field was to shift the city's growth to the far northeast quadrant of the city. Even at that, Montbello was already 30 years old before the first planes took off from the airfield.

On September 11, 1965, the city annexed a huge section to the northeast of Stapleton Airport, covering the area between approximately Havana Street and Chambers Road from Smith Road to 56th Avenue. In 1934, Joe Miller had acquired the land as his grazing farm. A Jewish immigrant, born in the Russian section of Poland, he had immigrated to the United States in 1877 at age 16. Arriving in Colorado, he started out raising and selling one cow at a time. Succeeding, he was soon a cattle baron. From there he expanded into the feed business. Eventually, he dominated the field, moving into real estate. One and all knew his spread to the northeast of Stapleton Airport as the Miller Ranch.

Joe Miller died at age 91 in December 1952. A grandson, Myron "Micky" Miller, took charge of the family land empire. Micky Miller came to collaborate with Aetna Insurance and such major Denver investors as Marvin Davis, Philip Anschutz, and Jordon Perlmutter in numerous efforts. Miller partnered with Sam Primack of Perl-Mack, a prime builder and developer, in forging Montbello on the Miller Ranch as an idyllic planned community combining industry and housing. The developer particularly aimed to attract military veterans, naming major arterials after such Air Force bases as Andrews, Maxwell, and Bolling. The first houses went up in the mid-1960s.

From the beginning, Montbello was something of a lower-middle-class enclave. Rather than storm sewers, waste waters flowed down culverts in the center of the medians of arterials. Promoters insisted Montbello was a thriving, self-sustained community, both part of the City and County of Denver and a world in and of itself. They stated it would be naturally racially integrated, a modern community for the post-civil rights era. Before long, the neighborhood had a large black population. Some settled there, having left Five Points and areas north and east of City Park. Additionally, it was the home of many members of the service stationed at Lowry and Fitzsimons.

Montbello encompassed about six square miles. It was the largest annexation Denver had undertaken since the 19th century. Full-scale development began in 1969. From the beginning, Montbello promoters emphasized the neighborhood as an abode of affordable homes, primarily drawing in sturdy wage workers and members of "families of modest income." Initial plans called for seven elementary schools in addition to a joint junior high/high school. The children of the early settlers had to ride the bus to get to school.

The building of schools were epoch events as Montbello emerged. Settlers demanded schools to serve them. The presence of schools, in turn, attracted young families. District #1 paid for the cost of procuring land and erecting the schoolhouses, often closely working with developers. The latter, seeing schools as necessary for Montbello's success, sometimes donated land. The supposedly visionary plan for Montbello did not include specific development costs to assure the area paid its own way for schools, parks, utilities, and roads.

Even before residential development started to sweep Montbello, the forerunner of Oakland School opened for the area in 1966 in a leased house at 4920 Troy Street. Initially known as Montbello School, it quickly expanded, taking over a nearby apartment complex at 4651 Tulsa Court, a place designated Montbello School #2. At times, the district referred to Montbello #1 as the Cottage and #2 as the Apartment. As the demand for classroom space expanded, in 1974 DPS leased two warehouses in the Montbello Industrial Park at 4845 and 4865 Oakland Street. It installed partitions in the buildings for classrooms. The next year it added a third building at 4825 Oakland Street, Montbello School #3. Officially, the complex was Oakland School. The third building was offices, the gymnasium, the cafeteria, and the location of health services.

About that time, plans were underway for McGlone School at 4500 Crown Boulevard. Initially, DPS announced it would close Oakland on the completion of the new building. By the time students entered McGlone in January 1978, the district saw the need to keep Oakland open given the soaring student population of the area. McGlone was part of the Next Six Years building program.

A real schoolhouse supplanted the Oakland School warehouses in 1984 at 4580 Dearborn Street. The firm of Hoover Berg Desmond designed it on plans

Photo by Phil Goodstein

Oakland School got a real home in 1984 at 4580 Dearborn Street.

Photo by Phil Goodstein

In the early 21st century, DPS built an annex to McGlone School, 4500 Crown Boulevard, for students in their first years of learning.

virtually identical to Marrama School, 19100 40th Avenue in Green Valley Ranch. Dignitaries dedicated the 26-classroom schoolhouse with 870 seats, on November 7, 1984. The old facility had had 273 students in kindergarten and first grade in 1978.

After some controversy about the designation of the Dearborn Street building, DPS decided to stick with the name Oakland School. During part of the busing era, Oakland had classes from kindergarten through second grade. Some of the older students went to McGlone. Others found themselves bused far across town to Samuels School at 3985 South Vincennes Court. Prior to the construction of the new building, Oakland had not been paired. Even at that, given its location in an isolated warehouse district, virtually all of its pupils arrived via bus.

Amesse School was Montbello's first true schoolhouse, opening in 1973 at 4330 Scranton Street. The board authorized it in the summer of 1971, initially stating it would have the capacity to educate 850. The school opened two years later with 615 seats. In 1978, Amesse stated it had 800 students with classes from kindergarten through sixth grade. All pupils lived in walking distance of the school, which escaped busing.

The building recalled pediatrician John H. Amesse. In 1965, as a mainstream Republican, he gained a place on the school board. On the body, he backed the initiatives of Rachel Noel and Ed Benton, pushing for racial accommodation and equal educational opportunity. Amidst the turmoil in the schools and in failing health, Amesse did not seek re-election in 1971. A heart attack killed him in October of that year.

The cornerstone of McGlone School reads 1977. The academy celebrates Roy "Dolly" McGlone. Born in western Nebraska on July 9, 1886, he grew up in West Denver, being part of a gang which vandalized the area. Along the way, he emerged as a tough guy, becoming an excellent boxer. Eventually, rather than fighting the system, he became part of it, serving for 33 years as a DPS instructor. Included was working at Byers Junior High, where he taught boys how to box, and supervising community recreation programs at West High. In the process, McGlone was a leader in shaping outdoor recreation for the district.

After retiring from DPS in 1951, McGlone was a renowned educator for the next 22 years at Laradon Hall, dealing with developmentally disabled children. The pedagogue passed away on November 11, 1974, when he was 88. The board authorized naming the Montbello academy for him at its September 18, 1975, meeting.

The schoolhouse opened at the beginning of the second semester in January 1978 with about 750 children and 36 teachers for grades two through six—Oakland School then educated those in kindergarten and first grade. Before long, Oakland had classes for kindergarten through third grade with McGlone being an intermediate school.

The district officially dedicated McGlone School on May 10, 1978. During part of the busing era, McGlone was paired with Fairview, near West 11th Avenue and Decatur Street, a place primarily educating Hispanos and Asians living in nearby housing projects. Around the time of the demise of court-ordered busing in the fall of 1995, CBS broadcaster Dan Rather visited McGlone as part of a feature "Courtroom to Classrooms." The 1996 DPS census stated McGlone had three students who were Native Americans, 398 blacks, 22 Asian-Americans, 136 Latinos, and 53 whites.

Besides Dolly McGlone, Charles T. McGlone was a major figure in the district after World War II. Born in North Platte, Nebraska, on April 16, 1906, in 1935 he joined the faculty at East High after having taught at St. Joseph's Catholic High School. At East, he was the baseball and swimming coach for the next 15 years. Prior to his retirement in 1971, he had served for some years as the joint principal of Sherman School and Alameda School. He was a relative of Dolly McGlone, part of a large family whose members stood out as athletes and community figures. Charles McGlone, who died from a heart attack on March 28, 1975, while on a vacation in Mexico, incidentally, was once a neighbor of another famed DPS principal, Leon Slavens.

Barney Ford School is at 14500 Maxwell Place. The board authorized it in March 1972, naming it that September for what it had simply described as Site 149. The school honors an escaped slave (1822–1902). Starting out as a barber, Ford succeeded as a restaurateur and hotelier while making a small fortune in real estate. Racist rules, he and his backers claimed, robbed him of a rich mining claim in the mountains near Barney Ford Hill in Summit County. A stained-glass window honors him at the Capitol. ABR Partnership was the architect of the 20-classroom structure with 855 seats. Students took their first classes in 1973 in what the administration called a "modified open space school."

The district did not bus Ford students. From 847 students in 1975, it counted an enrollment of 778 students in 1978, declining to 675 in the early 1980s. A decade later, DPS stated the academy had space for 601 students. The 1996 census reported a membership of 647. "We shall not fail our future by losing our past,"

Schools have come to hang banners advertising their academic achievement. Such is the case with Jessie Maxwell School, 14390 Bolling Drive. The facility honors the district's first African-American principal.

the school quoted Barney Ford as saying. It observed that, during his long career, he was always a stalwart champion of education. Barney Ford Park is adjacent to the school.

DPS authorized Maxwell School at 14390 Bolling Drive in 1998, naming it in honor of 88-year-old Jessie Whaley Maxwell. A native of Louisiana, born in 1909, she was the daughter of school teachers. She followed them in the profession, earning her degree from Bishop College in Marshall, Texas. Visiting a relative in Denver, she met and married pharmacist Hulett Maxwell, the business partner of the black Democratic boss of Five Points, Sonny Lawson.

In 1942, Jessie Maxwell started substituting at Whittier School. Before long, she was a full-time instructor. She moved up to the principal's post in 1955. As such, she was the first African-American principal in the district. The educator transferred to Columbine School in 1966, retiring in 1972. The civil rights pioneer passed away in 2002. At the behest of Montbello school board member Bennie Milliner, in 1998 DPS resolved that the building named in her honor was to be a fundamental academy with a strict program stressing old-fashioned discipline and basic reading, writing, and arithmetic.

Jessie Maxwell followed in the footsteps of Marie Anderson Greenwood, the woman honored by Greenwood School at 5130 Durham Court, a program opening in August 2001. A native of Los Angeles, born on November 24, 1912, the African-American Marie Anderson arrived in Denver with her family at age 13. After struggling at Morey Junior High, she had a miserable sophomore year at East High School where she suffered from racial discrimination. Transferring to

West as a junior, she excelled there, winning a scholarship to the forerunner of the University of Northern Colorado where she earned a teaching certificate.

Seeking a job, she caught the eye of Whittier principal Lila O'Boyle who also oversaw Gilpin School. Both places had substantial black enrollments. Around five feet tall, O'Boyle dominated the schools and those around her. She hired Marie Anderson in 1935 to teach first grade. This made Anderson the second black public school teacher in the city. The first had been Rufus Felton, a Civil War veteran who briefly taught in the late 1860s/early 1870s. Anderson was the inaugural African-American to gain tenure, achieving it in 1938 after finishing the standard three-year probationary period. After her marriage to Bill Greenwood in 1943, Marie Anderson quit the system to become a young mother. The couple settled in a developing section of southwest Denver where she sent her children to the newly opened Newlon School. There she actively involved herself in their education and school programs. On this basis, she started serving as a Newlon substitute teacher in 1953, rejoining the district as a full-time instructor two years later. As such, Marie Anderson Greenwood was the first black teacher in the district to teach at a predominantly white school.

Greenwood retired from DPS in 1974, going on to volunteer with the Denver Public Library. She reflected on her experiences, emphasizing the wonders of education in a book, *Every Child Can Learn*. Her family and champions of civil rights and education celebrated her centennial in 2012. She passed away on November 15, 2019, just before her 107th birthday. (Over the years, DPS has sometimes named schools for living people such as Dora Moore, Eugene Stevens, Aaron Gove, and William H. Smiley. For the most part, it has waited until after the death of an educator to memorialize the pedagogue.)

Greenwood School had a lion on its logo. In 2004, it officially became Greenwood Academy when it expanded to include a middle school. By the 2010s, 93 percent of its students qualified for free or discounted lunches. Seventy percent of them were from families that spoke a first language other than English. Before deciding on the name Marie Greenwood School, the board had pondered designating the schoolhouse for Lena Archuleta or "Daddy" Bruce Randolph. Within a few years, it honored those community figures with buildings.

Montbello High School

On August 29, 1980, Montbello came of age with the opening of the $10.5 million Montbello High School at 5000 Crown Boulevard. It was part of the Next Six Years. The school occupied a 40-acre campus. Adjacent to the school was the 40-acre Montbello Central Park. The location of the school and the park reflected the politics and economics of the development of the neighborhood. Back in 1975, developers Micky Miller and Sam Primack had clashed bitterly with DPS, refusing to sell the district land for the proposed McGlone School. This forced the district to buy property three blocks east of the preferred site for $136,750 from the Denver Catholic Archdiocese.

What Miller and Primack gained by not selling to DPS they lost in good will. By this time, realizing the high costs of annexations, including the price of new

Montbello High School opened at 5000 Crown Boulevard in 1980.

schools and parks, the city had amended its annexation laws to require developers to provide land for schools. Back in 1967, in the wake of the annexation of Montbello, DPS gained a say about annexations. Until then, the mayor and city council had the exclusive power to decide on including more land in the City and County of Denver. Seeing the need for developers to collaborate with the school district, Miller worked out a deal with the city and DPS. He donated 36.87 acres for the high school and another 36.87 acres for the park based on DPS and the city sharing the costs of developing the school and the park. (The rest of the land was acquired by vacating existing roads where the school and park emerged.)

Montbello High School was the city's tenth high school, the first to open since John F. Kennedy in 1966. Students were the Warriors. DPS commissioned the firm of Nixon Brown Brokaw Bowen in 1977 to design the structure with room for 2,100 learners. Reflecting the trend of the day, many classrooms had no or few windows. Until the new building opened, Montbello students were bused to Hamilton, Hill, or Place (7125 Cherry Creek Drive) for junior high. Most proceeded to Thomas Jefferson for grades 10, 11, and 12.

As was typical of schoolhouses of the era, Montbello High School was an incredibly bland building with none of the charm or features of North, South, East, and West. When it opened, the schoolhouse included classes from ninth through 12th grades. It added seventh and eighth grades the next year.

The joint junior high/high school never worked well. To accommodate everybody while assuring a separation between the younger and older students, those in 10th, 11th, and 12th grades started the schoolday at 6:45 AM. Their classes got out just after 1:00 PM. Those in middle school occupied the building from

Photo by Phil Goodstein

On Martin Luther King Day, January 14, 1987, DPS dedicated a middle school in memory of the civil rights activist at 19535 46th Avenue.

10:50 AM to 4:35 PM. They did not have a defined faculty or principal of their own. The result was confusion and turbulence. The solution in 1983 was to bus those in seventh and eighth grades elsewhere. The new Montbello building included a community school offering adult education and evening and weekend recreation and arts and crafts programs.

To educate those in seventh and eighth grades, the district opened Martin Luther King Middle School in 1986 at 19535 46th Avenue near Ceylon Street in Green Valley Ranch. On authorizing the building for Site 175 on May 19, 1983, the board had simply designated it the Northeast Middle School with a capacity of 1,680. Brooks Waldman Architecture designed it. Students became the Panthers. The place's slogan was DREAM: "Dignity, Respect, Excellence, Achievement — Martin Luther King Middle School." Work began on the building in early 1985. District leaders dedicated it on Martin Luther King Day, January 14, 1987.

According to a review conducted by the District School Improvement and Accountability Council in the mid-1990s, Martin Luther King School was "huge, spotless, and orderly." This came shortly after ABC Television had featured the school on "Prime Time Live" in November 1992. The network broadcast footage of a couple of raucous student altercations filmed by freelancers using hidden cameras. The place, the telecast declared, was illustrative of the dangerous lack of discipline in schools across the country. The superintendent's office responded by shaking up the administration and the school's disciplinary policies. By that time, with more than 1,100 students, King was the largest middle school in DPS. In 1996, the academy counted 934 pupils, 64.5 percent of whom were black compared to 14.3 percent Hispanic, 14.1 percent white, 6.3 percent Asian, and .7 percent Native Americans.

This was well in the future. Many of the Montbello schools opened in the 1970s and 1980s when busing overshadowed all educational considerations. During these decades, members of the school board continued to clash with each other while superintendents came and went.

A Note on Sources:

The February 1970, p. 2, *SRv* told of plans for a comprehensive building program. "Schools for Denver's Children: A Proposal for Many Urgent Buildings and Side Needs of the Denver Public Schools" was a district promotion brochure for the 1971 bond issue. A copy is in FF 13:13 of the Banks papers. Publicity for the 1971 bond issue, in FF 7:40 of the DPS papers, claimed that money to build Henry Junior High was part of the program. In contrast, the DPS PR of April 25, 1973, in FF 3:37, asserted the school was financed on a "pay-as-you-go" basis.

SN, October 26, 1970, pp. 15, 17, mentioned the five-year building program. *SN*, November 16, 1970, p. 21, outlined some of the projects. The flyer of the Neighborhood Schools Committee, in FF 1:30 of the DPS papers, includes an explicit call for pay-as-you-go financing by Bob Crider, Ted Hackworth, and Bert Gallegos.

SN, September 27, 1971, p. 8, October 25, 1971, p. 11, and November 8, 1971, p. 13, stressed the 1971 bond issue. The 1974 *DPS Report*, no pagination, outlined the district's building program with money from the bond issue.

A chapter on Wyman is in the unpaginated *Histories of the Denver Public Schools* (Denver: DPS, n.d.). FF 6:141–47 in the DPS papers are on Wyman. I outline the history of the school and the neighborhood in *Ghosts of Denver*, 190–92, and *School Book*, 61, 70, 112, 155, 206, 256, 268, 325, 384. (The index listing for Wyman was unwittingly omitted from *School Book*.) *Focus*, June 1980, p. 3, told about pods and the design of schools with flexible spaces. On January 23, 2020, Dorothy Gotlieb recalled the open classroom fad and its severe problems. Mike Davenport, who gained his architectural degree in the 1970s, has discussed the debate over windows and school heating and cooling systems in many conversations. *SCJ*, August 27, 1974, p. 5, blasted the architecture of the district's new buildings, particularly attacking Wyman. It argued that the lack of windows meant vandals could not break windows at the schools. A report in FF 21:40 of the Yasui papers lists the high number of suspensions at Wyman in the mid-1970s. Volume three will deal with the Center for 21st Century Learning.

FF 7:10–17 in the DPS papers focus on Gove. I deal with the school in *Park Hill Promise*, 107–08, and *Modern East Denver*, 55–61. FF 7:91 of the DPS papers mentions the Learning Bridge at Morey. I attended an August 16, 2012, gathering of Gove alumni who were mourning the demolition of the second Gove. They readily shared memories about both the old and new buildings and materials they had gathered on the history of the school. On April 24, 2018, retired teacher Dan Goe recalled his experiences at Gove in the 1950s and 1960s.

The 1976 *DPS Report*, 6, observed crowded classrooms and the work of the DCTA in redressing the problem. *Cmq*, January 1979, p. 4, and February 1979, p. 1, reported the move to close schools. On p. 3 of the February number, it observed the need for court review in shuttering any buildings because of the busing order.

The 1978–79 PTA Notebook in GP has statements about the administration's school closure and consolidation procedures. Included is a DPS PR, March 23, 1979. *RMN*, December 5, 1980, p. 5, and December 12, 1980, p. 106, looked at debates over school closings. *RMN*, March 16, 1979, p. 4, and April 17, 1979, p. 43, observed how dropping enrollment forced the district to close many of its schools. *SN*, September 25, 1978, p. 12, explained the district's budgetary problems in the face of the soaring cost of living.

FF 5:144 of the DPS papers has the resolutions closing and selling Perry School. *SN*, January 4, 1972, p. 21, tolled the end of Perry School. *SN*, April 8, 1974, p. 35, reported plans to lease or sell the building. *School Book*, 237, 261, 262, 271, 423, outlines the history of the program. Catlett, *Farmlands*, makes no mention of the place. She touches on Barnum School, 61. On occasion, Roger Dudley has shared his memories of growing up in Barnum in the 1950s and 1960s and the nature of Perry and Barnum schools.

School Book, 422, traces the origins of Belmont School. *SN*, May 29, 1973, p. 39, reported plans to close Belmont. It observed the board's reconsideration of the decision, June 4, 1973, p. 41. *CPB*, January-February 1975, p. 6, observed the 100-percent PTA membership at Belmont. *Cmq*, May 1979, p. 4, outlined the closing of Belmont and the dispersal of its students. Also see *RMN*, April 18, 1979, p. 1, and *DP*, April 18, 1979, p. 3. Catlett, *Farmlands*, 95, makes passing mention of Belmont. She stresses the role of the Denver Indian Center, 109. On December 3, 2019, Rick Waters, the director of the Indian Center, discussed the program and the building's origins as a schoolhouse.

DPS announced the Citizen Advisory Commission on School Closures in press releases on February 22 and March 16, 1977. FF 3:45 of the DPS papers, in the file on Belmont School, discusses the fate of Emerson. *HDN*, Spring 2012, p. 5, and Fall 2013, pp. 4–5, told of Historic Denver's occupation of the building.

Materials on school consolidation are in an envelope in GP of miscellaneous clippings and reports of DPS for the "1950s, 1970s, and 1980s." Also see *Cmq*, June 1979, p. 4, and January 1981, p. 3. Meadow, "Hard Years," *CJ*, May 8, 1974, pp. 23–26, links the push to close Moore School to DPS's integration schemes. On August 14, 2019, Margaret Benton recalled attending Moore School in the mid-1960s and the natural integration and diversity of the student body.

Cmq, January 1978, outlined the emergence of the Friends of Dora Moore. The minutes of the January 19, 1978, school board meeting, p. 7, observed the district's commitment to save and renovate Moore School. In 1988, Carole McCotter chatted about the origins of the Friends of Dora Moore.

The 1977–78 PTA Notebook in GP has many unidentified clippings on school closings and consolidations. It includes an October 3, 1977, DPS PR on public meetings on school closings. The holding also has a June 14, 1977, article from the *Wall Street Journal*, p. 1, "Books vs. Bricks." *Cmq*, September 1977, emphasized the debate. *Cmq*, January 1979, p. 3, and April 1979, p. 7, listed schools DPS was pondering closing and the work of the committee on school consolidations and closings. In passing, the PTA publication observed, January 1974, p. 4, that DPS materials about the schools the district wished to close were of "dubious value."

SN, April 14, 1982, p. 47, reported the impending closing of many schools. FF 4:80 of the Ash Grove PTA Papers has a March 1979 DPS report on school closings. *RMN*, November 12, 1983, p. 10, outlined the collapsing enrollment in DPS and the numbers at various schools.

SB, January 31, 1949, p. 4, observed problems with the tower at Ashland School. In 2010, Wally Ginn shared the story about the wrecking of the landmark. I touch on Ashland's fate and the emergence of Valdez School in *North Side Story*, 217–19. FF 6:104–09 of the DPS papers are on Ashland. *NDT*, October 4, 2012, pp. 4, 7, and August 21, 2014, p. 2, looked at the renovation of Valdez School. There are files on Ashland and Valdez at NSAC. Materials on Joe P. Martinez and the painting of him are in FF 8:9 of the CCR papers at DPL.

I touch on the emergence of Del Pueblo School in *West Side*, 297–300. Records on it are FF 4:20–23 of the DPS papers. The dedication book, FF 4:21, has the specifications of the building and the school board minutes on its naming. FF 4:22 deals with the groundbreaking. FF 4:23 observes ties between Kaiser School and Del Pueblo and the changing attendance borders of the West Denver academy. The West High Alumni Room has materials on Elmwood and Del Pueblo. *DP*, September 22, 1972, p. 31, and *RMN*, September 22, 1972, p. 12, told of the name Del Pueblo over Elmwood.

RMN, August 27, 1982, p. 1, stressed DPS's policy of not leasing or selling empty schoolhouses to religious or private schools. Nelson, *Flights of Angels*, 20, 63, celebrates Ralph Pitts. FF 5:152–61 of the DPS papers deal with Pitts School. Included is a biography of Ralph Pitts by his son Malcolm, FF 5:154. GP includes a notebook filled with Pitts PTA records. *Cmq*, October 1984, p. 4, reported leasing Pitts School to the Colorado Association of School Executives. I glance at Temple Sinai's presence in the old school in *Exploring Jewish Colorado*, 49. FF 5:160–61 of the DPS papers deal with the congregation's occupation of Pitts School. On January 23, 2020, Dorothy Gotlieb discussed the synagogue.

A copy of "The Next Six years," is in FF 21:22 of the Yasui papers. On p. 20, the document condemned six of the historic junior high school buildings as "educationally obsolescent." A January 13, 1976, DPS PR, *SN*, January 26, 1976, p. 24, and the February 4, 1976, special issue of *SN*, p. 1, outlined the six-year pay-as-you-go plan. *RMN*, May 27, 1976, p. 6, observed the school board delaying the launch of the effort.

Colorado Year Book 1959–61 (Denver: Colorado State Planning Division, n.d.), 243, outlines the changing nature of state mill levies. Peltier, "Newlon," 80, 83, has passing mention of the relationship between District #1 and the state tax commission. *DP*, November 6, 1974, and *SN*, December 16, 1974, p. 19, told of the defeat of the November 5, 1974, mill levy request.

SN, June 7, 1976, p. 39, and October 3, 1977, p. 11, mentioned the new DCTA contract and the efforts to relieve overcrowding. *SN*, September 1, 1971, p. 2, reported the authorization of Samuels School. *Cmq*, October 1977, looked at the pairing between Samuels and Cheltenham schools. FF 5:15–22 of the DPS papers focus on Holm School. Also see *School Book*, 354, 411, 415, 416.

FF 6:52–57 of the DPS papers deal with Southmoor. *SRv*, February 1963, p. 3, touched on the impact of annexations on DPS. *SN*, December 16, 1974, p. 19, observed the board authorizing the construction of Southmoor. The 1975 *DPS Report*, 28, heralded the impending completion of the building. An April 12, 1977, DPS PR outlined the scope of Southmoor School and announced its planned dedication on April 18. Also see FF 5:68 of the DPS papers. *BN*, September 18, 1998, and November 20, 1998, observed the neighborhood push to reopen Southmoor as an elementary. The publication celebrated the relaunching of the school, August 20, 1999. *BN*, March 3, 1999, reported the gifted and talented program at Southmoor. Volume three will discuss the gifted and talented program and the Rocky Mountain School of Expeditionary Learning.

DPS records on Centennial School are FF 3:110–12. *SN*, April 8, 1974, p. 35, observed plans to sell Alcott and Berkeley schools. I deal with all three schools in *North Side Story*, 89, 457–59, 461, 497, 498.

DP, February 6, 1976, p. 14, reported plans to phase out Thatcher and McKinley schools. FF 5:68–82 and 6:85–90 of the DPS papers look at the new combined Thatcher-McKinley building. They stress the ecological emphasis of the schoolhouse and outline the programs at the academy. DPS PR, February 14 and February 15, 1977, emphasized plans for McKinley-Thatcher and solar energy. The 1976 *DPS Report*, 19, heralded the proposed schoolhouse. Also see *Focus*, September 1979, p. 1. A January 13, 1976, DPS PR, p. 2, told of plans for McKinley, Thatcher, Lincoln, and Washington Park schools. FF 4:59 of the DPS papers is on the sale of the old Thatcher building. The South High History room has files on all elementary schools feeding into the high school. *DP*, September 28, 2019, p. 5A, reported the $5 million renovation of McKinley-Thatcher. I give my take on McKinley and Thatcher schools in *University Park*, 102, 118, 165–71, 224, 241.

School Book, 113, 114, 326, 406–08, glances at Boulevard School. DPL WH 2103 is a one-box holding about Boulevard, especially PTA records. Additionally, there is a small collection about it at NSAC. I drew on the latter for my mention of Boulevard School in *North Side Story*, 176–77. In 2013, Walter Keller recalled attending Boulevard School in the 1970s.

The story of Globeville School is in *School Book*, 121, 128, 129, 258, 259, 354. *DP*, February 28, 2019, p. 5C, discusses Laradon School. Most of all, see George V. Kelly and Harry Farrar, *Garden of Hope: Laradon Hall* (Boulder: Pruett, 1980). Chalkbeat, October 7, 2019, told of the opening of a preschool in the old Globeville School at Laradon Hall. *Schools for a New Century* will probe the links between DPS and preschool programs.

DP, June 17, 1983, mentioned the leasing of Washington Park School to Denver Academy. *Cmq*, April 1984, p. 2, told of the sale of the schoolhouse. *GCCC*, January 2019, p. 19, heralded Denver Academy. In *Washington Park*, I look at Myrtle Hill and Washington Park schools, 84–88, Lincoln School, 59–62, and Steele School, 174–78. FF 6:115–19 are the DPS records on Washington Park School.

SN, May 30, 1972, p. 50, observed plans to phase out Alameda School. *SN*, May 29, 1973, p. 39, reported plans to close and raze the building. *SN*, April 8, 1974, p. 35, announced the intention to sell the structure. I touch on its fate in

South Broadway, 105–06. DPS files on it are FF 3:2–3. An undated article features Sherman School as a center of art programs is in the 1984–85 clipping notebook in GP. *School Book*, 34, 35, 36, 173, 184, 261, 386, 391, outlines the history of Sherman School. *South Broadway*, 109–10, talks about the Art Students League.

SRv, June 1924, p. 3, hailed the new Elyria School. Frances Melrose reviewed the history of the neighborhood, *RMN*, August 10, 1986. A copy is in FF 4:58 of the DPS records. FF 4:59 is on the sale of the schoolhouse. Also see Elizabeth L. MacMillan, *Elyria: Denver's Forgotten Suburb, 1881–1941* (n.p.: n.p., 2004), 21, 26, 47–48, Jerome Smiley, *History of Denver* (Denver: *Denver Times*, 1901), 651, *Cmq*, May 1979, p. 4, and Forrest, *Schools*, 35.

Jean Sidinger remembered teaching in the old Swansea School during a discussion on September 28, 2019. In November 2018, Leanne Vargas reminisced about attending the new building and being bused to Holm in the late 1970s/early 1980s. FF 6:76–81 of the DPS papers deal with the replacement Swansea School. *RMN*, September 16, 1975, pictured the destruction of the old building. *BN*, March 15, 1996, complained about overcrowding at the school. *BN*, February 16, 2001, told of the authorization of an addition to the building. FF 6:79 has an undated newspaper clipping about lead contamination at Swansea. Chalkbeat, *DP*, July 14, 2019, p. 3B, discussed how air pollution threatened students. It also mentioned the monitoring of the impact of I-70 on Garden Place School.

RMN, June 20, 1992, p. 4N, looked at Tony Garcia and the renovation of Elyria School as the home of Su Teatro. I trace the troupe's move to Santa Fe Drive in *West Side*, 390–92. *DP*, November 15, 2012, p.4C, reported plans for the apartment complex at the old Elyria School.

A January 13, 1976, DPS PR, p. 2, outlined its plans for Columbian School. *Cmq*, December 1983–January 1984, p. 3, told of the board awarding the construction contract for the new schoolhouse. FF 3:131–35 of the DPS papers focus on the 1984–85 Columbian building. *Coloradan*, January 1, 1893, p. 9, featured the 1892 schoolhouse. *DP*, June 6, 1983, reported the drive to save the old Columbian building. An undated article from the *News*, in the in the 1985–86 PTA Clipping Notebook in GP, observed the immediate overcrowding of the school. *BN*, March 19, 1999, mentioned the authorization of the new roof. There is a file on Columbian at NSAC.

In informal conversations between 2010 and 2016, the late Wally Ginn recalled his clashes with members of the school board, especially Omar Blair, on trying to save vintage DPS schoolhouses. *BN*, March 22, 1996, emphasized the achievements of the landmark process. *DP*, March 17, 1991, celebrated East as an official landmark.

NSAC has a file on Smedley, including materials on the campaign of Save Old Smedley. I mention the effort in *North Side Story*, 90. *School Book*, 111, 236, 379, 404, traces the origins of the school.

My *Civic Center*, 275–78, 280–83, deals with Evans School. Also see *School Book*, 117, 145, 161, 162, 245–46, 273, 396. Articles on the possible future use of Evans School include *GCCC*, August 2019, p. 9 and *DP*, August 7, 2019, p. 15A.

The online version of *DBJ*, December 10, 2019, reported the sale of Evans School and the hopes of the new owners.

There are numerous articles about overcrowded schools and the need for action in 1985–86 PTA Clipping Notebook in GP. All are from the *Post* or *News*. They lack dates and page numbers. So did a letter to the editor by a teacher from Montbello High School, John Dellinger, complaining that the increased number of administrators was more a nuisance than a help to instructors. These were officials who endlessly looked over the shoulder of teachers during the 1980s.

The 1918 *DPS Report*, 98–99, glanced at the district warehouse at West 13th Avenue and Fox Street. The 1927 *DPS Report*, 66–67, mentioned its expansion. FF 1:73 of the DPS papers has plans for what became the Hill Top facility. *SB*, May 15, 1967, p. 140, told of the district leasing warehouse space at 2705 West Fifth Avenue. *BN*, November 20, 2000, reported plans to buy land as part of the Hilltop Service Center. *SN,* April 8, 1974, p. 35, announced the intention to sell 1278 Fox Street.

SRv, January 1961, p. 3, observed that the growth of administrators did not match the expansion of the district. *SRv*, November 1967, p. 2, emphasized that a new administration building was part of that year's bond issue. *SN,* March 11, 1974, p. 31, and April 8, 1974, p. 35, reported the decision to buy 900 Grant Street for $3.75 million. CANS, *Judicial Fiat*, 12, lists the vote on buying the midrise. FF 1:40 of the DPS papers, advertising the sale of 900 Grant Street, claims it was built in 1968, stating DPS bought it for $3.2 million. *SN*, February 3, 1975, p. 27, told of the exit from 414 14th Street and the sale of that edifice. *School Book*, 216, 277–78, 348, 354, 359, reviews the construction and evolution of 414 14th Street.

A supplement to the September 14, 1969, Empire section of *DP*, "City within a City," outlines the hopes of Montbello. Kelly, *Old Gray Mayors*, 185–87, heralds the annexation of Montbello as a far-sighted achievement. Pearson, "Denver Case," 173, observes the power DPS gained in 1967 in having a say on annexations. FF 8:39 of the DPS papers includes a copy of *Montbello Portfolio*, a 1979 promotion guide to the area by the Montbello Citizens' Committee. It outlines the origins of the community, pp. 1–2, and the push for schools, p. 3.

A file on Montbello is in the Micky Miller papers at the Beck Archives at DU. Drawer 16 of the Branscombe papers had files on Montbello and Green Valley Ranch. *RMN*, December 4, 1966, p. 74, announced Montbello development plans. *DP*, September 14, 1999, p. 1C, and *RMN*, September 6, 1996, p. 32A, looked back on 30 years of the community. A 50-year retrospection was in *DP*, September 22, 2016, p. 4C YourHub. On November 28, 2017, Angel Garcia recalled being among the pioneer settlers of Montbello in 1967. Over the years, Bettina Basanow has shared her memories as a longtime resident of Montbello who has participated in many community ventures. *Pioneer Press*, December 3, 1986, in FF 5:59 of the DPS papers, discusses the development of Montbello schools.

The October 1985 issue of the *Green Valley Gazette* outlined the hopes of Green Valley Ranch and the firms promoting it. *RMN*, February 23, 1985, sketched the aspirations of the area. It told about the development of the enclave, September

16, 1993, p. 1B; cf. *RMN*, July 18, 1998, p. 7. *RMN*, September 15, 1984, had a special advertising section "G" on Green Valley Ranch.

Forrest, *Schools*, 48, discusses early Montbello schools, including the evolution of Oakland School, 49. *SB*, May 15, 1967, p. 137, reported leasing space for Montbello School. *SN*, September 2, 1975, p. 3, mentions the Montbello Cottage and the Montbello Apartment. FF 5:130–34 of the DPS papers focus on the Oakland School replacement building. DPS PR, November 1, 1984, touted the dedication of the new Oakland School on Dearborn Street. Also see *Pioneer Press*, November 19, 1986.

FF 1:21 of the Noel papers has reports about the push for Montbello High School and the development of schools in the area. An unidentified January 18, 1983, clipping in the 1982–83 PTA Historian's Notebook in GP observed problems at Montbello schools.

SN, September 1, 1971, p. 2, reported the authorization of Amesse School. I briefly mention John Amesse in *Mayfair*, 179. Volume three will discuss Amesse and other schools in Montbello and Green Valley Ranch in the 21st century.

A file on Dolly McGlone is in the DU Archives in the collection on honorary degrees. I mention him in *West Side*, 187–88. Kelly, *Garden of Hope*, 89–119, stresses his work at Laradon Hall. FF 6:53 of the DPS papers tells of the push to name what became Southmoor School for McGlone. *DP*, April 2, 1975, p. 40, and April 4, 1975, p. 71, reviewed the life of Charles McGlone.

FF 5:58–65 of the DPS holdings are on McGlone School. *SN*, October 6, 1974, p. 9, reported naming the new school. It told of the planned opening, December 12, 1977, p. 25, and the impending dedication, April 25, 1978, p. 54. The 1975 *DPS Report*, 28, and the 1976 *DPS Report*, 19, observed progress on the school. A January 13, 1976, DPS PR mentioned McGlone School was modeled on Kaiser School. *SN*, November 17, 1995, observed Dan Rather's visit to McGlone.

SN, October 10, 1972, p. 9, reported the authorization of Barney Ford School. FF 4:90–93 of the DPS papers deal with the academy. *DP*, March 28, 1999, p. 29A, related the lore about Barney Ford. Marian Talmadge and Iris Gilmore, *Barney Ford, Black Baron* (New York: Dodd, Mead, 1973), is the major study of him. Annette Student, *Denver's Riverside Cemetery* (San Diego: CSN Books, 2006), 139–41, celebrates him. The April 7, 1997, report of the DPS department of planning on "School Accreditation Guidelines," p. 16, has a copy of the Ford School improvement plan. DPS web sites of most uneven quality discuss achievement and enrollment at Ford School and its links to the Denver Center for International Studies, a program I will deal with in *Schools for a New Century*.

DP, July 20, 1998, observed the naming of Jessie Maxwell School. FF 5:56–57 of the DPS collection deal with the academy. *BN*, January 22, 1998, announced plans for the building and the intention of making it a fundamental school. I touch on Jessie Maxwell in *Curtis Park*, 353–54. Thomas Hornsby Ferril remembered her in *RMH*, January 4, 1969, p. 8. *SN*, March 10, 1981, p. 52, celebrated her as a retired principal. Tollette, *CBLP*, 74–75, Grant, *Growing Up in Black Denver*, 71–72, and *RMN*, May 8, 1958, p. 53, heralded her achievements.

Our Neighborhood Schools in Alweis, *Rebels Remembered* celebrates the leadership of Lila O'Boyle. There is a holding on Marie Greenwood at BCL, ARL56. She laments the discrimination she encountered at Morey and her views of the schools in an interview in *Our Neighborhood Schools*. Her granddaughter and namesake, Marie L. Greenwood, celebrated the educator on her reaching her centennial, *By the Grace of God: The True Life Journey of 100 Years* ([Denver]: Greenwood & Associates, [2013]). *DP*, April 17, 2012, p. 4A, celebrated her 100th birthday. Stephens, *African Americans*, 106, and Mauck *Five Points*, 83, observe her importance. I touch on her in *Curtis Park*, 352–54. 9News reported her death on November 16, 2019; the *Post* followed on November 19, 2019, p. 1A.

BN, October 6, 2000, announced plans for what became Greenwood School, and the naming of the building, March 2, 2001. Also see *RMN*, April 1, 2001, p. 26A. *DP*, January 1, 2017, p. 2A, observed the poverty of students attending the academy.

DPS PR, February 15, 1977, and July 22, 1977, outlined plans for Montbello High School and the district's collaboration with the city for the adjacent park. Also see *SN*, October 4, 1976, p. 7, and *Focus*, March 1980, p. 8. A four-page DPS bulletin of April 21, 1980, celebrated Montbello High School. *SN*, September 16, 1980, p. 7, heralded the ribbon-cutting.

FF 5:59 of the DPS papers explains the problems DPS had in obtaining the site for McGlone School. FF 8:33 looks at the development of Montbello High School. Included are articles from *DP*, March 5, 1976, and *RMN*, March 5, 1976, p. 20, outlining the deal with Micky Miller.

FF 8:33–44 of the DPS records focus on Montbello High School. *RMN*, January 10, 1983, p. 8, and *RMN*, February 11, 1983, p. 10, told of challenges at the building and problems with the middle school. Additionally, there are scattered, mostly undated and unidentified, articles in the 1982–83 PTA News Notebook in GP on difficulties at Montbello High School. Materials on Martin Luther King Middle School include FF 7:57–60 of the DPS papers, DPS PR, January 9, 1987, and October 31, 1991, and *BN*, January 14, 2000, and January 21, 2000.

Chapter Fourteen

Transformations

I n May 1977, voters needed to fill three seats on the school board. As the polling approached, Ted Hackworth announced in March that he was not going to try to keep his place on the body. Three years earlier, he had failed in a run for the state Senate, 9,665, against Arch Decker, 11,926, a conservative Democrat who later became a Republican. Hackworth remained active in neighborhood politics, especially the Harvey Park Improvement Association.

Hackworth successfully ran for an open seat on city council in 1979, representing far southwest Denver. In the city legislature, he often opposed trendy proposals and was frequently on the losing end of measures that passed by 11–2 or 12–1 margins. Term limits forced him to retire in 2003. DPS subsequently dubbed the playing fields at Sabin School, 3050 South Vrain Street, in his honor. The former champion of neighborhood schools died at age 83 on November 9, 2009.

Incumbent Bob Crider led the polling in the 1977 school elections with 22,317 votes. A newcomer, Marion Hammond, 16,706, was second. Kay Schomp kept her seat, coming in third, 15,569. The DCTA had enthusiastically backed all three victors. This was the first time it had swept a race since it started intervening in school board contests in the 1960s.

Crider stated he was pleasantly surprised by the size of his triumph. A key to his political success was an ability to project the wisdom of the everyday citizen opposed to fancy schemes of experts and improvers. The board member endlessly stressed his humble roots. He claimed to have affiliated with the Democrats as the party of the poor and workers. On the side, he was a Rotarian, Elk, and a member of the Knights of Columbus.

Hammond was the pastor of St. Thomas Episcopal in Park Hill at 22nd Avenue and Dexter Street. Born in Gardner, Kansas, in 1927, he grew up in and around Kansas City. After earning his bachelor's degree from DU in 1948, he gained his ordination in 1951 after attending the Berkeley Divinity School in New Haven, Connecticut. His first pastorate was at St. Barnabas Church in Cortez, Colorado. He took charge of St. Thomas in 1963, becoming a central figure in the church-based Park Hill Action Committee.

Listening to a leading member of the congregation, Bea Branscombe, Hammond sent his five children to Denver Public Schools. The preacher became a close personal friend of her husband, Art, the school reporter for the *Denver Post*. The preacher was also a colleague of Fred Thomas, the civil rights activist behind the desegregation lawsuit. The parson conducted the funeral of another companion, former district attorney and mayoral aspirant Dale Tooley at the church in April 1985. The preacher invited blacks to St. Thomas, introducing jazz and African masses. The congregation additionally had outreach programs to teenagers and homosexuals. St. Thomas was a pioneer in pushing the ordination of women.

The school board victor followed in the tradition of clerics seeking places on the DPS governing agency. In 1961, for example, C. Elroy Shilkles of First Baptist Church failed in a run for the board. John Gerberding of Epiphany Lutheran suffered defeat in 1965. Park Hill Congregational minister Richard Kozelka likewise failed in 1967. Ramiro Cruz-Ahedo, the pastor of Inner City Parish, a Methodist-oriented congregation by West High School, lost in the 1975 school board campaign.

On November 7, 1976, six months before running for the board, Hammond had celebrated a mass for DPS. He specifically invited the superintendent, members of the school board, teachers, and administrators. This was his personal way of saying thanks for the job they had been doing. The preacher held the service shortly after he had lost his bid to gain election as the Episcopal bishop of Hawaii.

"A Time to Reach Out" was Hammond's election slogan. He managed to raise about $30,000 for his run. Key supporters included Dale Tooley and state treasurer Roy Romer. Schomp and Hammond were something of an unofficial team, sharing facilities and volunteers.

Dorothie Clark, an educator and civil rights veteran who was the head of the black studies department at UNC, was the candidate of the black caucus for the board. During the mid-1970s, she had been on the Community Education Council (CEC), the court-appointed panel that was supposed to assure that desegregation worked. In 1983, she came in fourth in a run for the two open at-large seats on city council. She did not do as well in her 1977 school board bid, placing seventh, 9,804.

Crider ran on the School Committee Ticket, an ad hoc coalition trying to keep alive the anti-busing success that had led him to victory in 1971. He failed to carry his running mates into office, housewife and educator Dorothy Gotlieb, 13,613, and contractor Alan D. Sortone, 10,887. Gotlieb and Sortone had joined Crider in making it clear they opposed busing. Simultaneously, Crider gained the nod of the Democratic Party.

Attorney Richard J. Callahan was the number-five finisher, 12,811. CANS leader Nolan Winsett was far behind, 5,141. Other candidates in the field of 18 included Lee Tafoya. The custodian at Schmitt School, he was the president of the DPS Association of Building Operating Employees. He gathered the support

SN

In 1977, Reverend Marion Hammond, right, joined the school board. He was part of a new pro-integration majority on the body with Kay Schomp who is standing next to him. Bob Crider was the third person elected to the board that year. They are sworn in by Judge Zita Weinshienk, left.

of 3,174 voters. DU student and DPS graduate Meyer Kadovitz, received 1,407 votes, trailed by Socialist Workers Party contender Miguel Pendas, 585.

On the board, the preacher was a firm fourth vote for the liberal wing with Blair, Schomp, and Rockwell. Bernie Valdez often joined them against Crider and Naomi Bradford. The new board elected Blair president. Rockwell was vice president. The two remained the leaders of the board for the next four years.

As head of the board, Blair announced he wanted to open up its meetings. To do so, he ordered the removal of the barrier separating the public and members of the board in the agency's meeting room. Ideally, this showed the board was indeed ready to listen to members of the everyday public rather than treating them as nuisances.

Besides dealing with Denver issues, Blair was most active in the Council of Great City Schools. This was a national organization of large urban school districts. Its conventions were excellent places to make connections. Executives looking for work often frequented them. Back in the early 1970s, for example, Louis Kishkunas met Jim Perrill at a gathering of the group. The encounter eventually led to his appointment as DPS superintendent. Blair won election as the group's president in 1982. That year, he also gained the presidency of the Colorado Association of School Boards.

On June 15, 1978, about a year before the expiration of his term, Bernie Valdez quit the board, citing his numerous other commitments. Dr. Fernie Baca-Moore, a professor at the UCD School of Education, replaced him. After having received her

BACA–MOORE BELIEVES:

- Denver is a vital city. Part of this vitality is dependent upon a first class school system. Our schools need to meet the challenges ahead through positive thinking leaders.

- Quality education for all Denver's children is their right and our responsibility. Education in the "basics" is where it starts.

- Taxpayers should get full value for every dollar invested in schools.

- Discipline must be fair and effective -- schools free from disruption.

In 1978, Fernie Baca-Moore, right, gained appointment to succeed Bernie Valdez on the school board. She failed in her bid the next year to stay on the body.

bachelor's from the forerunner of UNC, she had gained her master's and doctorate from CU. The new member had served on various appointive boards such as the Colorado Commission on the Status of Women. In 1970, she was a Centennial State representative to the White House Conference on Children and Youth. The new board member had taught at Merrill from 1961 to 1967 before joining the DPS administration. Sworn in on August 10, 1978, she was the board's first Latina.

After Valdez retired from his city post in 1979, both Latinos and the mainstream political establishment heralded him. Many Hispanic civic and business associations came to have their quarters in the Bernard Valdez Heritage Center in the old West Side Courthouse at West Colfax Avenue and Speer Boulevard. The Latin American Research and Service Agency handed out annual Bernie Valdez awards. On March 18, 1996, Denver Public Library opened a new branch, the Valdez–Perry Library, at 4690 Vine Street in the overwhelmingly Hispanic Elyria neighborhood. It saluted Valdez and the John Perry family which had donated the land for the athenaeum. The former school board member passed away in November 1997.

William Schroeder and Franklin Mullen

Fernie Baca-Moore was unable to hold her place on the board in the 1979 election when voters had to fill two seats. That year Omar Blair, who failed to answer a PTA questionnaire asking for his views, came in second, holding his seat with 28,557 votes. The integration establishment supported him. Key endorsers included Ed Benton, Bernie Valdez, Bruce Rockwell, Marion Hammond, Rachel Noel, Paul Sandoval, and Minoru Yasui. Blair trailed the 55-year old William R. "Bill" Schroeder Sr., 31,465.

Preservationist and park advocate Carolyn Etter was third, 27,536. For 15 years, she had been most active in education issues. Included was leadership in the PTA and serving as an observer for the Community Education Council. In the early 1970s, she was the PTA representative on a committee getting the city to adopt a series of bicycle routes. With her husband Don, who was once a partner with the powerful law firm of Holland & Hart, she was subsequently the city's manager of parks and recreation. Former board member James Voorhees was a co-chairman of her school board bid.

Alberta Jesser, something of Schroeder's running mate as an anti-busing candidate, followed, 24,539. She was a retired DPS teacher and administrator who had been principal of Fallis School for 16 years. Baca-Moore, whom the DCTA endorsed, came in fifth, 22,725. Other candidates were teacher Joan Baucher, 11,736, Schmitt School custodian Lee Tafoya, 7,582, instructor Carney Crisler, 5,713, Meyer Kadovitz, a college student who grew up in North Denver, 4,572, and counselor Mark Mandler, 4,021.

DPL

Schroeder was in the pattern of those who opposed busing. A native of Faribault, Minnesota, born on May 20, 1923, his affluent family lost almost everything in *In 1979, Bill Schroeder, a former police officer, won a seat on the school board. Here he looks at a Garden Place School scrapbook with an eager young learner.*

the Depression. They came to Denver to start again. He dropped out of school at age 14 to help support his mother after the sudden death of his father. Eventually, he returned to school and earned his general equivalency degree from Opportunity School. He subsequently took classes at DU and CU. The future board member tried his hand at a number of jobs from being a police officer to a bouncer to a truck driver to a ditch digger to a delivery man.

Around the end of World War II, Schroeder built his home at 1620 South Perry Street, then mostly an open, undeveloped area. While on the police department, he founded Schroeder & Company, a real estate agency in 1947. After simultaneously running the brokerage and being on the force, the contender left the police department to devote himself to real estate. For years, Schroeder & Company was at 3738 West Colfax Avenue. It was later at 4393 West Florida Avenue. Schroeder was most active in junior sports programs and the Boy Scouts. Over the years, he held offices in the Denver Board of Realtors and had been president of the Optimists Club.

From the beginning, Schroeder was among those opposed to busing, seeing it as a scheme that destroyed neighborhood schools while it did not help children ordered onto the bus. During the 1970s, he was frequently on the ballot as

Contractor Franklin Mullen spent freely in 1981 in winning a seat on the school board.

a Republican stalwart. While cynics stated he hoped that people might vote for him in confusion with the city's popular Democratic Congresswoman Pat Schroeder, he had already run for mayor in 1971 when he received 3,473 votes, projecting himself as a tough law-and-order former policeman. This was a year before Pat Schroeder's entry into politics. Anti-busing board member Naomi Bradford backed Bill Schroeder in 1979. So did Republican state Senator Sam Zakhem, a longtime financial contributor to the anti-busing cause. In 1982, Bill Schroeder briefly sought the Republican nomination for Congress against Pat Schroeder.

The 1979 school board candidate presented himself as a personal example of the trauma of busing and the decline of DPS. He observed he had sent his five children through District #1 schools. When it came time for them to enroll their children in school, all moved to the suburbs, not wanting to be part of a court-ordered system whereby abstract integration, not quality education, was at the heart of DPS. He built on this, campaigning right when Judge Matsch was again ordering around the district because it did not precisely comply with the court's rigid bean-counting approach to integration. On the school board, the new member allied himself with Crider and Bradford.

Those opposed to busing regained control of the board in 1981 when contractor/real estate investor Franklin "Frank" Mullen, 54, defeated Ginny Rockwell at the same time Naomi Bradford gained re-election. As much as the contests a decade earlier, the balloting focused on forced busing. The victors made it clear they still did not like federal court oversight of the schools. With Ronald Reagan in the White House, they hoped this would soon end.

Born on March 31, 1927, Mullen grew up in a small town in New Mexico where his mother oversaw a one-room schoolhouse. He reminisced about her discussing, over the dinner table, the toils of teaching. This convinced him he had to do his all to advance education. The victor was a relative newcomer to the community, having arrived in Denver in the early 1970s. He was proud of having been a Marine during World War II. After the fighting, he briefly sought to make his way in Hollywood, re-enlisting during the Korean War. Out of the service, he turned to real estate, eventually expanding into construction. In the Mile High City, he flourished as a developer and broker. He lived by the Polo Club at 2552 Alameda Avenue, later dwelling in an elite downtown residential highrise.

After surviving a private plane crash in 1961 and a heart attack in 1979, Mullen dedicated himself to education reform. He poured $100,000 of his personal funds into winning the school board race. The contender effectively employed the money for television advertising. He led the field with 18,351 votes. Bradford received 16,597. Carolyn Etter, who had also come in third in the 1979 polling, trailed at 12,619. Rockwell showed little dynamism in the election, finishing a distant fourth, 10,364. Armando Atencio, the city's manager of social services, was the Hispanic contender. He was far behind, 3,614, followed by John Ragan, 2,495, the assistant dean of admissions at DU. Gretchen D. Carmen Palmer, a self-avowed Christian who was a businesswoman living in southwest Denver, received 1,621 votes. Angeline Heaton, a multi-lingual physician from Park Hill, was last, 1,081. Around 15 percent of eligible voters participated in the contest. There was no specific black contender in the balloting.

Already on the night of his victory, Mullen announced that he was backing Bob Crider as the new president of the board. In an unusually gracious statement, Naomi Bradford, who became vice president, saluted Omar Blair, the outgoing president. He had, she observed, fairly treated the previous board minority. Blair sourly responded that the triumph of Mullen and Bradford had set back the city by at least 20 years. On the board, Mullen insisted the governing body take an active hand in the day-to-day management of the schools. Additionally, he called for upgrading teacher salaries while having the district promote itself to parents and the business community.

The 1983 Election

Crider did not seek re-election to the school board in 1983. Back in the 1970s, he had moved from northwest Denver to 5998 West Columbia Place in southwest Denver. His new home was close to Ted Hackworth. They remained political and personal friends. At the same time Hackworth gained the seat on city council in 1979 to represent far southwest Denver, Crider successfully campaigned for an at-large seat on council. He later stated it was "fun" simultaneously being on both council and the school board.

Besides these two posts, Crider was a real estate salesman. He entered that profession in 1974 when the trucking firm for which he had worked went out of business. He joined the agency of Nolan Winsett, the founder and head of the anti-busing Citizens Association for Neighborhood Schools. Crider later was a salesman for a couple of meat packing firms, pulling on his links with Hackworth. In reflecting on his school board service, Crider stated that court intervention had "ruined" District #1. As a member of the agency overseeing DPS, it had been his duty to try to mitigate the damage. He defined an integrated school as a place where everybody was welcome.

On council, Crider often voted with Hackworth, being part of a fading conservative block on council through the 1980s. Quite a friendly man, he emerged as president of council in 1986–87. At times, he lost control of the meetings, particularly during public hearings. All the while, it was obvious that he had greater political ambitions.

For the most part, city council left school issues alone, seeing them as the purview of the board of education. Nor did success in a race for one body translate

Paul Sandoval projected himself as being everywhere and concerned with everything when he unsuccessfully ran for city council in 1971. He joined the school board in 1983.

into victory in a contest for the other. Illustrative is how back in 1965, Houston "Hoot" Gibson, who had won election to council in 1963 to represent southwest Denver, unsuccessfully sought a place on the board while he still had two years on his council term. Former city councilman Larry Perry, from far northwest Denver, lost in his 1983 bid for the school board. Happy Haynes, who represented Park Hill and Montbello on city council at the turn of the century, gained a seat on the board of education in 2011. Marcia Johnson, who was on the school board from 1989 to 1995, won a seat on council in 2003 for southern Park Hill and much of the area east of Colorado Boulevard to the north of Cherry Creek.

In 1991, Crider won the open race for auditor. This is the city official who is supposed to be the taxpayers' watchdog. A duty is to intervene in controversial issues if he believes something is amiss in their funding. For the most part, Crider never exercised such power. In particular, he was auditor right when problems and costs exploded at the arising Denver International Airport. The former school board member failed to investigate what was happening there. Even so, he continued to project himself as a voice of common sense and opposition to a smug and sterile political elite. This was his message in 1995 when he challenged incumbent Wellington Webb for mayor. His campaign never gained traction. The auditor was a distant third in the polling with about 10 percent of the vote. Crider subsequently moved to Canon City where he died on August 16, 2017.

Kay Schomp also stepped down from the school board in 1983. She remained active in educational issues. She was a co-chairwoman of a 1985 effort to overhaul the state's school finances. Most of all, she was a loud proponent of keeping and enhancing DPS classes on art and music. After the district had cut many of them, she was a central actress in creating a magnet school for artistically gifted youngsters, the Denver School of the Arts, in 1991. She died at age 83 on November 20, 2000. Her funeral was at Montview Presbyterian Church, a place closely tied with many other leaders of DPS. At one time, Denver Public Schools had the Kay Schomp Commitment to Excellence Award. The School of the Arts dubbed its recital hall for her. The academy also had an endowment fund named in her memory. The main branch of the Denver Public Library included the Kay Schomp Elevators.

Schomp's close associate, Ginny Rockwell, also remained politically active after her 1981 defeat for re-election to the school board. She was among the many wealthy individuals rallying to the mayoral campaign of Federico Peña in 1983. He named her to the library commission right when Denver Public Library was in massive transformation. From being the university of the people that stored yesterday's volumes, it more sought to serve as something of a bookstore featuring bestsellers while it disposed of old stock. Additionally, Rockwell was active in the Junior League while being a visible supporter of the Denver Art Museum and the Colorado Symphony. A stroke felled her on April 13, 2003, at age 79.

Back in 1985, turbulence rocked Colorado National Bank, headed by her husband, Bruce Rockwell. Taking responsibility, he stepped down from the post. He moved over to lead the Colorado Foundation, a newly formed philanthropy focusing on improved health care. He passed away on July 13, 2004.

Like Schomp and Crider, Marion Hammond left the school board in 1983. He retired as pastor of St. Thomas Episcopal five years later. The preacher subsequently moved to an Episcopal community in Santa Fe, New Mexico. The result was three open seats in the 1983 balloting. Paul Sandoval, Judy Morton, and William R. "Bill" Schumacher filled the posts.

In the early 1970s, Sandoval was an aspiring young Chicano politician. Born on June 29, 1944, the ninth of 11th children, he came to Denver with his family when he was six. (In some accounts he was born in Denver.) His father was a butcher. The young man grew up near Annunciation Church at 36th Avenue and Humboldt Street. By this time, it had a large Hispanic membership.

With his siblings, Sandoval attended the parish school. A sympathetic nun tutored him, helping him learn English. He went on to marry a former nun who was a school teacher. After getting his diploma from Annunciation High School, he gained a bachelor's from the University of Colorado, going on to do graduate work in political science and economics.

For a while, Sandoval worked for the city in its section dealing with youth services. Social service, he explained, was a passion. Included was being active in a program seeking to reduce the dropout rate. When he launched his first political campaign at age 26 in 1971, seeking a seat on city council, he was a counselor at Community College of Denver. By that time, along with other members of his family, he was living on the North Side. His campaign literature declared he had lived in the council district his entire life. In asking for votes, he stated he was a young father who was deeply committed to community uplift and self-help.

Sandoval's bid for council came at a time when the politics of race and ethnicity were burgeoning. Some Latinos, not trusting the racist system, formed a militant Hispanic third party, La Raza Unida, in 1970. Against them, others, including Sandoval, insisted it was necessary to work within the Democratic Party. He was an also-ran in the field of eight for the council post.

In 1974, Sandoval easily brushed aside a challenge from West Denver state Representative Betty Benavidez to gain the Democratic nomination to the state

Senate, sweeping the contest in November. In the legislature, he stood out as a voice of the rising Latino population that wanted recognition. A cousin, Don Sandoval, also served in the state Senate. Another cousin, Joe Sandoval, became a DPS principal. Personally, Paul Sandoval claimed to embrace the improvement of the schools for his people, chairing a Chicano Education Project.

After easily winning re-election to the Senate in 1978, Paul Sandoval gained a place on the powerful Joint Budget Committee. He did not seek to stay in office in 1982. A redistricting, during which Denver lost a seat in the Senate in the wake of the 1980 census, threw him in the same constituency with incumbent Dennis Gallagher. A widely known politician with an excellent gift of gab who showed up at most community events and campaigned endlessly, Gallagher had seemingly unlimited political reach in North Denver. Though a plurality of those living in the district were Latino, Sandoval knew he probably could not win the election as an ethnic candidate against Gallagher, a man who especially had a lock on the vote of senior citizens. Back in 1978, Gallagher had kept his seat in Senate District #1, 11,247, over Republican Ray Fenster, 3,204. Sandoval, who had faced no opposition, gathered 6,702 votes. A problem was that many Latinos failed to register and vote.

After leaving the Senate, Sandoval ran for the school board in 1983. This was the same time when another young Hispanic politician, Federico Peña, gained election as mayor. In the process, Sandoval's victory in the school board contest was an indication that people of Latino heritage were finally asserting themselves politically.

Gaining a place on the school board also reflected the political nature of the board. While school elections remained nonpartisan, at times political aspirants treated service on the board as a half-way house as they sought another position. Those serving on the board do not receive any compensation. To do the job right, an incumbent has to devote plenty of time to the post. Many members put in more than 40 hours a week in meetings, studying documents, and connecting with constituents. While officeholders receive some rewards, such as being invited to many receptions, having expense accounts, and being compensated for travel to conferences, most have seen service on the board as a position of public responsibility. By shaping the schools, they have been convinced they are forging the city's future.

Sandoval was outspoken on this point. In running for the board, he stressed he knew budgets. He also emphasized he sent his daughters to Bryant–Webster School at 3635 Quivas Street. The politician lived close to it at 1744 West 36th Avenue.

Besides politics, Sandoval devoted himself to business. In association with Sal Carpio, in December 1983 he gained possession of Carbone's, a combination bar, bakery, and pizzeria at West 36th Avenue and Tejon Street. His partner had been La Raza Unida's candidate for Congress in 1970. Five years later, Carpio gained election to District #9 on city council. It had a serpentine shape, connecting Hispanic sections of downtown, Old East Denver, North Denver, West Denver, and South Denver. Once a teacher at Cole Junior High who went on to become an adjunct professor of sociology at Metro, Carpio had a mastery of federal urban assistance programs. Years after the Great Society and War on Poverty had faded,

School board member Paul Sandoval lived near Bryant–Webster School, West 36th Avenue and Quivas Street. At one time, Patricia Carpio was the principal, She was the wife of Sal Carpio, Sandoval's business partner and the local member of city council.

he managed to get Washington to pay for many new facilities for District #9. Back in the mid-1970s, he had been on the board of the Community Education Council, the court-appointed body working to see DPS successfully implemented busing. Carpio's wife, Patricia, was a teacher who became a DPS principal. She headed such schools as Cheltenham, Fairview, and, eventually, Bryant-Webster. Patricia Carpio was later in the front office.

Carpio and Sandoval renamed Carbone's "Papa Rox." The moniker honored Roxie Carbone, the father of Richard Carbone, the man from whom they had acquired Carbone's. Once a member of city council, Roxie Carbone was something of a father figure in the area who had brought together Hispanos and Italians. Many had called him Papa Roxie.

In 1983, Carpio passed on running for mayor in favor of Federico Peña. As he consolidated himself in office, the new mayor stood out as a foremost exponent of the corporate establishment. Increasingly, Carpio became alienated from the administration. He turned his attentions to Papa Rox. He realized he needed to build a business and a financial foundation for his family.

William Schumacher and Judy Morton

The 38-year-old Sandoval swept the 1983 school board election. He received 49,589 votes in a field of 12. William R. Schumacher came in second, 38,494. Last on the ballot, his name was next to Sandoval—far and away, Sandoval had the best name recognition of all the candidates.

Schumacher was the son of German immigrants, born in Denver on September 19, 1921. Soon after his birth, his father, a railroad fireman, died in a crash. The future board member graduated from Manual in 1939 where he was an all-star football player. This earned him a scholarship to the University of Denver. He left school in 1942 to serve in the Army Air Forces. After the end of the war, Schumacher returned to DU, earning his bachelor's in social science and physical education in 1946. Four years later he received a master's in school administration.

Originally Schumacher taught social studies and history at South High where he doubled as a coach and a physical education instructor. Before long, he was a counselor. In 1960, he emerged as the inaugural assistant principal at the new Thomas Jefferson High School. Then he was principal of Lake Junior High. From there, he took charge of George Washington in 1967, holding the post for two years where he established himself as a no-nonsense administrator. Along the way, Schumacher was among those helping forge the Latin American Research and Service Agency as an uplift program for Hispanic Denver. Additionally, he was a strong supporter of Junior Achievement.

In 1969, Schumacher took a break from DPS when he moved to Brussels, spending three years as the superintendent of an international school that primarily catered to the children of American citizens living in Belgium. He returned to DPS in 1972 as principal of Place Junior High. Schumacher retired in the spring of 1979, when he was the district's supervisor of personnel services. In 1982, the DPS Athletic Hall of Fame enshrined him. By the time he ran for the school board, the former principal operated a travel agency.

Like Sandoval, Schumacher was a registered Democrat. He ran for office stressing the need for more discipline while touting his background whereby a professional educator would have a say in the direction of the school board. In many ways, the candidate was a traditional conservative, quite the opposite of Sandoval who projected himself as a sophisticated ethnic liberal businessman.

The 40-year-old Judy Morton joined Sandoval and Schumacher in the winner's circle. Born in suburban Chicago in 1942, she had been a cheerleader in junior high school—she seemed to be the perpetual cheerleader, always urging on her fellows. Following her graduation from Iowa State University, she came to Denver as a junior high school teacher. Marriage led her to concentrate on raising her family. Active in school issues, she gained election as the head of the Denver PTA. With her husband, she ran a small college textbook publishing company. Among her ventures was creating a "My Heart is in the Denver Public Schools—and so are my Children" bumpersticker when she headed the PTA image committee in 1982.

The image committee had emerged in the 1970s as a way of selling the schools to an extremely skeptical public amidst the turbulence of court-ordered busing. Since at least 1974, the PTA worked with others in the community in trying to paint a positive picture of DPS. During the late 1970s, Morton was the PTA leader of the paired Wyatt and Slavens schools. A registered Republican, she built on her PTA activism, coming in third in the 1983 contest, 34,862. She dwelt at 2700 Bates Avenue in the Southern Hills neighborhood close to Slavens School.

Sandoval and Morton had been something of an unofficial team in the campaign. They received the backing of both the DCTA and the Chamber of Commerce. The two groups also endorsed a third candidate, William E. Richardson, 48, the manager of the East Denver YMCA who was active in the Adopt-a-School program. Back in January, an unofficial black caucus had nominated Richardson as the African-American contender in the race. He came in fifth in the balloting with 25,189 votes, behind Mary Baca, 34,249, who had been a community volunteer for 25 years. Included had been membership on the board of the Denver Urban Renewal Authority. As much as anything, Baca ran in the hope of supporting President Ronald Reagan's vow to redress the country's supposed educational crisis. The fourth-place finisher trailed Morton by about 600 votes.

NSAC

In 1983, retired DPS teacher, coach, principal, and administrator William Schumacher gained election to the board of education.

The 18-year-old James Ortega, got 12,827 in the polling. He was a West High student. Primarily, he ran to protest the hideous way he had been shoved into special education classes for the emotionally disturbed because he dared speak out on school issues. Sharron Frank, a former teacher, got 22,269 votes, just behind Sharon Clark, a DPS employee, 22,431. Former city councilman Larry Perry won 17,218 votes. A graduate of Manual, he sent his children to parochial schools. At the time he ran he was active in the improvement council at the Career Education Center, a DPS program providing high school students with a vigorous vocational education. Realtor Dick Peterson had 15,428 ballots. Ruth Miller, whose husband was a school custodian, followed with 14,254. Calvin Brott, a part-time janitor at the convention center trailed the field, 3,682.

On the board, Morton and Sandoval became personally quite close. More often than not, she voted with Sandoval. Franklin Mullen generally joined with them. Gossip claimed other things went on between Sandoval and Morton. The former state senator had divorced his first wife, Mary Helen, in 1982. She unsuccessfully sought to succeed Sal Carpio on city council in 1987 when the incumbent did not run for re-election.

Financial Problems

Before long, Sandoval clashed with Superintendent Joseph Brzeinski. So did Franklin Mullen. The head of the district projected himself as a master educator, insisting that he was in charge of all academic issues. To help others learn more about education, he sponsored regular Superintendent's Seminars, sessions where leading pedagogues addressed the DPS hierarchy. Brzeinski was also active in national

Photo by Phil Goodstein

*From its origins in 1889, Denver Public Library has had a close
relationship with Denver Public Schools. Here Tara Bannon Williamson,
the chief librarian of the Park Hill branch, marches in 2012 to advertise
the summer reading program the library conducts with the schools.*

educational organizations. On May 7, 1980, with Omar Blair, he was a guest in
Washington, D.C., for the inauguration of the new federal Department of Education.

The NEA had lobbied for a cabinet-level Department of Education since the
19th century. It used its clout with President Jimmy Carter to make it a reality.
As critics predicted, the new branch of the federal government did not change
anything of substance. Though the Republicans vowed to abolish the Department
of Education, they kept it going once they were in power.

In dealing with the day-to-day operations of DPS, Brzeinski was an acute
enough educator to realize the severe limitations of tests. He openly admitted that
when students did well on them, the district was quick to take credit, observing
the administration inevitably found excuses when test results were disappointing.
Even at that, he observed that in the course of the 1982–83 schoolyear, DPS
scholars exceeded the national norm on 42 of the 44 standardized tests they took.
Additionally, the system had a successful reading program. From the beginning
of Denver Public Library in 1889, DPS closely worked with the athenaeum in
promoting childhood literacy.

The standardized tests did not always go over easily. Teachers informed students
ahead of time when the exams were to be administered. In some cases, there was a
high absence rate on those days. In 1982, some pupils, complaining that the tests
were the be-all and end-all of the system, walked out of testing rooms. Eventually,
DPS used computer labs as places where students could practice taking online
standardized tests.

Brzeinski heavily stressed public relations. He held receptions to meet members of the community, staff, and instructors. Despite his outreach, many still distrusted the system. Typical were loud complaints by the PTA when the superintendent transferred numerous principals at the semester break in early 1978. The result was mass discontinuity in the schools. The criticism forced the district to cut back on such midyear moves.

All the while, severe financial problems haunted DPS. Denver was in a frenzied boom during the late 1970s/early 1980s. The city projected itself as the emerging energy capital of the world. Numerous skyscrapers arose as the offices of international petroleum corporations. Simultaneously, the suburbs sprawled. Nationally, inflation soared. Despite the creation of the Department of Education, which was supposed to assure better federal financing of schools, District #1 continually found itself lacking funds. Part of the reason Brzeinski sought to close schools was because DPS simply did not have the money to operate and maintain them.

Budget problems were particularly severe during the 1982–83 year. On a couple of occasions, the system was broke. This led it desperately to borrow $2.5 million

Author's collection

Even while community confidence in DPS dropped amidst court-ordered busing, the district insisted its students achieved superior results on standardized tests. It had already touted the results in 1956.

to cover an eight-day gap. No sooner had it paid off the high-interest loan than it had to borrow another $6.9 million to pay for ten days of operations. To prevent further borrowing, it increasingly slashed offerings. This had already been the case in 1977. As part of its borrowing $13 million that January, it drastically reduced the district's sponsorship of Head Start, closing 18 such programs in March.

In explaining the causes of the budget shortfall, the superintendent's office was amazingly imprecise in giving taxpayers exact numbers about the district's spending. This came out when it approached the voters on November 30, 1982, to hike the mill levy. The DCTA collaborated with the administration, mobilizing teachers to call voters to urge the passage of the measure. Some of the money was to pay for a 8.7 percent hike in instructor salaries. On this basis, the populace granted the mill levy request, 25,011–17,626.

The extra taxes were not enough. So the district soon complained. It was once more in the hole in 1983. Those dissatisfied with the system argued the money problems illustrated that either the superintendent had not been honest with the electorate or he was incompetent. They observed that while the cost of living in the area had escalated by 93.5 percent over the past decade, the district was spending nearly 220 percent more per pupil than it had in the early 1970s. This hinted that something more than inflation explained the budget shortages. It might be that the district was terribly mismanaged.

Financial conditions became even worse when the oil bubble burst in the mid-1980s. This included the collapse of assessed property valuations whereby tax revenue plummeted. Added to this were federal budget cuts under President Reagan that badly impacted public schools everywhere. As a sign of their distrust in DPS, as well as wishing to hold on to every penny they could in financially hard times, voters said no to a hike in the mill levy in a special election in November 1985. By then, the school board had forced out Brzeinski as superintendent.

The Dismissal of Brzeinski

Given the way Joseph Brzeinski had gained the superintendent's office in 1977 from a divided school board, he always had to look over his shoulder. Members of the board continued to squabble. Factions changed after each election. Added to the financial problems and the endless difficulties stemming from busing, this meant that the superintendent often treaded water.

Personally, Brzeinski was close to Omar Blair. The district's chief constantly squabbled with Blair's prime nemesis on the board, Naomi Bradford. On joining the agency in 1981, Mullen was also soon quite critical of Brzeinski. The body, the new member insisted, must be vigilant, supervising the superintendent.

Among Mullen's initiatives was having DPS acquire the land across the street from 900 Grant Street at the southwest corner of 10th Avenue and Grant Street for $75,000 in 1986. The property included the Henry M. Porter Manor. A 20-room mansion dating from 1912, it was then six modest residential units. A six-unit apartment house was next to it. DPS demolished the latter for more parking. It pondered tearing down the Porter House. Preservationists managed to save the building, getting it declared a landmark in 1989. Nothing ever came of Mullen's suggestion that DPS build a bridge over Grant Street to link the mansion with the administration headquarters. Nor did the board listen to the proposal of member Paul Sandoval that the house become a daycare facility for DPS employees. The district sold the residence in 1996 for $380,000.

The 1983 election of Sandoval tipped the scales against Brzeinski. Outgoing board president Bob Crider had specially supported Brzeinski, arranging for a year's extension of the superintendent's contract in February 1983, three months before the school board election in which Crider did not seek to retain his seat. The measure also extended by a year the contracts of Brzeinski's top aides. There was no advance notice of the proposal. Crider and the superintendent's supporters had sprung it on the other board members. The

Author's collection

During the 1980s, Judy Morton was president of the board of education. She usually allied herself with Paul Sandoval. They led the move to oust Joseph Brzeinski as superintendent in 1984.

extension, comparable to the deal Kishkunas had received from departing board members, was designed to handcuff the new board if its majority did not like the superintendent.

A sign that Brzeinski was out of favor came soon after the 1983 balloting when the board paid $25,000 to create a conference room on the seventh floor of 900 Grant Street. The table had space for only seven chairs. The design exiled Brzeinski to a nearby seat. Previously, the superintendent had sat next to the president at board committee meetings. Sandoval judged Brzeinski a weak leader when the superintendent failed to protest the snub.

(Besides the seventh floor room, the board also had a meeting room on the first floor where it held its public sessions. At times, members there sat in a three-part table whereby they looked at both each other and the audience. Board members made many of their crucial decisions at the work sessions on the seventh floor where there was limited space for outside observers. Not until the 1990s did the board start making tape recordings of such committee sessions.)

The superintendent, seemingly, had no idea why he provoked such opposition. He projected himself as low key, a compromiser who was able to work with everybody. In seeking accommodation, he failed to observe the highly charged disagreements on the board. Nor did he realize that his close association with Omar Blair led Blair's opponents on the school board to target him.

In February 1984, by a four-to-three majority, the board announced it was calling in outside consultants to evaluate the quality of the superintendent's performance. Those supporting the move explained that the district's budget was incomprehensible with a looming multi-million dollar shortfall. Amidst this, rumors swirled that the board was going to fire Brzeinski at a March 15 session. During a tense meeting, the members decided, four-to-three, to keep him in office.

Bradford was the swing vote. Apparently, Blair pressured her to keep the superintendent since the district was then engaged in a hearing before Judge Richard Matsch about the desegregation order. The ouster of Brzeinski, Blair implied, would assure DPS lost the case. As it turned out, this did not matter. Matsch ruled the United States District Court must retain oversight of the district.

As tensions mounted, the DCTA came to the defense of Brzeinski. The superintendent, it stated, was entitled to due process. The board stated this was the case. Before the ouster of Kishkunas, it had evaluated him and found him wanting. It did the same with Brzeinski. The study showed the superintendent's faults.

Meanwhile, it was obvious that Bradford had joined the three other critics of the superintendent who had called on Brzeinski to quit. Seeing what was coming, on April 27, 1984, he resigned as of the end of the schoolyear with two years remaining on his contract. He received an excellent settlement with the district. His wife, Willow, was a teacher at Opportunity School. His son, John, was once an administrator in Jefferson County Schools. A daughter, Judith, taught in Aurora. The former head of DPS passed away at age 90 on March 26, 2016.

Carle Stenmark took charge as interim superintendent on Brzeinski's departure. He was a senior administrator. A Denver native born on December 7, 1924, Stenmark made his way through Moore, Morey, and East. From there, he went to the religiously based Wheaton College in Illinois. During World War II he served with the Navy in the South Pacific. Staying in the reserves, he was proud to have also served during the Korean and Vietnam wars. The educator returned to Denver, going to work for DPS, teaching math in elementary schools. Within a few years, he was an elementary principal. Around 1960, he transferred to 414 14th Street. For a while, he was a key cog in the district's public relations office, helping issue the weekly *Superintendent's Bulletin*.

In 1970, Stenmark had been a candidate to replace Robert Gilberts as superintendent. When he lost out to Howard Johnson, he was the superintendent's administrative assistant before becoming assistant superintendent in charge of general administration. The board again passed him by in 1973 when Johnson retired. The next year, it named Stenmark deputy superintendent under Kishkunas. The board again said no to him in 1977 following the dismissal of Kishkunas when it selected Brzeinski to become the district's leader. Stenmark claimed this was because he had gotten on the wrong side of Omar Blair. The assistant superintendent had defended the staff against vindictive policies of some on the board. Now, with the ouster of Brzeinski, Stenmark finally appeared to have his chance.

James Scamman

The 60-year-old Stenmark was among the three finalists to become the next DPS superintendent in 1984 out of 77 who applied for the post. Nobody more pushed his candidacy than board president Naomi Bradford. This earned the wrath of vice president Franklin Mullen. Right as Bradford heavily lobbied in Stenmark's behalf, the acting superintendent withdrew his application. He explained that "compelling" personal reasons had led him to step down.

It quickly came out that the "compelling" personal reasons were problems within the district that Stenmark failed to specify. The acting superintendent stated he hoped to remain a top DPS executive under the district's next leader. Even at that, Bradford continued to campaign for Stenmark. On January 31, 1985, she lost on the matter after a lengthy public and executive session when, by a four-to-three vote, the board hired the 46-year-old James Pierce Scamman.

DPS

James P. Scamman, once a music teacher, disharmoniously led DPS when he was superintendent from 1985 to 1988.

The victor beat out a black assistant superintendent of the Baltimore school district, Lewis H. Richardson Jr., 55, who had recently been demoted from deputy superintendent of the Maryland city's system. Blair championed Richardson, stating DPS should have a black superintendent. Bradford, Schroeder, and Schumacher opposed him.

In a convoluted deal, Bradford, Schroeder, and Schumacher offered Blair the chance to make Richardson superintendent. In exchange for his vote to name Stenmark as the district's chief, they promised DPS would bring Richardson to Denver as deputy superintendent and the designated successor to Stenmark. The deal collapsed when Schumacher refused to go along. The board rejected Richardson's nomination five to two with Sandoval supporting Blair in backing the black pedagogue. Before long, Stenmark left DPS, going on to serve as president of Swedish Hospital. The former administrator passed away at age 88 in July 2012.

A possible woman successor to Brzeinski, La Rue Belcher, had left the district before the hiring of Scamman. She quit as assistant superintendent in charge of secondary education in July 1983, shortly before the Brzeinski situation exploded. Then 57, she had been with DPS for 38 years. She became the first woman assistant superintendent in the district in 1977 when she moved to the central administration after having been principal of Thomas Jefferson High School. Belcher, once principal of Gove, had started teaching in 1945 at the old Westwood High School, a program DPS eliminated in 1947 when it annexed the land that included Westwood School near South Lowell Boulevard and West Kentucky Avenue. Belcher's administrative service included being on the Ad Hoc Committee of 1980–81.

(Lore in Catholic Denver has celebrated Westwood High School as a place of opportunity. While early on there were numerous Catholic instructors and a few Catholic members of the school board, some of the faithful believed DPS discriminated against members of their religion. In particular, District #1 was highly hesitant to hire young instructors with teaching degrees from the area's two

Catholic colleges, Regis and Loretto Heights. Most of those whom DPS hired as instructors had received their teaching degrees from either DU or the forerunner of the University of Northern Colorado. Among them were many Catholics. Very few DPS teachers were graduates of CU or other Colorado state teachers colleges. The Arapahoe County School District #18, Westwood, hired those with teaching certificates from Regis and Loretto Heights. The teacher shortage during World War II and during the baby boom era eliminated any vestige of religious discrimination in DPS hiring practices. Not until 1941 did Loretto Heights emerge as a four-year college. Only in 1952 did Regis become an accredited four-year college.)

The district's new superintendent, James Scamman, took office on January 31, 1985. Born in Missouri in 1929, he excelled as a musician, earning his degree in music from Central Missouri State College in 1952. For a while, he was a high school music teacher and band leader. In 1960, he gained a master's of music from Northwestern followed by a doctorate in education from Iowa State University in 1965. By this time, Scamman had moved out of the classroom, holding administrative posts in Minnesota, California, and Wisconsin. In 1973, he emerged as superintendent in Stevens Point, Wisconsin. There he clashed with the board. At one point, it put him on probation for six months. It heralded his service when he left in 1979 to take charge of schools in South Bend, Indiana. There he worked to desegregate the district.

Turbulence followed Scamman. Some disliked him for shaking up the system. Others praised him because he saw it necessary to cut out the deadly bureaucratic rot within the South Bend schools. More than coming across as a master educator, the superintendent projected himself as a virile sportsman, being a skier, swimmer, and scuba diver. As such, he fit in with the athletic cult of comparable young businessmen and aspiring executives.

Scamman, backers asserted, was "decisive," "strong" and someone who "knows what he wants to do." The pedagogue projected himself as an innovator. Judy Morton especially celebrated Scamman as "energetic, futuristic." Board president Naomi Bradford called him a "charmer" even as she dismissed him as "impetuous."

In hiring Scamman, the board failed to reach terms with him. He stunned the district when he asked for a salary of $80,000 in addition to a $20,000 tax-deferred annuity and an expense account. He had been receiving $59,300 in South Bend. DPS had paid former superintendent Brzeinski $74,530. Negotiations saw Scamman accept $75,000 in addition to a car and various expense accounts.

The superintendent pulled in a close assistant from South Bend, Joan Kowai, to become assistant superintendent of elementary education. He arranged for another South Bend cohort, Dean F. Damon, to take charge as assistant to the superintendent—Damon was then the superintendent of Bennett, Colorado, schools. The board authorized both appointments by four-to-three votes, reflecting that, almost from the beginning, Scamman faced a stormy tenure. Given his salary demands and the way the divided board selected him, Scamman never had a honeymoon period. No sooner was he in office that some members criticized him.

The arrival of the outside administrators also angered high-ranking figures at 900 Grant Street. Most of them had spent their entire careers at DPS and were unhappy with those seeking to change the everyday workings of the system.

Personally, the new superintendent was financially comfortable. He settled in the Country Club neighborhood at 141 Marion Street. A sign of his wealth is that he owned and frequently flew his own airplane. His wife, Marilyn, obtained a place as an instructor at the UCD School of Education. The couple had three children.

A New Busing Crisis

At first, Scamman reached out to the community. DPS, he lamented, had long had a siege mentality where it treated everybody and anyone as a potential enemy. Typical of his self-portrait as a can-do administrator is that when he discovered massive maintenance problems with the district's buses, requiring the grounding of a third of the fleet because of safety violations, he personally worked as a driver and a mechanic in trying to alleviate the problem. This did not help. Buses were all too frequently involved in accidents stemming from mechanical failures.

During the fall of 1985, much of the bus fleet was dysfunctional. A bus fell on its side on September 30, when its rear axle collapsed. In another case, 10 children had to be taken to the hospital when a bus from Holm School filled with smoke. Seven other youngsters were taken to the hospital about the same time when a bus

Photo by Phil Goodstein

Even after the United States District Court released DPS from the busing order at the end of the 1995–96 schoolyear, buses remained part and parcel of the district. Back in 1983, bad management forced the system to pull about a third of its fleet from operation since they were not safe to drive.

crashed into a car after the bus's brakes failed. Outside inspections showed that 209 of the district's 340 buses were not safe. Nor was the busing division well supervised. According to a review by the Colorado Department of Education, this part of District #1 was "in total disarray." The problems stemmed from "bad management." In upwards of 40 percent of the cases, mechanics had to repair buses for a second time after they initially failed to fix problems.

As the crisis mounted, the district announced it was suspending bus transportation for 3,000 high school students. They needed to get to school by themselves for the next week. Additionally, they had to arrive 30 minutes earlier than usual: DPS moved the start of the high school day to 7:30 AM so enough buses were available to transport younger students. As a consequence, the number of tardy students soared. George Washington, where about half of the 1,600 students had arrived on school buses, found its absentee rate doubling from 100 to 200 a day. The district gave no account that often adolescents were deprived of sleep when the schools imposed ever earlier opening times on them.

DPS found money to lease 100 buses at $53.90 per vehicle per day for the rest of the school year. As part of his publicity campaign, Scamman led a caravan of seven buses brought in from Grand Junction. No sooner had the new buses arrived that there were more problems, including buses with drained batteries which would not start on cold mornings. In other instances, maintenance was so poor that the buses ran out of fuel.

To probe the reasons the administration had so allowed the bus fleet to decay, DPS commissioned the accounting firm of Price Waterhouse to survey that part of the system. Newspapers reported DPS spent $30,030 a year on each bus compared to an average of $17,658 elsewhere in the metropolitan area. Members of the board of education and business community talked about privatizing school busing to an outside contractor. The drivers and mechanics, represented by local #1563 of the Amalgamated Transit Union, successfully fought this measure. They pointed to the findings of the Price Waterhouse study: privatization might well increase the actual cost of the transportation program while reducing the wages of the workers.

While going along with paying the consultant $49,000 to review the bus fleet, Scamman stated the obvious—the dysfunctional bus fleet was a legacy of poor supervision. It was illustrative of the need to shake up the central administration. For that matter, he complained the DPS central office was utterly bloated. Though student membership had decreased from nearly 100,000 to 58,000 since the late 1960s, DPS still had about the same number of administrators as it had during the peak of enrollment. The front office was filled with encrusted bureaucrats who lacked any sensitivity to a changing city and the way members of racial and ethnic minorities desperately sought recognition as they worked to rise through the school system. Change, Scamman promised, had to come from below. His role was to encourage it. Even at that, he presided over a central administration consisting of two deputy and five assistant superintendents, a greater number than when DPS had been at its peak membership.

Not surprisingly, the hierarchy fought back. Senior administrators circulated bumperstickers criticizing Scamman's management of DPS. Foes insisted that

As part of its financial retrenchment in the 1980s, DPS eliminated many of its music classes. Many students greatly enjoyed them, including the social dimension of performing. Pictured is the trombone section of the South High band in 1940.

far from being an effective administrator in South Bend, the superintendent had bailed out of that post to come to Denver, leaving behind a morass in the Indiana city. Right as the controversy was soaring, Scamman unsuccessfully applied to become superintendent in both Baltimore and Omaha. Arguing that this showed the district's chief had no loyalty to Denver, his foes escalated their attacks.

While the superintendent alienated the old order, he failed to build a new one. As the breakdown in the bus fleet illustrated, bad management swamped DPS. Far from changing it, Scamman was constantly at the center of commotion. Additionally, he was frequently out of town on endless trips.

From the beginning, Scamman angered people with his blunt comments. For example, he enraged supporters of magnet schools when he stated all schools should offer all programs. Besides, magnets were extremely expensive, costing the district about $600 more per student than everyday district schools. Even at that, he wanted to create a demonstration school as a model of the best DPS could offer. He pointed with pride to the establishment of such an academy in South Bend.

The superintendent inflamed professional minorities when he failed to advance ranking black and Hispanic administrators. A group of Spanish-Surnamed professionals, Hispanics of Colorado, particularly decried him for slighting assistant superintendent Albert "Al" Aguayo, the top Latino at 900 Grant Street.

Aguayo had been principal at West before becoming the DPS official in charge of high schools. Backers heralded Aguayo as a success story, the executive who had visibly acted to reduce dropout and suspension rates among Hispanos. He subsequently left DPS to serve as a superintendent in California before returning to the district. In 1993, clashing with Superintendent Evie Dennis, whom he accused of being biased against Latinos, he found himself exiled to Thomas Jefferson High School as an assistant principal.

Aguayo's achievements seemed transitory. DPS had struggled with its high dropout rate for decades, particularly among the sons and daughters of blacks, the Spanish-Surnamed, and those from low-income families. Time and again, it launched programs to redress the problem. Back in 1977, for example, it had emphasized its Holding Power Advisory Committee. This was a citizen group working with numerous branches of the district to keep adolescents in school. As with many other efforts, it faded away.

Nor did Scamman encourage community peace when the district moved sixth graders to middle schools in the fall of 1988. Rather than relying on the district's staff, he sought to bring in another associate from South Bend to oversee the transition. Even at that, the superintendent gained support from the business community, foundations, and other education executives. He emphasized "outcome-based education." It did not matter, he argued, how many specific classes a student took or even the grades he earned. The crucial issue was whether the youngster learned. Additionally, the superintendent repeated the traditional mantra that a prime purpose of the schools was to build character among the new generation.

As tensions soared, critics repeatedly blasted Scamman for a lack of sensitivity. At times, he tended to behave as a dictatorial conductor of an orchestra who simply expected everybody to play their assigned parts and never question his direction, beat, or interpretation. The superintendent won community and teacher favor when he stated he did not need an increase in his salary at the time of financial shortages. Nevertheless, some board members wanted to hike his pay, claiming a higher salary indicated a more prestigious, more qualified incumbent. The superintendent's compensation stayed the same.

For years, DPS emphasized its public relations department, often issuing upwards of a dozen press releases a week.

Nor was the board united. Judy Morton served as president from 1985 to 1987; Franklin Mullen was then vice president. Despite tensions, in 1986, as a sign of confidence in Scamman, the board voted five to two to extend his three-year contract to June 1989. Before long, however, Scamman particularly got on the wrong side of Morton's cohort, Paul Sandoval, the board member who had done the most to hire him.

The upshot was an extremely critical performance review of Scamman in May 1987. In response, the board stated it had no plans to extend his contract for another year; on the contrary, it was subjecting the superintendent to another performance evaluation before the end of 1987. The study showed no improvements. Consequently, on January 20, 1988, the board ousted Scamman by a four-to-three vote.

Officially, the bureau's action was a response to the superintendent's request for a "voluntary" demotion whereby he stayed with the district as the director of curriculum. A year later, the board pushed Scamman over to the newly created post of music coordinator. In a sense, this was a return to his old job as a band director. By this time, the district had drastically cut its music program in response to funding shortages.

Scamman soon left DPS for a post with the Colorado Department of Education. He was something of a favorite of both Governor Roy Romer and state Commissioner of Education Bill Randall. The music instructor frequently took special assignments for the department, flying around the state in his own plane. This was the situation around 10:00 PM on Tuesday, May 25, 1993, when the former superintendent was flying back to Denver from Durango in his four-seat aircraft. It plowed into the Crestone Needles at a 13,000-foot elevation. Scamman died with his only passenger, Dave D'Evelyn. His companion was a foremost champion of charter schools and school choice, having been among the founders and leaders of the pro-free market Independence Institute in 1985.

On the departure of Scamman, James B. "Jim" Bailey took over as interim superintendent, staying in charge until the beginning of the new schoolyear on August 31, 1988. A Denver native born on January 17, 1930, he made this way through DPS, graduating from South High School. He went on to get his bachelor's degree and teaching certificate from the forerunner of the University of Northern Colorado in 1951. Bailey joined DPS as an elementary science teacher in 1953. After five years in that post, he rose to become an assistant principal. Between 1959 and 1961, Bailey was among the teachers on KRMA. After being the district's science supervisor from 1961 to 1966, he took over as its director of federal aid programs.

Bailey was especially close to Superintendent Robert D. Gilberts, emerging as the executive in charge of staff relations in 1968. As such, he served as the district's chief negotiator in dealing with the DCTA until 1977. Included was being the DPS official in the negotiations leading to the 1969 teachers' strike. Along the way, Bailey gained first a master's and then a doctorate in education from DU in 1974—he had first entered the program in 1961.

When Brzeinski became superintendent in 1977, Bailey emerged as associate superintendent in charge of education. He replaced the departing Roscoe Davidson.

Carle Stenmark prepares to get his script right. A veteran, high-ranking administrator, he repeatedly failed to become superintendent.

The latter, long a rival of Brzeinski, left the system to lead the suburban Englewood district. Then, in 1978, Bailey gained promotion as deputy superintendent, a position he shared with Stenmark. He and Stenmark were both collaborators and rivals. When he emerged as acting superintendent on Scamman's ouster, Bailey stated he had no desire to be superintendent.

Despite the turmoil in the superintendent's office, DPS was actually doing an excellent job. It had simply failed to present its achievements. This was the message of an October 1991 school survey. Principals were most positive about the schools' achievements. Parents, teachers, and outsiders were not nearly as optimistic about the district's attainments, bemoaning the high dropout rate and the inability of graduates to master simple tasks. All the while, DPS churned out ever more documents about the guaranteed success of its programs. It continually tinkered with the specific requirements and classes students had to take.

New programs and promises of achievement were endless. Typical was a pamphlet issued in the early 1990s, *Putting Kids First*. The title implied that this had not been previous DPS practice. Not shy about their ambitions, those behind the effort described themselves as "thirty brave souls" who had "vision" in 1989 when they launched the effort. Soon upwards of 200 community activists embraced the initiative, volunteering for numerous subcommittees. The study came up with such seemingly revolutionary postulates as that it was necessary to reach out to parents of poor children, including those who were homeless. The Denver Foundation participated with DPS in formulating *Putting Kids First*. Right when the internet was starting to become part and parcel of American life, the study called for online classes. It also insisted the district needed more magnet programs. Not idealistic statements, but politics, continued to guide DPS, including the choice of the next superintendent.

A Note on Sources:

On March 31, 1977, p. 6, *RMN* reported Ted Hackworth was not seeking re-election to the school board. Catlett, *Farmlands*, 175–76, heralds him. In 2016 and 2019, during informal conversations, Cathy Donohue remembered serving on city council with Hackworth and his ties to lobbyists. *DP*, November 10, 2009, p. 2B, and November 11, 2009, p. 3B, reported his death.

There were profiles of Bob Crider in *DP*, April 10, 1979, p. 14, May 22, 1979, p. 2, December 2, 1982, and November 20, 1994, p. 6C, and *RMN*, June 15, 1981, p. 6, and December 13, 1986, p. 14. I mention the 1995 mayoral race, *DIA*, 423–26. Cathy Donohue has likewise remembered him.

Park Hill Promise, 49, 146, glances at Marion Hammond. *DP*, March 2, 1963, p. 4, told of his call to St. Thomas Episcopal. *DP*, May 31, 1986, p. 8B, looked at him when he was a candidate to become bishop of Hawaii. A November 3, 1976, DPS PR announced Hammond's plan for a mass to celebrate DPS. In 2011–12, Meredith Branscombe, the daughter of Bea and Art Branscombe, shared stories about her parents, their involvement at St. Thomas Episcopal, and Hammond. In 2019, Phil Campbell, the retired pastor of Park Hill Congregational Church, remembered his interactions with Hammond.

DP, March 20, 1977, p. 45, stressed that Dorothie Clark was the candidate of the black caucus. *RMN*, March 17, 1977, p. 26, looked at her career. *DP*, March 3, 1977, p. 15, and *RMN*, March 6, 1977, p. 36, portrayed Lee Tafoya. *RMN*, March 31, 1977, p. 25, told of candidate debates. *DP*, April 2, 1977, p. 2, and *RMN*, April 2, 1977, p. 23, profiled the contenders. *RMN*, May 18, 1977, p. 5, and *DP*, May 18, 1977, p. 1, reviewed the returns. On January 23, 2020, Dorothy Gotlieb recalled the race.

A May 31, 1977, DPS PR celebrated Omar Blair's action in removing the barrier in the board room. *SN*, August 24, 1982, p. 3, outlined the purpose of the Council of Great City Schools and Blair's role in it. *SN*, December 14, 1982, p. 29, observed his election as president of the Colorado Association of School Boards.

Bernie Valdez allowed me to interview him on December 30, 1996, about a year before his death. *DP*, April 4, 1976, p. 20, profiled him. *RMN*, July 16, 1978, p. 6, and August 1, 1978, p. 9, and *DP*, August 1, 1978, p. 3, observed efforts to fill the vacancy on the board created by Valdez's exit. *DP*, August 10, 1978, p. 2, and *RMN*, August 10, 1978, p. 6, told of Fernie Baca-Moore joining the school board. I mention the Valdez Heritage Center in *West Side*, 174, 430, and *DIA*, 167–73. *DIA* also looks at the Valdez–Perry Library, 170, 173.

A special issue of *Cmq*, May 1979, lists the contenders in that year's school board race. A copy is in the 1978–79 PTA Notebook in GP. The same holding has an LWV survey of the candidates and many undated press clippings about the contest. Typical of the newspaper coverage was *DP*, May 2, 1979, p. 69. *RMN*, March 26, 1981, p. 163, looked at Carolyn Etter. I focus on her achievements in *University Park*, 131–32. DPS has a large unprocessed collection of her papers with her husband Don, WH 1974. A review of the 1979 school board election is *RMN*, May 16, 1979, pp. 5, 8.

A 1977 LWV tour itinerary of southwest Denver featured 1620 South Perry Street and the work of William Schroeder. DPL has a video, C-24, a 1979 candidate debate aired on Channel Six. *SN*, June 4, 1979, p. 71, told of Schroeder's election to the school board, describing him as someone who had run for various offices. A sympathetic look at Schroeder's wife, Pauline, was in *DP*, May 13, 1971, p. 33. There is no date on a *DP* article about Schroeder in the 1984–85 clipping notebook in GP. It outlines his tumultuous early life.

Focus, November 1978, p. 1, outlined the organization of the school board amidst Blair's presidency of the body. *DP*, May 20, 1981, p. 1, and *RMN*, May 20, 1981, p. 1, listed the 1981 school board polling. Judge Matsch observed the anti-busing dimension of the 1981 school board election in his ruling on the Keyes case on May 19, 1982; a copy is in 1983–84 PTA Notebook in GP. The 1984–85 clipping notebook in GP has an unidentified article from the *Post* outlining the career and views of Franklin Mullen. Fishman, "Endless Journey," 210, reviews school board politics at that time. The May 1981 *PPV* included interviews with candidates in that month's school board race. It especially focuses on Carolyn Etter, 5–8, Virginia Rockwell, 12–15, and Franklin Mullen, 21–26. It observed that Naomi Bradford refused to sit for an interview, but gave a statement about her views, 31–32.

DP, April 15, 2003, p. 11C, and *RMN*, April 16, 2003, p. 16B, reviewed the life of Ginny Rockwell. The *News'* article was a paid advertisement. *DP*, July 14, 2004, p. 10C, observed the passing of Bruce Rockwell.

Fishman, "Endless Journey," 218, reports Crider's view that court intervention had "ruined" the district. Meadow, "Hard Years," *CJ*, May 8, 1974, pp. 23–26, quotes Crider's definition of an integrated school. *DP*, March 23, 2000, recalled Kay Schomp. *Front Porch Stapleton*, March/April 2004, p. 3, linked her to the School of the Arts, observing the presence of its Kay Schomp Theatre.

Richard Gould, *The Life and Times of Richard Castro* (Denver: CHS, 2007), 70–87, emphasizes the striving Hispanos living on the East Side in the 1950s and 1960s, including Paul Sandoval. I review the political roles of Sal Carpio and Sandoval in *North Side Story*, 64, 111–13, 234. The 1984–85 clipping notebook in GP has a undated *DP* article profiling members of the school board, including Sandoval.

DP, September 16, 1966, p. 19, mentioned Bill Schumacher's appointment as principal of GW. *RMN*, May 25, 1973, p. 94, reviewed his stint as the superintendent of the International School in Brussels. There is no date on a *DP* article in the 1984–85 clipping notebook in GP profiling him. In informal chats, CJ Backus remembered him as the principal when she was a student at GW. She pulled up an obituary of him from *DP*, November 30, 2005.

A list of the membership of the 1979 Image Committee of the PTA is in an envelope in GP of miscellaneous clippings and reports of DPS entitled "1950s, 1970s, and 1980s." *Cmq*, October 1982, p. 5, had an article by Judy Morton promoting the PTA image committee and the bumpersticker. Her February 11, 1983, resignation from the image committee to run for the school board is in the 1984–88 PTA President's Notebook in GP. An undated article in *DP* in the 1984–85 PTA clipping notebook in GP profiles her as a cheerleader.

There are numerous clippings on the 1983 school board race in the 1982–83 PTA News Notebook in GP and the 1982–83 PTA Historian's Notebook in GP. Included is a PTA survey of the candidates. *RMN*, December 15, 1982, p. 8, outlined the push for the black caucus. *DP*, January 18, 1983, and *RMN*, January 16, 1983, p. 13, mentioned the black caucus and the campaign of William E. Richardson. *RMN*, May 18, 1983, p. 10, focused on the contest. *DP*, May 22, 1983, p. 1A, reported the results.

Wesley, *NEA*, 243–47, looks at the many efforts of the NEA since the 19th century to form a federal Department of Education. *SN*, May 22, 1980, p. 59, stressed the presence of Joseph Brzeinski and Omar Blair in Washington at the launching of the agency. Sinclair, *Goslings*, 272, observed the push for a Department of Education in the 1920s, predicting it would not achieve any great results; compare, Murphy, *Blackboard Unions*, 132.

The 1982–83 *DPS Report*, 2, candidly discussed problems of tests even while observing the district's achievements. *RMN*, February 22, 1983, p. 1, noted some students had walked out of testing rooms in 1982, giving no details. *Cmq*, March 1982, discussed the problems with the mid-year transfers of principals in early 1978 and their legacy.

There is passing mention of the severe DPS budget problems in the 1970s in FF 1:32–36 of the Ash Grove PTA Papers. FF 3:63 has 1974 documents from DPS outlining the role of the district's budget advisory committee and various other citizen councils.

Cmq, December 1981, p. 3, reported mass spending cuts because of the looming shortage of funds. A budget folder for 1981–83, in GP, has district documents moaning about inflation while failing to cite specific budget numbers. *Focus*, May 1983, p. 2, told of the district's funding shortfall and emergency borrowing. *RMN*, August 16, 1983, p. 10, observed the financial crisis. The daily reported continuing economic problems, October 21, 1983. The 1982–83 PTA Historian's Notebook in GP is filled with clippings about the DPS budget crisis. There are comparable articles in the 1983–84 PTA Historian's Notebook and the 1986–87 PTA clipping notebook.

DP, January 7, 1977, p. 2, and March 11, 1977, p. 36, mentioned DPS eliminating Head Start programs. *DP*, January 21, 1977, p. 52, and *RMN*, January 21, 1977, p. 20, told of the district borrowing money to pay its immediate bills.

RMN, October 26, 1982, p. 13, outlined the push for a tax hike to cover the district's financial shortages. *RMN*, November 18, 1982, observed opposition to the measure. Also see *DP*, November 6, 1982, and *RMN*, November 30, 1982. *DP*, December 1, 1982, p. 1B, reviewed the results.

On June 27, 2019, former school board member Rita Montero recalled the work sessions on the seventh floor of DPS headquarters. She claimed the board started recording them at her insistence. On February 27, 2018, Montero chatted about Franklin Mullen, including his proposals for the Grant Street bridge.

FF 1:34 of the DPS papers look at the acquisition of the Porter House. *RMN*, May 26, 1986, was a rather superficial article about the deal. Nancy Widman, *Sherman-Grant Historic District* (Denver: Preservation and Public History Research, 1997), 44, traces the history of the house. *DP*, September 29, 1996, p. 14E, listed the sale of the property.

RMN, February 22, 1983, p. 1, reported the extension of Brzeinski's contract. *DP*, February 17, 1984, p. 1, and February 18, 1984, p. 6, observed the board ordering the evaluation of the superintendent. *RMN*, March 26, 1984, p. 1, looked at the tensions on the board and told the story about the remodeling of the conference room; cf. *DP*, June 17, 1983. *DP*, March 30, 1984, p. 4A, and

RMN, March 30, 194, p. 11, mentioned the DCTA's demand for due process for Brzeinski. *RMN*, April 27, 1984, p. 1, and *DP*, April 27, 1984, p. 1, reported the superintendent's resignation. Clippings on Brzeinski's ouster are in the 1983–84 PTA Historian's Notebook in GP. There was a private obituary of Brzeinski in *DP*, March 31, 2016, p. 14A.

Jimi O'Connor recalled that Carle Stenmark was a math teacher and the editor of the *Superintendent's Bulletin* during a November 17, 2018, discussion. Taylor, "Leadership Responses," 190, touches on Stenmark. *RMN*, March 31, 1977, reported his clashes with Omar Blair. *DP*, April 28, 1984, p. 9A, profiled Stenmark when he became acting superintendent on the ouster of Brzeinski. *DP*, July 4, 2012, p. 2A, July 8, 2012, p. 7B, and July 9, 2012, p. 14A, recalled the interim superintendent. *DP*, July 2, 1983, saluted La Rue Belcher. *SN*, August 29, 1977, p. 2, had told of her appointment as assistant superintendent.

During a lecture I delivered at the Gardens at St. Elizabeth on September 12, 2019, a senior citizens home administered by the Catholic Church, a member of the audience discussed Westwood's hiring of Catholics compared to DPS's reluctance to employ those with teaching certificates from Regis and Loretto Heights. *School Book*, 139, 171, 178, 179, 181, 298, 301, mentions anti-Catholicism and the Catholic influence on DPS prior to World War I. Ibid., glances at Westwood School, 376, 420, 421, 423.

The 1984–85 PTA clipping notebook in GP is filled with undated and unidentified articles about the superintendent search and the hiring of James Scamman. DPL has a clipping file on the man. *DP*, May 3, 1985, p. 1B, reported his selection. A puff piece praising him was in *DP*, March 30, 1986, p. 1B. The *Post*, May 2, 1986, p. 13, looked at the question of hiking his salary. It told of the contract extension, May 23, 1986, p. 13. There are additional articles about Scamman, mostly undated and unidentified, in the 1985–86 PTA Clipping notebook in GP. They observe the anti-Scamman bumperstickers and the superintendent's ability to mesmerize the press and supporters. The notebook also has articles about the numerous problems with the bus fleet and consulting contract to Price Waterhouse.

Dick Koeppe recalled Al Aguayo during an August 26, 2019, interview. *DP*, November 20, 1993, chronicled Aguayo's complaints about Evie Dennis and his demotion to assistant principal of Thomas Jefferson. There is a report on the Holding Power Advisory Committee in the 1978–79 PTA Notebook in GP.

Undated articles in the 1986–87 Clipping Notebook in GP report the critical evaluation of Scamman. *RMN*, May 28, 1987, p. 6, and *DP*, May 29, 1987, p. 1B, analyzed turbulence on the board and criticisms of the superintendent. DPS PR, February 1, 1988, reported Scamman's "voluntary" demotion. *Pueblo Chieftain*, May 27, 1993, and *RMN*, May 27, 1993, p. 6A, tolled Scamman's death in the plane crash.

An August 15, 1977, DPS PR, mentioned the rise of James B. Bailey to associate superintendent; compare *SB*, August 29, 1977, p. 3. DPS PR, February 1, 1988, outlined the background of Bailey. *RMN*, November 13, 2008, p. 11B, recalled his life. A copy of the school survey of October 1991 is in the 1992–93 notebook in GP. The 1992–93 notebook of GP has a copy of *Putting Kids First*.

Chapter Fifteen

More Changes

In 1985, Omar Blair decided two terms on the school board were enough, not seeking re-election. He passed away at age 85 on March 24, 2004. This was right when Denver Public Library was building a new branch in Five Points that included a research collection focusing on the African-American West. The facility became the Blair–Caldwell Library, recalling the school board member and Elvin Caldwell, the city's first black city councilman, who also had recently died. In 2004, DPS dubbed a new charter school at 4905 Cathay Street in Green Valley Ranch "Omar Blair School." Blair's daughter, Deborah "Debby" Blair-Minter, went on to serve as its principal.

Edward J. Garner gained election to the school board in 1985, when he was something of the official black candidate to succeed Blair. By this time, an increasingly well-organized caucus of African-American politicians, clerics, and community activists led by then state Representative Wilma Webb, usually gathered in January or February of school board election years to name a contender for the post. Those whom it backed had uneven electoral success.

Garner was also something of the PTA contender. Prior to his election, he had been most active in the group. Constantly attending school board meetings, he reported on them for the PTA's monthly newsletter *Communiqué*. He described himself in election materials as an education consultant.

In a low turnout in which only 7.4 percent of the electorate participated, Garner led the field with 9,589 votes. Carole H. McCotter came in second, 8,653, defeating incumbent Bill Schroeder, 7,449. Mary E. Baca, who called herself a "professional" volunteer, was fourth, 6,936. Far behind were Dennis Hand, 1,114, Keith James, 871, Rosalyn Miller, 836, James Ortega, 466, and Harvey Swan, 284.

Ed Garner won election to the school board in 1985 as both the black and the PTA candidate.

A native of San Augustine, Texas, born on October 5, 1942, Garner had come to Denver during his service in the Army. The victor held a bachelor's from Prairie View A&M in the Lone Star State, having done graduate work at UCD. He was part of Kappa Alpha Psi, a foremost black college fraternity with an extremely strong and influential alumni group. With his wife and three children, he settled in Montbello.

Prior to his election to the board of education at age 42, Garner had held numerous community posts, including on the Denver Council of the PTA, the DPS Black Education Advisory Council, and the Montbello Community School Advisory Committee. Additionally, he was a trustee of Community College of Denver. Fran LeDuke, a crucial white figure in forging the Greater Park Hill Community Incorporated who was a close political associate of Roy Romer, was Garner's campaign manager. The candidate worked as a salesman for Proctor & Gamble. In 1987, Ed Garner gained the presidency of the school board, holding the post for the next four years.

Born in California on June 25, 1943, Carole L. Hand McCotter, earned her bachelor's and a teaching certificate from San Jose State University, spending five years in the classroom. She went on to do graduate work at Boulder and UCD. The victor was the wife of a leading business executive who was involved in utilities and oil. Dwelling at 345 Lafayette Street in the Country Club neighborhood, the couple was in the social directory. McCotter was in tune with such previous Country Club members of the board as Kay Schomp and Ginny Rockwell. Like Schomp, McCotter had been active in the Moore School PTA, serving as its president. In 1977, she had been the inaugural president of the Friends of Dora Moore, the organization working to preserve and enhance the academy.

In addition to her experience as an elementary school teacher, the board candidate had been an instructor for the Colorado Migrant Council. Governor Richard Lamm had appointed her to the state Commission on Children and Their Families. The victor was also involved with in the Junior League and was part of the Leadership Program of the Chamber of Commerce. Among her many school efforts was serving as the educational coordinator of the Denver Juvenile Court.

In her well-financed bid, McCotter effectively employed radio advertising. She plastered the city with yard signs declaring "because." She and Garner ran as something of a ticket. McCotter announced she hoped their victory would convince the United States District Court that the school board was completely committed to integration and so end its oversight of the district. Her triumph did not achieve this result.

The 1987 Election

The 42-year-old Dorothy Gotlieb won a place on the board in 1987, replacing Franklin Mullen. She came in second in the balloting, 35,384, to incumbent Naomi Bradford, 58,629. By that time, Bradford was part of the establishment. Or so the *Denver Post* claimed when it endorsed her and Gotlieb.

Mullen had at first declined to seek re-election before conducting a lackluster race. He came in third with 22,673 votes. Lois Court received the fourth highest total, 22,012. She was a Democratic Party stalwart who was once on the Denver election commission and went on to serve in the General Assembly. The school board aspirant was active in many DPS ventures. Included was serving on the board of the District School Improvement and Accountability Council (DSIAC), a group of concerned teachers, parents, and community figures reviewing school policies. Additionally, she had chaired the district's Health Advisory Committee and been president of the Denver Association for the Gifted/Talented. Her two sons attended Bromwell Elementary—she lived nearby at 780 Elizabeth Street. Art Branscombe, a longtime *Denver Post* educational reporter who, in retirement, was on the board of the DSIAC, was another of the also-rans. The Chamber of Commerce endorsed him. He got 16,511 votes.

Born in Cambridge, England, on July 31, 1944, to parents who had fled the Nazis from Austria, Gotlieb had previously lost a 1977 bid for the school board. The mother of three DPS students, she lived in far southeast Denver at 4123 South Rosemary Street. Worried about how the busing order impacted them, she attended school board meetings during the mid-1970s. There she found herself treated with contempt by the board led by Bernie Valdez. Under him, she claimed, the board was not nice to anybody. In 1978, drawing on support she had gathered in her run for the DPS governing board, Gotlieb won the Denver seat on the Colorado board of education as a Republican.

In office, Gotlieb worked closely with Governor Richard Lamm in calling for an educational system geared to the needs of business. She failed in a bid for city council for an open seat in far southeast Denver in 1983. Typical of Gotlieb's wide outreach in her 1987 campaign for the Denver board of education, she received the backing of both the Board of Realtors and the Denver Area Labor Federation. After one term on the DPS agency, Gotlieb went on to gain a seat in the state House of Representatives in 1996, winning re-election in 1998. This was when members of the GOP still had a strong influence in parts of southeast and southwest Denver. In 2000, Gotlieb lost her bid for the state Senate. Her defeat was something of the end of the Republican electoral presence in that part of town. She went on work for the Colorado Department of Education. After moving out of town, she became the chair of the Arapahoe County Republican Party in the late 2010s.

Back in 1983, at the behest of board president Naomi Bradford, Gotlieb became DPS ombudsman. Part of her responsibilities was being the district's representative in working with its various advisory councils. Included was serving as the administration's representative on the DSIAC. In part, she ran for the school board after the DPS governing bureau, as the behest of Judy Morton, had dismissed her from the post as a way of attacking her sponsor, Naomi Bradford.

In 1977, Dorothy Gotlieb unsuccessfully ran for the school board. She won a seat a decade later.

Back in the 1970s, Gotlieb sent her children to Cole, Samuels, and Cheltenham. This required a great deal of commuting on her part to keep up with school activities. Such transportation problems were among the many issues the United States District Court never considered in the busing order. In the course of 1991–93, Gotlieb was president of the DPS governing body.

Paul Sandoval's Fate

Meanwhile, Paul Sandoval had troubles both on and off the school board. Despite claiming to be a liberal Democrat from a family that had been deeply involved in the labor movement, he continually clashed with members of the DCTA. Nor was his bar, Papa Rox, doing well. The board member and his partner Sal Carpio had drinking problems. This especially came out when the police arrested Sandoval for drunk driving around 12:25 AM in early October 1988. They stopped him after he had run a red light at West 38th Avenue and Tejon Street. He could not show proof of insurance. A test showed he had a blood alcohol level of more than .15, well above the .08 limit defined as driving under the influence. The school board member stated he had had four or five beers that night while taking painkillers. The drugs were necessary since he had been badly hurt in a car accident three months earlier. This was the third time Sandoval had been picked up for drunk driving.

Two days after his latest stop, Sandoval quit the school board. He stated he no longer had the fire to serve. Besides, he was facing a week in the hospital and six to ten weeks of recuperation from injuries stemming from his accident. Nor was he happy about having received threats during a recent clash with the DCTA. The bar owner was also most pressed for time. In addition to running Papa Rox, in April 1988 he had accepted an appointment from Governor Roy Romer to serve on the Colorado Commission on Higher Education. Sandoval also had to devote himself to the family business, Tamales by La Casitas.

Rita Montero, who served on the school board from 1995 to 1999, gave a different version of what happened. Sandoval had had financial problems in acquiring Carbone's/Papa Rox. As a member of the school board, he managed to finagle a loan from the district to help buy the place. Payment on the sum was past due. Rae Garrett, the president of the DCTA, who had repeatedly quarreled with Sandoval, was aware of this. She stated if Sandoval did not quit the board, she would publicize the problematic loan. When Montero was on the board, the district's lawyers refused to allow her access to the financial records which would confirm the accusation.

Besides the bar business, Sandoval also was a founder and partner in Western Services System, a non-profit educational reform group that dated from 1973. It challenged what it believed was the unfair, illegal nature of the state's school finance system. At the same time he was on the DPS board, Sandoval arranged for his partner in Western Services, Bill Rosser, to sign on as District #1's school-community officer. His $51,000 a year salary was $13,000 more than Rosser's predecessor in the job.

While newspapers and critics sniped at such a seeming conflict of interest, Sandoval was among those emphasizing that, as much as anything, DPS needed better press. Working with the district's director of publicity, Bob Gould, a former Smiley teacher who had been president of the DCTA in 1968–69, Sandoval was at the center of a campaign during the 1985–86 schoolyear to emphasize the system's achievements. Ideally, Gould stated, that with the help of 500 volunteers, especially parents satisfied with the job DPS was doing, the district could overcome negative perceptions, particularly by affluent parents who had the choice of whether their children enrolled in the district, went to private schools, or moved to the suburbs.

Mayor Federico Peña signed on to the publicity effort. Assistant Superintendent Al Aguayo was a foremost figure in urging a better image of the schools through the volunteer effort. Nonetheless, critical stories about the district were unending. As they had since the 1970s, many white parents found other options than seeing their children bused across town, especially during their elementary years.

Sandoval also projected himself as a philanthropist. In 1985, he announced the creation of the Jerry and Camilla Sandoval Fellowship Foundation in honor of his parents. He was endowing it with $500,000 to $1.3 million from the sale of stock in Mile Hi Cablevision. This was the firm that had recently won the contract to provide Denver with cable television. Back in 1981, when the firm was bidding for the contract, it found itself having to establish a minority ownership group to achieve it. In the process, it offered stock to about a dozen politically active members of the black and Hispanic communities. After Mile Hi won the franchise, the stock price soared, particularly when Comcast bought out the Denver operation. The result was a tidy profit for Sandoval and others who had been part of the ownership group.

The Jerry and Camilla Sandoval Foundation, the school board member explained, was designed to assist Hispanos seeking to earn graduate degrees in education as part of an effort to increase the number of Latino administrators. Among the first to receive a fellowship was the 28-year-old Ronald Cabrera. Then a teacher at North, he went on to serve as the district's interim superintendent from October to December 2018 after Tom Boasberg quit in the middle of the term as the district's leader. The foundation was not registered with the Colorado secretary of state's office.

Carpio and Sandoval lost Papa Rox near the end of 1989. The former school board member remained politically active. His second wife, Paula, once the chairwoman of DPS's Hispanic Education Advisory Council, went on to serve in the state Senate before winning a vacancy election to represent northwest Denver on city council in 2010. By this time, Sandoval's Tamales by La Casitas was a simple Mexican restaurant at the southwest corner of West 36th Avenue and Tejon Street. Once filled with cartoons about the Denver Broncos, it was across the road from what had been Papa Rox (then Lechuga's). The firm dated from the early 1980s. Republican colleagues of Sandoval on the Joint Budget Committee had helped finance Tamales by La Casitas. At one time, the business had its headquarters at the southeast corner of West 44th Avenue and Tennyson Street. The company once sold tortillas to supermarkets.

In 2011, after a year on city council, Paula Sandoval did not seek to hold the seat. That February, as the balloting approached, doctors diagnosed her husband as suffering from terminal cancer of the pancreas. The former school board drew on ties with Secretary of the Interior Ken Salazar to get preferential treatment at the University of Colorado Hospital. The two had politically collaborated for years. As much as anybody, Sandoval had helped Salazar rise in state politics. Before joining the cabinet of Barack Obama, Salazar had been Colorado attorney general and a United States senator. With Sandoval, he was often quick to denounce as racists those who disagreed with his policies. At least that was the version given by school board member Rita Montero.

During a rededication of the renovated 1911 North High School building in the summer of 2011, the school dubbed a second-floor seminar room in honor of the deadly ill Sandoval to host a prestigious Sandoval Lecture. The politician passed away in April of the next year. DPS memorialized him by branding a multi-school complex in the Northfield section of the old Stapleton Airport as the Paul Sandoval Campus near 56th Avenue and Central Park Boulevard. Money from a 2012 bond issue paid for it. The first buildings opened three years later. Paula Sandoval came to serve on the board of the Emily Griffith Foundation, a charity dating from 1991 designed to link Opportunity School with the corporate sector while assuring students graduated without debt. In 2019, Paul Sandoval's daughter, Amanda, gained election to city council, winning the seat her stepmother had once held.

Rich Castro

At its November 17, 1988, session, the school board selected Richard H. "Rich" Castro to fill the vacancy stemming from Sandoval's resignation. The new member was a product of parochial schools. Born in Denver on September 29,

1946, he graduated from Annunciation High School in 1964, being a
fellow student with Paul Sandoval.
Originally, Castro hoped to become a
priest, enrolling at the local Catholic
St. Thomas Seminary. The young
man soon realized this was not his
calling, leaving Denver to attend
Trinidad State Junior College. Castro earned his bachelor's from Metro
in 1970. From there he went on to
the University of Denver, gaining a
master's of social work in 1972.

By that time, Castro was part
of the turbulent world of Chicano
politics, working as a community
organizer in the highly polarized
West Side. In 1969–70, he led a
successful neighborhood drive to
keep the city from transforming 11th

Courtesy Gregorio Alcaro

and 12th avenues into busy one-way
streets going from Lincoln Park at
Mariposa Street to Cheesman Park
at Humboldt Street. Simultaneously,
he was among those in the Chicano
movement who insisted on the
absolute necessity of working within

*In November 1988, Rich Castro gained
appointment to the school board seat previously held by Paul Sandoval. His failure
to keep it in the 1989 balloting helped
trigger the creation of districts for school
board members.*

the Democratic Party. This led to his election to the legislature in 1974. He
succeeded Betty Benavidez, the woman whom Paul Sandoval defeated in the
Democratic primary for the state Senate. She was the wife of Castro's political
mentor and boss, Waldo Benavidez.

Castro stayed in the House until 1983 when he resigned to become the head of
the Denver Agency on Community Relations under recently elected Mayor Federico
Peña. This was a new incarnation of the Commission on Community Relations. It
was later the Agency on Human Rights. While retaining that post, Castro agreed
to serve on the school board.

The incumbent sought to hold his position in the May 1989 balloting. This
campaign was simultaneous with a referendum on whether the city should build
Denver International Airport. He endorsed the initiative. In the process, he and
others running for the school board had to gain attention amidst the incessant
drumbeat of the corporate-political establishment that the airport was the city's
salvation.

Castro failed to stand out in the contest. The former state legislator ran a lax
campaign, coming in fourth in a field for 14 for three seats. Sharon Ruth Brown
Bailey, who lived near City Park at 2701 Race Street and was a 1971 graduate of

East High, was the candidate of the black Democratic establishment. She led the balloting, 40,763. Marcia Johnson, a resident of affluent white Park Hill at 1922 Locust Street who was linked with many improvement efforts, came in second, 38,663 — she had once been the president of the Smiley PTA. The 41-year-old Thomas M. "Tom" Mauro, who lived in far southeast Denver at 7834 Colgate Place, grabbed the third spot, 36,686. He was vice president of United Bank Service Company. This was the data processing branch of United Bank of Colorado, the state's largest financial institution. Backing from the Republican Party helped him win the race. Castro trailed Mauro by 281 votes, 36,405.

The triumph of Bailey and Johnson was indicative of the continuing vigor of Park Hill integration activists. The two victors ran as an informal team. Their backers loudly called for supporters to cast only two votes compared to the three they were allowed. Ideally, this gave a boost to the ticket. It might have helped Mauro eke by Castro.

The Park Hill turnout in the election was also greater than usual. No neighborhood more supported the airport than Park Hill with the promise the field would reduce the endless drone of jet airplanes over the enclave. Johnson was on the election commission from 1995 to 1999, going on to win a place on city council in 2003 where she served two terms.

Before gaining election to the board of education, Sharon Bailey had been closely involved in school issues and black politics. After getting out of high school, she headed to Princeton where she received her bachelor's in 1975. She gained a master's from CU in 1980. UCD awarded her a doctorate in public administration in 1998. Her dissertation, "Journey Full Circle," was "A Historical Analysis of *Keyes v. School District #1*." The victor's five-member committee reviewing the thesis included former DPS superintendent Richard Koeppe and then superintendent Irv Moskowitz. For some years, Bailey was a policy analyst for the Western Interstate Commission on Higher Education.

Bailey served a stint as the chairwoman of the Colorado Black Roundtable. Her husband, John T. Bailey, had played in the American Basketball Association in the 1970s. Eventually, he was a political activist in his own right. With him, she worked as the coordinator of the Joint Effort Youth Foundation, an effort to enhance education in the African-American community. Back in 1984–85, she had been among those lobbying for DPS to hire Lewis H. Richardson of Baltimore, the black candidate for superintendent. The mother of three children, in 1985 she failed in seeking the endorsement of the black caucus to run for the board of education.

While on the DPS governing bureau, Bailey faced a dilemma when her daughter received a scholarship from Graland School. This was an elite private Hilltop academy that educated children of the city's wealthy. The school board member had urged her daughter to apply for the grant, accepting it. She explained that no matter how good DPS programs were, they did not match the aristocratic inside connections offered by a place like Graland.

In the course of 1993 to 1995, Bailey and Marcia Johnson shared the post of vice president of the board under Tom Mauro. Bailey did not seek to keep her place on the school board in 1995. She subsequently was DPS research director, later becoming the district's manager of diversity, unity, and inclusion. As such, she was something of an informal civil rights compliance officer for the system, highlighting what she believed were racially discriminatory policies.

At times, Sharon and John Bailey switched as to who was the politician in the family. In 1991, he failed in a run for city council for District #8, covering Five Points and much of historic black Denver. Eight years later, he unsuccessfully sought an at-large position in the city legislature. As the executive director of 100 Black Men of Denver Incorporated, he was actively involved on March 13, 1996, when around 100 to 150 black students walked out of George Washington High School. They protested the absence of a black culture program, the administration's lack of concern about them, and its resort to suspensions and expulsions rather than working to resolve problems suffered by African-American youngsters.

Courtesy Jeff Hersch

Sharon Bailey was on the school board from 1989 to 1995.

In 2007, Sharon Bailey ran for an open place on city council seat for District #8 — an African-American had held the seat since 1955. Carla Madison also sought the office. She was a white artist and nurse who was allied with city hall and the Democratic Party while leading the City Park West Neighborhood Association. The area, she observed, was rapidly changing. A modification of District #8 borders brought in a good deal of white Park Hill. Bailey gained a plurality in the May voting, winning 36.65 percent of the vote compared to Madison's 28.34 percent. Two other candidates received the rest of the ballots. During the runoff campaign, John Bailey literally sought to demonize Madison. He screamed that she had pagan idols on the porch of her house at 2145 York Street. In the process, he came across as a raging demagogue, aliening supporters whereby Madison triumphed in the runoff, 2,816 to 2,636.

While Park Hill had mobilized behind Bailey and Johnson in 1989, Castro did not reach out to Hispanic neighborhoods. He failed to turn out his supporters. Instead of conducting a hands-on campaign where he was everywhere, he primarily relied on his reputation and the way the media portrayed him as the essence of Latino success.

About two years after he lost his bid to stay on the school board, Castro died from a brain hemorrhage at age 44 in April 1991. The district subsequently renamed Westwood School in his honor when it opened a replacement building at the end of spring break in 1993 at 845 South Lowell Boulevard. Money from a 1990 bond issue paid for it. Roybal & Associates, an architectural firm that had worked closely with DPS and Jefferson County Schools on many projects, designed the new building. (Roybal later sued DPS, claiming the district discriminated against minority business enterprises.)

Castro School went up at the southwest corner of South Lowell Boulevard and West Ohio Avenue in 1993, replacing Westwood School. It remembers Rich Castro who was on the board of education from 1988 to 1989.

Castro School included a couple of terra cotta reliefs over the Ohio Avenue entrance taken from the old Westwood — wreckers brought down the old Westwood building in January 1994. Working with the city, DPS created a large playing field/ community park where the old structure had stood. A 1998 bond issue reserved $2,143,791 for a six-classroom addition to Castro. The district also spent $1,499,420 to add four labs for deaf and hearing-impaired students to the school.

The Castro family gave a bust of the deceased board member to the building. An interior mural highlighted the contributions of Rich Castro. Eventually, the school painted over the mural and locked the bust and other Castro memorabilia in a closet. At the behest of Castro's widow, past and present Hispanic members of the legislature saved the materials, seeing them moved to a display on the Auraria campus. (Castro's widow, Virginia, incidentally, was a social worker who was once the program manager of DPS's social worker services.)

Castro pupils were the Cheetahs. Back in 1996, the enrollment had been about 500, 77 percent of whom were Hispanos. The membership by late 2010s hovered between 500 and 600. About 88 percent were Latinos, 4 percent were Asian, 4 percent black, 2 percent white, 1 percent Indian, and about 1 percent a scattering of mixed and other races. Virtually all of the students qualified for free or reduced-price lunches.

The Nita Gonzales Challenge

Politically active Hispanos yelled that the results of the 1989 contest were not fair. Given the heavy Latino enrollment in DPS, there should be at least one

Spanish-Surnamed individual on the board. They sought to learn from black Denver by husbanding their resources and lining up behind a candidate who could win. On this basis, the 41-year-old Nita Gonzales asserted herself in 1991 as the Chicana contender.

More than anything, the challenger was best known as the daughter of Corky Gonzales. After he was badly injured in a car accident in the fall of in 1987, she took charge of the remnants of the Crusade for Justice and its private school, Escuela Tlatelolco. This angered others within the Chicano community. The Crusade, they insisted, belonged to the activists who had built it, not the Gonzales family.

Nita Gonzales paid this no heed. By this time, she had a master's in education from Antioch, had served as a manager of Servicios de la Raza, and had been on the board of Denver Community Corrections. The candidate put together a strong coalition, gaining the support of foremost Democratic Party functionaries.

Swanee Hunt was among her backers. She was the daughter of a reactionary Texas oil billionaire. Shunning the limelight for some years after arriving in Denver in 1977 as a preacher's wife, Hunt had worked with Caroline Schomp, the daughter of school board member Kay Schomp, in running a half-way house for troubled indi-

Author's collection

Nita Gonzales touted her wide-ranging ties with the establishment when she unsuccessfully sought to gain a place on the school board in 1991 and 1993.

LYNN COLEMAN
FOR
DENVER BOARD OF EDUCATION

The Parent's Voice

"The school should be seen as part of the extended family by design. As partners, parents, teachers and principals need to determine the educational focus of their schools.

When elected, I'll use my vote as a Board member to help bring about effective changes resulting in a better education for all Denver children. I have the time and skills to be your representative on the Board of Education. Please give me your support by voting for me on May 21, 1991."

Lynn Coleman

Lynn Coleman was an upset winner for the school board in 1991.

viduals. Eventually, Democratic feminists, who wanted recognition and power within the political system, convinced Hunt of the justice of their views. In 1992, she was the number-one donor to the Bill Clinton campaign. The president rewarded Hunt by naming her United States ambassador to Austria.

Hunt was among many community figures endorsing Nita Gonzales for the school board. Les Franklin, a black business executive who directed the Governor's Job Training Office, was among them. So were J. Langston Boyd, the politically influential pastor of Shorter African Methodist Episcopal Church, and Denise Edwards, a lobbyist for the Colorado Coalition of 100 Black Women. Such stalwarts of Latino Denver as businesswoman Veronica Barela and Katherine Archuleta, a top aide of Federico Peña who later worked for Swanee Hunt, likewise backed Gonzales. The Denver Area Labor Federation endorsed the Chicana. Former black state representative and city councilman King Trimble was the treasurer of her campaign.

Despite such widespread support, Gonzales came in third in the 1991 contest selecting two members. Incumbent Carole McCotter kept her place on the board in the May 21 balloting. She led the pack of nine candidates with 19.2 percent of the total ballots cast, 30,739. The head of her finance committee, Sherry Eastlund, soon emerged as the chairwoman of the District School Improvement and Accountability Council. Eventually, Eastlund spent more than 40 years working for DPS or serving on an array of citizen committees advising the schools.

Lynn Coleman, 38, an insurgent, claimed the second seat in the balloting, 26,570, 16 percent. She was very much a product of DPS. Both of her parents had taught in the system—her mother was the librarian at Opportunity School. After attending Lincoln, Bromwell, and Byers, Coleman graduated from East in 1971. From there she went to Berkeley. After dropping out of the University of California, she worked as a buyer for a Berkeley bookstore for four years. In 1978, she joined the carpenters union. After returning to Denver in 1981, she was a self-employed carpenter who taught carpentry for women through DPS community schools. Coleman shifted fields in 1989 when she established an independent photo studio.

The mother of three children whom she enrolled in DPS, Coleman was outspoken on school issues. The victor lived to the east of Park Hill at 8630 Montview Boulevard. Rob Hernandez, a member of the General Assembly, was Coleman's campaign manager.

Gonzales, who had the backing of outgoing Mayor Federico Peña, had $16,000 in her war chest—all of it was donations. She narrowly trailed Coleman, 25,664. Close behind was incumbent Ed Garner, 25,201. Coleman had spent $2,100 of her own funds in a race that cost her campaign $45,500. Garner stated he paid for about one-third of the $25,000 of his bid for re-election. The DCTA had especially campaigned against him in response to his attacks on the union during the 1990–91 contract negotiations.

Park Hill resident James E. Culhane, a partner in the powerful law firm of Davis Graham & Stubbs, got 15 percent of the vote, 24,056. Robert Leland Johnson, a landlord and a self-proclaimed educational expert, won 9,764 (6.1 percent). Psychologist Curtis C. Dotson trailed with 6,818 (4.1 percent), just ahead of teacher Michelle O. Serries, 6,590 (4 percent) who had previously run in 1989. Another teacher, Frank E. Deserino was at the bottom, 5,066 (3.2 percent).

Turnout in heavily Latino neighborhoods was miserable. Gonzales decried this. Fellow Hispanos, she insisted, should have had the wherewithal to troop to polls to put the only Chicana on the ballot into office. Politically active Spanish-Americans who hated Corky Gonzales and his legacy, responded by noting Latino Denver did not vote for Nita as a way of saying no to the Gonzales family.

The establishment ignored this perspective. If anything, Gonzales had been its candidate. The politically correct moaned about her defeat and the previous loss by Rich Castro. To assure a Latino was on the school board, they argued it was necessary to change the way voters elected members of the DPS governing agency. In particular, it there must be school board districts. This, they insisted, would guarantee representation from the different parts of the city.

The idea had been in the air since at least the early 1970s. At that time, advocates of black Denver and integration had called for districts after their supporters lost three school board elections in a row whereby the board was seven to zero against busing after the 1971 balloting. The call for districts faded when advocates of a unitary, integrated district won posts on the board in 1973 and 1975. Even so, when Omar Blair retired from the board in 1985, black state Senator Regis Groff announced he would push a district-election scheme in the legislature if another black did not win the school race that year. The effort collapsed when Ed Garner emerged victorious. There was never any discussion about having proportional representation on the school board or run-off elections.

After Gonzales went down to defeat, the political establishment eagerly lined up behind the district scheme. Without asking the voters what they thought about the idea of dividing the school board into districts, during the 1992 session of the General Assembly, the city's legislative delegation pushed Senate Bill 175. Members of the Republican Party backed it along with the Democrats.

The statute amended the state's school board law. As of January 1, 1993, it specified that the seven-member Denver school board was to consist of two at-large members in addition to five people elected from districts. The act reduced the term of board members from six years to four years. It made no provision for requiring candidates to receive a majority of the votes. The sitting school board defined the new districts as one seat each for the southeast, southwest, northeast, and northwest sections of the city. The fifth district was the center of the community, including Capitol Hill and parts of Park Hill.

The 1993 Election

In 1993, Nita Gonzales once more ran for the board, filing for the at-large seat held by Naomi Bradford who sought to stay in office. The Latina gathered the most funds of all the contenders. Voters again said no to her. The victor for the one open at-large seat was Aaron Gray in a contest where incumbent Dorothy Gotlieb declined to seek re-election. Another resident of Park Hill, dwelling at 2830 Eudora Street, Gray was a black minister who held the pulpit at Scott United Methodist, a historically African-American church. His triumph showed that seemingly "minority" groups could put their members in office in city-wide elections. This had already been the case in 1983 when Federico Peña won the mayor's race as a Latino. Four years later, Wellington Webb, a black, gained election as auditor before he triumphed in the 1991 mayoral contest. For that matter, such Latinos as Bert Gallegos, Bernie Valdez, and Paul Sandoval had won election to the at-large school board. Had there still been the traditional two at-large seats in 1993, Gonzales might have gained a place on the board.

Gray triumphed by winning Montbello, then largely a black enclave. None of the other candidates actively campaigned there. He gained 8,195 votes, 39.2 percent of the total. Gonzales was second with 5,332, 25.5 percent. The race saw the defeat of incumbent Bradford, 5,143, 24.6 percent, who had been on the board since 1975. Rita Montero and Josie Sanchez were also on the ballot as Latina candidates. Montero, who had complete contempt for Gonzales, stated she ran to take votes away from the woman who was the establishment's favorite Chicana for the school board. Montero got 429 votes, 2.1 percent, and Sanchez, 358, 1.7 percent. Other candidates were Carrie Bailey-Woods, 949, 4.5 percent, and Connie Ellis, 499, 2.4 percent.

Despite the loss, Nita Gonzales continued to lobby DPS. She was a backer of Hispanics of Colorado in its push for a full recognition of her people. Included was the demand for appointing and advancing Latinos as DPS principals and administrators. In September 1994, she was co-chairwoman of the Latino Education Organization. To show its dissatisfaction with the schools, it arranged for around 1,000 students to stage a one-day walkout on the 16th of the month, Mexican Independence Day. The action was in tune with her father's efforts to make September 16 a Chicano holiday. The walkout was also supposed to show Latino Denver's displeasure with the continuing racism of the district. Students participating in it were sacrificing valuable classtime to enhance their educational

Escuela Tlatelolco, a school created by the Crusade for Justice, occupied by old St. Dominic's School near the northwest corner of West 29th Avenue and Federal Boulevard. Nita Gonzales, who failed in runs for the school board in 1991 and 1993, oversaw it, arranging for DPS to finance Escuela Tlatelolco as a contract school.

futures. Others dismissed this as nonsense, observing many students were always ready for an excuse to ditch classes.

Most of all, Gonzales continued to push Escuela Tlatelolco. After her father stepped down as the head of the Crusade, she emphasized Escuela's origins as a private school focusing on Chicano history and culture. "Educating children, liberating minds," it promised. By the early 1990s, she insisted it was a private alternative high school. It was open to dropouts and others who had not succeeded in traditional schools. Additionally, the school had elementary-level classes.

After the Crusade left its old quarters at 16th Avenue and Downing Street, Escuela relocated to West 41st Avenue and Tejon Street where Servicios de la Raza, an agency linked to the Gonzales family, had its office. In 1995, with the help of a city loan, the school acquired the former home of St. Dominic's School, next to St. Dominic's Catholic Church at the northwest corner of West 29th Avenue and Federal Boulevard. The city financing was another sign that Gonzales was essentially part of the establishment against which she so raged. The money came shortly after her promotion of the September 16, 1994, student walkout from DPS.

About the time Escuela moved to the St. Dominic's location, Gonzales reached an accommodation with DPS. The district made Escuela Tlatelolco a contract school. This was something of a modified charter school where, basically, Gonzales and her cohorts had a free hand in running the DPS-funded academy. Part of the program was social activism where the students often participated in protests. They annually marched on Martin Luther King Day.

Escuela emphasized the success of the students. Those having no truck with Gonzales insisted academic performance was hideous. Time and again, the district demanded improved test scores from Escuela Tlatelolco. The school repeatedly managed to stave off ultimatums. In 2005, at the behest of Mayor

John Hickenlooper, the administration forgave $305,000 of the $350,000 loan the Crusade/Escuela had received ten years earlier.

During the next decade, DPS repeatedly issued warnings about the lack of academic performance at Escuela. Despite them, it kept extending the school's contract. Finally, the administration had had enough in December 2014. It observed that the school's performance remained miserable after repeated probationary periods. The district so announced that it was terminating the contract at the end of the schoolyear. The daughter of Corky Gonzales said this was just as well. Now she did not need to worry about oversight from bureaucratic busybodies. The school would go its own way, keeping alive the spirit of the Crusade for Justice. Henceforth, she announced, Escuela would be a bilingual Montessori. Gonzales managed to get DPS to keep funding Escuela to the end of the 2015–16 schoolyear. The program failed to open at the beginning of the 2016–17 term. By the summer of 2017, its building was on the market. A buyer vowed to transform the old St. Dominic's School into residences. It was unclear whether Escuela repaid its loan to the city after receiving money for the building.

Jay P. Hemming was the other victor in the 1993 contest. He was the first district representative on the board, winning the seat for southwest Denver. A sheet metal worker, he invariably went by his initials as JP. His big push on the board was calling for DPS to adopt a personalized learning plan for each student. He had gained 1,743 votes over dentist Efren Martinez, 1,593. Hemming won by personally soliciting voters in contrast to the much better-funded Martinez who relied on advertising. The new member sometimes showed up at board sessions right from the factory, seemingly embodying a hands-on approach to DPS business.

For the most part, Hemming was among the members who assumed the superintendent was always right. Superintendents came and went amidst the transformation of the school board. Between 1988 and 1995, James Scamman, James Bailey, Richard Koeppe, Evie Dennis, and Irv Moskowitz all held the post.

A Note on Sources:

My *Curtis Park*, 200, 206, 208–09, 210, tells about the origins of the Blair–Caldwell Library. *DP*, April 12, 2018, p. 4C YourHub, heralded Blair Charter School. On September 13, 2019, Buddy Noel chatted about Blair.

The 1988 Black History Calendar features Ed Garner for August. *DP*, January 18, 1983, told about the black caucus meeting to decide on a candidate for the school board. There is also an unidentified article in the 1984–85 clipping notebook in GP talking about the black caucus for the 1985 board race. *RMN*, February 10, 1985, p. 10, mentioned Garner winning the caucus' endorsement. *DP*, May 14, 1991, p. 5F, profiled Garner when he sought re-election. Also see Doug and Wallace Yvonne McNair, *Colorado Black Leadership Profiles* (Denver: Western Images, 1989), 19.

RMN, May 15, 1985, p. 8, looked at Carole McCotter's school board race. It reported her victory, May 22, 1985, p. 6. *DP*, May 14, 1991, p. 5F, profiled her. Ellen Kingman Fisher, *Junior League of Denver* (Denver: CHS, 1993), 60, mentions McCotter's influential role in the Junior League. The school board member shared her views with me, particularly her role at Moore School, during a 1988 phone interview. Sherry Eastlund discussed McCotter's activism during a conversation on March 6, 2018.

DP, May 20, 1987, p. 5A, reviewed the 1987 school board election. *DP*, November 1, 1978, p. 80, profiled Dorothy Gotlieb in reporting the race for the state board of education. She shared her views and memories during a long phone interview on January 23, 2020. Gotlieb donated her papers from her school board experiences to CHS. *SN*, February 10, 1981, p. 41, had glanced at Gotlieb when she emerged as the president of the state board of education. *RMN*, August 26, 1983, p. 32, had reported her becoming DPS ombudsman. There are numerous undated articles on the 1987 school election in the 1986–87 Clipping Notebook in GP.

DP, April 9, 1988, p. 3C, observed the appointment of Paul Sandoval to the Colorado Commission on Higher Education. *RMN*, October 7, 1988, p. 7, and *DP*, October 7, 1988, p. 1A, reported Sandoval's arrest for drunk driving and his resignation from the school board.

The 1986–87 Clipping Notebook in GP has undated articles about Western Services Systems, Paul Sandoval, and the hiring of Bill Rosser. The 1985–86 PTA Clipping Notebook in GP includes undated stories from the *Post* and *News* about Bob Gould and how he worked with Sandoval in urging volunteers to participate in the campaign to get the district better public relations.

An undated article from *RMN*, in the 1985–86 PTA Clipping Notebook in GP, announced the formation of the Jerry and Camilla Sandoval Foundation. A press release from the foundation in 2018 observed that Ron Cabrera had been the first recipient of its largess back in the mid-1980s. Miller Hudson, who had served in the legislature with Sandoval and knew the politician well, chatted about the Mile Hi Cablevision deal on December 17, 2019. In the course of the interview, he observed the financing of Sandoval's tamale business. He also emphasized Sandoval's links with Ken Salazar. *DP*, June 26, 2011, p. 1A, looked at Sandoval's career and his ties with Salazar. The *Post*, April 25, 2012, p. 4A, mourned Sandoval's death.

On August 9, 2017, Rita Montero shared memories of her time on the school board and the political clout of Paul Sandoval. She mentioned the story about Sandoval's clashes with the DCTA and the real reason he quit the school board. Additionally, she blasted him for describing his opponents as racists to deflect merited criticisms of his policies.

A review of Tamales by La Casitas was in *NDT*, August 3, 2006, p. 12. The paper, April 21, 2011, had Paula Sandoval's statement of why she did not seek re-election to city council. *DP*, March 3, 2011, p. 4B, reported her leaving the race. It had told about her triumph in the vacancy contest, May 5, 2010, p. 1B. *DP*, July 17, 2014, p. 7C, glanced at the Paul Sandoval Campus. *GPHN*, January 2017, p. 1, mentioned debates on the development at Northfield and the campus.

Cmq, December 1988–January 1989, p. 5, chronicled Rich Castro filling the school board vacancy. Gould, *Richard Castro*, 222–23, touches on Castro's role on the school board and the 1989 election. The politician's papers are at the Auraria archives. I examine his political role, especially in West Denver, in *West Side*, 250–53, 256. *Naysayer*, June 2009, was my review of Gould's book.

DP, May 6, 1989, pp. 5–6B, looked at the candidates in that year's school board race. *RMN* May 17, 1989, p. 27, reviewed the contest, observing how the question of building the new airport overshadowed it. The official precinct-by-precinct returns are in Box 35 of the Castro papers.

DP, March 14, 1996, p. 3B, and *RMN*, March 17, 1996, p. 18, reported the walkout at GW and the role of John Bailey. In 2007, Paul Weiss, the husband of Carla Madison, discussed the city council race and John and Sharon Bailey. Marcia Johnson reflected on the schools in *GPHN*, August 2019, p. 10. I touch on her career in *Park Hill Promise*, 322, 334, 336.

FF 6:121–23 of the DPS papers deal with the replacement of Westwood by Castro School. *BN*, January 21, 2000, observed a planned addition to Castro School. *Daily Journal*, September 23, 1993, stressed the relationship between Roybal & Associates and DPS. *DP*, October 10, 2016, p. 2A, mentioned the Roybal suit against DPS. On June 15, 2019, David Hill shared the story about the bust of Rich Castro and the events at Castro School leading to the display about the legislator on the Auraria campus.

RMN, May 19, 1991, p. 57, profiled school board candidates. So did *DP*, May 14, 1991, p. 5F, of an election supplement. On June 27, 2019, Sherry Eastlund recalled her participation in the schools, work at administration headquarters, and involvement with DSIAC. Box 12 of the DCTA papers has a file on the 1991 board election, including candidate answers to the group's survey. *DP*, May 23, 1991, p. 15, listed the results.

I touch on the controversies surrounding Nita Gonzales in the Chicano community in the January 2005 and July 2016 *Naysayer* and *DIA*, 165–66. Also see Vigil, *The Crusade for Justice*, 369–71. *WW*, January 29, 1998, p. 28, reviewed continuing tensions in the Hispanic community about Nita Gonzales and the Crusade.

A copy of Senate Bill 92–175, calling for Denver school elections via districts, is in the 1992–93 notebook in GP. The *Naysayer*, November 2001, reflected on the problematic achievement of electing board members by district. An undated article in the 1984–85 clipping notebook in GP tells of the African-American push to keep a black on the school board and Regis Groff's urging school elections via districts if a black did not succeed Omar Blair on the board. A file in the 1994–95 notebook in GP outlines procedures for school board elections.

In numerous conversations, Rita Montero has given me her extremely negative views of Nita Gonzales and the academic failure of Escuela Tlatelolco. On June 27, 2019, she mentioned how she had been unable to discover if the city had demanded repayment of the school's loan after Escuela had closed and sold its building. *DP*, February 22, 2008, p. 4B, mentioned DPS placing Escuela Tlatelolco on probation. *DP*, December 7, 2014, p. 4A, told of DPS ending its contract with the Crusade program. The paper plugged the school's new orientation, June 4, 2016, p. 1A. It failed to report the shuttering of the program. Also see *NDT*, September 15, 2016, p. 4, and the *Naysayer*, July 2016.

DP, May 19, 1993, p. 1A, and *RMN*, May 19, 1993, p. 4A, reviewed the results of the school board race. I touch on Aaron Gray in *Park Hill Promise*, 86–87. Volume three will look at his service on the board. The 1995 notebook in GP includes a January 6, 1994, memo from JP Hemming calling for individual learning plans. On February 27, 2018, Rita Montero remembered being on the board with him.

Chapter Sixteen

Evie Dennis

On taking office as acting superintendent in 1988, James B. Bailey did not seek to become the permanent leader of the district. In part, he bowed out when the school board launched a national search to fill the post. From DPS, he became the legislative liaison of the Colorado Department of Education, holding the post until 1997. He was subsequently a consultant to school districts across the state. The pedagogue passed away at age 78 in November 2008.

Bailey left DPS when he realized he did not have a future in the district. The school board made it clear that DPS once more needed new perspectives and leadership. In part, that was why the agency had brought in James Scamman as superintendent in 1985. An outsider, DPS directors hoped, would not be bogged down in the internecine bureaucratic squabbling at the center of the hierarchy. Even at that, the board landed up hiring a man who once had close connections with the administration, Richard Koeppe.

To find the right person to head District #1, the school board commissioned Floretta McKenzie, the former superintendent of Washington, D.C., and her McKenzie Group in the federal capital to conduct a national search. By July 1988, 77 had applied, 53 of whom completed the application. The board stated it was going to get input from school and community groups at open sessions once it had selected the finalists. No sooner had it promised as much than it postponed the forums on July 20. Something was wrong with the process and many who were seeking the job.

Richard "Dick" Koeppe was among those consulting on the effort. A disciple of Robert D. Gilberts, he had been DPS assistant superintendent for instruction from 1968 to 1972. Included was essentially serving as deputy superintendent once

Howard Johnson took leadership of the district in 1970. Koeppe was never happy under Johnson, claiming the superintendent showed no initiative or leadership. Nor did Koeppe enjoy the endless meetings and continual clashes over busing. He was sure that, after the 1969 election, the school board was more interested in sabotaging the court integration order than seeing DPS provide equal educational opportunity. In 1972, he left DPS to take charge of the prestigious suburban Cherry Creek School District.

In his new post, Koeppe excelled as a politician, mixing with the school board and the community. He made it known that he wanted to hear dissident opinions, hiring aides who were willing to tell him when they thought he was wrong. His deputy, Donald K. "Don" Goe, handled much of the day-to-day administration of Cherry Creek schools. An East High alumnus who was once the president of the DCTA when he taught social studies at Gove, Goe had gone on to serve as principal of Cherry Creek High. In 1987, after 15 years as Cherry Creek superintendent, Koeppe retired to become a professor of education at the University of Colorado Denver. He dwelt at 8679 Kenyon Avenue in the far southeastern part of the city, a house he stayed in for more than 50 years while his children made their way through DPS.

Koeppe was a key part of the effort to find the new superintendent. While the McKenzie Group scoured the country, he focused on the Mile High aspect of the hiring process. This led him to talk to numerous community groups, teachers, and business interests about what they were looking for in the district's next leader.

The national search was a dud. Much to the surprise of the board, candidates were often seeking to leave behind bad experiences and troubled relationships. (A keynote of personnel searches is that people whom recruiters interview about the qualification of candidates frequently make highly positive comments about those seeking positions elsewhere. In part, they do so in the hope of getting rid of administrators whom they consider bungling idiots or tyrants.)

After reviewing the qualifications of the eight semifinalists selected to become District #1 superintendent, the board nominated two finalists. In pondering which person to choose, the DPS governing body concluded neither was fit for the job. By this time, some of the semifinalists had withdrawn amidst negative publicity. No candidate was able to gather unanimous support of the board. Ed Garner, president of the board, and vice president Judy Morton wanted at least a six-to-one vote for the new superintendent in view of how the polarized divisions on the board had been partially responsible for the ouster of Scamman.

On August 14, 1988, with the beginning of the schoolyear looming, the board offered the 57-year-old Koeppe a one-year contract as superintendent from September 1, 1988, to August 31, 1989, while it continued its search. He stated he would accept the unexpected offer, announcing he planned, after the year, to go back to his job at UCD.

The son of German immigrants, Koeppe had grown up in La Crosse, Wisconsin, with German as his first language. Eventually, he made his way through Wisconsin State University La Crosse, going on to get a master's in American diplomatic history from the University of Wisconsin. After being drafted, he returned to the

University of Wisconsin on his discharge from the military. His doctorate was in education with a minor in the history of Rome. He insisted history was a most valuable pursuit in understanding the present.

By the time he had gained his doctorate in 1961, Koeppe had spent five years in the classroom in an inner-city school in Milwaukee. At the same time he received his Ph.D. from the University of Wisconsin, so did Robert Gilberts. The two had connected at the school. Gilberts invited Koeppe to join him as the director of student services in the Oconomowoc school district where he was superintendent. Koeppe, who developed a close personal friendship with Gilberts, moved with the superintendent to Madison where he

Drawing by Daniel Lowenstein

Dick Koeppe was superintendent in 1988–90.

likewise was the director of student services. From there, he relocated to Denver to maintain his ties with Gilberts.

In part, Gilberts wanted Koeppe in Denver because he knew that Koeppe was often blunt, openly telling the superintendent when he thought he was mistaken. The two especially stuck together in District #1 where they found themselves having to fight the inbred system of administrative loyalists who had been nurtured by Kenneth Oberholtzer. The new superintendent recalled that out of approximately 400 DPS administrators when Gilberts had taken charge, all but a handful had risen in the system.

Compared to the intent clashes and close press scrutiny Koeppe had seen in DPS, he found being superintendent in Cherry Creek a manageable, thriving position. Yes, he admitted, Cherry Creek bused students. Officially, it "transported" them via buses simply to get them to school as opposed to "busing" referring to transporting students in the name of integration.

Looking back on DPS during the Gilberts era, Koeppe described the period as "hectic times" and the "war years." He saw the role of the superintendent as primarily a communicator who brought together all school constituencies. As such, it was necessary for the administrator to be fiercely honest, calling the shots as he saw best.

On taking office as DPS superintendent in September 1988, Koeppe's number-one priority was pushing through a mill levy hike in November. As the head of the district, Koeppe acted much like his forerunners, appointing numerous study committees. Among his public relations gestures was volunteering for the district's homework hotline. Operated out of George Washington High School, it emerged in the fall of 1985 as a phone service students could dial when they were stumped on assignments. Besides Koeppe, volunteers included Mayor Federico Peña and

District Attorney Norm Early. Personally, Koeppe had excellent ties with Peña. One month he visited the mayor at city hall; the next Peña traveled to 900 Grant Street to see Koeppe.

By the end of the 1988–89 schoolyear, Koeppe stated he was "extremely pleased" with what he had accomplished as superintendent. Right after he made the announcement, the district received the results of that year's the standardized Iowa Tests. They were worse than expected.

Working with the school board, Koeppe aimed to redress the declining test scores in the district. To achieve this end, in September 1989 DPS announced it was eliminating remedial classes. Henceforth, it would mix low-performing students with those in regular classes. It was unclear how this was to help students struggling to master subjects. Putting them in with normal learners might lead them to be left even further behind in their studies. No one, critics of the approach observed, called for placing untalented youngsters on sports teams next to star athletes. Test scores did not improve under the new approach.

Already on October 29, 1988, the board had extended Koeppe's contract to the end of the 1989–90 schoolyear when its search for a new leader appeared hopeless. The superintendent later regretted accepting the offer. Unlike his post in Cherry Creek, where he had a smooth working relationship with the board, he found himself continually at odds with the directors of DPS. He gladly exited the superintendent's seat at the end of his second year. By this time, those unhappy with the direction of the schools blasted him for his secrecy and failure to turn around the district.

Photo by Phil Goodstein

In 1988, the University of Colorado dedicated the North Classroom Building on the Auraria campus as the prime location of its Denver program. Dick Koeppe, superintendent of DPS from 1988 to 1990, was a member of the faculty of the UCD school of education during the 1980s and 1990s.

During his last year, Koeppe groomed his successor, Evie Garrett Dennis. On taking charge as superintendent, he had found himself swamped by the many uncompleted tasks that had been left hanging since the dismissal of Scamman. As such, he needed an efficient assistant. After James B. Bailey refused Koeppe's offer to stay with the district as deputy superintendent, he asked East High principal Jim Tracy to take the job. A 1950 graduate of East, Tracy stated he preferred to stay at East. Koeppe thereupon turned to Dennis, a high-ranking functionary who was most articulate and always let people know exactly where she stood.

Impressed by her skills and candor, in November 1988 Koeppe named Dennis deputy superintendent as of January 1, 1989. She had the reputation of getting things done. According to her daughter, Dennis was able to do one thousand things at once. Koeppe stated no one had pressured him to make the choice. The board approved Dennis' nomination on December 15, 1988. On August 15, 1989, the board unanimously stated she was to take charge of the district on September 1, 1990, awarding her a three-year contract.

After leaving as superintendent, besides returning to the UCD education program, Koeppe served for a while as a consultant with DPS, particularly helping train those volunteering for the district's collaborative decision-making bodies in the early 1990s. By 2020, he was among the few survivors of the school busing wars of the late 1960s/early 1970s when he shared memories of them.

Evie Dennis

The new superintendent was extremely well-known among DPS insiders. Evie Garrett Dennis always stood out in a crowd and readily called attention to herself and her achievements. In some ways, her hiring was the product of sexual and racial politics. Amidst the dismissal of Scamman, loud voices in the black and Latino communities insisted the district needed a minority as its head. By this time, as a legacy of busing, 63 percent of the students were either African-American, Hispanic, or of some other ethnic or racial minority while the city as a whole still had a majority of "Anglos." As had been the case since the 1970s, affluent white denizens often did not send their children to DPS, especially when they were subject to busing during elementary years.

As the firing of Kishkunas, Brzeinski, and Scamman had shown, traditional white men had not succeeded as administrators. DPS needed a new approach. Many African-American and Hispanic champions of education had dismissed the national search for a successor to Scamman as a costly charade. Instead of wasting money on it, DPS should find its next leader among the many well-qualified Mile High black and Latino pedagogues. Paul Sandoval, who had been the real leader of the board at the time of Scamman's exit, had both backed the national search and the hiring of a local minority.

Among black and Hispanic educators, none more fit the bill to lead DPS than Dennis. She was a veteran of the system, an excellent publicist, and had an assertive personality. The district's new leader had a reddish tint to her face and an attractive blonde head of hair. Insiders debated whether it was natural, a dye job, or a wig. (Pictures of Dennis in the 1960s and 1970s show her with a gorgeous head of black

GP

Evie Dennis was the first woman and first black to head DPS, serving as superintendent from 1990 to 1994.

hair.) The new superintendent was a master of a royal wave of greeting, particularly when she drove by teachers and staffers in her chauffeured limousine.

Born Eva Garrett in Canton, Mississippi, on September 8, 1924, Dennis was the daughter of a preacher who ran a small saw mill. The eighth of nine children, she lost her mother while in high school. Her father saw that seven of his children made it through college. The future superintendent moved to St. Louis after graduating from high school. In 1950 she married Philip Dennis of Chicago, a medical student in St. Louis. The couple divorced in 1951, the same year Evie Dennis gave birth to her only child, Pia.

After working in a potato chip factory, the young woman was a hospital attendant at St. Louis City Hospital from 1947 to 1953 while attending St. Louis University, receiving her degree in biology in 1953. On graduating, she was a lab technician at the Washington University School of Medicine. Subsequently a research assistant on allergies at the St. Louis Jewish Hospital, she relocated to Denver in 1958 as a research assistant at the Children's Asthmatic Research Institute and Hospital (CARIH) at West 19th Avenue and Lowell Boulevard. It was the successor to the Jewish National Home for Asthmatic Children. Along the way, Dennis received additional training at prestigious national hospitals and universities. The future superintendent frequently helped physicians and researchers put together papers for medical journals.

In September 1966, Dennis joined DPS as a math teacher at Lake Junior High—it was directly to the south of CARIH. She claimed the principal of her daughter had recruited her for the post. At that time, DPS bused some students living close to Barrett to Lake in the name of relieving overcrowding at Smiley and Gove.

Before long, Dennis was a counselor at Lake. During this period, which saw the intense clashes between the Denver Federation of Teachers and the Denver Classroom Teachers Association, she lined up with the DFT. She was among those who went out on strike in 1969.

After having done graduate work at DU from 1964 to 1966, in 1971 Dennis gained a master's in education from CU. The same year she joined the administration as what the district called a "community specialist." About that time, she became DPS's coordinator of the newly established Black Education Advisory Council. As such, she connected the concerns of the citizens serving on it with the school board and the superintendent's office.

On May 22, 1973, Dennis was near the ladies' room on the third floor of 414 14th Street close to the point of explosion when a bomb racked the building. She was not injured. In retrospection, she later said she might have been the target of the device since she had written a statement about busing that Judge Doyle used in his integration order. In 1976, Dennis emerged as administrative assistant to Superintendent Louis Kishkunas. As such, she frequently represented him at community meetings. Included was being the superintendent's representative on the board of the Denver Council of the PTA.

After the school board ousted Kishkunas and installed Joseph Brzeinski as superintendent in 1977, Dennis found herself exiled to a newly created post as the director of human relations and student advisory services. Among her duties was submitting annual reports to the United States District Court about the status of the busing order and DPS's efforts to become a unitary district. In 1979, the administrator was a prominent supporter of the re-election of Omar Blair to the school board. Dennis was a members of the Ad Hoc Committee in the course of 1980–81.

By the mid-1980s, Dennis was the district's executive director. This was something of the equivalent of being its chief operating officer. The aspiring superintendent had an excellent knack for gaining publicity. The *Superintendent's Newsletter*, the inside DPS publication, frequently listed the many honors she reaped and her numerous international trips.

Even before she became a ranking figure in DPS, Dennis had asserted herself. Soon after moving to Denver, she settled in the flourishing middle-class black section north of the City Park Golf Course, living at 3072 Cook Street. Her daughter, Pia, was bused to Park Hill School for first and second grades where she was a stellar student. Pia Dennis was among the many black children who landed up in the new Barrett Elementary in 1960. This did not please Evie Dennis who was among those outraged by the opening of Barrett as something of a Jim Crow academy.

The tall, long-legged Pia Dennis was a track star. To help assure her daughter had opportunities to compete, Evie Dennis helped form the Mile High Denver Track Club. It was part of the Amateur Athletic Union (AAU). Evie Dennis rapidly rose in the national federation, gaining election as its vice president in 1978, when she was its first black woman officer. This was part of the pedagogue's wide-spread involvement in sports.

Back in 1972, Dennis was part of the crew accompanying the United States Women's Track and Field Team to the Summer Olympics in Munich. The next year, she joined the woman's AAU Track and Field Team on its summer tour. The future superintendent played a key role in coordinating the women's Olympic team at the 1976 games in Montreal. The National Association for Girls & Women in Sport gave her its highest honor in 1983. While superintendent, Dennis served on the National Defense Advisory Committee reviewing athletic programs at service academies. In 1988, she was the delegation chief of the United States team to the Summer Olympics in Seoul, South Korea. Four years later, she became a member of the elite International Olympic Committee, the inaugural black woman on its board. Eventually, she was enshrined in the Colorado Sportswoman's Hall of Fame.

Dennis had a knack for receiving awards. Among the groups heralding her was the International Olympic Committee. It granted her distinguished recognition during the 1992 Summer Olympics in Barcelona. She was a past vice president of the United States Olympic Committee who had been a premier promoter of the games.

In a way, this was a strong political statement. Many of the people becoming politically active and visible in Colorado politics in the last quarter of the 20th century had cut their teeth on shooting down Denver's bid for the 1976 Winter Olympics. In contrast, Dennis had supported the games at a period when many leading black athletes boycotted the Olympics or sought to make political protests at them. Personally, she was close to Jerome Biffle, an East High alumnus, who had won a gold medal in track at the 1952 Summer Olympics. He went on to be a teacher and coach at East.

Additionally, Dennis retained her interest in medicine, serving on a wide array of boards dealing with health issues. For a while, she was the president of the foundation promoting awareness and treatment for lupus. Politically involved, she had close ties with leading Democrats, being invited to the White High for the 1997 inauguration of President Bill Clinton. In 1999, the Rocky Mountain chapter of the American–Israel Friendship League specially honored the then retired superintendent—for a while Mayor Wellington Webb was president of that group.

By the time the school board tapped her to lead DPS, Evie Dennis held a doctorate. Those dissatisfied with the appointment immediately carped that it was a bogus degree. She received a doctorate of education from Nova University in Nova, Florida, in 1976. Located near Fort Lauderdale, the school had started in 1964 as Nova University of Advanced Technology. It had but 377 regular students in 1974 when it was rapidly growing. The school especially emphasized learn-while-you-earn programs where it gave students credit for life experience. Additionally, it reached out to educators. Having a national scope, it adopted clusters of administrators seeking advanced degrees. They took classes once a month in their home city for three years in addition to attending a week-long summer institute on the Nova campus. Dennis' 85-page dissertation, "Developing and Implementing a Viable Intergroup Educational Program in the Denver Public Schools," was based on her work in overseeing the court-mandated inservice instruction of teachers in 1974–75 in the wake of the court order that DPS employees take classes to assure their sensitivity to the requirements of the latest busing order. For the most part, the study is filled with academic jargon. Instead of focusing on how the program actually worked, the dissertation primarily looked at surveys Dennis and other supervisors had made of the effort. She concluded the initiative was a great success and a national model of how a district could successfully implement an integration plan. In contrast, Maurice Mitchell, who had headed the Community Education Council during the time Dennis administered the inservice program, dismissed the initiative as most ineffective. Rather than actively engaging teachers about ways by which they could assure that integration worked, it primarily showed them movies.

Harold A. Stetzler, once the DPS director of personnel, coordinated the Denver cluster for Nova. Having the doctorate gained Evie Dennis additional pay as a DPS administrator. At the same time Nova awarded the future District #1 superintendent a doctorate of education, other school districts refused to honor the Florida school's degrees.

Photo by Phil Goodstein

Evie Dennis, superintendent between 1990 and 1994, was a big supporter of athletics. The initials "DPS" decorate the football field on the Evie Dennis Campus, a huge educational park at 4800 Telluride Street in Green Valley Ranch.

Dennis fiercely defended the integrity of her doctorate, being proud to have left the doctoral program at CU for the Florida school. She was loyal to Nova University, supporting it when academic publications and daily newspapers attacked it as a diploma mill. The school pointed to its great success, observing its alumni had leading positions in schools across the country. Among them was the chancellor of the New York Public Schools. Nova advertised that five of the board members of the Council of Great City Schools, an organization bringing together the largest urban districts in the country, were alumni.

After Dennis gained her doctorate, Nova University rapidly grew. Upon merging with the Southeastern University of the Health Sciences in 1994, it became Nova Southeastern University. By the end of the 2010s, it had upwards of 20,000 students on multiple campuses when it was renowned for a program for those seeking positions in healthcare.

When Dennis took charge of DPS, she earned around $100,000 a year at a time when an average teacher received $31,254. In office, she projected herself as being tough but fair. A prime achievement as superintendent was getting voters to authorize a $199.6 million bond package on May 8, 1990. Since approving a bond in 1971, paid off in 1985, DPS had operated on a pay-as-you-go basis. Now, it argued, its buildings were again getting old. First-class education required a mass investment in upgrading them. Besides, the district had to prepare for growth. After years of declining enrollment, it believed it had turned the corner. New schoolhouses were needed for a new generation.

Originally, the school board planned to hold the bond election in 1989. As DPS sought the money, it found itself up against the ambitions of Mayor Federico Peña. The city was convulsed with debates over whether it should build Denver International Airport. The city's leader made it clear he would readily sacrifice anybody and everything to achieve this goal. Not wanting to compete with the airport or ask voters for more taxes too soon after a successful municipal bond election in November 1988, the district delayed its bond issue until 1990.

In explaining the need for the money, DPS stated it actually required $350 million to $400 million to pay for new construction and the upgrades of existing facilities. As it was, it was simply requesting the most basic revenue to enhance the schools. Included was a computer fixation. The district argued it was necessary to rewire buildings so computers were a central part of instruction. The issue set aside $93 million for four new elementaries, $35 million for the refurbishment of existing buildings, $20 million for the removal of asbestos and other building repairs, and $29 million for the computers. With the promise of money for almost every school, 16 percent of the electorate went to the polls, narrowly supporting the measure, 23,056–22,131. Barbara Grogan, a key figure in the Chamber of Commerce, was the head of the "citizens" committee promoting the bond issue. She stated it did not matter how small the majority was—DPS now had the money for future progress.

Even while seeing the district pass the bond issue, Dennis faced severe opposition within the administration. Some of her top staff members, particularly Deputy Superintendent George Starface and Assistant Superintendent Patricia Baca, moaned that Dennis failed to consult them on many key matters. Recognizing the obstacles she faced, on October 5, 1993, Dennis, who was approaching her 70th birthday, announced she was stepping down as superintendent at the end of the 1993–94 school year. By that time, her contract was set to expire while she faced severe criticism from members of the school board, especially Lynn Coleman. Though board president Tom Mauro fervently backed Dennis, rumors swirled she faced a fight to stay as superintendent. For the most part, it was business as usual during Dennis' years in office: constant controversies, sporadic achievements, and the unending complaints that the schools were not performing as well as they should.

Shortly after Evie Dennis retired, her daughter, Pia Dennis Smith, got in severe trouble as principal of East High. An alumna of the school, Pia Smith had joined DPS as a teacher after graduating from Washington University, a Jesuit school in St. Louis for which her mother had worked. The younger Dennis went on to receive a master's from UNC in 1987. A most dynamic young woman, Pia Smith emerged as principal of East in 1990—the district announced the appointment during the 20th reunion of her class of 1970. There she quickly bonded with students; many of whom often simply called the principal "Pia."

Over the years, the younger Dennis had held administrative posts, including being the director of the district's Advanced Placement program. To prepare students for it, she called for math teachers to channel students into calculus, avoiding lower forms of mathematics. This might have reflected an inability to keep track of money. Or so her detractors claimed.

Pia Dennis married a former football star. They had a son and a daughter. They sent their son Alex, who was six foot five and about 220 pounds, to the Catholic Mullen High School, where he was a top athlete. Excelling in football, basketball, and track, he was also an outstanding student. Upon his graduation in 2000, he headed to Stanford on a football scholarship.

Debt plagued Dennis' husband. Some around the district whispered he had a severe gambling addiction; others hinted at drugs. To help him pay his bills, she embezzled about $9,000, including money East had received for a study of the historic renovation of its landmark home. She pled guilty to one felony and one misdemeanor on May 10, 1995, for the misuse of school funds. The principal conceded she had written checks from the school to herself

1991 *Angelus*

Pia Dennis Smith was the brilliant daughter of Superintendent Evie Dennis. In 1990, Pia Smith became principal of East High.

and had cashed a Colorado Historical Fund check for personal use. The court sentenced her to four years probation and ordered her to repay the stolen sums.

Superintendent Irv Moskowitz, Evie Dennis' successor in office, stated he would retain Pia Smith as East's principal. Other than for her crimes, she had an excellent record in the district. His announcement came at the same time three members joined the school board on May 11, 1995. Among the first actions of the new board was taking up the case of the East High principal. On being sworn in, Rita Montero observed that DPS had fired six employees for theft since 1990, including a janitor who simply took an unopened carton of milk and drank it rather than discarding it. Smith did not deserve any special privileges because of her past service or who her mother was. DPS should not employ a felon who had stolen district money. Seeing what was coming, Smith quit DPS. In the wake of her departure, DPS conceded it had lax accounting and banking practices. Pia Smith went on to be the educational director of Botanic Gardens, later being an adjunct professor of biology at Community College of Denver.

Personally, Evie Dennis had a gambling problem. On her retirement, she owed considerable sums to casinos. Nothing was said about this when the school board met in secret session in late 1993, shortly after she had announced her impending retirement. With no public discussion or vote, it awarded her a bonus for $400 a month for the rest of her life as "deferred compensation" for her 28 years with the district. The board officially affirmed the action, five-to-two, in March 1995. JP Hemming and Lynn Coleman opposed it. About a year later, a Central City casino extolled Evie Dennis' gambling luck when she won jackpots of $1,140 and $1,200.

In 2008, the Colorado Women's Hall of Fame enshrined Evie Dennis. She died early the next year. DPS celebrated her in August 2010 when it named its new educational park, at 4800 Telluride Street in Green Valley Ranch, the Evie Dennis Campus. Pat Hamill, the kingpin in Oakwood Homes, the prime developer of Green Valley Ranch, eagerly supported the creation of the complex. Consisting of numerous buildings with different programs offering classes from early childhood education through 12th grade, the campus promised to assist students from "cradle to career." Most of all, the Dennis years saw the reshaping of the administration of the schools. In part, this stemmed from labor strife, an endemic problem during her administration.

A Note on Sources:

On November 13, 2008, p, 11B, the *News*, recalled the career of James B. Bailey. DPS PR, March 2, 1988, emphasized the DPS committee to choose the national consultant to pick the superintendent. A July 11, 1988, DPS PR told of the role of Floretta McKenzie. DPS PR July 19, 1988, mentioned the eight semifinalists and listed the groups invited to participate in the selection of the superintendent. With no explanation, the DPS PR of July 20, 1988, stated the district had postponed the planned forums.

Richard Koeppe shared his memories on August 26, 2019. Taylor, "Leadership Responses," 98, 190, touches on his career. *RMN*, October 20, 1967, p. 56, told of DPS hiring Koeppe as assistant superintendent. *DP*, April 21, 1972, p. 88, observed him quitting DPS to take the Cherry Creek post. *RMN*, August 15, 1988, p. 6, and *DP*, August 15, 1988, p. 1A, and August 21, 1988, p. 1B, reported him becoming superintendent. Also see *Cmq*, August-September 1988, p. 7. In April 2017, Charles Angeletti reflected on his long career in academia and the cynical nature of many search committees, emphasizing the false praise given to candidates for jobs. Dan Goe, who worked under Koeppe in Cherry Creek, discussed the superintendent on April 24, 2018.

DPS PR, September 30, 1988, told of the homework hotline. Also see *Cmq*, November 1986, p. 6. A district announcement on May 16, 1989, listed Koeppe's achievements during his first year as superintendent. *Cmq*, November 1988, p. 6, observed the extension of Koeppe's contract. DPS PR, May 22 and May 23, 1989, reported the result of the Iowa Tests. *RMN*, September 20, 1989, p. 6, mentioned the plan to eliminate remedial classes as a means of hiking test scores. *RMN*, December 3, 1989, p. 10, chronicled criticisms of Koeppe for failing to inform the public of his plans to ax 119 teachers.

RMN, August 15, 1988, p. 6, observed pressures for DPS to hire a minority as superintendent. *Cmq*, December 1988–January 1989, p. 5, and February 1989, p. 5, mentioned Evie Dennis becoming deputy superintendent and Koeppe's endorsement of her. On August 26, 2019, Koeppe recalled his impressions of Dennis and how he came to select her as deputy superintendent.

Tollette, *CBLP*, 62–63, includes Dennis. *Inside DPS*, May 1994, profiled her. BCL has a holding on Dennis, ARL 152. Box one has materials on her background and involvement with DPS. Much of the rest of the collection is filled with awards and certificates, especially from her athletic ventures.

Taylor, "Leadership Responses," 180, looks at Dennis' role during busing controversies. *SN*, September 7, 1976, pp. 2–3, observed her appointment as administrative assistant to the superintendent. *RMN*, June 19, 1977, p. 6, mentioned Joseph Brzeinski's purge of Dennis as an assistant to the superintendent. *SN*, August 29, 1977, p. 2, observed her becoming the head the Department of Human Relations. *Cmq*, August-September 1984, p. 3, reported her role as DPS executive director.

DP, August 13, 1989, p. 1A, reported Dennis was the prime candidate to be the district's next superintendent. DPS PR, August 15, 1989, heralded the naming of Dennis as superintendent for the 1990–91 schoolyear. It included her résumé. A copy of her résumé is also in FF 1:79 of her papers. *RMN*, August 16, 1989, traced Dennis' background in reporting her selection for the job.

Materials on Dennis were in drawer 32A of the Branscombe papers. Dennis recalled the bombing of the main administration building in an interview in *Our Neighborhood Schools* in Alweis, *Rebels Remembered*. *RMN*, August 28, 1994, pp. 6–9M, and August 31, 1994, profiled Dennis on her leaving office as superintendent. In informal conversations, especially on June 24, 2017, Jimi O'Connor, has recalled Dennis, her flamboyant hair, royal wave, and gambling problem.

SN, December 15, 1972, p. 20, and January 12, 1976, p. 22, observed Dennis' links to the Amateur Athletic Union and the United States Olympic Committee (USOC). On March 12, 1973, p. 30, *SN* told of her selection to accompany the AAU team on its tour. The publication, March 31, 1975, p. 34, stressed her role in the 1976 Summer Olympics, and the award of the National Association for Girls & Women in Sport, March 23, 1983, p. 56. Miller Hudson recalled the politics of the Olympics and Dennis' role on the IOC during a December 17, 2019, interview. *RMN*, September 12, 1988, p. 10, and *DP*, February 6, 2006, p. 2D, stressed Dennis' close ties with the USOC. DPS PR, July 14, 1992, told of her appointment to the National Defense Advisory Committee. *DP*, December 5, 1978, p. 29, observed Dennis' leadership position with the AAU. *RMN*, September 12, 1988, p.10, stated she was the first black woman on the USOC.

There is a blurb recognizing Dennis' support of the Olympics in the 1992–93 notebook of GP. *DP*, September 5, 2002, p. 1D, observed the ties between Dennis and Jerome Biffle. I review the fight over the 1976 Denver Winter Olympics in *Our Time*, 146–69.

RMN, August 20, 1989, pp. 8, 10, profiled Dennis, calling her tough but fair. FF 1:79 of the Dennis papers has materials documenting her involvement with a variety of committees promoting better health. FF 1:108 of the Dennis papers focuses on her presidency of the Lupus Foundation. FF 1:57 has a certificate of her attendance at the 1997 Clinton inauguration. FF 1:52 is the program of the American–Israel Friendship League honoring Dennis.

Dennis, "Developing and Implementing a Viable Intergroup Educational Program," is her dissertation. She argues the DPS inservice and integration program was a great success and a national model, especially compared to contemporary developments in Boston, 46–47. Mitchell, "Desegregation," p. 73, is highly critical of the inservice program. Even at that, he agreed Denver's implementation of desegregation was a national exemplar, p. 76.

WW, September 20, 1989, pp. 6–7, discussed the problematic nature of Evie Dennis' doctorate even while stating she was eminently qualified to lead DPS. In passing, it examined the questionable character of Nova University, especially its educational graduate program. The article stung Dennis. She complained mightily, including to some whom *Westword* had quoted. Her correspondence on the piece is in FF 1:89 of her papers. FF 1:88 has materials on Nova, emphasizing the influential scope of its alumni in school systems. Included is the school's November 1989 *Alumni Network*, p. 3, featuring Dennis on her appointment as DPS deputy superintendent.

The web index of the holdings of the library of what became Nova Southeastern University references a small collection on Evie Dennis, including a couple of the studies she wrote for DPS, notably "An Exploratory Analysis of School Climates: Facts Affecting Morale in the Schools." On August 1, 2019, Jodi Welch discussed Nova University and its programs for those seeking careers in healthcare.

The February 20, 1996, "Proposed Pupil Assignment Plan, 1996–97," p. 3, reviewed the 1990 bond issue; cf. DPS PR, January 19, 1990, and DPS PR, March 5, 1990. *Cmq*, October 1988, p. 5, told of the impending effort to ask for a mill levy hike and the bond issue. *Cmq*, March 1989, p. 7, and May-June 1989, pp. 3, 7, discussed the decision to delay the bond issue so as not to interfere with the campaign for Denver International Airport. *RMN*, March 19, 1990, p. 14, looked at Barbara Grogan and the push for the 1990 school bond. It reported the results, May 9, 1990, p. 6.

Ronald Emerson, "Denver Public Schools and Decentralization: An Implementation Game" (Ph.D. dissertation, UCD, 1996), 141, 165, cites the complaints of George Starface and Patricia Baca about how Dennis operated as superintendent. *RMN*, October 6, 1993, p. 5A, observed Evie Dennis' announcement of her impending retirement. In the process, it looked at school board politics. *RMN*, April 2, 1994, reported lobbying to hire a black to succeed Dennis. She reflected on her career as superintendent in an interview in *DP*, August 7, 1994, p. 1C.

FF 1:97 of the Dennis papers features the athletic achievements of Alex Smith, the son of Pia Smith. *RMN*, May 11, 1995, p. 4A, May 12, 1995, p. 4A, and May 13, 1995, p. 4A, and *DP*, April 5, 1995, p. 1B, May 11, 1995, p. 1A, May 12, 1995, p. 1A, May 14, 1995, p. 2C, and May 21, 1995, p. 1D, and *WW*, July 25, 1996, discussed the problems of Pia Dennis Smith. Jimi O'Connor remembered his clashes with Pia Smith during a conversation on November 17, 2018, when he informed me about the debts of her husband. On February 27, 2018, Rita Montero gave me quite a different version of the ouster of Pia Smith, stating the board fired her because the East principal had embezzled funds from student organizations. I attended East High with Pia Dennis Smith.

DP, February 25, 1995, p. 1A, exposed the secret meeting of the school board and its award to Evie Dennis of $400 a month as "deferred compensation." *For the Record*, April 1995, p. 17, listed the vote on the measure. *WW*, July 25, 1996, reported Evie Dennis' gambling wins in Central City. *DP*, January 19, 2013, p. 10A, mentioned the Dennis Campus. Volume three will deal with that complex.

Chapter Seventeen

Collaborative Decision-Making

E ven while Evie Dennis convinced voters to approve the 1990 bond issue for more construction, the district claimed it did not have enough money for teachers. As DPS launched its new building program, its contract with the DCTA was up for renewal at the beginning of the 1990–91 schoolyear. Initially, the school board was sure it would have no trouble reaching an agreement with the association. This was so much the case that it announced negotiating sessions were open to the public, a sign of the district's transparency. Far from proceeding smoothly, the bargaining quickly bogged down. (Traditionally, collective bargaining is held in private where both sides often threaten and bluff. When it is staged in the open, at times negotiations are something of theater, more designed to win the backing of the audience than achieve an equitable contract.)

By the time of the negotiations, the DCTA represented all but 1,000 of the district's 4,500 instructors. Those who did not wish to belong, including members of the DFT and individuals opposed to unions, had an annual opportunity to opt out of mandatory membership. Even so, as required by the collective bargaining agreement, the district deducted fees from their paychecks to cover the costs of the DCTA providing them with basic benefits.

The union labeled its negotiating document a "Revitalization of Denver Public Schools." Besides the obvious demand of guaranteeing its place as the exclusive bargaining agent in 1993–94 when the proposed three-year agreement was to expire, the DCTA also wanted to use the negotiations to have a greater clout in classroom decisions vis-à-vis the administration. In particular, the organization's proposal called for a form of school-based management where the teachers, working with the principal, parents, and staff, would have a prime say in how the school operated. Superintendent Dennis made it clear that this was unacceptable. Under her orders, DPS issued press releases blasting the demands of the DCTA.

447

The administration's comments were indicative. As negotiations stalemated, it was obvious teachers were extremely frustrated with the existing management. In light of the stagnant enrollment and plummeting test scores, nobody was happy with the schools. Given that none of the players had any larger vision to explain what had gone wrong, each sought power from the others. The superintendent wanted to break what she believed were union-imposed work rules limiting her ability to reorganize schools and reassign teachers. The DCTA wished to protect its members from administrative diktats.

Most of all, classroom instructors complained they had been left behind by budget cuts. Teacher frustration with the district and the DCTA came out in 1986 when 1,646 members of the union authorized a contract promising a 1 percent pay hike. Another 667 said no; 835 failed to cast ballots. (Usually members ratify union contracts by margins of more than 75 percent.)

Some who voted no were skeptical of the district's promise of a 6 percent hike in 1987 if funds were available—they were not. By this time, DPS had among the lowest starting salaries of any district in the metropolis. Not only did the cost of living increase while salaries were stagnant, but cutbacks in materials meant concerned teachers had to open their pocketbooks to pay for necessary classroom supplies.

The 1990 proposed contract failed to address these concerns. Before long the negotiations were at an impasse. The hope that open sessions would facilitate the agreement quickly faded. DPS and the DCTA agreed on an outside mediator. On December 15, 1990, after the facilitator failed to produce any understanding, members of the DCTA authorized a strike on the week after classes resumed following the winter break. Ed Garner, the president of the school board, thereupon threatened to break any such strike, complete with the firing of all teachers who dared stand up for themselves. In the process, he drew upon traditional anti-union rhetoric. As much as ever, teachers were supposed to be professionals who were too elevated to strike over wages and working conditions.

Nobody more agreed with Garner than Democratic Governor Roy Romer. Elected in 1986 with the support of the labor movement, he announced he would prevent the strike at all costs. By this time, Romer projected himself as the "education governor," the man undertaking bold initiatives to redress problems that had previously bogged down the schools.

Prior to his election, Romer had a checkered history on education issues. He had risen in Park Hill politics in the 1950s and 1960s when he was a member of the Park Hill Action Committee. First elected to the legislature in 1958, he had been a sponsor of the state's inaugural fair housing measure the next year. During the mid-1960s, when he was in the state Senate, Romer was a fervent champion of President Lyndon Johnson. Not only did he back civil rights, the Great Society, and the War on Poverty, but he was a strong advocate of the Vietnam War. On this basis, he was the Democratic candidate for the United States Senate in 1966. He badly lost the race to incumbent Republican Gordon Allott.

For a while, Romer dropped from the political scene. He enhanced a comfortable fortune in running his family's farm implement business while he expanded into

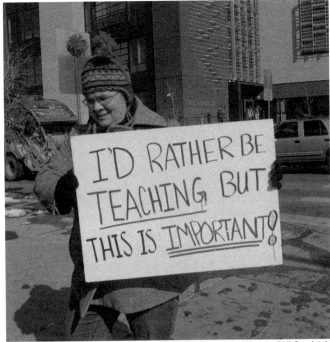

Photo by Phil Goodstein

Dedicated instructors would rather be teaching. On occasion, they have found themselves forced to walk out of classrooms in protest of poor pay and bad working conditions. Governor Roy Romer, a supposed friend of labor, used all of his clout to keep DPS instructors from striking in 1991.

real estate speculation and suburban shopping center development. Personally, he sent some of his six children to DPS; others attended private schools.

Romer's wife, Bea Miller, was especially active in pushing early childhood education. Included was hosting a private preschool at the family home at 4600 Montview Boulevard and the nearby Montview Presbyterian Church. Bea Romer's father, Reverend Arthur Miller, was pastor of the congregation from 1947 to 1967. Under him, it had been a premier part of the Park Hill Action Committee.

In 1974, Romer played a pivotal role in the Democratic campaign when the party, which had repeatedly lost state elections since 1962, gained control of the governorship, House of Representatives, and some other state offices. Newly elected Governor Richard Lamm rewarded Romer, making him his chief of staff. As such, the Park Hill politician often represented the state's leader on committees, including those dealing with education.

As governor, Lamm continually lambasted the schools while sending his son to the private Colorado Academy; his daughter attended DPS. The state's public schools, the governor lamented, were not turning out top scholars comparable to those graduating in the Soviet Union, Germany, and Japan. Romer echoed Lamm on education.

In 1977, when state treasurer Sam Brown quit to go to Washington to head ACTION under the Jimmy Carter administration, Lamm named Romer as the state's new treasurer. By this time, Romer stressed that he was essentially a Wall Street Democrat, a man who was liberal on social issues while affirming the mastery of the country's richest investors and corporations. When Lamm opted not to seek re-election in 1986, Romer was his hand-picked heir. The Republicans viciously red baited the treasurer during the campaign, targeting his strong civil rights record. Their tactic backfired. He easily gained the statehouse.

The new governor had an extremely brusque style. He often showed little interest in policies or people. At times, Romer rapidly flittered from program to program. When opponents of Denver International Airport asked questions about the wisdom of the field in 1989, the governor threatened to "roll over and crush" all who got in the way of the project. He endlessly touted development programs while offering generous subsidies to out-of-state investors to move to Colorado and reshape it in their image. In intervening in DPS labor negotiations, Romer insisted he was the man who would settle the dispute with no further squabbling on either

side. (Back during the 1969 teachers strike, Republican Governor John Love refused to become involved. He stated school matters were a local concern and he had no power over them.)

By the time of the negotiations, DPS financial problems were as bad as ever. Despite the bond issue and the governor's vows to improve education, increases in state financing for schools were less than the rate of inflation. Rather than seeing that the actions of the school board, especially its failure to raise the pay of teachers, might have left instructors with no choice but to strike, the supposedly pro-labor governor repeated there would be no strike. To prevent it, he turned to the 1915 statute creating the Colorado Industrial Commission. This was a viciously anti-union body formed in the wake of the Ludlow Massacre the previous year. Essentially, it kept unions from walking out without massive advance notice whereby employers had plenty of time to recruit replacement workers and break labor organizations.

1991 John F. Kennedy High School Annual

Teachers conducted informational picket lines in 1991 as they prepared to strike DPS.

Recognizing the governor's powers and threats, the DCTA voted to delay the strike. Members announced a work slowdown in grading papers and various tasks outside of the classroom. Romer, in turn, ordered the heads of the Colorado Department of Education and the Colorado Department of Labor and Employment to intervene in the contract negotiations. The leader of the latter body, Joe Donlon, a veteran of the union movement, oversaw the effort. When he failed to break the deadlock, Romer personally took charge. He called in all sorts of experts while holding endless hearings. During them, speaking for the school board, member Tom Mauro emphasized DPS had to operate ever more like a business compared to the restrictive work rules the DCTA had been able to achieve in past contracts. This was an open message that the board hoped to break the union's power.

Tensions lingered during the first months of 1991. The prolonged negotiations and hearings drained energy from the strike vote. Most teachers did not want to walk out. They were concerned about their students and the disruption of classes. Still, they realized that, given the refusal of DPS to concede key issues, if they were not ready to strike conditions could get worse. Meanwhile, as bargaining sessions continued to go nowhere, morale plummeted.

Finally, nearly 12 weeks after Romer had first intervened and had announced that a settlement was at hand, the governor dictated a contract on March 27, 1991. The DCTA accepted it. The deal expired on August 31, 1994. (Compared to Romer's active intervention into Denver school politics, neither outgoing Mayor Federico Peña nor any of the candidates wishing to succeed him in the May 1991 election paid much heed to the issue.)

Besides dealing with such traditional labor-management issues as pay, discipline, working hours, and the right to personal leave, Romer saw that section five of the contract created collaborative decision-making committees (CDM) for all District #1 schools. Not only were they a product of some of the union's demands and the suggestions of corporate educational champions, but the bodies were also something of a re-invention of the wheel. If nothing else, they highlighted the marginal role of school improvement and accountability councils.

School Improvement and Accountability Councils

In the early 1970s, "accountability" was a buzzword. Different people had vastly different definitions of what it meant concerning the schools. To make it a reality, the legislature passed House Bill 134 in 1971. It required all public schools be accountable to the community. To assure this was the case, the measure ordered each district to create an accountability committee. The bodies reported to the Colorado Department of Education.

In response to the legislation, the school board formed the District School Accountability Council, appointing its members on December 16, 1971. The new bureau, in collaboration with the superintendent's office, created an accountability committee at each school. It was to consist of the principal, teachers, concerned parents, members of the community, and a representative of the PTA to review the operations of the school. Such top DPS administrators as Carle Stenmark, Richard Koeppe, and Joseph Brzeinski were on the district body — all subsequently acted as superintendent. An immense amount of paperwork flowed from the effort.

452

THE DENVER SCHOOL BUSING WARS

Doris Banks Papers, Auraria Archives

In 1966, Roy Romer unsuccessfully ran for the United States Senate. He went on to serve as governor from 1987 to 1999. While in office he constantly tinkered with the public schools. Personally, he sent some of his children to private schools.

There was nothing new about the committees. As part of the post–World War II building effort, the district formed numerous bodies of citizens and parents to advise it about the location and scope of new buildings. DPS had had school advisory committees for decades. In 1967, for example, it had 96 such commissions in 117 schools. The district invited the bodies to comment twice a year about everything from teacher salaries to class sizes to the character of buildings to equal educational opportunity. School advisory committees waxed and waned, often reflecting activists among the parents. Unlike the accountability councils, they did not have a specific legal mandate.

The racial and ethnic pressures surrounding busing controversies led DPS to create advisory councils including for blacks, Hispanos, and Native Americans. At the same time it was pushing the new accountability committees, the district also had an Advisory Group on Educational Excellence. Private organizations, such as the Denver Coalition for Educational Priorities emerged. That group called for a community review of the DPS budget to assure that district's number-one priority was the education of students. In passing, it worked with accounting firm Arthur Andersen to review DPS's finances.

For the 1981–82 schoolyear, DPS totally reorganized the District School Accountability Council into the District School Improvement and Accountability Council (DSIAC). Initially, it had 34 members. There were now school improvement and accountability councils (SIAC) at each school. On September 30, 1982, the board incorporated existing parental advisory committees and individual school budget advisory councils into the SIAC framework. It charged the district council with reviewing reports and overseeing the committees at individual schools.

From the beginning, SIACs had extremely confused lines of command. Included was a built-in conflict of interest: the principal was a key player on the council which was to assure that the principal was accountable to the council. The DSIAC was to link the individual schools to the superintendent and the school board.

A prime responsibility of the DSIAC was to remind schools they had to create school improvement plans. These documents were filled with idealistic rhetoric. It is unclear whether such efforts had the slightest impact in actually increasing the academic achievements at the schools. Nor was there commanding evidence that SIACs accomplished anything in making the schools improved and more accountable. Other advisory commissions remained in existence, focusing on the district's budgeting procedures and employment policies. DPS likewise retained councils advising it about the specific outlook of racial and ethnic groups.

To encourage the SIACs and other advisory groups, DPS created a Department of School Advisory and Accountability Services. New bureaus constantly came and went. Included were modifications of the SIACs. A sweeping amendment of the school finance act in 1988 increased the role of the Colorado Department of Education in requiring annual reports from the councils. Ideally, the bodies reflected the demographics of the school attendance zones they served. Rules stipulated the reports include information about the racial, ethnic, and gender divisions of the learning community.

Despite constant reminders from the district council and goading from the administration, many local committees never produced the annual profiles of the schools they were supposed to write. There was often an extreme gap between the glowing suggestions spewed out by members and the ways schools sought to solve the day-to-day learning problems. At times, the reports appeared to be nothing more than busywork.

There were a wide variety of DSIAC subcommittees. They dealt with everything from academic standards to reviewing possible charter schools to probing the district's transportation system. At times, the leaders of the DSIAC complained the administration essentially ignored them, only consulting with the committee when it was sure the accountability board would agree with the superintendent's policies.

The SIACs depended on volunteers. Many concerned citizens served on them. Almost anybody who wanted to could find a place on a school council. Included were what the district called "non-parent" community members. Often these were men and women whose children had graduated from DPS. Among them was Art Branscombe, a longtime education reporter for the *Denver Post* who, with his wife Bea, was always a foremost champion of the district while advocating integration programs. Attendance at SIAC meetings was often miserable with more members being absent than present.

The SIACs reflected the socioeconomic composition of parents. Well-educated, affluent individuals were far more likely to volunteer for them than poverty-stricken individuals, many of whom were intimidated by teachers and principals. Though whites were a definite minority in DPS enrollment once the busing order rolled forward, they were a majority of SIAC members. A 1996–97 census totaled 1,608 people participating in the accountability councils. Included were 110 administrators. The count found 11 Indian, 148 black, eight Asian, 231 Hispanic, and 610 white members of in SIACs. As was typical of DPS numbers, the sum did not add up to the 1,608 who were part of the accountability councils.

The DSIAC was frequently a cheerleader for the schools. This particularly came out in the mid-1990s when its curriculum subcommittee reviewed the city's 18 middle schools. At a time when problems overwhelmed middle schools, leading some elementaries to expand through eighth grade, the DSIAC report was glowing. All the places, it declared, were excellent efforts that were orderly and well maintained.

Community Control

Despite the less than sterling achievements of SIACs, they were part of a rage for what the district branded "site-based management." This became official district policy in 1986. In some ways, it stemmed from fights for community control of the schools in New York City in the late 1960s. Seeing that schools, particularly in poverty-stricken areas, failed to produce magical results, reformers claimed the gigantic Gotham district needed to connect people living near the schools with teachers and administrators. This included allowing concerned parents, neighbors, and businesses a say in how the schools were run. The Ford Foundation especially pushed the measure, providing money for it. This was primarily the doing of the foundation's head, McGeorge Bundy, previously a foremost Vietnam hawk when he was national security advisor to presidents John F. Kennedy and Lyndon B. Johnson from 1961 to 1966.

Far from improving New York schools, community control produced chaos, including a bitter strike by the United Federation of Teachers in 1968–69. It was never clear exactly which community was controlling the schools — communities are internally divided by class, race, religion, and ethnicity. The teachers union decried community control as essentially a means of undermining the job security of instructors and subjecting them to the whims of power-hungry people who claimed to represent the community. Proponents were unable to point to any great achievements community control produced.

Nonetheless, community control appeared an idyllic alternative to a dysfunctional, hierarchical system. Likewise, proponents argued site-based management was the epitome of democracy. In 1989, the Los Angeles United School District adopted a form of it with no great success. It did so about the time the Denver school board, at its January 5, 1989, meeting, committed itself to a dialogue with the DCTA about site-based management. The goal was "shared-decision making." Already in 1985–86, Superintendent James Scamman insisted he was delegating more powers to individual schools. In part, this led to opposition from top administrators and, eventually, to his ouster.

Not all teachers embraced site-based management. They saw themselves as pawns being manipulated by grandmasters who might well interfere with their professional expertise in the classroom. As had been the case in wars over community control in New York City, they also feared they would be scapegoats if the program did not deliver as promised.

Schools are a central part of the community. Such was the idea behind community control in the 1960s and 1970s. On a more prosaic level, DPS has worked with neighbors and businesses in making school playgrounds part of communities. Such is the case at Knapp School, 500 South Utica Street.

Nor was the school board very clear about precisely what site-based management meant, particularly in regard to district-wide standards. Indeed, the more the district stressed site-based management, the more it increased its emphasis on standardized tests. This was a glaring contradiction since site-based management meant that schools were no longer bound to follow the district's curriculum. In the process, DPS's long-established, creative, flexible curriculum program, which dated back to the efforts of Superintendent Jesse Newlon in the 1920s, more or less went by the wayside. As opposed to efforts to permit teachers to work with students based on the youngsters' ability and existing knowledge, DPS, partially under pressure from Governor Romer, increasingly made the results of standardized tests the only measure of learning.

In part, the demand for community control also reflected a long-lingering controversy about the very essence of the schools. Some educational advocates projected schools as nothing more than service-delivery agencies, i.e., places which provided education for children whereby teachers were assembly-line workers pouring knowledge into the heads of students as measured by the tests. Others insisted the schools had to be a flexible partnership, bringing in members of the community while making sure parents were an everyday part of the learning experience. Romer paid no heed to the latter concept. As much as anything, the governor ignored existing means of citizen and parent input such as the SIACs through the creation of CDMs.

CDMs in Action

In settling the 1991 labor dispute, Romer's order specified that all schools, regardless of the enrollment, were to have a CDM consisting of the principal, four teachers selected by the faculty, three representatives of the parents and the community, one staff member, and a representative from the world of business. The DSIAC quickly went on record supporting site-based management. As much as anything, it hoped the governor's measure would allow members of SIACs more clout.

As had been the case with SIACs, participation in CDMs was extremely uneven. Some parents and community members eagerly volunteered for them. These were often the same people who showed up as leaders of PTAs and the precinct committees of the Republican and especially Democratic parties. Such individuals were also actively involved in neighborhood improvement associations. Some had served on SIACs. Those giving their time to the bureaus had been actively involved in the education of their children. They attended back-to-school nights and, when necessary, donated to provide school supplies and programs. The same people were often on both a school's SIAC and CDM.

There were many working-class members of CDMs. Few individuals mired in poverty, whose children performed poorly in school, joined the bureaus. Such parents, who struggled to make ends meet, frequently held two or three jobs. As had long been the case, some parents, including undocumented aliens, feared any encounters with the authorities. Especially after the end of busing in 1996, some schools, invariably in low-income neighborhoods, were unable to recruit enough parents and community members to have full CDM committees. All the while, cynics sniped at the governor's order. Ed Lederman of the Coors-financed free market Independence Institute mocked the program as "ersatz educational reform." The CDMs, he derogatorily stated, were nothing more than "student councils for adults."

The lack of participation by low-income individuals, educational champions observed, was indicative of the challenge public schools faced. Pedagogues repeatedly pointed out that success began in the home. As such, to improve education, it was necessary to motivate parents to assure students were engaged. The CDMs failed to breech this gap.

No more than the SIACs were CDMs reflective of the ethnic and racial composition of the student body. A 1998 count showed that out of 1,027 serving on the decision-making boards, 10 were Indian, 141 black, 10 Asian, 178 Hispanic, and 541 "other," i.e., whites or people who did not reveal their race/ethnicity. (The total added up to 870, typical of the unreliable numbers of DPS.)

The 1999 census listed 20 percent of the CDM members as Latino compared to a student enrollment of 50 percent; black students consisted of 22 percent of the district with 15 percent of CDM members being African-Americans. Whites, in contrast, composed 65 percent of the decision-making bodies while only 24 percent of the enrollment was white. All the while, backers of CDMs and SIACs emphasized the vital role of the Chamber of Commerce in backing this form of school democracy.

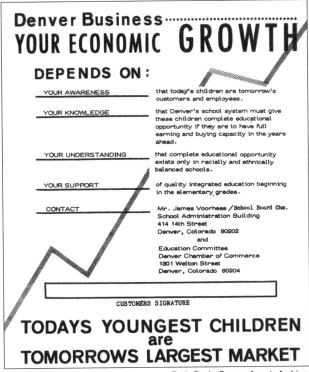

Doris Banks Papers, Auraria Archives

The Chamber of Commerce has constantly touted the school district. An excellent system, it has repeatedly stated, is vital to the area's economic vitality. This notice dates from 1969 when the business group endorsed the campaign for integrated education.

The Chamber announced its full support of the CDMs. The governor set up the decision-making bodies to assure an influential business role in the schools. The program called for the state commissioner of education to work with the corporate sector in helping select CDM members. The implication was that private money-making interests had an extra say in determining the nature of the schools.

According to enthusiasts, the CDMs were to have a direct link with the "city's major employers." Additionally, there was frequently a close overlap between the business representatives and the non-profit sector. Both the Denver Foundation and the Denver-based Charles Gates Foundation were active in nominating business voices to DPS committees. Major players on 17th Street, such as Del Hock of Public Service and Charles Steinbrueck, a one-time president of the Chamber of Commerce, showed up on key DPS advisory councils. Sue Burch, another figure with the Chamber who was a most active insider at the Capitol, served on DPS committees. There was often close communication between the administration, school board, and the education commission of the Chamber of Commerce. Additionally, a Public Education & Business Coalition loudly asserted itself, advocating funds and offering direction to the district. It was especially involved in helping train members of CDMs.

Having a business representative on the board revealed that there was to be no questioning of the economic establishment in the school curriculum. A further inference was that teacher seniority and the rights of labor interfered with education—there was no provision for representatives of trade unions to be on the boards. At the most, the president of the DCTA showed up as one of many community figures on various DPS advisory committees.

Despite such hype and support, many CDMs lacked a corporate or even a neighborhood business representative. While some who served on the committees in the name of representing business were concerned citizens eager to help the schools, others were representatives of major law firms, bond dealers, and comparable parts of 17th Street. In some cases, large firms urged employees to volunteer for the boards as part of virtually mandatory community service.

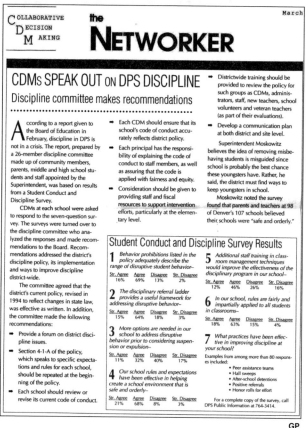

GP

A prime purpose of collaborative decision-making teams was to assist in school discipline. This newsletter, dating from about 1995, was co-sponsored by the Center for Quality Schools, a private organization bankrolled by the Piton Foundation, which was also a prime champion of CDMs.

Nor were teachers always eager to devote their time to CDMs. In some places, principals selected "volunteers" from the faculty whom they assigned to the committees. At times, this resulted in packing the bodies in favor of the head of the school.

CDMs at middle schools and high schools included two non-voting students, selected by student councils. The measure encouraged the participation of neighborhood organizations. Each CDM had the right to expand its size depending on the specifics of the school. Literature about both CDMs and SIACs made it clear that concerned individuals were welcome to volunteer for them. Virtually all who did so gained places.

At times, CDMs were a family affair. At Montclair, for example, Allan Kettlehut was the business representative; his wife, Rosemary, was the staff member on the board. Walden Silva was the community representative at Palmer School; his wife Mary was a teacher on the CDM.

Generally, those active in the school committees were advocates of community uplift. They readily embraced suggestions promising improvements. Surveys of the schools showed such individuals had overwhelmingly positive views about DPS. Some showed no grasp of why reforms never delivered as promised while there continued to be extreme public angst over the performance of the schools.

From the beginning, Superintendent Evie Dennis complained the CDMs undercut her role as superintendent. She also claimed she had severe enemies on the school board who favored the CDMs as a way of undermining her. The Colorado Education Association, she asserted, used its influence with Roy Romer to get the governor to create the bodies. In many ways, the implementation and the development of CDMs showed the maximum possible misunderstanding of what they were supposed to accomplish.

Illustrative of the problems with CDMs was that meetings were sometimes extremely tense. Disgruntled members thereupon appealed to the administration to resolve their differences. Seeing the need for solid direction and instruction of how CDM members should behave and what they ought to accomplish, the CDM Improvement Council oversaw the supposedly autonomous school-based collaborative decision-making bodies.

The CDM Improvement Council

The emergence of the CDMs did not simply stem from Governor Romer's order or the hopes of the DCTA contract. From the beginning, foundations asserted themselves, seeking to use their money to influence public policy. This was especially the case among business-connected non-profits that projected themselves as champions of childhood and education. Particularly visible were funds from the Annie E. Casey Foundation of Baltimore. Dating from 1948, it stemmed from the fortune of Jim Casey, the founder of United Parcel Service. It saluted his widowed mother who had raised him and his siblings. The goal was to assist unfortunate youths and give them an opportunity to advance within the business establishment. Ideally, CDMs helped make this possible.

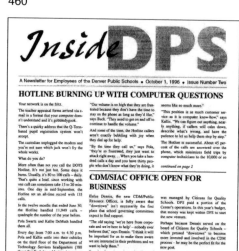

GP

DPS has issued a large number of short-lived publications, including Inside DPS. *The October 1, 1996, issue announced a new office to deal with problems with collaborative decision-making and school improvement and accountability councils.*

No non-profit played a greater role in CDMs and the operations of DPS than the Piton Foundation. Oilman Sam Gary created it in 1976 with earnings from his immense petroleum empire. Once an associate and disciple of Denver-based oil wildcatter Marvin Davis, Gary had holdings from Montana to Argentina. A self-professed liberal Democrat who had backed George McGovern for president in 1972 before lining up behind Ronald Reagan in 1980, Gary preferred to work from behind the scenes in charitable ventures through the Piton Foundation. The philanthropy aimed to help those mired in poverty have a chance to succeed within the system. The organization's name said as much, referring to the tool mountain climbers pound into the rock in the hope of having a firm grip as they make their way upward.

Eventually, the Piton Foundation was a foremost champion of charter schools while shouting "reform," i.e., destroying the traditional public school system for specialized, privately controlled but publicly funded academies. Its purpose, the organization stated, was "providing opportunities for children and their families to move from poverty and dependence to self-reliance." For a while, Gary's partner in Gary–Williams Energy, Ronald Williams, served on the board of the DPS Foundation, a corporate-dominated body emerging in 1992. He additionally liberally contributed to school board candidates backing "reform."

Virtually from the time CDMs started to function during the 1991–92 school year, the administration, backed by foundations, saw that the committees needed guidance and firm direction. CDMs were not free to run the schools as they wished, but had to operate under strict parameters. To make sure that those serving on the committees knew the scope of the bodies, DPS created a training program for volunteers. Key figures with the Charles Gates Foundation helped oversee it. (The Charles Gates Foundation stemmed from Gates Rubber. It had no connection with the Bill and Melinda Gates Foundation, an organization eagerly involving itself in school issues.) Del Hock, the head of the powerful Public Service Corporation of Colorado (soon part of Xcel) was a major corporate figure backing the initiative instructing members of CDMs.

The contract dictated by Governor Romer gave the CDMs the basic role in governing the school, including setting budgets and deciding whether to make textbooks a priority. The assumption was that there was a natural consensus whereby all parts of the community agreed that outstanding education benefited everyone. Some of the language defining CDMs sounded as if it had been taken from idealistic cooperative ventures of the 1960s. A prime purpose was to "work together toward the common good." There was zero reflection of why different classes and interests continually clashed. Also missing were the widely diverse approaches to education while there was no consensus about which approach was superior.

From the beginning, disharmony was part and parcel of CDM meetings. Often the bodies became quite bitter and dysfunctional. To redress the problem, the district created the CDM Improvement Council (CIC). This was a new layer of bureaucracy overseeing the CDMs. It was closely linked to the central administration. Each of the different clusters of DPS had a CIC to coordinate the school-based councils. Clusters were groups of schools centered around high schools. An assistant superintendent ran the CIC with two principals, three teachers, and three parents in each of the clusters. Overseeing them was the central CIC. During the late 1990s, members included Superintendent Irv Moskowitz, school board president Sue Edwards, and Leonard Fox, the president of the DCTA.

The CIC trained members of the CDMs on how they were supposed to behave. The district had a set of "consensus facilitators." They met with members of CDMs when dissent racked the school-based governing bodies. When those on a CDM were unable to reach an agreement, they were supposed to file an "impasse report" with the CIC. The supervising agency thereupon worked to clear up the problem. Additionally, to emphasize the importance of both CDMs and SIACs, DPS created a CDM/Public Resource Office in 1996. The district ordered CDMs to contact it when they needed assistance.

To reward those serving on the CDMs, the district staged an annual banquet for members. It was part of an incentive system. Near the start of the schoolyear, DPS hosted a "gathering" for people on CDMs. There it sought to provide direction and structure for the organizations. In many ways, the CDMs operated like mini-school boards. As much as members of the board of education, CDM activists sometimes sought to dictate specific ways a school was to be run rather than seeing that professional educators did an excellent job of running the school.

Quality Matters, the newsletter of the Center for Quality Schools, particularly emphasized CDMs and the CIC. The forerunner of the group, Citizens for Quality Schools, came together in 1991 during the labor tensions. Primarily, the organization pulled in key figures in the corporate and non-profit sectors. From the beginning, the Citizens for Quality Schools had the ear of Governor Romer. The group took credit for suggesting that he use his powers not only to prevent the strike, but to take advantage of the labor negotiations to transform the district via creating CDMs. The Piton Foundation bankrolled the Center for Quality Schools. The group operated out of the office of the Piton Foundation.

Collaborative decision-making committees, the Center for Quality Schools explained, were vital to help give schools a specific identity. Through site-based management, the private organization argued, schools would band with the surrounding community, so assuring they were reflective of the culture and character of the people living near them. It argued as much at the same time DPS was under the federal court order to become a "unitary district." From the beginning of the campaign for equal educational opportunity, exponents had insisted all schools must essentially be the same.

The Center did not pay any heed to this dichotomy. It initially was in charge of training members of CDMs. It also played a crucial role in forging the CIC. To encourage school board members to support CDMs, the Center worked with the PTA and the League of Women Voters in arranging school board candidate forums. Additionally, it projected itself as an ombudsman to which supporters of CDMs could turn if they found themselves stymied by the DPS hierarchy. Among its ventures was putting together a nine-part weekly television series in 1997–98, "Your Kids, Your Choice," broadcast on Channel Eight, the city hall frequency.

The Anschutz Family Foundation, Denver Foundation, Gates Foundation, Rose Community Foundation, and the Hunt Alternatives Fund joined the Piton Foundation in bankrolling the Center for Quality Schools. Representatives of 17th Street and city hall filled the Center's board. As much as anything, it was the voice of the establishment in promoting CDMs.

The Center for Quality Schools essentially liquidated itself at the end of the 1997–98 schoolyear when it ceased publishing *Quality Matters*. It argued that the CDMs had become so well established there was no longer a need for an outside lobbying group. The final issue of *Quality Matters* observed that there were no studies showing a link between decentralization, site-based management, and school performance. For that matter, CDMs quickly faded away, disappearing after they were not included in the 2003 contract between the DCTA and DPS. By that time, the district had suffered continued labor problems. This was especially the case in 1994 when the teachers again walked out of the classrooms.

The 1994 Strike

Not only was it highly questionable whether the creation of CDMs and Governor Romer's educational "reforms" did the slightest actually to enhance the learning climate in the schools, but his actions failed to improve labor relations. Tensions were especially taut in October 1993 when the agreement he had dictated for 1991–94 was nearing its end. At that time, the district announced it was virtually broke. Consequently, it could not pay teachers the promised 3.5 percent salary hike of the contract. In reaction, teachers staged a series of sick-outs that month. Compared to 250 to 350 who usually called in sick daily, during protest days 480 to 560 teachers stated that illness prevented them from coming to work. The result was to strain the DPS finances in paying for substitutes. If the administration actually cared about labor peace and the goodwill of the teachers, those participating in the sick-outs explained, it would find money for the promised wage increase. Instead of addressing what was wrong, the administration threatened students who announced they supported the teachers. It particularly targeted those who engaged in a solidarity walkout with the instructors at 9:15 AM on Monday, October 11, 1993.

By this time, DPS was swamped by endless budget shortages. No sooner had it seemingly balanced its books than new funding problems appeared. It continually asked voters to hike the mill levy. For the most part, they agreed. Still, the school board claimed there just was not enough money to go around.

To try to resolve the morass, in January 1993 the school board created the Budget Steering Committee. It was a combination of employees, administrators, and concerned citizens. Many of the last were also prime figures on CDMs and SIACs. Ideally, the Budget Steering Committee was part and parcel of the district's commitment to decentralization. For the most part, the council had no more impact on board policy than did the other advisory agencies. If anything, it was among the many programs the district added that did not directly deal with education.

The district's financial projections oscillated. At one time, it claimed it faced a $31 million shortage in 1994; a re-evaluation brought the figure down to $13 million. A suggested means of savings was cutting faculty and increasing class size. This was at the same time the school board asked voters for bond issues to construct new buildings, claiming they were necessary to redress overcrowded classrooms.

The DCTA bitterly protested the faculty cuts. Besides, it argued, the administration's numbers were untrustworthy. For example, in the name of saving funds, in 1993 Superintendent Dennis announced she was eliminating 26 of the top 80 administrative posts in the district. The union declared she had done no such thing. It was merely the appearance of action. An independent investigation by

Photo by Phil Goodstein

Militant actions by the Denver Classroom Teachers Association have inspired teachers through all of Colorado. Here a delegation of the Colorado Springs Education Association rallied for more pay near the Capitol in April 2018.

Denver Post education reporter Mark Stevens found only 14 eliminated positions. They saved the district $456,000 when it needed to find $31 million. Such clashes over numbers and DPS austerity sparked the 1994 teacher strike.

Morale in the classrooms was already low. Many teachers spent upwards of $500 annually in personal funds for classroom supplies. They worked an average 50-hour week. Instead of redressing the inequitable tax base, DPS hoped to balance its budget on the backs of the teachers. Even at that, the DCTA simply called for the public to open its purses since education was the best investment a community can make. In the process it repeated the lines of 19th-century advocates of public schools: it was much less inexpensive to educate youngsters than allow them to run loose whereby it was necessary to lock them up in prisons. The union gave no specifics about where DPS was to get the additional funds.

The union and administration eventually reached a creaky compromise in the fall of 1993. Bad feelings lingered. They exploded a year later in October 1994. By this time, the Romer contract had expired. The board and DCTA deadlocked over a new accord. By a two-to-one margin, members of the DCTA rejected a contract dictated by Joe Donlon, the head of the Colorado Department of Labor and Employment.

Donlon had acted at the behest of Governor Romer. The mediator's proposal did not deal with crucial issues. In particular, the teachers wanted essentially a 40-hour work week. This included more days for planning in addition to paid daily 45-minute lunch breaks. The upshot was 2,400 of the district's 3,800 instructors went out on strike on Monday, October 10, 1994.

Unlike the 1969 strike, when labor solidarity closed some deliveries to the schools, DPS managed to keep all of its buildings open with the help of 1,000 substitutes and 1,400 scabs — about 500 substitutes whom DPS called in honored the picket lines. Eventually, there were approximately 1,200 substitutes in the classrooms. Many students saw the strike as an ideal time for a break. About one-third of them supported the walkout by not going to school — around 20,000 of the 63,000 students were absent during the protest. On an average schoolday, approximately 90 percent of students were in classes.

Striking teachers staged frequent rallies. Included were boisterous picket lines in front of the administration building. The gatherings drew about 1,000 to 2,000 daily. The union arranged for members to have picket lines at all of the schools. Not surprisingly, there was a good deal of anger and name-calling between strikers and scabs. During the walkout, individual schools canceled many classes because of the lack of teachers. In places, such as at West High School, authorities herded the students into the auditorium, showing them Hollywood blockbusters.

Instead of probing why his intervention into DPS labor relations had so failed, Governor Romer resorted to brute force. As he had in 1990–91, he stated he was going to crush the strike. The attorney general threatened to fine strikers $100 a day in addition to getting the courts to order them to jail for up to 60 days. Consulting with the attorney general, Romer employed the Colorado Labor Peace Act. This was a measure dating from World War II designed to bust unions.

GP

Besides negotiating with DPS in behalf of teachers, the Denver Classroom Teachers Association has sought to elect its friends to the school board. Here is a 2019 vote solicitation it sent out in the wake of a successful strike it staged earlier that year.

When Romer announced that, under the provisions of the Labor Peace Act, teachers must not strike, the DCTA turned to the courts. After a hearing on the matter, Denver District Court Judge Larry Naves observed on October 12, 1994, that strikes by public employees were legal in Colorado. The governor had failed to cite any specifics as to how a walkout by the teachers would direly impact public safety. Consequently, the jurist upheld the right of the workers to leave their jobs.

Rather than accepting the judge's reasoning, the school board reacted to Naves' decision with mass bluster. It called for jailing striking teachers. There would be no further negotiations, it declared, as long as instructors were on the picket lines. The teachers replied that the board was responsible for the strike. Had it treated them with honor and kept its past promises, they would be in the classrooms. The administration had offered them such a pitiful contract they had no choice but to go on strike. Far from hurting children, they stated, their labor action actually improved the schools and so helped all students.

After Judge Naves upheld the legality of the strike and the teachers walked out, Romer again intervened. On the third day of the walkout, once more presenting himself as the super education governor, he personally took charge of the negotiators. Three extremely tense days of negotiations followed with Romer acting as mediator. After five days on the picket lines, the DCTA won. The teachers gained a 2.15 percent pay hike, worth about $5.1 million—the board had offered approximately $4.1 million. Besides getting the 45-minute lunch periods, the deal extended the teachers' year from 180 to 190 days. This allowed those who had gone out on strike to make up some of the time during which they were out as "inservice days." The agreement also specified that the contract was to overrule the power of CDMs in terms of specific staffing of schools. Members of the DCTA approved the agreement 1,953–125, on October 15, returning to work on Monday, October 17.

Labor haters blasted the teachers for daring to "strike against the children." They did not condemn the school board for policies that gave the teachers no option except to walk out. Solidarity was missing from the labor action. Unionized DPS workers, including clerks, custodians, and bus drivers, continued to report to their jobs. This reflected the decline of the Coalition of Employee Groups, an alliance of many of the unions representing DPS workers. For a while, it operated out of the DCTA headquarters at 1780 South Bellaire Street. That building was also the office of the Denver Association of Educational Office Professionals, the union representing DPS clerks and secretaries.

Despite the Coalition, most of the groups were on their own. Illustrative was the action of Local #1563 of the Amalgamated Transit Union. In 1993, it declined an offered 3.5 percent pay hike. The union, having about 400 members who drove DPS buses or maintained them, stated it recognized the district was suffering from a budget shortage. In exchange for giving up higher wages, it demanded DPS guarantee the members' jobs. This included rejecting privatization proposals, measures basically designed to destroy the union and reduce wages while allowing outside businesses to profit by providing school services.

In reaction to the 1994 teachers strike, members of the General Assembly pondered legislation to allow districts to fire striking teachers. Though the DCTA continued to insist it was willing to collaborate on virtually everything with the administration, bad blood continued to mark the relations between the union and the board. On occasion, negotiations during contract renewals collapsed.

A year after the 1994 strike, the CEA, the parent of the DCTA, occupied the former home of Silver State Savings at 1500 Grant Street as its headquarters. William Muchow & Associates designed the building, which opened in 1964, both to match the nearby Capitol and as a statement of modern architecture. It had cost the bank more than a $1 million. Back in the late 1970s, the Colorado Democratic Party rented part of the space as its headquarters.

The CEA committed itself to purchasing the new home in 1991. It paid $750,000 for the edifice, pouring $2.1 million into its renovation. Located catercorner from the Capitol, the complex included the headquarters of the DCTA. The Mile High union insisted it was working for "the schools Denver students deserve." For the most part, it had the affiliation of about three-fourths of the instructors. Besides classroom teachers, it had about 550 members among school paraprofessionals, psychologists, and social workers.

Other instructors belonged to the DFT. Some opted not to join a union. Among them were those who continued to insist they were "professionals." Many of the charter schools DPS increasingly opened beginning in the 1990s were non-union operations. By the late 2010s, the DCTA had around 2,940 members, about half

Photo by Phil Goodstein

In 1995, the Colorado Education Association moved to a new home at 1500 Grant Street. The structure went up in 1964 as the home of Silver State Savings. It came to include the offices of the DCTA.

of the total instructors in DPS, including those in charter schools. At that time, the CEA represented 38,000 to 40,000 teachers.

Evie Dennis had retired at the end of the 1993–94 schoolyear. As the subsequent strike showed, financial pressures remained on the district while it tried to make decentralization and site-based management a reality. At the same time it was pressed to pay for those initiatives, DPS estimated it spent about $12 million annually to meet the mandates of the federal court stemming from the Keyes case. Everything changed in 1995 when Judge Richard Matsch finally released DPS from court supervision.

A Note on Sources:

There were numerous press releases by DPS on the 1990–91 labor negotiations. Illustrative were those of August 27, August 30, September 11, and September 27, 1990. DPS PR, October 24, 1990, bitterly attacked the demands of the DCTA, upholding the power of the superintendent. In the process, it outlined the union's demands, including school restructuring and site-based management. The document includes a copy of "Revitalization of DPS."

Undated articles in the 1986–87 Clipping Notebook in GP outline the financial crisis of 1986–87 and how it impacted teacher salaries. *Cmq*, May-June 1987, p. 3, celebrated that year's contract between the DCTA and the district.

DPS PR, October 26, November 15, 16, and 30, December 11, 20, and 27, 1990, looked at the breakdown in negotiations. *Education Week*, December 5, 1990, analyzed the collapse of the talks. DPS PR, February 6, 1991, announced Roy Romer's intervention into the bargaining.

There are materials on Romer in the Branscombe papers. Included is the transcript of an interview with Romer discussing educational issues. In it, Bea Branscombe questioned Romer's sending his children to private schools. I review Romer's political background and role in boosting Denver International Airport in *DIA*, 101, 187, 195, 420, 422, 423, 458, 462, 463, 464, 473, 474, 491, 495, 503, 512, 523, *Our Time*, 69, 98, 99, and *Park Hill Promise*, 210–12. Schwartzkopf, "Collective Bargaining," 196, observes Governor John Love's hands-off position during the 1969 teachers strike.

The 1993–94 PTA Notebook in GP has the testimony from Evie Dennis and board representative Tom Mauro to the panel assembled by Romer in January 1991 to resolve the DPS contract impasse. The 1996–97 red BAC notebook in GP discusses the declining rate of state financing for the schools under Romer.

Ronald Emerson, "Denver Public Schools and Decentralization: An Implementation Game" (Ph.D. dissertation, UCD, 1996), is an academic look at the emergence of CDMs. It outlines the background of the 1990–91 union negotiations, 1–4. The study observes the strike vote, Romer's intervention, and the new contract, 5–10. The thesis is filled with mass statistical jargon and a meandering discussion of sociological methodology. It primarily relies on newspaper accounts and interviews with some of the key figures in the formation of CDMs.

A copy of the 1991–94 union contract is in the 1992–93 notebook in GP. Section five outlines the nature and scope of CDMs. In 5:3, the act encouraged civic involvement; 5:5 provided for the CIC; 5:6 outlined the on-going training requirements; 5:7 stressed the consensus goal. I commented on the creation of the CDMs in the April 1991 *Naysayer*.

The 1992–93 notebook of GP has a copy of DPS's *Collaborative Teams: An Interactive Model to Support Our Institution of Learning* (Denver: DPS, 1992). *Accountability*, which first appeared in January 1994, was a newsletter promoting CDMs and the accountability committees. Bill Winder, who was active in the accountability drive for CDE, was editor. It contains an immense amount of educational gibberish. Copies are in the 1994–95 notebook in GP.

SRv, November 1955, p. 6, emphasized the district's many citizen committees on its building plans. It told of school advisory councils, January 1958, p. 4. There is passing mention of SIACs in FF 21:33 Yasui papers. FF 21:35 refers to some school advisory committees prior to the state accountability mandate. *SRv*, March 1967, p. 4, looked at school advisory committees. *SN*, April 12, 1971, p. 47, mentioned the citizen advisory committee about the budget. FF 3:61 of the Ash Grove PTA Papers has 1974 DPS handouts about the various advisory councils. *SB*, October 17, 1960, p. 25, and October 31, 1960, p. 33, mentioned the school advisory committees.

CT, September 1971, p. 2, reviewed the state educational accountability law. *Cmq*, October 1983, p. 5, mentioned the Advisory Group on Educational Excellence.

Ibid., p. 2, and November 1983, p. 4, referred to the Coalition for Educational Priorities. A statement of the Coalition is in the 1982 PTA Notebook in GP. An undated article in the 1982–83 PTA News Notebook in GP mentions the clash between the PTA and the administration on district finances.

A CDE flyer, in the 1972–73 PTA History Notebook in GP, outlines the origins of accountability policies and councils. *SN*, February 14, 1972, p. 29, and March 16, 1972, p. 37, told about the emergence of the inaugural District School Accountability Council. A special March 1972 issue of *SN*, no pagination, listed the membership. The unpaginated 1974 *DPS Report* touches on community participation boards working with the district. *Focus*, April 1978, p. 3, emphasized the Department of School Advisory and Accountability Services and the wide variety of advisory committees.

The December 1996 report of the Instructional Focus Team, discussed the way DPS adopted site-based management in the fall of 1986. It traced the less than successful nature of the program. Diane Ravitch, *The Great School Wars* (New York: Basic Books, 1974), 329–36, 397, links the push for community control to McGeorge Bundy and the Ford Foundation. Also see Goldstein, *Teacher Wars*, 240–41, and Murphy, *Blackboard Unions*, 240.

Cmq, February 1989, p. 6, reported the January 5, 1989, board meeting and the commitment to "shared decision-making." On December 1, 2018, Jimi O'Connor stressed the irony of site-based management in view of the emphasis on standardized tests while he discussed the decline of the DPS curriculum program. Dorothy Gotlieb made the same point during a phone interview on January 23, 2020. *PTA Today*, March 1979, p. 12, dissected the push for standardized testing, arguing it was counterproductive to quality education. *Schools for a New Century* will review the rise of mandatory state-dictated standardized tests in the 1990s while Romer was governor.

"Colorado Families and School Project" was a June 1983 report by CDE. It was part of a national review of the links between school policy and families. In passing, p. 20, it emphasized the debate between schools as delivery agencies and as partnerships. A copy is in the 1983–84 PTA Notebook in GP.

The transformation of the School Accountability Council into the School Improvement and Accountability Council is in *Cmq*, October 1982. The newsletter mentioned DSIAC, February 1984, p. 3. An undated clipping from *DP* in the 1982–83 PTA News Notebook in GP outlines the new DSIAC.

Information about SIACs is overwhelming taken from GP. The collection includes about 15 big three-ringed notebooks filled with documents of the DSIAC from the early 1990s to the middle of the first decade of the 21st century. There are also scattered materials on SIACs in the Branscombe papers. During informal conversations in 2017–19, Sherry Eastlund and Dorolyn Griebenaw, both of whom chaired the DSIAC, recalled their experiences on the body and its impact.

The DSIAC report for the 1996–97 schoolyear, p. 10, listed the membership by race and ethnicity of those serving on the committees. A copy is in the 1997–98 notebook in GP. The November 1998 report of the DSIAC, p. 8, had a census of those serving on CDMs. It stressed the role of the Chamber of Commerce on the bodies, p. 1. Emerson, "Decentralization," 120, 125, deals with the relationship of CDMs and SIACs. A copy of the SIAC middle school review is in the 1994–95 notebook of GP.

The 1994–95 notebook in GP includes a December 2, 1993, DSIAC resolution supporting site-based management. On November 10, 1993, the body had heralded the "customers" of the district. The 1985 *DPS Report*, 4, emphasized the district was giving decision-making power to individual schools. Emerson, "Decentralization," 112, quotes Ed Lederman on CDMs.

There are mentions of the role of the Chamber of Commerce's education committee in the 1994–95 notebook in GP. The Chamber emphasized the ties in its legislative subcommittee report of December 1994. Fred Brown, *The Persistence of Vision: The Denver Metro Chamber of Commerce* (Golden: Fulcrum, 2011), is a subsidized book emphasizing the all-embracing role of the Chamber of Commerce and how it has operated as something of a shadow government.

BN, December 13, 1996, observes the role of the Public Education & Business Coalition. A DPS Staff Review, in the 1996–96 notebook in GP, links the Public Education & Business Coalition to training programs of CDMs. Sue Burch shows up on a list of the members of the 1994–95 DPS budget subcommittee. A copy of its report is in the 1994–95 notebook in GP. The 2000–01 notebook has a memorial to Burch who died on July 13, 2000.

The 1994–95 notebook in GP includes an outline on the nature of the DSIAC. The laws about accountability are in the February 1995 report of the DSIAC to the board of education. The holding also has a copy of *Strategic Plan, 1990–95* (amended version, June 17, 1993). Both are typical of the earnest uplift rhetoric of education supporters while they lack any larger vision.

Emerson, "Decentralization," 103, 139, 140, quotes Dennis' views about the CDMs, the CEA, and her problems with the school board. The study, 148, observes clashes between the administration, the board, and the community over the nature of CDMs, 148. The general conclusion of the study, chap. 5, is that the bodies were poorly implemented and understood.

I touch on the Annie E. Casey Foundation in *West Side*, 409–10. The *Naysayer*, February 2012, looked at the Piton Foundation; compare *NDT*, February 29, 1996, p. 3, *RMN*, April 7, 2001, p. 8C, and *DP*, April 26, 2010, p. 21A. *RMN*, December 11, 1983, p. 8, celebrated Sam Gary as among the country's richest men. *DP*, March 9, 1984, p. 1E, heralded him as a philanthropist, sketching his business empire. In informal discussions, Tom Torgove has praised Gary as a foremost donor to worthy causes. He also explained the symbolism of the name Piton Foundation.

There are copies of CDM impasse reports and rules for filing them in the 2000–01 CIC Notebook in GP, a volume including CIC materials dating from 1997. *BN*, April 7, 2000, told about the planned "gathering" for members of CDMs on September 23, 2000. *Inside DPS*, October 1, 1996, p. 1, emphasized the CDM/Public Resource Office.

The final issue of *Quality Matters*, May 1998, pp. 1–5, outlined the history of the Center for Quality Schools, emphasizing the group as the sparkplug in creating

CDMs. The sheet, p. 5, explained the financing of the operation, and p. 7, listed board members. Emerson, "Decentralization," 105, 110–11, 132, looks at corporate and non-profit funders of the group. The study also mentions the Public Education Coalition. *Schools for a New Century* will deal with the demise of CDMs.

DP, October 11, 1993, p. 1, glanced at the teacher sick-outs and the way the administration sought to punish students who supported the instructors. A copy is in FF 8:10 of the DPS papers. Materials in the 1992–93 notebook in GP outline budget pressures and the DCTA's demand that the district pay the promised salary increase of the Romer-dictated contract.

GP includes notebooks of BSC. They are filled with many financial statements and projections. Included are letters to the board suggesting specific changes in the district's spending. DPS PR, January 5, 1994, discussed the budget problems, stating a $13 million gap loomed. At that time, the district issued a monthly newsletter, *Putting Kids First—A Budget Update*. Copies are in the 1993 BSC Notebook in GP. *BN*, February 23, 1996, and March 15, 1996, emphasized the overcrowded condition of the schools.

The 1993 BSC Notebook in GP includes an April 12, 1994, press release from the DCTA denouncing the cuts in teacher positions. *Just the Facts*, a DPS newsletter, February 1975, emphasized the economy of spending for education over prisons. A Chuck Green column on the editorial page of *DP*, November 21, 1993, reviewed the controversy over whether the DPS administration had eliminated 26 top jobs, citing the research of Mark Stevens.

DP and *RMN* had front-page stories from October 10 to 16, 1994, about the teachers' walkout. None of the articles had any great depth, particularly about the position of the DFT or other school employees and organizations. *NYT*, October 15, 1994, had an overview of the strike and its settlement. Also see *Education Week*, October 26, 1994. *USA Today*, October 11, 1994, emphasized the school board's bluster and threats to jail striking teachers. I probed the 1994 walkout in the November 1994 *Naysayer*. *Legislative Link*, January 1995, reported the introduction of a Senate bill allowing the dismissal of striking teachers.

There is a file on the Coalition of Employee Groups in box one of the DCTA papers. On June 21, 2018, Ray McAllister shared memories of his involvement as the head of the group. A copy of the ATU's letter of March 10, 1993, about its contract and the threat of privatization, is in the 1992–93 notebook in GP.

Folder #252 in the Muchow papers at DPL, WH 1288, has plans for the building that became the CEA headquarters. Also see *DP*, January 14, 1962, and September 24, 1964, p. 31, *RMN*, February 24, 1963, p. 56, and June 24, 1965, p. 66, and *CJ*, February 27, 1963, p. 6. *CEASO Insider*, November 1991, p. 3, announced plans to buy 1500 Grant Street. The web pages of both the DCTA and CEA are relatively insubstantial. They list membership and the building at 1500 Grant Street.

Chapter Eighteen

The End of Busing

By the time Evie Dennis took charge as superintendent in 1990, the intense polarization over busing had faded. Blacks and Hispanos were on and off the board of education. Vehement foes of the court order had mostly left Denver or sent their children to private or religious schools. Even at that, as shown by the victory of such candidates as Naomi Bradford, Franklin Mullen, and Dorothy Gotlieb, Republicans and foes of busing still won elections through the 1980s.

Busing for racial integration faded everywhere during the decade before Dennis became superintendent. Courts increasingly realized that busing did not automatically provide quality education for all students. Still, there was no more ostensible Jim Crow. Other than for a lingering case in Charlotte-Mecklenburg, North Carolina, and the decisions by Judge Matsch, most jurists released school districts from busing orders.

Many proponents of the busing stuck to the Keyes case. Among them was Rachel Noel. She continued to insist that court oversight were vital in assuring equal educational opportunity. She was convinced that District #1 was so racist at its core that it would revert to its old practices without the constraint of the strong arm of the federal courts. While she conceded that busing never fulfilled her hopes, she blamed this on the way school board had sabotaged the effort. The reformer never pondered whether fundamental problems with the schools reflected social, class, and family divisions.

Gordon Greiner, the lead attorney for the plaintiffs, continued to insist on court oversight to preserve the perceived achievements of the legal battles of the 1970s. The result was an almost annual clash before Judge Matsch. The school board and many community figures argued DPS had turned the corner and had programs to assure equal educational opportunity without being subject to court rulings. Noel, Greiner, and others denied the assertions. For the most part, Judge Matsch sided with the original plaintiffs. Cynics argued the plaintiffs treasured their power whereby the court continued to listen to them over elected officials.

White flight haunted court decisions. Judge Matsch had continually to amend his order, especially concerning the percent of racial enrollment in schools, because the number of white students continued to decline vis-à-vis blacks and an ever larger Hispanic enrollment.

Still, busing continued. Anti-busing majorities knew better than to defy the court. The board kept promising new programs whereby Judge Matsch would grant DPS freedom from the busing order. What DPS needed to do, critics of court supervision agreed, was to convince the jurist that the district had complied with the order. In such a manner, it would gain the freedom to operate without a federal judge telling it what to do. This would improve education whereby learning, not abstract integration, was at the heart of the district.

To convince the court that it had complied with Judge Doyle's original order, on April 10, 1984, claiming it had made endless progress in submitting to the court order, the school board adopted Resolution 2233. It stated DPS had done its utmost to create a unitary district. The agency adopted the measure on the heels of Resolution 2228, a declaration that future school boards must be bound to respect DPS's commitment to equal educational opportunity. Observing it was ten years since the final DPS/court agreement on busing, the system argued it was time for it

Photo by Phil Goodstein

Old school buses are sometimes on the road performing a variety of other tasks. Included is hauling around people as part of Bronco Billy's, a local tour company.

At the orders of the United States District Court, DPS was forced to bus students between 1969 and 1996 in the name of abstract equal educational opportunity. Shown is the DPS bus facility along the east side of Federal Boulevard between West Severn Place and West Eighth Avenue.

to gain independence from court oversight. This would help it attract more students and provide better education to all.

The measure failed to convince Judge Matsch who ruled in June 1985 that DPS still had not done enough to overcome its past discrimination and assure equal educational opportunity. In the process, he ripped the district for bringing in new experts and counsel who cited endless statistics that had no bearing on the problems of DPS. Besides, the jurist observed, the district still had not come up with remedies to integrate schools in overwhelmingly black neighborhoods where there were few white students available from sister schools.

Matsch further observed problems with Resolution 2233. While the school board had unanimously passed the measure declaring DPS was a nondiscriminatory, unitary district, board member Omar Blair testified that he did not trust his white colleagues on the board to maintain an integrated district. Nor, the judge concluded, did Resolution 2228 mean anything. No future board could be bound by decisions of past boards. As such, DPS's arguments were essentially hollow.

In the wake of the failure of Resolution 2233, in 1985 under new superintendent James Scamman, DPS pushed for an out-of-court settlement with the plaintiffs. The district's leader did so after pro-integration forces once more gained a majority of the school board in May. By this time, there were few anti-busing zealots left in the city. On the contrary, the populace generally ignored the school contest whereby only 7 percent of the eligible voters went to the polls. Scamman's efforts to reach an accommodation on busing went nowhere.

Yet more programs followed to convince the court that DPS did not need judicial oversight. Seeing that at least District #1 appeared to be trying, on February 25,

1987, Judge Matsch relaxed court supervision, allowing the district more freedom in its day-to-day operations and adjustments of school borders as part of the "Interim Decree." He simultaneously urged that the plaintiffs and district engage in further negotiations. Ideally, they could reach an agreement whereby he could issue a permanent injunction settling the case.

In August 1988, the board passed Resolution 2314. As it had with Resolution 2228 of 1985, the measure bound all subsequent school boards to preserve and enhance integration. This included everything from assuring more minorities were involved in accelerated classes to making sure the district did not specially target them for infractions. Once more, the court said this was not enough. In 1990, the Tenth Circuit again upheld Judge Matsch when the jurist insisted on court oversight of the district. The United States Supreme Court declined to review the matter.

Despite this setback, the mantra remained the same. Especially after the creation of collaborative decision-making committees in 1991, DPS cited them as illustrating that the district actively involved the community in operating the schools. As such, CDMs allowed the citizenry and elected officials to rule the schools. That was not the role of the courts.

Meanwhile, enthusiasm for busing had faded everyplace. A generation after the upheavals of the 1960s and 1970s, proponents were not able to show outstanding achievements. There was still a gap between the performance of children of affluent, well-educated families—more often than not white—and those from poverty-stricken, poorly educated families where parents had not always finished high school. All the while, numerous ad hoc committees came and went, seeking to shape the district. There was, for example in 1992, United for Kids, an organization emphasizing the need for the ethnic diversity of the schools in tune with the ideals of the 1960s.

Opponents of court oversight once more brought the issue before Judge Matsch. They failed to convince him it was time to end busing in January 1992. Both Mayor Wellington Webb and Governor Roy Romer argued the time for court oversight had passed. A friend of the court brief filed by the city stated busing had badly hurt the community. The mayor echoed this: the best way to achieve integrated schools was by having integrated neighborhoods. In response, Judge Matsch authorized new settlement talks between DPS and a nebulous Black-Hispanic Coalition. It was quickly obvious that that body did not speak for all African-Americans or Latinos. After nearly a year, the negotiations collapsed. All the while, Judge Matsch expressed concern about the 1974 anti-busing amendment added to the state constitution. He wondered whether he could lift the busing order since he believed the amendment was an unconstitutional abridgment of the right to equal educational opportunity.

The jurist held another lengthy hearing on whether DPS was finally a unitary district beginning on August 22, 1994. The court showdown once more brought out problems in the system. "I don't know," testified outgoing Superintendent Evie Dennis as to why schools more punished black and Hispanic students than white students. As much as ever, her response showed the DPS leadership saw no link between socioeconomic divisions, race, and school achievement and problems.

But that did not matter, Dennis implied, as she argued DPS needed to be free of court oversight. The fact that she, a black woman, was superintendent, showed the nondiscriminatory nature of the district.

Having pondered the evidence for more than a year, on September 12, 1995, the jurist ruled in favor of DPS. He granted that the district had a legitimate point: voters had selected first a Latino, Federico Peña, and then a black, Wellington Webb, as mayor. The results showed the city was open and diverse. Most of all, Matsch concluded that, after 26 years, DPS had indeed become a unitary district. The busing order had achieved all it possibly could. As such, DPS was once more free of the court in deciding its destiny as of the end of the 1995–96 schoolyear. Even at that, Matsch warned, the court would readily intervene if it found DPS was returning to its old de facto racist policies. Besides, the massive drop in white enrollment since the beginning of the busing order meant there simply were not enough white children left in the system for court-ordered integration to be meaningful.

In part, the court order reflected Judge Matsch's view of the case. He saw himself as essentially a caretaker, reviewing developments in the district in the same way that federal judges keep their fingers on other long-lasting litigation such as a corporate bankruptcy or an anti-trust case. Far from wishing to prolong the lawsuit, he had stated he wanted to collaborate with the school board to resolve it. This was particularly the case in 1981–82 when he had worked with the board to develop what became the Consensus Plan as a way of ending the controversy.

At least friendly observers so painted Matsch. Others did not believe this, pointing out the judge constantly found problems with all of DPS's suggested remedies until his 1995 decision. During his long supervision of the case, he never dealt with the many problems caused by busing such as the way the court order isolated schools from where students and families lived. Rather than connecting school achievements with the class and educational backgrounds of families, Matsch had a most mechanical approach of judging everything by race. There was no reflection about whether busing indeed improved education.

Judge Matsch was not alone. His actions reflected court rulings across the country. In 1999, the United States District Court released the Charlotte-Mecklenburg, North Carolina, school district from a busing order, marking the end of the federal school integration orders. (Back in 1971, the Supreme Court had ruled busing was a legitimate means of achieving desegregation in deciding the Charlotte-Mecklenburg case.)

During the 26 years between the time the plaintiffs had first filed for relief in 1969 and Matsch's final order, the nature of the federal courts had substantially changed. The initial intervention came just after Earl Warren had retired as chief justice. Under him, the Supreme Court had seen the necessity of stepping into highly charged disputes amidst the mass upheavals of the day. In part, the Republicans asserted themselves during the post-Warren era in the name of pushing for a court that primarily upheld the status quo.

In the end, nobody was particularly happy with how the courts oversaw District #1. Even so, some of the plaintiffs looked at the case as a great civil rights victory. They argued it had forced the racist DPS to act to make equal educational

After the end of court-ordered busing in 1995–96, many children continued to attend schools miles from their homes. Often their parents drove them to magnet and charter schools. To help parents connect with children, some schools had designated pick-up areas, complete with cell phone applications. This banner was at Whiteman School, 451 Newport Street.

opportunity a reality. Former board member Bernie Valdez heralded the case insofar as it led the district to be more sensitive to the needs of Hispanic students. Advocates of brotherhood insisted that busing assured that all students realized the diversity of the city in which they lived. Ideally, this assured they grew up as tolerant adults.

Already on May 14, 1995, the board had adopted Resolution 2505. It vowed to involve the whole community in its decisions, working with one and all should the court finally end the busing order. After Matsch's decision, the board passed resolutions 2529 and 2530 in February 1996. The measures promised the system would maintain its operations as a unitary district that did not segregate. Around the same time, in the wake of the judge's ruling, the NAACP, Urban League, and other civil rights groups created Citizens Concerned about Quality Education, vowing to preserve pressure on the district. The organization quickly faded away.

Nobody more loudly opposed the ending of court oversight than Rachel Noel. As much as ever, she feared DPS would automatically revert to being a racist system. By this time, few listened to her. In contrast, both Aaron Gray, an African-American who was president of the school board, and Mayor Wellington Webb celebrated Matsch's decision. Black Denver, they argued, wanted to come home. African-Americans were as tired of endless busing as everybody else.

This did not sit well with some Montbello students. Adolescents living there, especially those who had been enrolled at George Washington High School, did not want to come home. They preferred attending George Washington over Montbello High School, a place they associated with the ghetto. In response, DPS worked with the Regional Transportation District to provide tokens/bus passes to those living in the Manual and Montbello attendance districts so they could continue to ride the bus to George Washington until they graduated.

The immediate result of the resolutions and Judge Matsch's decision was the depairing of 16 elementary schools. For the 1996–97 schoolyear, DPS modified the boundaries of 54 of its 78 elementary schools. The next year, it changed the borders of 17 of its 18 middle schools and nine of its ten high schools. The goal was to assure that, except for magnets, all buildings were once more neighborhood schools. DPS ended busing for middle schools and high schools after the end of the 1996–97 schoolyear.

Despite the termination of busing, whites remained a minority in DPS even while more than half of the city's population was white. A 1993–94 school census listed only eight elementaries as having more than 50 percent of the student body that was white: Asbury (52 percent), Bromwell (51.2 percent), Cory (51.9 percent), Lincoln

Photo by Phil Goodstein

Lincoln School, at the southwest corner of South Pearl Street and Exposition Avenue, was among the few elementary schools with a white majority by the time of the end of busing in 1995. As part of DPS's emphasis on business partnerships with the schools, it has displayed a banner advertising a local chiropractor.

(51.4 percent), Marrama (52.4 percent), McKinley-Thatcher (56.7 percent), Sabin (64.8 percent), and University Park (50.6 percent). None of the middle schools had at least a 50 percent white enrollment. North High was 76.9 percent Hispanic, West was at 81.1 percent Hispanic, and Abraham Lincoln at 58.2 percent Hispanic. There were also heavily black schools such as Amesse (61.7 percent), Ashley (61.8 percent), Barrett (69.1 percent), Hallett (63.3 percent), McGlone (71.9 percent), Oakland (61.3 percent), Smith (63.2 percent), and Stedman (80.1 percent). Gove, 59.5 percent, Cole, 51.7 percent, and Martin Luther King, 64.6 percent, were middle schools with a majority black enrollment. In ensuing years, the number of blacks and Hispanos in some schools soared.

DPS took a considerable budget hit in depairing schools. It also faced the problem of overcrowding. This was particularly the case at such places as Cheltenham and Swansea. Previously, about half the children in their attendance districts had been bused miles away while few white children had ridden the bus to them. Now, they had more students than DPS claimed the buildings could handle. To help coordinate the district's policies, a post-busing task force emerged. In the case of Cheltenham, busing continued for the 1996–97 schoolyear to Kaiser so the school could handle all who sought to attend while the district added classrooms to Cheltenham.

This was only the beginning of the legacy of the busing era and the changes wrought by the end of the court order. A year after Judge Matsch released DPS from supervision, Gordon Greiner, the plaintiffs' leader lawyer, retired from Holland & Hart. It was the only firm for which he worked during his career. In the course of the litigation, 18 attorneys from the firm had participated in the case. The firm's total cost was about $1 million. A 1992 estimate by the *Rocky Mountain News* claimed that by that time Greiner had earned about $800,000 alone from the busing litigation. Total legal bills, including to DPS's outside counsel, were then $4 million. Holland & Hart received considerable attorney fees for its pro bono contribution to the Keyes litigation. Back in 1974, Judge Doyle, as part of his ruling that DPS implement the Finger Plan, had ordered DPS to pay $360,000 for the legal costs of the plaintiffs. Much of the money went to the NAACP Legal Defense Fund. It had spent $35,000 to print the Keyes record as part of the appeal process. Holland & Hart, in turn, often billed LDF to pay for its costs in the litigation.

His involvement in the Keyes case saw Greiner develop close ties with the LDF, serving on its board for some years. He retired to Washington state. The litigator died just before his 72nd birthday on August 24, 2006, seven weeks after he had been diagnosed with cancer. So little was remembered of his days as a Goldwater Republican who wore a crew cut that obituaries described him as always having long hair and a wild, untrimmed beard.

After serving as chief judge of the United States District Court of Colorado from 1994 to 2000, Judge Matsch took senior status in 2003. This allowed him to sit on the cases he wished to hear. After 45 years on the federal bench, he died at age 88 on May 27, 2019.

Evie Dennis' years as superintendent were also filled with controversies over discipline. The release from busing allowed the district new freedom to explore different approaches to education. Not only did magnet schools notably expand in the 1990s, but charter schools also became part and parcel of District #1. Before long, "choice" was a mantra of the system. Included were experimental approaches including schools that were exclusively for girls or which were virtually all black. In a way, the new emphasis was a product of the failure of busing and integration to deliver as promised. All the while, the business-political orientation of DPS was highly visible. By the end of the 2010s, there were massive laments about the highly segregated nature of the district whereby some started to recall busing as a great success. All of these developments are part of volume three, *Schools for a New Century*.

A Note on Sources:

Resolutions 2233 and 2314 are reported in *BN*, February 9, 1996. Evie Dennis outlined them in her 1988 study, *Report on Resolutions 2233 and 2314*. It looks at the origins of the two measures, 1–2, 3, 7. The short work argues the district was making integration a reality. Bailey, "Journey Full Circle," 141, reviews Resolution 2233, printing it, 230, along with Resolution 2314, on 232. *RMN*, April 15, 1984, p. 1, mentioned DPS's appeal of the court order. Fishman, "Endless Journey," 209–10, gives his take on Resolution 2233 and Judge Matsch's rejection of it.

Fishman, "Endless Journey," 211, 214–15, overviews Scamman's efforts to reach an out-of-court settlement of the busing case. Ibid., 211, mentions the 1985 election, Judge Matsch's decision of February 15, 1987, 215–16, and hopes for a settlement of the case via a permanent injunction. Matsch's 1987 ruling is 670 FSupp 1513. Bailey, "Journey Full Circle," 148–50, emphasizes the Interim Decree. A flyer of United for Kids is in the 1992–93 notebook of GP.

RMN, January 4, 1992, p. 8, January 26, 1992, p. 7, and February 6, 1992, p. 8, looked at that year's court appeal while emphasizing the cost of busing. Bailey, "Journey Full Circle," 152–54, mentions new appeals of Judge Matsch's oversight and the changing demographics of DPS. The study, 156, glances at DPS's 1992 motion that Judge Matsch release it from oversight, tying it to the national end of busing. Ibid., 157–58, emphasizes the comments of Roy Romer and Wellington Webb in asking the court to end the busing order, and the negotiations involving the Black-Hispanic Coalition, 159–164. The dissertation, 165–65, likewise deals with the legacy of the 1974 anti-busing amendment. FF 1:31, 34, of the Noel papers have reports of the unsuccessful settlement conference in 1992–93.

A May 12, 1994, statement by Evie Dennis, in the 1993 BSC Notebook in GP, estimated the annual costs of meeting the desegregation order. *DP*, August 24, 1994, featured her testimony before Judge Matsch. *RMN*, August 23, 1994, p. 4A, reported on the hearing. *RMN*, August 25, 1994, p. 10A, told of Rachel Noel urging the court to keep busing in place. On May 1, 1995, p, 14A, it reported Noel's worries about the end of busing. *RMN*, September 13, 1995, p. 1A, announced Matsch's lifting the integration order. It is 902 FSupp 1275. Bailey, "Journey Full Circle," 171–78, reviews it, extensively quoting the text.

The minutes of the October 29, 1995, meeting of the DSIAC observed Matsch's decision and its impact. *QM*, February 1996, p. 15, emphasized the consequences of Judge Matsch's order. Ibid., also looked at the many magnet schools then in the district. *BN*, November 20, 1998, told of Resolution 2530.

Fishman, "Endless Journey," 219–23, a work published in 1987, reflects on the complex legacy of the Keyes case and how none of the parties was completely satisfied with the intervention of the courts. In passing, 202, the study observes the settlement of other school busing cases in the 1980s. The essay concludes that the litigation was worthwhile in that it increased district awareness of the problems of minority students.

Time, September 11, 2019, included an opinion article by Gloria J. Brown-Marshall. In it she emphasized the end of federal court-ordered busing with the termination of the Charlotte-Mecklenburg case in 1999. During a talk at the January 27, 2018, meeting of Park Hill Neighbors for Equity in Education, former school board Laura Lefkowits claimed the lack of white students in the district by 1995 was key to Judge Matsch's decision while she argued busing had been a success.

On June 27, 2019, Rita Montero, who was on the board at the time of Judge Matsch's decision ending busing, recalled the debates on the ruling, the positions of Aaron Gray and Wellington Webb, and DPS's collaboration with RTD to transport students to George Washington who wished to stay at the high school. Bailey, "Journey Full Circle," 236, prints Resolution 2529.

The 1995–96 *DPS Report*, unpaginated, discussed the changing attendance borders in the light of Judge Matsch's ruling; cf. the 1996–97 *DPS Report*, 14. The 1996 BSC Notebook in GP has documents reviewing the financial impact of the end of busing. It also reports, without details, the post-busing task force. FF 2:24 of the Noel papers has the DPS busing rules for 1996–97, the first year the district operated free from the court order.

Pearson, "Denver Case," 204, mentions the court awarding the plaintiffs legal fees. FF 6:6 of the Keyes papers has documents showing the basis on which plaintiffs were entitled to legal fees in civil rights cases. Box 7 of the collection is filled with billings from Holland & Hart to the LDF and the Equal Educational Opportunity Fund. *RMN*, May 23, 1982, p. 4, looked at the legal costs of the first dozen years of busing. *RMN*, January 26, 1992, p. 7, listed the $800,000 earned by Gordon Greiner in the busing litigation. Bailey, "Journey Full Circle," 155, states the cost of litigation was $4 million by that time. Orfield, *Must We Bus?* 376, 385, observes the cost of the Keyes litigation and the legal fees. FF 3:115–24 of the DPS papers deal with Cheltenham School.

DP, September 10, 2006, p. 6B, reported Greiner's death. *DP*, May 28, 2019, p. 6A, observed the passing of Judge Matsch. It was inferior to the obituaries in *NYT*, May 29, 2019, and *WW*, May 28, 2019.

Index

V1 refers to volume one, V3 to volume three, of schools and those who are central to DPS.